PAUL AND THE HERMENEUTICS OF FAITH

C.E. Shephard
4/2004

Paul and the Hermeneutics of Faith

Francis Watson

t &t clark

Published by T&T Clark International
an imprint of Continuum
© Francis Watson 2004

The Tower Building,   80 Maiden Lane
11 York Road,   Suite 704,
London SE1 7NX   New York, NY 10038

www.continuumbooks.com

First published 2004
Reprinted 2006, 2007

British Library Cataloguing-in-Publication Data
A catalogue record for this book is available from the British Library

Typeset by Tradespools, Frome, Somerset
Printed on acid-free paper in Great Britain by Biddles Ltd., King's Lynn, Norfolk

Contents

Preface

"What is the advantage of the Jew, or what is the value of circumcision? Much in every way! First, they were entrusted with the oracles of God ... " In Romans 3.1–2, Paul views the reception, preservation and propagation of the texts of scripture as the primary reason to reaffirm the unique significance of Jewishness. Jews are people who hold in trust the very words of God, and they do so on behalf of humankind as a whole. Paul continues no further with what might have developed into a list of Jewish privileges. Jews – including Paul himself and the hypocritical teacher he has just caricatured – are simply those who possess, cherish, study, teach, and argue about the scriptures. These Pauline Jews are people of the book.

This book is about Jewishness, and it is similarly limited in its scope. Many of the topics that might be anticipated in a study of Paul's relation to his Jewish heritage are absent here – or virtually so. In spite of the attention given to the scriptural interpretation especially of Galatians and Romans, nothing is said about either the immediate historical contexts of these letters, or their place within Paul's ministry or theology as a whole. No answer is given to the question what *kind* of Jew Paul may be said to have been – whether Hellenistic, Pharisaic, mystical, apocalyptic, apostate, or simply anomalous. On the non-Christian Jewish side, there is no attempt to survey the total phenomenon of Second Temple Judaism, or to advance any theories about it, or to trace key motifs across a range of texts. The later Judaism of the rabbis is entirely absent, and the vexed question of what if anything it can teach us about the earlier period is ignored. These necessary and important matters have been set aside in order to focus on a single point: the fact that *Paul and his fellow-Jews read the same texts, yet read them differently.* This is a book about readers and their divergent readings.

More precisely, my concern is with the act of reading. The hermeneutical assumption underlying everything that follows is simply that in the act of reading the reader is *changed.* Reading (even when "pre-critical") is not a one way process in which readers impose meanings on the text that merely express their own prior convictions and ideological prejudices. If that widely accepted view were correct, the scriptural text would be inert and mute, and we would have to focus on the convictions and prejudices themselves, revealed and reflected back in the mirror of the text. In contrast, it is the working hypothesis of this book that the act of reading entails an interaction between text and reader, analogous to a conversation between two people. That means that we must take seriously the agency not only of the reader but also of the text. In analysing the readings of early Jewish readers of scripture, we shall try to view them as divergent realizations of the text's own semantic potential. We shall be concerned not only with early readers of, say, Genesis, but also with Genesis itself.

Books tend to grow out of their authors' earlier work in ways that are neither wholly random nor predictable in advance. In my own case, the present work marks a return to the general area of my first book, *Paul, Judaism and the Gentiles* (1986), which was based on an Oxford University doctoral thesis submitted early in 1984, and which played its part in the attempt to rethink Paul's theology of justification and the law in historically plausible ways. That book gave expression to the disillusioning discovery that an earlier, explicitly theological approach to the Pauline texts was seriously and irredeemably flawed. The excitement that the work of Bultmann and Käsemann had generated in the preceding theological generation now seemed to be based on false premises. In my own case, this led on to a series of attempts to think through the relationship between theology and exegesis at a more general level. The facile assumption that exegesis is inevitably corrupted by theology has never seemed remotely plausible to me, and the emergence of new hermeneutical perspectives seemed to offer the prospect of a more nuanced and less antagonistic account of the relation between the two disciplines.

This book is not a work of theology, however, or of specifically theological hermeneutics. It is more ecumenical in its ambitions: I hope that it will be of interest to those for whom a Christian or Jewish identity is integral to their scholarship, but also to those for whom this is not the case. This in no sense marks a retreat from the commitment to practise a theologically oriented exegesis. What I hope to show is that an open-ended theological orientation is integral to any exegesis that engages seriously with the text and its subject matter. This theological orientation does not need to draw attention to itself as such, for issues of contemporary theological concern are bound to come to light whenever the scriptural texts are read with empathy and insight. In the present work, the attempt will be made not only to reread Paul but also to learn from Paul and others how to become better readers of texts that were their scripture and that remain ours: notably the Pentateuch, or Torah. If the quest for a better reading of the Pentateuch seems theologically irrelevant to Christians or to Jews, then something has gone wrong somewhere.

How are we to go about the task of recovering these early readings of scripture, which, although occurring in well-known texts, are still not sufficiently recognized or understood *as readings*? The format adopted here is to set a Pauline reading of, for example, the Abraham narrative or the closing chapters of Deuteronomy alongside one or more alternative readings of the same text. In this way, a critical dialogue opens up between the two (or more) readers. They read the text for themselves, but they also argue with one another about how it *should* be read. As they do so, appealing to the text itself in support of their proposals, it becomes clear how and why they have chosen to realize the text's semantic potential in such divergent ways. At points where additional readers are introduced, differences will come to light within the non-Christian Jewish side of the debate; and these may be at least as significant – within their own framework – as the differences generated by Paul himself. Texts have been selected simply on the grounds that they would make good dialogue partners for Paul. Other texts might have been chosen, and in two or three cases they initially were. If, after part I, there is a slight bias towards texts written in Greek, that does not imply any intention to favour "Hellenistic" over "Palestinian" Judaism as Paul's primary Jewish context. On the contrary, I regard this distinction as unimportant, and so devote a great deal of space in part I to the quest for a common context for Paul and the author of the Habakkuk pesher.

My eclecticism in the selection of texts is also a matter of methodological principle, however: I reject the assumption that the views of "real" Jews of the Second Temple period are better reflected in a text such as *Jubilees* than in the writings of, say, Philo. If Jews are people who argue together about a shared scriptural heritage, then Philo has as much right to participate in the discussion as anyone else. (The same is true of Paul.) An essentialist view of Judaism as a religion immune from difference and historical change has long been maintained by Jews and Christians alike – but it is simply wrong. Confident assertions about what every Jew believed, or what no Jew could have accepted, should be treated with scepticism.

Several years ago, the shadowy bureaucracies which now control British higher education came up with the expression, "lone scholar", which was supposed to characterize the research typically practised in humanities disciplines in contrast to the team- and project-based approach of the natural sciences. After a while, someone noticed that this expression was both inept and offensive, and it was consigned to the scrapheap of outworn managerial jargon. In reality, research in the humanities is typically conducted by individuals located within informal and often international networks of scholars. This is certainly true of the present work, and it is a pleasure as well as an obligation to acknowledge a few of my

indebtednesses. It is especially important for me to acknowledge the first
two, since the scholars concerned will each have their own reasons for
dissatisfaction with major elements in the case set out in this book.

During my postgraduate studies in the early 1980s, I had the good
fortune to meet Professor Ed Sanders following a paper that he delivered
in Oxford on the subject of Paul's view of the law. At that time, Professor
Sanders was on research leave at Trinity College, Cambridge, and was
putting finishing touches to his *Paul, the Law, and the Jewish People*. With
great generosity, he invited me to visit him for further conversation on
these matters, to which he gave up an entire afternoon. I am now more
aware than I was then that one does not go on research leave in order to
hold long conversations with postgraduate students. Professor Sanders
also gave me the invaluable gift of a copy of his forthcoming book in
typescript, and remained generously supportive during the early stages of
my career.

Further back still, I owe a debt of gratitude to Dr N. T. Wright for
introducing me to the exegesis of Romans in Greek during my
undergraduate years. This was a matter of weekly one-to-one "tutorials"
(in the Oxford nomenclature), which invariably extended far beyond the
single hour to which I was entitled. Over a period of many months, we
worked together through the Greek text of Romans, from beginning to
end. My abiding memory is of the sheer intellectual excitement of realizing
that one did *not* know in advance what the text must be saying, and that it
was full of possibilities which did not conform in the least to conventional
protestant assumptions. (I recall the exclamation, "Luther got Paul so
wrong!") At around the time when Sanders' *Paul and Palestinian Judaism*
was published (1977), Tom Wright was already independently thinking
through many of the ideas that later, after the completion of his own
doctorate, came to be known as the "new perspective on Paul". After such
an apprenticeship in the art of exegesis, postgraduate research on a Pauline
topic seemed the only future worth considering.

At a later date, Richard Hays' *Echoes of Scripture in the Letters of Paul*
(1989) was, for me at least, the first indication that insights drawn from
contemporary hermeneutics and literary theory could fruitfully be applied
to Pauline interpretation in general, and to Paul's reading of scripture in
particular. Here, for the first time perhaps, Paul emerges *as a reader*,
constrained by the texts and yet creatively free in his handling of them.
Conventional critical studies of Paul's scriptural interpretation shed light
on a number of incidental matters, yet sooner or later find themselves
compelled to admit that his manner of reading is alien to us, arising as it
does from his rabbinic background, his polemical strategy, or his unique
apostolic authority. The heart of Pauline theology has always been located
somewhere other than in his scriptural interpretation. *Echoes of Scripture*
changed all that, and raised the possibility that Paul's hermeneutic might

itself be the way into the heart of his theology. I have benefited enormously from many conversations with Professor Hays over the years, about these and other matters. Shortly after my move from London to Aberdeen, it was a suggestion from him that led me to abandon a research project that was probably doomed anyway, in order to return to the field of mainstream Pauline studies.

Other debts are more specific. A conversation with Lou Martyn helped me to clarify my thoughts on the relation between Christ and scripture in Paul. I would like to have done more justice here to Professor Martyn's remarkable Galatians commentary. Douglas Campbell helped me to see that Paul's use of an unassuming six-word fragment from Habakkuk raises issues of great hermeneutical and theological interest. This suggestion may well have been the origin of the whole of part I of this book (although, for better or worse, I cannot persuade myself that Paul finds in this text a reference to the faithfulness of Christ). Judith Lieu first raised doubts about the adequacy of a "parting of the ways" model for the relation of early Christianity to Judaism. Troels Engberg-Pedersen, Dale Martin and Seth Kunin posed questions about exegesis and theology that I found uncomfortable yet salutary. Simon Gathercole showed me that close reading of Second Temple Jewish texts creates real difficulties for the dominant "covenantal nomism" hypothesis. And some remarks of Jim Davila's alerted me to some of the pitfalls that await those who venture unprepared into the field of Qumran studies.

In conclusion, I must gratefully acknowledge the period of research leave funded by the Arts and Humanities Research Board which has enabled me to bring this project to completion. I would also like to thank Mr Christopher Richardson for his meticulous work on the indexing.

Francis Watson

21 February, 2004

Abbreviations

AB	Anchor Bible
AnBib	Analecta Biblica
AOT	*The Apocryphal Old Testament*
AOTC	Abingdon Old Testament Commentary
APOT	*Apocrypha and Pseudepigrapha of the Old Testament*
ATD	Das Alte Testament Deutsch
AThANT	Abhandlungen zur Theologie des Alten und Neuen Testaments
BBB	Bonner Biblische Beiträge
BHT	Beiträge zur historischen Theologie
BKAT	Biblische Kommentar, Altes Testament
BNTC	Black's New Testament Commentaries
BZAW	Beihefte zur Zeitschrift für die alttestamentliche Wissenschaft
CBQ	*Catholic Biblical Quarterly*
CBQMS	Catholic Biblical Quarterly Monograph Series
DJD	Discoveries in the Judean Desert
DSD	Dead Sea Discoveries
EDSS	*Encyclopedia of the Dead Sea Scrolls*
EKKNT	Evangelisch-Katholischer Kommentar zum Neuen Testament
FRLANT	Forschungen zur Religion und Literatur des Alten und Neuen Testaments
GMT	F. García Martínez and E. Tigchelaar, *The Dead Sea Scrolls: Study Edition*
HNT	Handbuch zum Neuen Testament
HThKNT	Herders theologischer Kommentar zum Neuen Testament
HTR	*Harvard Theological Review*
IBC	International Biblical Commentary
ICC	International Critical Commentary
JBL	*Journal of Biblical Literature*
JBLMS	Journal of Biblical Literature Monograph Series
JJS	*Journal of Jewish Studies*
JSJ	*Journal for the Study of Judaism*

JSNT	*Journal for the Study of the New Testament*
JSNTSup	Journal for the Study of the New Testament Supplement Series
JSOTSup	Journal for the Study of the Old Testament Supplement Series
JSPSup	Journal for the Study of the Pseudepigrapha Supplement Series
JTS	*Journal of Theological Studies*
KAT	Kommentar zum Alten Testament
KEKNT	Kritisch-exegetischer Kommentar über das Neue Testament
LW	*Luther's Works*
MTZ	*Münchener Theologische Zeitschrift*
NEBKAT	Die Neue Echter Bibel: Kommentar zum Alten Testament
NICNT	New International Commentary on the New Testament
NIGTC	New International Greek Testament Commentary
NovT	*Novum Testamentum*
NovTSup	Supplements to Novum Testamentum
NTS	*New Testament Studies*
OBT	Overtures to Biblical Theology
OTL	Old Testament Library
OTP	*Old Testament Pseudepigrapha*
RB	*Revue Biblique*
RQ	*Revue de Qumran*
SBLDS	Society of Biblical Literature Dissertation Series
SBLMS	Society of Biblical Literature Monograph Series
SJT	*Scottish Journal of Theology*
SNTSMS	Studiorum Novi Testamenti Societas Monograph Series
SNTW	Studies in the New Testament and its World
SP	Sacra Pagina
STDJ	Studies on the Texts of the Desert of Judah
TAPA	*Transactions of the American Philological Association*
TDNT	*Theological Dictionary of the New Testament*
ThHKNT	Theologischer Handkommentar zum Neuen Testament
ThStKr	*Theologische Studien und Kritiken*
TLZ	*Theologische Literaturzeitung*
TU	Texte und Untersuchungen zur Geschichte der altchristlichen Literatur
TynB	*Tyndale Bulletin*
WBC	Word Biblical Commentary
WMANT	Wissenschaftliche Monographien zum Alten und Neuen Testament
WUNT	Wissenschaftliche Untersuchungen zum Neuen Testament
ZAW	*Zeitschrift für die alttestamentliche Wissenschaft*
ZNW	*Zeitschrift für die neutestamentliche Wissenschaft*

Introduction

Paul was a Jew. He was not only a Jew – for identity is never determined by a single factor, however significant. After his encounter with Christ, Paul was perhaps an idiosyncratic Jew. Indeed, his Jewish identity may have been contested. But the fact remains that this apostle of Jesus Christ to the Gentiles was, at least by upbringing and in his own self-understanding, a Jew. Paul's Jewishness is now generally acknowledged, and indeed emphasized. But it is still a question how this factor can most fruitfully be put to use in the interpretation of his texts. And the answer, in general terms, is that a Jewish Paul must be shown to be engaged in critical dialogue with other Jews about a common heritage and identity.

If no evidence of such a dialogue can be uncovered, then Paul's Jewishness will lack any fundamental hermeneutical significance. It will be just a "fact" about him, to which one may appeal in order to clarify one aspect or another of his texts. There is, however, an obvious point at which we may expect to uncover traces of an inner-Jewish dialogue. However they otherwise differ, *Paul and his fellow-Jews read the same scriptural texts, the Torah and the prophets.* They interpret these normative texts in order to interpret the world of contemporary experience in and through them, and their readings of text and world are by no means the same. According to the principle of scriptural normativity, text and world must somehow be made to fit one another; and yet the vagueness of this "somehow" leaves scope for very different attempts to make the required connections. So Paul and other Jewish readers participate in an ongoing conversation about how to read the Torah and the prophets, and the fact that they read differently is just what makes the conversation possible and necessary. This is the point at which Paul's Jewishness becomes hermeneutically significant. As a Jew, Paul is a reader of scripture alongside other readers.

The importance of this simple observation has often been overlooked, owing perhaps to a tendency to see Paul as a unique and self-contained phenomenon. This tendency to isolate Paul is by no means universal, but it has proved remarkably persistent. Where it makes its presence felt, points of contact with the wider Hellenistic and Jewish spheres will be duly noted, but they will not encroach on the isolation of the "real" Paul, with his highly individual theology and vocation. Like his own experience on the Damascus Road, this Paul appears on the scene without preparation or precedent. Like the Melchizedek of the Epistle to the Hebrews, he has no father or mother or genealogy. He is, as it were, sovereign over his own discourse. Everything in it – his "view of the law", his "doctrine of justification", his "use of scripture" – is, precisely, *his*. The interpreter must therefore operate within an exclusively Pauline frame of reference, paraphrasing the texts, elucidating their obscurities and contradictions, reconstructing the logic of their argumentation, assigning them to a historical context, weighing and assessing the different parts that make up the whole. Important and illuminating though it may often be, this kind of Pauline interpretation fails to distance itself sufficiently from Paul's own intensely individual self-consciousness, and so perpetuates and heightens tendencies in his own discourse towards autonomy and self-containment. In the last resort, this intense focus on Paul's own individuality serves only to make him *uninteresting*. His texts need to be set within a wider perspective. Pauline monologue must be relocated within some form of dialogue.

If Paul's Jewishness is hermeneutically significant, and if Paul is a reader of scriptural texts alongside other readers, then it is no longer possible to read his own texts as monologues. Instead, they come to represent one voice within a three-sided conversation. As a Jew, Paul is engaged in animated and sometimes contentious debate *about* the scriptural texts, and *with* the scriptural texts.

A Three-way Conversation

This book is a comparative study in the early reception of Jewish scripture, with a primary Pauline focus. The aim is to explore the relationships between three bodies of literature: the Pauline letters, the scriptural texts to which they appeal, and the non-Christian Jewish literature of the Second Temple period which appeals to the same scriptural texts. These three bodies of literature are often studied in relative isolation from one another, with only a superficial sense of their interconnectedness. In contrast, the intention here is to get these texts talking to each other – or rather, to show how they are as they are by virtue of an ongoing conversation in which they all already participate.

The primary concern is with the Pauline texts. We shall identify and criticize the assumption that Paul's reflection on topics such as "justifica-tion" and "the law" can be treated in abstraction from his scriptural exegesis and hermeneutics – as though this reflection occurred in a textual vacuum. Paul's so-called "view of the law" is nothing other than his reading of a text; his "theology of justification" is in reality a scriptural hermeneutic; and the reading and the hermeneutic are intertwined, since the hermeneutic is itself an exegetical construct based on selected key texts. Like other Jewish theologies of this period, Pauline theology is *intertextual* in form, in the sense that it is constituted by its relation to an earlier corpus of texts that functions as communally normative scripture. This intertextual dimension becomes explicit in Paul's scriptural citations, and we shall therefore focus especially on the texts in which these predominate: above all, the Letters to the Romans and to the Galatians. As we shall see, Paul cites individual texts not in an *ad hoc* manner but on the basis of a radical construal of the narrative shape of the Pentateuch as a whole, highlighting and exploiting tensions between Genesis and Exodus, Leviticus and Deuteronomy. Many of the apparent contradictions within Paul's "view of the law" in fact originate within the pentateuchal texts themselves, at least as Paul reads them. Precisely in their canonical form, these texts are not at all the homogeneous and monolithic entity they are often taken to be.

A second concern is with other early Jewish texts that engage with, and are shaped by, the same scriptural material. Scriptural interpretations are to be found here that differ not only in relation to Paul but also among themselves, and it should not be assumed that the distinctiveness of a Pauline reading will be different in kind or degree from the distinctiveness of a non-Pauline reading. This makes it inappropriate to try to reconstruct from divergent sources a single "contemporary Jewish" reading of a particular part or aspect of scripture, which would then serve as a foil for the Pauline reading. Rather than attempting to generalize, individual texts must be selected which exemplify alternative interpretative possibilities to the ones that Paul draws out; and exegesis of these selected texts must be carried out with no less care and attention to detail than one devotes to Paul's own texts. Texts such as the Habakkuk Pesher, the *Wisdom of Solomon* and *4 Ezra* fully repay a "close reading", and each has a theological and hermeneutical interest of its own which must be brought to the fore if comparison with the Pauline readings is to be fruitful. Whatever other factors help to shape them, scripture is the generative matrix within which these texts come into being, and it is therefore possible to see both the Pauline and the non-Pauline texts as operating within the single intertextual field constituted by the communal acknowledgment of the earlier texts as "scripture", and by the expectation that, as they are interpreted, these texts will themselves interpret and shape the world of present experience. Difference and disagreement, even over matters such as christology, take place only on that common ground.

A third concern is with the scriptural texts themselves, in the canonical form(s) they assumed for their early readers. We must read these texts for ourselves if we are to interpret their interpreters. We cannot assess the contrasting readings of Habakkuk 2.4 by Paul and the Qumran pesherist without some sense of what this text might mean within Habakkuk and the Book of the Twelve as a whole, quite apart from what its early readers do with it. It is true that the differences between such readings expose the crucial part played by the presuppositions and commitments that individual readers bring to a text. Yet it is wrong to imagine that the text itself is no more than a blank screen onto which readers project their various concerns: it is normally possible to show that the text itself is implicated in the readings it occasions. To interpret is always to interact with a text, and it is also to be *constrained* by the text. If so, it is essential to retrace the way from the scriptural text to its Pauline and non-Pauline realizations, in a manner that allows the scriptural text a voice of its own within a three-way conversation. There are always a variety of ways in which the semantic potential of a scriptural text may be realized, and it will not normally be our place to adjudicate between the various readings. The point is simply that readers are not wrong when they ascribe semantic potential to a text, and that, in interpreting their interpretations, we must take seriously their claim to be realizing that semantic potential. If that is correct, it will no longer be possible to justify an approach to the scriptural text that abstracts it from its own history of interpretation – as though the only proper object of study were a text that remained unread. Text and interpretation lie on a continuum. To analyse early Jewish readings of the Pentateuch as interactions with the text is to contribute to the study of the Pentateuch itself.[1]

Three bodies of texts engaged in a three-way conversation: what this metaphor envisages is a dynamic process rather than a static juxtaposition of self-contained positions.[2] A three-way conversation is a fairly complex social practice, and this one has some additional complexities of its own. We shall be investigating interactions between scripture (S), the Pauline texts (P), and non-Christian Jewish texts (J) that may be formalized as follows:

(1) $P \leftrightarrow S$

(2) $J \leftrightarrow S$

(3) $P(S) \leftrightarrow J(S)$

---

1.   It is the great contribution of Brevard Childs to have shown how the "canonical form" of a text mediates between its circumstances of origin and its later usage. At a time when many older attempts to correlate the Old Testament/Hebrew Bible with the history of the ancient near east have broken down, Childs' proposal would seem to stand on the side of sociohistorical realism. It is mystifying that Childs continues to evoke such antipathy, at least among some British scholars.

2.   For the "conversation" metaphor I am indebted to Richard Hays, who describes the Letter to the Romans as "an intertextual conversation between Paul and the voice of Scripture" (*Echoes of Scripture*, p. 35). Hays acknowledges the desirability of including a third participant in the conversation, in the form of non-Christian Jewish exegesis: see his "On the Rebound: A Response to Critiques of *Echoes of Scripture in the Letters of Paul*", pp. 70–73.

Each of these pairings represents an interaction rather than a unilinear movement. In order to preserve the integrity of all three conversation partners, and to prevent any one of them from dominating the discussion, it will be necessary to move in both directions within each pairing. It is not enough to attend to what Paul says about the scriptural text; it is also important to attend to what the scriptural text might have to say about its Pauline appropriation. Granted that such an appropriation will never be a simple repetition of a given semantic content, how far can the text be said to lend itself to this appropriation? Yet it is equally important to acknowledge the constructive element in appropriation, and not to criticize Pauline or non-Pauline interpretation for attempting something more than the mere reproduction of a narrowly circumscribed "original meaning". The function of canonical scripture is to enable the interpreter to make sense of the world of contemporary experience, and not simply to assign an "original meaning" to a text: in the end, it is the world rather than the text *per se* that is the object of interpretation. It should also be noted that none of the three voices in the three-way conversation is straightforwardly singular. We will have to reckon with an $S^{1,2,3\cdots}$, a $P^{1,2,3\cdots}$, and a $J^{1,2,3\cdots}$, who may on occasion engage in debate among themselves.

The metaphor of the "three-way conversation" is an attempt to capture the dynamic of the intertextuality that is our concern. The basic hypothesis is that engagement with scripture is fundamental to Pauline and non-Christian Jewish theological construction, and that these "early Jewish" texts, Christian or otherwise, can therefore be located within a single intertextual field – not in spite of their interpretative differences, but precisely because of them. If the hypothesis proves correct, it would have profound implications for our understanding of "Christian" and "Jewish" identity, and of the relationship between the two.[3]

---

3. This concept of the "single intertextual field" may have a contribution to make to the wider discussion of Christian origins in relation to "Second Temple Judaism", and is broadly compatible with the reorientation called for by Gabriele Boccaccini (among others). As Boccaccini argues, "Jews and Christians have for centuries tacitly agreed on the idea of Judaism as an unchanging, unchanged (and perhaps unchangeable) system" (*Middle Judaism: Jewish Thought 300 B.C.E.–200 C.E.*, p. 8). It is also agreed on both sides that "Christianity" is to be sharply distinguished from this unchangeable system. According to Boccaccini, this consensus must be "recognized as a consequence of confessional bias" (p. 18). While Christianity and Rabbinism chose to disinherit one another, "a reciprocal excommunication cannot cancel the truth of their common origin" (p. 16) – an origin within a "plurality of groups, movements, and traditions of thought coexist[ing] in a dialectical relationship, which was sometimes polemical but never disengaged" (p. 14). It is the idea that this "common origin" is constituted *intertextually* that is my own focus. It should be noted that Boccaccini's analysis undermines the "parting of the ways" model, according to which a Gentile-dominated Christianity largely *abandoned* its "Jewish heritage".

At this stage, a critical engagement with related scholarly positions is the best way to clarify the rationale and potential of this model of intertextuality.[4] We begin, almost inevitably, with E. P. Sanders' influential account of Pauline Christianity in relation to its Jewish milieu.[5] For Sanders, there is little or no basis for dialogue between Paul and that milieu – only an assertion of incommensurable difference.

The Covenant and the Law of Life

The broad outline of Sanders' account of the "Palestinian Judaism" against which Paul reacted is well known. According to Sanders, the dominant, post-Reformation tradition of Pauline interpretation is seriously at fault. Taking its starting point in the Pauline antitheses of faith and works, grace and law, this tradition claims that Paul's intention is to contrast the Christian understanding of salvation with the Jewish one. On the Christian view, salvation or justification is by grace alone, wholly an act of God that is to be acknowledged as such in faith. In contrast, the Jewish view holds that it is only human obedience to the law that can secure salvation. This opposition between divine and human agency is, however, not at all what Paul intended. It cannot be, for, so far as they are known to us, the diverse forms of Judaism practised in the periods before and after 70 CE do not actually teach that human obedience to the law is the way to salvation. Fundamental to almost all of them is God's gracious election of Israel: the Jew who observes the law is already within the covenant, the sphere of God's mercy and grace. Law observance is a means not of "getting in" but of "staying in", in the sense that God's electing grace always precedes and grounds the human response required by the law. It is only very serious breaches of the law that could lead to exclusion from the covenant. Otherwise it is assumed that God is merciful and forgiving, that repentance is always a possibility, and that provision for repentance and forgiveness is made within the law itself in the form of sacrifices for sin. For Judaism, then, salvation is by God's grace, although a basic commitment to observe the law is also required. And this covenant-centred view of Judaism is attested even in the Pauline texts – for it is just such a Judaism of divine election and mercy that is the object of Paul's criticism. Paul rejects Judaism on the basis of an *a priori* christology, for

4. It will be clear that I understand "intextuality" to refer to interactions between texts, and imply no Derridean claim about the ultimacy of textuality. I am unimpressed by the suggestion that the term "intertextuality" should be used sparingly if at all, on account of its allegedly doubtful philosophical pedigree (see S. Porter, "The Use of the Old Testament in the New: A Brief Comment on Method and Terminology", pp. 84–85).

5. E. P. Sanders, *Paul and Palestinian Judaism: A Comparison of Patterns of Religion* (1977); *Paul, the Law, and the Jewish People* (1983).

which Christ is the sole means of salvation from the universal human plight. His objection to Judaism is simply that it is not Christianity.

Anyone tempted to think that Sanders' argument is superfluous might like to read the section entitled "Jewish legalism" in Rudolf Bultmann's *Primitive Christianity in its Contemporary Setting* (1949).[6] Here, with scant reference to any sources, Bultmann interprets the Judaism of the post-exilic period as a futile attempt to escape present historical reality. God's saving history is confined to the scriptural past and the fantastic future of the apocalyptists. For the present, "the nation lived outside history" and in "extraordinary isolation" from the outside world.[7] God's transcendence was now understood metaphysically; ritual was more important that morality, so that Jews "lost sight of their social and cultural responsibilities".[8] The Law had to be obeyed unquestioningly, even when its precepts had become obsolete and meaningless with changing circumstances; no attempt was made to determine their unifying principle. It is true that the Law would not have been subjectively experienced as a burden by those familiar with it from childhood, and that the Old Testament ethical tradition was still a living force. Yet "life makes demands which lie beyond the purview of the devout Jew, and Jewish morality became over-scrupulous and casuistical".[9] This legalistic conception of obedience meant that "the prospect of salvation became highly uncertain".[10] Oddly, however, this uncertainty coexisted with a high level of self-righteousness. Even repentance "became a good work which secured merit and grace in the sight of God. In the end the whole range of man's relation with God came to be thought of in terms of merit, including faith itself."[11] What is most striking in all this is the disapproving, judgmental tone. It is made unambiguously clear that Bultmann personally dislikes the historical phenomenon he is writing about, and that he intends to communicate that dislike to his readers.[12]

Sanders' account of "Palestinian Judaism" is still a valuable corrective to such misreadings. In particular, he successfully marginalizes the

---

6. Pp. 59–71. The English translation of this student textbook was reissued as recently as 1983.

7. *Primitive Christianity*, p. 60.

8. *Ibid.*, p. 62.

9. *Ibid.*, p. 67.

10. *Ibid.*, p. 70.

11. *Ibid.*, p. 71.

12. This is Bultmann at his worst. Bultmann at his best is another matter. I continue to think that he should be taken seriously, and that he should not simply be demonized – in spite of the strictures of Daniel Boyarin (*A Radical Jew*, p. 214). Frank Thielman rightly points out that Bultmann's view of Paul is seriously misread by Sanders himself, who fails to note that Bultmann too sees Paul as reasoning backwards from "solution" to "plight" (*From Plight to Solution*, p. 17).

previously dominant metaphor of "earning" or "meriting" salvation – salvation understood as the "wages" or "reward" for work done, a metaphor which is held to represent the quintessence of Jewish "legalism". In place of this model, Sanders proposes a "covenantal nomism", which rightly insists that the context or framework of law observance is always the gracious divine election of Israel. Yet the expression "covenantal nomism" leaves open the question as to how precisely covenant and law observance are related to one another. While Sanders favours one type of answer to that question, this may not be the only possibility.[13] For example, it is conceivable that, precisely within the covenant, future divine saving action might in some sense be conditional on faithful (though not sinless or graceless) observance of the law. That would still be "covenantal nomism", although not as Sanders understands it. If, for some Jews, law observance within the covenant was indeed a precondition of divine saving action, there is no longer any reason to deny that Paul *might* have contrasted this emphasis on certain modes of human action with an opposing emphasis on the radical priority of divine action. There is no reason why Paul should not have said that the way of righteousness is the faith elicited by *God's* prior saving action, rather than those human actions prescribed within the covenant that may be designated as "works of law".[14]

As Sanders himself understands "covenantal nomism", "covenant" always takes precedence over "nomism". Law observance is a secondary human response to the prior divine redemptive act of the election of Israel; it is the covenant rather than law observance that is fundamental for soteriology. Sanders does not intend to detach covenant from law observance, but he does maintain a clear order of precedence. Always and everywhere, the covenant is radically prior to law observance. God first elects, and only then does God command; God does not elect *in order* to command. Yet this is to underestimate the extent to which, in the

---

13.   The flexibility of "covenantal nomism" is noted by Richard Bauckham, who (unlike Sanders) finds no difficulty in applying it to *4 Ezra* ("Apocalypses", in *Justification and Variegated Nomism*, ed. D. A. Carson, Peter T. O'Brien and Mark A. Seifrid; pp. 173–74).

14.   The first third of Sanders' book is devoted to early rabbinic ("Tannaitic") literature, and it is here that the "covenantal nomism" model is developed. Turning to earlier material (the Dead Sea Scrolls, Ben Sira, *1 Enoch, Jubilees, Psalms of Solomon* and *4 Ezra*), Sanders is insistent that the same "covenantal nomism" is evident here, so that – with the exception of *4 Ezra* – the entire extant Palestinian Jewish literature from 200 BCE to 200 CE is based on a single soteriological model. Would Sanders have reached the same conclusions if (1) he had not started out from the Tannaitic period, and (2) he had been more open to the possibility of theological diversity among the texts of the Second Temple period? For nuanced discussion of Sanders' treatment of rabbinic theology, see H.-M. Rieger, "Eine Religion der Gnade: Zur 'Bundesnomismus'-Theorie von E. P. Sanders", and F. Avemarie, "Bund als Gabe und Recht: Semantische Überlungungen zu berît in der rabbinischen Literatur", in *Bund und Tora*, eds. F. Avemarie and H. Lichtenberger.

literature of this period, covenant and commandment are inseparable.
this literature, it is widely assumed that the Sinai event belongs to the *foundation* of Israel's election, together with the calling of the patriarchs and the exodus from Egypt. In contrast, Sanders gives divine election absolute priority over Israel's law observance, seeking to ground final salvation so far as possible in a gracious divine election that precedes and indeed relativizes the law and its practice. The clearest expression of such a view in Second Temple Jewish texts is to be found in Paul himself. As Paul puts it in Galatians 3.17, "The law, which came four hundred and thirty years afterwards, does not annul a covenant previously ratified by God, so as to invalidate the promise." Covenant is primary, commandment is secondary – chronologically, but above all soteriologically. Yet it is difficult to find convincing examples of such a distinction in non-Christian Jewish texts. If it is possible to generalize about these texts, there seems to be broad agreement that Israel's observance or non-observance of the law is fundamental to the covenant itself. The demand imposed on Israel by Israel's God, with the conditional promise attached that "the one who does these things shall live by them", is integral to the form and content of the covenant. The entire book of Deuteronomy is an amplification of that conditional promise, and there is ample evidence that the authors of early Jewish texts had read Deuteronomy.

We may take as an example an important passage in Ben Sira 17, which opens with reflections on God's creation of humankind in the divine image, and the bestowal of the gifts of dominion and understanding (vv.1–10).[15] At that point, the author suddenly jumps from Genesis 1 directly to Exodus 20, and we find ourselves standing with Israel at Mount Sinai. There, God

> bestowed knowledge upon them, and allotted to them the law of life
> *[nomon zōēs]*. He established with them an eternal covenant *[diathēkēn
> aiōnos]*, and revealed to them his decrees. Their eyes saw the greatness
> of his glory, and their ears heard the glory of his voice. And he said to
> them, Beware all unrighteousness! And he gave commandment to each
> of them concerning his neighbour. (Sir.17.11–14)

The reference to Sinai is clear, and the divine bestowal is described here both as "the law of life" and as "an eternal covenant". As elsewhere in the Greek version of this text, "law" and "covenant" are closely related, if not synonymous.[16] What is significant, however, is not the usage of the term

---

15. Here and elsewhere, citations from this work are from the Hebrew where available in full, otherwise from the Greek translation. For the Hebrew texts, see P. C. Beentjes, *The Book of Ben Sira in Hebrew*.

16. It is possible that, here as elsewhere in the Greek translation, *diathēkē* may represent not *bryt* but *ḥ(w)q*. On this, see the excellent discussion by Anna Maria Schwemer, "Zum

diathēkē but the assumption that the giving and observing of command-ments is fundamental to God's relationship to Israel. This giving and observing of commandments is not here set within a *prior* "covenant" characterized by pure divine electing grace. The law is the law of life in the sense that its commandments point the way to life, and this law is the concrete form of God's covenant with Israel. Of course, the author knows of divine mercy and forgiveness, of repentance and means of atonement, but these motifs do not in any way qualify his conviction that the law and its observance are fundamental to Israel's relation to its God.

This does not mean that the covenant is exclusively linked to the event at Mount Sinai, and that the scriptural use of this term in connection with Abraham in Genesis 15 and 17 is abandoned. In principle, the Abrahamic covenant (or the exodus, or the opening of the Sinai pericope) might serve as scriptural basis for the conviction that covenant or election is radically prior to the commandments and their observance. Ben Sira does not take this view, however. Rather, his view is that the covenant with Abraham and the Sinai event are both foundational to Israel's election, and that the two must be assimilated to one another so as to bring out their interdependence. Ben Sira has this to say about Abraham:

> Abraham was father of a multitude of nations, and no one has been found like him in glory; who kept the commandments of the Most High *[mṣwt 'lywn]*, and entered into covenant with him. In his flesh he cut for him an ordinance, and in testing he was found faithful. Therefore the Lord swore to him with an oath to bless the nations through his seed . . . (Sir.44.19–21)[17]

Here, the promise is confirmed not only on the basis of the offering of Isaac (cf. Gen.22.15–18) but also on the basis of the keeping of commandments and covenant. Abraham was indeed the privileged recipient of divine promises, but he received these promises as one who "kept the commandments of the Most High" – a general reference to a life of obedience to the law, closely associated with "entering into covenant with him". Here the promises are brought within the scope of the law given through Moses at Sinai. At Sinai, as we read in the following chapter, God

> made him hear his voice, and led him into the darkness, and placed commandments in his hand, the law of life and knowledge *[twrt ḥysym*

Verhältnis von Diatheke und Nomos in den Schriften der jüdischen Diaspora Ägyptens in hellenistisch-römischer Zeit", pp. 75–79. Schwemer shows that the Hebrew text already assumes the equivalence of *ḥ(w)q* and *bryt*.

17.   In the Greek translation, "the commandments of the Most High" is replaced by, "the law of the Most High"; "he cut for him an ordinance" by "he established a covenant"; and "to bless" by "to be blessed".

wtbwnh], to teach Jacob his ordinances, and his testimonies and judgments to Israel. (Sir.45.5)[18]

As in Deuteronomy, the promises to the patriarchs are inseparable from "the law of life and knowledge", God's "ordinances" or (in the Greek translation) his "covenant" with Israel. Observance of the law is fundamental to Israel's existence as the covenant people of God. Yet the law that is observed is the law of the God who in the giving of the law enters into covenant with Israel. "The law which Moses commanded us" is identical to "the book of the *covenant* of the Most High God" (Sir.24.23; cf. Ex.24.7). In this text at least, there is no prior covenant to serve as the foundation for a secondary giving and observing of commandments.

Ben Sira takes full account of Israel's elect status, the divine mercy, and the possibility of repentance and atonement. As Sanders says, "the heart of Ben Sirach's religion may be described as confidence in God's justice tempered by confidence in his mercy: pragmatic nomism modified by the assurance of compassion".[19] What is not quite clear, however, is how much this statement actually proves. No doubt it demonstrates that "Ben Sirach's nomism ... is not to be equated with works-righteous legalism in the pejorative sense, in which a man arrogantly thinks that his good deeds establish a claim on God".[20] In defending Ben Sira against such charges, does Sanders also wish to exclude the possibility that, for this author, the human observance of the commandments is the divinely appointed way to life? Presumably he does, for the central argument of Sanders' book is that obedience to the commandments "simply keeps an individual in the group which is the recipient of God's grace".[21] Yet, in an important passage unmentioned by Sanders, Ben Sira draws a rather different conclusion from a key passage in the Torah itself. Towards the end of his life, Moses summarizes the entire significance of the law he has handed down:

> I call heaven and earth to witness against you this day, that I have set before you life and death, blessing and curse. Therefore choose life, that you and your descendants may live... (Deut.30.19)

Ben Sira alludes to this text as he argues for the freedom of the human will, in opposition to the claim that our conduct is determined by God:

> If you wish *['m thps]*, you will keep the commandment, and to practise faithfulness is one's own choice *[rṣwn]* ... He has set before you fire and water: for whichever you will, stretch forth your hand. Before each

---

18. Greek: "...he gave him commandments in person *[kata prosōpon]*". The translator here passes over the allusion to the stone tablets. "Ordinances" is replaced by "covenant".
19. *Paul and Palestinian Judaism*, p. 334.
20. *Ibid.*, p. 345.
21. *Ibid.*, p. 420.

person are life and death, and whichever one chooses shall be given to him. (Sir.15.15–17)[22]

The allusion to Moses' appeal is clear and straightforward. "Life" and "death" represent the two opposing human destinies, understood here as in Deuteronomy in this-worldly terms. There are two respective ways to those two destinies, keeping the commandments or transgressing them; and the way that we take is a matter of our own choice, not of fate.[23] This does not contradict what is said elsewhere about mercy, atonement, repentance, and so on: if any Jews of this period thought in terms of lifelong sinless perfection, Ben Sira was not one of them. Yet the appeal to recognize one's own capacity to observe the commandments, and to find in them the divinely ordained way to true human flourishing, is meant to be taken seriously. What Moses and Ben Sira do *not* say, however, is that obedience to the commandments "simply keeps an individual in the group which is the recipient of God's grace". The group in receipt of God's grace may in some sense be a presupposition of these statements, but it is not what they are actually *about*.

Why, then, is the term "grace" supposed to be the best weapon with which to defend Ben Sira against ill-defined charges of legalism, self-righteousness, and the like? The answer is that Sanders' entire presentation of "Palestinian Judaism" is informed by an unexamined theological value judgment, according to which a religion (Christian or Jewish) *should* give priority to divine grace, while not neglecting consequent human conduct. A non-pejorative account of "Palestinian Judaism" and its "pattern of religion" *must* therefore show how it conforms to this normative principle. But the normative principle is itself the product of Pauline and (liberal) protestant Christianity, divested of christological trappings that are supposed to be inessential. In Sanders no less than in Bultmann, "Judaism" is subjected to a generalized Pauline norm. Without such a norm, there is no need for a non-pejorative account of a Jewish "pattern of religion" systematically to subordinate human law observance to a prior divine election of grace.[24]

---

22. Greek: "commandments" rather than "commandment" (the singular alluding to Deuteronomy 30.11). After "one's own choice", one Hebrew manuscript (A) adds: "If you are faithful in it *['l t'myn bw]*, you too will live" (reading *'m* for *'l*). This was probably also present in ᴾ ` is unattested in the Greek.

`s point is developed at length in *4 Maccabees*, a Hellenistic work in a quite `e. In spite of its Greek philosophical pretensions, the thesis that reason is master `ns seeks to demonstrate the possibility of faithful observance of the law. `vance is seen as the way to life, as the example of the martyrs demonstrates. `e" is eternal life; in *Ben Sira*, abundant life on earth.

`hilip Alexander, "Sanders belongs to a line of interpreters of Tannaitic `1 . . . to stress its 'liberal' side. It is surely significant that most of these

In this brief discussion of Ben Sira, the interpretative dimension of his text has turned out to be highly significant. The author sees himself – and is seen by his translator – as above all an interpreter of the Torah and the other sacred scriptures (cf. Sir.24.23–34; 39.1–3; Prol.). This crucial interpretative dimension is underplayed throughout Sanders' studies in Palestinian Judaism, where his selected texts are characterized by a common "pattern of religion" rather than by their interpretative engagement with the texts of the Torah. Even where the interpretative dimension might seem inescapable, as in the case of *Jubilees*, Sanders looks for evidence of the dogmatic priority of grace and ignores the writer's interpretative perspective on the biblical text.[25] If this were given a more prominent role in the analysis, it is likely that different construals of the relationship between election and law observance would come to light: for it cannot be said that the texts of the Torah itself unambiguously subordinate law observance to a prior election of Israel. The Torah would lead us to expect that some early interpretative texts might see the Sinai event and its aftermath as the culmination and fulfilment of the prior history that runs from creation to exodus. If there are ambiguities and tensions in the scriptural texts, one would expect a degree of interpretative diversity rather than an almost universal conformity to a single "pattern". Attention to the hermeneutical dimension of Second Temple Jewish literature, and to the dialogical relation between scripture and its early interpretation, will liberate both sets of texts from the normative criteria that so often predetermine how they are read.

scholars have either been Christians of liberal Protestant background or Jews arguably influenced by liberal Protestant ideas" ("Torah and Salvation in Tannaitic Literature", p. 271). For scholars such as Schechter and Montefiore, Moore and Sanders, it is "axiomatic that a religion of works-righteousness is inferior to a religion of grace... [N]owhere does any of them radically question the premise that there is something wrong with a religion of works-righteousness. Though they are better informed about classic Judaism and write about it in a more respectful and sympathetic way, scholars such as Moore and Sanders may also be in danger of distorting it by forcing it into a typology which it does not fit" (p. 272). While these comments are thoroughly apposite, there is a danger that, in adopting the traditional polarization of "grace" and "works-righteousness", one might revert to the older model of mutually exclusive soteriological principles. In the model proposed here, it is more a matter of the relationship between the Abraham narrative in Genesis and the Sinai covenant (and its aftermath) in Exodus-Deuteronomy.

25. A symptom of this neglect may be seen in Sanders' "Index of Passages", where references to the Pentateuch represent only about three per cent of the scriptural and non-scriptural passages cited (*Paul and Palestinian Judaism*, pp. 583–608; p. 583).

Christ and Scripture

For Sanders, Paul's claim that righteousness is "not by works of law" is directed against the view that "accepting and living by the law is a sign and condition of favored status" – a view which, "independently of Paul, we can know to have characterized Judaism".[26] While Paul's attack is based on an accurate description of its target, he does not criticize it for deficiencies that could be stated in abstract form – a tendency to promote legalism or self-righteousness, for example. According to Sanders, Paul has come to believe that God's plan of salvation is realized solely in Christ, for the benefit of Jew and Gentile alike, and that the possibility of salvation by an alternative route – through covenant, election and law – can therefore be ruled out. What Paul finds wrong with Judaism is simply that it speaks of something other than God's plan to bring salvation to the world in Christ. For Paul, two differing and incompatible claims are being made about the divine plan of salvation, and for one of these to be right is necessarily for the other to be wrong. While Paul is hypothetically prepared to countenance the possibility that righteousness is by the law and that Christ died in vain (Gal.2.21), in reality he knows that Christ died for our sins to deliver us from the present evil age (Gal.1.4), and that what is in vain is the pursuit of righteousness by works of the law.

At the heart of this proposal is a highly significant emphasis on the sheer concreteness of the positions polarized by the Pauline antithesis. On this view, "not by works of law" refers to a quite specific social praxis, and not to a human proclivity that could be stated in general terms. "By faith in Christ" refers to an equally specific and contingent social reality, irreducible even to a general statement about the priority of divine grace. The two positions are simply incommensurable; they are not open to debate with one another. Alternatively, it may be suggested that the general principle underlying the works/faith antithesis is that of ethnicity. The antithesis corresponds to opposing identifications of the community of salvation – on the one hand, the Jewish people in its covenant relationship with the God of Israel, on the other, a community in which ethnic origin is immaterial. On this basis, it is possible to argue (with J. D. G. Dunn and Daniel Boyarin) that Paul criticizes Judaism for its ethnic exclusiveness, holding as he does that exclusiveness is inherently bad and that an inclusive understanding of the divine–human relationship is inherently good.[27] In contrast, Sanders insists that Pauline christology is not reducible to a

---

26. *Paul, the Law, and the Jewish People*, p. 46.

27. "[W]hat Paul was concerned about was the fact that covenant promise and law had become too inextricably identified with ethnic Israel as such, with the Jewish people marked out in their national distinctiveness by the practices of circumcision, food laws, and sabbath in particular... [W]hat Paul was endeavoring to do was to free both promise and law for a wider

general preference for inclusiveness, any more than it is reducible to a general disapproval of self-righteousness. While Sanders has allowed his account of Judaism to be determined by a general principle relating to the priority of divine grace, no such abstraction is to be found in his presentation of Paul. Here, the difference is a matter of sheer contingent fact, and is established *a posteriori* rather than *a priori*, on the basis of what God has done in Christ. For Sanders, as also for J. L. Martyn, Paul opposes Judaism (and/or judaizing Christianity) on the basis of the purest "positivism of revelation".[28]

The emphasis in Sanders and Martyn on the irreducible concreteness of the Pauline antitheses represents a major conceptual breakthrough. This point is logically independent of the accompanying description of Judaism: for, on Sanders' premises, Paul would have rejected a non-Christian Judaism whatever its views on covenant and mercy, law and obedience. And yet it is over-simplified to see the relationship of Paul to Judaism in terms of sheer juxtaposition and confrontation. On this view, "Judaism" claims that salvation is through covenant and law, while Paul claims that salvation is through Christ alone; there is no scope for dialogue or debate but only for assertion and counter-assertion. This is problematic not because we know on general grounds that dialogue and debate are preferable to assertion and counter-assertion, but because Pauline antithesis formally preserves the possibility of dialogue by acknowledging a relation to the scriptural texts on both sides. Terms such as "faith", "Christ" and "grace" point to a divine saving action announced in the holy scriptures, attested by the law and the prophets (cf. Rom.1.2; 3.21). The expression "works of law" does not point to the same divine saving action, but it does point to the same scriptural texts: for "the law" is itself a

---

range of recipients, freed from the ethnic constraints which he saw to be narrowing the grace of God and diverting the saving purpose of God out of its main channel – Christ" (J. D. G. Dunn, *Romans 1–8*, pp. lxi–lxii). On Boyarin's extreme version of this position, see below.

28. I do not use Bonhoeffer's phrase with pejorative intent. Martyn develops Sanders' point in a more theocentric direction. According to Martyn, Paul "takes his bearings from the good news that in Christ... God has invaded the cosmos"; thus, he "does not argue on the basis of a cosmos that remains undisturbed, a cosmos he shares with the Teachers" – i.e. his opponents (*Galatians*, p. 22). In Sanders' terminology, Paul's thought moves from "solution" to "plight", not the reverse (p. 93n): Paul does not see Christ as the solution to a pre-existing deficiency within Judaism. Martyn's theocentric version of this point is indebted to Ernst Käsemann, the dedicatee of this exceptional commentary, and is perhaps its most significant contribution. In spite of reservations about Martyn's approach to Pauline scriptural exegesis, my own emphasis on the hermeneutical priority of the promise – unconditional divine self-commitment to future saving action on behalf of Abraham and the world – is indebted to his recovery of the concept of divine agency, and to his exegetical outworking of the theological insight that divine being and divine action are one and the same.

text, and its "works" are human actions and abstentions prescribed by this text. The Pauline antitheses encapsulate a disagreement about the interpretation of a text, and they thereby presuppose that there is a shared text about which to disagree.

While the common reference to scripture preserves the possibility of dialogue between Pauline and non-Pauline soteriologies, that does not prove that any such dialogue is actually presupposed in Paul's texts. It is, perhaps, not unusual for *a priori* dogmatic claims to present themselves in the guise of *a posteriori* exegetical results. According to Sanders,

> Most of Paul's arguments are based on Scripture, but we can hardly think that simply by reading the Scripture he came to the view that obedience to the commandments contained in it is not a prerequisite for righteousness. We see, rather, that he arrived at a position which led him to read Scripture and to understand God's intention in a new light.[29]

The implication here is that Paul's disagreement with Judaism derives from a christological conviction that is self-grounded and self-sufficient, and that the pervasive appeal to scripture is merely a secondary consequence of that primary conviction. In this account, the relationship between christology and scripture is a unilateral one: christology determines how scripture is read, but christology itself is not itself determined by the reading of scripture. In the last resort, that would mean that scripture is dispensable for Paul. His christology stands or falls on its own account, irrespective of whether it issues in plausible readings of scripture. It is only his polemical or apologetic concerns that lead him into extensive exegetical engagement, forcing him to defend his christological conviction on ground that is less than ideal for his purposes. If the light that illumines Paul shines upon scripture only from the outside, then the formal possibility of dialogue on scriptural terrain will remain unrealized and Pauline exegesis will be no more than a secondary application of Pauline dogmatism. Thus, as J. L. Martyn puts it, when Paul "hears" a messianic prophecy in a Genesis text, "the point of departure for his exegesis is the advent of Christ".[30] But is what Paul "hears" in the text no more than an echo of what he already knows, independently of scripture?

For Paul, it is more important that scripture should shed light on Christ than that Christ should shed light on scripture. Paul has no independent interest in the meaning of scripture as such: the meaning of scripture is identical to its significance, and both are to be found in its manifold, direct and indirect testimony to God's saving action in Christ. Scripture is not a secondary confirmation of a Christ-event entire and complete in itself; for

29. *Paul, the Law, and the Jewish People*, p. 46.
30. J. L. Martyn, *Galatians*, p. 340.

scripture is not external to the Christ-event but is constitutive of it, the matrix within which it takes shape and comes to be what it is. Paul proclaims not a pure, unmediated experience of Christ, but rather a Christ whose death and resurrection occur "according to the scriptures" (1 Cor.15.3–4). Without scripture, there is no gospel; apart from the scriptural matrix, there is no Christ. The Christ who sheds light on scripture is also and above all the Christ on whom scripture simultaneously sheds its own light. In Galatians 3, for example, Paul does not simply assert that scripture must be read differently in the light of Christ, so as to refute opponents who appeal to scripture on their own ground. Rather, Paul's rereading of scripture is determined by his single apostolic preoccupation with the Christ-event, which must be interpreted through the lens of the scriptural witness.

If there is no unilateral imposition of christological meaning onto scripture, and if the relationship of Christ and scripture is a circular one, then the possibility is reopened of dialogue with scripture, and with others about scripture. Of actual dialogues between the historical Paul and fellow-Jews (Christian or otherwise), we can know very little. Even in the case of Galatians, we can never be sure whether, in citing a text, Paul is countering his opponents' use of the same text. (Indeed, the more important scripture is for Paul, the less likely it is that his selection of texts is determined by his opponents.) Rather, "dialogue" (or "conversation") serves here as a metaphor for our own attempts to retrace the way between the scriptural text and its Pauline and non-Pauline interpretations, and to identify the resulting convergences and divergences.

Intertextual Dynamics

In Paul, scripture is not overwhelmed by the light of an autonomous Christ-event needing no scriptural mediation. It is scripture that shapes the contours of the Christ-event, and to discern how it does so is to uncover the true meaning of scripture itself. Pauline theology is thus intertextual theology: explicit scriptural citations are simply the visible manifestations of an intertextuality that is ubiquitous and fundamental to Pauline discourse. As Richard Hays writes,

> The vocabulary and cadences of Scripture – particularly the LXX – are imprinted deeply on Paul's mind, and the great stories of Israel continue to serve for him as a fund of symbols and metaphors that condition his perception of the world, of God's promised deliverance of his people, and of his own identity and calling. His faith, in short, is one whose articulation is inevitably intertextual in character, and Israel's Scripture

is the "determinate subtext that plays a constitutive role" in shaping his literary production.[31]

As Hays goes on to note, this is not at all "to deny or exclude the presence of nonscriptural influences on [Paul's] discourse".[32] Indeed, Paul's reading of scripture will itself be subject to nonscriptural influences, since this reading is not a mere reproduction of a given content but a dialogue in which the dialogue partners each retain their own culturally specific identity over against the other. Paul is, of course, a specifically Jewish reader of scripture, but neither he nor anyone else possesses a "purely" Jewish identity that can be abstracted from the broader historical and cultural contexts which always co-determine identity.[33] To highlight the intertextual formation of Pauline theology is not to succumb to the questionable dualism of "the Judaism/Hellenism divide".[34]

Hays notes that, unlike Matthew or John, "Paul shows relatively little interest in messianic prooftexts", although he does suggest that "the messianic exegesis of scripture might be assumed as the presuppositional background to Paul's interpretations".[35] How then does Paul use scripture, if not for messianic exegesis?

> What Paul finds in Scripture, above all else, is a prefiguration of the *church* as the people of God ... Paul uses Scripture primarily to shape his understanding of the community of faith; conversely, Paul's experience of the Christian community – composed of Jews and Gentiles together – shapes his reading of Scripture. In short, Paul operates with an *ecclesiocentric* hermeneutic.[36]

---

31.   *Echoes of Scripture*, p.16. The citation is from the literary critic Thomas M. Greene.
32.   *Ibid.*, p. 16.
33.   Illustration of this theoretical point may be seen in Martin Hengel's *Judaism and Hellenism*, with its well-known emphasis on the fact that "by the time of Jesus, Palestine had been under 'Hellenistic' rule and its resultant cultural influence for 360 years" (p. 1).
34.   On this point, see T. Engberg-Pedersen (ed.), *Paul beyond the Judaism/Hellenism Divide*. Engberg-Pedersen's insistence that scholars should "giv[e] up altogether using any form of the Judaism/Hellenism divide as an interpretive lens" (p. 3) is perhaps a little over-zealous; purged of essentialist presuppositions, this distinction can still be heuristically useful. Thus John Barclay can perceptively describe Paul as "an anomalous Diaspora Jew", who, "despite years of association with Gentiles", did not encourage his communities "to draw on the heritage of Hellenism, through which, as other Diaspora Jews had found, a universalized form of Judaism could come to expression ... Instead, we find in Paul a strongly antagonistic cultural stance, combined with a radical redefinition of traditional Jewish categories" (*Jews in the Mediterranean Diaspora*, pp. 387–88). Here, the categories of "Judaism" and "Hellenism" are a necessary means of identifying the "anomaly".
35.   *Ibid.*, pp. 85, 86.
36.   *Ibid.*, p. 86; italics original.

If this is correct, it may be that Paul's letters contain a christology essentially unmediated by scripture (as argued by Sanders and Martyn), alongside which is to be found an intertextually constituted ecclesiology (as argued by Hays). But this seems an unsatisfactory conclusion, for Pauline ecclesiology cannot be isolated in this way. If, for Paul, the church is "the community of people who confess that Jesus Christ is Lord",[37] it is also the community *created* by the exaltation of Jesus Christ as Lord. This exaltation occurs by way of Jesus' death and resurrection, which are the culmination of a life that embodies God's reconciling action on behalf of the entire world. Thus for Paul the divine saving action is the comprehensive context both of "christology" and of "ecclesiology". Christology and ecclesiology speak of different aspects of the many-sided and comprehensive saving event in which the cosmos finds itself "invaded" by God (J. L. Martyn). In that sense, Paul's exegesis is determined by his soteriology.

This soteriological orientation is broad enough to encompass both the christological and the ecclesiological emphases in Paul's scriptural interpretation. The fact that christological exegesis does not take a Matthean form in Paul does not mean that it is absent altogether.[38] Christ is announced not only in the water-producing and strangely mobile rock in the desert (1 Cor.10.4) but also and more importantly in the promise to Abraham of a singular seed (Gal.3.16). Indeed, the entire promise motif that Paul draws from Genesis represents an unconditional divine self-commitment to a future saving action that is universal in scope. Retrospectively, it is evident that the form of that saving action is Christ. The curse pronounced upon the one hung upon a tree has the crucified Christ in view (Gal.3.13). The Genesis depiction of a singular act with universal consequences is typologically applied to Christ (Rom.5.12–21).[39] The radiance that transfigures Moses' face is a type of the glory of God in the face of Christ (2 Cor.3.12–18). The Torah has Christ indirectly in view when it finally announces that its own conditional offer of life to the one who observes its prescriptions (Lev.18.5) issues only in the universality of the curse (Deut.27.26) – thereby creating space for the very different soteriological logic of "faith" (Hab.2.4; cf. Gal.3.10–12).

As for "ecclesiology", it is notable that, in Romans 9, the citations that inform Paul's reflection on the theme of the people of God all refer to God's *action* in salvation or judgment, mostly in the form of first person singular divine discourse:

37. *Ibid.*, p. 86.
38. As Hays of course recognizes. Indeed, Hays finds christological exegesis at one place where I would not, Habakkuk 2.4 (see his "'The Righteous One' as Eschatological Deliverer").
39. See the discussion in my "Is There a Story in These Texts?", pp. 235–39.

In Isaac shall your seed by called. (Gen.21.12; Rom.9.7)

At this time I shall come, and there shall be to Sarah a son. (Gen.18.10, 14; Rom.9.9)

The greater will serve the lesser. (Gen.25.23; Rom.9.12)

Jacob I loved and Esau I hated. (Mal.1.2–3; Rom.9.13)

I will have mercy on whom I have mercy, and I will have compassion on whom I have compassion. (Ex.33.19; Rom.9.15)

For this reason I raised you up, so that I might show forth my power in you, and so that my name might be proclaimed in all the earth. (Ex.9.16; Rom.9.17)

I will call him that is not my people, My people, and her that is not beloved, Beloved. And it shall be that, in the place where it was said to them, You are not my people, there they shall be called sons of the living God. (Hos.2.25, 1; Rom.9.25–26)

If the number of the sons of Israel is as the sand of the sea, the remnant shall be saved. For the Lord will accomplish upon the earth a word that completes and cuts short. (Is.10.22–23; Rom.9.27–28)

If the Lord Sabaoth had not left us seed, we should have become as Sodom and have been like Gomorrah. (Is.1.9; Rom.9.29)

Behold, I lay in Zion a stone of stumbling and a rock of offence, and the one who believes in it shall not be put to shame. (Is.28.16, 8.14; Rom.9.33)

The purpose of these citations is to trace the origin of the Christian community back to the double-edged electing act of God, as announced by God himself in scripture. It would be wise to avoid characterizing Paul's exegesis here in terms such as "ecclesiocentric" or "theocentric", since what is at issue is not the church or God *per se* but the people of God as constituted by the divine electing decision. The suggestion that Paul's scriptural interpretation finds its focus in soteriology appears to be comprehensive enough to cover Romans 9.[40]

---

40. Responding to criticism of his "ecclesiocentric" focus, Hays writes: "Granting that Scripture tells the story of *God's* activity, we must say in the same breath that God's activity is directed towards the formation of a *people*" ("On the Rebound", p. 77; italics original). While this is true, *Echoes of Scripture* and Martyn's *Galatians* probably have some things to learn from each other about, respectively, divine agency and intertextuality in Paul.

Relatively explicit christology is not entirely lacking in Romans 9. Christ is Isaiah's "stone" that marks the parting of the ways between offence and faith, the point at which the divine decision of election and rejection is concretely enacted. Yet Hays is right to find a marked christological reticence in Pauline exegesis. The reason for this reticence is not that Paul draws on scripture only when discussing topics unrelated to christology; for Paul, there are no such topics. Thus, the Isaianic "stone" passage serves to introduce a passage where references to "Christ" (Rom.10.4, 6, 7) and to Jesus as "Lord" (10.9, 12) are prominent. The divine electing decision is realized in the disjunction between non-Christian Israel, which continues zealously to pursue the soteriological programme of which Moses wrote in Leviticus 18.5 (Rom.10.1–5), and the community of Jews and Gentiles that acknowledges God's raising of Jesus to universal lordship (Rom.10.6–13). If Romans 9 focuses on the scriptural announcement of God's electing decision, Romans 10 speaks retrospectively of its concrete realization in the death and resurrection of Christ, and in the faith and the offence to which this gives rise.[41] In the light of Romans 10, it is possible to see that all of the texts cited in Romans 9 are christologically (and ecclesiologically) relevant. Yet, to repeat the point, the christological reference is highly indirect. Where Paul finds the figure of Christ hidden in the scriptural language of Deuteronomy 30.12–14, he consciously and explicitly rewrites the passage, so drastically that it is now ascribed not to Moses but to a personified "Righteousness of faith" (Rom.10.6–10). It seems that Paul respects the fact that the scriptural authors he cites – Moses, Isaiah, and the others – are *not* in a position to share in the distinctively Christian confession of Jesus as Lord. Their testimony to God's saving act in Christ can only be indirect. They anticipate something of the logic of the future divine action, but they know little or nothing of its concrete form.

It follows that, for Paul, what a prophet knows or says will differ from what the apostle knows or says. In this acknowledged difference lies the possibility of dialogue between the apostle and the prophet. The prophet is not simply a cipher for the apostle. Prophetic discourse is one thing, apostolic discourse is another, and, if the latter includes interpretation of the former, it does so in such a way as to respect its specificity and integrity. Scripture testifies to the gospel, but, since its testimony is indirect, it requires the apostolic interpreter to identify the conjunction of the two. Isaiah needs Paul as Paul needs Isaiah; yet Isaiah is not subsumed

---

41. This contrast between the scriptural testimony to election/rejection and its concrete realization in Christ seems a better way to integrate Romans 9.6–29 and 9.30–10.21 than the view that Paul here balances "divine predestination" with "Israel's responsibility" (so C. K. Barrett, "Romans 9.30–10.21: Fall and Responsibility of Israel", in his *Essays on Paul*, pp. 132–53 [pp. 132–37]; E. Dinkler, "Prädestination bei Paulus – Exegetische Bemerkungen zum Römerbrief", in his *Signum Crucis*, pp. 241–69 [p. 241]; J. Fitzmyer, *Romans*, p. 576).

into Paul, for the prophet and the apostle need one another precisely as partners in dialogue.[42]

As Hays argues, a text such as Romans should be read as "an intertextual conversation between Paul and the voice of Scripture".[43] The conversation metaphor preserves the distinctiveness of the two parties. On the one hand, it indicates that there is no question of Paul's effacing his own role as reader and concealing himself behind some rigid and absolutized "authority of scripture". Paul does not simply reproduce the "plain sense" of the text and can sometimes perpetrate a "strong misreading", drawing from it conclusions that can only be described as "outrageous".[44] We should consider that Paul's citations

> often function not as proofs but as tropes: they generate new meanings
> by linking the earlier text (Scripture) to the later (Paul's discourse) in
> such a way as to produce unexpected correspondences . . . [45]

For Paul as for any preacher, interpreting scripture is always a means to the particular ends he has in view, and this gives his interpretation or *use* of scripture a greater freedom and flexibility than those who see scriptural interpretation as an end in itself could ever permit themselves. Indeed, we can learn from Paul to question "the ideal of a perspicuous authoritative text that contains an unchangeable meaning" and that eliminates "the necessary contribution of the reader and the reader's community in the act of interpretation".[46]

On the other hand, the "conversation" model of (Pauline) scriptural interpretation also maintains the distinctiveness of the text over against the interpreter.[47] Paul respects the integrity of the text in his reticence over messianic exegesis, and above all in the fact that his readings derive from his construal of the narrative shape of scripture as a whole:

> Paul finds the continuity between Torah and gospel through a
> hermeneutic that reads Scripture primarily as a *narrative* of divine
> election and promise. God is the protagonist in the story, the one who

42. On this, see J. Ross Wagner, *Heralds of the Good News*. Wagner rightly asks *both* how "Paul's understanding of his gospel and of his own particular calling as an apostle shape his reading of Isaiah", *and* how "Isaiah's oracles help to form Paul's conception of his own message and mission" (p. 3).

43. *Echoes*, p. 35.

44. *Ibid.*, pp. 115, 111.

45. *Ibid.*, p. 24.

46. *Ibid.*, p. 189.

47. It is therefore disappointing that Brevard Childs can find in Hays' book a characterization of the Old Testament as no more than "a deposit of imagery which freely reverberates as 'echoes' within the New Testament" (*Biblical Theology of the Old and New Testaments*, p. 243).

> formed and sustained Israel from Abraham onward, the one whose
> promise of faithfulness stands eternally firm... [Paul] has selected
> fundamental themes of the biblical story as hermeneutical keys to the
> meaning of the tradition. The selection of key themes differs in
> important ways from the selection made in rabbinic Judaism, but Paul's
> claim of hermeneutical continuity is grounded no less thoroughly in the
> texts themselves.[48]

Interpretation as "conversation" guards against the danger that the
discourse of either text or interpreter will be absolutized into an
authoritarian monologue. The simple fact that the texts Paul cites are
also available to other readers, and cannot be "owned" by any one
interpreter, represents an openness in Paul's texts both towards the
scriptural texts themselves but also towards a wider reading community.
The difference Hays notes between Pauline and non-Pauline readings is
itself an opening towards dialogue.

Does Paul have a sense of the shape of the scriptural narrative as a
whole, or does he draw resources from it in an *ad hoc*, disconnected
manner? We might find support for the latter position in the apparent lack
of co-ordination between many of his readings. Within the space of a few
verses, Paul can move from the Abraham/law/Christ schema of Romans 4
to the Adam/Christ/law schema of Romans 5, without any attempt to
show how Adam and Abraham relate to one another. On the other hand, it
is striking that, in the catena of citations in Romans 9 (see above), Paul
follows closely the scriptural ordering of his texts from Genesis and
Exodus before moving on to Hosea and Isaiah. In chapters 4–10 of this
book, we shall locate Paul's interpretative statements on the grid or
template provided by the five books of the Torah, connected as they are by
a gradually unfolding narrative. If this strategy is successful, we shall have
shown that Paul's fragmentary exegetical statements do indeed stem from
a broad construal of the narrative shape of scripture, and that fundamental
scriptural themes function as hermeneutical keys.

The construal of scripture that will emerge is less smoothly linear, more
fractured, than Hays' reference to unfailing divine faithfulness might
suggest. In reading the Torah, Paul chooses to highlight two major
tensions that he finds within it: the tension between the unconditional
promise and the Sinai legislation, and the tension between the law's offer
of life and its curse. These are tensions between *books*: Genesis and
Exodus, Leviticus and Deuteronomy. As we shall see, Paul was by no
means the only early reader to notice such tensions, and to respond to
them. What makes him unusual is the fact that he *exploits* these tensions,
building his entire hermeneutic on them instead of finding ways to

---

48. *Echoes of Scripture*, p. 157; italics original.

mitigate and contain them. The Pauline hermeneutic is fundamentally antithetical; part I of this book will therefore explore the construction of Pauline antithesis, from texts drawn not from the law but from the prophets. This antithetical hermeneutic relates not only to tensions within scripture but also to the interpretative disagreements that they engender. The Pauline hermeneutic thus acknowledges the ongoing reality of interpretative conflict, and traces it back to tensions within the texts themselves. Non-Christian Israel, zealous for God, commits a hermeneutical error in pursuing its own righteousness, but nevertheless has scriptural warrant for its predestined error in the promise of Leviticus 18.5 (cf. Rom.10.1–5). Moses' veil stands for the fact that, in important respects, Moses' text conceals the truth about itself from the community in which it is read, week by week (cf. 2 Cor.3.12–18). Paul remains committed to scriptural coherence, but his antithetical hermeneutic puts it under severe strain. Or rather, as he himself might prefer to think, his hermeneutic is based on the *discovery* of the tension-laden dynamics of the scriptural narrative itself, in its diachronic unfolding – a discovery that serves to illuminate the logic of the gospel. Scriptural dissonance is both uncovered by the gospel and resolved by it, since its theological function is to testify to the gospel.

The Conflict of Interpretations

Paul's antithetical hermeneutic uncovers a dissonance within the text that is also the occasion of ongoing interpretative conflict. This means that our understanding of "conversation" will have to encompass the possibility of disagreement. For Paul, scriptural interpretation and theological controversy often go hand in hand. All too often, we might add. But it may be premature to conclude that Paul's theological and hermeneutical controversies are necessarily a matter of regret. Rather than deciding at the outset to minimize disagreement and to highlight possibilities of consensus, it seems more fruitful to ask what interpretative disagreement actually is, and whether we are right to worry about it.

Disagreement is a familiar social practice in which it is difficult not to engage on a regular basis. It arises from the fact that humans live not in solitude but in community, and that from time to time their respective norms, projects or goals come into conflict. Since interpreting texts is an extension of the interpretative activity that permeates all human interpersonal relations, it is hardly to be expected that the specialized activity will be immune from the disagreements endemic to the wider field. Indeed, the possibility of disagreement is inherent in the practice of textual interpretation: for if a text needs to be interpreted at all, its meaning is not self-evident and there is always room for more than one account of what that meaning is.[49] If it is possible to interpret, then it is also possible to misinterpret; and to claim that misinterpretation has taken place is to engage in the practice of interpretative disagreement. In itself, disagreement is an ethically neutral act. It does not necessarily imply that one party is doing violence to the other, that a human right to freedom of speech is under attack, or that there has been a failure to understand the other's point of view. The ethical risks that accompany disagreement are perhaps no greater than those attending other practices, such as the avoidance of conflict. Disagreement is always an act rather than just an occurrence, and those who engage in it do so on the basis of means and ends they regard as appropriate and rational. Most important of all, disagreement presupposes a shared concern and thus an acknowledgment of community rather than a retreat into isolation. It always intends its own resolution, even if this can only be attained in the form of a negotiated compromise or an agreement to differ.

There are special problems in the field of Pauline interpretation, however. The anxiety is that a Paul in interpretative disagreement with fellow-Jews helps to set in motion a long history of hostility and misunderstanding, and that to perpetuate the disagreement in any way is to ignore the lessons of its appalling modern outcome. This anxiety is not to be lightly dismissed. It is evident, for example, that the Bultmannian interpretation of the relationship between the Pauline gospel and Judaism is not unrelated to the discourse of nineteenth- and twentieth-century European anti-Semitism.[50] This interpretation remained influential until as recently as the 1970s, at which point a recognition of its ethical, historical and theological deficiencies began to establish itself. The more recent inclination to minimize disagreement and to highlight more conciliatory possibilities may be understood as a justified attempt to exorcize that particular ghost. Yet the assertion that disagreement is *necessarily* associated with violence is itself open to criticism – not least because it is itself a violent act that seeks to stifle dissent. In the case of textual interpretation as elsewhere, disagreement is in reality an acknowledgment of community, whereas a pluralism that seeks everywhere to replace disagreement with pure "difference" is actually destructive of community and dialogue.

If ancient or modern traditions of scriptural interpretation generate disagreement, that need not be a symptom of moral crisis. As Alasdair MacIntyre writes:

---

49. Unless an interpretation is (1) God-given, and (2) generally recognized as such – as in the case of Joseph and Pharaoh's dreams.

50. See my discussion of Bultmann in *Text and Truth: Redefining Biblical Theology*, pp. 153–76. "Not unrelated" does not imply that the relationship is straightforward.

> [W]hen a tradition is in good order, it is always partially constituted by
> an *argument* about the goods the pursuit of which gives to that tradition
> its particular point and purpose... Traditions, when vital, embody
> continuities of conflict.[51]

If Paul and the author of *Jubilees* disagree profoundly about the meaning
and significance of the Genesis Abraham narrative, they thereby show that
they participate in a common tradition in which the exegesis of the sacred
text is the way to normative saving truth. They agree (against sceptics then
and now) that a normative truth exists; they agree (against pessimists) that
this truth intends ultimate human well-being; and they agree (against
relativists) that this truth is to be found within the particular tradition for
whose proper articulation they contend. That does not mean that what the
two Genesis interpreters have in common is greater than what divides
them. It does mean that disagreement and agreement are not mutually
exclusive but mutually dependent. Indeed, even in the act of disagreement
unexpected convergences may come to light.

It is a limitation of some recent scholarly work on Paul that, in largely
justified reaction against the Bultmannian tradition, it does not sufficiently
allow for disagreement between Paul and his fellow-Jewish contemporaries. For example, it may be said that Paul was exclusively concerned with
the Gentile world, and that neither his gospel nor his understanding of the
law have any direct bearing on the beliefs and practices of the Jewish
community.[52] Or it may be said that Paul's strictures are directed primarily
at a form of *Christian* Judaism, and that he leaves the historically
dominant non-Christian variety to go its way unhindered.[53] Or it may be
said that Paul's christology is simply Christian superstructure erected on a

---

51. *After Virtue*, p. 222; italics added.

52. See, *passim*, L. Gaston, *Paul and the Torah*; S. K. Stowers, *A Rereading of Romans*; J.
G. Gager, *Reinventing Paul*. Gager formulates with great clarity one of the primary
methodological assumptions of this school of thought: "Any statement that begins with the
words, 'How could a Jew like Paul say X, Y, Z about the law', must be regarded as misguided.
In all likelihood Paul, the apostle to the Gentiles, is not speaking about the law as it relates to
Israel but only about the law and Gentile members of the Jesus-movement" (p. 44; original
italicized). Gager shares with his questioner the assumption that, on the basis of ahistorical
and essentialist notions of "Jewish identity", we can impose *a priori* limits on what first-
century Jews could say about the Torah. Gager's conservative agenda is further exposed when
he states that "we should always read [Paul] within the context of traditional Jewish thought,
not against it" (p. 46). "Traditional Jewish thought" is a poor description of the ideological
ferment of Second Temple Judaism, which one could hardly be "within" without taking up
positions "against" competing claims to articulate authentic Jewish scriptural tradition.

53. See J. L. Martyn, *Galatians*, p. 38; Galatians 1.13–14 is acknowledged to be
problematic for this view. Martyn's careful demarcation at this point is in some tension with
his claim that Galatians is concerned with "the polarity between apocalypse and religion"
(*ibid.*).

firm foundation of shared Jewish convictions.[54] In their different ways, these scholarly positions all register deep unease at the proposition that disagreement is a rather fundamental element in Pauline discourse. No such inhibitions are felt by Daniel Boyarin, however, who insists that "I *do* (unlike Davies and Sanders) believe that Paul was motivated by a critique of Judaism, if not by the slanderous libel that Luther accused him of."[55] For Boyarin, Paul is emphatically a Jew – and yet his Jewishness no longer consists in a conservative adherence to what "all Jews believed", but comes to expression precisely in his radicality. This Paul is "a radical Jew". To be radical is, by definition, to be in disagreement with almost everyone else; and to be a radical Jew is to be in disagreement with most fellow-Jews about a common heritage of scripture and tradition. Paul remains Jewish as he argues that righteousness is through faith rather than works of law – not because many other Jews were saying the same (they were not), but because Paul's claim is concerned wholly with intra-Jewish issues of scriptural interpretation and hermeneutics. It should also be noted that a more Jewish Paul is in no sense a less Christian one: the point is that these are not mutually exclusive categories.

In the present book too, Paul is a radical Jew. Here, however, Paul's distinctive reading of scripture produces a rather different interpretative disagreement to the one that Boyarin finds in him. Boyarin rightly emphasizes that the disagreement occurs within a shared tradition: for "Paul lived and died convinced that he was a Jew living out of Judaism", and he genuinely represents "one option which Judaism could take in the first century".[56] The disagreement is therefore a matter of hermeneutics. Unfortunately, the hermeneutic Boyarin ascribes to Paul is one that simply erases the concrete particularity of scripture: for Paul was "a Jewish cultural critic" who "was motivated by a Hellenistic desire for the One, which among other things produced an ideal of a universal human essence, beyond difference and hierarchy".[57] This led him to reinterpret "the

---

54. J. D. G. Dunn distinguishes between "the deepest level" of Paul's thought, that of his "inherited convictions", and the "middle, pivotal level", which was "the faith which came to him on the Damascus Road" (*The Theology of Paul the Apostle*, p. 713). At the deepest level, "Paul's faith remained in large measure the faith and religion of his fathers... He thought of his new faith in Jesus Christ not as a departure from that older faith, but as its fulfilment" (p. 716). Paul's beliefs about God "were Jewish through and through" (p. 29), and "God continued to be the bedrock and foundation of his theology" (p. 717). It is assumed that, insofar as it can be shown to be "Jewish", Paul's thought is non-contentious; a "more Jewish" Paul will therefore be an eirenical Paul. Does this allow Paul to be (in Boyarin's phrase) a "radical Jew", in a manner that gives equal weight to both terms? On Dunn's interpretation of Pauline God language, see my "The Triune Divine Identity".

55. *A Radical Jew*, p. 11; italics original.

56. *Ibid.*, p. 2.

57. *Ibid.*, pp. 2, 7.

physical, fleshy signs of the Torah, of historical Judaism ... as symbols of that which Paul takes to be universal requirements and possibilities for humanity".[58] Paul thereby sacrifices Jewish particularities to his quest for a universal humanity signified in the symbol of the "Christ". Boyarin finds this reading of Paul in a single proof-text, Galatians 3.28. And yet Paul's apparently universalizing conclusion that "you are all one in Christ Jesus..." is followed by a remarkably particularistic sequel: "... and if you are Christ's, you are Abraham's seed, heirs according to promise" (Gal.3.29). This ties the preceding verse back into the reading of Israel's scriptural history in terms of the dialectic of promise and law, which is the concern of the chapter as a whole. "Neither Jew nor Greek" no doubt has to do with Paul's elimination of the excised foreskin as the necessary signifier of participation in this history: but to be opposed to a specific particular is not to be opposed to particularity in general.

Paul's disagreement with fellow-Jews about scriptural interpretation is not primarily to do with the competing claims of universality and particularity. Where universalizing claims occur, they articulate a Jewish universalism that remains thoroughly particularistic – as in Paul's appeal to Adam, a figure known only to Jewish scripture. Boyarin's anti-particularist Paul is at odds with his own acknowledgment (following Hays) that Paul was "a consummate reader of the Bible", and that it is "impossible to assume that Paul, any more than the Rabbis, would have been content to falsify or manipulate Scripture (in his own eyes) to win his arguments".[59] If Paul finds in the scriptural texts little more than the platonizing ideology he brings to them, he is actually a rather poor reader of the Bible – one who reinforces the familiar stereotype of the (pre-critical) reader as imposing preformed meanings onto texts and learning nothing from them. It is just this account of pre-critical reading that the present work seeks to dismantle, substituting for it a *dialogical* under-standing of the act of reading.

So our concern will be with the consummate reader of the Bible, not with the essentialist who yearns for the One. We shall follow him in his reading of the Bible, alongside and over against other readers of the Bible who also disagree among themselves about how best to articulate the shared scriptural tradition.

Boyarin's pointed remark about Luther's "slanderous libel" compels me to add a slightly defensive postscript. In the course of these studies in the early interpretation of scripture, it may turn out that one major faultline between the Pauline and non-Pauline readings is not wholly unrelated to the exegesis and theology of Martin Luther. Among all other possible

58. *Ibid.*, p. 7.
59. *Ibid.*, p. 11.

interpretative differences, there does appear to be a distinction between a reading of the Torah that lays all possible emphasis on the promise to Abraham of unconditional divine saving action, worldwide in its scope, and a reading centred upon the demand emanating from Sinai for specific forms of human action and abstention. Luther would hardly have been surprised at the suggestion that the Pauline antitheses he exploits are grounded in divergent readings of the Torah: and he features accordingly in the pages that immediately follow. This will be virtually his only appearance in the book, however, and it is not part of my intention (conscious, subconscious, or whatever) to "rehabilitate Luther".[60] Many of the reasons for the current anti-Lutheran climate in Pauline studies are good ones, and the retractations I would now make of things I said on this matter in an earlier book are few and qualified.[61] Yet there is a potential danger that certain exegetical possibilities will be ruled out in advance merely because of their apparent proximity to Luther. Such an attitude is more suited to some heresy-hunting orthodoxy than to a critical scholarly discipline.

60. I leave that to the likes of Stephen Westerholm, who throws out the challenging if mystifying suggestion that "students who want to understand Paul but feel they have nothing to learn from a Martin Luther should consider a career in metallurgy" (*Israel's Law and the Church's Faith*, p. 173).

61. I refer to my *Paul, Judaism and the Gentiles* (1986), a work in a post-Sanders vein. In the present work, I reject the assumption that Pauline references to "works of the law" must always be relativized by appeal to a prior theology of election and covenant. On the other hand, the insistence that "works of the law" really does refer to a Jewish praxis centred upon a text – and not, for example, to morality in general or to questionable ecclesial practices – still seems to me to be valid. Despite a notable lack of nuance at certain points, I would also defend the "sect" model against the criticisms of, among others, Dunn (*Romans 1–8*, p. lvii: "astonishing") and Boyarin (*A Radical Jew*, p. 50: "quite astonishing"). The position developed in this book is broadly compatible with such a model.

Part One

Antithesis

Chapter 1

Justification and Hermeneutics

Half a millennium ago, there came into being a reading of Paul's letters – and especially of his letters to the Romans and to the Galatians – that continues to cast its long shadow over the present. According to Martin Luther, the Christian gospel itself is most fully and adequately articulated in these Pauline letters, in comparison to which even the Gospels according to Matthew, Mark and Luke are of only secondary importance – to say nothing of still more marginal texts such as the Epistle of James, that unfortunate "epistle of straw".[1] The Epistle to the Romans, we are told, "is really the chief part of the New Testament, and is truly the purest gospel"; every Christian should know it by heart, and find in it each day the food and drink of the soul.[2]

Negatively, Luther views this letter as a sustained attack on the assumption that righteous living is within our unaided grasp. Its chief purpose is "to break down, to pluck up, and to destroy all wisdom and righteousness of the flesh . . . "[3] This assault is directed not so much against our vices as against our virtues – a point that is crystallized in a stark reworking of the typology of exodus:

> The whole exodus of the people of Israel formerly symbolized that exodus which they interpret as one from faults to virtues. But it would be better to understand it as an exodus from virtues to the grace of Christ, because virtues of that kind are often greater or worse faults the less they are accepted as such . . . [4]

Positively, the Epistle to the Romans is full of comfort. In it there comes to expression "the chief article and foundation of the gospel", which is "that before you take Christ as an example, you accept and recognize him as a gift".[5] Luther and Paul alike "preach so strongly against works and insist

1. See Luther's "Prefaces to the New Testament" (1522), *LW* 35, pp. 361–62.
2. "Preface to the Epistle of St Paul to the Romans", *LW* 35, p. 365.
3. *Lectures on Romans* (1515–16), *LW* 25, p. 135.
4. *LW* 25, pp. 136–37.
5. "A Brief Instruction on what to look for and expect in the Gospels" (1521), *LW* 35, p. 119.

on faith alone, for no other reason than that the people may be offended, stumble, and fall, in order that they may learn to know that they are not saved by their good works but only by Christ's death and resurrection".[6] This last passage alludes to the Pauline text controversially rendered by Luther in the words: "So halten wir dafür, dass der Mensch gerecht werde ohne des Gesetzes Werke, allein durch den Glauben" (Rom.3.28).[7] If, in relation to the New Testament as a whole, the Epistle to the Romans is "the purest gospel", then this single statement, summarizing as it does the argument of Romans 1–4, is its definitive expression.[8]

For Luther, the Epistle to the Romans is the key to the New Testament. No less significantly, it is also the key to the Old. "It appears", writes Luther, "that [Paul] wanted in this one epistle to sum up briefly the whole Christian and evangelical doctrine, and to prepare an introduction to the whole Old Testament."[9] In reading the scriptures of both Testaments, the crucial distinction is the one between Moses and Christ, the Law and the Gospel; and it is Romans, and specifically its opening section, that inculcates this distinction – supported, of course, by material elsewhere in the Pauline corpus, notably Galatians. If the biblical canon is envisaged as a circle in which some texts stand closer to the centre while others are located towards the periphery, it is the Pauline texts that enable Luther to identify this centre and to determine the position of other texts in relation to it. However firmly we believe that Old Testament scripture is God's own Word, we will fundamentally misunderstand it if we have not learned from Paul that we are justified by faith, through the gift of God in Christ, and not by works of law. This is the thread that will guide us safely through the labyrinth of the sacred texts.

When, long after Luther's time, "Pauline theology" becomes an independent object of investigation, the opening chapters of Romans continue to shape the agenda. Scholarship either confirms that this opening section of Paul's least context-bound and most systematic letter provides the key to the edifice of Pauline theology; or it rejects this view, and seeks for some alternative construal. In either case, Luther himself is not far away, whether as a sheltering paternal presence or as a ghost to be exorcized. Indeed, the ghost that one seeks to banish may itself be no other than the repressed figure of the father – in which case we may have to

6. "On Translating: An Open Letter" (1539), *LW* 35, p. 196.
7. "And so we maintain that the human being becomes righteous without the law's works, solely through faith."
8. Romans 3.28 is ultimately more significant for Luther even than "the righteousness of God" in Romans 1.17, highlighted in the well-known (and historically problematic) autobiographical fragment of 1545.
9. "Preface to Romans", *LW* 35, p. 380.

acknowledge that this figure is inescapable, and learn to accommodate ourselves to his presence.

Of the many twentieth-century attempts to banish the ghost of Luther from Pauline exegesis, Albert Schweitzer's remains one of the most illuminating and insightful. In his initial study of the history of modern Pauline scholarship (1911), Schweitzer again and again attacks the enduring assumption that "Pauline theology can be divided into practically the same individual doctrines as that of Luther, Zwingli, and Calvin" – with the result that modern scholarship "continues to be embarrassed by a considerable remnant of the prepossessions with which the interpretation of Paul's doctrine was approached in the days of the Reformation".[10] The Reformation is here presented as the great obstacle that the modern scholarly study of Paul has so far failed to overcome. Although "the Reformation fought and conquered in the name of Paul", its appeal to him was of doubtful validity; for "Reformation exegesis reads its own ideas into Paul, in order to receive them back again clothed with Apostolic authority."[11] For Schweitzer, the Reformation's apostle of faith is a figure created in its own image and has little to do with the Paul of history.

In contrast to the individualistic tendencies of the Pauline concept of righteousness by faith, so beloved by the Reformers, Pauline theology is now said to be shaped by an intense, dogmatic conviction about the imminent end of the present world order, and by the belief that, in the interim between Jesus' resurrection and the general resurrection, Christians already participate with Jesus in the life of the age to come. In the opening pages of the belated sequel to the 1911 book, *The Mysticism of Paul the Apostle* (1930), Schweitzer describes as follows the "fundamental thought" of Pauline mysticism:

> I am in Christ; in him I know myself as a being who is raised above this sensuous, sinful, and transient world and already belongs to the transcendent; in him I am assured of resurrection; in him I am a Child of God.[12]

For Schweitzer, this "being-in-Christ" is the foundation of Paul's entire theology. Pauline mysticism differs from other mysticisms at two crucial points. First, it is a Christ-mysticism without a corresponding God-mysticism. We are "in Christ", but we are hardly ever said to be "in God". Second, this Christ-mysticism has its roots in Jewish eschatology. The

10. *Paul and his Interpreters*, p. 33.
11. *Paul and his Interpreters*, p. 2. Schweitzer had earlier accused modern protestant exegesis of doing something similar in the case of the historical Jesus.
12. *The Mysticism of Paul the Apostle*, p. 3; Schweitzer proceeds to list Galatians 2.19–20, 3.26–28, 4.6, 5.24–25, 6.14; 2 Corinthians 5.17; Romans 6.10–11, 7.4, 8.1–2, 9–11, 12.4–5; and Philippians 3.1–11, as the primary "utterances of Pauline mysticism" (pp. 3–4).

mystical experience of the eternal in the temporal is here an experience of the future in the present. On the basis of his belief that the resurrection of Jesus was the beginning of the general resurrection, Paul concludes that "the powers of death and resurrection which were made manifest in Jesus ... are now at work upon the corporeity of those who are elect to the Messianic Kingdom, and enable them to assume the resurrection mode of existence before the general resurrection of the dead takes place".[13] Thus the law loses its binding authority, for it can have no place in the age to come but belongs only to the age that Christ has now brought to an end.

This eschatologically conditioned mysticism is, Schweitzer argues, ultimately incompatible with the doctrine of "righteousness by faith" expounded first in Galatians, in close connection with the doctrine of life in Christ, and subsequently in Romans 1–4, in a "pure" form from which Christ-mysticism is absent. Here, in fundamental statements such as Romans 3.28 and 4.5, it is said that righteousness is obtained by faith as such, without any reference to being in Christ. And yet,

> Paul cannot mean that righteousness comes directly from faith in the strict sense, since this is in fact impossible. All the blessings of redemption which the believer possesses flow from the state of being in Christ, and from that alone. Faith in the abstract has no effective significance: it becomes operative only through that being in Christ, beginning at baptism, to which it leads.[14]

Thus, the texts that teach that we are justified by faith and not by works of law, and that we are to believe in the one who justifies the ungodly – precisely the texts that are so central for Luther – are for Schweitzer incompatible with Paul's most fundamental theological convictions. In ascribing righteousness to faith itself, and not to being in Christ, Paul says something other than what he really means. According to Schweitzer, this tension between conviction and articulation arises in part from purely linguistic considerations: Paul may have decided that "righteousness by faith" would be preferable to "righteousness in Christ" as an antithesis to "righteousness by the law", since "faith" represents the human action that corresponds to obedience to the law. More significantly, the terminology of "righteousness by faith" is determined by the scriptural texts that Paul cites. His doctrine of freedom from the Law

> can no doubt be derived with demonstrative clearness from the eschatological doctrine of redemption and the mystical doctrine of the dying and rising again with Christ. But what profits logical correctness when his opponents have scripture on their side? And the scripture is

---

13. *The Mysticism of Paul the Apostle*, p. 101; translation modified.
14. *Ibid.*, p. 206; translation modified.

theirs to use in all its utterances save two. These two passages were
Paul's brilliant discovery ... For Paul these two passages – Gen.xv.6
and Hab.ii.4 – express the real meaning of the scriptures. With them he
invalidates all others. But in order to be able to use them he must
formulate the doctrine of righteousness through being-in-Christ as the
doctrine of righteousness by faith.[15]

Constrained as he is by these scriptural texts, the Paul of Romans is
compelled to dispense with the eschatological-mystical explanation of the
end of the law's jurisdiction, and to find an alternative explanation in
factors inherent to the law and to human nature. The result is an
apologetically motivated, individualistic and intellectualistic understanding of salvation, in tension with Paul's own quasi-physical doctrine of
redemption as a cosmic event. It is impossible to derive the doctrine of
redemption from the doctrine of righteousness by faith; on the contrary,
the latter is a mere fragment of the former. "Once Paul has left behind the
discussion necessitated by his scriptural argument about faith-
righteousness and law-righteousness, it is of no more service to him."[16]

This, then, is the exegetical argument that leads to Schweitzer's well-
known claim that "the doctrine of righteousness by faith is therefore a
subsidiary crater, which has formed within the rim of the main crater – the
mystical doctrine of redemption through the being-in-Christ".[17] Allowing
for a little updating of the terminology ("participation" in place of
"mysticism", perhaps), the argument remains impressive.[18] But what of
that subsidiary crater, situated not at a distance but within the rim of the
main crater? What is the function of the subsidiary theme *within* the

---

15. *Ibid.*, p. 209.
16. *Ibid.*, p. 221.
17. *Ibid.*, p. 225. In *Paul and his Interpreters*, Schweitzer indicates that his "subsidiary
crater" claim is actually a variant of a position taken by others. For example, H. Lüdemann
(1872) had attempted to show that the tensions within Pauline theology "find their ultimate
explanation in the coexistence of two different doctrines of man's nature and two different
doctrines of redemption" – an "ethico-physical" doctrine and a "juridical" one (p. 30). The
juridical view is expressed in Romans 1–4, and derives from Jewish roots; the Hellenistic
ethico-physical view takes over from Romans 5 onwards, and for Paul is the more important
of the two (*ibid.*). Indeed, Schweitzer claims that this distinction was accepted by almost all
scholars of the later nineteenth century, and that "in general the ethical set of ideas is regarded
as the original creation of the Apostle, and is assumed to represent the deepest stratum in his
thought" (p. 32). Schweitzer's own contribution is to derive the "ethico-physical" strand from
Jewish apocalyptic.
18. When Schweitzer's *Die Mystik des Apostels Paulus* was belatedly published in 1930,
the title seemed to locate it within the dichotomy of *Die Mystik und das Wort* created by
Brunner's anti-Schleiermacher polemic of that title in 1924. Some resulting scholarly
misreadings are usefully though briefly discussed by Barry Matlock, *Unveiling the Apocalyptic
Paul*, p. 54. For a generally persuasive attempt to bring the term "mysticism" back into
Pauline studies, see Alan Segal, *Paul the Convert*, pp. 34–71.

broader context of Paul's "doctrine of redemption"? The distinction between the two is based wholly on Romans 1–8, where, from chapter 5 onwards, "righteousness by faith" gives way to the terminology of union with Christ.[19] How and why does this shift take place? Is Paul moving from the periphery to the centre, from the foundation to the superstructure, or just from one room to another?

It is understandable that, on the basis of the Pauline corpus as a whole, Schweitzer chose to emphasize the priority of participation in Christ over righteousness by faith. Pauline Christians experience a transformed life in union with Christ, through the Spirit, within the Christian community. The Christ with whom they are now united once died and rose for them and will one day return, and the present reality of union arises from the reality of that past and that future. Participation in Christ is fundamental for Paul; and yet this theme is strikingly absent from Romans 1–4, the very passage in which we were supposed to find the heart of the Pauline gospel. Indeed, references to Christ of any kind are extremely sparse here. In the long argument of Romans 1.16–4.25, Christ is briefly identified as the agent of judgment (2.16), as the origin and object of faith (3.22, 26), as the one whose atoning death secures redemption (3.24–25), and as the one who died and was raised for us (4.25). That is all. No other Pauline passage of comparable length is so sparing in its references to Christ. These references are almost as scarce when Paul is speaking of faith (1.16–17; 3.21–4.25) as when he is speaking of sin, guilt and the law (1.18–3.20). It is true that christological presuppositions and implications are often present even where they are not made explicit. As we shall see, that is emphatically the case here. And yet the paucity of direct references to Christ is very striking. Paul's reader is left in no doubt that we are justified by faith and not by works of law, but the christological basis of this faith is merely hinted at in statements that are concise to the point of obscurity (cf. 3.22–26).

As far as it goes, Schweitzer's solution to this problem is broadly correct. When Paul speaks here of "righteousness by faith" (1.16–17; 3.21–4.25), he does so on the basis of two crucial scriptural texts that associate righteousness with faith (Habakkuk 2.4, quoted in Romans 1.17; Genesis 15.6, quoted in Romans 4.3 and *passim*). In speaking as he does, Paul respects the fact that these pre-Christian texts cannot explicitly refer to Christ. The gospel was indeed promised beforehand through the prophets in the holy scriptures, and the content of this gospel is indeed God's Son (Rom.1.2–3); yet the direct way in which Paul as an apostle can speak of Jesus Christ differs from the indirect way of the prophet. Insofar as he

19. In Galatians and Philippians 3, "in Christ" and "righteousness" terminologies occur in the same contexts. With the exception of the transitional chapter 5, they are kept apart in Romans 1–8.

speaks on the basis of the prophets, Paul himself cannot directly speak of Christ. It is, then, the scriptural basis of Paul's argument in Romans 1–4 that limits the possibility of explicitly christological statements. Christology – God's act in Christ – is of course fundamental to this argument from beginning to end, and it will be totally misunderstood if its christological foundation is overlooked. And yet for the most part this remains implicit. Paul must speak of Christ with a degree of reticence and indirectness if he is to show that his gospel can be articulated through "scripture alone" – not only the two texts that speak of faith and righteousness, but also the other related Abrahamic material and the texts cited in Romans 3.10–18 as articulating the message of the law. Paul's doctrine of righteousness by faith is an exercise in scriptural interpretation and hermeneutics. This is the language he uses when arguing that his understanding of God's act in Christ conforms to scripture.

According to Schweitzer, such a doctrine of righteousness by faith cannot be made the basis of all Pauline theology. Paul needs this "subsidiary doctrine" to enable him to debate the meaning of the law and its relation to the gospel on inner-scriptural grounds. "More he does not ask of it."[20] Yet it is unsatisfactory to conclude that the conceptuality that lies at the heart of Galatians and major sections of Romans lies on the periphery of Paul's real theological concerns – as though, just at these points, Paul is responding to contingent problems that compel him to use a language fundamentally alien to him.[21] If Luther claimed that Paul was most himself in these texts, it is hardly convincing to reply that, on the contrary, Paul here is *least* himself, and that Romans and Galatians give a distorted view of his "real" theological priorities. "Real" by which criteria?

If the language of righteousness and faith has a specific, identifiable purpose, that is not to diminish its significance. In arguing that righteousness is by faith, Paul attempts to show *nothing less* than the conformity of his gospel to the fundamental dynamic of scripture, as articulated in his selected texts. If we restate Schweitzer's point in these positive terms, we find that we have unexpectedly returned to Luther – for whom, as we recall, Paul wrote Romans as "an introduction to the whole Old Testament". By a roundabout route, and without noticing where it has led him, Schweitzer actually confirms that Luther is right in at least this one crucial respect: the Pauline doctrine of righteousness by faith is indeed intended to serve as the hermeneutical key to scripture. Luther assumes that this hermeneutical role demonstrates the importance of the doctrine; Schweitzer, its unimportance. For Luther, the Pauline doctrine of

---

20. *The Mysticism of Paul the Apostle*, p. 225.
21. For a recent restatement of this Schweitzer-like position, see U. Schnelle, "Transformation und Partizipation als Grundgedanken paulinischer Theologie", pp. 70–75.

righteousness by faith has been given to enable us to read the Old
Testament aright. Without this thread to guide us, we fail to grasp how, in
the Old Testament writings, "Christ is wrapped in swaddling clothes and
laid in the manger".[22] For Schweitzer the Pauline appeal to scripture is
artificial and unconvincing, occasioned merely by immediate apologetic or
polemical needs. The swaddling clothes and the manger are now provided
by Jewish apocalyptic, and the Old Testament scriptures are folded up and
restored to their rightful place in an earlier phase of the history of religion.
Schweitzer's evaluation of the doctrine of righteousness by faith creates a
sharp disjunction between the scriptural and the apocalyptic strands of
Paul's Jewish heritage.[23] And yet the disjunction is untenable. A
Hellenizing Paul could perhaps be detached from his Jewish scriptural
heritage, but not a Jewish one.[24]

A hermeneutical understanding of Paul's doctrine of righteousness by
faith makes it possible to see the divine saving action in Christ as itself a
hermeneutical event. From this perspective, what takes place in Christ is
the emergence of a new reading of the scriptural texts. Texts that are
already authoritative, and that have long been read and interpreted as
such, are now read and interpreted *differently*. The nature of this difference
can only be determined by setting up a three-way conversation between the
scriptural text and its Pauline and non-Christian Jewish appropriations. In
this and the following chapters, the aim is to construct a conversation
along these lines, based on the first of the texts that Schweitzer rightly
identified as fundamental for Paul's hermeneutics of faith: Habakkuk 2.4.

The Rhetoric of Citation

Shortly after he begins to unfold the positive counterpart to the preceding
account of human existence under the law, Paul turns to the figure of
Abraham to confirm and amplify his thesis that righteousness is by faith
and not by law observance (Rom.4.1–25). A simple analysis of Paul's
argument in Romans 3.21–4.25 runs as follows:

22. "A Brief Instruction on what to look for and expect in the Gospels", *LW* 35, p. 122.
23. If Paul's doctrines of redemption and justification are shaped respectively by Jewish
apocalyptic tradition and by Jewish scripture, it should be possible to extend the concept of
intertextuality beyond the "righteousness" passages into the "participatory" ones: for
intertextuality becomes explicit in scriptural citation but is not to be reduced to it. This
possibility lies beyond the scope of the present work, however.
24. Schweitzer appears to regard the categories of "Hellenistic" and "Jewish" as mutually
exclusive. For an acute analysis of the cultural background to this assumption, see Dale
Martin, "Paul and the Judaism/Hellenism Dichotomy", pp. 32–44.

The Thesis (3.21–26)
Polemical Development (3.27–31)
Scriptural Proof from the Story of Abraham (4.1–25)

This is in fact the outline offered by Ernst Käsemann;[25] others are similar, if less succinct.[26] It is assumed that Paul *first* states his "thesis" about the righteousness of God in his own words, adding some preliminary clarifications in response to anticipated questions, and *then* turns to scripture to show that it supports the contentious position he has just asserted. Although the scriptural proof is over twice as long as the preceding section, it is the assertions of Romans 3.21–31 that are held to carry the greatest theological and rhetorical weight. These statements express the heart of Paul's doctrine of righteousness by faith, admittedly using cryptic and perhaps traditional language in doing so. For Käsemann, the scriptural argument is important and necessary for Paul, but overall it does not display the doctrine of justification as "the centre of his theology and of the present epistle" as effectively as "the thesis" and its "polemical development" at the close of chapter 3.[27] Indeed, in order to re-establish the doctrine of justification as the Pauline "centre", it may seem necessary to *minimize* its hermeneutical and exegetical dimension: for it is just this dimension that Schweitzer's "secondary crater" argument so strongly emphasizes.[28] If, in Romans 3.21–4.25, the trend of Paul's unfolding

---

25. *Romans*, pp. 91, 101, 105.

26. For U. Wilckens, Romans 3.21–31 ("Die Offenbarung der Gerechtigkeit Gottes") comprises (1) 3.21–26, "Die These: Die Glaubensgerechtigkeit aufgrund der Sühnetat der Gerechtigkeit Gottes im Tode Christi" (*Römer*, 1.182); and (2) 3.27–31, "Die Universalität der Glaubensgerechtigkeit für Juden wie Heiden" (1.244). This is followed by 4.1–25, "Begründung der Glaubensgerechtigkeit aus der Schrift" (1.257), which is divided into three further subsections. Dunn's analysis is similar. 3.21–31 outlines God's saving righteousness to faith in Christ Jesus, and comprises: (1) "The Decisive Demonstration of God's Righteousness in the Death of Jesus" (*Romans*, 1.161); and (2) "The Consequences for the Self-Understanding of the Jewish People" (p. 183). 4.1–25 is headed, "Abraham as a Test Case" (p. 194). A minority of commentators (e.g. Barrett and Schlier) treat 3.21–31 as a whole, without a subdivision at v.27.

27. Cf. Käsemann, *Romans*, p. 92. This evaluation is implicit rather than explicit in Käsemann's reading. His many references to "the justification of the ungodly" refer back to a text in chapter 4 rather than chapter 3, and he can claim that, in the allusion to creation out of nothing in Romans 4.17, the radicalism of the doctrine of justification is brought out "as hardly anywhere else" (p. 123). Yet he can also bluntly state, with reference to 4.9–12, that, "[w]hile it uses synagogue methods, Paul's argument from Scripture is worthless for us, since it ignores the historical meaning of the text" (p. 115). The theologically valuable elements in Romans 4 emerge only when its character as "scriptural proof" is subtracted.

28. Käsemann rejects Schweitzer's "secondary crater" thesis as a characteristic aberration of "critical Liberalism" (*Romans*, p. 24). "The doctrine of justification is the *specifically Pauline* understanding of christology, just as the latter is the basis of the former" (*ibid.*; italics added).

argument is to show that his doctrine of justification is not simply "his" but is taught by scripture, the tendency of Käsemann's interpretation – and of many others – is to put this argument into reverse. Irrespective of Paul's hermeneutical and exegetical concerns, the doctrine of justification is here understood precisely as *Paul's* doctrine, taught by him alone, its scriptural dimension merely an accommodation to current polemical requirements and exegetical conventions. In this exercise in *Sachkritik*, a judgment based on criteria external to the text serves only to obstruct the reading of the text on its own terms. If Romans 3.21–4.25 is read on its own terms, it becomes clear that, at least for Paul, the crucial question is whether his thesis about righteousness by faith can produce a plausible and persuasive reading of scripture.

Where the possibility of a hermeneutical account of the doctrine of justification is rejected or overlooked, the result is not only that Romans 4 is downgraded to a position of secondary importance. In addition, Romans 1.18–3.20 will be seen as an abstract demonstration of "the universality of sin", and little significance will be found in its culminating statements of and about the law, where it is precisely the meaning and significance of scriptural texts that is at stake (cf. 3.9–20). And, although Paul hastens to emphasize that his proclamation of the righteousness of God is "attested by the law and the prophets" (3.21), the scriptural grounding of this proclamation will be ignored. This scriptural grounding is to be found not only in Romans 4 and in the extensive exposition of Genesis 15.6 that lies at its heart. It is also to be found in Habakkuk 2.4, quoted in Romans 1.17b. Indeed, as we shall see, Paul's proclamation of the righteousness of God in Romans 1.17a and 3.21–31 is nothing more nor less than commentary on this text. It is understandable that Schweitzer could claim that the doctrine of righteousness by faith arises out of just two scriptural texts (Habakkuk 2.4 and Genesis 15.6), for it is these two texts that mark the beginning and the end of Paul's exposition of his doctrine in Romans 1–4, bracketing and enclosing it and ensuring that it operates throughout on scriptural terrain.[29]

For Paul, these two brief scriptural utterances articulate the scope and the dynamics of the whole of scripture. The role of the doctrine of

---

29. Following Schweitzer, Peter Tomson describes Paul's justification theology as a "midrash" based on two key verses (Gen.15.6; Hab.2.4), in which Paul "combined his gospel for Jew and Greek, spiritual descent from Abraham and the share in the world to come inherent in it, and the central concept of faith... This midrash appears in different forms, combined with various other verses, in two contexts, Gal 3 and Rom 1–4, according to the needs of the argument" (*Paul and the Jewish Law*, p. 65). Tomson seeks to limit the scope of Paul's justification theology in order to create space for Pauline *halakha*, and points to the absence of the characteristic justification terminology in "halakhic" passages such as 1 Corinthians 8–10 (p. 63).

righteousness by faith is to explain how and to what extent this can be the case. Scriptural interpretation is not a secondary addition to a freestanding doctrine of justification, propping it up with more or less dubious, superfluous and extraneous "proofs". Scriptural interpretation is constitutive of this doctrine; it is what it *is*.

Citation and antecedent

Elaborating the proposition that the gospel is the power of God unto salvation for everyone who believes, Paul writes:

> For the righteousness of God is revealed in it, by faith for faith [*ek pisteōs eis pistin*]. As it is written: "The one who is righteous by faith [*ho dikaios ek pisteōs*] will live." (Rom.1.17)

The relation of this scriptural citation to its antecedent (the statement about the righteousness of God) is often misunderstood. Far from being a secondary confirmation of a freestanding dogmatic assertion, the citation from Habakkuk 2.4 actually *generates* its antecedent. This prophetic text is the matrix from which Paul's own assertion derives. Conversely, the antecedent amplifies the citation: it is commentary, an expository gloss on the prophetic text. The exegetical problems posed by the antecedent should not be treated in abstraction from the citation; antecedent and citation are interdependent.

The key to this understanding of Paul's text is to be found in an unexpected place – in the conventional formula, "as it is written", which introduces the citation precisely by identifying it as a citation, derived from a normative though unspecified scriptural text.[30] This introductory formula serves also to connect the citation with its antecedent, the statement that precedes it in its new context; it asserts that the citation corresponds both to its exemplar and to its antecedent. In Romans 1.17 the relation of citation to antecedent is distinctive and significant.

In the Letter to the Romans, the introductory formula "as it is written" occurs sixteen times, with minor variations.[31] This standard introductory

---

30. From a rhetorical point of view, it is the introductory formula that constitutes the citation: so C. D. Stanley, *Paul and the Language of Scripture*, p. 37. An exception to this occurs when the effect of an argument depends on the audience's recognition of a citation, even in the absence of an introductory formula: the use of Habakkuk 2.4 in Galatians 3.11 is a case in point (on this see D.-A. Koch, *Die Schrift als Zeuge des Evangeliums*, pp. 12–14). In an "allusion", audience recognition is desirable but not essential.

31. *Kathōs gegraptai*, nine times (1.17; 2.24; 3.4; 9.13, 33; 10.15; 11.8, 26; 15.9); preceded by *alla*, twice (15.3, 21); followed by *hoti*, three times (3.10; 4.17; 8.36); *gegraptai gar*, twice (12.19; 14.11). In four of these cases, B and a few other mss. read *kathapēr* for *kathōs* (3.4; 9.13; 10.15; 11.8). There is no discernible difference between *gegraptai gar* and *kathōs gegraptai*.

formula occurs throughout the letter,[32] although alternative formulae are employed on no less than thirty occasions in chapters 4, 9–11 and 15.[33] These alternative formulae take a variety of forms. They may serve to identify the human author of a scriptural utterance,[34] or the human addressee of a divine utterance recorded in scripture.[35] Scripture itself may be the speaker in a specific utterance;[36] on one occasion, the speaker is even said to be Paul himself, on another "the righteousness of faith".[37] Of the remaining cases, a number are so brief that the intention is clearly to integrate the citation as fully as possible into the new context.[38]

The significance of the standard introductory formula, "as it is written", can be illuminated by comparing it with the alternative formulae.[39]

First, Paul's standard formula introduces citations anonymously. In contrast to Romans 4, where the texts cited are thoroughly contextualized, Romans 1.17 gives no indication of the source of the citation.[40] It does not

---

32. There are six occurrences in chapters 1–8 (1.17; 2.24; 3.4, 10; 4.17; 8.36), five in chapters 9–11 (9.13, 33; 10.15; 11.8, 26), and five in chapters 12–15 (12.19; 14.11; 15.3, 9, 21). The formula is traditional rather than distinctively Pauline, occurring (with variations) in Josh.9.2b (= 8.31); 4 Kgdms.14.6; 2 Chr.23.18; 4Q174 1.i.12; Test.Levi 5.4; Mk.1.2; Lk.2.23; Acts 7.42, 15.15, etc.

33. Rom.4.3, 6, 9, 18, 22, 23; 9.7, 9, 12, 15, 17, 25, 27, 29; 10.5, 6, 11, 13, 16, 18, 19, 20, 21; 11.2, 4, 9, 34; 15.10, 11, 12. In Romans 9–11, there are twenty instances of "alternative" formulae, as against five of the "standard" formula.

34. There are nine instances of this in Romans: 4.6 ("As David pronounces the blessing of the man to whom God reckons righteousness apart from works"); 9.27 ("And Isaiah cries out on Israel's behalf"), 9.29 ("And as Isaiah said before"); 10.5 ("For Moses writes [concerning] the righteousness which is by the law that..."); 10.16 ("For Isaiah says"); 10.19 ("First, Moses says"); 10.20 ("And Isaiah dares and says"); 11.9 ("And David says"); 15.12 ("And again Isaiah says").

35. Three instances: 9.12 ("... it was said to her [Rebecca] that..."); 9.15 ("For he says to Moses"); 11.4 ("But what does the divine word say to him [Elijah]?"). Four further instances of divine speech may also be mentioned: 4.18 ("in accordance with what was said") and 9.9, ("for this is the word of promise"), where the addressee of a divine word is identified by way of the wider context; 9.25, where the name given is that of the prophetic book and not the addressee ("as he also says in Hosea"); and 10.21, where it is clearly God who speaks in and through Isaiah ("But to Israel he says").

36. Four instances: 4.3 ("For what does the scripture say?"); 9.17 ("For the scripture says to Pharaoh"); 10.11 ("For the scripture says"); 11.2 ("Or do you not know what the scripture says in [the passage about] Elijah?").

37. 4.9 ("For we say"); 10.6 ("But the righteousness of faith speaks like this").

38. Seven instances: 4.22 ("therefore"); 9.7 ("but"); 10.13 ("for"); 10.18 ("indeed" [*menounge*]); 11.34 ("for"); 15.10 ("and again he/it says"); 15.11 ("and again"). Several of these instances might perhaps be described as allusions rather than citations.

39. For the contemporary background to Paul's use of the two types of introductory formula, see D.-A. Koch, *Die Schrift als Zeuge des Evangeliums*, pp. 25–32.

40. In Romans 4, the standard formula is used once (v.17), alternative formulae six times (vv.3, 6, 9, 18, 22, 23); four of these introduce repeated citations of Genesis 15.6 (vv.3, 9, 22, 23).

require its reader to recognize the text cited, or even to have heard of the prophet Habakkuk. All that is necessary is an understanding of the concept of a normative body of writings, and an acceptance that the words cited are to be found in it – somewhere. Anonymous citation does not confer any greater or lesser authority on a text, but it does affect the nature of the authority ascribed to it. If attribution to a specific author highlights the text's individuality and distinctiveness, anonymous citation emphasizes its representative character. In Romans 1.17, the words, "The one who is righteous by faith will live" are attributed simply to scripture as a whole – the body of writings to which the formula "as it is written" refers. It is scripture as a whole that speaks in these words.

Second, the standard introductory formula emphasizes the written character of the text cited, whereas the alternative formulae normally introduce a text as a spoken utterance – whether the speaker in question is a prophet, God or scripture itself.[41] In most cases, the verb of speaking occurs in the present tense,[42] and the effect is to make the scriptural statement a contemporary utterance. In what they once wrote, Moses, David and Isaiah still speak here and now. Even where divine speech occurred in a quite specific context, addressed perhaps to Moses or to Pharaoh (cf. 9.15, 17), it can still be introduced as contemporary speech. On the other hand, the standard formula presents a citation as a completed utterance that is definitive and permanently valid. A specific relation to the present is implied not in the formula itself but only in the connection it creates between the citation and its antecedent. As divine-human speech, scripture addresses us here and now; as writing, it confronts us in a definitive form handed down to us from the past. If speech connotes immediacy, writing connotes normativity.

Third, the standard and the alternative introductory formulae imply a different relationship between the citation and its context. The tendency of the alternative formulae and the corresponding citations is towards full integration into Paul's own discourse. Without them, this discourse would be incomplete and incoherent. If, for example, the six alternative formulae and corresponding citations were to be excised from Romans 4, the argument would at times be incoherent; for these citations (vv.3, 6–8, 9, 18, 22, 23) are not only fundamental to Paul's argument, they are also integral to his discourse. On the other hand, a citation introduced by the standard

41. Twenty-two cases in Romans: 4.3, 6, 9, 18; 9.9, 12, 15, 17, 25, 27, 29; 10.6, 11, 16, 19, 20, 21; 11.2, 4, 9; 15.10, 12. Only in 4.23 ("But it was not written for his sake alone that...") and 10.6 ("For Moses writes [concerning] the righteousness which is by the law that...") do alternative introductory formulae share the standard formula's emphasis on writing.

42. This is so in eighteen out of the twenty-two texts listed in the previous note (4.3, 6, 9; 9.15, 17, 25, 27; 10.6, 11, 16, 19, 20, 21; 11.2, 4, 9; 15.10, 12). Past tense verbs occur on only three occasions (4.18; 9.12, 29). In 9.9, nouns are used instead of a verb.

formula will not be integral to the discourse, however important it may be for the argument. In Romans 4, the standard formula is used only once, to introduce a citation from Genesis 17.5: Abraham is said to be "the father of us all – as it is written, 'Father of many nations/Gentiles have I appointed you' – before the God in whom he believed" (vv.16–17). Had Paul omitted the parenthetical citation and written, "... who is the father of us all before the God in whom he believed", the omission would not have been perceptible. Although the text would no longer say what Paul in fact wished it to say, it would not be incoherent. The reason is that the "as" of the standard formula implies a correspondence between citation and antecedent that entails a degree of repetition, and so, at the level of the discourse, of redundancy. In citations introduced by alternative formulae, no such repetition occurs. Here, the point at issue is stated once, not twice – except on the rare occasions when these formulae too begin with "as".[43] Since repetition serves rhetorically to create emphasis, the standard formula will tend to increase the argumentative and rhetorical force of quotations that it introduces.

In the case of Romans 1.17, the correspondence between the citation and its antecedent is especially strong. In most cases, the correspondence occurs on the semantic level but not on the lexical one. In Romans 3.9–10, Paul writes:

> We have already charged that Jews and Greeks are all under sin – as it is written: "There is no one righteous..."

In the antecedent, Paul speaks in his own words; in the citation, a similar point is made in different words. The scriptural statement, "There is no one righteous" may indeed serve to confirm that "Jews and Greeks are all under sin", but the correspondence here is at the semantic level only. In the absence of any lexical correspondence, the Pauline antecedent retains a degree of priority and independence in relation to the citation. In a minority of cases, however, correspondences on the lexical as well as the semantic level indicate that the antecedent has been formulated with the citation already in mind. This is so in Romans 9.32–33:

> They [Israel] stumbled over the stone of stumbling – as it is written: "Behold, I lay in Zion a stone of stumbling and a rock of offence..."

Here, lexical correspondence indicates that the antecedent is dependent on the citation. The citation is primary, and the antecedent is an interpretative gloss that applies the citation to the present situation. That is also the case in Romans 1.17:

---

43. This occurs in just three of the thirty passages in which alternative introductory formulae are used (4.6; 9.25, 29).

For the righteousness of God [*dikaiosunē theou*] is revealed in it, by faith for faith [*ek pisteōs eis pistin*]. As it is written: "The one who is righteous by faith [*ho dikaios ek pisteōs*] will live."

While the "as" of the standard introductory formula already indicates that the reader is to expect a degree of semantic correspondence, the degree of lexical correspondence here is highly unusual. Looking back at the antecedent from the standpoint of the citation, we see that the crucial formulation about "the one who is righteous by faith" is already foreshadowed in it, although in a more complex form involving, among other things, the substitution of an abstract noun and a genitive construction for the adjectival noun of the citation. While (in contrast to the example from Romans 9.32–33) the antecedent here amplifies and elaborates the citation, it remains dependent on it. The prophetic text is cited here as the matrix from which the Pauline language of "righteousness by faith" derives.[44] This language is indeed Paul's language, but it is introduced in such a way as to lead the reader to conclude that it is not only or even primarily Paul's. Originally and primarily, this is the language of scripture, cited here in the representative form of an anonymous prophetic text: that is what Paul wishes his reader to understand.[45]

This brings us to the point where the purely formal analysis of the Pauline "rhetoric of citation" can be shown to be exegetically fruitful. If Romans 1.17a is indeed an interpretative gloss on the Habakkuk citation, this must determine the way in which this text is understood.

The scriptural matrix

In Romans 1.17, the correspondence between antecedent and citation – already asserted by the standard introductory formula – is unusually close.

---

44. This view of Paul's citation is the exact opposite of D.-A. Koch's claim that Paul "restlos... die Zitataussage in die eigene theologische Gesamtkonzeption integriert" (*Die Schrift als Zeuge des Evangeliums*, p. 276).

45. Compare Douglas Campbell, "The Meaning of ΠΙΣΤΙΣ and ΝΟΜΟΣ in Paul", p. 101, who convincingly argues that the Habakkuk text was the historical origin of Paul's *ek pisteōs* phraseology. As Campbell shows, *ek pisteōs* occurs twenty-one times in Romans and Galatians, the texts in which the Habakkuk citation is found, and never in any other Pauline text. It is more likely that the phrase was derived from the prophetic text than that it was "originally used by Paul as a crucial catchphrase and that he then 'found' Hab 2:4 in the scriptures to undergird his phraseology. If this was so, we would expect him to use *ek pisteōs* in contexts where Hab 2:4 is not directly cited" (p. 101n). My own discussion focuses not on the historical origin of Paul's terminology but on its rhetorical origin within the discourse of Romans.

Nowhere else in Romans are lexical connections between antecedent and citation as significant as they are here:[46]

(A) Antecedent	For the *righteous*ness of God is revealed in it, *by faith* for faith
(B) Introductory formula	– as it is written,
(C) Citation	For the *one who is righteous by faith* will live.

If the supplementary words in the antecedent arise out of the spaces in the citation, then Paul is offering the following paraphrase of his text from Habakkuk:

> *The one who is righteous* (that is, with a *righteous*ness of God, revealed in the gospel) *by faith* (since this righteousness is received *by faith* and is intended for faith) *will live*.[47]

Later in his letter, Paul himself will use just such a format to paraphrase a passage from Deuteronomy:

> The righteousness of faith speaks thus: *Do not say in your heart, Who will ascend into heaven?* (that is, to bring Christ down), *or, Who will descend into the abyss?* (that is, to bring Christ up from the dead). But what does it say? *The word is near you, in your mouth and in your heart* (that is, *the word* of faith which we preach: for if you confess with *your mouth* that Jesus is Lord and believe *in your heart* that God raised him from the dead, you will be saved). (Rom.10.6–9, cf. Deut.30.12, 14)

While Paul does not employ this *pesher* format in Romans 1.17, the logical relationship of text to gloss is similar in the two cases.

Exegetically, the most significant implication of this hermeneutical approach to Romans 1.17 is that the much-disputed "righteousness of God" *(dikaiosunē theou)* cannot be understood in abstraction from the human figure of "the one who is righteous". Paul's point is surely that the righteousness of Habakkuk's "righteous person" is a righteousness approved by God. That the righteousness of which the prophet speaks is "of God" is already implied in the claim to normativity entailed by "it is written". These references to God and to scriptural status converge on the issue of the *truth* of the assertion that righteousness is by faith and for faith. Paul's claim that the righteousness of which he speaks is genuinely "of God" is supported by the fact that just such a righteousness is asserted

---

46. In addition to Romans 9.32–33, cited above, the only other passages in which lexical connections are evident are 4.6–8 (where an alternative introductory formula is used), and 4.16–17.

47. The lack of a gloss on "will live" may support the thesis of A. Nygren that Paul expounds the first part of the Habakkuk citation ("the one who through faith is righteous...") in Romans 1–4, and the second part ("... will live") in Romans 5–8 *(Romans*, pp. 28–32). On this point, see also note 61, below.

by the normative prophetic text – from which indeed Paul's claim derives. While Paul will later emphasize that this righteousness is a pure gift, and that God's saving action in Christ is summed up in the giving of this gift (cf. Rom.3.24–26; 5.15–17), that is not the point here. In Romans 1.16–17, Paul is concerned to establish an initial correlation of "righteousness" and "faith", as suggested by his Habakkuk text.[48] As Paul understands it, this text speaks simply of a righteous status and identifies the means (i.e. faith) by which this righteous status can be attained. It also implies a divine acknowledgment of this faith as righteous – an acknowledgment that *constitutes* the righteousness of faith. In that sense, Paul's gloss remains faithful to the text it interprets: the revelation of God's righteousness in the gospel corresponds exactly to the identification of true righteousness in the prophetic text. If the prophet speaks of a righteousness valid before God, it is the same righteousness that is revealed in the gospel. The righteousness of God in Romans 1.17 is the pattern of human conduct that God acknowledges as righteous.

If Paul's statement in Romans 1.17a is an interpretative gloss on the Habakkuk text, as he himself claims, then this understanding of "the righteousness of God" as "the righteousness valid before God" is virtually inescapable – even if the same phrase is later used with other nuances.[49] In the present context, it cannot refer primarily to righteousness as divine gift, and still less can it refer to the divine saving action in its entirety – the view that has dominated discussion of this phrase since Käsemann's influential article of 1961.[50] The debate has often focused on scriptural and post-scriptural evidence, in the questionable belief that this will prove decisive for Paul's own usage. The mass of parallels and influences from deutero-Isaiah, the psalms, and the Qumran *Hodayoth* ensures, ironically, that the scriptural origin to which Paul himself points (the Habakkuk text) is consistently overlooked.[51] And yet in Romans 1.17 Paul did *not* write:

---

48. To say that Romans 1.17 is "the fork in the road for all subsequent exposition [of Romans]" (Käsemann, *Romans*, p. 24) is simply to echo Luther's retrospective account of his "conversion", in which this text plays a crucial hermeneutical role in relation to scripture as a whole. There is no exegetical warrant for the assumption that, just at this point, the Pauline gospel must come to expression in its entirety.

49. This paraphrase is reminiscent of Luther's translation ("die Gerechtigkeit, die vor Gott gilt, welche kommt aus Glauben..."). The relevance of the Habakkuk citation for interpreting the *dikaiosunē theou* is rightly emphasized by Cranfield: if the citation "focuses attention on the justified man, not God's act of justifying him", the same is presumably true of its antecedent (*Romans*, 1.98).

50. "'The Righteousness of God' in Paul" (Eng. tr. in his *New Testament Questions of Today*, pp. 168–82).

51. For a recent example of this procedure, see Brendan Byrne, *Romans*, pp. 57–59.

> ... for in it the righteousness of God is revealed by faith for faith – as it
> is written: "The Lord has made known his salvation *[to sotērion autou]*,
> before the Gentiles he has revealed his righteousness *[apekalupsen tēn
> dikiaosunēn autou]*." (cf. Ps.97.2)

On Käsemann's reading, Paul's actual citation of Habakkuk 2.4 is a
wasted opportunity to make clear what he meant by "the righteousness of
God". On the reading proposed here, the citation makes it impossible to
detach the "righteousness of God" from "by faith".[52]

The main contextual argument for identifying "the righteousness of God"
with God's saving action is found in the relationship between 1.17a and the
preceding statement in 1.16 – which is then given precedence over the much
closer relationship with the citation. Paul is unashamed of the gospel,

> for it is the power of God unto salvation to everyone who believes, the
> Jew first and also the Greek; for the righteousness of God is revealed in
> it, by faith, for faith ...

The parallelism between "the power of God" and "the righteousness of
God" may seem to indicate that the two phrases are approximate
equivalents, and that "the righteousness of God" must refer to God's
powerful saving intervention in Christ.[53] But v.16 states that God's power,
operative in the gospel, brings about the salvation of everyone who has
faith; v.17 states that the righteousness of God is by faith (if the citation is
allowed to determine the interpretation of its antecedent). The righteousness of God is correlated not with the power of God but with
salvation – that is, with the outcome of God's action for humankind,
which is at the same time the rationale of that action. The human correlate
of the powerful, self-disclosive divine action is "salvation", interpreted
here as the righteousness that is finally valid before God, which occurs in
and through faith. "Salvation for everyone who believes" is equivalent to
"righteousness by faith". If Paul meant to say something like that in
Romans 1.16–17a, then it is understandable that he should cite Habakkuk
2.4 in its support. If he meant to say something quite other than that, he
would seem to have selected the wrong text.

In Romans 1.17, the Habakkuk citation must be allowed to determine the
sense not only of "the righteousness of God" but also of "by faith for
faith". If, as is likely, Paul understands the citation to be speaking of "the

---

52.   Having hypostatized the *dikaiosunē theou*, Käsemann is at a loss to know what to do
with *ek pisteōs eis pistin*, and has to concede that "it is related only loosely to the preceding
statement" (*Romans*, p. 31). Paul's point is evidently that "[t]he revelation of God's
righteousness, because it is bound to the gospel, takes place always only in the sphere of faith"
– in which case it can hardly be said that "Paul proves his point from Hab 2:4" (*ibid.*).
53.   The parallel between *dunamis theou, dikaiosunē theou* and *orgē theou* (1.16–18) is
emphasized by Käsemann, *Romans*, p. 27.

one who is righteous by faith",[54] then "by faith for faith" is an interpretative gloss which must be connected as closely as possible to "the righteousness of God". Apart from the citation, it would be possible to understand Paul's claim that "in it the righteousness of God is revealed, by faith for faith" as speaking of a *revelation* that occurs by and for faith. But if the citation speaks of the one who is righteous by faith, the interpretative gloss must also speak of righteousness by faith, rather than revelation by faith.[55] In the light of the citation, Paul's point must be that in the gospel the righteousness of God is revealed, a righteousness that is by faith and for faith (cf. Rom.3.21–22). Here, "by faith" is scriptural, whereas "for faith" must be a gloss intended to draw out a further implication of the scriptural language. If the prophetic "by faith" implies an instrumental relationship between faith and righteousness, the Pauline "for faith" hints at an intentional divine action – the acknowledgment of the one who has faith as righteous. In that sense, the righteousness of God is *for* all those who believe (cf. Rom.3.22). As in the case of Abraham, there is a human individual who believes, and there is a divine reaction to that fact which takes the form of a "reckoning" as righteous (cf. Rom.4.3, citing Gen.15.6). "By faith for faith" indicates that the instrumental relationship between faith and righteousness entails a free and intentional divine responsive action. The gloss, "for faith" rules out any suggestion that righteousness is somehow inherent to faith, without reference to the free divine decision.

Very different interpretations of Romans 1.17 would result if the "by faith" of the citation were taken to refer to the "faithfulness" either of God[56] or of Christ.[57] Such readings tend to detach "the one who is righteous" from "by faith", and understand the citation to say either that "the righteous one will live by my [i.e. God's] faithfulness" or "the Righteous One [i.e. Christ] will live by [his] faithfulness". The first person possessive pronoun is actually found in the Septuagintal version of Habakkuk 2.4, and it is possible to argue that Paul retains the sense expressed there even though the pronoun has dropped out of his own version.[58] In the christological reading, it can be argued that "the righteous

---

54. On the basis of Pauline usage elsewhere, most commentators agree that the citation is to be translated, "The one who is righteous by faith will live" rather than, "The righteous one will live by faith". Particularly relevant is the later usage of *ek pisteōs* in close conjunction with the verb *dikaioun* (Rom.3.26, 30; 5.1) or the noun *dikaiosunē* (3.22; 9.30; 10.6).

55. So Cranfield, *Romans*, 1.100; Moo, *Romans*, pp. 70–71. Dunn links *ek pisteōs* with *apokaluptetai* without discussing the syntactical issue (*Romans*, 1.44).

56. The view of L. Gaston, *Paul*, pp. 111, 170; with qualifications, Dunn, *Romans*, 1.43–46.

57. R. Hays, "'The Righteous One' as Eschatological Deliverer"; D. Campbell, "Romans 1:17", pp. 281–85.

58. Compare Dunn, who argues that omission of the pronouns found in both LXX ("my faithfulness") and MT ("his faithfulness") "does not necessarily amount to an exclusion of these other renderings" (*Romans*, 1.45).

one" *(ho dikaios)* is an established messianic title.[59] Yet it is not clear that either of these readings of the Habakkuk citation can give a coherent reading of its antecedent as an interpretative gloss. The claim that "the righteousness of God is revealed in it, by faith, for faith" is fully comprehensible as a paraphrase of *(i)* "the one who is righteous by faith will live" – but much less so as a paraphrase of *(ii)* "the righteous one will live by [God's] faithfulness", or *(iii)* "the Righteous One [i.e. Christ] will live by faithfulness". If Paul understood his citation along the lines of the second, Septuagint-inspired option, then the antecedent should have shown that the phrase "by faithfulness" in the citation refers to "the faithfulness of God". While the Greek *ek pisteōs* can certainly mean "by faithfulness", a reference here to divine faithfulness would require other indications in the context; and it is just these that Paul fails to provide in his interpretative gloss. He might have written that "in it the faithfulness of God is revealed...", or that "in it the righteousness of God is revealed, through the faithfulness of God..." – but, in the absence of an explicit "faithfulness of God" formulation such as is found in Romans 3.3, it is unlikely that this is intended in 1.17. Similarly, if Paul had understood his citation along christological lines, we would have expected a reference to christology in the antecedent – a clarification that Habakkuk's "righteous one" really is to be identified with "Jesus Christ the righteous" (cf. 1 Jn.2.1). The second and third readings require a reader who is hypersensitive to what is only implicit in the citation – that the "faithfulness" in question is God's, or Christ's – while ignoring the explicit contextual interdependence of citation and antecedent. A reading is to be preferred that can make sense of that interdependence.

In the antecedent, the phrases "the righteousness of God" and "by faith, for faith" are clearly derived from the Habakkuk citation, which they serve to clarify. Paul operates here within the constraints of his text and does not force it to say what it does not and cannot say, since his aim at this point is to demonstrate the harmony between his gospel and the prophetic assertion. Here at least, he observes the maxim, "Not beyond what is written" (cf. 1 Cor.4.6). Yet the citation in Romans 1.17 corresponds to the antecedent still more closely than these verbal connections suggest. The antecedent does not speak of the righteousness of God in isolation, it speaks of the disclosure of that righteousness in the gospel. The gospel's disclosure of the divine righteousness is confirmed by the prophetic text,

59. According to D. Campbell, the phrase *ho dikaios* occurs frequently in the NT as an early Jewish Christian christological title ("Romans 1:17", p. 282); the passages cited are Acts 3.14, 7.52, 22.14; Jas.5.6 [sic]; anarthrously in 1 Pet.3.18, 1 Jn.2.1; perhaps 1 Jn.2.29, 3.7, 2 Tim.4.8. The absence of any explicit Pauline attestation of this "christological title" is an embarrassment for this hypothesis, as is the failure of Hebrews 10.37–38 to extend a christologically oriented reading of Habakkuk 2.3–4 into the crucial v.4b.

which, in speaking of the righteousness that is by faith, is itself a disclosure of that righteousness. The apostolic gospel and the prophetic writing are at one not only in speaking of a righteousness that is by faith, but also in the disclosure that occurs by way of their speaking. In the citation, the introductory formula "it is written" is the functional equivalent of "in it is revealed" in the antecedent. The revelation that occurs *viva voce* in the proclamation of the apostle is at one with the revelation that occurs through the prophetic writing.

This analysis of the relation of citation to antecedent in Romans 1.17 has drawn attention to a methodological deficiency that impairs much of the modern discussion of Paul's "righteousness of God" language. In accordance with the conventions of the commentary genre, commentators simply follow the order of the words in Romans 1.17, beginning with "the righteousness of God", and proceeding to deal more briefly with "is revealed" and "by faith for faith" before concluding with the citation. The result is that the citation exercises little or no discernible influence on the interpretation of its antecedent, despite the lexical and semantic indications that this particular antecedent is an interpretative gloss on the citation.[60] The main point of the present discussion is not to offer support for one of the various well-established options in the "righteousness of God" debate, but rather to present Paul's language of righteousness and faith – at the very moment of its entry into the text of Romans – as the language of scriptural interpretation, arising out of the prior prophetic testimony. No one would dispute that, as a matter of fact, this Pauline terminology has a scriptural background. But what is persistently overlooked is the fact that it *explicitly presents itself* as arising out of a quite specific scriptural background, and that the implied author of Romans therefore speaks here as the interpreter of the prophet and not simply in his own name.[61] Paul's doctrine of righteousness by faith is an exercise in scriptural interpretation, and intends itself to be understood as such.

---

60. Thus Habakkuk 2.4 is at no point mentioned in the lengthy discussions of Romans 1.17a in the commentaries of Käsemann (pp. 23–31) or of Fitzmyer (pp. 257–63).

61. Among commentators on Romans, A. Nygren is unusual in emphasizing the importance of the Habakkuk citation, in which he finds "the whole message of the epistle" (*Romans*, p. 81). Paul elucidates the first part of the citation ("the one who through faith is righteous...") in chapters 1–4, the second half ("... shall live") in chapters 5–8 (pp. 28–32). Although Nygren's thesis is often rejected on the grounds that it diminishes the significance of chapters 9–11, that need not be the case. In its favour is the fact that the verb *zōn* in an eschatological sense occurs six times in Romans 5–8 (6.10 [× 2], 11, 13; 8.12, 13; cf. 8.11, *zōopoiein*), and only once elsewhere in the letter (10.5, a citation of Leviticus 18.5); similarly, the noun *zōē* occurs eleven times in Romans 5–8 (5.10, 17, 18, 21; 6.4, 22, 23; 7.10; 8.2, 6, 10), and twice elsewhere in the letter (2.7; 11.15). Dependence on the Habakkuk citation is evident in formulations linking righteousness and life (*eis dikaiōsin zōēs*, 5.18; *dia dikaiosunēs eis zōēn aiōnion*, 5.21), and in the declaration, "... you will live", in 8.13.

Antithetical Hermeneutics

The Habakkuk text is not only significant at the outset of Paul's argument in Romans. In Romans 1–3 as a whole, it plays as important a part as Genesis 15.6 does in Romans 4. While both texts enable Paul to establish his antithesis between righteousness by faith and by works of the law, it is the Habakkuk text that is given pride of place in this respect. As we shall see, the Pauline antithesis is to be understood as an antithetical *hermeneutic* – that is, as a paradigm for interpretation according to which the scriptural testimony to divine saving action is marked by a fundamental and irreducible duality.

The twofold scriptural testimony

Although righteousness terminology occurs in Romans 1.18–3.20, the crucial link between righteousness and faith, established by the prophetic text and emphasized by the Pauline paraphrase, is absent.[62] The prophetic announcement that the one who is righteous by faith will live is left in suspense, as Paul turns his attention to an extended argument that intends to show that the law is *not* the "power of God unto salvation". This argument concludes as follows:

> We know that what the law says it speaks to those who are in the sphere of the law *[en tō nomō]*, so that every mouth may be closed and the whole world may be accountable to God. Therefore by works of law shall no flesh be justified before him, for through the law is knowledge of sin. (Rom.3.19–20)

In these closing sentences, the emphatic fourfold reference to the law indicates that Romans 1.18–3.20 is arguing a case not just for the universality of sin but also for the role of the law in the divine exposure and judgment of this universal sin, in which Jews as well as Gentiles are implicated. In the series of citations in 3.10–18, the textuality of the law is underlined. This text, it is argued, does not teach that the way to a righteous standing before God is to perform the actions that correspond to its stipulations. On the contrary, its message "for the Jew first, but also for the Greek" is that "no one is righteous, not even one" (cf. 1.16; 2.9, 10; 3.9–10).[63] That is the human situation, but it is specifically *the law's*

---

62. *Adikia* (1.18, twice); *dikaiokrisia* (2.5); *dikaioun* (2.13; 3.4, 20); *dikaios* (2.13; 3.10); *dikaiosunē* (3.5). *Pistis* occurs only in the reference to the "faithfulness of God" (3.3), which is contrasted with human *apistia*.

63. In the light of its opening (3.9–12), and in spite of its conclusion (3.20), it seems unlikely that the catena is addressed *exclusively* to Jews (as argued by S. J. Gathercole, *Where is Boasting?*, pp. 212–15).

disclosure of the human situation, which is simultaneously a disclosure of the meaning and significance of the law itself. The law is that divine address to humankind which not only commands and prohibits, but also pronounces the divine verdict on those who transgress. Its sphere is universal. If, at an earlier stage of his argument, Paul distinguished between those who are "without law" and those who are "in the law" (2.12), his aim even there was to relativize this distinction by showing how the law is operative even in the Gentile world which does not know the Law of Moses (2.13–16; cf. 1.32). In 3.9–20, the gap between Jews and Greeks is finally closed: for Jews and Greeks alike are within the sphere of the law's address, which brings "knowledge of sin" by proclaiming that "there is no one righteous, not even one... "[64]

By the time Paul's argument reaches its conclusion in Romans 3.9–20, a hermeneutical dilemma has come to light. In the introduction to that argument in 1.16–17, we heard the prophetic testimony that the one who is righteous by faith will live. Yet this testimony, with its correlation of righteousness and faith, was thereafter left in suspense, and we have found ourselves listening instead to the testimony of the law, interpreted and summarized in words adapted from Psalm 13 LXX: "There is no one who is righteous, not even one" (Rom.3.10). Like the Habakkuk citation, this one too is introduced by the formula, "For it is written", which asserts a correspondence between citation and antecedent and presupposes the normative status of the text that is cited. It is written that the one who is righteous by faith will live, but it is also written that there is no one who is righteous, not even one. Paul has set up this dilemma with a view to its resolution. The negative statement is assigned to the voice of "the law", in accordance with its role in bringing about the knowledge of sin. In no sense has this negative testimony been superseded or consigned to the past. Although a written text, the law is still said to "speak", here and now in the present, and what it now says is what was once written (cf. 3.19–20). And yet this utterance of the law is not the whole of the scriptural testimony. Scripture also speaks of a human being who is indeed righteous, but with a righteousness that is by faith. It seems that the scriptural testimony is two-sided, double-edged. It is indictment and promise,

64. According to S. Stowers, Romans 3.20 refers only to Gentiles, who are the main targets of 1.18–3.20 as a whole: "[T]he minute one begins to imagine the books of Moses concretely and to think about how these writings functioned among Jews in Paul's time, the idea of Paul saying that the law, with its divinely ordained institutions, cannot make Jews acceptable to God becomes absurd" (*A Rereading of Romans*, p. 190). While the emphasis on the concrete function of the books of Moses is to be welcomed, it is undermined by the assumptions of (1) a uniform Jewish orthodoxy, which (2) Paul could not possibly have contravened. Fortunately, neither Paul nor other contemporary readers of the books of Moses were as uncritically conservative as Stowers thinks.

judgment and grace, law and gospel. This construal of the basic shape of
the scriptural testimony is distinguished sharply and polemically from one
in which scripture is law and nothing but law, understood not simply as
indictment but above all as positive, promising demand. That is what is
ruled out in the claim that "by works of law shall no flesh be justified
before him..." (3.20). To see the Law of Moses as defining the way to
righteousness and salvation, for the Jewish people but potentially for the
whole world also, is to misunderstand the testimony of the law and of
scripture as a whole.

The relevance of the Habakkuk text even at this later stage in Paul's
argument can be demonstrated by setting Romans 1.17 and 3.20 alongside
each other:

> For in it the righteousness of God is revealed, by faith, for faith; as it is
> written, the one who is righteous by faith *[ek pisteōs]* shall live.

> Therefore by works of law *[ex ergōn nomou]* shall no flesh be justified
> before him, for through law is knowledge of sin.

The later text is the conclusion and summary of a lengthy argument, but it is
so closely related to the earlier text that it might have been its immediate
sequel (cf. Gal.2.16). In both texts, there is a concern with "righteousness",
that is, with the human person's standing before God. In Romans 1.17, the
adjective "righteous" *(dikaios)* in the Habakkuk citation is paraphrased in
terms of "the righteousness of God" *(dikaiosunē theou)*, and in 3.20 the
same concern with human standing before God is expressed in the verb,
"shall not be justified" *(ou dikaiōthēsetai)*. The phrase, "by works of law"
(ex ergōn nomou) has apparently been constructed on the model of
Habakkuk's "by faith" *(ek pisteōs)*. In the Habakkuk citation and the
Pauline gloss, righteousness and faith are positively correlated: one is
"righteous by faith" with a righteousness that is the righteousness of God.
In the summary of the law's testimony, however, righteousness and law
observance are negatively correlated. By works of law shall no flesh be
righteous before God, for the testimony of the law is that there is no one
righteous, not even one. In both cases, righteousness is correlated with a
particular mode of human action: the contrast is only effective on the basis
of the parallel. Finally, the two texts both speak of a disclosure.
Righteousness by faith is what is disclosed in the prophetic text, echoed
in the gospel; human sin and guilt before God is what is disclosed in the law.

Romans 3.20 is not the immediate sequel of 1.17, but it might have been.
Confirmation of the close relationship between the two passages may be
seen in a parallel passage in Galatians, where Paul states:

> That no one is justified before God by the law is clear, for "the one who
> is righteous by faith shall live". (Gal.3.11)

Here, the Habakkuk citation is used to confirm the claim that no one is righteous before God by means of the law. If, as the prophet teaches, we are righteous by faith, then the logical corollary is that we are not righteous by the law. The negation is derived from the scriptural assertion; it belongs to the interpretation of the scriptural text. In Romans, despite the interval that separates the scriptural assertion from its negative corollary, a similar hermeneutical logic is operative. In Romans, however, the negation ("By works of law shall no flesh be justified before him") is no longer presented as a direct interpretative conclusion from Habakkuk 2.4. While the parallels between Romans 1.17 and 3.20 indicate that the relation between affirmation and negation remains close, the negation is now presented as a conclusion drawn not from the prophetic text but from the law's own utterance. If the voice of the law proclaims to the whole world that "no one is righteous, not even one", if through the law comes knowledge of sin, then the negation can be derived from the law itself. Faith and law are no longer simply juxtaposed, for the law itself makes way for faith. More convincingly than in Galatians, Paul can now claim that, far from undermining the law, the faith spoken of in the Habakkuk citation actually serves to establish the law (cf. 3.31). Paul can claim this because, in contrast to Galatians 3.11, the long argument of 1.18–3.19 has been inserted between the fundamental assertion (1.17) and the corresponding negation (3.20). Faith serves to establish the law because it enables us to hear the law's true voice not in the promise that those who observe it will live thereby but in the declaration that, "works of law" notwithstanding, "there is no one who is righteous, not even one".

In the discussion that follows, the texts that make up the catena in Romans 3.10–18 will be traced back to their scriptural roots, in order to clarify the Pauline hermeneutic that can find in them nothing less than the authentic voice of the law. What is already clear is that Paul speaks as an interpreter of scriptural texts in speaking as he does of righteousness and faith, the law and its works. In particular, the Habakkuk text provides Paul with a standpoint from which he can reread and rethink the entire scriptural testimony to the demand that God imposes on his people in the law. "The law" is a text to be read rather than an object about which one might have a "view". It seems that Paul can see this text as extending into later scriptural writings that offer authoritative commentary on the Law of Moses. The distinction between text and interpretation here becomes fluid.

The voice of the law

According to Romans 3.19, "Whatever the law says it speaks to those who are in the law, so that every mouth may be shut and the whole world may be accountable to God" (v.19). The reference here to the voice of the law *(hosa ho nomos legei)* summarizes the preceding verses, in which a catena of scriptural texts is cited to prove the thesis of v.9, that "Jews and Greeks are all under the power of sin". What the law says, which is that by works of law shall no flesh be justified, it says by way of such texts as these. None of the texts cited is actually derived from the Pentateuch. Paul hears scripture's negative verdict on human endeavour beyond the Law of Moses as well as within it, and, insofar as the later writers are all saying the same thing as Moses, they too articulate the voice of the law.[65] Indeed, Paul too plays an active part in this articulation, by shaping as well as selecting his scriptural texts.[66]

(1) Paul's catena opens with five emphatic assertions to the effect that the truly righteous person simply does not exist:

> There is no one who is righteous *[dikaios]*, not even one.
> There is no one who understands.
> There is no one who seeks God.
> All have turned away, together they have become worthless.
> There is no one who does good, not even one. (Rom.3.10–12)

The emphatic, rhetorically impressive repetitions are in fact Paul's own creation, based on Ps.13[14].1–3:

> The fool said in his heart, there is no God.
>   They are corrupted, they practise abominations,
>   there is no one who does good *[poiōn chrēstotēta]*, not even one.
> The Lord looked down from heaven upon the sons of men,
>   to see if there is anyone who understands or seeks God.
> All have turned away, together they have become worthless,
>   there is no one who does good, not even one. (Ps.13.1–3)[67]

Paul subjects this passage to a remarkably free handling. In Romans 3.12, Psalm 13.3 LXX is quoted verbatim (or almost so, depending on a minor textual problem), but the preceding verses of the psalm are treated selectively and with significant modifications.

---

65. According to Cranfield, the phrases "whatever the law says" and "to those who are in the law" (Rom.3.19) refer to scripture as a whole (cf. 1 Cor.14.21; Jn.10.34, 15.25); thus "law" here has a broader meaning than in the four occurrences of this term that follow in vv.20–21 (*Romans*, 1.195–96). Yet the repeated emphasis on "law" in its narrower sense must surely determine the meaning of "whatever the law says", and of its sequel. The writers cited in the catena are seen as commentators on the law.

66. For the following analysis, compare the excellent discussion of L. A. Keck, "The Function of Rom 3:10–18", pp. 141–47. Keck emphasizes that the catena is "carefully constructed", that divergences from LXX appear to be deliberate, and that the whole "suggests 'bookishness' rather than ad hoc recollection of OT texts" (p. 145).

67. References here and elsewhere are to the Septuagint enumeration of the psalms.

In Romans 3.10, the first of the four "there is no one..." statements in the first half of the catena is only loosely based on the text of the psalm. Paul takes the first of the psalm's two identical statements to the effect that "there is no one who does good..." (Ps.13.1c), and substitutes for it the statement that "there is no one who is righteous...". This substitution is motivated by the desire to avoid the repetition found in the psalm itself, and to place at the beginning of his catena a term that is of fundamental importance in the argument of Romans as a whole. It is also possible that Paul's wording has been influenced by Ecclesiastes 7.20:

> For there is no righteous person in the land, who does good and does not sin.

Here, the words "there is no righteous person" correspond exactly to the opening words of Paul's catena. Yet the emphatic "not even one" that follows in Paul's version of the citation reflects the psalm text, which remains the basis for Romans 3.10–12 as a whole.

The second and third of the series of "there is no one" statements are created by Paul out of a pair of participles in Psalm 13.2. The Lord looks to see if there is anyone who understands or seeks God, and the following verse describes the negative outcome of this quest. Paul reads the outcome into the quest itself, so that "... if there is anyone who understands or seeks God" becomes: "There is no one who understands, there is no one who seeks God". The structure of the negation in Psalm 13.1c (= v.3b) is extended into Paul's rendering of v.2b, by the simple device of substituting *ouk* for *ei* in the phrase, *ei estin suniōn*, and by repeating the *ouk estin* (in place of *ē*) in the phrase that follows. The resulting series of identically constructed negations aptly summarizes the psalm's negative verdict on "the sons of men", and the omissions and substitutions heighten its rhetorical impact.

(2) In the second section of the catena (Rom.3.13–14), fragments of three other Davidic psalms are stitched together. The negations of the first section have focused on an absence: the person who is righteous, who understands, who seeks for God, and who does good simply does not exist. A search for such a person will be in vain. But there has also been a brief characterization of the people who actually do exist: "All *[pantes]* have turned away, together they have become worthless" (Rom.3.12a). The second section of the catena develops this characterization of a distorted humanity by attending to their speech. To the reference to their "throat" and "tongue" in the first citation (Ps.5.10) Paul has added passages referring to their "lips" (Ps.139.4) and to their "mouth" (Ps.10.7). Despite the diverse origin of these passages, this second section of the catena is no less coherent than the first:

> An open grave is their throat,
> with their tongues they deceive.

> Poison of asps is under their lips,
>   whose mouth is full of cursing and bitterness. (Rom.3.13–14)

The first two lines of this composite citation are derived from Psalm 5.10. In this psalm, David's initial plea that prayer should be heard (vv.2–4) leads to a description of God as one who is utterly opposed to "transgressors", to "all who work lawlessness" and "all who speak falsehood" (vv.5–7). Distinguishing himself from such people, David announces his intention to worship in the house of God and prays for protection from his enemies' machinations:

> Lord, lead me in your righteousness because of my enemies,
>   make straight your way before me.
> For there is no truth in their mouth,
>   their heart is worthless,
>   *an open grave is their throat,*
>   *with their tongues they deceive.* (Ps.5.9–10)

The psalm concludes with a plea for judgment on such as these, so that all whose hope is in God may rejoice and exult in him (vv.11–13).

Paul draws from this psalm the characterization of David's enemies in terms of their speech. They speak falsehood, there is no truth in their mouth, and their deadly and deceitful speech is directed against David himself and against God (cf. Ps.2.3). As in the case of Psalm 13, however, Paul eliminates the ties that connect the cited words to their original contexts. In neither case is there an attribution to David – in contrast to Romans 4.6–8, where a citation from Psalm 31 is introduced with the words, "Just as David pronounced a blessing upon the person to whom God reckons righteousness apart from works..." (cf. also 11.9–10). The absence of an attribution of Psalm 13 or 5 to David is unremarkable, but what is more striking and significant is the absence of any demarcation between the cited texts. There is no indication that the cited words derive from the psalms, and there is also no indication that at Romans 3.13 we pass from one psalm to another.[68] This is in sharp contrast to Romans 15.9–12, where, in another catena of citations, the divisions between the citations are clearly marked ("And again he says...", "And again...", "And again Isaiah says...").[69] The effect of this lack of demarcation is to break all ties with the original context, so as to put the words of scripture to a new use within a quite different context. In the case of Psalm 5.10, Paul's citation does not deviate from the original wording. But the words, "An open grave is their throat, with their tongues they deceive" are no

---

68. This explains the scribal error that introduced the texts cited in Romans 3.13–18 back into the LXX text of Psalm 13.
69. Compare also Hebrews 1.3–13.

longer David's complaint about his enemies. They are a scriptural indictment of the whole of humanity, Jew and Greek alike, who are "all under sin" (Rom.3.9). David's complaint is anonymized in order to receive a universal application. Human unrighteousness and sinfulness come to expression in speech – and this is the case universally, whatever the differences that otherwise distinguish one group from another. "With their tongues they deceive" – and tongues are languages as well as physical organs, all of which are used to enable people to prey on one another and to falsify the truth of God (cf. Rom.1.32).

The citation from Psalm 5 leads smoothly into closely related, briefer citations from Psalms 139.4 and 9.28, again derived from David's numerous complaints against his enemies:

> Save me, Lord, from the wicked person,
>> from the unrighteous man deliver me,
> who plan unrighteousness in their heart,
>> all day long they prepare for war.
> They sharpened their tongue like a serpent's,
>> *poison of asps is under their lips.* (Ps.139.2–4)

> He [the sinner] says in his heart, I shall not be moved,
>> from generation to generation I shall be free from evil.
> *His mouth is full of cursing and bitterness* and deceit
>> under his tongue is trouble and distress. (Ps.9.27–28)

In the second citation, Paul changes a singular relative pronoun into a plural in order to assimilate it to its new context; there are also minor omissions and alterations to the word order. The first citation is preserved verbatim. The quoted passages are selected because their references to "lips" and "mouth" cohere so well with the "throat" and "tongues" of the preceding citation. Indeed, Paul has also introduced elements of structural coherence into his composite citation:

> *a*   An open grave is their throat,
> *b*   with their tongues they deceive.
> *a*¹ Poison of asps is under their lips,
> *b*¹ whose mouth is full of cursing and bitterness. (Rom.3.13–14)

In *a* and *a*¹, distorted speech is referred to by way of metaphors of death (an open grave, poison of asps), whereas in *b* and *b*¹ the reference is to literal distortions of speech (deceit, cursing and bitterness). In *a* and *a*¹, the metaphor is placed first and is followed by the reference to the bodily organ, whereas in *b* and *b*¹ the bodily organ is mentioned first.[70] All this indicates

---

70. This accounts for a change to the Greek word order in the citation from Psalm 9.28: *hōn to stoma aras* rather than *hou aras to stoma autou*.

that these citations have not been selected at random and carelessly thrown together. As in the rewriting of Psalm 13, the construction of this new text out of scriptural material shows considerable rhetorical skill.

(3) The third and final section of the catena is linked to the second by its focus on specific bodily organs (feet, v.15; eyes, v.18; cf. Rom.6.13a), but moves beyond the realm of speech into that of violent action. The first three lines derive from Isaiah 59.7–8, the final one from Psalm 35.2:

> Swift are their feet to shed blood,
>   ruin and misery are in their ways,
>   and the way of peace they did not know.
> There is no fear of God before their eyes. (Rom.3.15–18)

In the following verse, Paul will claim that "what the law says it speaks to those who are under the law", and, in the original contexts of the passages cited, the address to Israel is unambiguously clear only in the Isaiah text. In the case of the psalms of complaint, David's enemies may easily be understood as Gentiles. Psalm 13 concludes with a prayer for the deliverance of Israel from captivity (v.7), which confirms that the "workers of iniquity" who "devour my people" (v.4) are Gentiles. In Psalm 9, the evildoers are explicitly identified as Gentiles (vv.6, 18, 37: "Let the sinners depart into Hades, all the Gentiles *[panta ta ethnē]* who forget God" [v.18]). All four of the psalms from which Paul quotes in Romans 3.10–14 refer not only to David and his enemies but also to the congregation of the righteous, who share his danger and who give thanks for his deliverance (Pss.5.12; 9.11, 19, 38–39; 13.5–6; 139.13–14). For nonsectarian Jewish readers, these and other similar psalms would most naturally be understood as speaking of Israel and the Gentiles, with Israel taking the role of the righteous, with whom the psalmist associates himself, and the Gentiles taking the role of the psalmist's enemies. These are indeed "nationalistic" texts, no less so than the later *Psalms of Solomon*, which constantly echo their language. Leaving aside for the moment the question why Paul selects just these texts to prove that Israel too is "under sin", we note that the original context of his Isaiah citation, unlike the others, does provide some support for his thesis.

In the Isaiah text, the prophet is speaking on the basis of his commission, which is to "lift up your voice and proclaim to my people their sins, and to the house of Jacob their transgressions" (Is.58.1). The hoped for salvation has not appeared, and it is Israel's sin that has delayed it:

> Is the hand of the Lord unable to save? or has his ear become deaf, so that he cannot hear? But your sins have separated you from God, and on account of your sins he has turned his face from you so as not to be merciful. (Is.59.1–2)

It is still "the house of Jacob" that is addressed here (cf. 58.14). In a vivid metaphorical depiction of their corrupt speech and conduct, it is said of them that they hatch adders' eggs and weave a spider's web (v.5):

> Their web shall not serve them as a garment,
>   nor will they be clothed with their works;
>   for their works are works of lawlessness.
> *Their feet* run to evil, *quick to shed blood,*
>   and their thoughts are the thoughts of fools;
>   *ruin and misery are in their ways,*
> *And the way of peace they do not know;*
>   and there is no justice in their ways,
>   for they have made crooked the paths on which they walk,
>   and they do not know peace. (Is.59.6–8)

It is because of this conduct that God's salvation remains far off (v.9). As the italicized words indicate, Paul's citation from this passage is highly selective. In addition to the omissions, there are minor differences from the LXX *(oxeis* for *tachinoi,* placed at the beginning of the sentence; *egnōsan* for *oidasin).* Once again Paul shows no interest in the broader context of this passage, and sets it alongside his psalm texts without any differentiation.

Finally, reference is briefly made to Psalm 35:

> The transgressor speaks sin in his own heart
>   *there is no fear of God before his eyes.*
> For he acts deceitfully to himself,
>   lest he should find his wickedness *[tēn anomian autou]* and hate it.
> The words of his mouth are wickedness and deceit,
>   he does not wish to understand or to do good.
> He plans wickedness on his bed,
>   he presents himself in every way that is not good,
>   evil causes him no offence. (Ps.35.2–5)

The rest of the psalm takes the form of a meditation on the Lord's mercy, truth and righteousness. The sentence quoted by Paul continues to explore the theme of the bodily members as "instruments of unrighteousness" (Rom.6.13). Its reference to God recalls "no one seeks for God" (Rom.3.11b), and its opening words *(ouk estin)* echo the fourfold repetition of this phrase at the beginning of the catena.[71]

---

71. According to Keck, the catena of Romans 3.10–18 was composed prior to Romans, not necessarily by Paul himself ("The Function of Rom 3:10–18", p. 147). The suggestion of a non-Pauline origin seems superfluous, however. The catena may have been put together during the preparation of a collection of scriptural excerpts prior to the composition of Romans (so D.-A.Koch, *Die Schrift als Zeuge des Evangeliums,* pp. 99, 179–84, pointing to comparable chains of citations in Romans 9.25–29, 10.18–21 and 15.9–12). As Koch writes: "Löst man sich von der Annahme, dass die Briefe des Paulus insgesamt erst im Augenblick

Having selected his texts, rewritten them where necessary, and harmonized them with one another, Paul has this to say about their scope: "We know that whatever the law says, it speaks to those under the law *[en tō nomō]* ... " These passages, which Paul turns into a single long scriptural citation of his own construction, articulate for him the voice of the law. In them, it is not a human author but the law itself that speaks; the names of the human authors (David and Isaiah) are eliminated, along with all other contextual factors that might detract from the universal applicability of the law's verdict on humanity. "Law" here is still the Law of Moses, but its verdict is articulated not in Moses' own words but in the words of later writers who serve here as his interpreters and commentators. It is nevertheless the law itself that utters this damning verdict on the people of the law, placing them in the same position of guilt before God that they assign to the Gentiles. Precisely in the texts cited in the catena, the law declares the guilt of the entire world – definitively, so that there can be no appeal (Rom.3.19b).

Paul's elimination of all links between the texts and their original contexts frees them to perform a new role in articulating the universal proclamation of the law – addressed as it is to Israel and indeed to "all flesh". This already mitigates the problem noted above, that, in at least four cases, the enemies to whom the texts originally referred are plausibly understood as Gentiles rather than Jews. But there is more to be said on this topic. Paul needs these texts to refer to Jews, and not only to Gentiles, in order to demonstrate his thesis that "by works of law shall no flesh be justified". If they refer only to Gentiles and not to Jews, then the law remains intact and Christ died in vain (cf. Gal.2.21). Responsibility for ultimate human well-being would remain in human hands, and the true voice of the law would be heard not in a negative verdict on all human action but in the exhortation to choose life and blessing rather than death and the curse. Can Paul offer any interpretative rationale for his decision to cause the psalms to say something that they originally did not say?

One possibility is that Paul assumes a christological reading of these psalms, in which David functions as a type of Christ, who is himself "of the seed of David" (Rom.1.3).[72] In the case of Psalm 68, for example, Paul will later identify the speaker with Christ. It is ultimately Christ rather than David who addresses to God the words, "The reproaches of those who reproached you fell upon me" (Ps.68.10; Rom.15.3). If, for Paul, the reference here is to "the Jews, who killed the Lord Jesus ... " (1 Thes.2.15–

---

des Diktierens enstanden sind, und setzt man ausserdem einen eigenständigen Umgang des Paulus mit dem Text der Schrift voraus, dann ist auch eine derart umfangreiche Zitatkomposition – jedenfalls im Römerbrief – nicht mehr überraschend" (p. 184).

72. So A. T. Hanson, "The Reproach and Vindication of the Messiah", in his *Studies in Paul's Technique and Theology*, London: SPCK, 1974, pp. 13–51; pp. 16–29.

16), that would explain how "enemies" whom previous Jewish readers would have understood to be Gentiles are now understood as non-Christian Jews. Thus, elsewhere in Romans, Paul can apply the violent imprecations of Psalm 68.23–24 to "Israel" (Rom.11.9–10) – although he immediately proceeds to limit their application. A christological hermeneutic along these lines appears to underlie the gospel passion narratives.[73] Yet there is no trace in Romans 3.9–20 of any such christological reading of the psalm texts that Paul cites. The speaker in these texts is neither David nor Christ but the law. The hypothesis that Paul here assumes a christological reading of the psalms he cites must be rejected.

A more plausible solution to the problem would be to understand David not as a type of Christ but as an example of a forgiven sinner. David's role in this capacity is underlined by Paul's citation from Psalm 31.1–2a in Romans 4.7–8:

> Blessed are those whose transgressions *[anomiai]* are forgiven,
> and whose sins *[hamartiai]* are covered.
> Blessed is the person to whom the Lord does not reckon sin.

In Paul's reading of this psalm, David shows his awareness that "transgression" and "sin" cannot simply be projected onto his and his people's enemies. It is not the case that some attain righteousness by practising the works of the law, whereas others remain in their transgression and sin, a difference that approximates to the distinction between Israel and the Gentiles. David himself was aware that sin is the universal human condition, and that what characterizes the people of God is not the absence of sin but the forgiveness of sin. If transgression and sin are no less evident among Israel than among the Gentiles, the voice of the law which brings the knowledge of sin may be heard even and especially in passages which might have seemed to speak only of the guilt of the Gentiles. When Jewish readers use these texts merely to condemn others, they condemn themselves – for they are guilty of the same things (cf. Rom.2.1). When it is said that "all have turned away, together they have become worthless" (3.12a), "all" must truly mean "all" – Jews as well as Gentiles (cf. 3.9, 23).

Paul's comment on the scope of the scriptural texts (Rom.3.19a) is a mirror-image of his interpretation of Psalm 31 in the following chapter. There, his concern is to show that the blessing David pronounces on the forgiven extends not just to Jews but also to Gentiles (4.9–12). In the present context, his concern is to show that the law's negative judgment on human conduct is addressed not just to Gentiles but also and primarily to Jews. The law's verdict makes the whole world accountable to God, and

---

73. So C. H. Dodd, *Historical Tradition in the Fourth Gospel*, pp. 31–49.

Gentiles are therefore included (3.19b, cf. v.9). Yet the law addresses especially those who are "in" or "under" the law (3.19a) – clearly a reference to Jews. Paul's reasoning is that, if the indictment summarized in 3.10–18 is addressed to Jews, then Jews must be included in this indictment. Taking Gentile guilt for granted, he argues that even those who seek to practise the law are in no way exempt from the law's universal verdict.[74]

The law's failed project

The juxtaposition of Habakkuk 2.4 and the catena of Romans 3.10–18 sets up an antithetical hermeneutic in which the voice of the prophet and the voice of the law represent the positive and the negative side of the total scriptural testimony to the Pauline gospel. The prophet announces that righteousness is by faith, the law brings the knowledge of sin, and between them they articulate the human situation before God in its pathos and its hope. This is a hermeneutical framework that is intended to make sense of scripture in its entirety, and we shall return to it in the concluding section of this chapter.

There is, however, a further dimension of Paul's antithetical hermeneutic that must be brought more clearly to light. In Romans 3.20, Paul makes two statements about the law. The second of these summarizes the message of the catena: "Through the law comes knowledge of sin." The first of them entails a denial: "By works of law shall no flesh be justified before him." The law, then, is associated both with the knowledge of sin and with "works" – the actions prescribed in its commandments. If the law prescribes a range of actions and abstentions, seeking thereby to regulate the lives of those it addresses, it cannot be said that it is *solely* an announcement of the universality of sin. When the law tells us to observe the sabbath, to honour parents, and to abstain from theft or adultery, it does not tell us that "there is no one righteous, not even one". On the contrary, it presupposes that righteousness is a genuine human possibility which it is its own role to enable. It seems that the law is in a certain sense divided against itself. Paul's antithetical hermeneutic claims to have uncovered a deep tension within the law itself, between an "optimistic" voice that assumes that its commandments can and should be obeyed, and a "pessimistic" voice that holds that this project of bringing righteousness into human life is doomed to failure. In Romans 3.19–20, it is the

74. As Sanders notes, the fact that the law speaks to those who are under the law (the Jews) does not in itself mean that the whole world is guilty before God (*Paul, the Law and the Jewish People*, p. 82). The solution to this apparent *non sequitur* is to see that the argument is also based on the *content* of what the law says, which is that "there is no one righteous" (Rom.3.10).

pessimistic voice that predominates. Yet the very negation of the law's "works" as marking out the way of righteousness acknowledges both that a very different construal of the law is possible, and that it has deep roots within the Torah itself.[75]

The assertion that "by works of law shall no flesh be justified before him" alludes to yet another Davidic prayer for deliverance, written (according to the LXX) at the time of Absalom's rebellion:

> Lord, hear my prayer,
>> give heed to my request in your truth *[en tē alētheia sou]*,
>> listen to me in your righteousness *[en tē dikaiosunē sou]*.
> And do not enter into judgment with your servant,
>> for no living thing will be justified before you
> *[hoti ou dikaiōthēsetai enōpion sou pas zōn]*.
> For the enemy pursues my soul,
>> he has humbled to the ground my life,
>> he has made me sit in darkness, like those long dead. (Ps.142.1–3)

In this prayer for deliverance, it is clearer than in any of the psalms explicitly cited (Pss.5; 9; 13; 35; 139) that the appeal to God's righteousness excludes any appeal to David's own righteousness. David participates in the guilt of all human beings, and so he cannot appeal to his own deserts as the basis for his plea. Indeed, his guilt potentially undermines his plea. If God chose to subject his conduct to a quasi-legal scrutiny, seeking out past sins and misdemeanours, God would undoubtedly prevail. No living being could withstand such a scrutiny. More clearly than in the other psalms, God's righteousness is identified here with God's mercy (cf. Ps.142.8, 11–12).[76]

In drawing on the language of this psalm to clarify the point of the preceding citations, Paul does not simply repeat its statement that "no living thing will be justified before you". The universal scope of the statement is preserved in the replacement of "every living thing" *(pas zōn)*

75. Romans 3.20a therefore ascribes a certain soteriology to the law itself, and not just to Paul's contemporaries (cf. Rom.10.5; Lev.18.5). Paul here tells us not only that "final salvation according to works is a belief of the Judaism with which he is in debate" (S. J. Gathercole, *Where is Boasting?*, p. 223), but also that this belief is rooted in the Torah itself. As Mark Seifrid states: "When Paul rejects the saving value of the 'works of the law' in Galatians and Romans, he does so with full recognition that he is dealing not merely with a misreading of the law, but with the law itself" (*Christ our Righteousness*, p. 105).

76. Richard Hays finds in this psalm the background for Paul's understanding of the "righteousness of God", the theme of the verses that follow (Rom.3.21–26): thus, Käsemann's understanding of this phrase in terms of "God's own active salvation-creating power" can be shown to be correct from within Romans itself ("Psalm 143 and the Logic of Romans 3", p. 108). Yet Paul's "righteousness of God" coinage presents itself in Romans 1.17 as a gloss on Habakkuk 2.4, and this text remains fundamental in Romans 3.21–31. There is a different usage in 3.4–5, where "God's righteousness" is derived from Psalm 50.6. The righteousness of God must be understood by way of the texts *actually cited* in Romans.

by "all flesh" *(pasa sarx)*; and, like the preceding citations, it is now seen as an utterance of the law, a summary of "what the law says" (3.19a). This particular utterance *of* the law is, however, also a statement *about* the law. Paul causes the law to speak not only about human sin but also about itself, by adding the phrase "by works of law" *(ex ergōn nomou)* to the language drawn from the psalm: "For *by works of law* shall no flesh be justified before him." What is excluded here is not justification *per se* but justification by works of law. That is the conclusion Paul derives from the law's own testimony, as previously cited. When the law declares the people of the law to be unrighteous, thereby communicating to them a "knowledge of sin", it is, crucially, making a statement not only about them but also about itself. The law declares that "works of law" – its own works, the observance of its commandments – are not the way to righteousness. But the observance of its commandments is precisely what the law enjoins from beginning to end, from the Decalogue in Exodus 20 to the eloquent exhortations of the book of Deuteronomy. Those who hear the commandments are exhorted to choose life rather than death, blessing rather than the curse (cf. Deut.30.19). Those who observe the commandments are promised that they will live by them (cf. Lev.18.5). Yet the law, whose very rationale is to engender the practices that lead to life, declares – according to Paul – that the possibility that it strove to exclude, that of death and the curse, has in fact been definitively realized. Certain works of law are practised, no doubt, but they occur only within a total context in which the members of the body – throat, tongue, lips, mouth, feet, eyes – have been converted into "instruments of unrighteousness" (6.13; cf. 3.10–18). The law has been unable to prevent a headlong plunge into iniquity, which is evident not simply in gross violations which cause a public scandal (cf. 2.21–24) but in the very texture of everyday life, where, for example, violent speech-acts against the other are so normal as to pass without comment (cf. 3.13–14). In asserting that works of law do not lead to righteousness, the law declares the failure of its own project.

Once the scriptural background to Paul's claim about the law has come to light, it is no longer possible to understand his exclusion of "works of law" as referring primarily to "boundary markers" that differentiate the Jewish community from the Gentile world and that generate pride in the divine election.[77] Works of law are the practices enjoined by the law,

---

77. Commenting on this passage, Dunn argues that *ex ergōn nomou* represents "the assumption that God's covenant with Israel gave them a special ground of justification, a special defense in the final judgment (*Romans*, 1.153–54). Paul's target was "the devout Jew who reckoned himself already a member of the covenant people ... " and who thought that his obligation under the law found characteristic expression in a distinctive religious lifestyle in which the distinctively Jewish rites inevitably came into prominence ... " (p. 155). Thus, the

understood soteriologically as representing the way to "life" (cf. 9.30–10.5).[78] Yet it is the testimony of the law itself that sinful human beings are incapable of attaining to life by this means.[79] In a context permeated by sin, the commandment that promised life leads only to death. As David himself recognized, salvation can only be the work of the divine righteousness and mercy.

The theme of Romans 1.18–3.20 is normally said to be "the universality of sin". It is striking, however, that this theme becomes fully explicit only at the conclusion of the argument, in the context of scriptural citations and of statements about the meaning and significance of scripture or "the law" (3.9–20). The universality motif is introduced in 3.4 ("Let God be true but every human false!"), and there too a scriptural citation immediately follows: " . . . as it is written, 'So that you may be justified in your words, and prevail when you are judged'" (Ps.50[51].6).[80] Here, God's "words" must refer to his indictment of the entire human race, and God's justification or judgment must consist in the human acknowledgment of the righteousness of the divine verdict which occurs when "every mouth" is "stopped" (cf. Rom.3.19). It is, however, *scripture* that announces in advance the final human acknowledgment of the divine verdict (3.4), and that proclaims here and now that all Jews stand

concept of "works of law" is "more narrowly and polemically focused" than, for example, the earlier comprehensive reference to "doers of the law" in 2.13 (p. 153). Dunn has derived the understanding of the covenant as "a special defense in the final judgment" from Romans 2, where the motif of divine impartiality is employed to criticize the assumption that membership of the covenant community guarantees salvation. In 3.1–20, however, this critique gives way to the theme of universal human guilt before God. In 3.20, "works of law" is to be taken at face value as a comprehensive expression that refers not only to circumcision (cf. 2.25–3.1) but also to the ten commandments (cf. 2.21–23) and to the practice of the law in general.

78.   No distinction is to be drawn between "doing" the commandments in Leviticus 18.5 and the Pauline "works of law". As S. J. Gathercole points out, the non-scriptural expression "works of Torah" *(m'śy htwrh)* is derived from the many scriptural references to "doing" *('śh)* the commandments of the Torah *(Where is Boasting?*, p. 92).

79.   On this reading, it remains the case that "works of the law" stands for "the way of life of the Jewish people, those who are within God's covenant with Israel", that Paul does not "regard the Jews as representatives of a more general phenomenon, 'religion', which involves human achievement and boasting before God", and that his argument entails "an implicit call for social reorientation" (see my *Paul, Judaism and the Gentiles*, p. 130, arguing against Käsemann). I would now add two points to this. (1) The "way of life of the Jewish people" is (for Paul) textually determined, and entails both a hermeneutic and a soteriology: "the Jews" are, above all, those who "were entrusted with the oracles of God" (3.1). (2) The implication should be avoided that "works of law" are subordinate to a prior covenant of pure divine grace; "covenant" and "works" should not be played off against each other.

80.   The antecedent to this citation itself alludes to scripture: "I believed, so I spoke *[episteusa dio elalēsa]*, I was brought very low; I said in my astonishment, 'Every human is a liar' *[pas anthrōpos pseustēs]*" (Ps.115.1–2; cf. 2 Cor.4.13). The citation itself is virtually identical to the LXX wording.

alongside all Gentiles in their manifold guilt before God (3.9–18); and these citations are in part self-referential, for in them the fundamental sense of the law itself comes to light (3.19–20). We also recall that to be a Jew is, first and foremost, to be "entrusted with the words *[logia]* of God" (3.1; cf. 2.17–20), and that the unfaithfulness of "some" (3.2) is determined by these same scriptural utterances. In the light of this, it is likely that the divine "words" *[logoi]* whose justice will be acknowledged on the Day of Judgment (3.4) are nothing other than the scriptural indictment of human sin as summarized in the catena that is to follow (3.10–18). The correspondence between "the words of God" and "in your words" (vv.2, 4) is too close to be coincidental.[81] In Romans 3.1–20, then, it is *the scriptural indictment* of universal human sinfulness that Paul seeks to articulate.[82] This follows on from the analysis of Gentile sin (1.18–32) and the anti-covenantal argument about the impartiality of the eschatological divine judgment (2.1–29) – relatively self-contained passages that nevertheless serve to establish important premises for the crucial argument that follows (3.1–20). Here, it emerges that precisely those divine scriptures that constitute the Jewish "advantage" over the rest of humankind (3.1) in fact set Jews in the same position of guilt before God as Gentiles: and this applies not just to "some" Jews (as in chapter 2), but to all. If Romans 1.18–3.20 is seen as a single argument whose thrust only becomes fully explicit in its conclusion, then its theme is "universal human sinfulness" not *per se* but as the true content of the scriptural testimony. Paul speaks here primarily of scripture and of the reality of human life as exposed by scripture.[83]

As we have seen, the law's indictment of humankind is at the same time an acknowledgment that its own project – of prescribing the actions or abstentions that constitute the way of righteousness for humans – has failed. The law exists in a state of self-contradiction. If for Paul it is its

81. The correspondence is rightly noted by J. Fitzmyer, *Romans*, p. 328.

82. In the light of the emphasis on scripture in 3.2–4, an integrated reading of 3.1–8 and 3.9–20 becomes possible. While vv.5–8 is in one sense a digression, responding to an accusation made against Paul himself (cf. v.8), the emphasis on judgment relates this paragraph both to what precedes it (v.4) and to what follows (vv.9–20). For further discussion of Romans 3.1–8, see chapter 9 below.

83. In most summaries of Romans 1.18–3.20, the scriptural dimension is of secondary rather than primary significance. Thus, according to G. Bornkamm, "Die Absicht der breiten Darlegungen von 1,18–3,20 ist ja eben, die Verlorenheit *aller* Welt an die Sünde und ihre Strafverfallenheit (3,19f.) unter dem Gesetz zu zeigen, wovon also niemand eine Ausnahme macht" ("Die Offenbarung des Zornes Gottes" [1935], repr. in his *Das Ende des Gesetzes*, pp. 9–33; p. 10). Criticisms of this standard view normally point to the absence of the universal sin motif in 1.18–2.29, but over-emphasize the independence of these sections at the expense of their contribution to an argument that culminates in 3.1–20.

pessimistic voice that predominates, the assumption that commandments can and should be obeyed cannot easily be eradicated from the texts of Exodus and Leviticus, Numbers and Deuteronomy. We shall return to this problem in chapters 6–9, where it will be crucial to take seriously Paul's claim that the contradiction occurs within the Torah itself, and is not just a figment of his own imagination.

The law and the prophets

Romans 3.9–20 concludes a long section (1.18–3.20) in which – as gradually becomes clear – the aim is to show, by the law's own testimony, that the law represents not the appointed way to salvation but the definitive disclosure of universal human sinfulness. Since it is the prophetic announcement of another way of salvation that enables Paul to hear this self-testimony of the law, the Habakkuk citation may be seen as the foundation for Paul's entire argument thus far. Its significance is confirmed by the long-delayed resumption of the language and conceptuality of Romans 1.17 in 3.21–31. If 1.17a may be seen as an interpretative gloss on the Habakkuk citation, 3.21–22 represents a carefully crafted expansion and development of that initial statement:

> For in it the righteousness of God is revealed, by faith, for faith; as it is written, The one who is righteous by faith shall live. (1.17)

> *But now apart from law* the righteousness of God has been manifested, *attested by the law and the prophets*, the righteousness of God through faith *of Jesus Christ* for all who believe. (3.21–22)

Here, the italicized phrases represent the new elements that did not occur in the original version of Paul's thesis about righteousness by faith. Without these phrases, the resumptive character of this passage stands out clearly. The righteousness of God has been manifested – the righteousness of God through faith, for all who believe. There are minor differences of phraseology: "has been manifested" *(pephanerōtai)* replaces "is revealed" *(apokaluptetai)*, "through faith" *(dia pisteōs)* replaces "by faith" *(ek pisteōs)*, "for all who believe" *(eis pantas tous pisteuontas)* replaces "for faith" *(eis pistin)*. The repetition of "righteousness of God" is not to be seen as a new element in this statement, since the same repetition is understood in the original statement: "in it the righteousness of God is revealed, by faith ... " means that there is in the gospel a revelation of that righteousness of God which is by faith. These alterations do not significantly affect the sense of the new statement, and are apparently motivated by the familiar stylistic concern for variation within repetition. Attempts to differentiate the meaning of "has been manifested" from "is revealed", or of "through faith" from "by faith", are unpersuasive.[84] The replacement of "by faith" by "through faith" means that the relationship to Habakkuk 2.4 is less explicit than in the original statement of Paul's thesis. But if the earlier statement is indeed a gloss on the Habakkuk text, then this second, expanded statement is also indirectly linked to that text. (We might compare the way in which, in Romans 4, Paul gradually assimilates the language of Genesis 15.6 into his own discourse.)

More significant than the elements of repetition are the three points at which Romans 3.21–22 amplifies the thesis of 1.17a, further developing the interpretation of the Habakkuk text.

(1) The phrase, "But now apart from law . . . " is the first additional element in the restatement of Paul's thesis in Romans 3.21–22. Following the four references to the law with which the previous section concludes (3.19–20), this confirms that the question of the law's meaning and significance is central to Paul's concerns here. The assertion that the righteousness of God is "apart from law" (v.21) corresponds to the assertion that this righteousness is "through faith of Jesus Christ" (v.22), and this makes it clear that the initial "by faith" of the Habakkuk citation carries for Paul the connotation, "apart from law". "By faith" *means* "apart from law", and the necessity of this "apart from law" arises from the fact that "by works of law shall no flesh be justified before him . . . ". In these brief, cryptic Pauline formulations, a radical new reading of Jewish scripture is coming to birth, over against a reading in which scripture consists most fundamentally in the commandments that point the way to righteousness and life. Paul here practises a specifically hermeneutical theology.

(2) This is confirmed by the second point at which Romans 3.21–22 represents an expansion of the original thesis of 1.17a. If the righteousness of God is manifested "apart from law", it is nevertheless "attested by the law and the prophets". The undifferentiated "as it is written" of the standard introductory formula (1.17; 2.24; 3.4, 10) here gives way to a formulation that acknowledges a certain distinction within the corpus of scriptural writings. Some writings are "law", others are "prophets". This formulation is itself traditional,[85] like Paul's standard introductory formula, although this is the only occasion on which he uses it.[86] While

---

84. A convincing case for regarding the "faith" formulations as synonymous is presented by Douglas Campbell, "The Meaning of ΠΙΣΤΙΣ and ΝΟΜΟΣ in Paul", pp. 91–99. Campbell rightly emphasizes that variations of usage may have a purely rhetorical significance.

85. References to "the law and the prophets" are found (with minor variations) in Sir. Prol.; 2 Macc.15.9; 4 Macc.18.10; Mt.5.17, 7.12, 11.13 (= Lk.16.16), 22.40; Lk.24.44; Acts 13.15, 24.14, 28.23; Jn.1.45.

86. As Dunn notes (*Romans*, 1.165).

it differentiates the Law of Moses from the "former" and "latter" prophets, the formulation is clearly intended to refer to scripture as a whole and need not imply any difference of function between its two main parts. In its Pauline usage too, the law and the prophets are at one with each other in attesting the righteousness of God through faith. Yet in its present context the traditional formulation may imply more than that. Like "apart from law", the phrase "attested by the law and the prophets" summarizes more detailed statements elsewhere, and these suggest that Paul finds an untraditional meaning in the traditional phraseology. For him, "law" and "prophets" represent not only the two generic categories of the scriptural writings, but also a fundamental distinction within the scriptural testimony to the righteousness of God through faith. In the preceding discussion, Paul has heard the voice of the law in the writings not of Moses but of David and Isaiah, cited anonymously in Romans 3.10–18 as embodying the voice of the law. In the words of its early commentators, the law announces that "no one is righteous, not even one" (3.10): and this is testimony to righteousness by faith in the indirect and negative sense that it rules out the alternative possibility of a righteousness by law observance. On the other hand, when the prophet speaks as a prophet and not as a commentator on the law, he speaks directly of the righteousness by faith that is the positive corollary of the law's testimony. Habakkuk spoke clearly of this, but so too did Moses himself when he wrote Genesis 15.6, the text that is to be expounded in Romans 4. The attestation of the righteousness of God by the law and the prophets is, then, twofold in form, consisting of an affirmation and a corresponding negation. And if the righteousness of God is attested by the law and the prophets, then the righteousness of God itself has a hermeneutical function: it serves to disclose the meaning of the law and the prophets, which speak respectively of the bankruptcy of one way to righteousness and of the other way that God has now opened up. Texts that Paul has cited – "there is no one righteous, not even one", "the one who is righteous by faith shall live" – encapsulate the double-edged testimony of scripture as a whole.

(3) The final addition to the original form of Paul's thesis about righteousness by faith occurs in the reference to a "righteousness of God through faith *of Jesus Christ*" (v.22). Jesus Christ was not mentioned in the original thesis, presumably because, for obvious reasons, he was not mentioned in the citation. The righteousness of God was said to be revealed in the gospel, but nothing was said about Jesus Christ as either the object or the subject of faith. Here too Romans 3.21–22 seeks to expand and clarify the original thesis. A qualified antithesis has already been established between the "faith" referred to by Habakkuk and the practice

of the law (3.21); and now the term "faith" must be clarified from another angle by way of a linkage with Jesus Christ. The expansion of the prophetic "by faith" to "through faith of Jesus Christ" was perhaps suggested by its negative counterpart in 3.20, the phrase "by works of law".[87] In both cases, a preposition introduces a double genitival construction in which the second substantive ("law", "Jesus Christ") serves to define the scope of the first ("works", "faith"). The "works" or actions in question are defined by their relation to "the law"; the "faith" or belief in question is defined by its relation to "Jesus Christ". Despite their definitional function, however, these genitive formulations retain a degree of vagueness, and clarity about the exact relation of the respective pairs of substantives can only be derived from the wider context. The phrase "by works of law" is likely to mean "the works or actions prescribed by the law", rather than "the works or actions performed by the law". We learn this not from grammar but from our sense that law is most probably to be understood not as a personal agent but as a set of divinely authorized demands for specified actions or abstentions, such as the ones alluded to in Romans 2.21–25. In the case of "through faith of Jesus Christ", the same methodological principle should apply. Although the reference to Jesus Christ serves to define or delimit the scope of "through faith", the exact relation between the two substantives remains unclear. This vagueness can only be dispelled by the reader's sense of how the relation of faith and Jesus Christ might appropriately be construed, on the basis of the broader context.[88] As we have seen, the phrase "through faith of Jesus Christ" occurs in a context in which a thesis derived from a scriptural citation is restated in amplified form. Paul's original thesis – about the righteousness of God which is by faith – took the form of an interpretative gloss on the Habakkuk citation. Although the gloss sought to clarify and amplify the quotation at several points, there was no indication that the prophetic "by faith" was understood as referring to the faith or faithfulness of Christ himself. "The one who is righteous by faith" is not Christ but the believer (compare the reference in 1.16 to "everyone who believes, the Jew first and also the Greek"). If in 3.22 the phrase "through faith of Jesus Christ" derives from the "by faith" of the original thesis and the citation (1.17), then it must be understood in a way that harmonizes with that earlier usage. "Through faith of Jesus Christ" indicates that the earlier "by faith"

---

87. So Barry Matlock, "Detheologizing the ΠΙΣΤΙΣ ΧΡΙΣΤΟΥ Debate", p. 21. This point does not undermine the derivation of *ek pisteōs* from Habakkuk 2.4, as Matlock assumes.

88. There is no initial presumption, on the basis of "the simple meaning of the Greek", that *ton ek pisteōs Iēsou* in 3.26 means "the one who shares the faith of Jesus", i.e. "the one who has faith as Jesus had faith" (*contra* L. T. Johnson, "Rom 3:21–26 and the Faith of Jesus", p. 81). In 4.16, we know that *tō ek pisteōs Abraam* refers to a sharing in Abraham's own faith because this is clear from the context.

is to be understood in some unspecified relation to Jesus Christ, but it can hardly indicate that Jesus is himself the subject of that faith or faithfulness. If Paul did not understand the Habakkuk citation christologically, then he cannot be referring to the faithfulness of Christ in Romans 3.22. If he did understand the citation christologically, he should already have made this clear in Romans 1.17.[89]

Paul himself provides the necessary contextual clarification of the relation of "faith" to "Jesus Christ" in the assertions that follow the expanded restatement of the original thesis in Romans 3.21–22. The introduction of "Jesus Christ" into the restatement prepares for the claim that those who have sinned are nevertheless

> justified freely by his grace through the redemption which is in Christ Jesus, whom God set forth as an atoning sacrifice, through faith *[dia tēs pisteōs]*, by his blood – as a sign of his righteousness on account of the remission of former sins in God's forbearance; as a sign of his righteousness in the present time, so that he might be just and the justifier of the one who is of the faith of Jesus *[ton ek pisteōs Iēsou]*. (3.24–26)

This passage is of course full of exegetical difficulties.[90] For our purposes, what matters is to see how it serves to clarify the relationship asserted in the phrase "through faith of Jesus Christ" (v.22). It is striking that this passage interprets Jesus' death not as the outcome of his own faithfulness but as God's saving action. While this action has its own particular time and place, it is not closed in upon itself but forms the basis of the ongoing divine action in which God justifies the one who responds to it in faith. Faith, and consequently righteousness, is what is intended in God's action in the death of Jesus: God set forth Christ as an atoning sacrifice by his blood, but with a view to the "faith" through which its benefits – righteousness, the remission of former sins – would be received. God justifies the one who is of the faith of Jesus, since the name "Jesus" denotes nothing other than the saving action that God accomplished in his death. If, however, God's action in Christ intends the faith that leads to justification, this faith is itself the recognition and acknowledgment of the divine saving action. In a two-way movement from Christ's death and back to it again, God's saving act in Christ seeks to elicit the answering faith that acknowledges it as what it truly is. Faith, then, is "faith of Jesus

---

89. On this argument, the translation "through faith in Jesus Christ" (e.g. Fitzmyer, *Romans*, p. 345) is hardly less misleading and paraphrastic than "through the faithfulness of Jesus Christ". Where a preposition is inserted in the one case or the definite article in the other, an interpretative decision is made that the Greek phrase leaves open.

90. On which see the clear and insightful analysis of Douglas Campbell, in *The Rhetoric of Righteousness*.

Christ" in the dual sense that Jesus Christ, the embodiment of God's saving action, is as such both the origin and the object of faith. In this way, the ambiguous genitive formulations – "through faith of Jesus Christ", "the one who is of the faith of Jesus" (vv.22, 26) – may be clarified, not by grammar but by context.

The expanded restatement of the original thesis about righteousness by faith (1.17) has related the new reality to the law, by way of a qualified antithesis (3.21), and to Jesus Christ (3.22a). Each of these points is further elucidated in what follows. The relationship between the new reality and Jesus Christ is the theme of Romans 3.22b–26, where God's saving action in Jesus' death is presented as both origin and object of the faith that leads to righteousness. The relationship between the new reality and the law is developed in 3.27–31, again by way of a qualified antithesis. In 3.21–22, then, the expansion of the original thesis has a programmatic function in relation to the remainder of this chapter.[91] And, since the original thesis was itself an interpretative gloss on the Habakkuk citation, that citation remains the foundation and presupposition of Paul's whole argument. It does not merely provide him with secondary scriptural support, rhetorically valuable but ultimately dispensable, for a freestanding argument of his own. As we have seen, the introductory formula "as it is written" serves in 1.17 not to confirm an independent statement but to identify the scriptural origins of that statement, and so to characterize the thesis-like antecedent as an interpretative gloss on the text cited. If the initial thesis is an interpretative gloss on the Habakkuk citation, then its further development in Romans 3.21–31 may similarly be traced back to the prophetic text.

In this chapter, we have begun to substantiate the claim that Paul's doctrine of righteousness by faith is an exercise in scriptural interpretation and hermeneutics. Paul seeks to persuade his readers that this language and conceptuality is generated by scripture, which thereby bears witness to its own fundamental duality. In its prophetic voice, scripture speaks of the (positive) outcome of God's future saving action; in the voice of the law, it speaks of the (negative) outcome of the human action that the law itself had previously promoted. This dual scriptural testimony is fundamental to the Pauline hermeneutics of faith, and we shall encounter a number of its variants in the chapters that follow.[92]

---

91. Romans 3.21–31 is therefore structured chiastically: A 3.21; B 3.22a; B^1 3.22b–26; A^1 3.27–31.

92. Paul's antithetical hermeneutic is developed especially in Romans 3, although its foundation is laid in 1.16–17. In Romans 4, as we shall see, Paul applies his hermeneutic to the

Although Paul has directed us to the testimony of the law and of the prophets, it is he himself who interprets that testimony. We cannot take on trust his claim that, while speaking in his own voice, he faithfully reproduces the (twofold) voice of scripture. We must also attend to those who understand the scriptural voice differently from Paul. In the case of the Habakkuk text, for example, a reading is possible which thoroughly integrates the prophetic testimony to God's saving action with the witness of the law. Such a reading will be the subject of the following chapter.

reading of Genesis. This analysis raises questions about the traditional distinction between 1.18–3.20 as "the problem" and 3.21–4.25 as "the solution" (so T. Engberg-Pedersen, *Paul and the Stoics*, pp. 179, 217, following Bultmann and Bornkamm).

Chapter 2

Reading the Twelve

The introductory formula, "as it is written", serves to authorize a new statement by asserting a correspondence with an older statement whose authority is already acknowledged. Where the lexical and semantic relationship between the new and the old statement is particularly close, the formula may also identify the source from which the new statement derives. In the case of Romans 1–3, Paul presents his doctrine of righteousness by faith as exegesis of Habakkuk 2.4, which generates and authorizes the fundamental statements of Romans 1.17a and 3.21–31.

"As it is written" has at least two further dimensions, however. First, it may be understood as an invitation to reread the text from which the citation is drawn, in order to confirm the supposed correspondence for oneself. Paul's text does not *demand* that its readers also read Habakkuk, yet it does present its own author as a reader of Habakkuk, understood as part of a collection of sacred and authoritative writings with a unique capacity to illuminate the present. Paul intends his readers to participate in his own attempts to make Christian sense of the scriptures. "Whatever was written in former times", he tells them, "was written for our instruction, so that through endurance and through the encouragement of the scriptures we might have hope" (Rom.15.4). If Paul's readers are to read his own texts critically and with understanding, they must join him in reading the scriptural texts to which he appeals. In the Roman Christian communities and wherever else Paul's letter is read, it will be necessary to pursue the dialogue with the scriptural texts along the lines that the letter has opened up. "As it is written" is an invitation to that dialogue.

Second, "as it is written" implies a reading community that not only acknowledges certain texts as normative but also concerns itself with the implications of that normativity. In the citation formula, the new text proposes an interpretation of an old and familiar text, and, in this case at least, it is assumed that former interpretations are inadequate or erroneous. "As it is written" is potentially a polemical statement: what the scriptural text really means is *this*, rather than *that*. When Paul asserts that the corollary of the scriptural "by faith" is "and not by works of law", he presents a *re*interpretation of a text already read and interpreted; a text on which he possesses no monopoly. A reinterpretation is achieved in dialogue not only with the text but also with the interpretative tradition. Thus, in citing a text, Paul engages in tacit dialogue with other readings no less than with the text itself.[1] A Pauline citation entails a three-way conversation.

Having traced the role of the Habakkuk citation in Paul's own discourse, we must now address these further dimensions of the citation formula. We are explicitly directed to a scriptural text in its canonical context, and we are implicitly directed to an interpretative context that makes reinterpretation a possibility. These are the two issues to be addressed in this chapter and the following one. In attending to them, we shall not be wandering away from the sphere of Pauline theology into other, only loosely related areas. If the Pauline "doctrine of justification" is in fact a scriptural hermeneutic, then it cannot be adequately understood apart from its relation to the scriptural text on the one hand and the interpretative tradition on the other.

The Hermeneutics of the End

The Qumran commentary on Habakkuk 1–2 is the obvious point of comparison with Paul's use of the Habakkuk text. While the two interpretations of this text can quite straightforwardly be compared, it is harder to show that they both participate in a single interpretative tradition. At first sight, Paul and the Qumran commentator appear to read Habakkuk in complete isolation from each other, and with incommensurable presuppositions. The first step towards bringing them into closer proximity is to investigate the place of the book of Habakkuk within the prophetic collection. Does this text already belong to a canonical "Book of the Twelve", with clearly defined content and order? If so, are there conclusions to be drawn about the significance of this composite book alongside the other prophetic books? Within the Book of the Twelve, was a special place assigned to Habakkuk? And, crucially, are there formal similarities between the Qumranic and the Pauline readings of Habakkuk, in and among the obvious differences? We shall see that all such similarities and differences are the product of the single intertextual field within which both readers are located. It is therefore no accident that two

---

1. This "tacit dialogue" with alternative readings occurs already in the act of positing one's own reading as the appropriate one. It is therefore unnecessary to show that any particular reading of a text was available to Paul, and that he had it in mind while writing. In the case of Galatians, for example, Paul's scriptural interpretation is dialogical in form whether or not he here responds to readings of texts already introduced by his opponents (as argued by J. L. Martyn, *Galatians*, pp. 302–306, 324–34, and others).

such different readers can both find a definitive summary of the message of the prophets within the same passage in Habakkuk.

The Book of the Twelve

In the section of his work devoted to the praise of the fathers, Ben Sira indicates that "the twelve prophets" could already be seen as a closed collection in the early part of the second century BCE. Isaiah, Jeremiah and Ezekiel are all duly commended (Sir.48.22b–25; 49.6–7, 8–9), alongside Hezekiah and Josiah, the only two righteous kings of Judah after David (48.17–22a; 49.1–5), and a brief summary of their respective messages is given. Of "Isaiah the prophet" it is said that

> he was great and faithful in his vision. In his days the sun went backward, and he lengthened the life of the king. In the great Spirit *[brwḥ gbwrh]* he saw the last things *['ḥryt]* and comforted the mourners of Sion. He showed what would take place until the end, and the hidden things before they came to pass. (Sir.48.22b–25)[2]

While Isaiah's ministry is linked with the reign of the righteous king Hezekiah, Jeremiah's ministry is the divine response to Judah's apostate kings, who

> gave their power to others, and their glory to a foreign nation – who burned the chosen city of the sanctuary, and made her streets desolate, by the hand of Jeremiah. For they persecuted him, although he was sanctified as a prophet in the womb, to uproot and afflict and destroy, and likewise to build and to plant. (49.5–7)

Next comes Ezekiel,

> who saw a vision of glory, which he showed him above the chariot of the cherubim. For he remembered his enemies with a storm, and did good to those who rightly directed their ways. (49.8–9)

In these depictions, the distinctive characters of the three main prophetic books stands out clearly, with obvious allusions to the respective texts (Is.1.1, 38.1–8, 40.1, 61.3; Jer.1.5, 10; Ezek.1). The twelve, however, are described as though they constitute a single book:

> And let the bones of the twelve prophets revive from their place; for they comforted *[parekalesan]* Jacob, and delivered them in the confidence of hope *[en pistei elpidos]*. (Sir.49.10)[3]

---

2. The first two sentences of this passage are extant only in Greek.
3. The Hebrew of Sirach 48.8–10 is defective.

For Ben Sira, the overall message of the twelve is essentially positive and echoes Isaiah's message of comfort. Thus the books of comfort precede and follow the books in which judgment predominates – above all Jeremiah, and also perhaps Ezekiel. In the case of the twelve, there is no clear allusion to any specific passage, although Ben Sira has previously shown a familiarity with Malachi, quoting the promise of Elijah's return at the book's conclusion (48.10; cf. Mal.3.23). While Ben Sira is praising famous men not famous books, his references to Isaiah, Jeremiah, Ezekiel and the twelve imply that the familiar Masoretic order was already in existence, and that it consists essentially of four books rather than fifteen.

The Qumran manuscripts from Cave 4 provide confirmation that the twelve minor prophets were already regarded as a single book in the second and first centuries BCE, and that they occurred in a fixed order corresponding to the later Masoretic one. This material, first published only in 1997, is admittedly difficult to interpret, and the analysis offered here is provisional and subject to correction.[4]

Eight manuscripts devoted to these texts survive in fragmentary form (4QMinor Prophets^{a-g} = 4Q76–82; 5QAmos = 5Q4). It is not possible to be certain that all of these manuscripts originally included all twelve writings. Yet most of them certainly contained more than one of these texts, and surviving fragments of a given manuscript tend to derive from texts contiguous to one another in the traditional Masoretic order. In two manuscripts, fragments survive of only a single prophetic text (4QXII^{d} = Hos.1.7–2.5; 5QAmos = Am.1.2–5). 4QXII^{b} comprises fragments of Zephaniah and Haggai (including the transition between the two), 4QXII^{e} of Haggai and Zechariah, 4QXII^{f} of Jonah and Micah,[5] 4QXII^{a} of Jonah, Zechariah and Malachi. More substantial fragments survive of the two remaining manuscripts. 4QXII^{c} contains material from Hosea, Joel, Amos, Zephaniah and Malachi(?), fairly extensive in the case of the first three.[6] 4QXII^{g} contains material from Hosea, Joel, Amos, Obadiah, Jonah, Micah, Nahum, Habakkuk(?), Zephaniah and

---

4. Information about the contents of the fragmentary minor prophets manuscripts is conveniently summarized in García Martínez and Tigchelaar, *The Dead Sea Scrolls*, 1.273–77, which in turn derives from the editorial work of R. E. Fuller, C. M. Murphy and C. Niccum, in *DJD* XV, pp. 221–318. The editors generally assume the Masoretic order in enumerating and listing the surviving fragments, and do not fully engage with the question whether these manuscripts actually followed this order. For additional information and analysis, see R. E. Fuller, "The Form and Formation of the Book of the Twelve".

5. It is plausible but not certain that a surviving fragment of Micah 5.1–2 belongs to 4QXII^{f} (*DJD* XV, p. 270). It was formerly identified as "4QMicah".

6. The editors of *DJD* XV conclude that a fragment of Malachi 3.6–7 "probably belongs to a separate, otherwise unknown manuscript of the Twelve" (p. 251).

Zechariah, including the transition between Amos and Obadiah. It also includes a fragment consisting of several layers in which texts from Hosea, Joel and Amos can be identified (frg.30), and a fragment of Nahum in which a term seemingly deriving from Micah has impressed itself in mirror image on the verso from the layer above (frg.97).[7] Thus, two transitions between one text and another are preserved (Amos-Obadiah in 4QXII^g; Zephaniah-Haggai in 4QXII^b); two layered fragments also give clear evidence of the ordering of the texts (4QXII^g); and the survival patterns also suggest the contiguity of Hosea, Joel and Amos (4QXII^c), Jonah and Micah (4QXII^f), Haggai and Zechariah (4QXII^e), and Zechariah and Malachi (4QXII^a; on the alleged presence of Jonah in this manuscript, see further below). If the evidence of the 4QXII manuscripts is assembled into a composite picture, the order that emerges is as follows:

> Hosea-Joel-Amos-Obadiah, Jonah/Micah, Micah-Nahum, Zephaniah-Haggai, Haggai/Zechariah, Zechariah/Malachi

Here, a hyphen represents clear evidence of order (a surviving transition, a layered fragment); a forward slash represents probable contiguity (survival patterns); and a comma represents the non-availability of evidence for a connection. This composite picture can be further refined by combining the unambiguous evidence of order with the indirect evidence of contiguity. The transition from Zephaniah to Haggai is preserved in one manuscript; and Haggai and Zechariah are contiguous in another, Zechariah and Malachi in a third. This would appear to confirm that the order of the final four books of the traditional collection was already represented in these manuscripts of the second and first centuries BCE. A similar situation exists in the case of three books in the middle of the collection (Jonah, Micah and Nahum). The hypothetical order would now be as follows:

> Hosea-Joel-Amos-Obadiah, Jonah-Micah-Nahum, Zephaniah-Haggai-Zechariah-Malachi

This order is fully consistent with the Masoretic order, and suggests that this may predate the alternative order attested by the Septuagint:

> Osee, Amos, Michaias, Ioel, Abdias, Jonas, Naoum, Ambakoum, Sophonias, Aggaios, Zacharias, Malachias

In this order, Amos and Micah have been "promoted" from third and sixth place to second and third place respectively; the order is otherwise identical to the Masoretic one. The Septuagintal order looks like an attempt to improve on an earlier order, by giving a more prominent place

---

7. Details in *DJD* XV, pp. 290 (frg.30), 315–16 (frg.97 verso and recto).

to Amos and Micah in relation to Joel and Obadiah in view of their greater length and significance and their links to Hosea.[8]

Habakkuk is the only one of the twelve who remains so far unaccounted for. With the doubtful exception of fragment 102 of 4QXII^g, which may derive from Habakkuk 2.4, this prophet is unrepresented in the Cave 4 texts.[9] In the light of the high value ascribed to Habakkuk in the pesharim, it is inconceivable that Habakkuk should have been omitted from the collection(s) represented by these texts. It is presumably a matter of chance that, among the twelve, only Habbakuk and Malachi are unattested in the identifiable fragments of 4QXII^g – although their unrecognizable remains may still lie scattered among the mass of unidentified fragments. Without this manuscript, other minor prophets would have been unrepresented in the Cave 4 material: Obadiah and Nahum are absent from 4QXII$^{a–f}$, and only a tiny fragment of Micah survives, probably belonging to 4QXII^f. Strong although indirect evidence for the original presence of Habakkuk in these manuscripts may be found in the hypothetical reconstruction of the order of the eleven attested minor prophets as given above. As we have seen, these writings fall into three groups: Hosea-Joel-Amos-Obadiah, Jonah-Micah-Nahum, Zephaniah-Haggai-Zechariah-Malachi. There are just two points in the chain where no links can be found, and where there is therefore space for another writing. There is no direct evidence that Jonah followed Obadiah (however probable this may seem), and there is also no evidence that Zephaniah followed Nahum. The likelihood is that this second gap in the Cave 4 manuscripts was originally occupied by Habakkuk.

It should not be taken for granted that all of these manuscripts would have included the entire Book of the Twelve prophets, however plausible this may appear in principle.[10] It seems certain that 4QXII^g would have done so, since fragments of ten of the twelve can be identified here, but of the other manuscripts the next most comprehensive is 4QXII^c, whose identifiable fragments represent just four or five of these writings (Hosea, Joel, Amos, Zephaniah, Malachi[?]). Yet in all six manuscripts whose fragments show evidence of more than one writing, traces of the standard order can be found. Even if some of these manuscripts did not contain the complete collection, they still presuppose its standard order and thereby

8. The claim that the LXX order derives from a Hebrew *Vorlage* (so B. Richards, *The Formation of the Book of the Twelve*, pp. 170–220) is undermined by the lack of evidence for such an order in any of the extensive minor prophets texts from the Judean desert. On this point, see R. E. Fuller, "The Form and Formation of the Book of the Twelve", pp. 92–93.

9. If fragment 102 of 4QXII^g reads *yśrh npš[w]*, as the editors conjecture, then this derives from Habakkuk 2.4a. However, four of the seven letters of this fragment are regarded as doubtful (*DJD* VIII, p. 316).

10. This is apparently assumed by the *DJD* editors.

confirm the existence of a "Book of the Twelve". If there was no standardized collection, we would expect more anomalies in the surviving evidence, which would have made it impossible to reconstruct any single order.

The only possible anomaly occurs in the location of the book of Jonah in 4QXII^a, in which (according to the reconstruction in *DJD* VIII) Malachi 2.10–3.24 (columns I–IV) is followed by Jonah 1.1–2.1 (columns V–VI). This manuscript has been dated to the early Hasmonean period (*c.* 150–125 BCE), and, if the reconstruction is valid, it would attest a version of the collection in which Jonah was treated as an appendix – perhaps on account of its distinctive character. In fact, however, the grounds for locating the Jonah fragments after Malachi appear to be tenuous, and are acknowledged by the *DJD* editors to be so.[11] If this possibility is disregarded, the Qumran minor prophet scrolls from Cave 4 confirm the existence of a single Book of the Twelve, already in its Masoretic order, as early as the second and first centuries BCE. Since several of these texts diverge considerably from the later Masoretic text, it would appear that the establishment of a proto-Masoretic order for the Book of the Twelve predates the establishment of the Masoretic text.[12]

Two other ancient manuscripts provide further confirmation that a Book of the Twelve already existed, in the familiar order, at the turn of the

---

11. As plate XLI in *DJD* XV indicates, the suggestion that the Jonah fragments of 4QXII^a followed the Malachi ones rests on a possible connection between fragment 9 of column IV (Malachi) and fragment 15 (Jonah), which would then belong to a column V. Fragment 9 consists of material from Malachi in a right-hand column (frg.9 i), together with a few traces of a left-hand column (frg.9 ii) which in the *DJD* plate has been connected to fragment 15 (= Jon.1.4–5). It is not clear either that these two fragments should be connected, or that connecting them in this way can justify the reconstruction of the Jonah text given on p. 229. The editors acknowledge that the order Malachi-Jonah, is uncertain (p. 222). In fact, even their more cautious claim that Jonah was probably placed in the final third of the collection (p. 222) seems to go beyond the evidence. All that can safely be said is that "remnants of three letters are visible on frg.9 ii, indicating that something followed the Book of Malachi" (p. 228). The evidence that this "something" was Jonah, or any other text from the Book of the Twelve, is inconclusive. Discussion of "the meaning of the placement of Jonah in 4QXII^a" (B. Jones, *The Formation of the Book of the Twelve*, pp. 129–69) is therefore redundant.

12. *DJD* XV does not discuss the text-critical significance of the fragmentary manuscripts it presents. A summary is given by R. Fuller, "Minor Prophets", *EDSS* 1.555–56. 4QXII^a (4Q76, *c.* 150 BCE) is a "non-aligned manuscript" which "agrees sometimes with the Masoretic Text, sometimes with G [the Septuagint], and frequently does not resemble either". 4QXII^b (4Q77, mid-second century BCE) "stands relatively close to the proto-Masoretic textual tradition in the readings which are preserved". 4QXII^c (4Q78, *c.* 75 BCE) "stands relatively close to the textual tradition represented by the Septuagint". 4QXII^d (4Q79, late first century BCE) "seems to stand relatively close to the proto-Masoretic textual tradition". 4QXII^e (4Q80, *c.* 75 BCE) "stands very close to the textual tradition represented by the Septuagint". 4QXII^f (4Q81) is too fragmentary for conclusions about its textual affiliation to be drawn. 4QXII^g (4Q82, late first century BCE) "disagrees frequently with both the

eras. Both of them belong to a varied collection of manuscripts and other artefacts deposited during the Bar Kokhba revolt, when parts of the Judean desert served as a refuge. The remains of a Greek minor prophets scroll were discovered in 1952 and 1961 at Wadi Ḥabra (Naḥal Ḥeber).[13] The initial find included larger and smaller sections of Jonah, Micah, Nahum, Habakkuk, Zephaniah and Zechariah, to which fragments ascribed to Hosea, Amos, Joel, Jonah, Nahum and Zechariah were subsequently added.[14] This manuscript (8HebXIIgr) has been dated to the late first century BC or early first century CE[15], and is said to represent a revision of the Septuagint which brings it into closer line with the current proto-Masoretic form of the text.[16] In addition, another fragmentary Hebrew minor prophets scroll was discovered in 1955 at Wadi Murabba'at, about eleven miles south of Khirbet Qumran, containing parts of Joel, Amos, Obadiah, Jonah, Micah, Nahum, Habakkuk, Zephaniah and Haggai. This manuscript (Minor Prophets (Mur 88)) has been dated to the second half of the first century CE, and is said to conform more closely to the Masoretic text than the Qumran manuscripts.[17]

In the Greek manuscript of the Book of the Twelve, the order is that of the Masoretic text rather than the Septuagint – so far as this order can now be reconstructed. In the Septuagint, Amos and Micah occupy the second and third places respectively, in the Masoretic text the third and the sixth places – so that Amos follows Joel and Micah follows Jonah. Although the concluding verses of Jonah are missing from 8HebXIIgr, there would have been space for them in the missing top half of the column in which Micah 1.1–7 is found.[18] The link between Nahum and Habakkuk can be secured in the same way.[19] In the case of Habakkuk and Zephaniah, the sequence of columns can still be traced.[20] While the links between Micah and Nahum, Zephaniah and Haggai, and Haggai and Zechariah are missing, the sequence Zephaniah-Haggai-Zechariah makes more sense of the

Masoretic Text and the Septuagint", but "stands close to the proto-Masoretic textual tradition in most readings". For the classifications employed here, see E. Tov, *Textual Criticism of the Hebrew Bible*, pp. 114–17.

13. *DJD* VIII (1990).
14. *DJD* VIII, p. 1.
15. *DJD* VIII, pp. 22–26.
16. *DJD* VIII, pp. 102–58, esp. pp. 145–46.
17. R. E. Fuller, "Minor Prophets", *EDSS*, 1.556. The text was published in *DJD II, Les Grottes de Murabba'at*, pp. 181–205; photographs are published in a supplementary volume (plates LVI–LXXIII).
18. *DJD* VIII, pp. 30–33.
19. *DJD* VIII, pp. 48–51.
20. See *DJD* VIII, plate XVIII, which gives a synoptic view of columns 17–23 (Hab.1.14-Zeph. 3.7).

surviving evidence than the sequence Zephaniah-Zechariah, with Haggai placed elsewhere.[21] The sequence of the books from which fragments survive was therefore as follows:

> . . . Jonah-Micah, Nahum-Habakkuk-Zephaniah-Haggai-Zechariah.

While it is possible that this manuscript has deliberately reverted to a traditional Hebrew order in preference to an already traditional Greek one, it is more likely that the order attested in the fourth- and fifth-century Codices Vaticanus, Sinaiticus and Alexandrinus represents a later, Christian revision of the older Hebrew order preserved in the Masoretic text and already attested in the pre-Masoretic manuscripts.[22]

Of the approximately 170 lines of the book of Habakkuk, fragments of around 100 survive, ranging from single letters to almost complete lines. Habakkuk 2.4 is fairly well preserved in column 17, lines 29–30:

> *id[ou] skotia, ouk eutheia psuchē autou [en]*
> *[autō. kai di]kaios en pistei autou zēset[ai.]*
> Be[hold], darkness, not straightforward is his soul [within]
> [him. And the righ]teous person shall liv[e] by his faithfulness.[23]

At several points, this reading is much closer to MT than to LXX. In the first line, the Hebrew *'yph* ("darkness") would account for *skotia*, in place of MT's difficult *'plh* (1QpHab: *'wplh*), perhaps meaning "puffed

---

21. *DJD* VIII, pp. 8–9.

22. Two further witnesses to the Septuagintal order may also be mentioned. (1) It is attested in 2 Esdras 1.38–40, which belongs to the Christian framework (2 Esdr.1–2 = 5 Ezra; 2 Esdr.15–16 = 6 Ezra) of an original Jewish apocalypse (2 Esdr.3–14 = 4 Ezra) found only in the Latin version of this text. In a statement that may derive from Matthew 8.11, and in an emphatically supersessionist context, Ezra is told: "And now, father, look with pride and see the people coming from the east; to them I will give as leaders Abraham, Isaac and Jacob – and Hosea and Amos and Micah and Joel and Obadiah and Jonah and Nahum and Habakkuk, Zephaniah, Haggai, Zechariah and Malachi, who is also called the messenger of the Lord." Here, the sequence of the twelve is that of the Septuagint. If the conventional dating of 2 Esdras 1–2 to the second century is correct, this would be relatively early evidence of the Septuagintal order. But the dating of this material is difficult. (2) The problem of dating also makes it hard to assess the evidence of *The Lives of the Prophets*, a Greek text of probable Jewish rather than Christian origin which gives brief accounts of the canonical prophets in the order: Isaiah, Jeremiah, Ezekiel, Daniel, Hosea, Micah, Amos, Joel, Obadiah, Jonah, Nahum, Habakkuk, Zephaniah, Haggai, Zechariah, Malachi (ch.1–16). Apart from the reversal of Amos and Micah, the order is that of the Septuagint. D. J. A. Hare's first-century dating for this text rests on a doubtful appeal to Luke 11.47 and to supposedly accurate topographical information, and plays down possible evidence for a date after 70 or 135 CE (*Lives*, 12.11; 10.11), or even after Constantine's conversion (2.13); see *OTP* 2.381.

23. *Skotia* might derive here from the adjective *skotios*, "dark" or "secretive", which would fit the context well. I take it to be a noun on the basis of the probable underlying Hebrew reading.

up" or "arrogant". Otherwise this line is close to MT, unlike LXX, which here states: "If he withdraws, my soul takes no pleasure in him." In the second line, *en pistei autou* is a striking alternative to the familiar Pauline *ek pisteōs*, but again corresponds to MT rather than LXX, for which "the righteous person will live by *my* faithfulness". It is notable that MT's two third singular possessives ("his soul", "his faithfulness") are replaced in LXX by two first singular possessives ("my soul", "my faithfulness"): both readings probably stem from the misconstrual of a *waw* as a *yod*. The LXX reading appears to predate the Letter to the Hebrews, where Habakkuk 2.4 is quoted in a form almost identical to the LXX, but with the two lines reversed for christological reasons (Heb.11.38). The reading of this text in 8HebXIIgr may represent an attempt to bring the Greek text into closer conformity to the proto-Masoretic Hebrew.

The Murabba'at minor prophets manuscript is better preserved than those of Qumran and Nahal Heber, and much of the original format can still be traced. This manuscript too follows the familiar Masoretic sequence. Columns II and III are still partially attached, demonstrating the link between Joel and Amos;[24] the link between Jonah and Micah is still visible in column XI.[25] Although nothing from Hosea and Malachi has survived at the beginning and end of this manuscript, the links between all ten intermediate texts are clear.[26] Unfortunately, very little of Habakkuk 2 has survived. There are just six words from vv.2–5, four of them conjectural, and none from v.4.[27]

The manuscripts from the Judean Desert confirm that, between the second century BCE and the second century CE, the minor prophets were already being read not as purely individual texts but as a collection and in a standardized sequence.[28] Habakkuk 2.4 is thus the utterance not only of an individual prophet but also of the entire Book of the Twelve. The question is whether this situation had, or has, any hermeneutical significance. Is it the case that, already in antiquity, the Book of the Twelve was read "as a whole", in the expectation of a coherent train of

24. *DJD* II (supplementary volume), plate LVI.
25. Plate LXI.
26. Amos-Obadiah, cols.VIII–IX (plates LVIII–LIX); Obadiah-Jonah, cols.IX–X (plates LIX–LX); Jonah-Micah (plate LXI); Micah-Nahum, col.XVI (plate LXVI); Nahum-Habakkuk, cols.XVII–XVIII (plates LXVII–LXVIII); Habakkuk-Zephaniah, col.XIX (plate LXIX); Zephaniah-Haggai, col.XXI (plate LXXI); Haggai-Zechariah, col.XXIII (plate LXXII). The plates should be compared with the transcriptions in *DJD* II, pp. 184–205.
27. *DJD* II, p. 199.
28. It is relevant here to note that the Qumran biblical manuscripts betray no "narrowly sectarian" features, and are to be seen as "thoroughly representative of... Palestinian Judaism generally" (George Brooke, *"E Pluribus Unum:* Textual Variety and Definitive Interpretation in the Qumran Scrolls", p. 109.

thought?[29] In fact, there is little evidence of this, and considerable evidence that the distinct identity of each of the twelve was maintained. It seems that the collection of the twelve into a single book affected their *status* more than their interpretation.[30] The Book of the Twelve seems to have held a status second only to Isaiah among the prophetic writings, with Jeremiah and Ezekiel in positions of subordinate importance.[31]

The status of the Twelve

Among the discoveries at Qumran and its neighbourhood, the minor prophets are represented by seven Cave 4 manuscripts, a fragment of Amos from Cave 5, and the manuscripts of Murabba'at and Naḥal Ḥeber: a total of ten manuscripts. Isaiah is represented by two manuscripts from Cave 1, eighteen from Cave 4, one from Cave 5, and one from Murabba'at: a total of twenty-two, exceeded only by Psalms (thirty-six manuscripts) and Deuteronomy (twenty-nine).[32] In the case of Jeremiah, one manuscript was discovered in Cave 2 (Jeremiah (2Q13)), containing substantial fragments of chapters 42–49, whereas Cave 4 yielded two extensive sets of fragments (Jeremiah[a] [4Q70] and Jeremiah[c] [4Q72]), containing parts of the first half of the book, and three small fragments initially thought to derive from a single manuscript (Jeremiah[b]) but more recently assigned to three separate manuscripts (Jeremiah[b,d,e] [4Q71, 71a, 71b]).[33] The arguments for this last conclusion do not appear to be compelling,[34] and the safest assumption would seem to be that Jeremiah is represented by three (or more) Cave 4 manuscripts, together with one from Cave 2. In the case of Ezekiel, fragments from Caves 1 and 3 yield parts of the text of Ezekiel 4.16–5.1 and 16.31–33, respectively (1QEzekiel [1Q9]; 3QEzekiel [3Q1]). Of the three Cave 4 manuscripts, the five fragments of Ezekiel[a]

---

29. As argued by A. Schart, *Die Entstehung des Zwölfprophetenbuchs*, p.28 – on the basis, however, of very slender evidence.

30. The status of the Twelve at Qumran is briefly discussed by R. E. Fuller, "The Form and Formation of the Book of the Twelve", pp. 96–98.

31. So J. Trebolle-Barrera, "Qumran Evidence for a Biblical Standard Text and for Non-standard and Parabiblical Texts", pp. 89–98; G. Brooke, "Prophecy", *EDSS*, 2.696.

32. Details of the Isaiah manuscripts in *EDSS*, 1.384–85.

33. See Emanuel Tov's discussion in *DJD* XV, pp. 171–72.

34. The three fragments represent different parts of the text: Jeremiah[b] = 9.22–10.21, Jeremiah[d] = 43.2–10, Jeremiah[e] = 50.4–6. The editor concedes that differences of (reconstructed) column width are not conclusive evidence for different manuscripts (*DJD* XV, p. 171), and that, even if written by different scribes, 4QJer[b,d] could have belonged to the same scroll (p. 172). An alleged distinction between the textual affiliation of 4QJer[b,d] on the one hand and 4QJer[e] on the other (p. 172) is apparently undermined by the later concession that "the textual character [of 4QJeremiah[e]] cannot be analyzed because the fragment is too small" (p. 207).

(4Q73) contain passages between Ezekiel 10.6 and 41.6; Ezekiel[b] (4Q74) contains six fragments from Ezekiel 1; and Ezekiel[c] (4Q75) preserves just five complete words and six additional letters from Ezekiel 24.2–3. Only small fragments could be salvaged from an Ezekiel scroll found in Cave 11 (11Q4); in addition, fragments from Ezekiel 31.11–37.15 were found at Masada.[35] Assuming that Ezekiel[b,c] derive from complete texts of this prophetic book, this would result in a total of seven manuscripts. Overall, the comparative figures for Qumran manuscripts are: minor prophets, eight (Caves 4, 5); Ezekiel, six (Caves 1, 3, 4, 11); Jeremiah, from four to six (Caves 2, 4). Discoveries from elsewhere in the Judean desert raise the first two figures to ten and seven respectively. While this evidence is compatible with the hypothesis that the Book of the Twelve was more highly regarded than the other two, a comparison with Isaiah might rather suggest an approximate parity between the other three texts. In itself, this evidence is ambiguous.

The relative significance of the Book of the Twelve in relation to Jeremiah and Ezekiel can be clarified by comparing the interpretative literature that they generated. The surviving Qumran pesharim comment on Isaiah, the Psalms, and six texts from the Book of the Twelve (Hosea, Micah, Nahum, Habakkuk, Zephaniah, Malachi).[36] No pesharim exist for Jeremiah and Ezekiel, but there are several fragmentary copies each of an *Apocryphon of Jeremiah*[37] and a *Pseudo-Ezekiel*.[38] These texts represent different modes of interpretation which may correspond to a difference in status.

The surviving fragments of the *Apocryphon of Jeremiah* indicate a predominantly biographical interest focusing on the period following the fall of Jerusalem to the Babylonians.[39] In the largest surviving fragment, "Jeremiah the prophet" visits the exiles in Babylon and tells them "what they are to do in the country of [their] exile" (4QApJer[c] [4Q385b], 16 I 5–7). Since it is said that he "[went out] from the presence of YHWH" (16 I 2), the implication is that Jeremiah went to Babylon by divine command. The hope is expressed that the exiles "will keep the covenant of the God of their fathers in the land of [their exile, and not do] as they and their kings and priests did..." (16 I 9–10). Shortly after this mission to the exiles in Babylon, Jeremiah is in Taphnes in Egypt, where he is requested to inquire of God on behalf of the exiles there. According to the word that he receives

---

35. Further details in *EDSS*, 1.280–82.

36. Isaiah: 3Q4, 4Q161–65. Psalms: 1Q16, 4Q171. Hosea: 4Q166–167. Micah: 1Q14, 4Q168. Nahum: 4Q169. Habakkuk: 1QpHab. Zephaniah: 1Q15. Malachi: 5Q10.

37. 4Q383; 4Q384 (?); 4Q385b; 4Q387b; 4Q389a.

38. 4Q385; 4Q386; 4Q387; 4Q388; 4Q391.

39. On this text see Devorah Dimant, "An Apocryphon of Jeremiah from Cave 4 (4Q385[B] = 4Q385 16)". Dimant rightly notes that the non-biblical motifs in this work are shared with other non-Qumranic texts relating to Jeremiah (pp. 26–30).

from the Lord, "the children of Israel and the children of Judah and Benjamin" are to "study my laws day by day, and keep my commandments", avoiding the example of those who followed "the idols of the nations" (16 II 2–9). Another fragment confirms the importance of this Egyptian connection. It opens with a reference to an enquiry of which "all who remained in the land of Egypt" are either the object or the subject; Jeremiah himself is said to be "from the land of Egypt" (4Q389a 3 3–5) – in striking contrast to the reference to "Anathoth in the land of Benjamin" as the prophet's homeland in Jeremiah 1.1. Jeremiah here appears to speak of Israel's exile as lasting for sixty-six years (3 6), a figure that is also found in the later Jeremianic tradition.[40] There is no trace of the utterly negative account of Jeremiah's Egyptian ministry found in Jeremiah 43–44.

This text seems to have focused on the biography of the prophet following the destruction of Jerusalem, emphasizing his role in teaching and encouraging the exiles especially in Egypt but also in Babylon. This is in broad agreement with the image of Jeremiah in the Greek *Letter of Jeremiah* (a fragment of which was found in Qumran Cave 7), where the prophet offers the exiles an extended critique of the idols of Babylon, arguing that "we have no evidence whatever that they are gods" (v.69). In 2 Maccabees 2, similarly, we are told that the prophet gave a copy of the law to the departing exiles and instructed them

> not to forget the commandments of the Lord, nor to be led astray in their thoughts upon seeing the gold and silver statues and their adornment. And with other similar words he exhorted them that the law should not depart from their hearts. (2 Macc.2.2–3)

In these texts, Jeremiah has become the preacher of the law to Israel in dispersion. The *Apocryphon of Jeremiah* shows no sign of any specific connection with the Qumran community and its characteristic preoccupations, and we may assume that its presentation of the prophet was a representative one. The prophet is honoured as an outstanding pillar of the exilic communities, and there is no trace here of the remarkable tendency in later Greek writings to allow Jeremiah's position to be usurped by Baruch the scribe.[41] Yet there is no indication in any of these texts that Jeremiah is honoured for the *book* that bears his name. On the contrary,

---

40. See the *Paraleipomena of Jeremiah*, 5.30; 6.5; 7.24. In the light of the Qumran fragment, the use of this figure to date the *Paraleipomena* before 136 CE (sixty-six years after the destruction of the temple) should now be rejected.

41. See the *Paraleipomena of Jeremiah* (= 4 Baruch), the *Syriac Apocalypse of Baruch* (= 2 Baruch, evidently originally written in Greek), and the *Greek Apocalypse of Baruch* (= 3 Baruch). Baruch's enhanced role here may go back to the Septuagintal book of *Baruch*, which functions as one of several appendices to the book of Jeremiah. In that text, however, Baruch is in Babylon; in the later texts, he remains in Judea.

the book of Jeremiah is treated with considerable freedom: the exilic ministry assigned to the prophet is only loosely connected to anything in the book itself. Of course, at Qumran and elsewhere, the book functions as scripture and can be cited as such.[42] Yet it does not receive the intensive attention accorded to Isaiah and the Book of the Twelve.

Also discovered in Cave 4 were fragments of a *Second Ezekiel* (or *Pseudo-Ezekiel*), evidently a rather different kind of work to the *Apocryphon of Jeremiah*. It appears to have opened with a prophecy of the destruction of Egypt and neighbouring nations, drawn from Ezekiel 30.1–5. In the fragment concerned, an introductory reference to "[... the wor]ds of Ezekiel" is followed by the statement that "the word of YHW[H] came to [me]" (4QpsEz^a [4Q385], frg.1). That this work did not open with the biblical account of Ezekiel's inaugural vision is confirmed by a fragment in which an account of that vision is preceded by a passage apparently describing the future salvation of Israel (4Q385 4). Ezekiel's vision of the valley of dry bones is represented by fragments of three distinct manuscripts. In the fullest of these, the (biblical) instruction to prophesy to the bones and to the wind (cf. Ezek.37.4–10) is occasioned by the prophet's own questioning. Ezekiel says to YHWH:

> I have seen many in Israel who love your name and walk on the paths of [righteousness.] When will these things happen? And how will they be rewarded for their loyalty *[hsdm]*? And YHWH said to me, I shall make the children of Israel to see, and they shall know that I am YHWH. (4Q385 2 2–4)

The vision of the dry bones, which follows immediately, indicates how Israel is to know YHWH and how the righteous in Israel are to be rewarded: they are to be raised from the dead. Thus, when the winds blow upon the reassembled bodies, "a great multitude of men will r[i]se and will bless YHWH Sebaoth ..." (4Q385 2 8). Asked when this will take place, YHWH gives a mysterious sign: "And YHWH said to [me ...] A tree will bow down and rise up" (4Q385 2 10). The author intends to show that Ezekiel's prophecy really is concerned with the resurrection, understood as the reward of righteousness. The passage was of interest to Christians as well as Jews. A Greek translation of *Second Ezekiel* seems to have been in circulation in the early church:[43] a citation in the *Epistle of Barnabas* appears to derive from this passage,[44] and there is also a possible citation in

---

42. 4QpIsa^c (4Q163) 1 4; 4QCatena^b (4Q182) 1 4.

43. This may explain Josephus's claim that Ezekiel "left behind two books" (*Ant.* x.79).

44. *Barnabas* 12.1 gives a citation from an unnamed prophetic text: "And when shall all these things be accomplished? The Lord says: When the tree shall fall and rise, and when from the tree blood flows forth." While it is uncertain whether or not the final phrase was found in

the *Apocalypse of Peter*.[45] This interpretation of a scriptural promise of "life" as referring to the resurrection is also relevant to the Qumran interpretation of Habakkuk 2.4. The sequel to the passage on the resurrection is found in column ii of *4Q Second Ezekiel*[b] (4Q386), frg.1, where, in response to a question about the land, YHWH promises that "a son of Belial" who "will plot to oppress my people" is to be put to death in Memphis, and that this will make it possible for "my sons" to return to the land. The exodus typology is clear. Like the *Apocryphon of Jeremiah*, *Second Ezekiel* seems to have a special concern with Jewish communities in Egypt. Also characteristic is the format of dialogue between YHWH and the prophet, which anticipates the later Ezra and Baruch apocalypses. In a further example of this, Ezekiel expresses his concern at the delay to the fulfilment of God's promises: "And the days will pass rapidly until [all the sons of] men say: Are not the days hastening on so that the children of Israel can inherit [their land]?" (4Q2Ez[a] [4Q383] 3). YHWH's fragmentary response appears to speak reassuringly about the divine control of time.

In contrast to the *Apocryphon of Jeremiah*, the Ezekiel text appears to keep relatively close to its scriptural exemplar. It is striking, however, that approximately half the surviving material is devoted to just two passages in Ezekiel, the inaugural vision of chapter 1 and the vision of the dry bones in chapter 37 (which occurs in fragments of three of the five manuscripts). If this text had been of similar scope to the scriptural one, it would be surprising that so high a proportion of the surviving material derives from these two important chapters. One would expect something more like the random distribution of surviving material from the scriptural Ezekiel, in which brief passages from chapters 1–11, 16, 23–24, and 41–44 are partially extant. The shorter the pseudonymous book was, the easier it is to understand the concentration of the surviving material on two obviously important passages. The author's aim, it seems, was to present a selection of the most important material from this book in an accessible format. Although a creative author in his own right, he is above all an abbreviator. *Second Ezekiel* may stand in approximately the same relationship to the

---

Second Ezekiel (it occurs also in 4 Ezra 5.5), the Barnabas passage is otherwise a recognizable translation. For detailed discussion, see M. Kister, "Barnabas 12:1, 4:3 and 4Q Second Ezekiel".

45. According to Richard Bauckham, *Apocalypse of Peter* 4.7–8 is a quotation not directly from Ezekiel 37 but from *Second Ezekiel*[a] 2 5–6 ("A Quotation from 4Q Second Ezekiel in the Apocalypse of Peter"). In the later text, God says to Ezekiel: "Son of man, prophesy to the several bones and say to the bones: bone to bone in [their] joints, sinew, nerves, flesh and skin and hair thereon." Similarly, in *Second Ezekiel*[a] 2 5 the command to prophesy is again addressed to the prophet as "Son of man", the bones are commanded to rejoin one another, and there is a reference to "joints". These elements are not found at the equivalent points in Ezekiel 37.

scriptural Ezekiel as *2 Maccabees* does to the voluminous lost work of Jason of Cyrene (cf. 2 Macc.2.19–23). In both cases, the main reason for the abbreviation was no doubt the length and difficulty of the original (cf. 2 Macc.2.24–25). In both cases, perhaps, it was felt that the original text, however valuable, would not find many readers for itself. To abbreviate was among other things to popularize.

The Jeremiah and Ezekiel works from Qumran belong to different interpretative genres from the pesharim on the minor prophets, Isaiah and Psalms. In the one case, the text is treated with a considerable measure of interpretative freedom; in the other, it is treated line by line, with all possible care. In conjunction with the biblical manuscript findings, the evidence suggests that the Book of the Twelve was accorded a high status at Qumran. The question is whether this was also the case within the wider community.

At this point, the evidence of the *Damascus Document* is significant, since the communities for whom this text legislates continue to live alongside their nonsectarian neighbours in the cities and villages of the Land of Israel. Unlike the members of the Qumran community, these people "reside in camps in accordance with the rule of the land *[srk h'rs]*, and take women and beget children" (CD vii.6–7).[46] This probably refers to normal communal life in cities and villages, not to separate settlements.[47] The laws in this text and the associated Qumran material imply a way of life in which there are houses, slaves, marriageable daughters, childbirth, divorce, agriculture, lost property, and the service of the temple. The evidence of this text harmonizes with Philo's claim that the Essenes "live in many cities of Judea and in many villages and in large communities with many members" (*Hypothetica*, 11.1).[48] Elsewhere, Philo recounts how, on the sabbath, "they proceed to holy places which they call 'synagogues'", where "one person takes and reads the books, and another

---

46. It is, however, an implication of xii.1–2 that "if a D [Damascus Document] settlement existed within Jerusalem, its members were necessarily celibate" (Philip Davies, "The Judaism(s) of the Damascus Document", p. 34). In Davies' view, the Damascus Document predates the Qumran community (*The Damascus Covenant*, p.2 and *passim*).

47. While the references in CD xii.19, 22 to a "rule for the assembly of the cities of Israel" and a "rule for the assembly of the cam[ps]" might suggest a distinction between cities and camps, a close relation between the two is implied in x.21–23, where the sabbath regulation that a person "is not to walk more than one thousand cubits outside his city" is followed by the regulation that sabbath food and drink is to be restricted to what is already "in the camp". In col.xiii, "the camp" appears to be synonymous with the local sectarian community. "Camp" probably implies a typological identification with Israel in the wilderness (so S. Talmon, "The Desert Motif in the Bible and in Qumran Literature").

48. Compare Josephus: "They occupy no one city, but they settle in each of them in large numbers" (*BJ* ii.124). Philo contradicts himself, however, when he states that Essenes avoided the cities and lived only in villages (*Quod omnis Probus*, 76).

of special proficiency comes forward and interprets what is not understood" (*Quod omnis Probus*, 82). If the *Damascus Document* is the authoritative "rule" for the non-celibate Essenes,[49] as the *Rule of the Community* is for their monastic counterparts at Qumran, it is likely that the scriptural hermeneutic it represents is broadly representative of the scriptural exposition practised in these "Essene" communities and their "synagogues".[50]

The *Damascus Document* is the most comprehensive extant example of the sect's scriptural exegesis, presenting pesher-type interpretations of a wide range of texts in the course of the reflections on the sect's history and significance that fill its first major section, the Admonition (i–viii, xix–xx). Of the prophetic texts that are explicitly quoted and discussed, three are from Isaiah, none are from Jeremiah, two are from Ezekiel, and eleven are from the Book of the Twelve. Quotations are drawn from seven of these twelve texts: Hosea (three times), Joel (once), Amos (twice), Micah (twice), Nahum (once), Zechariah (once), and Malachi (once). The *Damascus Document* offers clear confirmation of the special place of the Book of the Twelve within Essene ideology.[51]

Isaiah Three texts from the book of Isaiah are cited in the *Damascus Document*, one of them twice:

(i) "There shall come upon you, upon your people and upon your father's house, days such as have [not] come since the day Ephraim departed from Judah" (Is.7.17; CD vii.10–12, xiii.23–xiv.1). The text is understood to refer to the future divine punishment of the wicked, but also to an event in

---

49. While Essene celibacy is strongly emphasized by both Philo (*Hypothetica*, 11.14–17) and Josephus (*BJ* ii.121–22; *Ant.* xviii.21), Josephus also acknowledges the existence of a non-celibate order of Essenes (*BJ* ii.160–61). While there is no indication that this distinction corresponds to a difference of location, with non-celibate Essenes living in the cities and villages of Judea and celibates living a communal life in settlements near the Dead Sea, the evidence of the Damascus Document and the Community Rule makes it probable that this was the case. Further confirmation is provided by Pliny, who does link Essene celibacy with the Dead Sea settlements (*Natural History*, v.15.73). In the light of the parallels between the Greek and Latin texts and (especially) the Community Rule, the "Essene hypothesis" remains useful within its limitations; see Todd Beall, *Josephus' Description of the Essenes*, and the expanded and updated material in his article on the Essenes in *EDSS*, 1.262–69.

50. It is the duty of the "Inspector of the camp" *(mbqr hmhnh)* to "instruct the Many in the works of God, and to teach them his mighty marvels, and recount before them the eternal events" (CD xiii.7–8). This suggests that the scriptural interpretation practised in this text was widely propagated in Essene communities. On this see Albert I. Baumgarten, "The Perception of the Past in the Damascus Document", pp. 11–12.

51. In the following discussion, Cairo ms. A will be cited (where available) without referencing the parallel texts from Caves 4. Incorporation of these texts would at no point have made a material difference.

the past, "when the two houses of Israel separated". The author has in mind the early history of the sect rather than an event in the reign of King Rehoboam. Those who rejected the teaching of the sect ("Judah") cast themselves in the role of "Ephraim", and suffered the inevitable divine retribution: for at that time, "all the renegades were delivered up to the sword, but those who remained steadfast escaped to the land of the north" (vii.13–14, cf. vi.5). This retribution is simply a foretaste of the retribution that is yet to come, and the second citation of the Isaiah text emphasizes this future dimension (xiii.23–xiv.1).

(ii) "Terror, pit and trap against you, you who dwell upon the earth!" (Is.24.17; CD iv.14). This text is interpreted by way of a series of equations or substitutions which identify the "three nets" in which Belial "catches Israel and makes them appear before them like three types of righteousness" (iv.15–16). Practices that others believe to be consonant with the law are denounced by the sectarians as "fornication", excessive "wealth", and "defilement of the temple" (iv.17–18). The two groups differ over the issue of remarriage ("fornication", iv.19–v.6) and regulations concerning menstruation and incest ("defilement of the temple", v.6–11).

(iii) "He creates a tool for his work" (Is.54.16; CD vi.7–8). This citation refers to the Interpreter of the Law *(dwrš htwrh)*, and is an adjunct to the more important citation from Numbers 21.18, the "song of the well" (CD vi.2–9). The "princes" (the converts of Israel, who dwelt in the land of Damascus) dug the "well" (the Torah); the "nobles of the people" (subsequent members of the sect) dug with the "lawgiver" *(mḥwqq*, the interpreter of the law *[dwrš htwrh]*) and his "decrees" *(mḥwqqwt)*. The Isaiah citation emphasizes that the raising up of the Interpreter of the Law is the work of God (cf. CD i.11). This citation and two of the others are explicitly attributed to "Isaiah" (vi.8) or to "Isaiah the son of Amoz" (iv.13–14, vii.10).

Ezekiel There are two citations from Ezekiel, one of which may not be original to the text:

(i) "To set a mark upon the foreheads of those who sigh and groan" (Ezek.9.4; CD xix.11–12). The citation occurs in a passage from the *B* text from the Cairo Genizah (xix.7–12) which replaces a section from the *A* text (vii.10–21) which is also attested in the Qumran material (4Q266 3 iii). Since the *B* variants are unknown at Qumran, it is not certain how old they are; yet they appear to share the ideology of the document as a whole, and may well go back to an old recension of the *Damascus Document*. Here, the reference is to a "first visitation, when "those who remained [in Jerusalem?]

were delivered to the sword" (xix.13), whereas the righteous who received the divine mark escaped (cf. Is.7.17, above). Here again, the "first visitation" is a foretaste of a second, future one. As with the Isaiah citations, the prophet's name is given.

(ii) "The priests and the Levites and the sons of Zadok who maintained the service of my temple when the children of Israel strayed far away from me, they shall offer me the fat and the blood" (Ezek.44.15; CD iii.21–iv.2). In the introduction to this citation, the prophet's name is again given (iii.21). As with the passage from Numbers, the equivalences or substitutions are arranged in chronological order, with the three groups referred to in the text corresponding to "the converts of Israel who left the land of Judah", to "those who joined them", and to "the chosen of Israel... who stand at the end of days" (iv.2–4).[52] Thus the Ezekiel text speaks of the entire history of the community from beginning to end – a history of priestly service in the house of God. There is no reference here to an individual figure such as the Teacher of Righteousness, the Interpreter of the Law, or the Unique Teacher (who are probably one and the same). These figures are generally subordinated to the community in the *Damascus Document* – in contrast to the Habakkuk pesher, where the Teacher is consistently treated as an individual character in his own right.

The Book of the Twelve There are eleven citations from seven of the minor prophets:

(i) "There shall be no king, no prince, no judge, no-one who reproves in righteousness" (Hos.3.4; CD xx.16–17).[53] The speaker here is God, rather than the prophet. This text describes the forty-year period between the death of the Unique Teacher (the Teacher of Righteousness) and the final destruction of those who turned away from the new covenant, established in the Land of Damascus, in order to follow the Man of the Lie (xx.10–15).

(ii) "Like a stray heifer, so has Israel strayed" (Hos.4.16; CD i.13–14). This was written about the time when the Man of Mockery *('š hlswn)* arose as the archetypal opponent of the Teacher of Righteousness, leading Israel astray with his lies (i.11–16). Thus, Israel strayed from the way pointed out by the Teacher. This "Man of Mockery" (or "Scoffer") is probably to be distinguished from the "Man of the Lie", who seems to

---

52. The addition of "and" before "the Levites" and "the sons of Zadok" ensures that the text refers to three groups and not to one (as in MT).

53. MT here has: "... without king, and without prince, and without pillar, and without ephod or teraphim".

have been a rival leader of the sect (CD xx.15; cf. viii.12 = xix.25–26). The "Wicked Priest", so prominent in the later Habakkuk commentary and in scholarly reconstructions of sectarian history, is absent from the *Damascus Document*, at least under that name.

(iii) "The princes of Judah will be like those who move the boundary; upon them will he pour out his fury like water" (Hos.5.10; CD xix.15–16). The *B* text has here turned a scriptural allusion in the *A* text (CD viii.3) into an explicit quotation. God here speaks of those who entered his covenant but did not remain steadfast in it (xix.13–20).

(iv) It is written, "... to return to God in tears and fasting".[54] It is also written: "Rend your heart and not your garments" (Joel 2.12, 13; 4Q266 11 i.5). These passages describe the worship that God desires, in contrast to the current temple sacrifice that God rejects in the words of Leviticus 26.31: "... I shall not smell the aroma of your pleasant fragrances" (4Q266 11 i.4).

(v) "I will deport the Sikkut of your King and the Kiyyun of your images, away from my tent to Damascus" (Am.5.26–27; CD vii.14–15).[55] The characteristic equations follow: the text refers to the books of the law and of the prophets, and the king is the community. A reference to the "star of your god" is omitted from the quotation but included in the interpretation, in conjunction with a text from Numbers: "A star moves out of Jacob and a sceptre arises out of Israel" (Num.24.17). The star is "the Interpreter of the Law, who comes to Damascus" (CD vii.18–19). This passage appears to speak of an exodus of the community and its sacred texts from Jerusalem to "Damascus" (symbolizing exile?), and of the subsequent arrival of the Interpreter of the Law.

(vi) "I will raise up the booth *[swkt]* of David that is fallen" (Am.9.11; CD vii.16). This quotation is an adjunct to the preceding one, and is based on a wordplay between *skwt* (Am.5.26) and *swkt* (Am.9.11). In both cases, the reference is to the books of the law: God sends the books of the law into exile, but in doing so he also raises them up.

---

54. MT: "Return to me with a whole heart and fasting and tears."

55. MT: "And you shall take up Sikkut your king and Kiyyun your images, star of your god, which you have made for yourselves. And I shall exile you beyond Damascus." A simple transposition improves the sense: "... and Kiyyun, star of your god [your star-god], your images which you have made for yourselves..." In the *Damascus Document*, "I will deport" (Am.5.27) replaces "you shall take up" (Am.5.26); and "from my tent to Damascus" *(m'hly dmšq)* replaces "beyond Damascus" *(mhl'h ldmšq)*.

(vii) "They shall surely preach" (Mic.2.6; CD iv.20).[56] Despite the plural, this is actually a reference to a single preacher, *Zaw*, who numbers "the builders of the wall" among his followers (iv.19). This passage occurs immediately after the references to fornication, wealth and defilement of the temple, so it may be that *Zaw* was a leader in the priestly establishment. His name is actually derived from Hosea rather than Micah. In Hosea 5.11, we are told that "Ephraim is oppressed, crushed in judgment, because he was determined to go after *Zaw*",[57] probably meaning, "Command". That is just what the "builders of the wall" do: they "go after *Zaw*" (CD iv.19). Perhaps *Zaw* is just another name for the "Man of Mockery"? Be that as it may, it is clear that the sect's opponents are all identified in advance in the prophetic scriptures.

(viii) "Each one entraps his neighbour with a net/*ḥrm*" (Mic.7.2; CD xvi.15).[58] This citation occurs in a legal section devoted to *ndbwt* or "freewill offerings" (CD xvi.13–20), and supports the rulings that "no-one should dedicate anything obtained by unjust means to the altar", and that "no-one should consecrate the food of his mouth for God" (xvi.13–15). Only surplus produce is to be voluntarily dedicated to the service of the temple.

(ix) "He [God] avenges himself on his foes and bears resentment against his enemies" (Nah.1.2; CD ix.5). Here, the same verbs occur as in the preceding prohibition of seeking revenge: "Do not avenge yourself or bear resentment against the sons of your people" (Lev.19.18; CD ix.2). Vengeance is a divine prerogative, not a human one; it should be left to God. As in all but one of these citations from the Book of the Twelve, the prophetic text is introduced anonymously. What is unusual is the ironic tone of the introductory formulation: "Surely it is not written, ...!" *[w'yn ktwb ky 'm]* (ix.5). Everyone who makes an accusation against his neighbour without good cause (ix.2–4) is behaving as though the prophetic text did not exist.

(x) "Awake, sword, against my shepherd, and against the man who is my companion – says God – strike the shepherd and the flock will scatter, and I shall turn my hand against the little ones" (Zech.13.7; CD xix.7–9). Along with the text from Ezekiel 9.4, discussed above, this is cited in the *B*

---

56. MT: "You shall not preach, they shall preach."

57. *ṣw (= zaw)* means "command" (Is.28.9–10); this has been confused with, *šw'*, "vanity", which originally stood in the Hosea text (cf. LXX).

58. MT has "brother" for "neighbour", and understands *ḥrm* straightforwardly as "net" (Eccl.7.26 and elsewhere) rather than as an object devoted to the temple (Lev.27.28) and belonging to the priests (Num.18.14). CD exploits the ambiguity of the term.

text in a passage which replaces the exegesis of Isaiah 7.17, Amos 5.26–27 and associated texts in *A* (CD xix.7–12; vii.10–21). The Zechariah passage describes the eventual divine punishment of "all those who despise the precepts and the ordinances" (xix.5–6). This text is explicitly attributed to the prophet Zechariah, but the introductory formula has apparently been closely modelled on the introduction to the Isaiah text in vii.10 *(A)*: "... when there shall come to pass the word which is written by the hand of Zechariah the prophet ... ", rather than, "... when there shall come to pass the word written in the words of Isaiah son of Amoz the prophet ... ". While this illustrates the secondary status of the *B* text, it also indicates that it stands in the same hermeneutical tradition as the *A* text.

(xi) "Who among you will close my door? And you shall not kindle my altar in vain!" (Mal.1.10; CD vi.13–14).[59] Once again, God is the speaker here. As in Romans 1.17, the language of the citation is already taken up in the passage that leads up to it (CD vi.12–13). Closing the door may mean that the sectarians must absent themselves from the temple. Though it is God's temple, it is God who calls for sacrifices there to cease.[60]

The majority of these prophetic texts are interpreted as references to events in the early history of the sect. The raising up of the Teacher of Righteousness (Is.54.16; Am.5.26), the opposition of the Man of Mockery (Hos.4.16) and of *Zaw* (Mic.2.6), the break with "Ephraim" and the punishment that befell the latter (Is.7.17; Ezek.9.4), the exodus of the community and its sacred texts to Damascus (Am.5.26–27), the apostasy that split the sect (Hos.3.4, 5.10) – all these events were divinely determined in advance and revealed to God's servants the prophets and to their inspired interpreters.[61] In this fictionalized historiography, the Book of the Twelve plays a central role.[62]

---

59. Also to be noted is the paraphrase of Malachi 3.16, 18 in CD xx.17–21. This is not introduced as a citation, however.

60. The meaning of the sectarian interpretation of Malachi 1.10 is uncertain, in the light of laws which appear to assume continuing participation in temple ritual (11.17–21; 16.13–14). On this see Philip Davies, "The Judaism(s) of the Damascus Document", pp. 34–35.

61. As Philip Davies writes, "The cumulative force of the numerous quotations and allusions amounts to a statement that the 'plot' of CD can be read in the bible: the community, the time in which it lives, its laws, everything is anticipated, described, regulated in the bible" (*The Damascus Covenant*, p. 55).

62. If allusions were taken into account as well as citations, Isaiah, Jeremiah and Ezekiel would be in a more prominent position in relation to the Twelve (see the tables in Jonathan Campbell, *The Use of Scripture in the Damascus Document 1–8, 19–20*, pp. 180–81). Campbell argues that "there is no clear-cut dividing line between citation and allusion in the Admonition", and that all biblical references "are manifestations of an underlying and overriding usage of the scriptures" (p. 176). Since the text itself both alludes to scripture and

This evaluation of the Book of the Twelve is not unique to the Essene movement. A later sectarian historiographer has frequent recourse to it, alongside other prophetic texts, as he tells the story of his own community's origins. Luke-Acts and the *Damascus Document* are perhaps rather similarly located in the period after the death of the founder and the initial consolidation of the movement. Luke draws upon a text from "the prophet Joel" in order to explain the dynamism of the community (Acts 2.16–21; Joel 2.28–32). Like his "Essene" counterpart, he quotes Amos 5.25–27, which he attributes to "the book of the prophets" (Acts 7.42–43) – although for him this text plays a negative role within Stephen's indictment of the rulers of Judea. Again like the Essene writer, he finds a reference to sectarian history in a later Amos passage which promises the raising up of the booth of David (Acts 15.16; Amos 9.11). He knows how, according to the book of Jonah, the people of Nineveh repented in response to Jonah's preaching – in contrast to those who rejected the sect's founder (Lk.11.29–32). An ongoing history of rejection is also indicated in God's word through the prophet Habakkuk: "Behold, you scoffers, and wonder, and perish, for I do a deed in your days, a deed you will never believe, if one declares it to you" (Acts 13.41; Hab.1.5). The Twelve also spoke of the founder's predecessor, about whom it was written: "Behold, I send my messenger before your face, who will prepare your way before you" (Lk.7.27; Mal.3.1).

If we supplement these six references to five books with material supplied by Luke's contemporary, Matthew, further references to the Book of the Twelve come to light. The founder's birthplace was predicted by the prophet Micah (Mt.2.5–6; Mic.5.2). Hosea's saying, "I desire mercy not sacrifice" (Hos.6.6) is drawn into the polemic against rival religious groupings (Mt.9.13). The typological relationship between Jonah and the sect's founder is extended (Mt.12.39–41). Although a garbled citation from Zechariah is misattributed to the prophet Jeremiah (Mt.27.9–10; Zech.11.12–13), the Zechariah text that once spoke of the divine punishment of the older sect's enemies (Zech.13.7) is now applied to the death of the founder and the scattering of his followers (Mt.26.31). In addition to Luke's five (Joel, Amos, Jonah, Habakkuk, Malachi), Matthew adds citations from three more of the minor prophets (Hosea, Micah, Zechariah). By now it comes as no surprise to find that Luke and Matthew also cite frequently from Isaiah and hardly at all from Jeremiah or Ezekiel.

---

cites it, it seems less than helpful to ignore a distinction that the text itself has created. In themselves, the "allusions" might be no more than an extension of the pervasive intertextuality of the scriptural texts themselves. It is the explicit citation of scripture that is the novel and interesting feature of this text.

Pursuing these parallels one stage further, it seems that the "Essene" and the "Christian" writers use these prophetic texts in a broadly similar way. In both cases, these texts are used to show that the history of the sect's origins is at the same time the predetermined history of God's saving action in the last days, and of positive and negative human responses to it. Thus, the prophetic texts are heard to speak of "the last days", the time of the sect's existence and history, and of the divine work of salvation and judgment that is here enacted and that will shortly reach its culmination. The sectarian belief in present divine action provides the impetus for a rereading of prophetic texts in which the work of God receives its authoritative interpretation.

The *Damascus Document* confirms the high status accorded to the Book of the Twelve, both at Qumran and in the wider "Essene" community; and the early Christian texts suggest that a similar evaluation was assumed elsewhere. For our purposes, however, there has been a notable absence so far. As yet, we have seen little evidence that a high status for the Book of the Twelve necessarily meant a high status for Habakkuk. In turning next to the pesharim, we shall find not only that Habakkuk was indeed valued, but also that it plays a crucial hermeneutical role in relation to the Book of the Twelve and the prophetic corpus in general. The passage at the heart of the book that makes this role possible is precisely the passage from which Paul cites: Habakkuk 2.1–4. The parallel between Paul and the Habakkuk pesherist does not lie simply in the fact that they both interpret the laconic statement that "the righteous shall live by his faithfulness", in one or other of its variant forms (Hab.2.4b). The parallel extends further: for both readers of the prophetic writings, this text is of fundamental hermeneutical importance. As such, it is not just one text among many but is uniquely significant.

In order to clarify the distinctive role assigned to Habakkuk, a preliminary account will be given of the Qumran pesharim relating to the Book of the Twelve.

Interpreting the Twelve

The Habakkuk commentary happens to be the best preserved of the Qumran pesharim, but no firm conclusions can be drawn from that fact about its significance for the community.[63] In the pesharim as a whole, however, the prominence of the Book of the Twelve is striking. Pesharim are also devoted to Isaiah and to the Psalms: while it is not clear

63. The danger of giving undue prominence to *1QPesher Habakkuk* is noted by M. Bernstein, "Introductory Formulas for Citation and Re-citation of Biblical Verses", pp. 65–70.

whether the manuscript fragments represent multiple interpretations of
these texts or multiple copies of single interpretations (perhaps with
variants), the latter is perhaps more likely.[64] Otherwise the pesharim are
devoted to the Book of the Twelve, six of whose texts are covered:
Hosea, Micah, Nahum, Habakkuk, Zephaniah and Malachi.[65] With the
exception of the commentaries on Habakkuk and Nahum, the poor state
of preservation even of the surviving fragments permits only tentative
conclusions about the ways these texts were read. Since scriptural
citations may be reconstructed more easily than their interpretations,
however, it is often possible to deduce the probable general direction of
an interpretation by relating its surviving remnants to the text that
produced it.[66]

Hosea Two fragmentary manuscripts survive of interpretations of Hosea:
4QPesher Hosea^a (4Q166), and *4QPesher Hosea^b* (4Q167). These cover
material from Hosea 2.8–14 and 5.13–8.14, respectively. In the interpretation of Hosea 2, the role of the prophet's unfaithful wife is taken by "the
generation of the visitation" (4QpHos^a i.10) – presumably a reference to
the non-sectarian Jewish community. In the comment on Hosea 2.10 ("She
did not know that it was I who gave her wheat... and gold which they
used for Baal"), we learn that these people "cast behind their back [all] his
commandments *[mswwtyw]* which he had sent them [through] his servants
the prophets", since "they listened to those who led them astray, and
acclaimed them, and feared them in their blindness like gods" (4QpHos^a
ii.4–6). The scriptural statement that "I will put an end to her joys, her
feasts, her new moon and her sabbaths..." (Hos.2.13) leads to the
comment that "[in all their fea]sts they follow the feast-days of the
Gentiles, but a[ll joy] will be turned into mourning for them" (4QpHos^a

---

64. With one exception, multiple manuscripts (Isaiah: 3QpIs = 3Q4; 4QpIs^{a-e} = 4Q161–
65; Psalms: 1QpPs = 1Q16; 4QpPs^{a-b} = 4Q171, 173) do not overlap, making it impossible to
tell whether they represent different copies of a single pesher or independent interpretations of
the same text (or parts of it). The surviving fragments cover material from Isaiah 1.1–2 (3Q4),
10.20–11.5 (4Q161), 5.5–30 (4Q162), 8.7–31.1 (4Q163), 54.11–12 (4Q164), 21.9–40.12 (4Q165);
Psalm 68.13–31 (1Q16), 37.6–39+45.1–2, 60.8–9 (4Q171), 127.5+129.7–8 (4Q173), 118.20
(4Q173a). The one extant overlap occurs at Isaiah 10.22–24, where two fragmentary
manuscripts appear not to coincide: Isaiah 10.22 is cited as a whole in 4QpIs^a 2–6 ii.4–5,
whereas in 4QpIs^c 4–6 ii.11–12 the first half of the verse is immediately followed by an
interpretation. In both cases the scriptural text appears to be a re-citation introduced by the
same introductory formula. In the light of the similarities of exegetical technique in the Isaiah
pesharim, it is perhaps more likely that an existing Isaiah pesher was recopied with variations
than that an entirely new interpretation was composed.

65. See the survey in T. Lim, *Pesharim*, pp. 27–39.

66. As J. H. Charlesworth notes, it is frequently the case that "some of the meaning of the
pesher is embedded in the biblical citation" (*The Pesharim and Qumran History*, p. 85).

ii.16–17). In the fragments of the second manuscript, there is a reference to the "Lion of Wrath" or "Angry Young Lion" (*kpyr hḥrwn*) known from the Nahum commentary, and identifiable as Alexander Jannaeus (4QpHos^b 2 2; 4QpNah 3 + 4 i.5, 6). This is a good example of the methodological principle noted above – that the general trend of even a fragmentary interpretation may sometimes be deducible from its scriptural lemma. The commentator refers to the Lion of Wrath in connection with Hosea 5.13: "And Ephraim saw his sickness and Judah his wound, and Ephraim went to Assyria and sent to a king who contends, and he was unable to heal you, and he did not cure your wound." The commentator may have found here a critical reference to Jannaeus' dependence on foreigners – perhaps the foreign mercenaries he used to quell a popular uprising (Josephus, *BJ* i.88–89; *Ant.* xiii.372–74). The Lion of Wrath has been brought to the commentator's mind by the text that immediately follows: "I will be like a lion to Ephraim and a young lion *[kpyr]* to the house of Judah." This is applied to "the last priest who will stretch out his hand to strike Ephraim" (4QpHos^b 2 3) – another probable reference to Jannaeus, who had six thousand members of a hostile crowd killed when pelted by them as he presided over festival sacrifices in the temple (Josephus, *ibid.*). In the light of the lemma, in which the lion is YHWH himself, the commentator would understand this event as a divine judgment upon "Ephraim" (the non-sectarian Jewish community). In contrast to the somewhat general religious polemic of *4QPesher Hosea^a*, this second text (or second part of the same text) seems to share the concern of other pesharim to interpret their own world and the scriptural text in the light of each other.[67]

Micah Still less is preserved of the Micah commentary (*1QPesher Micah* = 1Q14) than of the Hosea one. Identifiable fragments of Micah 1.2–5 and 6.15–16 suggest that the commentary covered the whole biblical book; the interpretation of the latter states that it concerns "the [l]as[t] generation . . . ". The citation of a relatively long block of text (Micah 1.2–5) recalls the practice of the Isaiah pesher (or pesharim); an early date (*c.* 100 BCE) has been proposed for both.[68] The most notable surviving passage is an interpretation of Micah 1.5bc ("What is the transgression of Jacob but Samaria? And what are the high places of Judah but Jerusalem?"). The Jacob/Samaria reference is interpreted first, but little of this survives beyond, "Its interpretation . . . " and a concluding reference

---

67. T. Lim is rightly sceptical about attempts to relate *4QPesher Hosea^a* to events in the period immediately before the arrival of the Romans in 63 BCE (*Pesharim*, p. 30). If *4QPesher Hosea^b* belonged to the same text, however, a reference to this period would be plausible. Lim notes the reference to the "Angry Lion", but does not develop the point (*ibid.*).

68. See Lim, *Pesharim*, p.21, for estimates of the dates of the manuscripts.

to "[the] simple".[69] The Judah/Jerusalem reference is applied to the "Teacher of Righteousness" (1QpMic 8–10 6), and to "a[l]l who offer themselves to join the chosen of [God . . .] in the council of the community, those who will be saved on the day of [judgment]" (1QpMic 8–10 7–9). The interpretation of the passage as a whole probably found in it a contrast between the Teacher and some opponent, who led astray the "simple". In the surviving material from the pesharim on the Twelve, this indication of the sect's memory of its early history is most closely paralleled in the Habakkuk commentary.

Nahum Much more extensive material is preserved from the Nahum commentary (*4QPesher Nahum* = 4Q169), where interpretations of Nahum 1.3–6 and 2.11–3.14 are partially preserved. Here, the prophetic text is related to the sect's view of its own past, present and future in three main ways. First, the opening theophany is applied to the divine judgment of the "Kittim" (the Romans): YHWH "rebukes the sea . . . " (Nah.1.3a), and this refers to the divine intention "to exe[cute] judgment on them and to eliminate them from the face [of the earth]" (4QpNah 1+2 4).[70] The verse concludes, " . . . he dries up all the rivers" (Nah.1.3b), and this too seems to apply to the Kittim, "with [all their l]eaders, whose rule will end" (4QpNah 1+2 4). Second, Nahum 2.11–13 depicts the doomed Nineveh as a lion's den. The phrase, " . . . where a lion went to enter there" (2.11) is interpreted as referring to "[Deme]trius king of Yavan, who sought to enter Jerusalem at the advice of the Interpreters of smooth things *[dwršy hḥlqwt]*" (4QpNah 3+4 i.2).[71] The lion image is developed in Nahum 2.12 ("The lion catches enough for his cubs and strangles prey for his lionesses"), and the commentator applies this not to Demetrius but to one already known as the "Lion of Wrath", who avenged himself on the "Interpreters of smooth things" by hanging them alive (4QpNah 3+4 i.6–7). The references to the false interpreters (the Pharisees) confirm that the

69. Milik's attempt to identify "Samaria" in Micah 1.5 with the "Spreader of the Lie", one of the Teacher's archetypal opponents, appears to be unlikely (so Horgan, *Pesharim*, p. 60).

70. The commentator tells us that "the sea is all *hk[tyym]*" (4QpNah 1+2 3). The term *kittim* is known to be in his vocabulary (4QpNah 3+4 i.3), and the insertion of this term in the lacunae in lines 3, 4 and 6 is likely to be correct (see Horgan, *Pesharim*, pp. 167–69).

71. "Interpreters" is to be preferred to "Seekers" in the translation of this expression, which is drawn from Isaiah 30.10. In the *Damascus Document*, the *dwrš htwrh* is the "Interpreter of the Law" (vi.7, vii.19), and this supports a similar translation of *dwršy hḥlqwt*; CD i.18 already speaks of those who "interpret with smooth things" *(dršw bhlqwt)*, i.e. who offer plausible but false legal rulings. The term *halaqot* is probably a wordplay on *halakot* (first attested in *mHag* 1.8, *m'Orl* 3.9): so A. I. Baumgarten, "Seekers after Smooth Things", *EDSS* 2.857–59.

two incidents are closely connected.[72] Third, the description in Nahum 3 of the destruction of Nineveh is directed mainly against "the Interpreters of smooth things in the last days", who "walk in treachery and lie[s]" (4QpNah 3 + 4 ii.2). The text of Nahum 3.1–14 is divided into sixteen sections of varying length; comments on nine of these are relatively well preserved, of which five look forward to the destruction of the "Interpreters of smooth things", identified with "Nineveh" (4QpNah 3 + 4 ii.6–7). The prophet condemns Nineveh as a "well-favoured harlot, mistress of enchantments, betraying nations with her harlotries and peoples with her enchantments" (Nah.3.4). This inspires the commentator to new levels of polemical eloquence:

> Its interpretation concerns those who lead Ephraim astray, who with their false teaching, their lying tongue, and their deceitful lips lead many astray – kings, princes, priests, and people, with the sojourner joined to them. Cities and peoples will perish by their counsel . . . (4QpNah 3 + 4 ii.8–9)

When he wrote as he did, the prophet Nahum was attacking the Pharisees of the commentator's time, as well as foreseeing an incident in which their final doom would be anticipated.[73] The polemic is no doubt to be understood against the background of the Pharisees' return to political power after the death of Alexander Jannaeus.

Habakkuk As with other pesharim, the commentator believes his text (the first two chapters of Habakkuk) to be rich in references to the sect, its origins, and its wider historical context. When the text speaks of the *ksdym* (the Chaldeans), it is in fact referring to the *ktyym* (the Romans).[74]

---

72. This is also confirmed by Josephus (*Ant.* xiii.377–84; *BJ* i.90–98). Josephus tells how Alexander Jannaeus gained his revenge on those Jews who had fought against him alongside the Seleucid Demetrius Akairos: "While he feasted with his concubines, he ordered some eight hundred of [his opponents] to be crucified . . . " (*Ant.* xiii.380). Although the Qumran commentator does not say so, he probably associates the "lionesses" of the scriptural text with the "concubines". For the involvement of Pharisees in this incident, see *Ant.* xiii.401–10; *BJ* i.110–14.

73. In *4QPesher Nahum* 3+4 i.7–8, Horgan connects the end of the incomplete sentence about hanging with the beginning of the following citation: " . . . he would hang men up alive [upon the tree] in Israel before, for regarding one hanged alive upon the tree [it] reads: Behold, I am against you" (*Pesharim*, pp. 163, 178–79). For the likelihood that the sectarians took a positive view of Jannaeus's action, compare the discussion of *1QPesher Hosea*[b], above.

74. Kittim is originally the name of one of the sons of Javan, the son of Japheth (Gen.10.4, 1 Chr.1.7; cf. references to "the islands of the kittim" [Jer.2.10, Ezek.27.6]). According to 1 Maccabees 1.1, Alexander the Great "came from the land of Kittim *[ek gēs Hettiim]*"; his successor Perseus is said to be "king of the Kittim *[Kitieōn basilea]*" (1 Macc.8.5). In Daniel and the Nahum pesher, however, the Greeks and the Kittim are clearly differentiated, and the latter can refer only to the Romans. In Daniel 11.30, "ships of Kittim"

Although the Nahum pesher also refers to the Kittim, it is only in the Habakkuk pesher that a detailed description of Roman military power is discovered within the prophetic text. The prophet speaks not of his own time but of the present when he speaks of the invader's ruthlessness, his arrogance, and his apparent invincibility (Hab.1.6–17; 1QpHab ii.10–vi.12). When the prophet denounces the *bwgdym* (traitors) who do not believe in the work of God (Hab.1.5), he is actually speaking of the traitors who turned away from the Teacher of Righteousness to the Man of the Lie (1QpHab ii.1–2).[75] The "righteous one" who is hemmed in by the wicked (Hab.1.4) is the Teacher of Righteousness (1QpHab i.12–13), and the "wicked one who swallows up one more righteous than himself" (Hab.1.13b) is the Man of the Lie (1QpHab v.8–12). Overall, the commentator reads Habakkuk 1 as primarily concerned with the Kittim, but finds important references to the Teacher of Righteousness at two specific points (Hab.1.4c–5, 13b).

After his treatment of Habakkuk 2.1–4 (to which we shall return), the commentator proceeds to interpret the "woes" of 2.5–20 as a series of references to a "Wicked Priest" (or to the "last priests of Jerusalem" [1QpHab ix.4], or the "Spreader of the Lie" [1QpHab x.9]). While it has been argued that the commentator has in mind a succession of identifiable high priests, the primary intention is to create correspondences with the scriptural text and not to provide historical information.[76] Habakkuk 2 is

---

(LXX: *Rōmaioi*] end Antiochus IV's campaign in Egypt. In the Nahum pesher, it is said that Jerusalem was not given "into the hand of the kings of Yavan from Antiochus until the appearance of the rulers of the Kittiim *[mwšly ktyym]*" (4QpNah 3–4 i.3). The equation of Habakkuk's *kasdim* with the *kittiim* was perhaps suggested by Isaiah 23.12b–13 (so G. Brooke, *Exegesis at Qumran*, p. 328).

75. The reading here is *bwgdym* rather than MT's *bgwym* ("Look, traitors...", rather than, "Look among the nations..."). The term is derived from Habakkuk 1.13, and this reading is also attested in the LXX (cf. Acts 13.41). On this and other textual variants, see William H. Brownlee, *The Text of Habakkuk in the Ancient Commentary from Qumran*, and *The Midrash Pesher of Habakkuk*; M. Horgan, *Pesharim*, pp. 10–55.

76. According to A. S. van der Woude ("Wicked Priest or Wicked Priests?"), six Wicked Priests are presented in sequence in *1QPesher Habakkuk*: Judas (viii.8–13), Alcimus (viii.16–ix.2), Jonathan (ix.9–12), Simon (ix.16–x.5), John Hyrcanus I (xi.4–8), and Alexander Jannaeus (xi.12–xii.10). Van der Woude assumes that these high priests are differentiated by the relative clause introduced by *'šr* that follows the references to the (Wicked) Priest in all but the final case: we are to think not of a singular "Wicked Priest", but of "the wicked priest who...". However: (1) we are also told of "the Man of the Lie who..." and "the Spreader of the Lie who..." (1QpHab v.11, x.9; cf. also 1QpMic 8–10 6; 4QpNah 3+4 i.5; 4QpPsᵃ iii.15+iv.8; CD i.14–15, iv.19–20); (2) *hkwhn hrš'* occurs in absolute form in xii.2, 8; (3) the steteotyped use of the articles and the adjective suggests a single individual, on the analogy of "the Teacher of righteousness", "the Man of the Lie" or "the Spreader of the Lie"; (4) supposed inconsistencies over the circumstances of the Wicked Priest's death (ix.1–2, 10–12; x.3–5) may simply be intended to make the Wicked Priest's final sufferings as comprehensive

understood as a kind of composite portrait of the archetypal misleader(s) of the Jewish people. Thus Habakkuk states that "wealth *[hwn]* will surely corrupt *[ybgwd]* the man of pride" (Hab.2.5),[77] and pronounces a woe on "one who heaps up what is not his" (2.6). The scriptural text generates the following interpretation:

> This concerns the Wicked Priest, who was called by the name of truth at the beginning of his office, but when he ruled over Israel his heart was lifted up, he turned away from God and betrayed *[wybgwd]* the laws for the sake of wealth *[hwn]*. And he robbed and gathered wealth *[hwn]* from the men of violence who rebelled against God. (1QpHab viii.8–11)

Here, the interpretation either draws on the vocabulary of the scriptural text ("wealth", "corrupt/betray") or finds appropriate synonyms ("lifted up" for "pride"; "robbed and gathered" for "heaps up"), so as to create the image of an opponent of the sect out of scriptural resources as well as communal tradition. The scriptural construction of the Wicked Priest continues throughout the series of "woes" in Habakkuk 2.5–20. The fourth of these is directed against one who makes his neighbour drunk, "in order that he may gaze upon their festivals" (Hab.2.15; 1QpHab xi.2–3);[78] this last phrase generates the dramatic scene in which the Wicked Priest pursues the Teacher of Righteousness to his place of exile and unexpectedly confronts him and his followers as they observe the Day of Atonement (1QpHab xi.4–8).[79] While an independent historical recollection or legendary motif may be preserved here, the story of the encounter on the Day of Atonement could have been inspired primarily by the biblical text.[80] Here and throughout his treatment of Habakkuk 2.5–20, the commentator follows the scriptural lemma in finding a singular rather than

as possible; (5) the anti-Pharisaic Jannaeus seems to have been assessed positively in the Hosea and Nahum pesharim. For a critical assessment of van der Woude's hypothesis, see Timothy Lim, "The Wicked Priests of the Groningen Hypothesis"; Lim doubts the singularity of the "Wicked Priest", but is also sceptical about precise historical correlations.

77. The reading is *hwn* (wealth), rather than MT's *hyyn* (wine).

78. The reading is *mw'dyhm* (their festivals), rather than MT's *m'wryhm* (their nakedness, shame). While this may be an "exegetical variant" (a variant introduced specifically for its exegetical possibilities), it is often an open question whether "the interpretation generate[d] the variant or the variant the interpretation" (T. Lim, *Pesharim*, p. 18).

79. This passage has often been explained with reference to the calendrical difference between the Qumran community and the Jerusalem priestly establishment – a view that goes back to S. Talmon, "Yom Hakkippurim in the Habakkuk Scroll" (1951). Yet the high priest's absence from Jerusalem on the Day of Atonement is a problem for history but not for legend.

80. The assumption that the pesharim contain reliable historical information about the "Teacher", the "Wicked Priest" or the "Man of the Lie" has rightly been questioned by Philip Davies, who argues that the pesharim drew traditions about their protagonists from the references to plural opponents in the Hodayoth (*Behind the Essenes*, pp. 87–105).

a collective opponent in the consistently singular addressee of the "woes" (Hab.2.6, 9, 12, 15, 19; cf. also v.5).[81]

The Habakkuk commentary is not unique among the pesharim by virtue of its references to the Kittim, the Teacher of Righteousness, the Man of the Lie, or the Wicked Priest.[82] The hermeneutical theory and the soteriology derived from Habakkuk 2.1–4 is a more significant feature of this commentary than its (problematic) contribution to our knowledge of the early history of the community.

Zephaniah Two fragments of a *Pesher Zephaniah* (or of Zephaniah pesharim) have been identified (1Q15; 4Q170). In the Cave 1 fragment, the surviving material is mainly drawn from the scriptural lemma (Zephaniah 1.18–2.2), although the word *pšr* does at least identify this as a commentary (1QpZeph 4). The lemma speaks of the destruction of "all the inhabitants of the earth" in the fires of divine wrath (Zeph.1.18); it is characteristic of Zephaniah that the universal "day of the wrath of YHWH" (2.1) is directed primarily against YHWH's own people. This was no doubt also the main theme of the commentary, which probably interpreted "all the inhabitants of the earth *[h'rs]*" as "[... all the inhabitants of] the land of Judah *['rs yhwdh]*" (1QpZeph 5). Lines 4–5 have been plausibly reconstructed as follows: "The interpretation [of the passage with regard to the end of days concerns all the inhabitants of] the land of Judah... ", which makes clear the general focus of this comment.[83] In the Cave 4 fragment, the scriptural text tells how YHWH will search Jerusalem and punish those who say, "YHWH will not do good, nor will he do evil"; their wealth will be plundered, their houses destroyed (Zeph.1.12–13a). Of the interpretation, all that survives is "[they] shall not eat", followed by the important *pšrw* ("Its interpretation: ... "). Since the former must also belong to interpretation rather than scriptural text, the subsequent indication of an interpretation must refer to a new scriptural citation – or perhaps to a "re-citation" of part of the preceding passage, an exegetical technique found also in the Isaiah, Nahum and Habakkuk pesharim.[84] The commentator no doubt exploited the threatening

---

81. The only partial exception is in *1QPesher Habakkuk* ix.2–7, where the threat that "all the rest of the nations will plunder you [sing.]" (Hab.2.8a) is referred to a plurality, "the last priests of Jerusalem" who are to be despoiled by the Kittim. This is a "re-citation", however, from a passage that has earlier been applied to a singular "Priest who rebelled... " (Hab.2.7–8; 1QpHab viii.12–ix.2).

82. Kittim: 4QpNah 1+2 3, 3+4 i.3; 4QpIs^a 8–10 iii.3–8 (x4). Teacher of righteousness: 1QpMic 8–10 6; 4QpPs^a iv.27 ; 4QpPs^b 1 4, 2 2. Man of the Lie: 4QpPs^a i.26, iv.14. Wicked Priest: 4QpPs^a iv.8.

83. I.e. *pšr [hdbr l'hryt hymym 'l kwl ywšby] 'rṣ yhwdh* (Horgan, *Pesharim*, pp. 64–65).

84. See T. Lim, *Pesharim*, pp. 40–41.

scriptural reference to Jerusalem ("At that time I will search Jerusalem with lamps" [Zeph.1.12a]) in order to denounce contemporary opponents in Jerusalem. The book of Zephaniah as a whole lends itself to an interpretation in terms of the forthcoming divine judgment that will befall the whole world, but especially the ungodly majority in Judea and Jerusalem. That is likely to have been the main theme of the Zephaniah commentary (or commentaries).

Malachi Just seven complete Hebrew words are preserved in the single fragment of *5QPesher Malachi* (= 5Q10), in comparison to a total of thirteen in the Zephaniah fragments. One and a half words are sufficient to identify Malachi 1.14a: "[And cursed be the deceiver in whose flock is a male, and he vows and sacrifices] what is blemished to the L[ord]". On the second line, the two following words ("...the scoffers *[hlsym]* as animals...") must stem from an interpretation in which the "deceiver" of the text is linked with "the scoffers", followed by a comment on their defective practice of sacrifice (5QpMal 2). The commentator probably has in mind the Jerusalem priesthood; Malachi will therefore have been read in the context of the sect's hostility towards the contemporary ordering of the temple. Malachi 1.14b provides a reason for the prophet's attack on defective sacrifices: "For I am a great king, [says YHWH of hosts...]" The comment takes up the theme of the divine kingship: "He is a living God *['l hy]*... to appoint [a]ll things *['t hkwl]*". The latter phrase may refer to God's ongoing providential ordering of the universe. Worthy sacrifices are to be offered to the God who is the creator and sustainer of all things – and this is not happening in Jerusalem.

Fragmentary though they mostly are, the pesharim on Hosea, Micah, Nahum, Habakkuk, Zephaniah and Malachi allow us to draw further conclusions about the significance of the Book of the Twelve at Qumran.

(1) There is a high degree of continuity between these pesharim and the interpretations of texts from the Twelve in the *Damascus Document*.[85] As we have seen, the three Hosea citations in the earlier writing are applied to the time of the sect's origins, when Israel was led astray by the "Man of Mockery", when the "Man of the Lie" caused some to turn away from the new covenant and the Teacher of Righteousness, and when his followers eagerly awaited the divine visitation that would take place forty years after his death. In conjunction with Hosea 5.11, Micah 2.6 produces a reference

85. The continuity is evident irrespective of whether or not the *Damascus Document* is a pre-Qumranite text. Whatever its origins, the manuscript remains indicate that it was valued and widely read at Qumran.

to a false "preacher" by the name of *Zaw*, who may be identical to the Man of Mockery. Like the *Damascus Document*, the pesherist continues to find the conflict between the Teacher of Righteousness and one or other of his traditional opponents prefigured in the text of Micah. While other (later?) commentaries are concerned with more recent or contemporary events (e.g. the pesharim on Hosea, Nahum, Zephaniah), there is no tension between these orientations towards the present or the past. Thus, in *Pesher Habakkuk*, the "Kittim" or Romans represent present reality, whereas the duals between the Teacher and his opponent(s) represent the past. As the time of the sect's existence is extended, the pesharim seek to reassure their readers that the whole of this period is encoded in the scriptural texts. Indeed, longer historical experience makes it possible to understand the prophetic texts more fully; and conversely, new historical experience may still be interpreted through the texts in which it was already long ago envisaged. As in the *Damascus Document*, text and experience interpret each other in a Qumranic version of the "hermeneutical circle".

(2) The pesharim on the Twelve appear to imply a special status for this composite book. In comparison to the Isaiah pesharim (or pesher), these commentaries have a particularly high proportion of comment to text. The Isaiah tradition tends to cite longer blocks of text, and comments often appear to have been fairly brief. This different ratio of text to comment is in evidence in all but one of the extant texts,[86] and this may suggest some kind of literary relationship between them.[87] To take two relatively intact examples, a citation of Isaiah 5.11–14 is followed by the comment, "These are the men of mockery *['nšy hlswn]* who are in Jerusalem, who...", leading directly into Isaiah 5.24b–25, which is followed in turn by a similar comment (4QpIs^b ii.2–10). In what may be the oldest pesher manuscript (*c.* 100 BCE), a seven line citation of Isaiah 30.15–18 is followed by five lines of comment, including a reference to "the congregation of the In[terpreters] of smooth things who are in Jerusalem" and a supporting citation from Hosea; Isaiah 30.19–21 follows (4QpIs^c 23 ii.3–19). While particularly important scriptural statements may be repeated and given a specific interpretation, there is much here that passes without comment. There are two possible explanations for this discrepancy between the pesharim on Isaiah and the Twelve. First, the Isaiah tradition may derive from an earlier stage in the evolution of the pesher genre. As the signs of "re-citation" may indicate, it may have included detailed interpretation of

---

86. *4QPesher Isaiah^d* is an exception, perhaps because of the importance of the text discussed (Isaiah 54.11–12) for the community's self-understanding (cf. CD vi.7–8, where Isaiah 54.16 is applied to the "Interpreter of the Law".

87. See note 64, above.

certain selected passages, but in general the commentator guides the reader through the scriptural text fairly rapidly. At a later stage – so the argument would go – commentators attempt a more thorough coverage of a text in its entirety, not just of its high points. Second, there is an obvious practical consideration: a shorter text lends itself to detailed comment more readily than a longer one. It is probably no accident that the other examples of detailed pesher exegesis are devoted to the psalms. By treating only selected psalms (e.g. Psalms 37, 45 and 60 in *4QPsalms Pesher*ᵃ), the commentator can aspire to a similar level of exegetical coverage as in the case of the Twelve. Whatever the reason for the differing traditions of interpretation, the effect is to give a special status to the Twelve as the primary source of detailed scriptural anticipations and confirmations of the sect's ongoing historical experience. By about the mid-first century BCE, the Twelve seem to have enjoyed a privileged role as interpreters of "the end of the days" – the period in which members of the sect were living.

(3) There is more continuity than is often thought between the interpretations of the Twelve and the scriptural texts themselves – continuity of a particular kind. In spite of their predilection for scripture as coded message, the pesherists can often interpret the texts in surprisingly straightforward ways: the Habakkuk pesherist on the Kittim would be an example of this. Even the more specific coded messages can reflect an intensified sense of the *general* appropriateness of a scriptural rendering to a contemporary figure or reality – as in the case of the "man of pride" who seems to be the primary addressee of Habakkuk 2.5–17. Yet the continuity between text and interpretation is more than a matter of exegetical technique. Above all, text and interpretation both articulate what might be called an *oppositional ethos*. Hosea, Micah, Zephaniah and Malachi have no inhibitions about denouncing current religious and political power structures, and empower their commentators to do likewise. In that sense, the sect's oppositional ethos is a genuinely scriptural construct; in its interpretations, the prophetic voice from the past again becomes contemporary. Conversely, it is hard to imagine the members of a Jerusalem-based ruling elite as having much use for such texts as contemporary address. It is striking that, when pronouncing his benediction on "the bones of the twelve prophets", Ben Sira speaks of their ministry firmly in the past tense: " ... for they comforted the people of Jacob and delivered them with confident hope" (Sir.49.10). Here, the twelve belong to a revered, sacred past in much the same way as the other great figures of the times in which they prophesied: Hezekiah, Josiah, Zerubbabel, Jeshua son of Jehozadak, and Nehemiah (48.17–22; 49.1–3, 11–13). Their life and witness remain an inspiration to us – but in general

terms only.[88] They must be understood within the historical contexts to which scripture carefully assigns them. Ben Sira's readers are to see themselves as standing within the continuum of history and tradition to which the twelve prophets belong, but at a different point in the process. When Ben Sira celebrates the merits of a contemporary high priest, Simon son of Onias (50.1–21), he does not imagine that the career of this individual is already envisaged in prophetic texts that have been, as it were, awaiting his arrival. The twelve belong to the living past of Israel's sacred heritage: the continuity is that of *tradition*. In the case of the pesherists, the continuity is that of *contemporaneity*. The prophets did not write as they did for their own times. If, long ago, they comforted their hearers with the promise of deliverance, it is not there that their significance lies. The prophets wrote as they did for the sake of their own future and our present: for their main subject matter was the sect itself, in its long-running conflict with the political and religious establishment. In these texts and their interpretations, the word of YHWH sounds forth again to denounce the corruption at the heart of the national life.

We are now at last in a position to turn our full attention to Habakkuk. The argument is straightforward: that in the text of Habakkuk 2.1–4 the pesherist finds his and his community's "hermeneutic of contemporaneity" explicitly articulated in scripture itself. As we have seen, Habakkuk is not a freestanding text but is part of the Book of the Twelve, which itself belongs to a larger prophetic corpus. This passage may therefore be read as validating Qumran prophetic exegesis as a whole. At this unique point at the heart of the Book of the Twelve, the Qumran hermeneutic shows itself to be identical to the hermeneutic prescribed and presupposed in the prophetic texts themselves.

The Persecuted Interpreter

In Habakkuk 1, the prophet protests against the divine announcement of the coming invasion by the *Kasdim*. Although they have been divinely appointed for judgment, God should not stand idly by as the righteous suffer unjustly at the hands of the wicked (vv.12–17). That is the substance of the prophet's "complaint" (2.1), and at the opening of the second chapter he takes his stand on a watchtower to await YHWH's response. When it comes, the response takes the unexpected form of a commission to write, in order that the prophet's message may be preserved for the benefit of a reader able to run with it: "And YHWH answered me and said, Write

88. Ben Sira does on occasion refer to the prophets in connection with hopes for the future (cf. Sir.36.15–16; 48.10).

the vision, make it plain upon the tablets, so that its reader may run" (2.2). From a Qumranic perspective, we must imagine this running reader as belonging to the time of "the last days". It is assumed that the role of the prophetic writing – rather than the more normal prophetic speaking – is to bridge the temporal gap between the prophet's own present and that so far undisclosed future (cf. Is.30.8). On this view, the written vision is simply unreadable before its time comes (cf. Is.29.11–12). The reader of Habakkuk 2.2 is thus projected into the future of v.3, where it is said that "the vision still awaits its appointed time" – the time when the hope expressed in the vision comes to fruition, but also the time when the written text can at last be read with understanding. As the appointed time draws near, the text will become readable: such at least is the pesherist's construal of the cryptic divine oracle. While some conduct themselves as though there were no promised future, it is those who remain faithful to the vision who "will live" (v.4). This warning and conditional promise must also be projected into the future, for until the time comes the vision is simply a closed book. The reader, whose eyes run along the lines of the text and who understands them, belongs to the future; and so too do those who live faithfully in the light of the vision – not to mention their opponents. The written vision is the book of Habakkuk itself, understood as a divine pledge that the future it envisages will surely come to pass, and as a divine appeal to wait patiently for that promised fulfilment. And Habakkuk represents the Book of the Twelve and prophetic writing as a whole.

In the Qumran reading of the Habakkuk passage, the crucial interpretative move is the projection of both the reader and the community of the faithful into the future in which the vision is to be fulfilled. It might seem more natural to suppose that the reading and the faithfulness it engenders belong to the period between the prophet's own lifetime and the appointed time of fulfilment. Yet the text does not explicitly say that. It encourages its readers to associate themselves with the reader who runs, and it permits them to conclude that this reading with full understanding is only possible in the last days. At least in retrospect, it is clear that the text leaves itself open to something like the Qumranic reading.[89]

The pesherist has six interpretative comments to offer on Habakkuk 2.1–4, and they fall into two groups. The first three comments are based on vv.1–3a (vv.1–2, 2b, 3a), and they concern the relationship between the prophet Habakkuk, the prophets in general, and their definitive interpreter – the Teacher of Righteousness (1QpHab vi.12–vii.8a). The three

---

89. If the Habakkuk passage is fundamental to the Qumran prophetic hermeneutic, then this hermeneutic is more a matter of ideology than of "exegetical method" (on which see George Brooke, *Exegesis at Qumran*, pp. 283–92). Conventional critical focus on exegetical method at the expense of hermeneutics is rightly criticized by R. Hays, *Echoes of Scripture*, pp. 12–13; his comments are as apposite in the case of *1QpHabakkuk* as they are in the case of Paul.

remaining comments are based on vv.3b–4 (vv.3b, 4a, 4b), and they concern the praxis of the community during the extended end-time. The comments on Habakkuk 2.2, 4b will be the main focus of our discussion.

The reader who runs

Habakkuk is instructed by YHWH: "Write the vision, make it clear on the tablets, so that he shall run who reads it" (Hab.2.2). What this means, according to the commentator, is that

> God told Habakkuk to write what was coming to the last generation, but the end of the age he did not let him know. And as for what he says, "so that its reader may run", its interpretation concerns the Teacher of Righteousness, to whom God made known all the secrets of the words of his servants the prophets. (1QpHab vii.1–5)

The prophet's commission is to "write the vision". Habakkuk writes the future, he writes for the sake of the future, and yet he does so without knowing what he writes: for God "did not let him know the end of the age *[gmr hqs]*" (vii.2). But what exactly was the prophet ignorant of, and how does that affect the way we understand his text? One possibility is that "what was to happen to the last generation" (which Habakkuk did know) is differentiated from "the end of the age" (which he did not know). The prophet would be speaking of the period immediately preceding the end, but not of the end itself; his text would represent a kind of prolegomena to eschatology. Yet it is hard to see why the pesherist should have been interested in such a distinction.[90] Another possibility is that the pesherist intends to contrast the prophet's knowledge of *what* would happen with his ignorance of *when* it would happen. This might agree with the claim in line 7 that "the last age will be extended and will go beyond all that the prophets say ... ". Members of the sect (or their precedessors) appear to have believed, no doubt on the authority of the prophets, that the end would come forty years after the death of the Teacher of Righteousness (CD xx.13–15). The extension of the age beyond the forty years is therefore among the unsearchable mysteries of God, since it remains unattested in the prophetic writings (1QpHab vii.8). The fact that "the final age is extended beyond them" requires endurance and vigilance on the part of the "men of truth" who "observe the law" (vii.10–12). Yet the reflections on the extension of the final age in lines 7–14 seem to have been occasioned purely by Habakkuk 2.3: "For the vision has an appointed time ... Though it tarry, wait for it; it will surely come and not delay." The motif of

90. The phrase, *'t hb'wt 'l hdwr h'hrwn* (vii.1) also occurs in *1QPesher Habakkuk* ii.7, where it refers to the prophetic message about the end in its entirety.

the delay of the end is not relevant to Habakkuk 2.2, the text under consideration in lines 1–2.

It is more likely that "what was to happen ..." is synonymous with "the end of the age", and that the pesherist intends to contrast what Habakkuk *writes* with what he *knows*. Under divine inspiration, the prophet writes of the end-time, but he does not understand what he writes. This leads directly into the following comment on v.2b: the prophet is told to "write the vision ... so that its reader may run", and the pesherist explains that the latter phrase "concerns the Teacher of Righteousness, to whom God has made known all the mysteries of the words of his servants the prophets" (1QpHab vii.3–5). The two comments on Habakkuk 2.2 exploit the contrast in the text between the writer and the reader, and the implication that what is written is written for the sake of the reader. Thus the contrast between the writer (Habakkuk) and the reader (the Teacher of Righteousness) is also a contrast between one to whom God "did not make known" the appointed end and one to whom God "did make known" all the secrets of that end.[91] The Teacher knows more than the prophet, because the Teacher has been given full understanding of the prophet's divinely inspired words, whereas the prophet himself has not. When Habakkuk writes of the *Kasdim* (the Babylonians), he is unaware that he is really writing about the *Kittim* (the Romans). Only the Teacher knows that, for, in inspiring the prophetic writing, God had the Teacher in mind as its primary addressee. The same is true, indeed, of all the prophetic texts. Habakkuk's subordination to his divinely authorized reader establishes the model for all other prophetic writers, for God has made known to this reader "all the mysteries of the words of his servants the prophets" (vii.4–5). The mysteries and the written words are not identical. Enabled by God, the Teacher who is also the reader who runs can penetrate the written words in order to lay bare the mysteries they conceal and preserve. The prophets themselves had access to their own words, but not to the mysteries of those words: that is the prerogative of the reader alone. Since this reader is also a Teacher, he communicates the mysteries of the prophetic texts to others; and the pesherist sees himself as standing within the ongoing dynamic of that interpretative event. Habakkuk's commission to write for the reader's sake serves to validate the sect's most fundamental hermeneutical decisions.[92]

---

91. Line 2: *l' hwd'w*; line 4: *hwdy'w 'l 't kwl* ...

92. The pesherist takes "running" as a metaphor for comprehension, perhaps by way of the idea of rapid, assured reading. There is no need for speculation about a possible wordplay in which *yrws* is linked to *rss* (to crush), or to *rsh* (hiph., to discourse), or to *rz* (mystery): for these superfluous suggestions, see G. Brooke, *Exegesis at Qumran*, pp. 291–92, and the literature cited there.

The mysteries of the words of the prophets cover the entire contents of the pesharim, which find inscribed in the prophetic texts the realities of the extended final age in which members of the sect are living. Different pesharim focus on different aspects of that final age; or rather, the pesharim claim to reveal the differences in the subject matter of the prophetic texts themselves. The prophet Nahum wrote (unknowingly) of Demetrius, the Lion of Wrath, and the Interpreters of smooth things. The prophet Habakkuk wrote (again unknowingly) of the Kittim, the Man of the Lie, the Wicked Priest, and the Teacher of Righteousness. These texts appear to envisage an ongoing saving and revelatory dynamic, rather than a once-for-all, already completed event. Yet the Teacher retains a privileged position for the pesherists: he is spoken of not only in Habakkuk but also in Micah and the psalms, and no doubt elsewhere. In Habakkuk, as we have seen, the Teacher is also the supreme, definitive reader, the reader who runs. It is worth considering how this relates to the other things that Habakkuk tells us about the Teacher and his place within the mystery of the divine decrees. In all, there are seven occasions on which God speaks through Habakkuk of the Teacher (Hab.1.4, 5, 13; 2.2, 4b, 8b, 15).[93]

Throughout the Habbakuk commentary, references to singular figures are generated by the scriptural text itself. According to Habakkuk, "the wicked one surrounds the righteous one", he "swallows up the one who is more righteous than he" (Hab.1.4, 13). Although the Hebrew terms might have been understood as collectives, a singular interpretation is also possible: and this gives rise to a dramatic interpretation in which the wicked and the righteous represent two individual antagonists. The decision to realize the possibility of a singular interpretation is announced, as if programmatically, in the comment on Habakkuk 1.4, which is unfortunately incomplete: "[The interpretation: the wicked one is... and the righteous one] is the Teacher of Righteousness" (1QpHab i.13). Since the "Man of the Lie" is referred to just a few lines later (ii. 1–2), he is the most plausible candidate to fill this gap in the text.[94] Where the scriptural text mentions a plurality of opponents, however, the commentator normally does likewise. The "traitors" of Habakkuk 1.5 ("Look, traitors, and behold ... ") are identified primarily with "the traitors with the Man of the Lie" (1QpHab ii. 1–2): the plurality is here retained. A similar close attention to number may be seen in the comment on Habakkuk 1.13b

---

93.   Hab.1.4 = 1QpHab i.12–13; Hab.1.5 = 1QpHab i.16–10; Hab.1.13b = 1QpHab v.8–12; Hab.2.2b = 1QpHab vii.3–5; Hab.2.4b = 1QpHab.vii.17–viii.3; Hab.2.8b = 1QpHab ix.8–12; Hab.2.15 = 1QpHab xi.2–8.

94.   The assumption that the Teacher's protagonist was identified as the "Wicked Priest" in 1QpHab i.13 has been effectively criticized by T. Lim ("The Wicked Priest or the Liar?", pp. 45–51).

("Why do you stare, traitors, and remain silent when a wicked one swallows up the one more righteous than he?").[95] Corresponding to the collective and the two opposing individuals are the House of Absalom, the Man of the Lie and the Teacher of Righteousness, who duly fulfil the roles prescribed for them in the scriptural text (1QpHab v.8–12). In Habakkuk's anonymous references to a "righteous one", the divine author of scripture intends a reference to the Teacher of Righteousness.

In these references to the persecution of the righteous one, the prophet Habakkuk presents the Teacher in the role of the victim of the Man of the Lie, who "rebuked" or "chastised" him with the tacit support of the treacherous House of Absalom (v.8–12).[96] In his two later appearances in the "Wicked Priest" passages, the Teacher is again presented as the innocent victim – although without the textual support provided by the earlier references to "the righteous one". The Wicked Priest is to be punished "for the wickedness against the Teacher of Righteousness and the men of his council" (ix.9–10); the text on which this comments speaks only of a punishment occasioned by "human blood and the violence done to the country, the city, and all who dwell in it" (Hab.2.8; cf. v.17). In the second passage, the story of the Wicked Priest's pursuit of the Teacher "to the place of his exile" is occasioned primarily by the scriptural phrase, "to gaze on their festivals". The scriptural "woe" is directed against "the one who makes his neighbour drunk, pouring out his anger *[hmtw]* ...", and this may underlie the reference to the Wicked Priest's pursuit of the Teacher, "in order to swallow him up in the heat of his anger *[bk's hmtw]*" (1QpHab xi.5–6). If so, "swallow up" (cf. Hab.1.13b = 1QpHab v.9) has replaced "make drunk", and the Teacher is the "neighbour" who is "made drunk" – that is, "swallowed up" – by the Wicked Priest. In this way, the scriptural text confirms the Teacher's role as the Wicked Priest's innocent victim.

As we have seen, however, the Teacher of Righteousness is the reader who runs. He is not only or primarily a victim, he is above all the inspired interpreter of the prophets.[97] Everything hangs on whether or not his

95.   The reading here is *lmh tbytw bwgdym* (addressed to the traitors) rather than MT's *lmh tbyt bwgdym* (addressed to God). On this, see T. Lim, *Holy Scripture in the Qumran Commentaries and Pauline Letters*, pp. 98–104; Lim finds here an instance of "exegetical modification" (p. 98).

96.   The House of Absalom "kept silent at the rebuke of the Teacher of Righteousness, and did not help him against the Man of the Lie" (1QpHab v.10–11). In the light of the scriptural text (Hab.1.13b), it is likely that the Man of the Lie here rebukes or chastises the Teacher of Righteousness. The alternative, that the Teacher rebukes the House of Absalom, fits the context less well.

97.   T. Lim argues that the Teacher is not only an interpreter but is also himself a prophet (*Holy Scripture in the Qumran Commentaries and Pauline Letters*, p. 118). As understood by the pesherist, however, the role of interpreter appears to be higher than that of a prophet.

interpretation is believed. In Habakkuk 1.5, the prophet admonishes the "traitors" to gaze in wonder – "for I am doing a work in your days, [and] you will not believe when it is told *[l' t'mynw ky' yswpr]*". The ten line comment that follows is the longest in the commentary, and is concerned entirely with the address to the "traitors" and with the phrase, "you will not believe when it is told". Three groups of "traitors" are identified and paraded. First are those members of the sect who acted treacherously along with the Man of the Lie in rejecting the Teacher of Righteousness (ii.1–3; cf. CD i.11–15); they are followed by a more generalized group of apostates, those members of the new covenant who "did not believe in the covenant of God *[lw' h'mynw bbryt 'l]*" (ii.3–4; cf. CD xix.33–35). Finally, there are those

> who will not believe *[lw' y'mynw]* when they hear all that is com[ing t]o the last generation, from the mouth of the Priest whom God has placed wi[thin the congrega[tion], to interpret *[lpšwr]* all the words of his servants, the prophets, by [whose] hand God declared *[špr]* all that is coming to his people Is[rael]. (1QpHab ii.6–10)

If the traitors will not believe God's work when it is told, it follows that God's work is announced in advance. Although that announcement initially takes places through the prophets, the prophets require an interpreter: and God has provided such an interpreter, in the figure of the "Priest" who is also the Teacher of Righteousness. It is above all the Teacher who is referred to in the scriptural phrase, "when it is told". It is, however, the task of the commentary itself to tell of everything that is to take place in the last generation (cf. i.2–3): priestly misrule in Jerusalem, the encounters between the Teacher and his opponents, the coming of the Kittim, the foundation of the community. In this passage, then, the commentary derives its own possibility and legitimacy from the figure of the inspired Teacher, who created the tradition of prophetic interpretation in which the pesherist himself stands.[98]

In the *Damascus Document*, the Teacher of Righteousness is probably to be identified with the "Interpreter of the Law" *[dwrš htwrh]* (CD vi.7, vii.18; cf. xx.32–33).[99] The author practises his own interpretation of

---

98. The pesherist sees his own interpretations as ultimately inspired by the Teacher: so T. Lim, *Holy Scripture in the Qumran Commentaries and Pauline Letters*, pp. 119–20, who points out that "it is an unsubstantiated claim to suppose that the form of biblical commentary known in the pesharim was already practised by him" (p. 120).

99. Philip Davies has denied this identification, on the grounds that the Interpreter of the Law is distinguished in CD vi.7–11 from a future figure who will "teach righteousness *[ywrh sdq]* at the end of the days" (*The Damascus Covenant*, pp. 123–24). This conflicts with the references elsewhere to the Teacher as a figure of the past (i.11; xx.32); Davies explains the discrepancy on redactional grounds. Even if Davies' hypothesis is correct, it is still compatible with an identification of the Teacher and the Interpreter at the level of the redaction.

prophetic texts, and holds that members of the faithful remnant are directly instructed by the prophets: God "taught them by the hand of the ones anointed by his holy spirit and by seers of the truth" (CD ii.12–13).[100] For the author of the Habakkuk commentary, however, the Teacher is now the inspired interpreter of the prophets. There is no reference here to any ongoing interpretation of the law: what is required, and contested, is the interpretation of the prophets. The reason for this shift in the perceived significance of the Teacher is to be found in the prophetic text itself, where the Teacher is identified with "the reader who runs" (Hab.2.2), to whom the divine mysteries hidden in the text of Habakkuk and the other prophetic writings are disclosed. Once again, a singular figure in the comment is derived from a singular figure in the text itself. The commentator presents the Teacher as the interpreter of the prophets rather than of the law because he finds this predestined role already inscribed in the prophetic text.

The Teacher plays two roles in *Pesher Habakkuk*. He is the final, inspired interpreter of the prophets, and he is the righteous victim of the Wicked Priest (or of his *alter ego*, the Man of the Lie). These two roles are both foreordained in scripture. The Teacher is the righteous one who is encircled and swallowed up by the wicked one (Hab.1.4, 13), but he is also the reader who runs with the text, the one in whom God's final eschatological action is declared (Hab.2.2; 1.6). Scripture thereby attests the Teacher's triumph over his opponents, who, whatever harm they may have done to the Teacher's person or influence, fail to eradicate the interpretative event that is the Teacher's real significance. The Man of the Lie and the Wicked Priest are themselves encircled and swallowed up by this interpretative event, being anticipated in scripture and unmasked through its interpretation. The commentary enables its readers to participate in the Teacher's triumph, in which the meaning and goal of history is encapsulated. That is the true significance of what "God told Habakkuk to write" (1QpHab vii.1).

Practising faith and Torah

The life and ministry of the Teacher of Righteousness is the definitive divine revelatory act, and as such it also has soteriological significance for the community in which his memory is preserved. For members of the community who read the Habakkuk commentary, it speaks of the source of their own salvation. The relationship between the Teacher and the

---

100.   Following the widely accepted emendation of *mšhw* to *mšhy*: "the ones anointed by his holy spirit", rather than, "his anointed one, his holy spirit". Unfortunately there is a lacuna at this point in 4Q266 2 ii.

implied reader of the commentary is crystallized in the comment on
Habakkuk 2.4b, "And the righteous one will live by his faith." (As we shall
see, "faith" rather than "faithfulness" is the most appropriate rendering of
'm[w]nh as understood by the pesherist.) The comment corresponds
closely to the three Hebrew words of the lemma, "[1] And the righteous
one *[wsdyq]* [2] by his faith *[b'mwntw]* [3] will live *[yḥyh]*", although with
a change to the order:

> Its interpretation: this concerns [1] all who observe the law *[kwl 'śy
> htwrh]* in the house of Judah, [3] whom God will deliver from the house
> of judgment *[mbyt hmšpt]* [2] on account of their labour *['mlm]* and
> their faith in *['mntm b-]* the Teacher of Righteousness. (1QpHab
> viii.1–3)

Here, the "righteous one" *[sdyq]* of the text is identified not with the
Teacher himself (as in the comments on Habakkuk 1.4, 13) but with "all
who observe the law in the house of Judah". The "life" that is promised to
the righteous consists in the divine deliverance "from the house of
judgment", and the faith which secures this outcome is oriented towards
the Teacher of Righteousness. The order in which the three elements of the
lemma are treated has the effect of placing still greater emphasis on "by his
faith", understood soteriologically as the means of escape from "the house
of judgment" into "life". For the pesherist as for Paul, Habakkuk 2.4b
represents a fundamental soteriological statement in which the entire basis
of a particular form of communal existence is summed up.

  The Habakkuk text is heard to speak of "faith in the Teacher of
Righteousness", rather than of "loyalty" or "faithfulness" to him.[101]
Earlier, the prophet has addressed the "traitors" *(bwgdym)* as those who
"will not believe" *(lw' t'mynw)* in the work of God (Hab.1.5). In the first
of the three comments on this statement, the commentator refers it to "the
traitors with the Man of the Lie" – or, "those who acted treacherously with
the Man of the Lie" (1QpHab ii.1–2). Unfortunately there is a lacuna at
this point: "who did not [. . .] Teacher of Righteousness from the mouth of
God". Yet the verb from the lemma ("believe") recurs in the second and
third comments on this text. The text concerns the traitors of the new
covenant, "since they did not believe in *[lw' h'mynw b-]* the covenant of
God . . . " (1QpHab ii.3–4). It also concerns the violators of the covenant,

---

101. GMT translates *b'mwntw* in the lemma as " . . . because of their loyalty to him", and
the crucial phrase in the pesher as " . . . on account of their toil and of their loyalty to the
Teacher of Righteousness"; Vermes, " . . . because of their suffering and because of their faith
in the Teacher of Righteousness"; Burrows, " . . . because of their labor and their faith in the
teacher of righteousness" (*The Dead Sea Scrolls*, p. 368); Brownlee, "because of their patient
suffering and their steadfast faith in the Teacher of Right" (*The Midrash Pesher of Habakkuk*,
p. 125); Lohse, " . . . um ihrer Mühsal und ihrer Treue willen zum Lehrer der Gerechtigkeit".

"who will not believe when they hear *['šr lw' y'mynw bšwm'm]* all that is com[ing t]o the final generation" (1QpHab ii.6–7). The repetition of the verb from the lemma in the second and third comments strongly implies that it also occurred in the first comment, which would then have spoken of the "traitors" as those "who did not believe in the words *[lw' h'mynw bdbry]* of the Teacher of Righteousness from the mouth of God".[102] If that is correct, there is a close parallel between the traitors, who did not believe in the words the Teacher received from God, and the righteous, who will be delivered from the house of judgment by virtue of "their faith in the Teacher of Righteousness". In other words, the verb *h'mn b-* (hiph., "believe in") and the cognate noun *'mwnh* (normally, "faithfulness", "loyalty") have become assimilated to one another. This is confirmed by the fact that the noun as well as the verb can be followed by the preposition *b-*, in introducing the reference to the object of belief or faith (the Teacher of Righteousness, or his words).[103] Even without the conjectural reconstruction of column ii line 2, the phrase " ... did not believe in the covenant of God" *(lw' h'mynw bbryt 'l)* in lines 3–4 suggests a similar interpretation of the noun followed by *b-* in the comment on Habakkuk 2.4b (cf. also *1QPesher Habakkuk* ii.14–15, where it is said of the Kittim that they "will not believe in *[lw' y'mynw b-]* the precepts of [Go]d"). God, then, delivers the righteous from the house of judgment "on account of ... their faith in the Teacher of Righteousness". In this context, faith or belief in the Teacher and his words must refer primarily to his role as interpreter of the prophets. God set the Teacher within the community "to interpret all the words of his servants the prophets, through whom God declared everything that was to happen to his people Israel" (1QpHab ii.8–10). While the traitors "did not believe in the words of the Teacher of Righteousness from the mouth of God", the righteous are characterized by "their faith in the Teacher of Righteousness". If, as is commonly said, Paul's interpretation of *'mwnh* as "faith" rather than "faithfulness" diverges from the original meaning of the Hebrew, the same must also be said of the Qumran commentator. In both cases, the object of faith is a human individual in whom the final, eschatological meaning of the prophetic scriptures is brought to light.

---

102. On this, see W. Brownlee, *Midrash Pesher*, p. 55, who rightly argues that the context does not support the alternative reconstruction proposed by I. Rabinowitz in 1950, which would fill the lacuna with the words, "who did not hearken to the words *[šm'w ldbry]*" (cf. 2 Chron.35.22; CD xx.28, 32).

103. It is generally assumed that *'mwnh* in *1QpHabakkuk* as in the Hebrew Bible means "faithfulness" or "loyalty", and that it is the Pauline conception of *pistis* as "faith" that is the semantic innovation (so J. Fitzmyer, "Habakkuk 2:3–4 and the New Testament", p. 242). Yet there is no reason why semantic change should be a Pauline prerogative, and the parallel between *'mwnh b-* and *h'myn b-* seems to prove otherwise.

The other main translation issue in the comment on Habakkuk 2.4b concerns the translation of *'mlm* as either active in sense ("their labour") or passive ("their suffering"). Those who observe the law are to be delivered from judgment on account of their labour or suffering, as well as their faith in the Teacher. The term may refer back to the preceding reference to observing the law – in which case, "their labour" would be the appropriate translation. In the comment on Habakkuk 2.3b, which speaks of the possible delay in the fulfilment of God's purposes, the exhortation to "wait for it" is applied to "the men of truth who observe the law, whose hands will not desert the service of truth when the final age is extended beyond them..." (1QpHab vii.10–12). Continuing to observe the law in the unexpectedly prolonged period before the end is here presented as a laborious and demanding activity. In contrast, the Spreader of the Lie teaches his followers "works of deceit *[m'śy śqr]*, so that their labour *['mlm]* is in vain" (1QpHab x.12). The reference here is probably to a law observance based on the misinterpretation of the law propagated by the Spreader of the Lie *(mṭyp hkzb)*. In this passage, "their suffering" would make no sense as a translation for *'mlm*. The phrase, "their labour", which is common to both passages (viii.2, x. 12), is best understood as a reference to law observance, whether true or false: and it is therefore the labour of law observance that secures the "life" or deliverance from judgment promised by the prophetic text, as well as faith in the Teacher of Righteousness. "Their labour" refers back to "those who observe in the law", and characterizes their law observance as an exacting service.

In these references to the Torah, the commentator has supplemented the statement of the prophetic text. It is here that the contrast with the Pauline reading of Habakkuk 2.4 is most obvious. According to the text, the righteous person will live "on account of his faith/faithfulness". According to the commentary, "all who observe the law" will live "on account of their labour and their faith in the Teacher of Righteousness". This corresponds to a tendency throughout the commentary to introduce references to the Torah into the text of Habakkuk. When it is said that "law *[twrh]* is ineffective and justice *[mśpt]* never goes forth" (Hab.1.4), the commentator divides the statement into two, eliminating the parallelism, and finds in the first part a statement about those who "rejected the Torah of God" (1QpHab i.10–11). Similarly, the crime committed by the Man of the Lie against the Teacher of Righteousness was that he "rejected the Torah *[htwrh]* in the midst of their whole Council" (1QpHab v.11–12). Those exhorted to wait patiently for the fulfilment of the vision are "men of the truth who observe the law" (1QpHab vii.10–11), and the same is true of those who have faith in the Teacher (1QpHab viii.2–3). When the prophet speaks of "the violation of Lebanon" and "the destruction of animals" (Hab.2.17), "Lebanon" is identified with "the Council of the Community" and "the animals" with "the simple ones of Judah, who observe the Torah" (1QpHab xi. 17–xii.5). On these five occasions, the commentator introduces references to the Torah into the prophetic text. The righteous will live not "by faith alone" but by virtue of their practice of the law as well as their faith in the Teacher. It would be inappropriate to follow earlier scholarly references to "legalism" or "works-righteousness" at this point – expressions which are too loaded with pejorative connotations to be useful. Throughout much of the commentary, the primary emphasis is on the Teacher of Righteousness as the persecuted interpreter of the prophets in whom – according to Habakkuk 2.4 – the community is to have faith. Yet supplementary references to law observance indicate how important this topic is for the commentator. In contrast, Paul places all possible emphasis on the *absence* of any reference to the law in Habakkuk 2.4 (or elsewhere in this text, with the exception of 1.4). His is, in effect, an argument from silence. He and the pesherist part company over the question whether there is any material significance in the prophet's failure to mention the law in the context of a fundamental soteriological statement.[104]

For Paul, who uses Habakkuk 2.4 to advocate an antithetical understanding of the relation of faith and law, "faith" corresponds to the universal scope of God's address in the gospel, directed as it is to Jews and Gentiles alike (cf. Rom.3.29–30). For the Qumran commentator, on the other hand, the "righteous people" of the prophetic text are identified with the minority within Israel who observe the law and believe in the Teacher. The commentator therefore minimizes every indication of universal concern in the scriptural text. In Habakkuk 1.5, this suppression of the universal dimension of the prophet's message has already occurred within the prophetic text itself. In place of the exhortation to "look among the nations *[bgwym]*" in order to behold God's work, the text used by the Qumran commentator reads, "look, traitors *[bwgdym]*". This reading is not his own invention, since it was present in the Hebrew *Vorlage* of the Septuagint. On the other hand, the proto-Masoretic reading may also have been available to him, since it is present in the minor prophets manuscript from Wadi Muraba'at (Minor Prophets [Mur 88] xviii.3). Elsewhere, the commentator reveals the influence of a proto-Masoretic reading even

---

104. In comparing the two interpreters' readings of Habakkuk 2.4, it is inadequate merely to see one as a deviation from the norm represented by the other – as H.-W. Kuhn does when he states that "der schwerwiegendste theologische Schritt, den Paulus gegenüber seiner jüdischen Tradition – und hier geht es nicht um spezifisch Qumranisches – getan hat, darin liegt, dass er den "Glauben" von dem "Tun" der Tora trennt..." ("Die Bedeutung der Qumrantexte für das Verständnis des Galaterbriefes", p. 177). It would be preferable to see both readings as arising from interpretative decisions about the Habakkuk text in its immediate and canonical contexts.

where his own *Vorlage* diverges from it (cf. 1QpHab xi.8–14).[105] It may therefore be more than an accident of textual transmission that neither his text nor his comment refers to a work of God "among the nations". Similarly, the commentator passes in silence over the references to the nations or Gentiles in the series of "woes" in Habakkuk 2.5–17, where the nations are repeatedly seen as the victims of the (Babylonian) conqueror denounced there (vv.5, 6–8, 17). In the commentary, the main object of the denunciations is the Wicked Priest, whose victims are no longer "the nations" but rather "the Council of the Community" and "the simple ones of Judah who observe the law" (1QpHab xii.2–6). The promise of a time when "the earth will be full of the knowledge of the glory of YHWH just as water fills the sea" (Hab.2.14) is interpreted in terms of the knowledge attained by the sect (1QpHab x.14–xi.2): the universal scope of the prophetic text is again eliminated from the interpretation. On the other hand, when the prophetic text denounces idolatry (Hab.2.18–19), the commentator is quick to find here a straightforward reference to "the idols of the Gentiles *[hgwym]*", which "will not save them on the Day of Judgment" (1QpHab xii.12–14). When "all the earth" is commanded to keep silence in the presence of YHWH (Hab.2.20), the interpretation again refers us to "the Gentiles who serve stone and wood" and who will be destroyed from the earth on the Day of Judgment (1QpHab xii.17–xiii.4). The association between faith, Torah and the elect community makes the Pauline emphasis on faith's universal scope quite inconceivable for the Qumran commentator.

Yet it would be one-sided to emphasize the obvious differences between the Pauline and the Qumranic readings at the expense of the striking formal parallels.[106] According to the prophetic text, "The righteous one will live by his faith" – or, "The one who is righteous by faith will live". However the statement is construed, the pesherist and the apostle are agreed that it is of fundamental importance, speaking of the divinely ordained way to salvation with a clarity and brevity virtually unparalleled in the rest of scripture. Paul does not mention Habakkuk 2.2, where the subordination of the prophet who writes to the reader who runs is so important for the pesherist's eschatological hermeneutic. Yet Paul too holds to an eschatological hermeneutic: for him as for the Qumran community, scripture was "written for our instruction, upon whom the

---

105. See W. Brownlee, *Text of Habakkuk*, pp. 118–23, on this and other possible "dual readings".

106. The issue of parallels of exegetical technique will not be discussed here. On this, see the cautionary remarks of Timothy Lim, who argues that at Qumran there is no single model of "pesher exegesis" (*Holy Scripture in the Qumran Commentaries and Pauline Letters*, pp. 129–34).

ends of the ages have come" (1 Cor.10.11; cf. Rom.4.23–24, 15.4).[107] In both cases, the definitive, eschatological interpretation of scripture is focused on a singular figure, persecuted by the leaders of his own people yet vindicated by God, in whom the previously concealed meaning of scripture has now been disclosed. The two readings of the Habakkuk text both articulate the "oppositional ethos" of the sectarian communities in and for which they were produced. They both contrast sharply with the eirenical, ruling class ethos fostered by a Ben Sira, for whom the twelve have an honoured place within a rich common heritage. For sectarian readers of the prophets, that common heritage has been fractured, and the fracture may be located at the point where a rereading of scripture comes to light that is accepted by some and rejected by others.

Even the Pauline faith/works antithesis can be located within this formal parallelism between the two readings of the Habakkuk text. In both cases, the prophet's reference to "faith" represents a rejection of the majority interpretation of the law, its practice and its significance, as found in "Israel" (1QpHab viii.10, cf. x.9–11; Rom.9.31). The pesherist derives the false view of the law from stereotyped figures such as the Wicked Priest, whereas Paul traces it back to the revered yet ambivalent figure of Moses himself, whose claim that "the one who does these things shall live" (Lev.18.5) cannot be harmonized with the soteriology of Habakkuk 2.4 (cf. Gal.3.11–12; Rom.10.5). Thus, unlike the pesherist, Paul extends his conflict with "those who are of works of law" (Gal.3.10) into scripture itself, thus creating an "antithetical hermeneutic" that grounds the conflict in matters of fundamental theological principle. In both cases, however, the eschatological conflict over scriptural interpretation is traced back to the mystery of the divine predestination as attested in scripture (cf. Rom.9.6–33). If, drawing now from the Nahum commentary, we bring the "Interpreters of smooth things" into the picture, we find that Paul and the pesherists are agreed in finding an anti-Pharisaic message in the prophetic writings (cf. Phil.3.5; Gal.1.13–14).

The comparison could be extended, and further parallels and differences would no doubt come to light. What is now clear is that Paul and the pesherist do not read Habakkuk in isolation from one another. The earlier interpreter works his way methodically through the text of Habakkuk 1–2, no doubt in a scriptorium at Qumran; the later one places a single brief citation at the head of a letter written from Corinth to communities in Rome. Yet the resulting readings are not simply incommensurable. They occur within a single intertextual field, of which the fragmentary manuscripts of the Book of the Twelve are a material vestige and symbol.

---

107. On this see R. Hays, "The Conversion of the Imagination: Scripture and Eschatology in 1 Corinthians", pp. 394–402.

This single intertextual field is the precondition for all the proliferating differences and similarities – and the difference-in-similarity and similarity-in-difference – that come to light as variously located readers read the same normative texts.

Chapter 3

The God of my Salvation

The introductory formula "as it is written" invites the reader to acknowledge a correspondence between the new text and an old, normative one. The correspondence is asserted, but it is always open to contestation. Paul may claim that Habakkuk 2.4 implies a radical disjunction between faith and the law, but for other interpreters it will seem self-evident that "the righteous person" of that text is to be identified with "all who observe the law in the house of Judah" (1QpHab viii.1), and that Paul's reading is completely mistaken. Such interpretative disagreement does not neutralize or invalidate the appeal to scripture: on the contrary, the possibility of disagreement is a precondition of any such appeal. "As it is written" is a call to active participation in the task of interpretation – an invitation to the reader to revisit the scriptural text in order to subject the alleged correspondence to critical testing.

A well-known statement from the Book of Acts may serve as a model. When Paul and Silas preached in the synagogue at Beroea, it is said that their hearers "received the word with all eagerness, examining the scriptures daily to see if these things were so" (Acts 17.11). Here, "the word" asserts a correspondence between the new and the old, and this assertion is neither rejected out of hand nor taken on trust. Instead, it is verified or falsified by independent study of the texts. The word, then, is an invitation to reread with a view to its own scriptural verification – with transforming effect on the interpretation of the scriptural texts themselves if the intended verification actually occurs. If it does not occur, scripture will seem to have falsified the word; the proposed new reading will be rejected as a misinterpretation, and a reading will be preferred which conforms to the *status quo*. One way or the other, and on the basis perhaps of a variety of interpretative criteria, the Beroean readers strive to allow the scriptural texts to determine their own interpretation. Rather than remaining mute, the texts must have their say. They must be given a voice in confirming or denying what is said to be the case.[1]

---

1. Could the addressees of Paul's letters follow up his scriptural interpretation in this way, or even follow it at all? C. D. Stanley thinks not ("'Pearls before Swine': Did Paul's Audiences

When Habakkuk 2.4 is read independently of Paul's use of it, it is widely assumed that it will mean something quite different from what Paul thinks it means. The outcome of the critical testing is unambiguously negative. As John Barton puts it,

> there is little likelihood that Paul has reproduced the meaning Habakkuk had in mind; his interpretation of this prophet, however much it differs from that current at Qumran, is no less the product of his own *prior* convictions about theological truth.[2]

Here as always, the critical instinct is to differentiate sharply between what the text originally meant and what it was taken to mean by its later (pre-critical) readers. In this case, what the prophet actually wrote was, "The righteous person will live by his faithfulness": nothing is said here about a "righteousness-by-faith". The statement has a specific literary function within the book of Habakkuk, and it presumably had an intended historical function within the context of the prophet's ministry – which, despite the absence of historical information at the outset of the book, is normally dated to the period of the Babylonian rise to power in the late seventh century BCE.[3] It is one thing to articulate the principle that "the righteous person will live by his faithfulness" within the context of Babylonian imperialist aggression; it is quite another to assert on the basis of this text that righteousness is by faith and not by works of law, for the Jew first and also for the Greek. Despite the similar wording, the text that Habakkuk wrote and the text as Paul cited it seem fundamentally alien to one another. The citation in Romans 1.17 looks like a text from the book of the prophet Habakkuk, but the voice that speaks in it is really the voice of Paul. Like Jacob playing the part of Esau, Paul dons the mantle of the absent prophet and speaks in his name.

In the conventional critical understanding of the relationship of apostle and prophet, the emphasis lies on the irreducible semantic difference between the scriptural text and its New Testament citation. In the modern era, the traditional assumption that a New Testament citation is simply the repetition and reproduction of a text's original content has lost all credibility. As the scriptural texts are restored to their original literary and historical contexts, meanings come to light that are wholly other than the meanings ascribed to them by traditional Christian interpretation, from the New Testament onwards. The presumption of a semantic identity

---

Understand His Biblical Quotations?"). But it is reasonable to suppose that Paul (1) hoped that his letters would be studied and discussed, and not just read through once, and (2) assumed a reasonable level of readerly competence in at least some of his addressees (cf. Rom.15.14).

2. *Oracles of God*, p. 245; italics original.
3. See the summary of scholarly views in F. Andersen, *Habakkuk*, pp. 24–27.

between text and citation has been replaced by a presumption of non-identity. In many respects, indeed, this marks a genuine advance within biblical interpretation, making it possible for the first time to attend to the distinctiveness of the individual scriptural voices. The independent testimony of the prophet Habakkuk does need to be preserved from over-hasty assimilation to the Pauline proclamation of righteousness by faith.[4] Yet the assumption that interpretation must *either* reproduce an original meaning *or* impose a meaning created by the interpreter is hermeneutically naïve. It results in a fundamentally antagonistic picture: Habakkuk and Paul are engaged in a struggle for the meaning of the prophet's own statement, in which for one to win is for the other to lose. Within a less confrontational and more dialogical hermeneutic, a rather different picture might emerge.

In this chapter, we shall reread the Habakkuk text in the light of its Pauline interpretation, in order to "see if these things are so" – asking whether it might confirm and enrich Paul's interpretation when allowed to speak in its own voice. It is obvious that the original text and its Pauline citation are not saying exactly the same thing, and that Paul does not merely reproduce a given content. Yet it should still be possible to illuminate the hermeneutical dimension of Pauline theology by way of an extended detour through the texts that he cites.

Writing and the Book

The Twelve and the canonical history

Originating perhaps in the late seventh century BCE, the book attributed to the prophet Habakkuk was still being read centuries later – not for antiquarian reasons but in the expectation that as a normative scriptural text it would demonstrate its continuing relevance for the community of faith. It was able to play this role because of its inclusion in one of the major repositories of Israel's prophetic traditions – the "Book of the Twelve", the content and form of which in the era of Paul and the pesherist have been discussed in the previous chapter. In rereading Habakkuk in the light of Paul and the pesherist, the first task is to investigate the hermeneutical significance of its canonical context. It is possible that an original book of the prophet Habakkuk once circulated on its own, in order to address the political crisis confronting the kingdom of Judah in the last years of its independent existence. But we know nothing of any

---

4. Thus, W. Rudolph's assurance that the Pauline use of Habakkuk 2.4b is "keine Verkehrung, sondern nur eine Vertiefung" (*Micha – Nahum – Habakuk – Zephanja*, p. 216) should not be too readily accepted.

such precanonical form of the book. The (gradual?) formation of the Book of the Twelve may well have involved further redactional activity, an extension of the processes of redaction that may sometimes be traced within the individual books.[5] The result is that the quest for an "original" text, as it left the hands of the prophet's first scribes or editors, is doomed to failure – or at least to uncertainty. While it is true (and important) that the canonical process preserves a number of indications of an original historical situation, its primary concern is with the text's continuing relevance to the communities in which it is cherished as holy scripture. The past must be placed at the disposal of the present. To read the prophetic texts out of an interest in the past as past is to read against the grain of the process that brought them into being. And so the apparent gulf between the seventh century BCE and the era of Paul and the pesherist turns out to be illusory: for the canonical form of the prophetic texts creates a continuum, ensuring that what was said there and then can still be heard here and now. Whether or not such a hearing actually occurs, it is the intention of the canonical process that it should do so – an intention which is embodied in the very form in which the scriptural texts are handed down.[6]

And yet it is important to note that the canonical process does not convert the books of the minor prophets into timeless texts without a history. While it is a subsequent present that is to be addressed, this present is addressed by texts that have been assigned by their editors to specific moments in the past. In the Book of the Twelve, the individual writings are placed in what their editors take to be their historical sequence. They are spread out along the line of the final stages of the canonical history as narrated by the books of Kings, Chronicles, Ezra and Nehemiah. In six of the twelve writings, explicit allusions to that history are found in the superscriptions:

> The word of YHWH that came to Hosea the son of Beeri, in the days of Uzziah, Jotham, Ahaz and Hezekiah, kings of Judah, and in the days of Jeroboam the son of Joash, king of Israel. (Hos.1.1)

---

5. As argued by A. Schart, *Zwölfprophetenbuch, passim.* In my view, Schart is too confident of our ability to reconstruct the "schriftübergreifende Redaktionsschichten" that he postulates. It is difficult to determine whether or not specific intertextual connections are to be attributed to redactors.

6. This position is indebted to, and in fundamental agreement with, Brevard Childs' rehabilitation of the concept of the canon as outlined in his classic *Introduction to the Old Testament as Scripture.* In this work, Childs discusses the minor prophets individually and has nothing to say about the Book of the Twelve as a collection. For an introduction to recent (post-Childs) debate about the Book of the Twelve, see James D. Nogalski and Marvin A. Sweeney (eds.), *Reading and Hearing the Book of the Twelve.* Note, however, the scepticism of E. Ben Zwi ("Twelve Prophetic Books or 'The Twelve'").

The words of Amos, who was among the shepherds of Tekoa, which he saw concerning Israel in the days of Uzziah king of Judah and in the days of Jeroboam the son of Joash, king of Israel, two years before the earthquake. (Am.1.1)

The word of YHWH that came to Micah of Moresheth in the days of Jotham, Ahaz and Hezekiah, kings of Judah, which he saw concerning Samaria and Jerusalem. (Mic.1.1)

The words of YHWH which came to Zephaniah the son of Cushi, son of Gedaliah, son of Amariah, son of Hezekiah, in the days of Josiah the son of Amon, king of Judah. (Zeph.1.1)

In the second year of Darius the king, in the sixth month, on the first day of the month, the word of YHWH came by Haggai the prophet to Zerubbabel the son of Shealtiel, governor of Judah, and to Joshua the son of Jehozadak, the high priest. (Hag.1.1)

In the eighth month, in the second year of Darius, the word of YHWH came to Zechariah the son of Berechiah, son of Iddo, the prophet... (Zech.1.1)

The superscriptions to Hosea, Amos and Micah closely resemble Isaiah 1.1 (although Hosea and Amos also refer to the northern kingdom); the superscription to Zephaniah resembles Jeremiah 1.1–2; and the precise dating in the post-exilic superscriptions recalls Ezekiel 1.1–2. The prophetic texts were clearly edited in close conjunction with one another.[7] These superscriptions presuppose the canonical history of Israel and Judah that tells of the last days of the kingdom of Israel before its destruction at the hands of the Assyrians, the precarious survival of the kingdom of Judah, the destruction of Jerusalem, the Babylonian exile, the subsequent return, and the rebuilding of the temple – a period of around three centuries, according to the biblical chronology.[8] The Book of the Twelve

---

7. For a thorough analysis of these superscriptions, see A. Schart, *Zwölfprophetenbuch*, pp. 39–46. Schart rightly argues that the redaction of these superscriptions intended "dass die Prophetenschriften nicht isoliert für sich, sondern in ihrer Bezogenheit aufeinander gelesen werden" (p. 44).

8. 2 Kings and 2 Chronicles agree on the chronological information they offer on the reigns of the kings of Judah, from Azariah/Uzziah to Zedekiah – a period amounting to 223 years and six months. 2 Chronicles 36.21–22 states, on the authority of Jeremiah, that the exile lasted seventy years, and that this period came to an end in the first year of Cyrus. Ezra, however, does not purport to give chronological information about the reigns of Cyrus, Ahasuerus, Artaxerxes and Darius. Zerubbabel and Jeshua undertake the rebuilding of the temple during the reign of Cyrus (Ezr.3.8–13) and resume it in the second year of Darius, with the encouragement of Haggai and Zechariah (4.24–5.2): their continuing involvement suggests

explicitly claims to derive from various identifiable points in that extended and eventful period, marked above all by the disappearance of the northern kingdom and the later trauma of exile. Whatever the (possibly tenuous) relationship between this intracanonical history and the actual history of the ancient near east, the Book of the Twelve is in close agreement with the canonical history and is presumably dependent on it.[9]

Assuming the originality of the traditional Masoretic order, on the basis of the evidence presented in the previous chapter, it is clear that the six texts among the Twelve that are explicitly dated have been deliberately arranged in chronological order and at three distinct points on the historical time-line. Hosea, Amos and Micah are presented as contemporary, with the ministry of Amos corresponding to the earlier part of Hosea's much longer ministry (the reigns of Jeroboam and Uzziah) and the ministry of Micah corresponding to the later part (the reigns of Jotham, Ahaz and Hezekiah). The five royal names associated with Hosea are thus distributed between Amos and Micah, so that the ministries of Hosea and of Amos/Micah run as it were on parallel lines. Zephaniah, the next prophet to be assigned a specific date, is set in the reign of Josiah. Since the ministries of Hosea and Micah end (like Isaiah's) in the reign of Hezekiah, this second datable point occurs more than fifty years after the first, separated from it by the lengthy reign of Manasseh and the brief reign of Amon (2 Kgs.21, 2 Chr.33). A further interval, of over a century according to the biblical chronology, separates the pre-exilic Zephaniah from the post-exilic Haggai and Zechariah, whose ministries date from the second year of Darius and again run in parallel to one another (cf. Ezra 5.1–2, 6.14). Whereas the ministry of Hosea, Amos and Micah corresponds to Isaiah's, and Zephaniah's to Jeremiah's, there is no exilic prophet among the Twelve to correspond to Ezekiel.

---

that the narrator envisages a relatively brief period between Cyrus and Darius. I am concerned with this chronological material only in relation to intracanonical history, and without reference to historical realities outside the texts.

9. Scepticism about the entire project of writing a "history of Israel" on the basis of biblical "sources" has been expressed by a number of recent scholars (e.g. P. R. Davies, *In Search of 'Ancient Israel'*; K. W. Whitelam, *The Invention of Ancient Israel*). This school of thought shares the current preference for a later dating for the composition or final redaction of the biblical literature, and raises critical questions even about apparently fixed points such as "the exile" or "Israel" itself. Hermeneutical deficiencies in some of this work are trenchantly exposed by Iain Provan, "Ideologies, Literary and Critical". Nevertheless, it is not clear that this school of thought can simply be *reduced* to its hermeneutical shortcomings. My references to "intracanonical history" are intended to acknowledge this debate without taking up any particular stance within it.

Interspersed among the six explicitly dated texts are six undated texts: Joel, Obadiah, Jonah, Nahum, Habakkuk and Malachi.[10] Three of these prophets are identified by reference to their genealogical or geographical origins (Joel, Jonah, Nahum), in addition to their personal names; but no chronological indications are provided. Since the six dated texts have been set in chronological order, and at three distinct historical locations, it is likely that this format is preserved in the placing of the six undated texts. Joel, Obadiah and Jonah are placed among the three "early" texts, giving the order: Hosea, Joel, Amos, Obadiah, Jonah, Micah. It is therefore probable that, for the redactors of the Book of the Twelve, Joel, Obadiah and Jonah belong to the same historical period as Hosea, Amos and Micah. In the case of Jonah, the reason for this placement is clear. The protagonist in the prophetic book is "Jonah the son of Amittai" (Jon.1.1), which identifies him with a figure referred to in the canonical history. According to 2 Kings 15.25, King Jeroboam

> restored the border of Israel from the entrance of Hamath as far as the Sea of the Arabah, according to the word of YHWH the God of Israel, which he spoke by his servant Jonah the son of Amittai, the prophet, who was from Gath-hepher.

This association between Jonah and Jeroboam accounts for the presence of the prophetic book in the company of Hosea, Amos and Micah. The ministries of Hosea and Amos are associated with Jeroboam's reign (Hos.1.1; Am.1.1); the ministry of Micah begins a little later; and the book of Jonah is therefore placed alongside Hosea and Amos but before Micah.

Four of the first six prophetic writings in the Book of the Twelve are clearly assigned to the first of the three points on the time-line, and this suggests that the two remaining writings – Joel and Obadiah – are also assigned to this same point.[11] The starting-point of the book of Joel is the devastation of the land by locusts and drought (Joel 1.4–7, 19–20), in

10. According to J. Nogalski, the inclusion of Joel, Obadiah, Nahum, Habakkuk and Malachi in the developing collection served to unify two pre-existing corpora, consisting of Hosea, Amos, Micah and Zephaniah, and Haggai and Zechariah 1–8 (*Redactional Processes in the Book of the Twelve*, pp. 275–77). If this is correct, the internal evidence of these texts suggests that the order was determined by historical criteria.

11. One need not conclude from "the absence of chronological data in the book of Joel" that "those who arranged the Hebrew collection of the Twelve Prophets must have used other criteria to determine its position between Hosea and Amos" (*contra* H.-W. Wolff, *Hosea*, p. 3). The chronological framework established by six of the twelve texts (seven, if Jonah is included) appears to be firm enough to incorporate the others as well. A further confusion arises when Wolff concludes that "matters of content dictated Joel's position before Amos, and not some knowledge of the time the book was composed" (*ibid.*). The likelihood that the redactors lacked any real "knowledge" of the book's time of composition does not rule out the possibility of a conjecture about its date which has left its mark on the canonical order.

response to which the prophet calls for an act of repentance, prayer and fasting centred upon the temple (1.14, 2.12–17; cf. 1 Kgs.8.35–40). The absence of any reference to external threats posed by Assyria or Babylon may help to account for the canonical redactors' early dating of this text. The book of Obadiah consists of an oracle against the people of Edom, who have participated in the capture of Jerusalem by an unspecified foreign army (Obad.10–14). The canonical redactors might have chosen to connect this text to the fall of Jerusalem to the Babylonians, and placed it accordingly between Zephaniah and Haggai (cf. Ps.137.7 for a complaint about Edomite actions at this time). However, the canonical history tells of warfare between Judah and Edom in the reigns of Amaziah, the father of Uzziah (2 Kgs.14.7–14; 2 Chr.25.5–24), and of Ahaz (2 Kgs.16.6, 28.17). In the earlier episode, expanded considerably by the Chronicler, a successful war against the Edomites leads to a rash challenge to King Joash of Israel, resulting in the capture of Amaziah and the despoiling of Jerusalem. This might explain how the canonical redactors could associate Obadiah with the period of Hosea, Amos and Jonah, Uzziah and Jeroboam.[12]

A further clue to the canonical dating of Joel and Obadiah may be seen in their orientation towards Judah, Jerusalem and Mount Zion.[13] Joel and Obadiah are clearly prophets of the southern kingdom of Judah, in contrast to Hosea and Amos. Yet the superscriptions to Hosea and Amos point to a concern to "claim" these northern prophets for the southern kingdom, by associating them with kings of Judah as well as of Israel (Hos.1.1, Am.1.1) – a concern that is also evident elsewhere in the redaction of these texts.[14] A related concern may be seen in the ordering of the first six texts in the Book of the Twelve, which fall into three pairs: Hosea-Joel, Amos-Obadiah, Jonah-Micah. As we have seen, the link with 2 Kings 15.25 makes Jonah a prophet of the northern kingdom, alongside Hosea and Amos; Micah, however, is associated primarily with the south (Mic.1.1). In each case, then, a northern prophet (Hosea, Amos, Jonah) is paired with a southern one (Joel, Obadiah, Micah). The canonical "early dating" of Joel and Obadiah serves to emphasize that an orientation towards Judah and Jerusalem goes back to the earliest phase of this prophetic collection. The canonical ordering of the six texts is the logical

---

12. Compare the Chronicler's insertion of named and unnamed prophetic figures into the reigns of Jehoshaphat (2 Chr.20.14–20, 21.12), Joash (24.17–22), Amaziah (25.14–16), Ahaz (28.9–11) and Zedekiah (36.12, cf. vv.15–16).

13. Cf. Joel 2.1, 15, 23; 3.5; 4.1, 6, 8, 16–21; Obad.11, 12, 17, 21; Joel 3.5b closely parallels Obad.17a.

14. For a brief summary, see Childs, *Introduction*, pp. 378–79, 399–403. It is possible that the superscriptions are intended to suggest that Hosea and Amos directed their ministry towards the southern kingdom of Judah after the event narrated in Amos 7.10–17 (so A. Schart, *Zwölfprophetenbuch*, p. 43).

culmination of the process that began with the Judean redaction of Hosea and Amos.

These six texts are thus assigned to the earliest of the three points on the Book of the Twelve's time-line, which incorporates the reigns of Jeroboam in the north and Uzziah, Jotham, Ahaz and Hezekiah in the south. Three texts (Nahum, Habakkuk and Zephaniah) are assigned to the second point, identified in the superscription to Zephaniah as "the days of Josiah son of Amon, king of Judah" (Zeph.1.1). The book of Nahum is entitled, "oracle concerning Nineveh" (Nah.1.1), and proclaims the imminent downfall of Assyria. Habakkuk on the other hand announces the rise to power of the *Kasdim*, the Babylonians:

> Look among the nations, and see, and be amazed and astonished: for I am doing a deed in your days – you will not believe when it is told. For behold, I am raising up the *Kasdim*, that cruel and hasty nation, who march across the breadth of the earth to possess dwellings that are not theirs. (Hab.1.5–6)

Between them, Nahum and Habakkuk recount a shift in the balance of power marked by the downfall of the Assyrians and the rise of the Babylonians. This is also presupposed in the canonical history, which tells of an Assyrian invasion during the reign of Hezekiah (2 Kgs.18–19; 2 Chr.32), and of Babylonian invasions during the reigns of Jehoiachim, Jehoiachin and Zedekiah (2 Kgs.24–25; 2 Chr.36; cf. also 2 Kgs.20). The placing of these texts before Zephaniah is at first sight puzzling, since the reign of Josiah predates the emergence of the Babylonian threat. An explanation may be found in the content of Zephaniah, which announces the divine judgment on Jerusalem (Zeph.1.2–18, 3.1–7). Neither Nahum nor Habakkuk alludes to the fall of Jerusalem, and they are therefore placed before Zephaniah. Zephaniah concludes with a promise of return from exile:

> At that time I will bring you home, at the time when I gather you together; indeed, I will make you a name and a praise among all the peoples of the earth when I bring back your captives before your eyes – says YHWH. (Zeph.3.20)

This concluding reference to exile and return paves the way for the texts at the third and final point on the time-line: Haggai, Zechariah and Malachi.

This group of texts is associated with the restoration of the temple (Haggai, Zechariah) and the struggle to preserve its purity (Malachi). The first two books are carefully dated in relation to the reign of Darius (Hag.1.1; 1.15–2.1; 2.10, 20; Zech.1.1, 7; 7.1). Malachi, however, is undated. The arguments so far presented for a chronological ordering of the Book of the Twelve make it clear that, for the redactors, Malachi is the latest work in the collection, and that it is concerned with the priestly ministry of the second, restored temple whose rebuilding is announced by Haggai and Zechariah. Internal evidence for this setting may have been found in the attack on priestly marriages to foreign women (Mal.2.10–12), which is also a concern of the books of Ezra and Nehemiah (Ezr.9.1–10.44; Neh.13.23–31). For the canonical redactors, Malachi may have seemed a uniquely "contemporary" text – in contrast to the other eleven writings, which are located in contexts that long predate the assembling of the collection.

In the canonical redaction of the Book of the Twelve, prophecy is historicized.[15] The book tells how the word of YHWH came to various named individuals at three major turning-points in a history spanning three centuries or more: the last days of the northern kingdom, the events preceding the destruction of Jerusalem and the exile, the return from exile and the rebuilding of the temple. Malachi may be seen as a bridge connecting this latter event, as attested in Haggai and Zechariah, with the redactors' present. The word of YHWH continues to address each subsequent present in and through the reading of the Book of the Twelve, but it comes not "vertically, from above" but from various crucial moments in the past. It addresses the present, indeed, but with a degree of indirectness. It is not immediately evident from the book itself how the word of YHWH during the time of King Jeroboam or of the Babylonian rise to power can still be addressed to readers in the late Persian or early Hellenistic periods, when the final redaction of the book must have taken place. The book itself raises the question of its own interpretation. Its meaning and significance are not self-evident, but must be discerned in an ongoing process of interpretation. The texts it contains are set within a redactional framework that serves to historicize them, underlining the non-identity between the word of YHWH during the reigns of King Jeroboam, Hezekiah or Josiah and the word that might now be encountered within these ancient writings. The texts preserve the call to "hear the word of YHWH" as announced by the prophets (Hos.4.1, cf. 5.1; Joel 1.2; Amos 3.1, 4.1, 5.1, 8.4; Mic.1.2, 3.1, 6.1–2). But for the book and its readers the possibility of hearing YHWH speaking directly out of the mouth of Hosea or Amos lies in the past. The call to "hear" must be supplemented by the call to *interpret*; indeed, for the reader to "hear" *is* to interpret. That point was clearly understood by readers of the Book of the Twelve at Qumran and in the early church. In interpreting texts from this collection in the light of their respective sectarian histories, these readers offer their own

---

15. Since the "chronological order" of the Twelve is that of the canonical history, and not the order of composition, the chronological ordering is fundamental to a canonical reading of the Twelve. This point is missed by Paul R. House, whose understanding of the "plot" of the Twelve in terms of sin, punishment and restoration is developed without reference to the canonical history (*The Unity of the Twelve*, pp. 123–60).

answer to the interpretative question posed by the texts themselves. The interpretations they offer may not satisfy nonsectarian readers, but they at least understand that the texts pose a question and that an answer of some sort is required. As it issues forth from the hands of its redactors, the book is open to a future in which its meaning and significance will become clear. That meaning and significance are not immediately legible: they must be *deciphered*.

The call to interpret, posed by the book itself, may be more precisely analysed in terms of *non-fulfilment* and *hope*. The word of YHWH to Israel and Judah, from the times of Jeroboam and Uzziah to the fairly recent past, is in the first instance a word of judgment. The prophetic word exposes the sin of God's people and threatens them with punishment, and, from the perspective of the historical distance presupposed in the canonical text, it is clear that this threat has been repeatedly actualized. The fact that, in the oldest texts in the collection, no king of Israel is named after Jeroboam is a reminder of the subsequent fate of the northern kingdom, which perished just as the northern prophets foretold. The references in Zephaniah to the imminent destruction of Jerusalem are vindicated by the later concern for rebuilding in the aftermath of catastrophe, as voiced by Haggai and Zechariah. For the reader, there can be no doubt that the divine word of judgment has repeatedly been realized in the nation's history, and that the prophets of judgment have retrospectively been vindicated (cf. Deut.18.21–22; Zech.1.4–6). Yet, according to the canonical texts, these same prophets also proclaimed a message of hope. In spite of the annihilating message of judgment, it is always hope that has the final word – as the conclusions to all twelve texts (including Jonah) make clear.[16] What is hoped for is a final, definitive enactment of the covenantal relationship between YHWH and his people. From the perspective of the canonical collection, this promise of a definitive divine saving action has evidently not yet been fulfilled – unlike the threat of judgment. In spite of the historical realities of exile and return, the post-exilic writings in the collection are testimonies precisely to the deferral of a fulfilment which so often seems near at hand but never actually arrives.

This (unscheduled?) interval between the announcement of salvation and its fulfilment is the space of the written canonical text. Yet hope deferred is still hope: the hermeneutic entailed in the canonical form of the Book of the Twelve is above all a hermeneutic of hope. The interpretation

16. House's strictly sequential reading of the "plot" of the Twelve leads him to claim that the hope of restoration is first introduced only in the concluding chapter of Zephaniah (*Unity*, p. 151). In contrast, "[t]he rays of hope in Hosea, Joel, and Amos in no way alleviate the conviction expressed in these books that doom inevitably waits" (p. 136). On this view, it is hard to see what the function of these remarkably uniform concluding sections is supposed to be.

called for by the text is one that shows how its unfulfilled hopes will find the fulfilment they seek in a still future divine saving action. The Book of the Twelve marks the intersection between a past dominated by the divine judgment and a future characterized by the hope of salvation.

This canonical hermeneutic of hope in the face of non-fulfilment is explicitly articulated within the book itself, and is not superimposed on it from the outside. As the Qumran pesherist rightly noted, the crucial passage is to be found in Habakkuk 2.1–3. Here, the prophet receives a commission not to speak but to write.

Salvation in question

As chapter 2 opens, we overhear an interior monologue in which the prophet Habakkuk addresses not God or the reader, but himself:

> Upon my watchtower I will take my stand, I will station myself upon the rampart, and I will look to see what he will say to me and what answer I shall return, concerning my complaint. (Hab.2.1)

The prophet has privileged access to a high place between heaven and earth, from which it is possible to see far beyond the horizon of those who live at ground level. In a comparable passage in Isaiah 21.6–10, a watchman is appointed by the prophet at YHWH's command. Instructed to look out for approaching chariots and riders, the anonymous watchman announces that, after long waiting, the riders have appeared – thus triggering the divine proclamation, "Fallen, fallen is Babylon..." This watchman is the prophet Isaiah's *alter ego*. In the distinction here between the prophet and the watchman, "the historical distance from the prophet Isaiah to the actual fall of Babylon is covered, without doing violence to the integrity of Isaiah's known historical location".[17] Habakkuk on his watchtower is also concerned with the destiny of the Babylonians. It is the place where the prophet awaits YHWH's response to his Job-like complaint (Hab.1.2–17):

> How long, YHWH, shall I cry and you will not hear? or call out to you, "Violence!", and you will not save? Why do you make me see wrong and look upon trouble? (Hab.1.2–3a)

Whereas Isaiah's watchman is appointed to his post (cf. also Ezek.3.17), Habakkuk ventures both his complaint and his position on the watchtower on his own initiative. Elsewhere in the Book of the Twelve, the predominant direction of the prophetic word is from God to the people, with occasional examples of intercession for the people (Am.7.1–6) or of

17. C.R. Seitz, *Isaiah*, p. 166.

dialogue between God and the prophet (Jonah). The book of Habakkuk is unique in its focus on the human word addressed to God (Hab.1.2–4, 12–17; 3.1–19);[18] the human word precedes the divine word, and the divine word is a response to the human word. The human word in question is a "complaint" about the non-occurrence of divine saving action.

It is arguable that the "complaint" to which the prophet awaits a response is to be identified only with the concluding section of chapter 1. On one reading of this chapter, the prophet's initial complaint about divine inaction in a situation of violence and injustice (1.2–4) is already answered in 1.5–11:

> Look among the nations, and see, and be amazed and astonished: for I am doing a deed in your days – you will not believe when it is told. For behold, I am raising up the Chaldeans, that cruel and hasty nation, which marches across the breadth of the earth to possess dwellings that are not his. Dreadful and terrible is he, from himself his justice and his dignity go forth... Then he sweeps by like the wind and passes on, and makes his own strength his god. (Hab.1.5–7, 11)[19]

This divine speech is often understood as the answer to the prophet's complaint about a violence and injustice that is taking place among his own people (1.2–4). When it is said that "*torah* fails and justice never goes forth" (1.4), this would then refer to an internal failure to implement the social programme of the Torah, and not to an external aggressor.[20] According to this view, it makes no sense to see a reference to the Chaldeans here: for "Yahweh cannot answer the complaint about the

18. The secondary role of the divine word in this text is noted by C.-A. Keller, "Die Eigenart der Prophetie Habakuks", pp. 157–58. Explicit divine speech is confined to 1.5–6 and 2.2b–3.

19. In Habakkuk 1.6–17, the oppressor is presented as a singular figure – *kśdym* in v.6 and *bwgdym* in v.13 being the only exceptions. From KJV onwards, the English versions tend to replace the Hebrew singular with plurals, switching to the singular only in 1.15–17 and in 2.4–19 (RV is a partial exception). The effect is to obscure the connection between 2.4–5 and chapter 1. In 1.11, I prefer to read *wyśm* ("... and makes"), with 1QpHab iv.9, rather than MT's *w'śm* ("... and incurs guilt").

20. This is the majority view, held among others by W. Hayes Ward, *Habakkuk*, p. 4; W. Rudolph, *Micha-Nahum-Habakuk-Zephanja*, pp. 201–202; Ralph L. Smith, *Micah-Malachi*, p. 99; J. J. M. Roberts, *Nahum, Habakkuk, and Zephaniah*, p. 88. The coming of the Babylonians would then be the divine punishment for the sins of the people. Another possibility is that the prophet complains in 1.2–4 (and 1.12–17) of Assyrian oppression, to which the Babylonians are the divine response (O. Eissfeldt, *Introduction*, pp. 419–20). This view goes back to K. Budde ("Die Bücher Habakuk und Zephanja" [1893]), who suggests that 1.5–11 was originally located after 2.4. These theories are described by P. Jöcken as, respectively, the anti-Jewish/anti-Babylonian theory (*Das Buch Habakuk*, pp. 3–85) and the anti-Assyrian/pro-Babylonian theory (pp. 148–176). Jöcken's survey confirms that representatives of the anti-Jewish/anti-Babylonian theory "bilden die grösste Untergruppe innerhalb der traditionellen Interpretationen" (p. 77).

violence of the enemy by announcing the coming of precisely this enemy
(vv.5ff.)."[21] If the divine announcement of the coming of the Chaldeans
answers the prophet's first complaint, it only leads to a further complaint
(1.12–17): and it is this second complaint to which the prophet awaits an
answer on his watchtower (2.1). On this view, an initial concern about
internal oppression leads to an announcement of punishment in the form
of an external aggressor – which in turn generates a further complaint. It is
assumed that the divine speech in 1.5–11 can only be seen as an answer to
the prophetic complaint of 1.2–4. While the divine speech does not itself
present the coming of the Chaldean(s) as a punishment for the nation's
sins, the prophet's second complaint acknowledges that YHWH has
"ordained him for judgment" and "established him for chastisement"
(1.13). YHWH would then be punishing the sins to which the prophet
refers in 1.2–4 – although in a manner that the prophet finds unacceptable.

This reading of Habakkuk 1 is implausible, however. There are close
parallels between the evils described in vv.2–4 and those attributed to the
Chaldeans in vv.5–17.[22] The prophet cries, "Violence!" (vv.2, 3), and the
divine speech states that the Chaldean army "comes for violence" (v.9: *ḥms*
in all three cases). The question in v.13 ("... why do you look upon the
faithless, and are silent when the wicked man swallows up the one who is
more righteous than he?") corresponds closely to vv.3a, 4b ("Why do you
make me see wrong and look upon trouble?... For the wicked man
surrounds the righteous...."). When it is said that "justice [*mšpṭ*] never
goes forth" (v.4), this may be linked to the statement about the Chaldean,
that "from himself his justice and his dignity go forth" (v.7). If 1.5–11 is
really the divine answer to the evils complained of in 1.2–4, then God's
solution to the problem of oppression is to exacerbate it, through a new
agent. That would no doubt explain why the prophet feels he has grounds
for a second complaint (vv.12–17), but it would not explain why the speech
ascribed to YHWH is logically and rhetorically so defective. If YHWH's
response to the prophet's cry, "Violence!" (v.2) is simply that the Chaldean
"comes for violence" (v.9), then the deity can hardly have expected the
prophet to find such a response satisfactory. Indeed, since the divine
speech is purely descriptive in form, it is left to the prophet to suggest to
YHWH that his raising up of the Chaldeans was punitive and disciplinary
in intention (v.12). If, on the other hand, the "violence" of vv.2–4 is
identified with the violence of the Chaldeans, these problems disappear.

21. W. Rudolph, *ibid.*, p. 201; my translation.
22. As noted by R. Rendtorff, *Einführung*, p. 245. The coherence of the complaints (1.2–4,
12–17) with one another and with the situation described in the divine speech (1.5–11) is the
main strength of what P. Jöcken has described as "die konsequent antibabylonische
Interpretation" (*Das Buch Habakuk*, pp. 86–147; p. 107) – although this appears not to have
had any significant recent representatives.

On the standard interpretation of Habakkuk 1, the two prophetic complaints (vv.2–4, 12–17) are oddly detached from one another. The divine answer to the first complaint generates the second complaint, but there is no backward reference from the second to the first. The prophet does not acknowledge that, although he had complained about unrighteousness within his own people, he has now abandoned that complaint and wishes to complain about something else. Speaking in both contexts about the oppression of "the righteous" by "the wicked" (vv.4, 13), he does not explain how a nation that is an unrighteous oppressor (presumably of the poor) in the first complaint can become the righteous victim of a different unrighteous oppressor (the Chaldeans) in the second. Thus, his complaints do not cohere with one another. If in Habakkuk 1 there is dramatic development along these lines, it lacks the narrative framework (such as is found in Jonah 4) that would make it effective.

The solution to these difficulties is to abandon the assumption that the divine speech in vv.5–11 is to be read as an "answer" to the questions put by the prophet in vv.2–4, and that these passages are supposed to follow one another in chronological sequence. Rather, the divine speech with the corresponding prophetic complaint (vv.5–17) are to be seen as an *elaboration* of the situation presupposed in vv.2–4. The prophet's initial cry, "Violence!" is presented without any contextual information. We do not know who is perpetrating violence on whom, or where, or when, or why. In the main body of the chapter, the divine announcement (vv.5–11) and the prophet's complaint (vv.12–17) serve to fill in the background of this initially contextless cry. We now learn that the violence in question is that of the invading, seemingly invincible Chaldean armies, and that their cruelty has been ordained by YHWH himself. The Chaldeans' victims are not just the prophet's own people but rather "the nations" (vv.5, 17), and it is on their behalf that the prophet speaks. Thus, the action referred to in the divine speech – the raising up of the Chaldeans – predates the prophet's complaint in vv.2–4, and is not a response to it. The text opens with the complaint rather than the divine speech so as to ensure that the emphasis falls on the prophet's own initiative in raising the question about the absence of divine saving action. That is, indeed, the single topic of the entire chapter; there is no awkward and unacknowledged shift from internal to external oppression. Alongside three other texts in the Book of the Twelve (Obadiah, Jonah, Nahum), this one shows virtually no concern with the problem of the sin and guilt of the covenant people. This issue is absent from the other three books because of their limited concern with the fate of specific enemies (Edom, Assyria). While Habakkuk is also concerned with a specific enemy, the book focuses not on the Chaldeans *per se* but on the theological problem that they exemplify: the problem of the continuing non-occurrence of divine saving action. That alone is the issue which the prophet hopes to resolve as he awaits the divine word upon his watchtower.[23]

As we have seen, the non-occurrence or deferral of divine saving action is also the primary issue posed by the entire Book of the Twelve in its canonical form. As we survey the period of four centuries or so that it purports to cover, it becomes clear that the prophetic threats of various inner-historical divine judgments have been amply fulfilled. It also becomes clear that the prophetic promises of definitive and final divine saving action, which have the last word in every text, have not been fulfilled and are, so to speak, held in suspense. The problem of the promise of salvation and its deferral is *the* problem of the Book of the Twelve, and it is just this that is articulated in the question with which the book of Habakkuk opens: "YHWH, how long...?" (1.2).

On his watchtower, the prophet waits for an answer. When the answer comes, it speaks of a quite unexpected, apparently unrelated topic: the written text.

Writing and hope

The divine answer to the question, "how long?" addresses the question of the time of the end (2.3) only by way of a detour in the form of a command to write (2.2):

> And YHWH answered me and said: Write the vision, and make it clear upon tablets, so that one who reads it may run. For still the vision is for its time, it hastens to the end and it will not lie. If it lingers, wait for it; for it will surely come, it will not delay.

This passage poses questions about (1) the scope, (2) the purpose and (3) the content of the "writing" that is here commanded.

(1) "Write the vision" is an ambiguous instruction. It is often assumed that what is to be written is a brief message such as Isaiah was once commanded to write:

---

23. The unsatisfactoriness of 1.5–11 as an "answer" to 1.2–4 is rightly noted by F. Andersen, *Habakkuk*, pp. 142–43 – although the traditional distinction between the prophet's first and second complaints is unfortunately retained. Andersen makes the crucial point that "[t]he inference so frequently made by commentators that the Chaldeans are God's chosen instruments for judgment on the deserving wicked (Assyria, Egypt, or the godless in Judah) finds no support in the passage itself" (p. 143). (The prophet's own reference to the Chaldeans' disciplinary role [1.12] is not emphasized.) If the "answer" is so "unsatisfactory", however, are we compelled to see it as an answer at all? Note also Andersen's later qualification of his position (p. 224).

And YHWH said to me, Take a large tablet and write upon it in common characters: For Maher-shalal-hash-baz. (Is.8.1)

What Isaiah writes is, "Spoil speeds, plunder hastens", which is shortly to become a proper name (Is.8.3). If Habakkuk was commanded to write a similarly brief message, then the most likely candidate would seem to be the statement found in 2.4 (or 2.4–5), which announces that the salvation of the righteous lies in their faithfulness, and denounces the oppressor.[24] Yet, in contrast to Isaiah, there is no indication in Habakkuk that any specific passage is identified with the writing that YHWH here commissions. The command to "write the vision" is quite general, and the word translated "vision" *(ḥzwn)* serves elsewhere in the Book of the Twelve to refer to the entire content of an individual book. Whereas most books in the collection open with a reference to the word of YHWH that came to the prophet,[25] four of them differ. Amos 1.1 speaks of "the words of Amos ... which he saw *[ḥzh]* concerning Israel ... " Evidently the verb can refer to what was heard as well as to what was seen (cf. Hos.12.11). Obadiah is entitled "Vision *[ḥzwn]* of Obadiah", and proceeds to declare the divine word concerning Edom (Ob.1.1). Nahum has a double superscription, one part of which refers to its content, the other to its author: it is both "the oracle *[mś']* concerning Nineveh" and "the book of the vision *[ḥzwn]* of Nahum the Elkoshite" (Nah.1.1). The superscriptions to Obadiah and Nahum indicate that the word "vision" can refer to an entire prophetic book. Habakkuk opens with the words, "The oracle *[hmś']* which Habakkuk the prophet saw *[ḥzh]*" (Hab.1.1). Since the noun and the verb translated "vision" and "saw" are cognate, it seems that the introductions to Nahum and Habakkuk have been deliberately assimilated to one another.[26] Each book in its entirety can be described as an "oracle" and as a "vision", that which the prophet "saw".[27] Thus, when Habakkuk is commissioned to "write the vision" (2.2), the reference is most probably to his book in its entirety. Unlike other prophets, Habakkuk is called not to speak but to write. In its literary context, the

---

24. So R. L. Smith, *Micah-Malachi*, p. 107; W. R. Brownlee, "The Placarded Revelation of Habakkuk", pp. 320–21, 324; S. Schreiner, "Erwägungen zum Text von Hab 2 4–5", p. 538.

25. Hos.1.1; Joel 1.1; Jon.1.1; Mic.1.1; Zeph.1.1; Hag.1.1; Zech.1.1; cf. Mal.1.1.

26. So A. Schart, *Zwölfprophetenbuch*, pp. 46–47. Schart argues that the incomplete acrostic theophany of Nahum 1.2–8 and the theophany of Habakkuk 3.3–15 were intended as a "frame" around the two writings (pp. 244–45), which were linked at the time of their incorporation into the earlier "D-Korpus", consisting of Hosea, Amos, Micah, Zephaniah (p. 246). He also highlights the distinction between Nahum and Habakkuk as prophets of salvation, and the earlier prophets as messengers of judgment (pp. 247–49).

27. Compare Isaiah 1.1, where the superscription combines both the noun and the verb: "Vision *[ḥzwn]* of Isaiah son of Amoz which he saw *[ḥzh]* ... "

command to "write the vision" is self-referential: in it, the book of Habakkuk speaks of its own origin and basis.[28]

(2) The prophet is to write the book that contains his "vision" not primarily for his own benefit but "so that one who reads it may run".[29] In Isaiah 40.31, the same verb is used when it is said that "those who wait for YHWH shall renew their strength, ... they shall run and not be weary". This indicates the general semantic domain in which Habakkuk's use of this metaphor is to be located.[30] The metaphor can be more precisely located by relating it to the liturgical "prayer" in chapter 3. At the conclusion of his prayer, the prophet confesses his joy in YHWH even in the midst of deprivation (3.18–19), and adds:

> YHWH my lord is my strength, he makes my feet like hinds, and upon my heights he makes me tread. (Hab.3.20)

Since the simile of the hinds is closely related to the metaphor of the runner, this passage suggests that the "running" metaphor in 2.2 alludes to the joy, strength and surefootedness enabled by YHWH. Habakkuk 3.20 is virtually identical to Psalm 18.33 (= 2 Sam.22.34), where it again occurs in the context of a theophany. Thus, in the same context, the psalmist celebrates the fact that

---

28.   The nearest parallel is to be found in Jeremiah 36. In Isaiah 30.8, the prophet is commanded to "write it before them on a tablet, and inscribe it in a book, that it may be for the time to come as a witness for ever". The reference here is probably not to the book as a whole – the view of Watts (*Isaiah 1–33*, p. 396) and Childs (*Isaiah*, p. 222) – but simply to the (feminine) name, "Rahab sit still" (v.7), to which the feminine suffixes and verb in v.8 refer back. As in Isaiah 8.1–3, the message to be written is very brief.

29.   In this translation of v.3b, "running" is the metaphorical *goal* of reading, and thus, indirectly, of writing: cf. RSV's "so he may run who reads it," which harks back to KJV and RV. Against this, NRSV assumes that (literal) running and reading are simultaneous: "Write the vision; make it plain on tablets, so that a runner may read it". This rendering takes MT's *lm'n yrws qwr' bw* to mean, "so that one shall run [while] reading it." In other words, the prophet's message is to be written so clearly that even someone who happens to be running past the inscribed tablets (which have been erected by the side of the public highway, like an advertising hoarding) will be able to read them. (For criticism of this view, see F. Andersen, *Habakkuk*, pp. 202–4.) MT's *qwr' bw* is more plausibly taken as the subject of the verb, *yrws* (cf. LXX's *hopōs diōkē ho anaginōskōn*); for the anarthrous participial phrase referring to the reader, cf. Isaiah 29.11 *(ywd' hspr)*. NIV's "... so that a herald may run with it" is also unlikely (*pace* Andersen, pp. 204–205), since *qr' b-* meaning "to read in/from" is a well-attested idiom (Deut.17.19; Jer.36.8, 10, 13; Neh.8.3, 18, 13.1; 2 Chr.34.18).

30.   It is less likely that the reference is to quick, fluent reading ("... to be easily read" [JB]) – that is, to a reading with full understanding. This seems to have been the view of the Qumran pesherist (1QpHab vii.3–5).

by thee I shall outrun *['r(w)ṣ]* a troop, and by my God I shall leap over
a wall. (Ps.18.30 = 2 Sam.22.30)[31]

The verb is the same as in Habakkuk 2.2, and refers to the transforming
effects of the strength that comes from God – a concept deriving from
archaic ideas about charismatic endowment. (Compare 1 Kings 18.46:
"And the hand of YHWH was upon Elijah, and he girded up his loins and
ran *[wyrṣ]* before Ahab to the entrance of Jezreel.") This divinely
bestowed strength is what YHWH intends for the reader of Habakkuk's
text. The prophet is to "write the vision... so that one who reads it may
run". When, at the conclusion of his text, the prophet celebrates YHWH's
gifts of joy, strength and surefootedness, he writes as he does in order to
draw the reader into the celebration.

Indeed, the whole of this text is intended for the reader. When the
prophet opens his text with the question, "how long...?" (Hab.1.2), he
asks not on his own behalf but on behalf of an "implied reader" who shares
his anguish over the contradiction between the promise of salvation and the
facts of experience. (Why otherwise should he have *written* a question
addressed exclusively to God, thus making it permanently available to be
read by others?) Similarly, the divine assurance that the (written) vision has
its time of fulfilment (2.3) is addressed not just to the prophet but, through
the medium of writing, to his reader – enabling him or her to "run", in the
confidence that the question addressed to God in chapter 1 has been
answered. The role of the reader is not absolutized, however: the prophet
does not vacate his own text to allow the reader to take full possession of it.
Without an address proceeding from an other, the reader would have
nothing left to read.[32] The double reference to "Habakkuk the prophet"
(1.1, 3.1) alludes to the fact that the reader of this text is genuinely
addressed by an other whose otherness is at no point dissolved.[33] Yet it is
the *reader* who is addressed by this other: if the figure of the reader is not to
be absolutized, neither is the figure of the historical author. To study this
text with the primary aim of restoring it to a so-called "original historical
context" is to refuse the role that the text itself assigns to its own reader.[34]

31. Or perhaps, "by thee I shall run against a troop".
32. See Kevin Vanhoozer, *Is there a Meaning in this Text?*, for a cogent critique of the
absolutized reader of contemporary hermeneutical theory. Vanhoozer rightly argues that a
text is irreducibly "a communicative act of a communicative agent, fixed by writing" (p. 225):
only as such does the text intend its own reader.
33. The prophet's name can represent this textual otherness even if it is not only (or not at
all) the voice of a historical individual named "Habakkuk" that can be heard in this text. Even
the pesherist knows that "God spoke to Habakkuk..." (1QpHab vii.1).
34. As Childs rightly argues, it is no accidental deficiency of this book that "the changing
historical situation of the ancient Near East between 605 and 587 is not carefully registered"
(*Introduction*, p. 453).

(3) The command to "write the vision" can only truly answer the prophet's complaint if the content of the vision is relevant to that complaint. If the complaint is concerned with the non-occurrence of salvation, the divine answer must speak of a salvation that is yet to come. While the book that is to be written will encompass both the prophet's complaint and YHWH's answer to it, it is that answer that must now be distinctly heard. It comes in the form of an explanation of the command to write so that the reader may run:

> For still the vision is for its time, it hastens to the end and it will not lie.
> If it lingers, wait for it; for it will surely come, it will not delay. (Hab.2.3)

The reference must be to the future divine saving action towards which the "vision" is oriented, and in which it finds its fulfilment; it is not that the "vision" itself – YHWH's revelation to the prophet – is deferred to some unspecified time in the future. The divine action of which the vision speaks has its appointed time: the prophet and his reader are to live in the light of this assured future, and they are enabled to do so by the written text in which the vision is to be enshrined.[35] The writing of the vision presupposes that prophet and reader must live at a time in which the fulfilment is not yet. The written text transforms this present from a time of pure violence and oppression, flagrantly contradicting the promise of salvation, to a time whose end has been determined by God: the present is now illuminated by the light of God's future, definitive saving action. The prophetic writing fills the space between vision and fulfilment in such a way as to transfigure it.

The significance of this connection between the written text and the "not yet" of salvation may be clarified by analysing its opposite: the spoken promise of a salvation that is to take place immediately. In the book of Haggai, the prophet receives two messages that are carefully dated to "the twenty-fourth day of the ninth month, in the second year of Darius" (Hag.2.10, 18, 20). The first message is addressed by the prophet to the priests (2.11, 13), and concludes with a promise of immediate divine blessing in place of the present dearth:

> Is the seed yet in the barn? Do the vine, the fig tree, the pomegranate and
> the olive tree still yield nothing? From this day on I shall bless.
> (Hag.2.19)

The second message is still more comprehensive, although addressed to an individual:

---

35.   "The vision is a witness to what God is going to do at a set time in the future. Because God's intervention is to take place in the future, the testimony about it is to be written down and preserved as a witness until the events of that day confirm it" (J. J. M. Roberts, *Nahum, Habakkuk, Zephaniah*, p. 110).

Speak to Zerubbabel governor of Judah, saying: I am about to shake the
heavens and the earth, and to overthrow the throne of kingdoms... On
that day, says YHWH of hosts, I will take you, O Zerubbabel son of
Shealtiel, my servant, says YHWH, and make you like a signet ring; for
I have chosen you, says YHWH of hosts. (Hag.2.21–23)

The precise dates and names indicate that God's saving action is to take
place imminently. Indeed, the turning point in the fortunes of the "people
of the land" (2.4)[36] has already arrived (cf. 2.19). The immediate blessing
promised in the first oracle is to lead directly to the universal
transformation promised in the second, which is addressed to the chosen
individual who will shortly experience it for himself. Since they concern the
immediate future of the people and their ruler, these messages are
delivered orally. The author of this text highlights the historical
particularity of Haggai's prophetic ministry by setting it within a more
explicit narrative framework than anywhere else in the Book of the Twelve
(with the exception of Jonah). Yet the very existence of this text is
testimony to the non-fulfilment of the promises it records. Its form
subverts its content even as it preserves it. For text and reader alike, the
twenty-fourth day in the ninth month of the second year of King Darius is
receding ever further into the past, without any sign of the universal
transformation that was supposed to be imminent then.[37] Yet, in spite of
this correlation between writing and non-fulfilment, the writing of these
unfulfilled promises also preserves the hope that they will (one day,
somehow) be fulfilled. The writing of this text is a gesture both of
disappointment and of hope – in such a way, however, that the
disappointment is subsumed in the hope.[38]

It is this correlation between writing, disappointment and hope that is
articulated in Habakkuk 2.1–3, which speaks for the entire Book of the
Twelve in thematizing the significance of prophetic writing. In this passage,
the Book of the Twelve locates itself in a time in which the salvation of

36. In this text, it is not said that these are returned exiles (in contrast to Ezra 3.8; 4.1, 12).
In Zechariah 2.6–7, a return from exile is still future.

37. There would still be a historical distance between text and prophecy even if we imagine
that the book is the work of a disciple writing during or shortly after the life of Haggai (so
Eissfeldt, *Introduction*, p. 428). Whenever the book was written, its narrative structure serves
to *historicize* the ministry of Haggai (compare Ezra 4.24–5.2, 6.14, where, however, the hopes
associated with the rebuilding project are not mentioned).

38. In his study of the non-fulfilment of prophecy, R. P. Carroll asks whether the texts
relating to Zerubbabel show any awareness of the disconfirmation of the hopes associated
with this figure. He concludes: "The nature of the material is such that the expectations are
well delineated in it but little or no attempt was made to indicate the outcome of such
expectations" (*When Prophecy Failed*, p. 165). In fact, the very existence of Haggai *as a text*
expresses an awareness both of the disconfirmation and of the enduring significance of the
hopes of which the prophet spoke.

which it speaks is not yet, although it already impinges on the present in and through the book itself. In place of the despairing cry, "how long...?", the book enjoins its reader to "wait", in the confidence that "it will surely come, it will not delay" (Hab.2.3).

Living from the Vision

A new perspective

While Habakkuk 2.3 points ahead to a future fulfilment, the following verses revert to the oppression of the present as depicted in chapter 1. As we shall see, however, the prophet's attitude towards this present has been fundamentally altered by the divine answer that has come to him on his watchtower. The Masoretic text of 2.4–5 is difficult, but the sense is greatly improved by incorporating a reading from the Habakkuk pesher which may well represent the original text:

> Behold, presumptuous[39] and not upright is his soul within him[40] – but the righteous shall live by his faithfulness.[41] Yes indeed,[42] wealth shall betray[43]

---

39. As pointed in MT, *'plh* is a pual perfect 3rd fem. sg. from the root *'pl*. BDB suggests that the root meaning is "swell", and gives the cognate noun *'pl* the meanings "mound, hill", with reference to an acropolis (2 Kgs.5.24; Mic.4.8; Is.32.14), or "tumour" (Deut.28.27; I Sam.5.6, 9, 12; 6.4, 5). Both suggested senses are doubtful, however, and it is not clear how relevant this material is to Habakkuk 2.4. More important is the occurrence of a verbal form from this root in Numbers 14.44, which speaks of the Israelites' rash attempt to conquer the land in defiance of YHWH's prohibition: this begins when "they acted presumptuously in going to the top of the mountain" (*wy'plw l'lwt 'l r'š hhr*; MT points the verb as hiph.). This sense is confirmed by the parallel passage in Deuteronomy 1.43, where the verb *zyd* ("act presumptuously") is used synonymously.

40. Roberts translates "in it", with reference to the vision, the subject of v.3 (*Nahum, Habakkuk, Zephaniah*, p. 107). With the help of an emendation and an appeal to the use of *yšr* in 1 Samuel 6.12, Habakkuk 2.4a is thus translated: "Now the fainthearted, his soul will not walk in it" (p. 105). "In it" is not possible if *npšy* governs *'plh* as well as *l' yšrh*, as it does in the unemended text.

41. Andersen translates "its reliability", referring back to the vision (*Habakkuk*, p. 214); cf. LXX.

42. In this context, *'p ky* cannot mean "how much more/less", as elsewhere (Prov. 11.31; 2 Chr.32.15); cf. Ezek. 23.40.

43. Reading *hwn ybgwd* (so 1QpHab viii.3), rather than MT's *hyyn bwgd* ("wine is treacherous"): see the discussion in J. A. Emerton, "The Textual and Linguistic Problems of Habakkuk II. 4–5", pp. 6–9. A scribe may have misread the consonants *h-w-n-y* as *h-y-y-n*, and then transposed the *gimel* and the *waw* that follow. For *bgd* with a direct object, see Psalm 73.15 – although Emerton rejects this construal of the syntax on metrical grounds. LXX gives no support for either "wealth" or "wine" here; *ho de katoinōmenos* in the Rahlfs text is a conjectural emendation of *katoiomenos* ("conceited"). The LXX rendering of v.5a may be

the arrogant man,[44] and he shall not abide[45] – whose greed is wide as Sheol, and like death he is never satisfied, and he gathers to himself all the nations, and draws to himself all the peoples.

As the translation indicates, the two verses belong together. On an interpretation of the command to write different from the one adopted here, the brief message that the prophet writes on his tablets consists only in v.4, and thus concludes with the words, "The righteous shall live by his faithfulness."[46] But there is no justification for this ultra-Pauline view. In 2.4–5, the prophet begins to speak of the subject matter of his complaint – the oppression of the righteous by the wicked (chapter 1) – on the basis of the new perception of that subject matter that he has attained as a result of the divine answer he has received (2.1–3). When he took his stand upon his watchtower, he waited to see not only "what he will say to me" but also "what I shall answer [*'šyb*], concerning my complaint" (2.1). Although the first singular verb is often emended to a third singular, it is supported by LXX (*ti apokrithō*) and by the content of the whole chapter.[47] "What he will say to me" is contained only in the divine speech in vv.2–3; "what I shall answer" refers to the prophet's response to this divine speech, in vv.4–20. Now that God has spoken to him of the certainty of his future saving action, Habakkuk can speak confidently in his own voice of the security of the righteous and of the imminent downfall of the wicked.

On this interpretation of Habakkuk 1–2, the movement of thought is similar to that of Psalm 73. First comes the complaint about the prosperity or injustice of the wicked (Ps.73.1–16; Hab.1.2–17). This is followed by the transforming moment of encounter with God, in the sanctuary or on the watchtower (Ps.73.17; Hab.2.1–3), which makes it possible to see that the wicked are doomed to destruction whereas the righteous find in YHWH their true refuge (Ps.73.18–28; Hab.2.4–20). In Habakkuk 2.4–5, it is still the prophet and not YHWH who speaks; he does not claim that his speech is identical to YHWH's by employing a standard formula such as, "Thus

translated: "Conceited and haughty is the arrogant man, he accomplishes nothing." The first four Hebrew words may have been unintelligible to the translator, and he fills the gap by inserting synonyms for "arrogant".

44. *yhyr* occurs elsewhere only in Proverbs 21.24, where it is synonymous with *zd*, "proud" (a sense supported by LXX: *anēr alazōn*). S. Schreiner understands *yhyr* as a verbal form, identifying it with the Aramaic *tahawwara*, "to be over-confident" ("Erwägungen", p. 541). V.5a is thus to be translated: "Der Wein ist verführerisch, [wenn er ihn trinkt, dann] wird ein Mann übermütig..." The theme of pride has already occurred in v.4a, however; a reference to drink as its cause seems out of place here.

45. The verb occurs elsewhere only in Psalm 68.13, where it is said that "she that remains at home [*nwt byt*] shall divide the spoil". The cognate noun, *naweh*, is commonly used with the sense "habitation" or "home" (e.g. Jer.50.44, with reference to Babylon).

46. So Smith, *Micah-Malachi*, p. 107.

47. There is a lacuna at this point in *1QpHab* vi.14.

says YHWH". Yet, in contrast to the complaint in chapter 1, the prophet is now able to speak on the basis of the divine word that has come to him, and the new perception it has created. Although, unlike the psalmist, he does not reflect on the folly of his former point of view (cf. Ps.73.2–3, 21–22), it is still an experience of conversion or transformation that is narrated and enacted in this text. The statements of Habakkuk 2.4–5 are the first that the prophet ventures on this new basis.

In the prophetic text as in the psalm, a single reality is spoken of from two different perspectives. As in chapter 1, the prophet speaks of the wicked and the righteous, and the description of the wicked recalls the earlier image of the fisherman:

> ... whose greed is wide as Sheol, and like death he is never satisfied, and he gathers *[wy'sp]* to himself all the nations, and draws to himself all the peoples. (2.5b)

> He brings them all up with his hook, he catches them with his net, he gathers them *[wy'sphw]* in his drag-net ... (1.15)

Yet, similar though the two passages are, they occur in quite different contexts. Before the experience on the watchtower, the description of the oppressor occurs in the context of the despairing questions about the absence of divine saving action which constitute the prophet's complaint (1.2–3, 13, 17). After the transforming experience, a new note is heard. The initial description of the oppressor takes the form of a clear moral judgment, in which the reader is invited to share: "Behold, presumptuous and not upright is his soul within him ... " Tacit appeal is made to a moral order that will ultimately prove to be the downfall of the one who transgresses it – and, correspondingly, the salvation of the one who conforms to that order: "The righteous shall live by his faithfulness" (2.4b). In the end, the order that makes it possible to apply the term "wicked" to one and "righteous" to another (cf. 1.4, 13) will prevail.

The prophet's diagnosis of the oppressor's condition begins by under-lining his arrogant presumption (in contrast to the faithfulness of the righteous), and proceeds to analyse his lust for possession, in which is to be found the seed of his downfall:

> Yes indeed, wealth shall betray the arrogant man, and he shall not abide – whose greed is wide as Sheol, and like death he is never satisfied, and he gathers to himself all the nations, and draws to himself all the peoples. Shall not all these lift up against him a taunt, and mocking riddles, and say: Woe to the one who multiplies what is not his – but for how long? – and incurs heavy debts! ... Because you have plundered many nations, all the remnant of the peoples shall plunder you – because of the human blood, and the violence done to the earth, to the city and all who dwell in her. (2.5–6, 8)

The oppressor's greed has already been mentioned in the complaint (1.16), but now the cry, "how long?" is no longer a cry of despair but expresses an absolute confidence that his term of possession is strictly limited. The prophet envisages the oppressed nations as taking up their song of triumph at some unspecified point in the future, but at a time when the tyrant's overthrow is itself still future.[48] This contrasts with another scriptural song of triumph over Babylon, in Isaiah 14.3–21, where the song is introduced with the same idiom (*nś' mšl 'l*, to "lift up a parable against"), but where the future in which the song is to be sung is one in which suffering and oppression are already past (Is.14.3). In Habakkuk, those who take up the taunt against the oppressor do so even while he retains his power to oppress. Their taunt is a song of defiance, sung from between the jaws of Death and Sheol (cf. Hab.2.5b). Whereas in Isaiah it is "Jacob" or "the house of Israel" which is to celebrate the triumph over the king of Babylon (Is.14.1–4), in Habakkuk it is not Israel alone but all the oppressed peoples. The series of "woes" – directed against an oppressor who, after Habakkuk 1.6, is never explicitly identified – speaks not simply of his overthrow but, above all, of a time when "the earth will be filled with the knowledge of the glory of YHWH, as the waters cover the sea" (2.14). If we take the text at face value, it is "all nations" and "all peoples" who celebrate the triumph and who also declare the nullity of the idols (2.13, 18–19), anticipating even now the knowledge of YHWH that will one day be universal. And the prophet himself thereby anticipates the day when his own new knowledge of YHWH as the God of future salvation will be universally shared.

This, then, is the context of the laconic statement that will one day be taken up by Paul, not simply as confirmation of an independent doctrine of "righteousness by faith" but as the origin and basis of this doctrine: "The righteous person shall live by his faithfulness." What do these words mean in the context of the book of Habakkuk, within the Book of the Twelve? And does their meaning in that context bear any relation to the meaning and function assigned to them in the very different context of Pauline discourse?

Faithfulness divine and human

"The righteous person", it is said, "shall live by his faithfulness." In the complaint, the righteous person has been cast in the role of the victim: the wicked one surrounds the righteous one, he swallows him up (Hab.1.4, 13). But now, after the transforming encounter on the watchtower, the

48. For the present, the prophet is making this speech on the nations' behalf (Andersen, *Habakkuk*, p. 225).

prophet's perception of reality has been altered. Although threatened by the arrogance of the oppressor, the righteous person will not succumb to that threat. On the contrary, he or she will "live" – that is, survive. Already in the context of the complaint, it has been said that "we shall not die" (1.12). Now the basis for that confidence is made explicit, and it lies, perhaps surprisingly, in a *human* attribute or practice – "faithfulness".

In Habakkuk 2.4–5, as we have seen, the main subject is still the oppressor, in preparation for the song of triumph that begins at v.6. The statement about the righteous in v.4b is the second member of an antithetical statement that recalls the wisdom tradition:

> Behold, presumptuous and not upright is his soul within him; but the righteous person shall live by his faithfulness *[b'mwntw]*. (Hab.2.4)

> When the tempest passes, the wicked is no more; but the righteous is established for ever. (Prov.10.25)

> An abomination to YHWH are lips of falsehood; but those that do faithfulness *['śy 'mwnh]* are his delight. (Prov.12.22)

Although the Habakkuk passage is not a self-contained proverb, it easily might have been – had it read: "Presumptuous and not upright is the soul of the wicked ... " As it is, it shares the antithetical parallelism of these proverbs (apparent especially in the contrast between "not upright" and "righteous"), together with the corresponding concern to differentiate the wicked from the righteous in terms both of their conduct and their destiny. Nevertheless, the fact that v.5 is concerned wholly with the theme of the wicked has the effect of marking out v.4b from its immediate context, turning it into a parenthesis:

> Behold, presumptuous and not upright is his soul within him (but the righteous shall live by his faithfulness); yes indeed, wealth shall betray the arrogant man, and he shall not abide ...

V.4b can thus be identified both as the second member of a two-part statement in antithetical parallelism, and as a parenthesis within a passage devoted to an analysis of the oppressor and his destiny. Even as a parenthesis, however, the statement carries considerable rhetorical weight; indeed, its relative isolation within its context serves to enhance this. The statement asserts both that the destiny of the righteous is to live and not to die, in spite of the threat posed by the oppressor, and that the way to this destiny may be summed up in the single term, *emunah* – conventionally translated, "faithfulness". The question is what this word would mean in the present context.

As we have seen, the prophet speaks here on the basis of the new perspective created by the divine oracle of vv.2–3, which has transformed a situation of oppression and injustice by setting it in the context of God's future saving action. With its connotations of dependability and reliability, the term *emunah* might have been used in connection with the "vision" received by the prophet, which is both the origin of his own text and the promise of the definitive saving action that is to fulfil it. The vision is "for its appointed time", it "will surely come" (vv.2, 3): it is therefore "faithful", and its faithfulness is that of the God who speaks in it.[49] Similarly, in Psalm 89 the "vision" (*ḥzwn*, v.20) in which God promised a sure future for David and his descendants is the basis for the celebrating – and, in the final section, the questioning – of the divine *emunah* (vv.2–6, 9, 15, 25, 34–35, 50 MT). God's "faithfulness" is manifested above all in his upholding and fulfilling of his promises. In Habakkuk 2.2–3, nothing is explicitly said about the divine attributes manifested in God's speech, but, on the evidence of passages speaking of both divine and human *emunah*, it is divine faithfulness – God's upholding and fulfilling of his promise – that here comes to light.

It is therefore tempting to adopt the Septuagintal rendering of Habakkuk 2.4b, according to which "the righteous person will live by *my* faithfulness".[50] Whether the Hebrew is taken to mean "his faithfulness" or "my faithfulness" depends on how the single letter of the pronominal suffix is read: as a *waw* in the first case, as a *yod* in the second (two Hebrew letters that are easily confused). There is in principle no reason why the Septuagint should not derive from an exemplar preserving an original reference to *God's* faithfulness, subsequently corrupted into the reference to the faithfulness of the righteous person implied in other early manuscripts (1QpHab viii.1–3; 8Heb1 xvii.30). If a *waw* could be mistaken for a *yod*, shifting the sense from "his faithfulness" to "my faithfulness", there is no reason why the opposite mistake might not have been made. Here and elsewhere, it might seem that *God's* faithfulness is a much more reliable basis for the "life" of the righteous person than his or her own. It is true that the provenance of this Septuagintal reading is uncertain: it is clearly attested for the first time only in the third century CE.[51] Yet, even though it is confirmed neither by Paul nor by the author to the Hebrews,

---

49. The connection between *'mwnh* and reliable and trustworthy speech is indicated by passages in which the term can be translated "truth" or "honesty" (Jer.5.1–3, 7.28, 9.2; Prov.12.22).

50. For discussion of four distinct forms of this text in Greek, see Andersen, *Habakkuk*, pp. 210–12.

51. Cyprian, *Treatises* xii.1.5, 3.42. Cyprian seems to understand the Latin equivalent of *ek pisteōs mou* as an objective genitive.

the latter may well have been aware of it;[52] and the lack of any earlier patristic citation may simply reflect the influence of the New Testament variants.[53] The external evidence is consistent with a pre-Christian date for the Septuagintal reading, although it does not demand it. Consequently, the further possibility that "my faithfulness" rather than "his faithfulness" represents the original Hebrew text cannot be ruled out.

Yet internal evidence suggests that the Septuagintal reading should probably be rejected, despite its apparent appropriateness to the context. Habakkuk 2.4 LXX and MT may respectively be translated:

> If he draws back, my soul has no pleasure in him *[ouk eudokei hē psuchē mou en autō]*; but the righteous will live by my faithfulness. (Hab.2.4 LXX)

> Behold, presumptuous and not upright is his soul within him *[l' yšrh npšw bw]* – but the righteous shall live by his faithfulness. (Hab.2.4 MT)

In the Septuagint translation, the first person singular is employed in both parts of the verse; in the Masoretic text, the third person singular. A decision between "my" or "his" faithfulness in v.4b will have to take into account the parallel distinction between "my" and "his" soul in v.4a – which is again the difference between a *yod* and a *waw*. The two texts appear to agree on the verb form governed by these phrases (*ouk eudokei* is probably an attempt to render *l' yšrh*). But "not upright is his soul..." belongs within the normal semantic range of this term, whereas "my soul has no pleasure..." does not. The third singular Masoretic version is therefore more likely to be original, in which case the Septuagint's first singular version is a misreading. If the Septuagint translator has misread a *waw* as a *yod* in v.4a (replacing "his soul" with "my soul"), then that is probably what happened in the analogous case in v.4b: an original "his faithfulness" has mistakenly been read as "my faithfulness". However well "my faithfulness" appears to suit a context in which the emphasis is on the

---

52. Paul's rendering *(ho [de] dikaios ek pisteōs zēsetai)* does not include either pronoun, but the resulting sense is closer to MT than to LXX. In Hebrews 10.38, the majority reading follows Paul, although a significant minority of witnesses (including P[46], א and A) insert the pronoun *mou* after *ho de dikaios* (rather than *ek pisteōs*). If *ho de dikaios mou* is original in Hebrews 10.38, then the transposition of the pronoun from an LXX position after *ek pisteōs* could be part of the author's rewriting of Habakkuk 2.3–4 LXX. In any case, *ho de dikaios mou* is surely dependent on *ek pisteōs mou*, and may represent an attempt to harmonize the LXX rendering with Paul.

53. Habakkuk 2.4b is quoted in the short Pauline form by Irenaeus (*adv. Haer.* iv.34.2), and in the form of the minority reading of Hebrews 10.38 by Clement (*Strom.* ii.4); this reading is also attested among the LXX manuscripts themselves, in Codex Alexandrinus. On the other hand, Tertullian's citation of this text reflects the Masoretic tradition (*adv. Marc.* iv.18, v.3).

certainty of God's saving action, "his faithfulness" is more likely to be original.[54] The task remains of making sense of this expression in the context of the transforming experience narrated in the preceding verses.

In Habakkuk 2.4–5, a normative moral judgment is pronounced against the oppressor, and his downfall is declared. This prepares the way for the oppressed nations' anticipatory song of triumph in 2.6–20. The whole passage (2.4–20) derives from the experience on the watchtower as narrated in 2.1–3. If the statement in 2.4b had originally read, "The righteous shall live by *my* faithfulness", this would undoubtedly have been a reference to the certainty of the vision's fulfilment, emphasized in v.3. Since it probably read, "The righteous shall live by *his* faithfulness", this indicates that the divine announcement of the future fulfilment is intended to evoke a specific response from its human addressee:

> For still the vision is for its time, it hastens to the end and it will not lie.
> *If it lingers, wait for it;* for it will surely come, it will not delay. (Hab.2.3)

Ostensibly addressed to the prophet, the exhortation to "wait" is also addressed to the "reader" of v.2, who is enabled to "run" by the vision in its written form. As we have seen, the intention that "the one who reads it may run" applies to the whole text of Habakkuk, and the prophet on his watchtower is therefore a surrogate for the reader of his text. Although the time of fulfilment has been fixed, it seems from a human perspective to "linger", with one apparent postponement following another. The interval between the vision and its fulfilment is, as it were, solidified in writing, which, symbolizing both the certainty of the future fulfilment and the fact that it is not yet, embodies in itself the exhortation to "wait". It is, then, the reader who is enjoined to "wait", addressed by the divine voice in and through the text: the shift of focus from prophet to reader in v.2 is carried over into the following verse. "Waiting" represents the form of life that corresponds to the vision, and is the intended perlocutionary effect of the whole text. When, in v.4, it is said that "the righteous shall live by his faithfulness", this "faithfulness" is therefore synonymous with that "waiting". One who "waits" for the vision's fulfilment, living in the light of that certain yet absent future, is "faithful" or "steadfast". Since v.4 is not a self-contained proverb but is integrated into its wider context, *emunah* here cannot merely refer to a general ethical attribute, such as

---

54. It should be noted that the LXX tradition is not entirely uniform, and that some manuscripts place *mou* not after *ek pisteōs* but after *ho dikaios*, or omit it altogether. The second and third readings assimilate the text to the citations in Hebrew and Paul respectively (so D.-A. Koch, "Der Text von Hab 2.4b in der Septuaginta und im Neuen Testament", pp. 68–85; C. Stanley, *Paul and the Language of Scripture*, pp. 83–84).

"moral steadfastness and integrity".[55] It refers instead to the form of life intended by the entire text of Habakkuk. The statement that "the righteous shall live by his faithfulness" formalizes and universalizes the exhortation, "If it lingers, wait for it".

To "wait" *(ḥkh)* is to live in the light of a promised fulfilment, and thereby to live the life intended in the promise:

> Bind up the testimony, seal the teaching among my disciples. *I shall wait for YHWH*, who has hidden his face from the house of Jacob, and I will hope in him. (Is.8.17–18)

> Therefore YHWH waits to be gracious to you, therefore he exalts himself to show mercy to you. For YHWH is a God of justice; *blessed are all those who wait for him*. (Is.30.18)

> *Therefore wait for me*, says YHWH, for the day when I arise as a witness. For my decision is to gather nations, to assemble kingdoms, to pour out upon them my indignation, all the heat of my anger... (Zeph.3.8)

In all such passages, to "wait" is to live steadfastly, patiently and faithfully in the light of the divine action that is promised or implied in them, but not yet present.[56] The divine faithfulness seeks to evoke a human counterpart.

It is this faithful waiting that is articulated and exemplified at the conclusion of the book of Habakkuk, where, in the context of prayer (3.1, 19b), the prophet responds to the theophany he has recounted in the central section of the chapter (3.3–15):

> I heard – and my body trembles, my lips quiver at the sound, decay enters into my bones, I tremble where I stand – yet I shall quietly wait *['nwḥ]* for the day of trouble to come upon the people who invade us. If the fig tree does not blossom, and there is no fruit on the vine, and the olive harvest fails, and the fields yield no food, and the flock is cut off from the fold, and there is no herd in the stalls – still I shall rejoice in YHWH, I will exult in the God of my salvation. (Hab.3.16–18)

Here, the return to the first person singular usage with which the prayer opened (3.2) marks the conclusion of the theophany. The prophet speaks of the initial shock of this event, but is more concerned to articulate the ongoing form of life that corresponds to it. This is again characterized as a

---

55. S. R. Driver's paraphrase (*Introduction*, p. 337). In support of this interpretation is the fact that *'mwnh* normally refers to "ethical" rather than "religious" conduct. But a general ethical statement would be out of place in Habakkuk 2.4.

56. Compare also Psalm 33.20; Daniel 12.12. In more "secular" contexts, the verb can mean either "delay until" (2 Kgs.7.9; Job 32.4) or "long for" (Job.3.21); the latter is obviously integral to the "religious" usage.

life of "waiting" (although a different Hebrew verb is used), and the object hoped for is again the divine judgment of the oppressor.[57] The concluding statements about joy in the midst of suffering are an expression of this hope: the potential deprivations listed in v.17 are perhaps to be connected to the enemy invasion referred to in v.16 (cf. 2.17; Jer.4.26, 6.6), although they may be meant to depict a plight that is even worse than the present reality of invasion. The prophet directs his reader to look beyond suffering to the God of future salvation. In doing so, he gives voice to the "faithfulness" by which the righteous shall live.

The parenthetical statement that "the righteous shall live by his faithfulness" encapsulates the perlocutionary effect that the prophet's written "vision" intends for its reader. The text is written to enable its reader to "run" (2.2) and to "wait" for the fulfilment of its vision (2.3), and in doing so the reader will manifest that "faithfulness" or steadfastness that characterizes the righteous and assures their life (2.4b). Within its wider canonical context in the Book of the Twelve, Habakkuk 2.1–4 explains why texts that seem to speak of unfulfilled and indeed superseded hopes have nevertheless been written and preserved to nourish the hope of succeeding generations of the community of faith. It is the entire Book of the Twelve that is written "so that one who reads it may run". The assurance that "the righteous shall live by his faithfulness" lies at the heart of this book.

The prophet and the apostle

At the beginning of this chapter, we identified ourselves with those who heard Paul's proclamation at Beroea, who, it is said, "received the word with all eagerness, examining the scriptures daily to see if these things were so" (Acts 17.11). Starting from Paul's proclamation and its explicit appeal to scripture, we have attempted to allow the prophet Habakkuk to speak in his own voice, from within his canonical context among the Twelve – that is, in his own voice as it was heard by the unknown editors and scribes responsible for the canonical process. If the point of this preoccupation with the prophet was "to see if these things were so", what is the outcome of the enquiry? We are, perhaps, still sceptical about Paul's appropriation of the prophetic statement – believing that "there is little likelihood that Paul has reproduced the meaning Habakkuk had in mind", and that "his

---

57. "[E]ven in his terror, the prophet recognizes the promise implicit in the vision, and the response of his will to the vision is precisely what God demanded in Hab.2.3. In light of the vision, Habakkuk is willing to cease from his complaints and to wait quietly for the vision's fulfillment, for the day of judgment to come upon the Babylonian oppressor" (J. J. M. Roberts, *Nahum, Habakkuk, Zephaniah*, p. 157).

interpretation of this prophet... [is] the product of his own *prior* convictions about theological truth".[58] Or does that opinion now have to be revised?

If it seems self-evident that the apostle and the prophet can have little or nothing in common, this betrays the continuing influence of a hermeneutic according to which texts are addressed to and contained by their immediate circumstances of origin, and that all subsequent usage marks a deviation from their "original meaning". In the present discussion, the limitations of this hermeneutic have become clear at point after point. The text of Habakkuk explicitly presents itself as written for a future of unknown duration; it privileges the reader over the author, and confines its reference to an identifiable historical situation to a single allusion to the "Chaldeans". It is the same "canonical process", but at a more advanced stage, that leads to the incorporation of this book within the larger collection of the Book of the Twelve. While the arrangement of the book is designed to reflect the unfolding canonical history, it also expresses the conviction that these products of earlier historical situations continue to lay claim to the present, and that their pastness is to be subsumed in the message they address to the present. There is clear continuity between the text's orientation towards its future reader and the logic of the larger canonical collection. Indeed, since we possess the text of Habakkuk only within the canonical Book of the Twelve, and as part of that larger book, the attempt to restore the entire book to a *Sitz im Leben* within the obscurity of "pre-exilic" Judah can only be regarded as historically naïve and hermeneutically perverse.

This canonical principle has its strikingly material counterpart in the form of the physical remains of copies of the Twelve from the Judean desert, discussed in the previous chapter. In the centuries around the turn of the eras, the book was valued highly enough to be copied, preserved, transported, translated – presumably in order to be read and interpreted. The book seems to have found the readers it sought for itself, and not just at Qumran. The pesherist's belief that "the one who reads it" refers exclusively to a single inspired reader did not bring the process of reading and interpretation to an end. And this is as it should be, for the book is intended for all of its readers, in whom it seeks to evoke a faithful and unyielding adherence to the vision it contains. If Paul turns out to be a poor reader of Habakkuk, the reason is not that he is historically far removed from this text: for historical distance has already been acknowledged and overcome in the canonical process.

As cited by Paul, the prophetic text states that "the one who is righteous by faith will live". From this seed there grows the Pauline doctrine of

---

58. John Barton, *Oracles of God*, p. 245; italics original.

righteousness by faith, as developed in Romans 1.16–3.31. It is the prophetic statement that allows Paul to correlate the terms "righteousness" and "faith" and to build an argument on that correlation – to the effect that, according to the scriptures, salvation is not dependent on law observance but on the acknowledgment of God's saving action that takes place in faith. Yet what the prophetic text appears to mean is, "The righteous shall live by his faithfulness". When this is read as, "The one who is righteous by faith will live", the possibility already arises that Paul is reading his prior theological convictions into this text, and is therefore failing to read the text itself. Paul would then *not* be the reader for whom this text is intended (cf. Hab.2.2).

On closer investigation, that conclusion turns out to be premature. When he finds in this text a testimony to "righteousness by faith", Paul can exploit the word-order both of the Hebrew and of the Greek, which runs: "The righteous by [his/my] faith[fulness] shall live." Yet Paul's construal also has its own exegetical logic. If "the righteous shall live by his faithfulness", the question might be raised as to what *constitutes* the righteousness of the righteous. Elsewhere in scripture, "righteousness" and "life" are correlated, the one being the way to the other. "If a person is righteous and does what is lawful and right... he is righteous, he shall surely live, says YHWH the Lord" (Ezek.18.5, 9). If the wicked turns from wickedness to righteous living, "on account of the righteousness which he has done he shall live" (Ezek.18.22). Granted the axiom that "righteousness" leads to "life", the Habakkuk text turns out to be ambiguous. In it, a third element comes into play alongside "righteousness" and "life": that of "faithfulness" as the way to life. The question is whether "righteousness" and "faithfulness" are to be distinguished from each other. The pesherist believed that they should be. In his interpretation, "The righteous" of the scriptural text is identified with "all who observe the law in the house of Judah", whereas "by faith[fulness]" refers to "their faith in the Teacher of Righteousness" (1QpHab viii.1–3). Those who observe the law and those who have faith in the Teacher are no doubt the same people, but their "righteousness" or law observance may be distinguished from their "faith". But for Paul, the text entails no such distinction between "righteousness" and "faith". It does not say that, contrary to Ezekiel, righteousness in itself is not enough, and must be supplemented by something else – that is, by faith. Rather, "by faith" serves to *define* the righteousness that leads axiomatically to life. If "the righteous shall live by faith", then it is their faith alone that constitutes them as righteous. In finding testimony to "righteousness by faith" in this text, Paul is not simply exploiting the word-order; underlying his exegesis there is a genuine theological logic. While he does not simply reproduce the meaning intended by the prophet, nor does he impose upon the prophet's words an entirely unrelated meaning of his own. Rather, he seeks to uncover the deeper logic of a text which does indeed intend nothing other than the "faithful" adherence to the vision contained in it.

Paul's second interpretative decision is to construe "faithfulness" (steadfastness, loyalty) as "faith" (belief, giving credence to). In this, he follows the pesherist, for whom the prophetic statement speaks of "faith in *['mnh b-]* the Teacher of Righteousness" (1QpHab viii.2–3). As we noted in the previous chapter, this phraseology derives from a Hebrew verb form from the same root which, together with a preposition, means "to believe in". The pesherist uses this idiom in expounding the phrase "you shall not believe" *(l' t'mynw)* in Habakkuk 1.5: this phrase is said to refer to "the apostates of the new covenant" who "did not believe in the covenant of God *[lw' h'mynw bbryt 'l]*" (1QpHab ii.3–4). In the Habakkuk pesher, the (biblical) idiom "to believe in" is extended to the cognate noun *emunah*, which thus comes to mean "faith". To believe in is the same as to have faith in, for the pesherist (writing in Hebrew) as well as for Paul (writing in Greek). Thus, a century or so before Paul, the prophetic statement could already be understood as referring not to faithfulness but to faith: "The righteous shall live by his faith." It seems that the pesherist here reflects a post-biblical idiom in which the noun acquires an additional usage under the influence of the verb.

It is striking that Paul does not follow the pesherist in interpreting the prophetic "by faith" as referring to an individual object of faith. For the pesherist, "by faith" refers to "faith in the Teacher of Righteousness"; but Paul does not claim that it refers to "faith in Christ". On the contrary, he is remarkably restrained in his christological references, both in Romans 1.16–3.31, where the Habakkuk text determines the argument, and in Romans 4, where its place is taken by Genesis 15.6. It is true that Paul paraphrases the prophetic "by faith" as "through faith of Jesus Christ" (Rom.3.22, cf. v.26): as we have argued, the genitive construction indicates that "faith" and "Jesus Christ" are correlated, without specifying the nature of that correlation any more precisely. Yet this explicit correlation with Christ occurs on only two of the eleven occasions in Romans 1–3 on which Paul speaks of "faith" on the basis of his citation from Habakkuk 2.4.[59] The influence of the citation is apparent not only in the recurrence of the prepositional phrase, "by faith" *(ek pisteōs:* Rom.1.17, 3.26, 30; cf. 3.28) and the analogous "through faith" *(dia [tēs] pisteōs:* Rom.3.21, 25, 30, 31), but also in the absence of an explicit christological reference in most of these instances. Paul of course assumes that "faith" is entirely and

---

59.   Rom.1.17 (× 3, including the citation); 3.22, 25, 26, 27, 28, 30 (× 2), 31. In the light of this christological reticence, it is hard to agree with J. A. Sanders' claim that "the real difference between Paul's exegesis of Hab.2.4 and Qumran's is Paul's application of the passage to Christ's atoning death" ("Habakkuk in Qumran, Paul, and the Old Testament", p. 112).

exclusively bound up with God's saving action in Christ, but he nevertheless exercises the christological restraint appropriate to his scriptural text and does not simply impose his christological convictions on it. The gospel speaks explicitly of Christ, but scripture does not; in this respect, the speech of the apostle differs from that of the prophet. This distinction between gospel and scripture, apostle and prophet, may be compared to the pesherist's claim that "God told Habakkuk to write about what was to happen to the final generation, but the end of the time he did not reveal to him" (1QpHab vii.1–2). For Paul as for the pesherist, the prophet does not fully comprehend the divine saving action of which he speaks, and his text therefore speaks of it only indirectly and as if at a distance (cf. also 1 Pet.1.10–12). The shift from "faithfulness" to "faith" is not motivated by any desire to impose an explicit christology on the scriptural text.

If, following the pesherist's lead, we translate Habakkuk 2.4b, "The righteous shall live by his faith", that would not greatly affect our interpretation of that text within its original canonical context. Assuming that *emunah* should be translated "faithfulness", we understood this as a reference to the faithful, enduring adherence to the still unfulfilled "vision" implied in the exhortation: "If it lingers, wait for it..." (Hab.2.3b). If we substitute a reference to "faith", that would highlight the fact that, if one is to "wait for" the vision, one must regard it as credible and trustworthy. One must believe that God really did answer the prophet's complaint about the absence of divine saving action, in the form of the written promise that is the canonical text. In fact, the two readings of the text are not so far apart. "Faithfulness" speaks more adequately of the way of life that corresponds to the vision, whereas "faith" speaks of the fundamental orientation towards the vision presupposed in this way of life; but each clearly entails the other. Within the text of Habakkuk, there is no faithfulness without what Paul and the pesherist call "faith" – just as, for Paul, there is no faith without faithfulness. If "faith" has been substituted for "faithfulness" in the citation of Habakkuk 2.4, the semantic loss is minimal.

Whether they think in terms of "faithfulness" or of "faith", the prophet and the apostle are at one in their assumption that *emunah* or *pistis* refers to the human response to the divine promise of definitive, eschatological saving action. The apostle's message is "gospel", in which human speech is the bearer of "the power of God unto salvation" to those in whom it evokes the response of faith (cf. Rom.1.16). The prophet likewise seeks to evoke a response in which the entire life of his reader is reoriented towards the future divine saving action of which he writes. His book begins with a despairing question about salvation: "YHWH, how long... shall I cry to you, "Violence!", and you will not save?" (Hab.1.3). It concludes with a theophany which tells how God "went forth for the salvation of your people, for the salvation of your anointed ones" (3.13), so that YHWH can be simply identified as "the God of my salvation" (3.18). From beginning to end, the book of Habakkuk is concerned with salvation – God's future saving action, which already impinges on the present in the form of the divine word of a promise put into writing. And it is concerned *only* with salvation – both its current absence and the certainty of its future realization. It is not concerned, for example, to address the problem of unrighteous conduct among the covenant people. It does not criticize their idolatry, like Hosea, or their social injustice, like Amos: for it is concerned most fundamentally with divine action rather than human, and with human action only on the basis of divine action promised and realized.

When Paul cites his proof-text in the form, "The one who is righteous by faith shall live", he shares with his scriptural source the conviction that all human life is to be lived in the light of God's final, comprehensive act of salvation.[60] For Paul, the prophetic "by faith" entails the corollary, "not by works of law"; that, and not an explicit christological reference, is the point he seeks to establish on the basis of Habakkuk 2.4, in order to bear witness to the radical priority of divine saving action even over the human action enjoined in the law itself. God's eschatological act of salvation is to be the foundation, origin and goal of all human living and acting. The term "faith" speaks of the human recognition and acknowledgment of God as "the God of my salvation", elicited by the divine word of the gospel and prefigured in the written prophetic vision. The antithesis between "faith" and "works of law" entails an entire scriptural hermeneutic, according to which the core of the scriptural message is to be found in the prophetic proclamation of the infallible, unconditional certainty of God's eschatological saving action. From that perspective, a hermeneutic which binds God's future saving action to a prior law observance represents a radical misreading of scripture, however deeply entrenched such a view may seem to be within the scriptural texts themselves. Indeed, although "faith" and "law" are ultimately in harmony with one another (cf. Rom.3.31), there is a deep faultline within scripture itself:

> That no-one is justified before God by the law is clear – for "the one who is righteous by faith shall live". But the law does not operate on the principle, "by faith": rather, "the one who does these things shall live by them." (Gal.3.11–12)

60. Thus there is no need to distinguish, as J. L. Martyn does, between what Paul "hears" in the scriptural text and what Habakkuk himself said and meant. "In Hab 2:4 Paul hears God promising the prophet that in the good news of Christ... God will one day make things right by creating eschatological life" (*Galatians*, p. 312). On the other hand, "For Habakkuk, faith is life lived in accordance with the life-giving commandments of God" (*ibid.*). Martyn's interpretation of Habakkuk is what one would expect from "the Teachers" (his term for Paul's opponents), but has no basis in the prophetic text itself.

If Habakkuk 2.4 represents one side of this faultline, Leviticus 18.5 represents the other. In the one case, the emphasis falls on the human acknowledgment of God's eschatological saving action; in the other, it is human action in obedience to the law's prescriptions that constitutes the scriptural path to life.[61] Paul tacitly acknowledges that it is only in the light of the revelation of Jesus Christ that he has uncovered this inner-scriptural disjunction (cf. Gal.1.12–17); but he also claims that this disjunction is "clear" *(dēlon)* on the basis of the literal sense of scripture itself.

It is also clear (at least to us) that the prophet himself does not consciously and explicitly intend to establish a new understanding of the way to salvation, in polemical opposition to Leviticus or Ezekiel. Paul does not rest his case on a single text, but rather on a network of interconnected texts. Yet it has been shown in these chapters that Paul places much greater weight on the Habakkuk text than is usually recognized, developing his doctrine of "righteousness by faith" by way of an extended exegesis of it; that his recognition of its significance was shared with other readers of the Twelve; and that, within its canonical context, the Habakkuk text itself answers to these readers' sense of its fundamental significance. In their different yet analogous ways, Paul and the pesherist draw on the semantic potential of the scriptural text itself – while not allowing themselves to be confined self-effacingly within its limits, as though they had nothing of their own to contribute. The scriptural text was created by its redactors for the sake of just such readers as these. Text and interpretation are located on a continuum, and the idea that the proper object of study is an essentially unread text is exposed as a modern scholarly fiction.

---

61. "Leviticus promises life to those who *do* the Law while Habakkuk proclaims that the just one lives *from faith*" (F. Matera, *Galatians*, p. 124; italics original). Matera tries to harmonize the conflicting citations as follows: "Since no one... fulfills the Law perfectly, the true source of life must be faith" (*ibid.*). If that is correct, then the key point in Paul's argument – that no-one fulfils the law perfectly – has had to be added by the commentator. Paul, on the other hand, is content to leave the two scriptural texts in stark juxtaposition. It is a central concern of the present work to identify the hermeneutical assumptions which lead him to do so – which have to do not with a "canon within the canon" or a proto-Marcionite rejection of the law, but with the unfolding narrative of the Pentateuch.

Part Two

Promise

Chapter 4

Genesis (1)

As he develops his argument in Romans 1–3, Paul at the same time constructs a hermeneutic – that is, an answer to the question how the scriptural texts are to be interpreted; how, at the most general level, sense is to be made of them. His hermeneutic purports to be grounded in scripture itself. Its scope is "the law and the prophets", scripture in its twofold entirety, and the individual texts cited serve to represent that twofoldness. In the brief dogmatic statement from Habakkuk (whose anonymity Paul preserves), it is the prophets who speak. They do not speak directly of Jesus the Christ, who is unknown to them by name. They do speak, indirectly, of a future divine saving act, universal in its scope, and of the human praxis that corresponds to this great hope. Their writings exist for the sole purpose of fostering that hope and that praxis among those who read or hear them. They are themselves the divine pledges of that hope. Scripture is not only a message of hope, however. It is also law, and for Paul its twofold form signifies an irreducibly twofold content which cannot be contained within the differentiation of the Torah or Pentateuch from the rest of scripture. Thus the voice of the law can be articulated through David or Isaiah, just as the voice of the prophets can be articulated through Moses (as we shall see). Like Habakkuk, however, David and Isaiah are anonymized. Their words are removed from their particular contexts and fused into a single summary of the law's verdict on the Jewish people, and so on humankind as a whole: there is no-one righteous, not even one. Scripture, it seems, is hope and indictment. It speaks of hope where there ought not to be hope, in a place where even the members of the body – lips, tongues, feet, eyes – have been corrupted into instruments of violence, rather than being employed in the service of God and the neighbour. Scriptural utopianism is held in check by a realism tinged with a deep pessimism. In particular, scripture refuses to validate the claims of the very community in which it is preserved and read and acknowledged as the oracles of God. Scripture does not recognize this community as a light to those who are in darkness – even though the purpose of scripture itself as Torah was surely to kindle such a light in the world. On the contrary, the world's darkness has invaded the community. As the prophet Isaiah foresaw, hostile outsiders unwittingly testify to the truth when they observe the conduct of the chosen people and mock its pretensions. The community has not put behind it the harsh prophetic denunciations of which its own scriptures are full to the point of monotony. These denunciations represented the divine word to earlier generations of the community, and they are still absolutely valid. In them, it is the voice of God's own law that speaks. Precisely here, however, in the very scriptures which are so at odds with their own community, there is also announced the hope of a transforming act of the divine sovereignty whose light illuminates a present that is otherwise without hope.

As this paraphrase shows, the Pauline reading of scripture is a reading in black and white. It finds in scripture only darkness and light, and the darkness is human and the light is divine. The boundary between the two is sharply defined. In scripture, God *divides* the light from the darkness, and – taking no interest in the various shades of grey or of other colours that appear as day turns to night or night to day – God pronounces this arrangement to be good. Scripture, Paul might say, is to be read in black and white because scripture just *is* black and white. Admirers of the various shades of grey or of other colours will not feel at home in these texts.

As Paul presents it, this construal of scripture is intended to displace an existing construal of scripture which is no less black and white in form. In this earlier hermeneutic, the boundary between light and darkness has been set at the border between the holy people and the idolatrous realm of the Gentiles. The boundary is here located *within* the human social sphere, although it also extends into the sphere of deity, in the form of the absolute antithesis between the living God and the idols. On this reading, scripture speaks – or rather, God speaks through scripture – of a people chosen by God to manifest the divine light in the world by walking in the way of God's commandments. The divine light takes humanly accessible form in the Torah, and a community is thereby created "through whom the imperishable light of the law was to be given to the world" (Wis.Sol.18.4). The world rejects the gift, and persists in its idolatry. In the enduring existence of the chosen people, however, an area of divine light does exist in the midst of the world's darkness.

Paul's displacement of this construal of scripture is fundamentally very simple. With the assistance of a prophetic critique directed primarily against the chosen people itself, the boundary between light and darkness is redrawn. It is not relocated at the border between the *church* and the world, however, as a naïve supersessionism might suggest. Instead, it is relocated at the border between God and humankind. If the people that walked in darkness have seen a great light, the darkness is their own whereas the light is purely divine. The distinction between the chosen people and the Gentiles is not abolished, but it is confined to the fact that the chosen people has been entrusted with the oracles of God, in which the true division of light and darkness takes place. Paul's reading of scripture in black and white is a radical revision of an earlier such reading. Scripture speaks of the darkness into which humankind has plunged itself, but it also speaks of the light kindled by the certainty of God's decisive saving action. Despairing of all human capacity, we must place our hope in God alone: that for Paul is the sum of the law and the prophets. And this means that we are not to be misled by a construal of scripture according to which human capacity remains intact, sanctioned by God. As the prophets tell us, the human conduct sanctioned by God is simply "faith". In a way that is both like and unlike Habakkuk, Paul sets faith on the border between despair and hope and sees it as facing in both directions. Faith is both despair of human capacity and hope in saving act of God.

In these opening chapters of Romans, Paul constructs a *hermeneutic* of faith. He does so by way of his selected prophetic texts, wishing to show that this hermeneutic of faith is prescribed by scripture itself. Yet the real test of this hermeneutic lies in the Torah. Can Paul's antithetical hermeneutic make sense of this composite yet monolithic foundation of Jewish identity? Can Paul actually *read* the Torah, or can he merely make unsubstantiated dogmatic claims about it?

Faced with this challenge, Paul begins – naturally enough – with the Book of Genesis (Romans 4). With the help of some other Pauline texts, we shall follow him as he makes his way through the first book of the law and on into Exodus, Leviticus, Numbers and Deuteronomy.[1]

Deconstructing the Hero

In Romans 4, a new proof-text is brought into play, which speaks of God's relationship not to the "righteous" in general (as in Habakkuk) but to a single individual: Abraham, who "believed God, and it was reckoned to him as righteousness" (Gen.15.6).[2] Paul's engagement with this text shows

1. The division of the Torah into five relatively distinct though interconnected books is the most obvious feature of its "canonical form" (so B. S. Childs, *Introduction to the Old Testament as Scripture*, pp. 129–30). This means, among other things, that "the final form of the Pentateuch... cannot be simply derived from the combination of literary sources" (p. 132). Judging from the fragmentary evidence of his letters, Paul appears to have had a strong sense of the individual identity of each of the five books, each of which makes its own distinctive contribution to his construal of scripture as a whole.

2. As U. Wilckens has argued, Romans 4 makes it clear that Paul "positiv und grundsätzlich an Abraham interessiert ist" ("Die Rechtfertigung Abrahams nach Römer 4" [1961], in his *Rechtfertigung als Freiheit*, p. 39). The reason for this interest is simply that – for Paul, if not for the Bultmannian theology that Wilckens here opposes – the Old Testament is necessary in order to understand the Christ-event: "Die Gottesgerechtigkeit könnte ohne das Zeugnis von Tora und Propheten nicht 'offenkundig' sein (3,21)" (p. 43). Wilckens' emphasis

two distinct though related concerns, and they correspond precisely to the two-sidedness of his understanding of "faith".

In Romans 4.1–12, the Genesis text is discussed with relatively little attention to its immediate context. In 4.13–25, however, the text is reconnected to the divine promise that precedes and occasions it in Genesis 15.5 (Rom.4.13–25). This distinction is evident in the vocabulary characteristic of the two parts of this chapter. While the terms "believe" or "faith" are evenly distributed in Romans 4, always with clear reference to Genesis 15.6, "promise" is confined to the second half of the chapter, whereas "works" (or "to work") is confined to the first.[3] The term "works" is used to characterize a hypothetical interpretation of the Abraham narrative that Genesis 15.6 serves to exclude:

> If Abraham was *justified by works*, he has occasion for boasting – but that is not his position before God. For what does the scriptural text say? "Abraham believed God and it was reckoned to him as righteousness." *To the one who works*, the reward is not "reckoned" as a matter of grace but as due recompense. But *to the one who does not work* but who believes in the one who justifies the ungodly, his faith "is reckoned as righteousness". In the same way, David too pronounces a blessing on the person to whom God "reckons righteousness" *apart from works . . .* (Rom.4.2–6)

Here, the initial reference to a hypothetical justification by works (v.2) is counteracted by the scriptural claim (v.3), and this sequence is repeated in the verses that follow (vv.4–5). In the second half of the chapter, however, the emphasis falls on the relationship of faith and promise:

> For not through law was *the promise* to Abraham or to his seed, that he should be heir of the world, but through righteousness of faith. For if those who are of the law are heirs, faith is in vain and *the promise* is void. Therefore it is by faith, so as to accord with grace – in order that *the promise* might be certain for all the seed . . . (4.14–16)

> He did not waver by disbelief *in the promise of God*, but was strengthened by faith, giving glory to God, fully confident that *what was promised* God was also able to accomplish. (4.20–21)

In these passages, the faith/promise correlation takes the place of the faith/works antithesis of the earlier part of the chapter. In vv.15–16, the promise

---

on "erwählungsgeschichtliche Kontinuität" (*ibid.*) should be qualified, however, by the observation that this (scripturally mediated) history may be characterized as much by disruptions and anomalies as by continuity.

3. "Believe", x6: Rom.4.3, 5, 11, 17, 18, 24; "faith", x10: 4.5, 9, 11, 12, 13, 14, 16 [x2], 19, 20; "promise", x5: 4.13, 14, 16, 20, 21; "works", "to work", x4: 4.2, 4, 5, 6.

in question is the one referred to in v.13 – that Abraham would inherit the world. In vv.20–21, on the other hand, it is the promise of Abraham's fatherhood, which will extend from the birth of a son to encompass "many nations", or "Gentiles" (vv.16–19). There is, however, a tendency here to conflate the various promises recorded in Genesis into a singular "promise of God" which Abraham believed.

In spite of their distinct subject matter, the two parts of Romans 4 run in parallel to one another. Paul's denial that the promise to Abraham was "through law" (vv.13–15) corresponds to the denial that his righteousness was "by works" (vv.1–8). The correlation between fatherhood and promise (vv.16–18) is anticipated in the earlier discussion of the scope of this fatherhood (vv.9–12). This latter passage completes Paul's first reading of Genesis 15.6, and it corresponds to the conclusion of the chapter (Rom.4.23–25). In both cases, it is argued that what is said about Abraham – that his faith was reckoned as righteousness – applies also to others: to Gentile and Jewish believers (vv.11–12), and to "us... who believe in the one who raised Jesus our Lord from the dead" (v.24).[4]

Most significantly, Abraham and God are characterized differently in the two parts of the chapter. The difference is highlighted by the use of participial clauses descriptive of the divine being and action (vv.5, 17). In vv.13–25, the object of Abraham's belief is the God of the promise, who "gives life to the dead and calls non-beings into being" (v.17, cf. v.24). Abraham himself is correspondingly characterized in terms of hope: "Against hope yet in hope he believed that he would become father of many nations in accordance with what was said: Thus shall your seed be" (v.18). In vv.1–12, however, Abraham believes in "the one who justifies the ungodly" (v.5). Abraham himself, elsewhere the outstanding scriptural exemplar of piety, is here assimilated to David, the scriptural exemplar of the forgiven sinner (vv.6–9). At this point, it becomes clear how the two treatments of Genesis 15.6 relate to one another. In the scriptural statement that "Abraham believed God", the word "God" refers to the one who releases Abraham from a past determined by Abraham's own guilt, in order to open up to him a future determined by God's creative and saving action. The faith/works antithesis of the first part and the faith/promise correlation of the second amount to a two-sided characterization

---

4. On the basis of this symmetry, Romans 4 should be divided into two parts rather than the more conventional three (faith not works [vv.1–8], justification prior to circumcision [vv.9–12], faith and the promise [vv.13–25] – so J. Fitzmyer, *Romans*, pp. 369–84). The passage on circumcision has to do with the *scope* of righteousness by faith, and is not primarily concerned with circumcision as a possible meritorious deed, as Fitzmyer still believes (*ibid.*, p. 378). Most importantly, Romans 4 should not be seen as merely "illustrating" what Paul has just said about "boasting" in 3.27–31 (*ibid.*, p. 369). Rather, 3.27–31 should be seen as *introducing* the argument of Romans 4.

of the divine being and action, and of the human being (*anthrōpos*, v.6) in the light of it. As we shall see, the purpose of both the negation and the affirmation is to identify the God of the promise as the primary agent in the Abraham narrative, rather than Abraham himself.

Our first task is to investigate the hermeneutical logic of Paul's appeal to Genesis 15.6 to show that righteousness is not "by works" (Rom.4.1–8). This is not a dogmatic claim imposed on the text from above, oblivious to the text's own concerns. Rather, it represents a reading of the story of Abraham as recounted by the Genesis narrator.

Modelling piety

For Paul, the scriptural assertion that "Abraham believed God, and it was reckoned to him as righteousness" eliminates the possibility that "Abraham was justified by works" and therefore possesses "grounds for boasting" (Rom.4.2–3). Those who "work" receive their reward as a due and not as a gift; but righteousness is reckoned to the one who does not "work" but rather "believes in the one who justifies the ungodly" (4.4–5). Where faith is reckoned as righteousness, righteousness is a gift and not an acknowledgment of merit or achievement. There is, Paul claims, a qualitative difference between the statement, "Abraham believed ... " and all other scriptural statements in which specific actions are attributed to Abraham. If "works" are in the first instance simply human actions (cf. Rom.2.6), and if the "works" that might conceivably justify are those human actions that conform to the revealed will of God, then the Genesis narrator ascribes "works" to Abraham in statements such as the following:

> So Abram went, as YHWH told him. (Gen.12.4)

> So he built there an altar to YHWH, who had appeared to him (12.7)

> So Abram went down to Egypt to sojourn there, for the famine was severe in the land. (12.10)

> When Abram heard that his relative had been taken captive, he led forth his trained men, born in his house ... and went in pursuit as far as Dan. (14.14)

> And Abram gave him a tenth of everything. (14.20)

> Then Abraham fell on his face and laughed, and said to himself, "Shall a child be born to a man who is a hundred years old?" (17.17)

Then Abraham took Ishmael his son and all the slaves born in his house or bought with his money... and he circumcised the flesh of their foreskins that very day, as God had said to him. (17.23)

When he saw them, he ran from the tent door to meet them, and bowed himself to the earth, and said, "My lord, if I have found favour in your sight, do not pass by your servant..." (18.2–3)

Then Abraham prayed to God, and God healed Abimelech, and also healed his wife and female slaves so that they bore children. (20.17)

So Abraham rose early in the morning, saddled his ass, and took two of his young men with him, and his son Isaac... (22.3)

Abraham buried Sarah his wife in the cave of the field of Machpelah east of Mamre (that is, Hebron) in the land of Canaan. (23.19)

In all such statements, a specific action is attributed to Abraham. In some cases Abraham acts in response to a specific divine command, in others he acts on his own initiative. Yet the narrator presents his entire life-story as unfolding within his relationship to YHWH, and so creates the presumption that even those actions without a specific divine mandate nevertheless conform to the divine will.[5] In a few cases, perhaps, it is open to the reader to construe Abraham's action as inappropriate. Yet the narrator never implies a criticism: Sarah is criticized for disbelieving laughter (18.12–15), but Abraham is not (17.17). In the story of Abraham, there is no such episode of rebellion against YHWH as there is in the case of Moses (Num.20.2–13) or David (2 Sam.11–12). While the Genesis narrator also exempts Jacob and Joseph from direct criticism, the relationship with YHWH is in both cases a more distant one, and the possibility of ethically questionable actions is clearer than in the case of Abraham (cf. Gen.27.1–29; 37.2–11). Abraham would seem to be the outstanding scriptural exemplar of pious conduct. If the scriptural testimony to his "works" consists in the sum of the sentences in which he is the subject of a verb, and if the narrator implies a more or less unqualified approval of his actions, then the narrative itself would appear to "justify" Abraham, declaring him to be righteous on the basis of his "works". Abraham would then have "grounds for boasting": and if self-glorification seems out of keeping with his characteristic modesty and reserve, there will surely be readers of his story who will "boast" on his behalf, exalting him as the pattern of every religious virtue.

---

5. In Romans 4.2, "works" is not an exact synonym of "works of law" (cf. 9.11–12; *contra* Dunn, *Romans*, 1.200). As we shall see in the following chapter, it is not the view even of *Jubilees* that Abraham's lifelong faithfulness to God was exclusively a matter of Torah observance.

Whatever such readers may think, Paul insists that this is not Abraham's position before God. God does not look upon Abraham as the pattern of every religious virtue, and that is not at all the message that God intends his story to convey to its readers. We know this on the basis of a single statement that occurs in the text itself: the interjection, " – but not before God!" (Rom.4.2) leads directly to the rhetorical question, "For what does the scripture say?" (4.3). What the scriptural text says is that "Abram believed God, and it was reckoned to him as righteousness" (LXX) – or that "he believed YHWH, and he reckoned it to him as righteousness" (MT). Paul believes that he has found here the point in the narrative where the "pious exemplar" reading is shown to be utterly untenable. This single sentence is the lever he needs in order to overturn a reading of the Genesis text which appears to be so entirely natural, straightforward and unproblematic. The isolated statement about Abraham's righteousness-by-faith shows that his story does not mean what it seems to mean.

Paul's point can be clarified by way of a comparison with the only other scriptural figure to whom "righteousness" is said to have been "reckoned". That figure is Phinehas.

Moments of decision

Unlike Abraham's, Phinehas's story is quickly told. At a time when the people of Israel are provoking YHWH's anger by participating in Moabite worship of the "Baal of Peor", Phinehas makes a decisive intervention:

> And behold, a man from the sons of Israel came and brought a Midianite woman to his family, before the eyes of Moses and before the eyes of all the assembly of the sons of Israel as they wept at the door of the Tent of Meeting. And Phinehas, son of Eleazar, son of Aaron the priest, saw it – and he arose from the midst of the assembly and took a spear in his hand, and followed the man of Israel into the tent, and pierced the two of them, the man of Israel and the woman through her womb. Thus the plague was stayed from the people of Israel. (Num.25.6–8)[6]

The downward thrust of Phinehas's spear violently parodies the act of sexual intercourse that it interrupts – a point that is covered up in Josephus's paraphrase, where Phinehas kills first the man and then the

---

6. According to the LXX version, the Israelite man "came and brought his brother to the Midianite woman, before Moses..." (v.6). Here, *'l* and *'t* have been exchanged, and "brothers" (i.e. "family") has been replaced by "brother". The difficult *'l hqbh* (probably, "into the tent") is translated as, *eis ton kaminon*: Phinehas enters "into the furnace", interpreted by Philo as referring to the furnace of human life, "burning and flaming with the excess of our misdeeds, impossible to extinguish" (*de Ebr.* 73).

woman with a sword (*Ant.* iv.153). His action recalls the Levites' slaughter of worshippers of the Golden Calf (Ex.32.25–29), and the non-violent atoning interventions of Aaron (Num.16.46–48) and Moses (Num.21.8–9). Phinehas's spear, Aaron's censer and Moses' bronze serpent all serve to halt the spread of a plague among the people. Just as the Levites' action is their ordination for YHWH's service (Ex.32.29), so Phinehas is appointed to an eternal priesthood:

> And YHWH spoke to Moses, saying: Phinehas, son of Eleazar, son of Aaron the priest has turned away my anger from the sons of Israel, in that he was zealous with my own zeal among them *[bqn'w 't qn'ty btwkm*; LXX, *en tō zēlōsai mou ton zēlon en autois]*, so that I did not destroy the sons of Israel in my zeal. Therefore say: Behold, I give him my covenant of peace, and it shall be to him and to his seed after him the covenant of a perpetual priesthood, because he was zealous for his God and made atonement for the sons of Israel. (Num.25.10–13)

The story of Phinehas's action serves to confirm the priestly legitimacy of a particular branch of the family of Aaron;[7] it is to be understood in the light of a concern with priestly – and specifically high priestly – genealogy.[8] Phinehas's legitimatory act of atonement provides a positive counterpart to the illegitimate action that led to the deaths of Aaron's eldest sons, Nadab and Abihu, who "offered unholy fire before YHWH, such as he had not commanded them" (Lev.10.1–7), and to the Levitical rebellion against the Aaronic priesthood, led by Korah (Num.16.1–40).

For later readers, the story of Phinehas acquired a broader exemplary function in addition to its legitimatory one. Phinehas was enlisted alongside other scriptural heroes whose actions provide inspiration for

7. The Phinehas episode is "intended to legitimatize the descendants of Phinehas, in the face of any possible opposition, as the true heirs to 'Aaronite' privileges" (M. Noth, *Numbers*, p. 199).

8. For high priestly genealogies from Aaron, Eleazar and Phinehas to Zadok, and from Zadok to the exile, see 1 Chronicles 6.3–15, 49–53. The last pre-exilic high priest is identified as Jehozadak, elsewhere referred to as the father of Jeshua or Joshua, the first post-exilic high priest (cf. Ezr. 3.2; Hag.1.1; Zech.3.1, etc.); thus, the high priestly line of Aaron, Phinehas and Zadok was believed to have survived the exile. The Chronicler's genealogies omit to mention the high priestly succession from Eli to Abiathar, and Josephus preserves what may be a traditional attempt to harmonize the divergent scriptural material. According to Josephus, the house of Phinehas surrendered the high priestly office to the house of Ithamar (Phinehas's younger brother), when, in the fourth generation after Phinehas, Eli became high priest (*Ant.* v.361–62). When Zadok the priest sides with Solomon and Abiathar with his unsuccessful rival Adonijah (1 Kgs.1.7–8), Josephus finds here the occasion for the recovery of the high priesthood by the house of Phinehas from the last representative of the house of Ithamar and Eli – in accordance with the divine announcement of its overthrow in 1 Samuel 3.11–14 (*Ant.* viii.10; cf. 1 Chron.24.3). Thus, between Eli and Zadok, the descendants of Phinehas "lived as private persons" (*Ant.* viii.11–12; cf. 1 Chr.6.5–12).

martyrs and all others who seek to realize reason's sovereignty over the passions (4 Macc.18.12). Phinehas could also be seen as an image of the soul zealous to excise the source of wickedness and folly from within itself, receiving from God the twofold portion of peace and priesthood as its reward (Philo, *Leg. All.* iii.242). Although Josephus ascribes Phinehas's action simply to his remarkable "courage" (*Ant.* iv.153), other interpreters echo the scriptural reference to his divine "zeal" or "jealousy" – his active participation in the divine wrath evoked by the people's rebellion and apostasy.[9] In the earlier period, however, the connection between this story and a particular claim to priestly legitimacy was still fundamental. Thus Ben Sira connects Phinehas's "zeal" to the ongoing high priestly office, and presents him as the third member of a triumvirate alongside Moses and Aaron:

> Phinehas son of Eleazar is third in glory, because of his zeal *[en tō zēlōsai auton]* in the fear of the Lord, and because he stood firm when the people turned away, in the willing goodness of his soul; thus he made atonement for Israel. Therefore a covenant of peace was established with him, that he should be leader in the sanctuary and over his people, so that to him and to his seed the dignity of priesthood might belong for ever. (Sir.45.23–24)[10]

In this passage, the original legitimatory role of the Phinehas story remains intact. Phinehas's zeal legitimates both the priesthood of all his male descendants and the high priesthood of the individuals chosen from among them to be "leader in the sanctuary". Ben Sira assumes a direct connection between Aaron and Phinehas on the one hand and his contemporary, Simon son of Onias, on the other: "May he establish his grace with Simon, may he confirm for him the covenant of Phinehas, which shall not be broken for him or his descendants, as long as the days of heaven" (Sir.50.24 Heb.).

At some point between the composition of the Phinehas episode and the time of Ben Sira, the author of Psalm 106 offers his own reflections on this story:

> And they joined themselves to the Baal of Peor, and they ate the sacrifices of the dead. They provoked anger with their doings, and a

---

9. M. Hengel argues that Josephus omits to refer to Phinehas's "zeal" because of its importance for "Zealots" and other revolutionaries (*Zealots*, p. 155; see also N. T. Wright, *The New Testament and the People of God*, p. 180). This is uncertain, however, as Josephus's brief reflections on the term "Zealot" do not suggest any specific scriptural background (*BJ* vii.268–70). Josephus's extensive treatment of the Phinehas episode does not otherwise suggest that he regarded it as politically sensitive.

10. "The dignity of priesthood" renders *hierōsunēs megaleion*. Here the Hebrew reads, *khwnh gdwlh* (Ms B XV), meaning "high priesthood". In this passage the Hebrew is incomplete.

plague broke out upon them. Then Phinehas stood and intervened, and the plague was stayed. And that has been reckoned to him as righteousness *[wtḥšb lw lṣdqh]*, from generation to generation for ever. (Ps.106.28–31)

At several points, the language here is close to Numbers 25.[11] That is not the case, however, when the psalmist comes to speak of the divine response to Phinehas's action. The eternal "righteousness" bestowed on Phinehas clearly alludes to the "covenant of peace" which is also a "covenant of perpetual priesthood" (Num.25.12–13). Here, the psalmist continues to think in terms of priestly legitimacy, although this is less explicit than in Numbers or Ben Sira. What is striking is that he speaks of this in language derived not from Numbers but from Genesis 15.6 – the only other occasion when "righteousness" is said to be "reckoned". It is true that the psalmist's phraseology is not identical to the Genesis narrator's. In the case of Abraham, it is said that "he reckoned it to him [as] righteousness *[wyḥšbh lw ṣdqh]*." In the psalm, the active verb has become a passive. Even this minor difference disappears in the Septuagint, however, where the passive formulation in the psalm text is seemingly retrojected into Genesis. The wording of the two passages is now identical: "And it was reckoned to him as righteousness *[kai elogisthē autō eis dikaiosunēn]*" (Ps.105.31a; Gen.15.6b).

It is possible that this close connection between Genesis and the psalm is coincidental, and that the psalmist did not derive his phraseology directly from Genesis, or the Genesis translator from the psalm. Even if the similarity is coincidental, however, the case of Phinehas's "righteousness" can still shed light on Abraham's. In both passages, righteousness is reckoned in consequence of a single, decisive action. Phinehas "stood and intervened" (or perhaps, "stood and made atonement *[exilasato]*" [LXX]). The psalmist here summarizes a train of events in which Phinehas "arose... and took a spear in his hand, and followed the man of Israel into the tent, and pierced the two of them, the man and the woman, through her womb" (Num.25.7–8). Whereas Phinehas "intervened", Abraham "believed God" – and in each case "it was reckoned to him as righteousness". In both cases, righteousness is constituted by a single action – just one out of the many actions that make up their respective life-stories. The single action that constitutes their righteousness has the

---

11. "And they joined themselves to Baal Peor" (Ps.106.28a) = "And Israel joined himself to Baal Peor" (Num.25.3). "And the plague was stayed" (Ps.106.30b) = "And the plague was stayed from the sons of Israel" (Num.25.8b). In Numbers, the first reference to the plague follows the account of Phinehas's action (Num.25.8, 9); earlier references to YHWH's anger do not mention the specific form it took (25.3, 4). The psalmist resolves the ambiguity by making the plague the background to Phinehas's action.

paradoxical effect of putting all their other actions into the shade. Elsewhere in the scriptural record, Phinehas participates in a military expedition against the Midianites (Num.31.6), leads a delegation to investigate an altar of doubtful validity (Josh.22.13–34), and officiates as high priest at Bethel (Jd.20.26–28). Yet, from the psalmist onward, readers of scripture have remembered Phinehas for just one of his actions – the single "intervention" that constituted his righteousness. In response to a situation of crisis, Phinehas performs a unique, unrepeatable priestly action in which the two-become-one are sacrificed for the well-being of the many. This action alone constitutes his eternal righteousness.

In the case of Abraham, his righteousness is constituted by his "believing God".[12] This action is no less singular than Phinehas's. Abraham no doubt believed all the other divine words that he heard on other occasions, but his righteousness is constituted by his believing acceptance of a single divine word uttered on a specific occasion, relatively early in his unfolding story.[13] The statement that "Abram believed God..." (Gen.15.6 LXX) is the sequel to the promise, "Thus shall your seed be" – with reference to the innumerable stars of the night sky (15.5). As with Phinehas, righteousness is reckoned to Abraham in consequence of a singular action. Yet the parallel with Phinehas makes the Genesis text all the more puzzling. It is not clear that the relation between the singular action and the other recorded actions is comparable in the two cases. Within its own terms of reference, Phinehas's action possesses a heroic quality that sharply differentiates it from the other actions ascribed to him. In the case of Abraham, the situation is the exact opposite. The singular action that constitutes his righteousness is devoid of any heroic quality, and this differentiates it from other actions ascribed to him in which

---

12. In the Hebrew *yḥšbh*, the feminine verbal suffix serves as a demonstrative pronoun referring back to the statement that "Abram believed YHWH" – compare the use of *z't* in Exodus 10.11 (so GK §122q). Similarly, Abram's believing God is the implied subject of *elogisthē*. The LXX passive is probably stylistically motivated, as in the similar case in Genesis 15.13 *(kai errethē pros Abram ...)*. The cultic instances of the verb "to reckon" (to which G. von Rad draws attention, *The Problem of the Hexateuch*, pp. 125–30) are characteristically passive in form.

13. LXX translates the perfect consecutive *wh'mn* with the aorist *episteusen*; BH emends accordingly to the imperfect consecutive *wy'mn* (cf. Ex.14.31: *wy'mynw*). Retaining the perfect consecutive, Gunkel argues that it should be translated, "he believed repeatedly" (*Genesis*, p. 179), citing the usage identified in GK §112e: "... a frequentative tense to express past actions..., i.e. actions repeatedly brought to a conclusion in the past." Examples given include Genesis 2.6 and 1 Samuel 2.19. In the case of Genesis 15.6, however, neither of the verbs that precede or follow the perfect consecutive (*wy'mr* [v.5], *wyḥšbh*) entail continuous or repeated action. *wh'mn* in Genesis 15.6 should be classed with a large number of cases in which the perfect consecutive is semantically indistinguishable from the imperfect consecutive (e.g. Gen.21.25, 28.6, 34.5, 49.23).

greatness and heroism is far more evident. Abraham is, so to speak, a photographic negative of Phinehas.[14]

There is nothing obviously heroic about Abraham's act of "believing God". To say that God spoke to Abraham and that Abraham believed what God said is to say no more than that God spoke credibly to Abraham. Since, within this story's terms of reference, divine speech is necessarily credible speech, Abraham does no more than recognize divine speech as what it is, enabled to do so by the divine speech itself. The speech in question is a promise, in which the speaker commits himself to future action on the addressee's behalf, seeking thereby to establish a relationship of trust on the basis of this commitment to future action. Unlike many of the divine utterances to Abraham, this one is not a command. When YHWH commands, Abraham habitually obeys – whether he is instructed to forsake his homeland or to sacrifice his son. But the statement, ". . . and he reckoned it to him as righteousness" is not attached to any of these acts of heroic obedience but to an act of consent to another's self-commitment. This is still an "act", and is distinguishable from the absolute passivity of the "deep sleep" to which Abraham succumbs a few verses later (Gen.15.12). Yet this act is almost invisible as such, since it is oriented entirely to the divine promise that has evoked it and to which it responds. A small thing in itself, its greatness lies entirely in the greatness of the promise. The speech-act of making a promise requires the addressee to acknowledge the promise as a promise and to regard it as dependable: when Abraham does this, his response simply marks the successful completion of the divine act of promise-making. YHWH "reckons righteousness" to Abraham when he believes the promise because YHWH intends that his relationship to Abraham should in future be exclusively determined by that promise. If Genesis 15.6 is understood as the hermeneutical key to the Abraham narrative, its effect will be to underline the centrality of the God of the promise. Abraham himself becomes a secondary figure in his own story. Indeed, his significance lies precisely in his secondariness.[15]

14. As von Rad points out, the narrator here communicates important theological statements, but "without describing the actual occurrence upon which these statements are founded, either in the case of Abraham or in the case of Yahweh" (*Genesis*, p. 184). Genesis 15.6 "state[s] programmatically that belief alone has brought Abraham into a proper relationship to God"; this text "almost has the quality of a general theological tenet" (p. 185). According to C. Westermann, Genesis 15.6 represents a "retrojection" of post-Isaianic ideas into the patriarchal narratives (*Genesis 12–36*, pp. 222–23).

15. In taking Genesis 15.6 in this way, Paul may be said to exploit its semantic potential, rather than correctly reproducing an original meaning – which is probably beyond full recovery. John Van Seters sees here a retrojection of Deuteronomic land theology, which insists on "righteousness" as the precondition for possession of the land (*The Yahwist as Historian*, pp. 250–51). Yet Ezekiel 33.23–29 (cited by Van Seters) speaks neither of

The works of the fathers

In the case of both Phinehas and Abraham, the singular action that constitutes their righteousness has the effect of downgrading all their other actions to a position of relative unimportance. For readers of their stories, this creates no difficulty in the case of Phinehas but great difficulty in the case of Abraham. In 1 Maccabees, both of these figures are to the fore in the speech of the dying Mattathias to his sons. The heroic deeds of the brothers Judas (3.1–9.22), Jonathan (9.23–12.53) and Simon (13.1–16.24) are inspired by the scriptural exemplars recalled by their father.[16] The exhortation, "Remember the works of the fathers" (2.51) implies that the scriptural exemplars form the invisible substructure of the entire narrative that is to follow:

> Now, my children, be zealous for the law *[zēlōsate tō nomō]* and give your lives for the covenant of our fathers. And remember the works of the fathers *[ta erga tōn paterōn]*, which they accomplished in their generations, and receive great glory and an everlasting name. Was not Abraham found faithful *[pistos]* when he was tested, and it was reckoned to him as righteousness *[kai elogisthē autō eis dikaiosunēn]*? Joseph at the time of his distress kept the commandment and became master of Egypt. Phinehas our father through his great zeal *[en tō zēlōsai zēlon]* received the covenant of an everlasting priesthood... (1 Macc.2.50–54)

Here, the description of Phinehas summarizes the divine commendation in Numbers 25.10–13, from which its language is drawn.[17] Although all of the scriptural heroes can loosely be described as "our fathers" (1 Macc.2.51), it is striking that only Phinehas is identified individually as "our father". Mattathias and the narrator claim that the Maccabees participate in the "covenant of everlasting priesthood" by virtue of their descent from Phinehas. They are therefore qualified for the high priestly office (10.21; 13.42; 14.41, 47) on the basis of their descent as well as their Phinehas-like

---

"righteousness" nor of "faith". When Van Seters states that, in Genesis as in Ezekiel, "obedience to the law comes before possession of the land" (p. 251), one has some sympathy with the Pauline insistence that this is just what the Genesis text does *not* mean.

16. The structural significance of this speech is unfortunately overlooked by David S. Williams, *The Structure of 1 Maccabees*, in spite of his (otherwise welcome) emphasis on 1 Maccabees as a book, and not a mere historical source. Williams' chiastic patterns tend to overlook the linear unfolding of the narrative.

17. In 1 Maccabees 2.54, *en tō zēlōsai zēlon* is derived from *en tō zēlōsai mou ton zēlon en autois* (Num.25.11); and *elaben diathēkēn hierosunēs aiōnias* is derived from *estai autō... diathēkē hierateias aiōnia* (Num.25.13). The parallels between Mattathias and Phinehas are discussed by J. Goldstein, *I Maccabees*, pp. 6–7.

acts of "zeal for the law".[18] Of all the scriptural exemplars, only Phinehas is commended for an act of violence directed against apostates, and this underlines his special affinity with Judas and his brothers (cf. 3.5–6).

In the case of Abraham, the language is again scriptural, or at least traditional (1 Macc.2.52). The phrase "when he was tested" refers back to the occasion when "God tested Abraham" by requiring him to offer up his son Isaac (Gen.22.1). The words, *en peirasmō heurethē pistos* (literally, "in testing he was found faithful") are drawn from Sirach 44.20, where the sequel ("Therefore the Lord assured him by an oath . . . ", v.21) confirms that the reference is specifically to Genesis 22, and not to the general course of Abraham's life. The language of the divine endorsement (". . . and it was reckoned to him as righteousness") is obviously drawn from Genesis 15.6, but is detached from the occasion when Abraham "believed God" and connected instead to the later occasion when Isaac was offered up. It is assumed that, as in the case of Phinehas, Abraham's righteousness must be constituted by a single heroic action. The Genesis narrator seems to present the offering of Isaac as the culmination of all Abraham's acts of obedience to God's command, and, for the author of 1 Maccabees, it can only be *this* action that evokes the divine commendation. In defence of this exegetical move, it might be said that the statement, " . . . and it was reckoned to him as righteousness" is an apt summary of the longer divine commendation in Genesis 22.15–18. We have already seen that just this phrase was used by the psalmist to summarize the divine commendation of Phinehas (Ps.106.31; cf. Num.25.10–13). The result, however, is that Abraham is assimilated to Phinehas, and Genesis 15.6 is deprived of its potential role as the hermeneutical key to his story. Abraham's righteousness is now constituted by a heroic act of obedience, and this is here recalled as one of the "works of the fathers" which can inspire the present generation to acquire "great glory" for themselves by emulating them (1 Macc.2.51).[19]

On this reading, "Abraham was justified by works" and has "grounds for boasting" (Rom.4.2).[20] Or rather, he is justified – as Phinehas was – by

18. Mattathias is identified as "a priest of the sons of Joarib" (= "Jehoarib", 1 Chron.24.7), and thus as descended from Eleazar and Phinehas (cf. 1 Chron.24.1–7). It is possible that the author of *1 Maccabees* responds here to "partisans of the Oniad line" who viewed the Hasmonean high priests as usurpers (so J. Goldstein, *1 Maccabees*, p. 8). For the Oniad appeal to Phinehas, see Sirach 50.24 (Heb.), cited above.

19. The phrase, "it was reckoned to him[them] as righteousness", is also attested in *Jubilees* in connection with Isaac's symbolic recognition of Levi and Judah (21.23), and the massacre of the Shechemites by Simeon and Levi (23.17). A paraphrase of this statement occurs in 23.19, where it is said of Levi that "blessing and righteousness were written down for him in the heavenly tablets before the God of all". See the discussion in S. J. Gathercole, *Where is Boasting?*, pp. 60–63.

20. The term "works" refers to actions carried out in conformity to the divine will in both Romans 4.2 and 1 Maccabees 2.51. In neither case is the concern merely with "the obligations

the single "work" or act that constitutes his righteousness, which may plausibly be understood not as an isolated event but as the culmination of a career of unquestioning obedience to divine commands. Here, Abraham is the primary figure in his own story. As Paul is aware, it is all too possible to read the Genesis narrative along these lines. The imaginary questioner who appeals to "Abraham our forefather according to the flesh", in order to counter Paul's dogmatic claim that justification occurs "apart from works of law" (Rom.4.1, 3.28), has a strong case. Indeed, for Paul, there is just one scriptural text that stands against such a reading of Genesis. As a simple matter of fact, and however it came about, the definitive divine verdict – " . . . and it was reckoned to him as righteousness" – is *not* attached to any of the available statements about Abraham's obedience, but to the report that he believed the divine promise. If those who read his story find inspiration in his heroic actions, they will not get to the heart of the matter – which lies instead in his own *secondariness* in relation to the God of the promise, who calls him out of nothing and makes him who he is (cf. Rom.4.17).

In order to understand Abraham's story aright, the divine endorsement in Genesis 15.6 must be allowed to put all his "works" or deeds of obedience into the shade. Indeed, it poses the question whether the reader is right to find in this story an image of total dedication to God. It appears from this text that God, unlike the reader, does *not* see in Abraham an image of total dedication and unwavering obedience. In Romans 4, Abraham is assimilated not to Phinehas but to David, who pronounces a blessing on those whose sins are forgiven by the God who justifies the ungodly (Rom.4.4–8).[21]

which marked off [the Jewish people] most clearly as the seed of Abraham, the children of Israel, the people of the law (circumcision, food laws, Sabbath, in particular . . .)" (Dunn, *Romans*, 1.201). The food laws and the Sabbath are not relevant to Abraham's story, and yet the possibility that Abraham was "justified by works" is for Paul a serious (though false) interpretative option. In the case of 1 Maccabees, the works of zeal for the law inspired by the fathers consist in the actions of the three brothers, as narrated in chapters 3–16. The fact that circumcision and food laws are important in the earlier account of martyrdoms (1 Macc.1.41–64) tells us nothing about the scope of the term "works", as used either by the author of 1 Maccabees or by Paul.

21.   While Paul shows no interest in defining Abraham's "ungodliness", the one thing he cannot mean is that Abraham "sought to be righteous as a result of his works" (H. Hübner, *Law in Paul's Thought*, p. 121). In Romans 4, the faith/works antithesis represents contrary *readings* of Genesis, and not a conflict within the experience of Abraham himself.

The Narrated Promise

Although Genesis 15.6 is singled out in Romans 4.1–12 as the hermeneutical key to the Abraham narrative, Paul does not isolate it from its scriptural context. In the course of the unfolding arguments of Romans and Galatians, he appeals to a number of crucial points in the Abraham narrative in such a way as to demonstrate the priority of the God of the promise. In that sense, his is a radically theocentric reading of the Genesis narrative, in which Abraham is who he is purely on the basis of the divine creative and communicative action. It is to this interpretation of the promise motif in Genesis that we must now turn. The aim will again be to reconstruct the hermeneutical and exegetical logic that leads Paul to read Genesis as he does, and not to measure his readings against some notional standard of exact conformity to an original authorial intention. Like the rejected reading in terms of Abraham's "grounds for boasting" and his "works" (to which we shall return in chapter 5), the Pauline reading can justly claim to realize something of the semantic potential of a complex and polysemic text. It is, precisely, a *reading*, arising from the interaction of reader and text; it is neither the exact reproduction of a given content nor the product of alien, non-negotiable dogmatic convictions.

The blessing of Abraham

In Genesis 12.1–3, Abraham's call to leave country and kin for a land that is yet to be disclosed is accompanied by divine promises that unconditionally guarantee not only his own future but also the future of the nation that is to spring from him, and ultimately the future of the world itself. Although he and his wife are childless (Gen.11.30), he receives the promise that "I will make you a great nation" (12.2a). The journey to the land is a journey on behalf of that nation, to whom the land will eventually belong; Abraham journeys as the ancestor of the nation. Yet the promise that follows – that "I will bless you and make your name great, so that you will be a blessing" (12.2b) – appears to refer not to the nation but to Abraham as an individual, and specifically to his prosperity and his reputation.[22] In fulfilment of that promise, it can later be said that "YHWH blessed Abraham in everything" (24.1). In the same chapter, Abraham's servant tells Laban, Bethuel and Rebekah how

> YHWH has greatly blessed my master, and he has become great; he has given him flocks and herds, silver and gold, male and female servants,

22. "So that you will be a blessing" might be rendered, "Be a blessing" (P. R. Williamson, *Abraham, Israel and the Nations*, pp. 221–23).

camels and asses. And Sarah my master's wife bore a son to my master when she was old... (24.35)

The language here echoes the promise that "I will bless you and make your name great", and confirms that this is fulfilled not in a distant future but within Abraham's own life.[23] YHWH's blessing of Abraham is comprehensive: Abraham is blessed "in everything", and this includes the gift of a son but is not confined to it. Abraham, then, will be "a blessing" in that his name will be invoked in blessings seeking the good fortune of the one who is blessed (cf. 24.60; 27.28–29; 48.15–20).

A divine blessing is promised to Abraham, such that his own name will be invoked in human blessings; and a divine blessing is also promised to others insofar as they receive him in friendship. "I will bless those who bless you, and him who curses you I will curse" (12.3a): this divine promise adapts a traditional formula of blessing and cursing (cf. Gen.27.29; Num.24.9).[24] In a fourth and final variation on the theme of "blessing", it is also said that "by you shall all families of the earth bless themselves" – or, "be blessed".[25] Even the reflexive reading presupposes the universal acknowledgment of the God of Abraham.[26] So great will Abraham's name become, so far will his reputation spread, that the whole world will invoke his name as they pray for blessings like his. The passive reading is represented by the Septuagint, where it remains constant in later parallel passages: "In you/your seed shall all tribes/nations of the earth be blessed" (Gen.12.3; 22.18). For the translator, the calling and destiny of Israel is to bring blessing to the entire world, and his

23. If the language of the "great name" is drawn from royal ideology, there is no hint here of an attempt to legitimate the monarchy of David or Solomon. According to John Van Seters, the royal terminology represents "a democratization of royal ideology in the exilic period" (*The Yahwist as Historian*, p. 270). As this comment illustrates, Van Seters sees the promise motif as a late development, in opposition to the traditional emphasis on its antiquity (Alt, Noth, Westermann). From the perspective of this work, late datings have the advantage of bringing scriptural texts into closer proximity to their postbiblical history of interpretation.

24. So C. Westermann, *Genesis 12–36*, pp. 150–51, emphasizing that J's reshaping of the old formula "made Yahweh the active party and related Yahweh's action to Abraham's posterity in the history of Israel" (p. 151).

25. This promise is repeated on four further occasions in Genesis (18.18; 22.18; 26.4; 28.14), addressed not only to Abraham but also to Isaac (26.4) and to Jacob (28.14). Of the five versions of this promise, the verb is in the reflexive *hithpael* on two occasions (22.18, 26.4; cf. also Ps.72.17, Jer.4.2) and the reflexive or passive *niphal* on three (12.3; 18.18; 28.14). Variations among these passages occur not only in the verb but also in the subject ("tribes" [12.3; 28.14]; "nations" [18.18; 22.18; 26.4]) and the indirect object ("in you" [12.3]; "in him" [18.18]; "in your seed" [22.18; 26.4]; "in you... and in your seed" [28.14]). With the possible exception of the verb, none of these variations appears to affect the sense.

26. Westermann, *Genesis 12–36*, p. 152. Compare Genesis 48.20, where, in an analogous case of a blessing that invokes individual names, the scope is confined to Israel.

rendering seeks to bring this out as clearly as possible. The passive rendering is reflected in the Greek translation of Ben Sira, which clearly alludes to the promise of universal blessing in its Septuagintal form (Sir.44.21; Gen.22.18). Yet Ben Sira's original Hebrew understood the Genesis promise in a similar way. God, we are told, swore to Abraham "to bless the nations by his seed *[lbrk bzr'w gwym]*".[27] Between them, the Septuagint translator and Ben Sira indicate that this promise was taken to refer to the blessing of the nations – perhaps because knowledge of an earlier idiom – "to bless oneself by" – had been lost.[28]

The promises to Abraham speak of his own prosperity, of the nation, and of the world's acknowledgment of God's action on his behalf. For the Genesis narrator, these promises are the enduring foundation of Israel's present existence and its future hope. They are the nucleus from which the story of God's covenant with Israel will unfold, drawn onward by future divine acts announced in advance. At the outset, it is entirely unclear to Abraham how the promised future will work out, and even for the narrator the people of Abraham are still on the way to a future that has yet to be actualized. From the narrator's perspective, it is still hardly conceivable how the whole world will acknowledge the God of Abraham.[29] He knows that this will be the end of the story he is telling, but he is only able to narrate the beginning of that story. Precisely because the story must be left open to an end lying beyond its own limits, it can only be a fragmentary story, without closure. Yet Israel's existence as the "great nation" promised to Abraham derives from that end, and the end is therefore anticipated even at the beginning.

Writing to the Galatians, Paul argues that this end, anticipated at the beginning, is taking place here and now in his own apostolic ministry to the Gentiles. In the Abraham narrative, scripture anticipates "that by faith God would justify the Gentiles"; the promise to Abraham that "in you all Gentiles shall be blessed" is an anticipatory proclamation of the gospel (Gal.3.8). The promise of universal blessing is read in the light of the statement of Genesis 15.6, that "Abraham believed God and it was reckoned to him as righteousness" (quoted in Gal.3.6). To understand the logic of this exegetical move, we must look more closely not only at Paul's interpretative statements but also at the texts he cites.

27. Ms B XIV. In the Greek translation, the passive rather than active infinitive *(eneulogēthēnai ethnē en spermati autou)* derives from recollection of the Septuagint.

28. For a summary of arguments for the passive and the reflexive sense, see P. Williamson, *Abraham, Israel and the Nations*, pp. 223–28.

29. Against Gunkel, who claims that "this passage does not involve matters still to come in the time of the narrator" (*Genesis*, p. 165).

Paul cites Genesis 12.3b in the form, "All Gentiles *[panta ta ethnē]* shall be blessed in you." This deviates at two points from the Septuagint's rendering, "All the tribes of the earth *[pasai hai phulai tēs gēs]* shall be blessed in you." First, "Gentiles" (or "nations") is substituted for "tribes". The substitution is derived from the repetition of the original promise in Genesis 22.18, which refers to "all the nations of the earth" rather than to "tribes" or "families" (cf. also 18.18). Only in Genesis 12.3 is this promise directly addressed to Abraham, however; in the later passage the nations are said to be blessed "in your seed". Second, the phrase "of the earth" is omitted. The result of these two modifications is that non-Jews are referred to not as collectivities ("tribes", or "nations") but as an aggregate of individuals ("Gentiles"). These "Gentiles" do belong to different nations; for example, they include "Galatians" (Gal.3.1). Yet God justifies not nations but individual Gentiles by faith, and the scriptural text is cited in a form that avoids unnecessary misunderstanding at this point.

In Paul's interpretation, the emphasis falls not on the Gentiles *per se* but on the claim that it is "by faith" that Gentiles are blessed in Abraham. It is those who are "of faith" who are "sons of Abraham" (v.7); it is "by faith" that the Gentiles are justified (v.8); it is those who are "of faith" who are blessed with believing Abraham (v.9). In all three cases, it is Habakkuk's phrase *(ek pisteōs)* that is used. This "faith" is the human acknowledgment of the divine saving action announced in the gospel and, in anticipatory form, in the promise.[30] What is at stake here is not simply the question of Gentile membership in the people of God, but the priority and unconditionality of divine saving action in its universal scope. In Paul's reading, the promise of Genesis 12.3 is first of all a statement about God and God's action, and only as such a statement also about Gentiles. Thus the passive "shall be blessed" of the scriptural quotation, echoed in v.9, is replaced in v.8a with an active verb of which God is the subject ("The scripture, foreseeing that by faith God would justify the Gentiles..."). When scripture says that "in you shall all Gentiles be blessed", it foresees and announces a future event in which God will justify the Gentiles by faith.

In Galatians 3.8–9, the Genesis quotation is preceded by one interpretative paraphrase – "The scripture, foreseeing that by faith God would justify the Gentiles..." – and followed by another. According to

30. The priority of God's promise over Abraham's faith is rightly emphasized by J. L. Martyn, *Galatians*, pp. 297–99. "In Abraham's faith God sees and recognizes the true effect of his own promise, and that recognition is the climax of the integrated event in which God set Abraham fully right" (p. 299). This correlation of promise and faith (or word and faith) ensures that faith as a human action is different in kind to "the works of the law"; that is the valid point underlying the old concern that "faith should not become a work", i.e. a condition of salvation.

this second paraphrase, the scriptural text means that "those who are of faith are blessed with believing Abraham *[sun tō pistō Abraam]*" (v.9). Two further paraphrases are given in v.14, according to which Christ's death under the curse of the law took place "so that the blessing of Abraham might come to the Gentiles in Christ Jesus, so that we might receive the promise of the Spirit through faith". While these purpose clauses are not explicitly presented as further interpretations of Genesis 12.3, that is clearly what they are: the Genesis text is here employed to explain the rationale and goal of Christ's death. Thus a single scriptural promise is said to mean four things, or the same thing from four different angles. "In you shall all Gentiles be blessed" means that:

(i)   "... those who are of faith are blessed with believing Abraham" (v.9)
(ii) "... by faith God would justify the Gentiles" (v.8)
(iii) "... the blessing of Abraham might come to the Gentiles in Christ Jesus" (v.14a)
(iv) "... we might receive the promise of the Spirit through faith" (v.14b).

These four interpretative statements presuppose four distinct although interconnected exegetical decisions. First, "in you" is interpreted as "with Abraham" (v.9; the exegetical logic is clearer if vv.8, 9 are considered in reverse order). The blessing of the Gentiles is thereby identified with the blessing bestowed on Abraham himself. Second, Abraham's blessing is his being justified by faith (v.8). Thus the Gentiles who are blessed alongside believing Abraham are justified by faith, as he was, and the faith by which he and they are justified is elicited by the divine word of promise or gospel. Third, "in you" also means "in your seed", and the seed of Abraham is Christ: the blessing of Abraham therefore comes about "in Christ Jesus" (v.14a, cf. v.16). Fourth, the blessing of Abraham is a *promise*, the fulfilment of which is the gift of the Spirit (v.14b).[31]

A more detailed presentation of these exegetical decisions will show how far they are grounded not just in Paul's own theological commitments but in the text of Genesis itself.

(1) "In you" is interpreted as "with Abraham" (v.9): the blessing which the Gentiles are to receive is a blessing initially bestowed on Abraham himself.

---

31. Paul does not here seek "to demonstrate in all seriousness that his concept of faith is true because it is found in the Scriptures" (H. D. Betz, *Galatians*, p. 141). Rather, he seeks to uncover the scriptural concept of faith, which, as clarified in Christ, is also his own concept of faith. It is misleading to suggest that there are initially two distinct "concepts of faith" which are secondarily shown to harmonize.

The promise that "in you shall all Gentiles be blessed" is therefore based on the prior promise that Abraham himself will be the object of the divine blessing: "I will bless you and make your name great, and you shall be blessed [*eulogētos*]" (Gen.12.2b LXX). This is "the blessing of Abraham" (Gal.3.14), an expression derived from Gen.28.4 LXX, where Isaac is addressing Jacob: "May he give the blessing of Abraham my father [*tēn eulogian Abraam tou patros mou*] to you and to your seed with you." The blessing of all Gentiles "in him" is identified with the blessing of Abraham himself: they are blessed *with* him, they are blessed as he was. Paul assumes that in the Genesis passage the word "bless" is used in a relatively univocal, homogeneous way. In order to interpret the reference to God's blessing of the Gentiles, we must look more closely at God's blessing of Abraham himself.

(2) What is meant by the promise, "I will bless you" (Gen.12.2)? As we have seen, this is primarily a statement about Abraham himself, and not about his descendants. It does not refer to any one specific blessing, such as the gift of a son, but to Abraham's entire life as blessed by God in all its aspects. Although material prosperity is an important element in this blessing (cf. 24.35), Paul takes it for granted that the promised blessing of Abraham cannot refer primarily to his material situation. Israel's covenant relationship with God is not a mere means to the end of prosperity and well-being; Abraham does not obey God's command and believe God's promise *in order to* enrich himself. If he did so, he would expose himself to Satan's critical question about another pious man blessed with material prosperity and personal well-being: "Does Job fear God for naught?" (Job 1.9). Abraham must obey and believe for God's sake, and thereby show himself to be a true and faithful servant of God (cf. Gen.18.17 LXX: "Abraham my servant [*tou paidos mou*]").

For Paul, the blessing of Abraham cannot be something extrinsic to the God who blesses; the blessing of Abraham is to be found in his relationship with God. In Genesis, that relationship can on occasion be characterized in terms of Abraham's obedience to the divine commands (17.1–2, 18.19, 22.16–18, 26.4–5). Although these passages might seem to make the divine promises contingent on Abraham's observance of the commandments, that is not the case in reality. Even in these later chapters of the Abraham narrative, there is never any doubt about Abraham's obedience. There is no statement to the effect that *if* Abraham observes the commandments, *then* he will be blessed – but otherwise not. Abraham's obedience is retrospectively acknowledged and connected with the fulfilment of the promises, but at no point is the future opened up by the promises seen as uncertain and conditional. The reason, as Genesis 12–15 shows particularly clearly, is that in this narrative promise is a more fundamental mode of divine discourse than command. Abraham obeys the command to journey to Canaan on the basis of God's promises, which constitute God's unconditional commitment to future action on Abraham's behalf. If "the blessing of Abraham" is to be found in his relationship to God, and if the God of this relationship is most fundamentally the God of the promise, then Abraham's blessing is identical to his relationship to precisely *this* God.

The Genesis narrator provides an explicit statement to this effect. Abraham was shown the stars in the sky, and received the promise: "So shall your seed be" (Gen.15.5). Hearing this divine word, "Abram believed God, and it was reckoned to him as righteousness" (15.6 LXX). The promise that "I will bless you" is, then, most fundamentally a promise of the divine acknowledgment of his belief in the promise as constituting his "righteousness". Fundamental to every other divine blessing is the blessing of being acknowledged as righteous before God; and if the God who acknowledges as righteous is most fundamentally the God of the promise, who unconditionally commits himself to future action on Abraham's behalf, then righteousness before this God will consist in belief and trust in promise and promiser. To secure such a trust, and a pattern of life corresponding to it, is precisely what is intended in this promise (like any other promise). To make a promise is to enable the addressee to live henceforth in the confidence of specified future action on his or her behalf, thereby creating a relationship with the addressee deriving from that shared and certain future. And that is what happens in God's promise to Abraham.

Although Genesis 15.6 is for Paul the most important scriptural statement about Abraham's relationship with God, it does not fully articulate the significance of this relationship for others. By linking this statement to Genesis 12.2–3, Paul shows that "the blessing of Abraham" is his righteousness by faith, but he also shows Abraham's righteousness by faith to be a pattern for others: for the blessing of Abraham is identical to the blessing that God will bestow on the Gentiles. If the blessing of Abraham is the same as the blessing of the Gentiles, and if the blessing of Abraham is his righteousness by faith, then the Gentiles will also be blessed in being made righteous by faith. Paul quotes from Genesis 12.3 in order to demonstrate the universal scope and normativity of the crucial statement about Abraham's relationship with the God of the promise in Genesis 15.6.[32]

---

32. If this analysis is correct, Pauline exegesis is both more creative and more responsive to the possibilities of the scriptural texts than is commonly perceived. The effect is to problematize the conventional distinction between Paul's culturally conditioned scriptural interpretation and what is permissible for "us", as articulated by J. Rohde in his comments on this passage: "Natürlich ist die Art der Beweisführung des Paulus aus der Schrift für uns nicht ohne weiteres nachvollziehbar, aber wir müssen berücksichtigen, dass Paulus als Schüler der rabbinischen Schriftauslegung des AT dies Buch nicht historisch-kritisch las wie wir, sondern es mit den ihm geläufigen Auslegungsmethoden interpretierte" (*Galater*, pp. 136–37).

(3) The promise that "in you shall all Gentiles be blessed" is the promise of a future divine action with universal scope. That promised action has, for Paul, now become reality in the death of Christ under the law's curse, which took place "so that the blessing of Abraham might come to the Gentiles in Christ Jesus..." (Gal.3.14a). Paul has already stated that Gentiles are blessed as Abraham was blessed (v.9), and the point is now repeated – with one highly significant difference.

The argument of Galatians 3.6–9 is a scriptural proof which derives certain logical conclusions from the two Genesis texts (Gen.12.3, 15.6). The reality of the Christ event does not directly impinge upon this proof, and the present tense verbs ("these are sons of Abraham" [3.6], "those of faith are blessed" [3.9]) refer, formally speaking, to a timeless possibility which could still be validly deduced from the texts even if no believing Gentiles actually existed. According to Galatians 3.13–14, in contrast, the promise of Genesis 12.3 has now been realized in the death and resurrection of Christ, the event in which the curse of the law gives way to the blessing of Abraham. Thus it can now be said – as it could not be said purely on the basis of scripture – that the blessing of Abraham comes to the Gentiles "in Christ Jesus". This is a further interpretative paraphrase of the scriptural statement that "in you all Gentiles shall be blessed", but on this occasion the statement is reinterpreted in the light of the event in which the blessing was actually bestowed on the Gentiles. Here, "in you" is no longer paraphrased simply as "with Abraham", although that interpretation is still valid, but rather as "in Christ Jesus". In the background here may be the exegetical observation that "the promises were spoken to Abraham and to his seed", which Paul takes as a reference to Christ (v.16). If this observation is applied to Genesis 12.3, "in you" would apply not only to Abraham but also to Christ, Abraham's seed. In the light of the actuality of God's act to justify or bless the Gentiles, the scriptural promise must mean that "in Christ Jesus shall all Gentiles be blessed". According to the version of the promise of universal blessing found in Genesis 22.18, "all the nations of the earth [*panta ta ethnē tēs gēs*] shall be blessed *in your seed*", and this may confirm that the identification of Christ as Abraham's seed (Gal.3.16) already underlies the claim that "the blessing of Abraham" comes about "in Christ Jesus". "In you" (Gen.12.3) means "with believing Abraham" (Gal.3.9), but it also means "in your seed" (Gen.22.18), and thus "in Christ Jesus" (Gal.3.14a, 16).

An important hermeneutical distinction comes to light at this point. There is for Paul a difference between a scriptural interpretation which proceeds deductively on the basis of the texts (Gal.3.6–9), and one that proceeds inductively on the basis of the actuality of Christ (3.14a). The two approaches complement each other, and neither can exist in a pure form without the other. The deductive approach keeps the inductive one from interpretative arbitrariness by insisting that it remains accountable to the texts; the inductive approach keeps the deductive one from abstraction by insisting that it remains accountable to the actuality of Christ. Both together constitute the twofold hermeneutic whereby Paul as a Christian rereads Jewish scripture.[33]

The two approaches are combined in Galatians 3.16. Until the final phrase, this statement is a simple deduction or observation from scripture:

> The promises were spoken to Abraham and to his seed. It does not say: "And to seeds...", as referring to many, but as referring to one: "And to your seed..."

This much misunderstood statement probably means that of the many "seeds" or children of Abraham – by Hagar (Gen.16), Sarah (Gen.18) and Keturah (Gen.25) – only one is the true heir to the promises: Isaac, Abraham's son by Sarah. Paul's interpretative paraphrase derives from scriptural statements such as Genesis 21.12: "Through Isaac shall your seed be named" (cf. Rom.9.7). It reflects the difference between Abraham's offspring, only one of whom was chosen, and the offspring of Jacob, who were also born to a number of wives or their surrogates but who were all chosen. The distinction between the many seeds and the one promise bearing seed (Gal.3.16) is closely related to the later statement that "Abraham had two sons...", one born according to the flesh, the other by promise (Gal.4.22–23).[34] The fact that Genesis itself does not speak of Abraham's many sons as his "seeds" is no more relevant than its lack of the term "promise". In both cases, Paul develops his own vocabulary in interpreting the scriptural text, and his interpretative claims are in principle distinguishable from the claims of his gospel. From the perspective of Christian faith, however, Paul sees a further significance in the figure of the one individual selected from the many to represent Abraham's true seed. Isaac is a type of

---

33.   In chapter 1 we noted another example of the same distinction in Romans 3.21–31, understood as a continuation of the interpretative engagement with Habakkuk 2.4 that began in Romans 1.17. When Paul refers to God as *ton dikaiounta ton ek pisteōs Iēsou* (Rom.3.26), the naming of Jesus indicates an inductive approach to the Habakkuk text informed by the actuality of divine saving action. When, however, he states that "we consider a person to be justified by faith apart from works of law" (3.28), the conclusion is drawn deductively from the text.

34.   It is usually assumed that the equation of "seeds" and "many" refers to the Jewish people as descended from the patriarchs, and that in referring the singular "seed" to Christ Paul is at odds with the Genesis text, in which "seed" is normally collective in sense: so Burton, who claims that there is no interpretation "which will satisfy the requirements both of the Gen. passages and of the context here" (*Galatians*, p. 182). Burton correctly notes that the identification of the seed with Christ is "an assertion of the apostle, for which he claims no evidence in O.T. beyond the fact that the promise refers to one person" (*ibid.*); but he fails to see the implied reference to Isaac.

Christ – just as the oneness of Adam and of his deed can make him too a type of Christ (cf. Rom.5.12–21).[35] In that typological sense, "And to your seed ... " is ultimately a reference to Christ. That conclusion can be drawn not from scripture alone but from the conjunction between deduction and induction, scriptural exegesis and the Christian gospel. In a slightly more complex form, the references to Abraham in Galatians 3.6–14 illustrate the operation of this same two-sided hermeneutic.

(4) The death of Christ under the law's curse takes place "so that the blessing of Abraham may come to the Gentiles in Christ Jesus", and "so that we may receive the promise of the Spirit through faith" (Gal.3.14). The second purpose clause appears to be in apposition to the first, and the blessing of Abraham would then be identified with the promise of the Spirit, received by faith. The reference to "the promise" connects this statement too to the promise of Genesis 12.3; it does not refer to scriptural passages such as Joel 2.28–32 in which the future outpouring of the Spirit is announced.[36] The promise that "in you shall all Gentiles be blessed" is fulfilled in God's act of justification by faith, in which those who are of faith are blessed alongside faithful Abraham (Gal.3.8–9); it is fulfilled in the death and resurrection of Christ, who redeemed us from the curse of the law so that the blessing of Abraham might come to the Gentiles (3.13–14a); it is fulfilled in the reception of the Spirit through faith (3.14b); and all this constitutes the single though complex act of God who justifies, Christ who redeems, and the Spirit who is received. As in the preceding interpretation of "in you" as "in Christ Jesus", Paul here rereads the Genesis text inductively, from the perspective of Christian faith and experience. The text is clearly a "promise", but only in the light of Christian faith and experience can the content of the promise be identified

35.   Romans 5.12–21 is not simply an "Adam-Christ parallel", it is a piece of typological exegesis in which the scriptural figure of the single individual whose single act has universal scope establishes a "type of the coming one" (5.14) – admittedly, a type whose unlikeness to its antitype has to be stressed more strongly than usual (vv.15–17). Whether the emphasis is on unlikeness or likeness, the singularity of the individual and his action is repeatedly emphasized in both halves of each statement (vv.15, 17, 18, 19). On the hermeneutics of this passage, see the discussion in my article, "Is There a Story in These Texts?", pp. 235–39. The link between typology and singularity in Romans 5 confirms that, in Galatians 3.16 too, the singular scriptural figure is seen as a type of Christ.

36.   The two *hina*-clauses of v.14 are parallel in form and meaning (so Betz, citing the analogous syntax of 1 Corinthians 4.6 [*Galatians*, p. 152n]). Against this, N. T. Wright argues that the first person plural in Galatians 3.14b is a reference to Jewish Christians, and that Paul therefore differentiates between "blessing for the Gentiles ... and new covenant for Israel" (*The Climax of the Covenant*, p. 154). The problem Wright raises – that this passage would otherwise lack all reference to the salvation of Israel (p. 153) – would be better addressed by taking *ta ethnē* (Gal.3.14a) as inclusive of Jews, as *panta ta ethnē* (3.8) may already suggest.

as the giving of the Spirit. Paul expects the Galatians to acknowledge that they received the Spirit not by works of law but by the hearing of faith (3.1–5), and it is the actuality of the outpouring of the Spirit among the Gentiles that is identified with the realization of Abraham's blessing.

Genesis 12.3 enables Paul to identify Abraham's faith in the divine promise (Gen.15.6) with the Gentile faith evoked by the gospel – with Jesus' redeeming death as the connecting link between the two. Word and faith are bound up with one another, and this relationship is rediscovered also in the ancient scriptures. The word of the gospel announces that the definitive divine saving action has now taken place, in accordance with the word of the promise; and faith is the acknowledgment intended in the announcement itself, an acknowledgment that issues in righteousness, blessing and the gift of the Spirit. "Faith" is foundational to the divine–human relationship because faith alone is the human act that corresponds to the prior divine communicative action and is intended in it.[37] The structure and rationale of this "faith" come to light only through Paul's dialogue with the scriptural text, and the theological and exegetical conclusions to which he is led cannot simply be dismissed as a violation of the "literal sense" of the text.

The inheritance

The promise of the blessing of the Gentiles exercises no discernible influence on the Genesis narrative, since it represents a future that lies far beyond the limits of the narrated present. The narrative itself is moved by two closely related promises whose fulfilment seems to lie nearer to hand: the promise of seed, and the promise of the land. The land is first promised in a theophany shortly after Abraham's arrival in Canaan:

> And the Lord appeared [*ōphthē*] to Abram and said to him: To your seed [*tō spermati sou*] I will give this land. And Abram built there an altar to the Lord who appeared to him. (Gen.12.7)

After Abraham and Lot have parted company, the promise of the land is renewed. The land initially promised "to your seed" is now promised "to

37. As Bultmann rightly emphasizes, "faith" for Paul is not "trust in God in general", but rather "acceptance of a word" (*Theology of the New Testament*, 1.318). "The word is *kerygma*, personal address, demand, and promise; it is the very act of divine grace... Hence its acceptance – faith – is obedience, acknowledgment, confession" (1.319). Recent emphasis on "the faith of Christ" has tended to lose sight of this crucial word/faith correlation. In the case of Galatians, the "subjective genitive" interpretation has been advocated most influentially by Richard Hays, in his *The Faith of Jesus Christ*, pp. 139–91; see also J. L. Martyn, *Galatians*, pp. 263–77.

you and to your seed for ever" (13.15). In addition, the "seed" to whom the land is promised now becomes the content of a second promise:

> And I will make your seed like the dust of the earth, so that if one can count the dust of the earth your seed too shall be counted. (13.16)

The promise that Abraham's seed or descendants will possess the land is obviously dependent on the future existence of these descendants, and this later passage (13.14–17) therefore begins to address the question left open by the earlier one (12.7). In light of the fact that Sarah is barren (11.30) and that Abraham is seventy-five years old (12.4), how is the promise, "To your seed I will give this land" to be fulfilled? A second promise must be added if the first is to make sense. In the Genesis narrative, the divine promises are not disclosed all at once but are clarified and expanded as Abraham's story unfolds.

The twofold promise of seed and land (in that order) is the theme of Genesis 15, where it is acknowledged for the first time that the promise is a *problem*. Source criticism finds indications of disunity in this chapter.[38] Abraham's complaint that he remains childless is repeated (vv.2, 3). His doubt about the gift of land (v.8) is in tension with the preceding statement that "he believed YHWH" (v.6). Although it is already night in v.5, where Abraham looks up at the starry sky, the covenant sacrifice that follows takes place at sunset (v.12). In the outline of future history in vv.13–16, Abraham's descendants are to be oppressed in Egypt for four hundred years (v.13) but are to return to Canaan in the fourth generation (v.16). The promised land belongs to the Amorites, whose iniquity is not yet complete (v.16), but it also belongs to no less than ten peoples, of whom the Amorites are only one (vv.18–21). Paradoxically, these indications of disunity actually serve to enhance the unity of the chapter. For the narrator, the promises of seed and land are so significant that material from a range of different traditions must be enlisted in order to bear witness to them. This divergent material enables us to overhear the testimony of many witnesses to the single theme of this chapter, which is the divine promise.

These indications of literary disunity are in any case superficial in comparison to the evidence of conscious literary structuring. The chapter is

---

38. See von Rad, *Genesis*, pp. 182–83, 189–90, for a summary. Von Rad makes a questionable distinction, however, between vv.7–18 ("perhaps ancient tradition from the patriarchal period itself") and vv.1–6, which are said to belong to a later and more reflective period (p. 190). Vv.13–16 are seen as an insertion, possibly from E. For the more recent view that the chapter is late rather than early, see J. Van Seters, *The Yahwist as Historian*, pp. 248–51. Here, "J has made an important shift in emphasis from the barrenness of the matriarch and her plight – the basic form of the ancestral tradition – to that of the patriarch and his problem of having a son as heir" (p. 249).

constructed as a dialogue between Abraham and YHWH (cf. 18.22–33), and a number of verbal and thematic parallels serve to connect its two major sections, which narrate the divine confirmation of the promise of seed (vv.1–6) and of land (vv.7–21). These parallels are as follows:

(i) Both sections open with a divine self-disclosure entailing a promise. Abraham is not to fear, for "I am your shield and your very great reward" (v.1). After promises relating to Abraham's descendants (vv.4–5), a new divine self-disclosure begins in v.7: "I am YHWH [LXX: *egō eimi ho theos*], who brought you from Ur of the Chaldeans to give you this land to possess [LXX: *klēronomēsai*]."

(ii) In both parts of this divine–human dialogue, divine self-disclosure is followed by a human expression of doubt, addressed in both cases to *Adonay YHWH* (LXX: *despota* [v.2], *despota kurie* [v.8]). How can there be talk of a very great reward when Abraham has no offspring, and a slave is his heir (vv.2–3)? How is Abraham to know that he is to possess the land, and that the promise is therefore true (v.8)? These doubting questions are linked verbally by their concern with the theme of inheritance. Abraham is anxious that his slave will inherit from him (*klēronomēsei me* [v.3]), and is informed by the word or voice of the Lord that this will not be the case (*ou klēronomēsei se houtos* [v.4]). When assured that he will be given the land to inherit (*klēronomēsai* [v.7]), Abraham asks: "How shall I know that I will inherit it?" (v.8). These are virtually the only occurrences of inheritance terminology in the Abraham narrative.[39]

(iii) In both cases, Abraham's expression of doubt is answered not only by further divine words but also by a visible sign: the starry sky (v.5a), and the smoking oven and flaming torch that pass between the remains of the sacrificial victims (v.17). Although otherwise rather disparate events, they both take the form of light shining in the darkness (cf. v.17), and they both serve to confirm a divine promise which is then restated (vv.5b, 18–21).

Genesis 15 as a whole underlines the fundamental significance of the promise motif for the Abraham narrative; that is the reason for Paul's interest in both parts of this chapter. In Romans 4, Paul interprets the promise of seed in the light of Genesis 17, where it is said that Abraham will become the father of many nations. His treatment of this theme is best discussed in connection with the later chapter. In both Galatians 3 and Romans 4, however, Paul also reflects on the promise of the land or the

---

39. The exception being Genesis 21.9; 22.17 and 24.60 are not concerned specifically with inheritance from Abraham.

"inheritance" in the second part of Genesis 15, emphasizing above all the promise's irreversibility and unconditionality. His aim is to show that scripture confirms the gospel's claim that in Christ and his Spirit God has assumed total responsibility for human salvation.

In Abraham a blessing was promised to all Gentiles; the law, on the contrary, brings a curse; in his death Christ entered into the law's curse, so that the promised blessing might be poured out on the Gentiles in the gift of the Spirit (Gal.3.8–14). The death and resurrection of Christ here form the second half of a chiastic structure, correlated with the fundamental scriptural themes of promise and law. But Paul's gospel does not only speak of Christ's act. God justifies, Christ redeems, the Spirit is received: humankind is encompassed on every side by a singular yet threefold divine saving action, which brings to an end the human saving initiative ostensibly promoted by the law. Because salvation is wholly God's act, salvation is certain; even "faith" is not so much a condition of salvation as the human acknowledgment intended and elicited by God's communicative action. According to Genesis 15.6, such was the faith of Abraham: for it was only as the addressee of the divine promises, committing God unconditionally to future saving action on his behalf, that Abraham is said to have believed and to have been justified. Thus the proper name "Abraham" most naturally occurs not in the nominative but in the dative case, in sentences in which God is the implied or actual subject of an act of promising:

> Scripture... proclaimed the gospel beforehand to Abraham...
> (Gal.3.8)

> To Abraham the promises were uttered, and to his seed. (3.16)

> To Abraham God gave it through a promise. (3.18)

The scriptural testimony to the promise confirms the gospel's claim that salvation is wholly God's act. If salvation were contingent on human self-salvific action, how could salvation be promised? Paul hears in the scriptural texts God's absolute, unconditional and irreversible commitment to the future salvation of humankind. And he hears this especially clearly in Genesis 15.7–21, where God confirms the promise of the land or "inheritance" by making a unilateral "covenant" with Abraham (Gen.15.18).

One preliminary indication that Paul has Genesis 15 in mind may be seen in the unusual passive, "the promises were uttered *[errethēsan]*" (Gal.3.16), which may derive from Genesis 15.13 LXX: "And it was said *[kai errethē]* to Abram, You shall surely know that your seed will be a sojourner in a land not their own..." (The LXX has similarly substituted a passive verb for an active one in Genesis 15.6 *[elogisthē]*.) More significantly, the statement that "to Abraham the promises were uttered, and to his seed" (Gal.3.16) appears to refer primarily to the promises of the land. The question is whether a specific concern with Genesis 15.7–21 can be demonstrated. The relevant passages are as follows:

> And God said to Abram after Lot had departed from him, Lift up your eyes from the place where you now are, north and south and east and west, for all the land which you see, to you I will give it and to your seed *[kai tō spermati sou]* for ever. And I will make your seed as the dust of the earth – if anyone is able to count the dust of the earth, then your seed shall be counted. Get up, go through the land, the length and the breadth of it, for to you I will give it. (Gen.13.14–17)

> And he said to him, I am the God who brought you from the land [MT: from Ur] of the Chaldeans so as to give you this land to inherit. And he said, Master, Lord, how shall I know that I shall inherit it? (15.7–8)

> In that day God made a covenant *[dietheto diathēkēn]* with Abram, saying, To your seed I will give this land, from the river of Egypt to the great river, the river Euphrates... (15.18)

> And I will establish my covenant between me and between you and between your seed after you for ever, as an eternal covenant, to be God to you and to your seed after you. And I will give to you and to your seed after you the land in which you sojourn, the whole land of Canaan to be an eternal possession, and I will be God to them. (17.7–8)

Of these promises, the reference to "Abraham and his seed" (Gal.3.16) is clearest in Genesis 13.15 and 17.7–8. In Genesis 15, however, it is said both that God will give "you" this land to inherit and that he will give it "to your seed" (vv.7, 18), so that there is no essential difference between the different versions of this promise – although the conjunction in the phrase cited by Paul *(kai tō spermati sou)* is lacking here. In observing that "to Abraham the promises were uttered, and to his seed", Paul seems to have all these passages in mind. In the following verses, however, the plural "the promises" (Gal.3.16) is replaced by a reference to a singular "covenant" which is identified with an equally singular "promise" whose content is the divine gift of "the inheritance":

> My point is this: a covenant *[diathēkēn]* earlier ratified by God cannot be annulled by the law, which came four hundred and thirty years later: that would be to invalidate the promise. For if the inheritance *[klēronomia]* is by law, it is no longer by promise. But God gave it to Abraham by way of a promise. (Gal.3.17–18)

The use of this terminology makes it certain that Paul has Genesis 15.7–21 specifically in mind. According to Genesis 15, God promised to give

Abraham "this land to inherit" (v.7), and "made a covenant" with him (v.18). "Covenant" and "inheritance" are also central to Paul's concerns in Galatians 3.

(1) The "covenant" of which Paul speaks was ratified unilaterally by God. Since it consists in a "promise", in which God binds himself unconditionally to future action on behalf of Abraham and his seed, it cannot later be replaced by a conditional arrangement in which divine action is contingent on prior human action. Even a human legal document such as a will (*diathēkē*, again) is relatively immune from the arbitrary treatment of those who would set it aside or rewrite it (Gal.3.15). How much more is this the case when the *diathēkē* in question is God's!

Genesis 15 is the basis for this Pauline theme of the unilateral, unalterable covenant of pure promise which cannot be emended even by the law. In that chapter, the confirmation of the promise in a solemn act of divine self-disclosure – "I am YHWH, who brought you out from Ur of the Chaldeans, to give you this land to possess" (v.7) – is not good enough for Abraham, who demands an absolute guarantee that the promise is valid. In response to his demand, he is required to prepare for a covenant ceremony by dividing the carcases of sacrificial animals and setting the two parts opposite each other with a passage between them (vv.9–10). Abraham drives away the birds of prey that come to feed on the carcases (v.11), but is afterwards reduced to a state of complete passivity. There is no more dialogue, but only a divine monologue as Abraham sleeps (vv.12–16), and this is followed by the spectacle of the fiery symbols of the divine presence passing between the remains of the sacrificial animals (v.17). In the monologue, an outline is given of the future history that will lead to possession of the land; this future history centres on an act of liberation after four hundred years of slavery in Egypt. The promise of the land is repeated, but in the context of a binding covenant ceremony which now *guarantees* the truth of the promise (vv.18–21; compare the oath of Genesis 22.16, as interpreted by Hebrews 6.13–18). Abraham now knows exactly *how* the promise will be fulfilled, and he also knows for sure *that* it will be fulfilled.[40]

Comparison with a similar ritual as described by Jeremiah brings out the unilateral character of this covenant with Abraham. Jeremiah tells how, in the last days of the kingdom of Judah, King Zedekiah

> made a covenant with all the people in Jerusalem to make a proclamation of liberty to them, that everyone should set free his

---

40. What is distinctive about this passage "is that God himself enters a communal relationship with Abraham under the forms which among humans guarantee the greatest contractual security" (G. von Rad, *Genesis*, p. 187).

> Hebrew slaves, male and female, so that no-one should enslave a Jew, his brother or sister. And they obeyed, all the princes and all the people who had entered into the covenant that everyone would set free his slave, male or female, so that they would not be enslaved again; they obeyed and set them free. (Jer.34.8–10)

The prophet complains that these freed slaves have now been re-enslaved, but for our purposes it is his reference to the original covenant ceremony that is of interest. Speaking through Jeremiah, YHWH says:

> The people who transgressed my covenant and did not keep the terms of the covenant which they made before me, I will make [like] the calf which they cut in two and passed between the parts – the princes of Judah, the princes of Jerusalem, the eunuchs, the priests, and all the people of the land who passed between the parts of the calf; and I will give them into the hand of their enemies and into the hand of those who seek their lives. Their dead bodies shall be food for the birds of the air and the beasts of the earth. (Jer.34.18–20)

Those who pass between the two halves of the carcase bind themselves to a particular course of action, on pain of a fate like the slaughtered animal's if they fail to carry it out. The ceremony is an impressive though not infallible demonstration of an unconditional commitment to act – in this case, by liberating Jewish slaves. In Genesis 15, however, it is YHWH who passes between the pieces. YHWH commits himself unconditionally to liberate those who will endure four hundred years of slavery in Egypt, and to bring them to the land promised to Abraham and his seed. There is no corresponding commitment on Abraham's part (unlike the two-sided covenant of Genesis 17, where Abraham must perform the covenant ceremony of circumcision). Abraham does not pass between the pieces. He is in a deep sleep (Gen.15.12).

From Paul's perspective, this archaic story attests the fact that even God *cannot* annul or modify the unconditional commitment to future saving action enacted in the covenant ceremony (cf. Gal.3.15–18). God is so totally identified with his promise that he would cease to be God if the promise were invalidated. And that is also to say that God is God in the *fulfilment* of the promise through Christ and his Spirit, in the unconditional action in which God assumes total responsibility for the salvation of the world.

(2) Paul draws from Genesis 15 not only the identification of promise and covenant but also the theme of the "inheritance". According to Genesis 15.7, God called Abraham from the land of the Chaldeans "so as to give you this land to inherit". For Paul, the "inheritance" is the true *content* of the promise of the land: what matters is not the land of Canaan, in which he shows no theological interest, but the fact that the promise concerns an

"inheritance". This term is presumably linked in his mind to the divine "covenant" which he has just compared to a human will or testament (Gal.3.15, 17) – that is, to a legal document in which property is unilaterally transferred to the one designated as "heir", whose "inheritance" it thereby becomes. Indeed, the "inheritance" motif in Genesis 15 suggests an analogy between Abraham and God. Abraham is promised a son who will inherit his property from him (Gen.15.4; cf. 21.10, cited in Gal.4.30). Similarly, God makes a *diathēkē* with Abraham and his seed, who will inherit the land. For Paul, the promised inheritance transcends the land no less than it transcends Abraham's property. Here too, he interprets the scriptural texts not only deductively, from within, but inductively, on the basis of the reality of a salvation that has nothing to do with the land. Yet the concept of the inheritance is valuable for him as illustrating the character of salvation as a gift unconditionally promised in the divine *diathēkē*.

The confirmation of the promise by way of this covenant or testament preserves it from an arbitrary rewriting in which the gift of the inheritance comes to be hedged around with conditions. That is the problem with the law, which removes salvation from the sphere of the unconditional divine promise and makes it contingent on observance: the one who does what it commands will live thereby (Gal.3.12; Lev.18.5). Paul so emphasizes that a promise is a promise as to rule out on principle the validity of the law's conditional offer of salvation.[41] If the inheritance is by law, then it is no longer by promise – but a promise is what God gave to Abraham, and that promise must stand (Gal.3.18).[42] Yet (Paul continues) the law is not really opposed to the divine promises, for its own conditional offer of life turns

41. Crucial to this interpretation is the claim that covenant and law represent unconditional and conditional understandings of divine saving action, and that Paul's point is that these are mutually exclusive. J. L. Martyn finds here only an *assertion* of the incompatibility of covenant and law: "What the Teachers see as a monolith Paul sees as an antinomy, for the advent of Christ has removed the term 'covenant' from the Law and has attached it solely to the Abrahamic promise" (*Galatians*, p. 341). On this account, Christ simply rewrites scripture. In fact, the detachment of covenant from law occurs within the texts Paul cites or alludes to: Genesis 15 on the one hand, Leviticus 18.5 on the other. Both speak of a future divine action – the gift of the land, the bestowal of life; but in one case that action is unconditional, in the other it is dependent on observance of the commandments. This inner-scriptural antinomy is fundamental to Paul's construal of the entire shape of the Pentateuch, and it helps to shape his view of the advent of Christ.

42. When Paul writes that, "if the inheritance is from law, it is no longer from promise" (Gal.3.18), he "stakes his case on the theological axiom that salvation is always, first to last, a matter of divine initiative and grace" (J. D. G. Dunn, *Galatians*, p. 186). So the problem with the law is that it sees salvation as something other than "a matter of divine initiative and grace"? Disappointingly, "from law" is glossed as "a mind-set too narrowly focused on the law and an identity too much understood in terms of the law" (p. 187): and so a chance for

out to be unreal. If Leviticus 18.5 were to be taken at face value, so that the divine commandments were taken to be the only way to life, without the drastic corrective of Deuteronomy 27.26, the text that "shut up everything under sin" – then, and only then, the conditional law would be opposed to the unconditional promise and there would be an insoluble contradiction (Gal.3.21–22).[43] Yet, as a matter of fact and contrary to initial appearances, the law creates space for the fulfilment of the promise. Its true role is to demonstrate the impossibility of the human salvific initiative that it appears to promote, subverting its own project in order thereby to witness to the salvation of God (cf. Gal.3.21–22).

Closely related points are made in another Pauline passage dependent on Genesis 15, Romans 4.13–16. Paul here states that

> not through law was the promise to Abraham or to his seed *[ē tō spermati autou]*, that he should be heir of the world *[klēronomon kosmou]*, but through righteousness of faith. For if those who are of law are heirs, faith is nullified and the promise is destroyed. For the law works wrath; but where there is no law there is no transgression. Therefore it is by faith, so that it might be according to grace, so that the promise might be sure for all the seed...

Here, the motif of the "covenant" has disappeared. Although the law's threat to the promise is expressed in language closely resembling Galatians 3.18, the point is no longer to declare promise and law to be incompatible in principle. Rather, promise and law are incompatible in practice, because the dire effect of the law is to "work wrath". The theological point is the same as in Galatians, however: to protect the original promise from every suggestion that it has been subjected to later qualifications and stipulations – and so to affirm the unconditional certainty of a salvation that is "according to grace" *(kata charin)*, solely the act of God.

Despite the absence of the covenant theme, the link with Genesis 15 is close. In Romans 4.13, the promise is now addressed "to Abraham *or* his seed" – "or" not "and", as in Galatians 3.16 (following Genesis 13.15, 17.8). This brings Paul's statement into line with Genesis 15, where the promise of the land is addressed first to Abraham (v.7) and only later to his seed (v.18). It is primarily Abraham who is "heir to the world" (Rom.4.13), for it is he who was called forth by God "so as to give you this

---

real insight into the Pauline antithesis is missed. Dunn concludes that the scriptural basis for Paul's "theological axiom" is actually rather weak: "Paul could just about hope to get away with it" (p. 185).

43. Allusions here to the previously cited Leviticus and Deuteronomy texts are rightly noted by F. F. Bruce, *Galatians*, p. 180. Paul's construal of these texts will be considered in chapters 7, 9, where it will again be important to uncover his exegetical reasoning, rather than tracing everything back to an *a priori* christology unmediated by scripture.

earth *[tēn gēn autēn]* to inherit (Gen.15.7): Paul takes the word *gē* to refer
not to the land but to the world *(kosmos)*.[44] Finally, Abraham receives the
promise "through righteousness of faith" in the sense that his faith has just
been reckoned to him as righteousness, in the preceding verse (Gen.15.6);
Paul here seeks to hold together the two halves of Genesis 15. The first half
of the chapter shows that the promise is "by faith" (Gen.15.1–6), the
second that it is "according to grace" (Gen.15.7–21). It is the same thing
that is said from these two perspectives: that the unconditional promise is
final and definitive, and that it can never be rewritten in conditional form.

The child of promise

As with the promise of the land, the Genesis narrator allows the meaning
and scope of the promise of "seed" to unfold gradually. In Abraham's
initial call, there is no reference to his seed. Abraham is told, "I will make
you a great nation" (Gen.12.2), but it is left open how that promise is to be
fulfilled. Then, in a theophany at Shechem, he receives the promise: "To
your seed I will give this land" (Gen.12.7). The "great nation" will be
descended from Abraham himself, and not from his wider household.
When this promise is repeated at Bethel (13.3–4, 15), reference is made for
the first time to the extraordinary number of Abraham's descendants, who
will be as innumerable as the dust of the earth (13.16). In Genesis 15, the
problem of Abraham's continuing childlessness is addressed. In a further
theophany, a son is promised: "This man will not inherit from you, but one
who shall come forth from your own loins, he shall inherit from you"
(Gen.15.4). The innumerability motif is repeated, this time with a reference
to the stars in the night sky (15.5), and Abraham himself is invited to
perform the impossible task of enumeration ("Look toward heaven, and
count the stars...") – in contrast to the indefinite "... if anyone can count
the dust of the earth" (13.16). The visible existence of the innumerable
stars gives special emphasis to the promise that follows: "*Thus* shall be
your seed" (15.5). The statement that "Abraham believed God..."
confirms that the promise has here been stated in definitive form – a long-
term promise of innumerable descendants that also entails the more
immediate promise of a son and heir (15.4).

From this point on, with the exception of the Sodom and Gomorrah
episode (18.16–19.38), the Genesis narrative will be preoccupied with the
problem of Abraham's promised son (Gen.16–21). More specifically, the
question posed by the narrative is this: will the promise of a son be fulfilled
by an action undertaken on human initiative, or by a miraculous divine

---

44.   The term *kosmos* therefore has some basis in Genesis 15, and need not be explained
solely out of texts such as Sirach 44.21 (cited by Cranfield, *Romans*, 1.239, and others).

action? Abraham and Sarah both assume the need for human initiative. The narrative will show that they are mistaken.[45]

In Genesis 16, the promise of a son is seemingly fulfilled in the birth of Ishmael to Hagar and Abraham. The surrogacy arrangement is proposed by Sarah herself:

> Sara the wife of Abram did not bear to him. And she had an Egyptian slave-girl, whose name was Hagar. And Sara said to Abram, Behold, the Lord has prevented me from bearing. Go into my slave-girl, so that you may produce a child by her. And Abram obeyed the voice of Sara. (Gen.16.1–2 LXX)

Abraham was promised a son and heir (15.4) – yet Sarah still did not bear a child (16.1). Sexual intercourse may have taken place, in accordance with Abraham's belief in the divine promise (15.6), but the conception which would vindicate his believing action still did not occur. The same Lord who pointed Abraham to the stars and promised, "So shall your seed be", had closed up Sarah's womb (cf. 16.2). The narrator does not imply any criticism of the proposed surrogacy arrangements, which Sarah and Abraham enter into precisely because they believe the promise and seek its fulfilment. Similar proposals from Rachel and Leah will later produce legitimate children for Jacob (30.1–13), and – in spite of the tension between Sarah and Hagar – there is no initial reason to suppose that the child Hagar bears to Abraham will be anything other than the child of the promise. That Ishmael will be the promised son is apparently confirmed by the angelic command that Hagar should return to Sarah, although ill-treated by her, and by the extension to Hagar of the promise of innumerable descendants: "I will so greatly multiply your seed that it cannot be numbered for multitude" (16.9–10). It is natural to suppose that this multitude is the same as the multitude promised to Abraham. Abraham himself "called the name of his son, whom Hagar bore, Ishmael" (16.15) – thereby acknowledging the child as the fulfilment of the divine promise. Indeed, since it is no longer the case that "you have given me no seed" (15.3), it seems clear that the promise has been fulfilled in Ishmael.[46]

---

45. Genesis 16.1 refers to childlessness without specific reference to the promise. Yet, as von Rad notes, "the reader who has read chs. 12; 13; 15 perceives the real problem at once: the delay... of the promise that was proclaimed with such emphasis" (*Genesis*, p. 191). Genesis 16 describes an attempt to resolve this problem through human initiative and insight (p. 196). The narrator "does not want the reader to judge or condemn but simply to see and hear" (*ibid.*) – and, we may add, to reach a conclusion about the events of Genesis 16 only retrospectively, in the light of the actual fulfilment of the promise in the birth of Isaac.

46. It is therefore misleading to find here an anticipation of Genesis 17, according to which Abraham "is the father of many peoples, not only of Israel" (C. Westermann, *Genesis*

In this context, Genesis 17 has a crucial role in the unfolding of the narrative, and is not just an intrusive priestly account of the origin of the rite of circumcision. In this chapter it is shown that Ishmael is not the promised son and that the promise will instead be fulfilled by way of a miraculous divine act. Despite the great age of both parents, Abraham will be the child's father and Sarah the mother (17.15–21). It is one thing for the eighty-six-year-old Abraham to become the father of Hagar's child (16.16); it is quite another for him to become the father of a child, thirteen years later, by his wife, the ninety-year-old and previously childless Sarah. The miracle is signified by the child's name, "Isaac" ("He laughed"), which recalls the incredulous laughter of each parent on the two occasions when the birth was announced (17.17, 18.12–15) – together with Sarah's joyful laughter after the child's birth, and the mocking laughter of Ishmael (21.6, 9).[47] At the announcement that "I will bless her, and moreover I will give you a son by her", Abraham falls on his face and laughs – and appeals for Ishmael's position as the firstborn to be recognized by God (17.17–18). Sarah too laughs when, listening at the door of the tent, she overhears the Lord promising her husband that she is to give birth (18.9–15). On both occasions, the motif of incredulous laughter serves to heighten the character of the divine promise as announcing an impossibility which is nevertheless possible with God:

> And the Lord said to Abraham, Why did Sarra laugh in herself, saying, Shall I truly give birth? I have grown old! Surely no word is impossible with God *[mē adunatei para tō theō rēma]*? At this time I shall return to you at the hour, and there shall be to Sarra a son. (18.13–14 LXX)

This promise is duly fulfilled when

> the Lord visited Sarra as he said, and the Lord did for Sarra as he spoke. And, having conceived, Sarra bore to Abraham a son in his old age, at the time, as the Lord spoke to him. (21.1–2)

Isaac, then, is the child of the promise that "I shall return to you at the hour, and there shall be to Sarra a son" (18.14). As such, he is the child of the miraculous divine action that fulfils the promise. Only the divine action is referred to; there is nothing here to correspond to the earlier statement

---

12–36, p. 245). Only in retrospect does it become clear that Genesis 16 does *not* describe the fulfilment of the promise of a son (15.4); Abraham himself accepts that conclusion only with reluctance (cf. 17.18).

47. In Genesis 21.9, Sarah sees Ishmael *mṣḥq*. Since this verb refers to laughter in v.6 (x2), it must surely do so here too (so F. F. Bruce, *Galatians*, p. 223). LXX, however, has Sarah seeing Ishmael "playing *[paizonta]* with Isaak her son". Assuming that the verb has negative connotations, Paul takes this to mean that "the one born according to the flesh persecuted *[ediōken]* the one born according to the Spirit" (Gal.4.29).

that Abraham "went in to Hagar, and she conceived" (16.3). Abraham's act is subsumed in the Lord's (cf. 18.10–14, 21.1–2). In contrast, Ishmael is retrospectively seen as the child of a purely human, fleshly, non-miraculous action in which Abraham and Sarah sought to secure the fulfilment of the promise by their own initiative. Yet Abraham is at first reluctant for Ishmael to be supplanted in his role as the firstborn (17.18). Even after Isaac's birth, Sarah's demand that Hagar and Ishmael should be expelled needs the confirmation of a divine oracle:

> And Sarra saw the son of Hagar the Egyptian, whom she had borne to Abraham, playing *[paizonta]* with Isaak her son. And she said to Abraham: Throw out this slave-girl and her son; for the son of this slave-girl shall not inherit with my son Isaak. And this saying about his son seemed very hard to Abraham. But God said to Abraham, Let not this saying about the child and about the slave-girl seem hard to you. Everything that Sarra tells you, hear her voice, for in Isaak shall seed be called to you *[en Isaak klēthēsetai soi sperma]*. (21.9–12)

The child of the divine action must be clearly distinguished and separated from the child of the human action. Thus, the initial promise of a son and heir (15.4) introduces a narrative which depicts the overtaking of a human initiative in relation to the promise by the divine initiative that was always intended in the promise. The human initiative served to make the promise conditional upon itself, in response to apparent divine inaction and silence. The actuality of the divine initiative in *these* circumstances, in which a false assumption about the promise and its fulfilment seems so plausible to Abraham and Sarah, testifies to the unconditional character of the promise and the divine action that fulfils it. Ishmael represents human falsification of the divine promise – although this can only be seen retrospectively, through the promise's fulfilment in Isaac. In Ishmael, divine action is subsumed in human action; in Isaac, human action is subsumed in divine action. Yet, since Ishmael, contrary to appearances, is *not* the child of the promise, he testifies indirectly to the unconditional and irresistible divine initiative embodied in the name and person of Isaac. The expulsion of Ishmael makes it finally clear that he and Isaac are incompatible and that the fundamental difference in the circumstances of their origins cannot be evaded and must be exposed. This is the theological point expressed in Sarah's harsh demand for Ishmael's expulsion, together with its divine confirmation. Abraham must learn from Sarah, and through Sarah from God, that flesh and promise are to be differentiated.[48]

---

48. In this reading, an "allegorical" dimension is already built into the Genesis redaction, in the form of an overarching theological perspective on the traditional narrative material. A different kind of allegorical reading is proposed by Phyllis Trible, for whom "[Hagar's] story depicts oppression in three familiar forms: nationality, class, and sex" (*Texts of Terror*, p. 27).

"Flesh" and "promise" are the terms used by Paul to interpret the theological significance of Abraham's two sons:

> It is written that Abraham had two sons, one from the slave-girl and one from the free woman. But the one from the slave-girl was born according to the flesh, the one from the free woman through promise... But you, brothers and sisters, are with Isaak children of promise. But just as the one born according to the flesh persecuted the one according to the Spirit, so it is now. But what does scripture say? "Cast out the slave-girl and her son. For the son of the slave-girl shall not inherit with the son of the free woman". (Gal.4.22, 28–30)

> Not all who are of Israel are Israel, nor are all the children of Abraham his seed, but "in Isaak shall seed be called to you". That is, it is not the children of the flesh who are children of God but the children of the promise are reckoned as seed. For the word of promise is this: "At this time I shall come and there shall be to Sarra a son." (Rom.9.6b–9)

Paul here cites passages that show Isaac to be the child of the promise, and that thereby show Ishmael to be something other than that – the child of the flesh (Gen.21.10, 12; 18.10, 14).[49] In the light of the Genesis narrative, it is clear that the terms "promise" and "flesh" articulate the contrast and the conflict between divine and human initiative. Indeed, in the final expulsion of Hagar and Ishmael (Gen.21.10), the narrative *enacts* this distinction – as Paul rightly sees when he attributes the expulsion to "scripture", and not to Sarah or to God (Gal.4.30). His "allegorical" interpretation of this narrative is in fact grounded in a plausible construal of its fundamental theological intention.[50] In finding here a contrast

---

Hagar is "the faithful maid exploited, the black woman used by the male and abused by the female of the ruling class, the surrogate mother, the resident alien without legal recourse", and so on (p. 28): of course, these identifications also establish the allegorical identities of Abraham and Sarah. The question is whether the redactional subordination of traditional narratives to the overarching promise motif already makes the story of Hagar something other than a "text of terror".

49. Galatians 4.30 reproduces Genesis 21.10 LXX with only minor adjustments ("the" rather than "this" slave-girl [x2]; "the son of the free woman" rather than "my son"). In Romans 9.7, the citation from Genesis 21.12 corresponds exactly to LXX. In Romans 9.9, the first part of "the word of promise" is drawn from Genesis 18.10: Paul's *kata ton kairon touton eleusomai* abbreviates LXX's *epanastrephōn hēxō pros se kata ton kairon touton eis hōras*. The second part *(kai estai tē Sarra huios)* is identical to the conclusion of the second version of the promise, in Genesis 18.14. The conflation and the omissions are intended to make the promise as clear and unambiguous as possible. In addition, the omission of the "return" motif serves to detach the promise from its narrative context in Genesis 18.

50. In Galatians 4.21–31, Paul does not identify "flesh" with genealogical descent (which is irrelevant for his Galatian readership), and his "allegory" does not enact a platonizing erasure of Jewish particularity (contra D. Boyarin, *A Radical Jew*, pp. 32–36). In Romans 9.6–

between two different "covenants" or construals of the divine–human relationship, Paul is proposing simply that the Genesis narrative be read with full theological seriousness. When he asks his readers, "Tell me, you who wish to be under law, do you not hear the law?" (Gal.4.21), he is inviting them to participate with him in a responsible interpretation of this text. He does not regard the text as a pretext for a free interpretative fantasia. He does not draw from it cheap debating points, in the hope of persuading impressionable readers to return to a gospel that is in principle independent of the scriptural texts to which appeal is made.[51]

The slave-girl who gives birth according to the flesh and the free woman who gives birth through promise are, allegorically speaking, two covenants – "one from Mount Sinai giving birth into slavery, which is Hagar" (Gal.4.24). "Hagar", or the Sinai covenant, gives birth according to the flesh (vv.23, 28) and into slavery (vv.24, 25). In Genesis 16–21, she and her son represent the possibility that human initiative is a necessary precondition for the fulfilment of the promise – a possibility that the narrative initially appears to endorse (Gen.16) but subsequently excludes, as it becomes clear that God's promise is an unconditional commitment to specific future action on behalf of the addressee. If that is what is intended in Paul's contrast between birth "according to the flesh" and "through promise", then the Sinai covenant must represent human action as the precondition for divine saving action, as Hagar does. That point is not explicitly made here, where it is said of the Sinai covenant only that it results in slavery (vv.24, 25). This failure to provide an adequate explanation of the Hagar/Sinai correspondence is perhaps responsible for the mistaken impression that this allegorical interpretation is arbitrary and artificial.

Yet Paul does provide the necessary explanation elsewhere in Galatians. Ishmael was born "according to the flesh" (4.23, 28), and a correlation between the Sinai covenant and "flesh" is suggested by Galatians 3.2–3:

9, genealogy is more to the fore – but in the context of a rethinking of the biblical concept of election. Inability to find Plato in Romans 9 is not just a product of theological prejudice (see *ibid.*, p. 28).

51. It is unlikely that Paul here responds to the use of the Hagar story made by his opponents, as argued by C. K. Barrett ("The Allegory of Abraham, Sarah, and Hagar in the Argument of Galatians", reprinted in his *Essays on Paul*, pp. 154–70). Barrett claims that "this is a part of the Old Testament that Paul would have been unlikely to cite of his own accord", since "its plain, surface meaning supports not Paul but the Judaizers" (p. 162). It is not explained why the Judaizers should have wished to identify the Galatians as descendants of Abraham through Ishmael, thereby undermining the crucial distinction between Jew and Gentile. The reference to Arabia (Gal.4.25; cf. 1.17) may suggest that the Isaac/Ishmael relationship is a distinctively Pauline concern. For the connection between Ishmaelites and Arabs, see also *Jubilees* 20.13.

> This is what I want to learn from you: did you receive the Spirit by
> works of law or by the hearing of faith? Are you so foolish? Beginning in
> the Spirit, are you now completed in the flesh?

This contrast between "faith" and "works of law" leads to the assertion
that "the law is not of faith, but 'the one who does these things shall live by
them'" (Gal.3.12; Lev.18.5). The Sinai covenant announces that human
observance of its requirements is the necessary precondition for the "life"
that God intends for his people. God's promise remains hypothetical and
inert until it is activated by appropriate human conduct: that for Paul is
the claim of the Sinai covenant, and it is already represented in the figure
of Hagar.[52]

Naturally, the typological parallel is not exact. Unlike the advocates of
"works of law", Abraham and Hagar are not impelled by a divine
command in acting as they do. Indeed, the parallel would hardly be
apparent at all, were it not for a common relation to the unconditional
divine promise. As we have seen, Paul believes that in Christ God has now
fulfilled the unconditional promise given to Abraham. It follows that, in
scripture, "promise" rather than "law" is the definitive mode of divine
address: for "law" would make the promise's fulfilment contingent on the
practice of "works of law", and would thereby undermine its unconditional character. The scriptural problematic of promise and law is thus the
story of Abraham and his two sons writ large; conversely, the Genesis
narrative encapsulates the inner-scriptural anomaly of the two incommensurable covenants. One covenant represents the beginning and the end, the
promise and its fulfilment, whereas the other occupies the space in
between, seeking the promise's fulfilment in a human initiative that ends
only in exclusion. The structure of salvation history, as outlined in
Galatians 3, is already foreshadowed in Genesis 15–21.[53]

---

52. Paul's "allegorical" interpretation of the Hagar story (Gal.4.24–31) follows a
summary of its "literal" sense in which the two basic antitheses – slave/free, flesh/promise –
are introduced (4.22–23). In Genesis 16, Hagar's status as "slave-girl" (*paidiskē* or *šphh*: 16.1,
2, 3, 5, 6, 8) always corresponds to that of Sarah as her "mistress" (*kuria* or *gbrh*: 16.4, 8, 9). It
is hardly the case that "the emphasis on [Sarah's] free status . . . is brought to the story by Paul
himself" (R. Hays, *Echoes of Scripture*, p. 113). Similarly, the promise/flesh antithesis is
recognizably a summary of precisely the passages that Paul cites or alludes to, here or
elsewhere (cf. Gen.15.4–6, 16.1–4, 18.9–15, 21.1–2). There is nothing inherently implausible
about the idea that a particular scriptural narrative might encapsulate a pattern writ large in
scripture as a whole. For these reasons, Paul's interpretation of the story of Abraham's two
sons should not be regarded as a "strong misreading" that can only have derived from an
"ironic sensibility" (*ibid.*, pp. 115, 112). Underlying that assessment is the assumption that the
Torah itself is a monolith, and that a somewhat perverse readerly ingenuity is the true source
of the anomalies Paul claims to find in it.

53. While Galatians 4.21–31 can be seen as a summary of chapter 3, it also continues to
preserve the scriptural order in its use of Genesis material. In Galatians 3–4 Paul "begins . . . ,

Father of many nations

In Genesis 17, the promise of the land – solemnly confirmed by the unilateral covenant of chapter 15 – is again repeated, with the additional promise that it will be "an everlasting possession" (17.8). Similarly, the promise of a son is repeated, although it is now added that the ninety-year-old Sarah is to be the mother (17.15–17), and that the child's name is to be Isaac (17.19, 21). Ishmael is thus disqualified from being Abraham's heir, as Eliezer of Damascus was in the earlier chapter (17.18–21, 15.2–4). The promise of a son is again closely connected to the motif of the innumerable descendants (cf. 15.5, 13.16).

At this point, however, a remarkable and unexpected development takes place – one that is seized on by Paul, in Romans 4. In the earlier chapters of the Abraham narrative, the promise of seed and the promise of land are closely correlated (12.7, 13.15–16, 15.1–21). In the outline of future history disclosed to Abraham in a vision (15.12–16), his descendants are clearly identified as the people who are to leave Egyptian oppression and return to claim their rightful heritage in the land of Canaan. The promises are seen as the underlying dynamic of the ongoing scriptural narrative, culminating in the conquest of the land under Joshua; they are expounded by, and contained within, the unfolding of the narrative. It is all the more remarkable that in Genesis 17 the innumerability motif breaks out of this narrative containment, as the descendants like the dust of the earth or the stars in the sky come to be identified not with the people of Israel but with the "many nations" of which Abraham is now said to be the father. This relationship is so fundamental to Abraham's identity that it is inscribed in the new name now bestowed on him, by which in future he is to be known:

> I will make my covenant between me and you, and I will multiply you greatly... As for me, my covenant is with you, and you shall be father of a multitude of nations/Gentiles *[patēr plēthous ethnōn]*. And no longer shall your name be called Abram, but your name shall be Abraham, for a father of many nations/Gentiles have I made you *[patera pollōn ethnōn tetheika se]*. And I shall increase you exceedingly, and establish you as nations *[eis ethnē]*, and kings shall come forth from you. And I will establish my covenant between me and you and your seed after you, to their generations, as an eternal covenant, to be God to

as Abraham begins, with promises, and he ends..., as Abraham ends, with sons" (C. A. Stockhausen, "The Principles of Pauline Exegesis", p. 149); compare also Romans 4.1–25, 9.6–9, and note the insertion of a "mid-point" into the story in Galatians 3.15–18 (alluding to Genesis 15.7–21) and Romans 4.9–12 (alluding to Genesis 17.9–14). If there is a "narrative substructure" in Galatians 3–4, it is to be found in the use of scriptural material and not in Paul's "narrative christological formulations" (*pace* R. Hays, *The Faith of Jesus Christ*, pp. 85–137).

you and to your seed after you. And I will give to you and to your seed after you the land in which you sojourn, all the land of Canaan to be your everlasting possession, and I will be their God. (Gen.17.2, 4–8)

This passage is anomalous in at least three ways. (1) The repeated reference to the "many nations" is left unexplained; (2) this new motif conflicts with the already established link between "seed" and "land", which is also found here; and (3) it also conflicts with the institution of the exclusive covenant sign of circumcision, which reinforces the identification of Abraham's seed with the people of Israel (17.9–14, 22–27). It is as if the innumerable seed motif has been divided down the middle, like the sacrificial animals of the earlier covenant ceremony. A "seed" is still promised, which will inherit the land of Canaan, but "innumerability" now takes the form of the "multitude of nations" of which Abraham will be the "father". According to Paul, it is the gospel that can make these anomalies fruitful for interpretation.

(1) No explanation is given of the repeated reference to the "many nations" of which Abraham is to be father.[54] A connection might perhaps be made with the promise of Genesis 12.3 that "in you shall all families of the earth be blessed/bless themselves" – looking forward as it does to an eschatological horizon that still lies beyond the Genesis narrator. The "multitude of nations" cannot be linked with Abraham's children by Hagar or Keturah (Gen.25.1–6, 12–18), for Sarah is identified as the "mother of nations", her own new name corresponding to the unanticipated role just as Abraham's does (17.15–16).[55] From the standpoint of the history of traditions, it is possible that the universalizing trend of this language developed out of statements of more limited scope, corresponding perhaps to the promise to Ishmael: "I will bless him and make him fruitful and multiply him exceedingly; he shall be the father of twelve princes, and I will make him a great nation" (17.20, cf. 25.12–18). If so, however, the universalizing development of this more limited language of blessing and fruitfulness would still not be

---

54. LXX's *patēr plēthous ethnōn* (v.4) and *patera pollōn ethnōn* (v.5) correspond to MT's *'b hmwn gwym* (*hmwn* = "crowd", "throng", "host"). In v.5, the etymology (*'brhm* = *'b-hmwn*) is hardly any more intelligible in Hebrew than in Greek. The "many nations" motif cannot be derived from Abram's new name.

55. This rules out Westermann's claim that Abraham is "the father of nations including the nation of Ishmael" (*Genesis 11–36*, p. 261). The suggestion of a gradual expansion in the scope of Abraham's significance is, however, apposite: "In the old patriarchal narratives he is the father in every aspect of the family realm; he then becomes the father of a people, and P elevates this further to the father of nations ..." (*ibid.*).

explained.[56] The closest analogy is to be found in the blessing, "Be fruitful and multiply", addressed to the first humans at their creation and renewed after the Flood (1.28, 9.9).[57] Abraham and Sarah inherit the blessing of Adam and Eve, Noah and his sons – but there is no explanation as to how this can be the case. Abraham's new name is a riddle awaiting a solution.[58]

(2) In the canonical form of the Genesis text, it is the innumerability motif of chapter 15 that provides the immediate background to the "many nations" theme of chapter 17. Although the two accounts of a divine covenant with Abraham represent originally independent traditions or distinct strata, it is the text in its final, canonical form that is the object of interpretation; it is therefore appropriate to see the earlier and the later texts as representing successive stages in the gradual unfolding of the promises. When Paul claims that the promise, "Thus shall be your seed" means the same as, "A father of many nations I have made you" (Rom.4.17–18; Gen.15.5, 17.5), he can justifiably argue that, in the text as it stands, God's pointing Abraham to the innumerable stars in the sky anticipates the universalizing promise of Genesis 17. The problem with this interpretative move is that it breaks the link between the promises of seed and of land. But this link is placed under severe strain within Genesis 17 itself. The first reference here to Abraham's "seed" follows without a break from the announcement that Abram is henceforth to be "Abraham", the father of a multitude of nations. In this context, the promise that "I will establish my covenant between me and you and your seed after you . . ." (v.7) would seem to identify Abraham's "seed" with the "many nations" of which he is to be the father. The terms "father" and "seed" obviously correspond to one another: if *A* is the father of *B*, then *B* is the seed of *A*. Yet, however obvious and inescapable this correspondence might seem, it is undermined by the reassertion in the following verse of the connection

56.   According to Paul Williamson, this motif may be a variant of the universal blessing theme elsewhere (Gen.12.3; 18.18; 22.18) – a view that "enjoy[s] the support of apostolic exegesis" (*Abraham, Israel and the Nations*, p. 166. This would not solve the anomaly of the relationship between the many nations, the seed and the land. The text has the semantic potential for "apostolic exegesis", but this potential can also be realized in other ways – as we shall see in the following chapter.

57.   As W. Eichrodt notes, the Priestly writer's account of the covenant with Noah "shows the universalist character of his faith" (*Theology of the Old Testament*, 1.58). Eichrodt speaks of the covenants with Noah and with Abraham as concentric circles, "the Noah covenant for the whole human race and the Abraham covenant for Israel alone" (*ibid.*). In the "father of many nations" motif in Genesis 17, an element that might seem to belong to the outer circle unexpectedly occurs in the inner circle.

58.   This element in the older tradition "is given by P conscientiously but as though under seal" (G. von Rad, *Genesis*, p. 200).

between seed and land: "I will give to you and to your seed after you the land in which you sojourn, all the land of Canaan to be your everlasting possession" (17.8). It is as if the "seed" motif (v.7) is pulled in two opposite directions, by the "many nations" motif on the one hand (v.6) and the "land of Canaan" motif on the other (v.8).[59]

(3) In Genesis 17, the promise that "you shall be the father of a multitude of nations" (v.4) is an elaboration of the initial promise that "I will make my covenant between me and you, and I will multiply you exceedingly" (v.2). The new name (v.5) appears to confirm that the covenant will concern the "many nations". Yet, in later references to this "covenant", it is linked not with the many nations but with Abraham's seed, who will possess not only the land of Canaan (vv.7–8) but also the mark of circumcision as the normative sign of the covenant (vv.9–14). The initial apparently universal scope of God's covenant with Abraham gives way to a covenant sign which radically demarcates Abraham's seed from all other nations. The anomalous differentiation between the many nations and Abraham's seed is reinforced by the addition of circumcision to possession of the land as a distinguishing characteristic of the seed of Abraham. Divergent usage of the term "covenant" underlines the contradiction. The covenant is embodied in the bestowal of the new name, "Abraham", that makes Abram the father of many nations (vv.4–5), but it is also embodied in the rite of circumcision:

> This is the covenant which I make between me and you and your seed after you, to their generations: every male among you shall be circumcised. And you shall be circumcised [in] the flesh of your foreskin *[tēn sarka tēs akrobustias humōn]*, and it shall be as a sign *[en semeiō]* of the covenant between me and you ... An uncircumcised male, who is not circumcised in the flesh of his foreskin on the eighth day, that person shall be cut off from his people, because he has destroyed my covenant. (Gen.17.10–11, 14)

This covenant appears to assign contradictory roles to Abram. He is to be "Abraham", father of a multitude of nations; but he is also to institute the "sign" of circumcision, thereby differentiating his own household, and the embryonic nations it contains, from all other nations. The name and the sign are at odds with each another.

Unlike other contemporary Jewish readers of Genesis, Paul noticed these anomalies and found them theologically significant. Reference is made to Genesis 17 in each of the two main sections of Romans 4, and in both cases the point at issue is the universal scope of the pattern established by

59.   John Van Seters notes that the writer of Genesis 17 "take[s] for granted the emphasis on the land promise in Gen.15.7–21 and merely summarize[s] it in 17.8 in his own way" (*Abraham in History and Tradition*, p. 289).

Abraham's righteousness-by-faith. In the second part of the chapter, where faith is correlated with the divine promise that evokes it, the promise, "Thus shall your seed be" (Gen.15.5; Rom.4.18) is assimilated to the later promise, "I have made you father of many nations/Gentiles" (Gen.17.5; Rom.4.17). The text from Genesis 17 here points to the universal implications of God's dealings with Abraham, much as the promise of universal blessing (Gen.12.3) does in Galatians. In the first part of Romans 4, where Abraham's righteousness-by-faith is differentiated from a righteousness-by-works, Genesis 17 poses a problem, since it appears to confine Abraham's blessing to those who are circumcised as he was (Rom.4.9–12). This chapter proves to be a positive resource in Romans 4.13–25, where Genesis 17.5 demonstrates the universal scope of the earlier reference to Abraham's "seed", but a problem in Romans 4.9–12, where the institution of circumcision as the "sign" of the covenant (Gen.17.11) is an obstacle to be overcome. In both cases, Paul's exegetical argument turns on the relationship between Genesis 17 and Genesis 15 (Rom.4.9–12, 17–18). The result is an exegetical *tour de force*.

In more detail, Paul's specific exegetical decisions may be analysed as follows:

(1) The institution of circumcision as the sign of the covenant has the effect of dividing Abraham's life into two parts, the period when he was uncircumcised *(en akrobustia)* and the period when he was circumcised *(en peritomē)*. Since circumcision as the signifier of the covenant has the effect of marking the foreskin as the signifier of that which is outside the covenant, the divine absence as opposed to the divine presence, the sign of circumcision retrospectively reconstitutes Abraham's past as standing under the signifier of the foreskin. In Genesis 17, the connotations of the term "foreskin" are overwhelmingly negative. "The flesh of the foreskin" is what must be destroyed if one is not to be destroyed oneself. It must be surrendered as a vicarious sacrifice for the well-being of the rest of the body. To be *en akrobustia*, then, is not to be in a state of nature which must subsequently be perfected by the grace of circumcision. To be *en akrobustia* is to be in a state opposed to grace and subject to the wrath of God. Thus, the early chapters of the Abraham narrative must be reread from the perspective of Genesis 17, which retrospectively imposes the negative sign of the foreskin on the protagonist of those chapters. If Abraham becomes a Jew in Genesis 17, then his former life becomes that of a Gentile. What is astonishing, for Paul, is that it is precisely this uncircumcised Gentile of whom it is said that "he believed God, and it was reckoned to him as

righteousness". This is remarkable above all for what it implies about God. God, it seems, is "the one who justifies the ungodly" (Rom.4.5).[60]

To put this point differently, Paul as a reader of Genesis is struck by the *belatedness* of the institution of circumcision (Rom.4.10). Circumcision does not stand at the beginning of the journey that Abraham undertakes with God, it occurs twenty-four years after he has obeyed the divine call to leave family and homeland (Gen.12.4, 17.1). It cannot be said that circumcision marks the culmination or completion of this journey, as though what had previously been imperfect were here perfected. On the contrary, the perfection of what had previously been imperfect has already taken place, not less than thirteen years earlier (cf. Gen.16.16), on the occasion when Abraham, contemplating the starry sky, heard the divine word, "Thus shall be your seed", and believed it – and God reckoned it to him as righteousness. From the chronology of Genesis Paul learns that uncircumcision does not debar one from righteousness. The circumcised Abraham does not become more righteous than he had been before, for righteousness is not a matter of degree but issues from a definitive, unsurpassable divine declaration.

If it was an uncircumcised, ungodly Gentile whom God justified, then it is no longer so implausible to suppose that the blessing that David pronounces on the forgiven extends beyond the circle of the circumcised (cf. Rom.4.9–12).

(2) Abraham received the "sign of circumcision" as a "seal of the righteousness of faith which occurred in uncircumcision" (Rom.4.11). The term "sign" (*sēmeion*) alludes to Genesis 17.11, where it is said that "you shall be circumcised [in] the flesh of your foreskin and it shall be as a sign of the covenant [*en sēmeiō diathēkēs*] between me and you". For Paul, the "covenant" of which circumcision is a "sign" is the covenant that God made with Abraham when he was justified by faith (Gen.15.6, 18) – an event that he will shortly refer to as "the promise to Abraham [and] to his seed, that he should be heir of the world" (Rom.4.13; cf. Gal.3.15–18). So belated is the sign of circumcision, in relation to the righteousness of faith that it signifies, that it does not undermine the primary association between the righteousness of faith and uncircumcision *(akrobustia)*, asserted no less than four times in Romans 4.10–12. This interpretation of the "sign" of circumcision might seem to conflict with the text of Genesis 17, in which the "covenant" is simultaneous with the "sign" and is quite distinct from the covenant of Genesis 15, with its reference to the

---

60. As B. Byrne notes, "Paul has depicted Abraham in such a way as to make the 'Gentile' stance before God the norm rather than the exception" (*Romans*, p. 148).

righteousness of faith. Paul's point, however, is that – whatever the text may seem to say – the rite of circumcision *cannot* establish a fundamentally new basis for the divine–human relationship, since this new basis has already been established *en akrobustia*. Circumcision cannot change Abraham's status before God, because that status has already been determined once for all.[61]

(3) In Genesis 17.4–5, Abraham receives his new name as "the father of a multitude of nations". Nowhere else in the Abraham narrative is there any reference to his role as "father" of his descendants, and the seven references to Abraham as "father" in Romans 4 all derive from this chapter of Genesis. Having rejected the possibility that Abraham's circumcision altered his relationship with God, Paul now discovers a more positive correlation between Genesis 15 and 17.

Abraham, according to Paul, is "the father of us all – as it is written: I have made you father of many Gentiles..." (Rom.4.16–17; Gen.17.5). That was essentially the promise that Abraham believed when his faith was reckoned as righteousness: for the promise of a seed as innumerable as the stars in the sky must be identified with the promise that he would be father of many Gentiles (Rom.4.18). Abraham is "father of us all" in the sense that he is

> the father of all who believe in a state of uncircumcision, so that righteousness is reckoned to them, and the father of circumcision to those who are not of circumcision alone but who also walk in the footsteps of the faith of our father Abraham while he was uncircumcised. (4.11–12)[62]

In these references to Abraham's fatherhood, Paul connects his initial association of the righteousness of faith and *akrobustia* with the promise of Genesis 17.5, that "I will make you father of many Gentiles" – so anomalous in a passage that identifies Abraham's "seed" by reference to the land and circumcision, and yet so important that Abraham must receive a new name which identifies him with this role. Abraham can be "father of many Gentiles", of a seed as innumerable as the stars in the sky, because, as a Gentile himself, he believed the promise that announced God's action on his behalf – and it was reckoned to him as righteousness. It is as the ungodly, uncircumcised Gentile who was justified by faith that

61. The chronology of the Abraham narrative can also lead to non-Pauline conclusions, however. According to *Genesis Rabbah* 46.2.2, circumcision was instituted "so that Isaac in particular [as opposed to Ishmael] should be born of holy seed" (cited by P. Williamson, *Abraham, Israel and the Nations*, p. 28).
62. The translation ignores the impossible *tois* preceding *stoichousin*; on this point see Cranfield, *Romans*, 1.237.

Abraham can be a "father" – the normative scriptural exemplar – to other Gentile believers. As one who subsequently submitted to circumcision, Abraham can also be father and exemplar to circumcised believers. These Christian Jews must acknowledge that the decisive event in his life took place while he was still uncircumcised. Yet this does not deprive their circumcision of significance: it remains the case that the value of being a Jew and circumcised is "much in every way", and that being entrusted with the oracles of God is the primary indication of that value (cf. Rom.3.1–2).[63]

(4) Paul argues on the basis of Genesis 17 that Abraham's justification by faith is unaffected by his subsequent, belated submission to circumcision, and that this decisive earlier event enables him to serve as "father" or normative exemplar to both Gentile and Jewish believers. A correlation is discovered between the *content* of the divine promise that Abraham believed and the *scope* of the pattern that he thereby established. He believed that he would become the father of many Gentiles, and it is precisely this believing that actually makes him the father of many Gentiles. The promise is already fulfilled in principle in the belief that it elicits. Yet for Paul the promise to Abraham must also be an anticipation of the gospel, in which what is proclaimed is not the human act of believing but the definitive divine act for the salvation of the world, which is the resurrection of Jesus. The promise that God will make Abraham father of many Gentiles must anticipate the gospel's announcement that God has raised Jesus from the dead.

Paul finds the basis for this connection in the scriptural reference to the great age of the parents to whom the child Isaac was promised (Gen.17.17). Although Abraham's fatherhood of many nations is a non-physical relationship, Paul retains the scriptural assumption that the birth of a child to Abraham and Sarah is crucial to the fulfilment of the promise of "seed" or of "many Gentiles". Thus the deadness of Abraham's own

---

63. In Galatians, unlike Romans, Paul does not integrate the issue of circumcision into his scriptural argument – although this argument (Gal.3.6–5.1) is enclosed within passages relating to circumcision (Gal.2.3–12; 5.2–12; 6.11–16). There is no evidence that Genesis 17 played any part in the Galatian debate – in spite of repeated assertions to the contrary (*e.g.* B. Longenecker, *The Triumph of Abraham's God*, pp. 129–30). In Galatia the issue of circumcision seems to have been symptomatic of a general desire to conform more closely to Jewish practices (cf. 4.10, 21; 5.4), whether this was inspired by Christian Jewish teachers from outside Galatia or by Galatian Christians wishing for better relations with local Jewish communities. For the latter possibility, compare the view of Mark Nanos that "the influencers are involved in welcoming non-Jewish guests into Galatian Jewish communities within which the Christ-believing subgroups assemble" (*The Irony of Galatians*, p. 14). It is perhaps more likely that it is Galatian Gentile Christians who are advocating circumcision (so J. Munck, *Paul and the Salvation of Mankind*, pp. 87–134) – but with a view to relations with local Jews, as Nanos suggests.

body and of Sarah's womb must be overcome by the divine life-giving action. When Abraham believes the divine promise that "I will make you father of many Gentiles", he thereby believes in the God who gives life to the dead – as is evident from two parallel paraphrases of "Abram believed God" (Gen.15.6):

... before the God in whom he believed, who gives life to the dead and calls non-beings into being... (Rom.4.17)

... who, against hope and in hope, believed that he would be father of many Gentiles... (Rom.4.18)

The dead to whom God gives life are in the first instance Abraham and Sarah themselves (cf. v.19), and this establishes a crucial analogy between Abraham's faith and Christian faith in the God "who raised Jesus our Lord from the dead" (v.24).[64] The scriptural reference to the advanced age of Abraham and Sarah establishes that the birth of the promised child must be a miracle of divine creativity (Gen.17.15–21) – which Paul interprets as a raising of the dead.

There is therefore a christological component in Paul's complex appeal to Abraham as exemplar, as well as an ecclesiological and a soteriological one. Genesis 15.6 is the fundamental and unsurpassable soteriological statement that Paul finds in the Abraham narrative, and its ecclesiological implications come to light as he demonstrates its universal normativity. But the normativity of Abraham does not rest in his faith *per se* but in his faith as the acknowledgment elicited by the promise of future divine saving action on his behalf. The promise that Abraham believed refers most directly to the universal scope of the future divine action, but as the promise of the God who gives life to the dead it also anticipates the message of the God of the gospel. Those who follow in the footsteps of Abraham believe as he did, in the sense that they believe in the same God: the God of the promise who is also the God of the life-giving action that fulfils the promise.[65]

In Paul's reading of the Abraham narrative, its fundamental theme is the divine promise that elicits Abraham's believing response. Abraham's belief was reckoned as righteousness not because of an arbitrary divine decision but because belief is the response intended in the divine promise itself – as with any other promise. For the act of promise-making to occur at all, a promise must be regarded by its addressee as *credible*; and it is the

---

64. So Barrett, *Romans*, p. 99. The double reference to "deadness" in v.19 already has Jesus' resurrection in view.

65. In that sense, Abraham's faith is already Christian faith (so K. Berger, "Abraham in den paulinischen Hauptbriefe", p. 72).

responsibility of the promiser to ensure the credibility of his or her promise. A promise must ensure its own credibility because its intention is to establish a relationship between promiser and addressee based on the addressee's confidence in the future action on his or her behalf declared in the promise. Abraham's faith, then, is nothing other than his acknowledgment of a divine address in which God commits himself unconditionally to future action on his behalf, with the intention that he should henceforth live in the light of that assured future. All of the themes that Paul derives from the Abrahamic promises – the opening to Gentiles of Abraham's blessing, the inheritance, the child of promise, the promise of the "many nations" – converge on this single point: that Abraham exemplifies the way of life enabled by a divine speech-act in which unconditional divine saving action is announced. This way of life is normative for all people, Gentile and Jew alike, because the original promise and the divine communicative action that has now fulfilled it are addressed to all people alike. Human life is to be lived on the basis of the gospel's announcement that Jesus is Lord of all and that God raised him from the dead: that is the divine word that Paul hears in the Genesis narrative. The "ecclesiological" reference to the inclusion of the Gentiles is not an independent theme but is a consequence of the universal scope of the once promised and now realized divine saving action. Paul does not emphasize the reference of the promise to the Gentiles because he knows in advance that a more inclusive Judaism is to be preferred to an exclusive one. The inclusiveness that Paul proclaims is not an abstract principle but a divine action with universal scope: the raising of Jesus.

Paul's "theocentric" focus on the unconditional divine saving action announced in promise and gospel does not exclude human action – as though divine activity necessarily entailed human passivity. Abraham's faith is far from passive. It represents a way of life enabled by, grounded in, and responsive to the divine announcement of an act in which God takes total responsibility for ultimate human well-being. For that reason, however, the divine promise definitively excludes all possibility that its realization may be contingent upon human action or "works", even if these are in themselves desirable and appropriate. God's promise is truly a promise: it is "of faith" *(ek pisteōs)* and "according to grace" *(kata charin)*, and it is therefore certain, a sure foundation rather than a probable or doubtful hypothesis (cf. Rom.4.16). Its unconditional character is highlighted within Genesis itself by the theme of Abraham's two sons, one born of human initiative and the other by divine power. Paul finds in this story an allegory or parable that legitimates his own attempts to present the promise as genuinely prior to and other than the law.

Although Paul's reading of Genesis can claim to be grounded in the realities of the scriptural text, it is of course possible to read the text differently. It might be read in such a way that the divine promise fades into the background in order to highlight the faithfulness, piety and heroism of Abraham himself. Paul's attempt to differentiate promise and law in his reading of this text takes place in full awareness of an alternative reading – from his standpoint, a misreading – in which promise and law are not so sharply differentiated. Indeed, his own reading may be characterized as a *counter-reading*, a reading directed against a prior reading in which Abraham is *not* seen primarily as the addressee of the divine promise. In Paul's reading of Genesis, the scriptural text is read *against* some at least of its former readers. It is to this characterization of Paul's reading as a reading-against that we turn in the chapter that follows.

Chapter 5

Genesis (2)

According to one possible telling of Israel's story, the Genesis narratives trace Israel's existence back to the obedience and faithfulness of the original addressee of God's command and promise. This might be described as an anthropocentric reading of Genesis, in which attention is focused on the actions of Abraham himself, in response to the divine word. In Paul's theocentric reading, the fundamental dynamic of these stories is that of the divine agency.[1] The possibility of the alternative, anthropocentric reading of the Abrahamic narratives is alluded to at the beginning of Romans 4:

> What then shall we say that Abraham, our forefather according to the flesh, has found? For if Abraham was justified by works, he has grounds for boasting – but not with God: for what does the scripture say? "Abraham believed God, and it was reckoned to him as righteousness." (Rom.4.1–3)

Paul here acknowledges, if only hypothetically, that his claim that Abraham exemplifies a righteousness without works and without boasting might be contested. The questioner who asks about "Abraham, our forefather according to the flesh" is "of the seed of Abraham", like Paul himself (Rom.11.1), and he invokes Abraham as a potential scriptural disproof of the Pauline thesis of a righteousness by faith and without works or boasting.[2] For his questioner or critic, Paul's thesis is refuted by the case of Abraham, whose righteousness before God was established by

---

1. The terms "anthropocentric" and "theocentric" are used here for heuristic reasons, and do not imply a value judgment. These terms are only approximations, and they identify general tendencies in the texts rather than inflexible dogmatic positions.

2. Assuming that "Abraham our forefather according to the flesh" is the correct reading, the phraseology of Paul's objector is a variation on the more common "Abraham our father". By the time of the *Mishnah*, this has become the standard appellation for Abraham: see *mTaan.* 2.4, 5; *mKidd.* 4.14 (x2); *mAb.* 3.12; 5.2, 3 (x2), 6, 19 (x4); cf. *mNed.* 3.11 ("seed of Abraham"); *mBaKa* 8.6, *mBaMe* 7.1 ("sons of Abraham"). Apart from two scriptural citations, there are in the *Mishnah* only two unqualified references to "Abraham" (*mAb.* 5.2, 6.10). Particularly relevant to Romans 4.1–5 are *mKiddushin* 4.14: "We find that Abraham our father had performed the whole law before it was given, for it is written, 'Because Abraham

works of obedience and faithfulness that give him legitimate grounds for glory and pride, and who thereby serves as a model for those who are privileged to name him as "our forefather". Abraham's righteousness is his endorsement not merely by human opinion but by God, and his endorsement by his own children echoes that divine endorsement. That God acknowledged Abraham's righteousness was no more than his due – unlike the more normal case of the next scriptural figure to whom Paul refers, David, who was righteous only on the basis of the forgiveness of sins. In the exceptional but still exemplary case of Abraham, there was no sin to be forgiven, no forgiving mercy to be exercised.

What were Abraham's "works"? Paul does not identify them specifically as "works of law". Although "works" is correlated with "law" in Romans 3.20–28, the references in Romans 4.2–5 to "works" and "working" stand on their own, and "law" does not recur until 4.13–16. The hypothesis that "Abraham was justified by works" sees his life as a series of acts of obedience to divine commands addressed specifically to him, and not just as anticipating the pattern of life revealed to Moses at Sinai and required of all Israel. Thus in Romans 4.4 the concept of "working" is analysed without specific reference to the Mosaic law:

> To one who works the reward is not reckoned as a gift but as his due.

In this quite general, everyday image, "working" takes place at the behest of another, who must recompense work satisfactorily accomplished in accordance with the initial specification. Applied to Abraham, the image suggests that Abraham accomplishes tasks imposed on him by his divine employer and is therefore entitled to "reward" or payment – which consists here simply in the acknowledgment of his righteousness in doing what he is commanded to do. Some of the actions or abstentions required of him may coincide with the Law of Moses, but others will not.

If Abraham's works are his acts of obedience to divine commands addressed specifically to him, then the claim that he was justified by works represents a specific reading of the scriptural narrative. On this reading, the Abraham narrative tells a story of human obedience to the divine command; only on that basis is it also a story of promise and fulfilment. At every point in the narrative from which Paul draws a divine promise, his critic might have found an act of obedience. The Genesis narrative will be read one way if its theme is taken to be the divine promise, another way if its supposed purpose is to commemorate the faithful obedience of Abraham. In turning now to some actual non-Pauline readings of the

---

obeyed my voice and kept my charge, my commandments, my statutes, and my laws' [Gen.26.5]"; and *Aboth*, 5.3: "With ten temptations was Abraham our father tempted, and he stood steadfast in them all, to show how great was the love of Abraham our father."

Abraham narrative, we shall ask how far they correspond to the hypothetical reading that Paul rejects.

Works of Faithful Obedience

Like Paul, the author of *Jubilees* seeks for a single key to this part of the scriptural narrative, but finds it not in Genesis 15.6 but in Genesis 22.1: "After these things God tested Abraham..." In Genesis, Abraham passes the test by demonstrating his willingness to sacrifice his son, and his faithful obedience is acknowledged: "Now I know that you fear God, seeing that you have not withheld your beloved son from me" (Gen.22.12). In *Jubilees*, however, the binding of Isaac is not a genuine "test" at all, but a divine demonstration of Abraham's faithfulness in order to confute "the prince Mastema", who plays here exactly the same role as Satan in Job 1–2. The reason why this cannot be a genuine test is that the Lord has already found Abraham faithful in so many earlier tests; from the divine standpoint, further testing is superfluous. In an exegetical move corresponding to Paul's use of Genesis 15.6, the motif of the test is detached from its original context in Genesis 22.1 and applied to Abraham's entire life:

> And it came to pass in the seventh week, in the first year of it, in the first month in this jubilee, on the twelfth of this month, that there were words in heaven concerning Abraham, that he was faithful in everything he told him, and that he loved the Lord, and that in every affliction he was faithful. And the prince Mastema came and said before God, "Behold, Abraham loves Isaac his son, and he delights in him above all things else; bid him offer him as a burnt-offering on the altar, and you will see if he will do this command, and you will know if he is faithful in everything in which you test him." And the Lord knew that Abraham was faithful in all his afflictions; for he had tested him through his country and with famine, and had tested him with the wealth of kings, and had tested him again through his wife, when she was abducted, and with circumcision, and had tested him through Ishmael and Hagar, his slave-girl, when he sent them away. And in everything in which he tested him, he was found faithful, and his soul was not impatient, and he was not slow to act; for he was faithful and a lover of the Lord. (Jub.17.15–18)[3]

---

3. Here and elsewhere, the translation is based on that of R. H. Charles (*APOT*, 2.1–82); I have also consulted the revision of Charles' translation by C. Rabin (AOT, pp. 1–139) and O. S. Wintermute (*OTP*, 2.35–142). Translations are primarily dependent on the Ethiopic version, described by Charles as "most accurate and trustworthy and indeed as a rule servilely literal..., singularly free from the glosses and corrections of unscrupulous scribes" (*APOT*, 2.2–3). Extant sections of the Latin version relevant to this chapter are 13.10b–21, 15.20b–31a,

Here, the life of Abraham is read as a series of occasions for the display of his faithfulness. The narrator uses the motif of the "test" to generate the related motif of "faithfulness", which he understands as the key to Abraham's exemplary significance. Thus Abraham's faithfulness is referred to no less than six times in this passage. There are words or voices in heaven proclaiming Abraham's faithfulness to every divine command and in every affliction. The prince Mastema proposes his new test to see whether Abraham's faithfulness to the divine command really knows no limits. But the Lord already knows that Abraham was faithful in everything; and the Lord's view is echoed by the narrator.[4]

The reference here to the occasions on which Abraham proved his faithfulness by obeying the divine command is closely related to the view that Abraham "was justified by works". Abraham's "works" are his acts of faithfulness and obedience to the will of God. Paul's reading of Genesis in terms of the promise motif is opposed to a reading which finds here a celebration of the faithful works of Abraham.

In quest of the true God

In Galatians 3.8, Paul quotes the promise of Genesis 12.3 that "in you shall all Gentiles be blessed".[5] Abraham here is simply the privileged addressee of the divine promise, and responds with faith to this anticipatory preaching of the gospel. But if "Abraham was justified by works", the emphasis will fall on the divine command that underlies the promises, and

---

16.5b–17.6a, 18.10b–19.25; other Abraham-related passages are only loosely attached to the text of Genesis (20.5b–21.10a, 22.2–19, 23.8b–23a). The Ethiopic and Latin versions are based on a Greek translation; extensive Qumran fragments show that, in this case, the hypothesis of a Hebrew original was correct – as was the judgment about the reliability of the Ethiopic and (lost) Greek versions (see J. C. VanderKam, *Textual and Historical Studies in the Book of Jubilees*). Of the material relating to Abraham, Hebrew fragments are extant only for parts of *Jubilees* 21–23, largely unrelated to Genesis (details in *EDSS*, 1.435). See also Charlotte Hempel, "The Place of the Book of *Jubilees* at Qumran and Beyond".

4. The author's rewriting of Genesis aims to enhance Abraham's exemplary significance, and is not directly motivated by soteriological concerns. E. P. Sanders seeks to show that "the soteriology of the book of Jubilees" corresponds to the pattern he finds in "Palestinian Judaism" as a whole, but does not reflect on the methodological difficulty of isolating a "soteriological" strand in a text of this nature (*Paul and Palestinian Judaism*, pp. 370–71). *Jubilees* opens with a scenario inspired by the disobedience-punishment-repentance-salvation pattern of Deuteronomy 30.1–10 (Jub.1.5–18); see also the judgment scene inspired by Genesis 6.1–4 as interpreted by the Enochic tradition (Jub.5.7–18). While both passages indicate the broad soteriological context within which the author's rewriting of Genesis unfolds, there is little in them that conforms to Sanders' claim that, in *Jubilees*, "salvation is given graciously by God in his establishing the covenant with the fathers" (p. 371).

5. Compare *Jubilees* 12.23; 18.16 (= Gen.12.3; 22.18); the passive "will be blessed" reflects the influence of the LXX on the Greek translator.

on Abraham's obedience to that command: "Go from your country and your kindred and your father's house to the land that I will show you" (Gen.12.1). Abraham is required to act, and he does act: "So Abram went, as YHWH had told him ... " (Gen.12.4).

Abraham's obedience to the divine call is highlighted in Hebrews 11, where the attempt is made to harmonize this theme with Paul's emphasis on promise and faith. The later writer summarizes Genesis 12 as follows:

> By faith Abraham, being called, obeyed and went forth to the place which he was to receive as an inheritance; and he went forth not knowing where he was going... (Heb.11.8)

Repeated references to the promise in vv.9–12 do not dispel the impression that the divine promise is here subordinated to human faith, obedience and patience (cf. Heb.6.13–15; Gen.22.16–17).[6] In contrast even to this Christian writer, who is clearly familiar with Paul's understanding of faith, Paul himself finds in Genesis 12 not a human act of obedience but the gospel's promise of the divine act in Christ through which all Gentiles will be blessed. With the exception of Paul, Christian and Jewish readers of Genesis take it for granted that the primary theme of the Abrahamic narratives is Abraham's obedience.[7]

According to *Jubilees*, Abraham's obedience to the divine call is his first demonstration of faithfulness when tested: he was tested "through his country" (Jub.16.17), a reference probably to the entire story that this narrator has to tell about Abraham's relationship to the place of his birth. The city of Ur, we learn, was named after its founder, who was the father-in-law of Reu, Abraham's great-great-grandfather (Jub.11.1–3). At this time, the prince Mastema and his armies of evil spirits were seducing humankind to manufacture and worship idols, which had previously been unknown;[8]

---

6. This may account in part for Luther's view that Hebrews is "a marvellously fine epistle", in which the author builds on the apostolic foundation with gold, silver and precious stones – so that "we should not be deterred if wood, straw or hay are perhaps mixed with them" ("Preface to the Epistle to the Hebrews" [1522], *LW* 35.395). Luther's comments help to establish the protestant hermeneutical principle that deviation from the Pauline norm is a sign of theological degeneracy – a principle that should (usually) be resisted.

7. Compare *1 Clement* 10.1–7, where Abraham is introduced as one who "was found faithful in his obedience to the words of God" (10.1); this is followed by extensive citations from Genesis 12.1–3, 13.14–16, and 15.5–6 (*1 Clem.* 10.2–6). Following a *verbatim* citation of Genesis 15.6, the author continues: "By faith and hospitality *[dia pistin kai philoxenian]* there was given to him a son in his old age, and through obedience he offered him as a sacrifice to God on the mountain which he showed him" (10.7).

8. This view of the origins of idolatry may be contrasted with the naturalistic account given in *Wisdom of Solomon* 14.12–21. The evil spirits are the progeny of the Watchers (Jub.10.5), and represent the immortal, heavenly part of the giants born to the Watchers and their human wives (1 En.15.8–16.1; cf. Jub.5.1, 7.21–22), and subsequently put to death (1

and so Reu's son, Serug, was renamed "Seruk" – "for everyone turned aside after all kinds of sin and transgression" (11.4–6). Seruk was the father of Nahor (11.7–8), who was the father of Terah – whose name speaks of the poverty to which people had been reduced by the ravens sent by the prince Mastema to devour their seed as soon as it had been sown (11.9–13). Terah was the father of Abram, who even as a child

> began to understand the errors of the earth, how all went astray after carved images and uncleanness... And when he was two weeks of years old, he separated himself from his father, so that he might not worship idols with him, and he began to pray to the creator of all things, that he might save him from the errors of humankind, and that it should not be his lot to go astray after the unclean and the degrading. (Jub.11.16–17)

Fourteen years later, after solving the problem of the ravens, Abram challenges his father over his worship of idols, but abides by Terah's plea that he should not make public his views on idolatry (12.1–8). It is not until Abram is sixty-seven years old that he acts on his principles by setting fire to the idols' temple – an act that brings about the death of his younger brother, Haran, consumed by the flames as he tries to rescue the gods (12.12–14; Genesis 11.28 says simply that "Haran died before his father Terah in the land of his birth, in Ur of the Chaldeans"). Although Abram's responsibility for the fire is not suspected, he and Terah leave Ur for Canaan, but settle initially in the land of Haran (Jub.12.15; Gen.11.31). Abram now abandons the practice of astrology, handed down to him by family tradition, and enquires of God whether he is to listen to the urgent pleas of those who wish him to return to Ur (Jub. 12.16–21, cf. 11.8). The divine command, "Leave your country and your kinsmen and your father's house, and go to a land that I will show you..." (Jub.11.22; Gen.12.1) is presented here as a response to this enquiry of Abram's. The command is therefore introduced with the words, "And [Abram] finished speaking and praying, and behold the word of the Lord was sent to him through me [the angel of the presence], saying..." (Jub.12.22).[9] Two years later, Abram sets off for Canaan with his father's blessing (12.28–31).

Abram is "tested through his country" (17.17), and found "faithful", in the sense that his obedience to the divine command completes his lifelong

En.10.9, 12.6, 14.6, 15.3; 86.3–88.2; Jub.5.7–10). After the Flood, which they appear to have survived, most of the evil spirits were imprisoned as punishment for their destructive behaviour; but at Mastema's request some were spared in ordered to inflict merited harm on the human race (Jub.10.1–13). The motifs of the mutual slaughter of the giants and the survival of their spiritual substance derive from Genesis 6.3 (Jub.5.9; cf. 1 En.10.10): so G. W. E. Nickelsburg, *1 Enoch 1*, p. 73.

9. In Abram's reference to the possibility of return, the narrator no doubt seeks to explain why it is that, in Genesis, Abram is only now told to leave his country and his wider family, although he and his father have long since already done so (Gen.12.1, 11.31).

rejection of the idolatry of his native place. Although there is no explicit basis in Genesis 11–12 for this interpretation of Abram's migration as a decision for the true God and against the idols, it goes back at least to the reference in Joshua 24.15 to "the gods that your fathers served in the region beyond the river" (cf. v.2).[10] Unlike the Pentateuch itself, the *Jubilees* narrator undertakes to explain the origin of the Gentile idolatry already presupposed in the Sinai revelation (Ex.20.3–6, 23), tracing it back to the malevolent activity of Mastema and the evil spirits during the period of the genealogy of Genesis 11. Thus Abram is presented as the first great opponent of idolatry. His first "test" is the idolatry of his birthplace, and his obedience to the command to finalize his breach with it is the first great demonstration of his faithfulness. In Pauline terminology, this is the first of the "works" of obedience to the divine command that constitute Abraham's righteousness or justification.

Affliction and triumph

The Lord tested Abraham "through his country and with famine, and he tested him with the wealth of kings, and he tested him again with his wife, when she was abducted... And in everything in which he tested him, he was found faithful" (Jub.17.17–18). The *Jubilees* narrator traces the paired motifs of testing and faithfulness throughout the narrative of Genesis 12–14 (= Jub.13). Both narrators refer only briefly to the famine in the land of Canaan, which (according to *Jubilees*) occurred after Abram had stayed in Hebron for two years (13.10). The nature of this test by famine is indicated by the preceding reference to the fruitfulness of the land:

> And he looked, and behold, the land was spacious and good, and everything grew there – vines and figs and pomegranates, oaks and ilexes, and terebinths and olive trees, and cedars and cypresses and frankincense trees, and all the trees of the countryside; and there was water in the hill-country. And he blessed the Lord, who had led him out of Ur of the Chaldeans and brought him to this land. (Jub.13.6–7)

The narrator has drawn this picture of Eden-like abundance from later Pentateuchal depictions of the land of promise,[11] and it serves to draw out the significance of the famine (13.11) as a test. Abram can give thanks for his migration from Chaldea to Canaan while the land is fruitful, but will he remain faithful to his calling in time of famine? Rather than returning to

10.   Compare also the references in Genesis to Laban's *teraphim* or images (Gen.31.19, 34, 35; cf. 35.2). The significance of Joshua 24.2 as an occasion for the later view is noted by Gunkel, *Genesis*, pp. 163–64.

11.   Cf. Ex.3.8; Num.13.23–27; Deut.8.7–9, 10.11–15.

Chaldea, he takes refuge in Egypt, although he believes this to be a place of danger (cf. Gen.12.11–13); and so, when tested, he again proves himself faithful.

Abram was tested "with the wealth of kings". The narrator has in mind not the gifts that Abram receives from Pharaoh (Gen.12.16), which he does not mention, but the spoils of war that result from Abram's military expedition to rescue Lot from the four kings (Gen.14). The text of *Jubilees* is incomplete at this point, but it must have presented Abram's offering of a tithe to Melchizedek as a precedent for the later practice of tithing (Jub.13.25–27).[12] More directly relevant is Abram's refusal of the king of Sodom's offer that he should keep the spoil:

> And the king of Sodom came and prostrated himself and said, Our lord Abram, grant us the people you have rescued, but let the spoil be yours. And Abram said to him, I lift up my hands to the Most High God, that I will take nothing that is yours, so that you cannot say, I have made Abram rich... (Jub.13.28–29; cf. Gen.14.21–24)

The narrator appears to regard this as a test which again demonstrates Abram's faithfulness. Abram has not been called from Ur of the Chaldeans in order to enrich himself by military exploits. By rejecting the spoil of war, he shows himself faithful to his vocation.

Abram was also tested "through his wife, when she was abducted". The narrator omits all reference to Abram's plan to pass Sarai off as his sister (Gen.12.11–13, 18–19), confining himself to the terse statement that "when Pharaoh seized Sarai, Abram's wife, the Lord struck Pharaoh and his entire household with severe diseases because of Sarai, Abram's wife" (Jub.13.13). In the Genesis narrative, Pharaoh's complaint highlights the questionableness of Abram's conduct; in *Jubilees*, his conduct throughout his five-year stay in Egypt is blameless, and he is held in high esteem on account of his wealth (13.11–14). On his return to Canaan with Sarai, it is said that he "blessed the Lord his God, who had brought him back in peace" (13.15). During his years in Egypt, he has not forgotten that Canaan is where he belongs. As in the related case of the famine, the story presents Abram as faithful to his vocation under adverse circumstances – incidentally eliminating features of the original story which might seem to detract from his exemplary role.

---

12. Westermann sees in the original Genesis narrative (14.18–20) an aetiological legend in which "a current practice, the deliverance by the Israelite farmers of a tenth part of their produce to a former Canaanite sanctuary, is explained and legitimated by an event in former times" (*Genesis 11–36*, p. 206). The author of *Jubilees* reapplied the episode to the practice of tithing in his own time (cf. Lev.27.30–33; Num.18.21–32; Deut.14.22–29; Neh.10.32–39; Mal.3.6–10).

Priesthood

In Romans 4, as we have seen, Paul sets his own reading over against the hypothesis that Abraham was justified by works and has legitimate grounds for boasting before God (v.2). This rejected reading of Genesis is also alluded to in Romans 4.13, where it is said: "Not by law was the promise to Abraham or his seed, that he should be heir of the world, but by the righteousness of faith." This statement differs from the earlier one in its reference to "law", rather than to "works" – the latter being a more general term in this context. Here, an interpretation of the Abrahamic narrative based on Genesis 15.6 is set in opposition to one in which the law provides the hermeneutical key. In this reading, acknowledged although rejected by Paul, the law is projected back into the life of Abraham. The association between Abraham and circumcision – the founding rite of the covenant more fully disclosed at Sinai – suggests that a law-oriented reading of the Genesis narrative may be possible, and that the backward projection from Sinai cannot be dismissed as mere anachronism. Once again, *Jubilees* illustrates how such a reading might work.

For the *Jubilees* narrator, Abraham's faithfulness to the divine commandments addressed specifically to himself is of a piece with his attitude towards the commandments in general, insofar as they were already made known to him. Before the law, Abraham is already a man of the law; only as such is he also the recipient of the promises made to himself and to his seed. For this narrator, the Abraham narrative must be reread in the light of the divine words addressed to Isaac:

> I will multiply your seed as the stars of heaven, and will give to your seed all these lands; and by your seed shall all the nations of the earth bless themselves; because Abraham obeyed my voice and kept my charge, my commandments, my statutes, and my laws. (Gen.26.4–5; cf. Jub.24.10–11)

Two aspects of the *Jubilees* portrayal of a law-observant Abraham have already been noted. First, Abraham was opposed to idolatry even during his earlier life in Ur of the Chaldeans. Second, Abraham's tithing anticipates the later practice as enjoined by the law. A third aspect, his submission to circumcision, will be considered shortly, in connection with Genesis 17. In addition to these points, the narrator also portrays Abraham as a priestly figure who anticipates the actions of the later Aaronic priesthood in his worship of God.

Like Noah, Isaac and Jacob, Abraham is already a priestly figure in Genesis itself.[13] On arriving in Canaan, he builds an altar at Shechem,

---

13. After the flood, Noah builds an altar and offers burnt offerings on it (Gen.8.20). Isaac builds an altar at Beersheba and calls upon the name of the Lord (Gen.26.25). Jacob builds one altar at Shechem (33.20), and is commanded by God to build another at Bethel (35.1–7).

where the Lord appeared to him, and a second altar near Bethel, where he calls upon the name of the Lord (12.6–8). Later, he returns to Bethel from Egypt (13.3–4). After that, he "moved his tent, and came and dwelt by the oaks of Mamre, which are at Hebron; and there he built an altar to the Lord" (13.18, cf. 12.6–7). The oaks of Mamre are Abraham's permanent place of residence at this point in the narrative; he is still living there in Genesis 14.13 and 18.1, although he later resides at Beersheba (22.19).[14] Thus the altars at Bethel and Hebron are built at locations where Abraham makes his home, and each of them represents a relatively permanent place of worship. The *Jubilees* narrator has a particular interest in these altars. The altar at Bethel was built "on the new moon of the first month"; Abram invoked the Lord there as "my God, the eternal God", and offered a burnt offering (Jub.13.8–9, cf. 13.16). The construction of the altar at Hebron is linked to the sacrifices described in Genesis 15.7–20, where, after the promise of offspring in vv.1–6, Abraham is reassured about his future possession of the land by means of covenantal rites. The later narrator follows closely the instructions about sacrificial animals and birds in Genesis 15.9, but has deferred his reference to the Hebron altar (Gen.13.18) until this point, so as to make it clear that the animals and birds were duly sacrificed upon it (Jub.14.9–11). After the covenant promise of the land has been solemnly ratified (Jub.14.13–18; Gen.15.12–18), the later narrator tells how "Abram offered the pieces and the birds and their cereal offerings and their drink offerings, and the fire consumed them" (Jub.13.19). In filling in the gaps in the Genesis narrative, the narrator also brings it into closer conformity to the later legislation for the Aaronic priesthood. In so doing, however, he attests the remarkable absence of any such concern in the Genesis text itself. If Genesis had been in complete harmony with the later Mosaic legislation, it would not have needed to be rewritten.[15] And to rewrite is, however indirectly, to criticize.

If there was an altar at Hebron, then, for the author of *Jubilees*, it must have been in regular use – even though Genesis itself does not mention this fact. It is also reasonable to suppose that its use was in broad conformity to the law. Thus, when the Lord appeared to Abraham to renew the promises and to establish circumcision as the sign of the covenant (Jub.15.3–24; Gen.17.1–27), Abraham was celebrating the feast of

---

14. Mamre – which is also a personal name (Gen.14.13, 24) – is later described as the place "where Abraham and Isaac had sojourned" (35.27). Sarah is buried in a field "east of Mamre (that is Hebron)" (23.19, cf. 49.30, 50.13).

15. The striking difference between "the religion of the patriarchs" and "Mosaic Yahwism", as represented in Genesis and Exodus respectively, is helpfully analysed by R. W. L. Moberly, in his *The Old Testament of the Old Testament*, pp. 79–104. Since his focus is on the final form of the text, the differences Moberly identifies could in principle have occurred to a premodern reader such as the author of *Jubilees*.

firstfruits (Jub.15.1–2). Genesis fails to make this clear, however, and has to be rewritten accordingly. More alarmingly, the Genesis narrator also speaks of Abraham as planting a sacred tree at his third main place of residence in Canaan, Beersheba, the Well of the Oath (cf. Gen.22.19), in spite of the later legislation prohibiting such things (cf. Ex.34.13; Deut.16.21).[16] This sacred tree is therefore replaced by an altar, at which Abraham celebrates the Feast of Tabernacles following the birth of Isaac (Jub.16.19–31). The timing and the nature of this Feast was already ordained on the "heavenly tablets" (16.28–29), the heavenly original of which the Law of Moses is the copy. According to this narrator, that is how the law can be observed even before its full revelation at Sinai.[17] Yet the priestly Abraham of *Jubilees* is not simply the product of this theory or dogma, he is a development from indications already present in the Genesis text. If Abraham built altars at Shechem and the oaks of Mamre so as to worship the Lord there, if he performed sacrificial rites on the occasion of the covenant promise of the land, then a reader familiar with the rites of the Aaronic priesthood is likely to make the connection.

Together with his rejection of idolatry and his submission to circumcision, Abraham's priestly service establishes him as faithful to the law even before the law's full revelation.[18] This is the figure to whom the promises were given; in that sense, "the promise to Abraham and to his seed" was indeed "through law" (cf. Rom.4.13). "Abraham was perfect with the Lord in all his works, and well-pleasing in righteousness all the days of his life" (Jub.23.10). He was justified by works, and among those

---

16.   On this point, see W. Moberly, *The Old Testament of the Old Testament*, pp. 92–93.

17.   The heavenly tablets represent the archetype of the Law of Moses, but also the book in which human destiny is recorded; the latter view is prominent in *1 Enoch* (e.g. 81.1–2, 103.2–3, 106.19) whereas in *Jubilees* it is the former that is emphasized (so S. K. Davis, *The Antithesis of the Ages*, p. 84). In *Jubilees*, laws written on the tablets include the prohibition of murder (Jub.4.5; cf. Deut.27.24) and intercourse with one's father's wife (Jub.33.10–12; cf. Lev.18.8, 20.11; Deut.27.20); and instructions relating to the Feast of Weeks and other major festivals (Jub.6.17–31), and to tithing (Jub.32.9–15). These passages do not necessarily imply an "eternal law" (as Davis argues), since in each case the law is inscribed on the heavenly tablets only *in consequence of* something that has taken place on earth: respectively, the murder of Cain, Reuben's intercourse with Bilhah, the covenant with Noah, and the exercise of the priestly office by Levi. In the cases of circumcision and the Feast of Weeks (15.25, 16.28–29), the heavenly prescription precedes the earthly performance. The author of *Jubilees* is primarily interested in correlations between the Genesis narrative and the prescriptions of the Torah, rather than in dogmatic beliefs about the Torah.

18.   Other relevant passages include *Jubilees* 18.17–19 (celebration of a festival), 20.4–9 (prohibition of fornication, intermarriage and idolatry), 21.1–23.32 (a "testament of Abraham"). In 21.5–10 instructions about sacrificial procedures are derived not from the "heavenly tablets" but from "the books of my forefathers", i.e. Enoch and Noah (21.10). On *Jubilees'* depiction of Abraham's last days (chs.19–23), see John C. Endres, *Biblical Interpretation in the Book of Jubilees*, pp. 18–50.

acts of obedience to divine commands were works of law. This is the reading of the Genesis narrative that Paul contests when he insists that Abraham's significance lies not in his works but in the fact that he believed God's promise, and was thereby accounted righteous.

Circumcision

Abraham was tested through his country, through famine, the wealth of kings, the abduction of his wife – and through circumcision (Jub.17.17). At the age of ninety-nine he willingly subjected himself to this rite, in obedience to God's command, and this is seen as further proof of his unwavering faithfulness. The *Jubilees* narrator follows Genesis 17 quite closely, but adds a long passage in which the angel who is dictating the book to Moses instructs him to lay particular emphasis on the importance of circumcision on the eighth day (Jub.15.25–34):

> This law is for all generations for ever, and there can be no reduction in the number of days, nor omission of even a single day out of the eight, for it is a rule for all time, ordained and written on the heavenly tablets. And everyone that is born, the flesh of whose foreskin is not circumcised on the eighth day, does not belong among the sons of the covenant which the Lord made with Abraham, but is marked out for destruction. There is no sign on him that he is the Lord's, and he is to be destroyed and to perish and to be uprooted from the earth, because he has broken the covenant of the Lord our God. For all the angels of the presence and all the angels of holiness have been so created from the day of their creation; and before the angels of the presence and the angels of holiness he has hallowed Israel, that they should be with him and with his holy angels. And you, for your part, command the sons of Israel to observe the sign of this covenant in every generation as a rule for all time, so that they are not uprooted from the land. (Jub.15.25–28)

Circumcision is the indispensable sign that one is a member of Israel, the holy people, and that one therefore belongs to the Lord. Continued possession of the land that God promised to Abraham is dependent on maintaining the practice of circumcision on the eighth day. Those of the sons of Israel who "have treated their members like the Gentiles" are guilty of the unforgivable sin: "There will be no more pardon or forgiveness to them ... for all the sin of this eternal error" (Jub.15.34). Here if anywhere, the promise to Abraham and his seed is "through law".[19]

---

19. Citing this passage, E. P. Sanders points out that there are for *Jubilees* a number of transgressions for which there can be no atonement: these include flouting the Sabbath (2.19–33), eating meat with the blood in it (6.11–14), giving a daughter or sister in marriage to a Gentile (30.7), having intercourse with one's father's wife (33.13–20), devising evil against

From a Pauline perspective, the *Jubilees* narrator's link between circumcision, people and land evades the anomalies of the biblical text. In Genesis 17, the land is indeed promised to Abraham's seed, and circumcision is indeed the sign of the divine covenant with Abraham and his seed (17.7–14). Yet, as we have seen, it is precisely here that Abraham is identified as the father not of the one, holy nation but of a multitude of nations (vv.4, 5, 6); and that is what his new name means. The same is true of Sarai, whose new name, Sarah, signifies her vocation to be "a mother of nations" (v.16). Twice, indeed, the covenant is explicitly linked with Abraham's universal role (vv.2, 4). Only with the third reference to the covenant is there a mention of Abraham's "seed" (v.7), and in this context – leaving out of account the promise of the land that follows – it seems clear that Abraham's "seed" is to be identified with the "many nations" of which he is the father. The covenant, the many nations, and the seed of Abraham would seem to be indissolubly linked; the very name "Abraham" is the guarantee of this link. Yet, in the following verses, this link disappears without trace. Abraham's seed is that part of his progeny to whom the land of Canaan is promised as an everlasting possession (v.8) and that practises male circumcision as the sign of the covenant (vv.9–14). The text seems to be pointing in two opposite directions, in one of which the Abrahamic covenant is for all peoples, in the other of which it is confined to the people of Israel. The author of *Jubilees* follows the text in one direction, Paul in the other.

For *Jubilees*, the institution of circumcision was another of the "tests" to which Abraham was subjected, and in which he proved himself faithful (Jub.17.17). As in Genesis, the narrator tells how Abraham immediately "did as God had told him" and circumcised every male in his household and was circumcised himself (Jub.15.23–24 = Gen.17.22–23, 26–27). Abraham's instant, unwavering obedience contrasts with the shameful behaviour of those of "the sons of Israel" who "neglect the circumcision of their sons", thereby provoking the wrath of God by forsaking his covenant (Jub.15.33–34).

one's brother (36.7–11), and failure to keep the Passover (49.8–9) (*Paul and Palestinian Judaism*, pp. 368–69). According to Sanders, "Rejection of any one of these commandments, like transgression of the commandment to circumcise, was regarded by the author as forsaking the covenant and thus forfeiting one's status as a member of Israel and one destined for eternal salvation" (p. 368). In fact, these passages are speaking primarily about capital punishment, and do not indicate that it is *only* those who commit capital offences who will (also) be punished eschatologically. In the depiction of the final universal judgment in *Jubilees* 5.7–18, members of Israel will have their sins forgiven if they "turn to [God] in righteousness", or "turn from all their guilt once each year" (5.17–18; cf. 34.18–19).

The two sons

Abraham's sixth and seventh tests consist in the expulsion of Ishmael and of Hagar (Jub.17.17). There follow two final tests, relating to the command to sacrifice Isaac (Jub.18) and the death of Sarah (Jub.19). When Abraham was mourning for Sarah, the angelic narrator recounts how "we tested him to see if he was patient in demeanour and free from bitterness in what he said, and he was found patient too in this" (19.3). After describing the negotiations for a burial-place, the narrator continues:

> This is the tenth test by which Abraham was tested; and he was found faithful and consistently patient. And he said not a single word about the rumour in the land, how God had said that he would give it to him and to his seed after him, but begged a place in it to bury his dead; for he was found faithful and was recorded on the heavenly tablets as the friend of God. (19.9)

Even if Ishmael and Hagar represent separate tests, the number of tests specified amounts only to nine. The author has perhaps failed fully to integrate a traditional schema into his own work. Yet this schema does enable him to clarify the nature of Abraham's exemplary significance as a model of faithfulness and obedience to divine commandments which often require him to make painful sacrifices. Two of these commandments concern his sons, Ishmael and Isaac, and at this point too the contrast with the Pauline reading of Genesis is clear.

The narrator introduces Sarah's surrogacy proposal by way of a link with Genesis 15. After the conclusion of the covenant ceremony of that chapter, "Abram rejoiced and told his wife Sarai everything; and he believed he would have seed, although she had not borne a child" (Jub.14.21). The story of Ishmael's birth is greatly abbreviated (14.22–24), since the narrator's only concern with him is to differentiate him from the one true son, Isaac:

> For Ishmael and his sons and his brothers and Esau, the Lord did not cause to approach him, and he chose them not, although they were the children of Abraham, because he knew them; but he chose Israel to be his people. (15.30)

> And in the sixth year of the fourth week we went to meet Abraham at the Well of the Oath, and we appeared to him ... and we blessed him and told him everything that had been decreed concerning him – that he should not die until he was the father of six more sons and that he should see them before he died, but that in Isaac should his name and seed be called; and that all the descendants of his other sons would be Gentiles, and be reckoned with the Gentiles, although one of Isaac's

sons would become a holy seed, and not be reckoned with the
Gentiles... (16.15–17)

These statements prepare for the account of the expulsion of Ishmael and
Hagar, in which the narrator follows Genesis fairly closely (Jub.17.1–
14 = Gen.21.8–21). Isaac is Abraham's legitimate offspring, the one
through whom Abraham is the ancestor of the elect people of God,
whereas Ishmael and the other sons are simply Gentiles. As in Genesis,
Abraham is distressed by the divine endorsement of Sarah's jealous demand
that Hagar and Ishmael should be expelled (Jub.17.4–7), but his obedience
to this command is again immediate and unquestioning. If Abraham's two
sons have any allegorical significance here, it lies in the differentiation not
of promise and law but of Jew and Gentile. Ishmael must be expelled so that
the holy race should not be contaminated by his presence.

It is the divine command to sacrifice Isaac (Gen.22.1) that provides
the narrator with the testing motif that he applies to the whole of
Abraham's life. Abraham's habitual obedience to the divine commands
is by now so well established that this greatest of all the tests is not
strictly necessary. Thus, after the expulsion of Ishmael and Hagar,
"there were words in heaven concerning Abraham, that he was faithful
in everything he commanded him, and that he loved the Lord, and that
in every affliction he was faithful" (Jub.17.15). The command to
sacrifice Isaac is issued only at the suggestion of the prince Mastema,
who is ultimately put to shame by Abraham's conduct (18.11). As in
Genesis, the earlier promises of blessing and innumerable seed are now
presented as the reward for Abraham's conduct. They are given,
confirmed now by a divine oath, "because you have obeyed my voice"
(Gen.22.18). *Jubilees* states this new basis for the promises still more
emphatically, and with an additional reference to Abraham's lifelong
faithfulness. The promises are given "because you have obeyed me, and
I have made known to all that you are faithful in everything I have said
to you" (Jub.18.16). In *Jubilees* as in Genesis, the divine promises are
here made contingent and conditional on Abraham's obedience – even if
only retrospectively.

In the light of this, it is understandable that Paul does not discuss this
passage. The omission is rectified, however, by other early Christian
interpreters:

> Was not Abraham our father justified by works when he offered
> Isaac his son upon the altar? You see that faith was active with his
> works and by the works the faith was perfected; and the scripture
> was fulfilled which says, Abraham believed God, and it was reckoned
> to him as righteousness; and he was called friend of God. You see
> that a person is justified by works and not by faith alone. (Jas.2.21–
> 24)

In this passage, the divine declaration of Abraham's righteousness by faith is seen as an anticipation of the full righteousness that Abraham attained by his works, culminating in the offering of Isaac. Although the author of *Jubilees* prefers to speak of Abraham's "faithfulness" rather than his "works", the underlying thought is similar.[20] It does not occur to either of these readers of Genesis that the primary theme of the Abraham narrative is divine action rather than human, and both of them therefore celebrate the Abraham of Genesis 22, whose obedience to even the most painful divine commands seems to know no limit.[21]

But it is not quite true to say that Paul is silent about this chapter. In Genesis 22, the new rationale for the promises is most fully stated at the beginning of the angel of the Lord's second address, which opens with the words:

> By myself I have sworn, says the Lord, that because you have performed this word *[to rēma touto]* and did not spare your beloved son, for my sake *[kai ouk epheisō tou huiou sou tou agapētou di' eme]*, that blessing I will bless you... (Gen.22.16–17)

This passage, with its divine oath, particularly impressed the author to the Hebrews, who concluded from it that Abraham "having patiently endured obtained the promise". The promise, guaranteed by a divine oath and the basis of our own hope, is the divine response to Abraham's exemplary conduct. Paul, however, hears something quite different in this language.

Who was it who "did not spare his own son"? In truth, it was not Abraham but God.[22] And God did not give up his own son as just one of a

---

20. In James 2.23, the reference to Abraham as "friend of God" recalls *Jubilees* 19.9, where Abraham "was recorded on the heavenly tablets as the friend of God" (cf. also Is.41.8; 2 Chr.20.7). The statement in James reads almost like an abbreviation of the longer statement in *Jubilees*.

21. That this passage is responsive to Paul is persistently denied by many commentators (e.g. L. T. Johnson, *James*, p. 249; P. Davids, *James*, pp. 130–32). Yet it is hard to read James 2.24 as anything other than an attempt to refute the Pauline thesis of righteousness by faith, as summarized in Romans 3.28. To claim that "the writer is on Paul's side in this verse", and that followers of James here seek "to rehabilitate the authentic notes of Pauline *sola gratia sola fide*" (R. P. Martin, *James*, p. 96) is to allow an *a priori* conception of canonical unity to override exegetical integrity. It should also be noted that the question, "Was not Abraham our father justified by works...?" (Jas.2.21) recalls Romans 4.1–2, where the question is raised whether "Abraham our forefather" was "justified by works"; the phrase, *ex ergōn edikaiōthē*, is common to both passages. In both cases, Abraham's potentially justifying "works" are his acts of obedience and faithfulness: the claim that "neither the works which James cites nor the justification which results are related to Paul" (Davids, *James*, p. 127) cannot be substantiated.

22. That Romans 8.32 alludes to Genesis 22.16 is denied by Schlier, who asks pointedly: "Was sollte es auch besagen, dass Gott wie Abraham handelt? Möglich wäre doch nur, dass Abraham wie Gott handelte" (*Römer*, p. 277). Fitzmyer is sceptical on the grounds that the

number of more or less striking divine actions, but in such a way as himself to be *identified* by this action. God is "the one who did not spare his own son but gave him up for us all" (Rom.8.32): the agent is identified by the action, and cannot be identified apart from it. When Paul reads of Abraham's supreme act of faithfulness, he is less inclined than other readers of Genesis to celebrate this act or to ascribe to Abraham grounds for boasting before God (cf. Rom.4.2). For Paul, scripture is not a collection of inspiring tales about heroes and heroines of obedience and piety. He does not approach his readers with the proposal, "Let us now praise famous men, and our fathers in their generations" (Sir.44.1). Scripture consists simply of "the words of God" (Rom.3.2). So concerned is Paul to praise only the work of God, announced in promise and gospel and realized in the raising of Jesus, that even Abraham at Mount Moriah is seen not as a heroic or tragic figure in his own right, but as an image of the God who is who he is supremely and definitively in the death of Jesus.[23]

Nature and the Patriarch

As readers of the same scriptural texts, Paul and the author of *Jubilees* both address the same fundamental problem: that the formation of the elect people of God, beginning from Abraham, long predates the giving of the law at Mount Sinai. The problem comes into sharp focus when the five books of the Law of Moses are understood as a whole, and when their narrative substructure is seen primarily as a vehicle for the divine commandments which determine for all time the manner of life of the chosen people. If the commandments are fundamental and foundational for the life of the chosen people, how is it that this people could come into being without them?

For Paul, the belatedness of the Sinai event discloses that the law is subordinate to the promise, which is where the true basis of God's dealings with his people and world is made known. God is more fundamentally the God of the promise than the God of the commandment. The unconditional divine commitment to future saving action on the world's behalf cannot be called into question by a law given four hundred and thirty years later, and by angels (Gal.3.17, 19). This radical solution to the interpretative problem

Jewish *Aqedah* tradition is late (*Romans*, pp. 531–32). Neither point is decisive, and the verbal overlap is too close to be coincidental. Wilckens rightly notes that "in Röm 8,32a kommt von Gen 22 einzig das Motiv des Nicht-Schonens zum Tragen, und gerade nicht das des Opfers" (*Römer*, 2.173).

23. In Romans 8.32, the roles of Abraham and Isaac are taken by God and Jesus. This may be compared with the martyrological rendering of the Genesis story in *4 Maccabees*, where the Abraham role is taken by the mother of the martyrs (14.20; 15.26–28), the Isaac role by her sons (9.21–22; 13.12; 16.20).

stems from Paul's conviction that the promise motif is the primary scriptural attestation of God's saving action in Christ, and, conversely, that in Jesus' death and resurrection God has now fulfilled his unconditional promise. In the promise, scripture preaches the gospel in advance (cf. Gal.3.8). And yet, other readings of the Genesis texts remain possible, as Paul himself is well aware. The priority of the promise and the belatedness of the Sinai covenant are real features of the scriptural text, but the explanation for this disjunction does not have to take a Pauline form. The author of *Jubilees* can claim that his emphasis on Abraham's faithfulness and Torah-obedience also has roots in the Genesis text itself.[24] For readers of Genesis, the belatedness of the law need not have the extraordinary significance that it has for Paul. The story of Abraham may be read as anticipating not the Christ-event but the event of Sinai, and Abraham may be presented as embodying the way of life that is subject to the divine command. Each interpretation will tend to emphasize certain texts and to downplay others, and there is no neutral standpoint from which one might arbitrate between the two.

What can be demonstrated, however, is the internal logic and the distinctiveness of the Pauline reading, in a context in which Abraham was widely understood as a model of pious conduct, and in which the divine role is simply to validate this model. At this point, the author of *Jubilees* is essentially at one with Philo of Alexandria. From a Pauline standpoint, the difference between the nomistic perspective of the one and the universalizing tendency of the other may be less significant than what they have in common. The difference remains significant, however, and Philo's reading of the Abraham narrative has its own contribution to make to our understanding of Paul.[25]

The first book of the laws

In response to the perceived problem of the belatedness of the law, the author of *Jubilees* presents an image of a Torah-observant Abraham, created from a variety of resources. Scriptural references to the altars that he built make it possible to see him as a priestly figure who offers sacrifices

24. On this point see B. Ego, "Abraham als Urbild der Toratreue Israels". Ego discusses Genesis 22.15–18, 26.3b–5, and 18.19, under the respective headings of "Abrahams Gehorsam als Verdienst" (p. 28), "Abrahams Toratreue" (p. 31) and "Abraham als Gesetzeslehrer" (p. 32). These passages probably represent different redactional layers, and the otherwise rather different images of Abraham in *Jubilees* and in Philo may therefore be seen as the extension of an inner-biblical process of tradition (pp. 37–39).

25. Comparisons between *Jubilees*, Philo and Paul become possible and illuminating if all three are understood primarily as interpreters of scripture. This would entail a shift of scholarly perspective in the case of Philo as well as of Paul; on this point, see Peder Borgen, *Philo of Alexandria: An Exegete for his Time*, pp. 1–13.

that accord with later legislation. Scripture also presents an Abraham who tithes, practises circumcision, and obeys all of God's commandments. An implicit rejection of idolatry can be discovered in the scriptural account of the departure from Chaldea. The author also employs the traditional concept of the "heavenly tablets" so as to claim that written laws already existed in heaven long before they were fully disclosed on earth – whether Abraham's actions are understood as conforming to a pre-existing heavenly law (cf. Jub.16.28–29) or as the basis for a law consequently enacted in heaven (cf. 18.18–19). Abraham was also instructed by earthly texts, in the form of "the books of my forefathers", Enoch and Noah (21.10); and he wrote down commandments of his own, which Jacob read to his sons and which Joseph later recalled at a moment of crisis (39.6). There is here no single, coherent theory about the Torah prior to Sinai – only the conviction that, as a matter of fact and in a variety of ways, the patriarchs practised it so successfully as to become the supreme models of Torah observance, despite knowing nothing of Moses or Sinai.

In *Jubilees*, the stipulations of the Sinai covenant are projected back into the patriarchal era – as if to pre-empt the Pauline thesis that the law did not exist before Sinai, so that there was once a time and place where there was no law and no transgression (Rom.4.15, 5.13; Gal.3.15–18). Philo of Alexandria is also concerned to connect the patriarchal age with the revelation at Sinai. Rather than interpreting the patriarchs in the light of Sinai, however, Philo seeks to interpret Sinai in the light of the patriarchs. For him, it is essential that the patriarchs precede the enactment of the written law, for in this precedence the key for interpreting the written law is to be found. Like Paul but unlike the author of *Jubilees*, Philo holds that the written law was given exclusively through Moses; it is not anticipated by any fictitious heavenly or earthly writings. Unlike Paul but like the author of *Jubilees*, Philo does believe that the written law has its antecedents. There is no time or place "where there is no law" (cf. Rom.4.15), since the law is embodied both in the universe and in the lives of holy men (and women), pre-eminent among whom are the patriarchs.

In spite of his predilection for allegorical interpretation, Philo has a clear sense of the overall shape of the Pentateuch. In the series of treatises known as *The Exposition of the Law*, Philo retraces the ground covered by Moses himself – a "Life" of whom, in two books, he had already written.[26] A treatise on the creation of the world is followed by treatises devoted to two triads of patriarchs: Enosh, Enoch and Noah (*Abr.* 7–47), and

---

26.   This work is referred to in *On the Virtues*, 52 and *On Rewards and Punishments*, 53 (the works that conclude the *Exposition*). The work on the decalogue follows directly after the treatises on the lives of the patriarchs (*Dec.* 1), and the *Life of Moses* presents itself as a free-standing work and not as part of the series (*Mos.* i.1).

Abraham (*Abr.* 48–276), Isaac and Jacob. The works devoted to the latter two have not survived.[27] A treatise on Joseph as the model politician leads to a treatment of the decalogue, the individual commandments of which are then used to structure the treatment that follows of the individual or "special" laws, in four books. A treatise on the virtues – a topic introduced in *Special Laws*, book iv – identifies the virtues common to all law observance, and the series concludes with a treatment of *Rewards and Punishments* loosely based on the blessings and curses of Leviticus 26 and Deuteronomy 28. These works on the creation, the patriarchs and the laws reflect the structure of the Pentateuch itself. At the beginning of the summary that opens the final treatise in the series, Philo writes:

> Of the oracles delivered through the prophet Moses, there are three types: the first concerns the creation of the world, the second is historical, and the third is legislative *[nomothetikēn]*. The creation of the world *[kosmopoiia]* is recounted throughout with an excellence worthy of the divine theme, beginning from the creation of heaven and concluding with the framing of humankind... The historical part is a record of good and evil lives, and of the judgments passed on each – whether of punishment or of honour – in each generation. As regards the legislative part, one division is more general *[katholikōteran]*, while the other consists in the ordinances of specific laws *[nomimōn entolai]*. (*Praem.* 1–2)[28]

Moses is here said to be a "prophet", but, more precisely, he is pre-eminently the "lawgiver" or "legislator" *(nomothetēs)* whose laws derived not from himself but from divine inspiration, and may therefore be regarded as divine oracles.[29] The question is why this lawgiver chose to preface his laws with the accounts of the creation of the world and its early history. What is the Book of Genesis doing within a law-code? A partial answer is implied in the reference to the "good and evil lives" whose stories are here narrated, with the ensuing honour or punishment as determined by the deity. Mosaic history is intended to instruct and warn and not merely to entertain, and the stories it contains are therefore narrative embodiments of principles and laws which will become more explicit in the "legislative" part of the law-code. For example, the story of Joseph's

27. They are summarized in *Rewards*, 31–51. On the *Exposition*, see E. Schürer, *History of the Jewish People*, III.2, pp. 840–54; M. E. Stone (ed.), *Jewish Writings of the Second Temple Period*, pp. 233–41.
28. Compare the similar passage in *Life of Moses*, ii.46–47, where the Pentateuch is divided into two parts, historical and legislative, with the historical part further subdivided between a section dealing with creation and a section dealing with particular individuals.
29. Thus the *Life of Moses* opens with the statement: "Of Moses, regarded by some as the lawgiver of the Jews, by others as the interpreter of the holy laws, I propose to write the life..." (*Mos.* i.1).

refusal to commit adultery with Potiphar's wife (Gen.39) harmonizes perfectly with the seventh commandment (Ex.20.14). Yet such stories do more than merely reinforce the decrees of the law: they belong not just to the rhetoric of law but to its substance. They derive from a period when there was no written law – an observation that raises two questions. How was it that someone could obey the seventh commandment before the ten commandments had been formally enacted? And what does this tell us about the nature of the written law?[30]

At the outset of the treatise *On Abraham*, it is stated that "the holy laws" are written "in five books", of which the first is named "Genesis" (*Abr.* 1). Purposing to discuss these laws in their scriptural sequence, Philo follows Moses in postponing discussion of the particular laws until the more general laws have been fully treated, since these are the originals or "archetypes" while the particular laws are the copies or "images" (3). The later distinction between the "general" laws of the decalogue and the "special" laws that follow is, as it were, writ large across the whole structure of the Pentateuch. The more general laws are the specific concern of the Book of Genesis, and they are to be identified with

> the men *[andrōn]* who lived irreproachably and well, whose virtues *[aretas]* have come to be inscribed in the most holy scriptures, not just for their own praise *[epainon]* but also to inspire the readers and to lead them to show the same zeal. For laws endowed with souls and reason are what these men have become – whom he [Moses] extolled for two reasons. First, he wished to show that the explicit commandments *[ta tetheimena diatagmata]* are not inconsistent with nature; second, that there is no great difficulty for those who wish to live by the established laws, since, before any of the particular laws had been written down, the first men practised the unwritten law *[agraphō te nomothesia]* easily and straightforwardly – so that one might properly say that the explicit laws are nothing but memorials of the lives of men of old, preserving a record of their works and words *[erga kai logous]*. For they were no one's students or pupils, nor were they taught by teachers what should be done or said; but, hearing and learning for themselves, gladly accepting conformity to nature *[akolouthian phuseōs]*, rightly holding nature to be the most ancient of statutes, they practised the law *[ēunomēthēsan]* all their lives long... (*Abr.* 4–6)

---

30. It is no doubt true that, "[o]n any Greek understanding of philosophy, it is hard to imagine any less philosophical text than the Pentateuch..." (John Barclay, *Jews in the Mediterranean Diaspora*, p. 165). Yet even an unphilosophical text can pose philosophical questions – or at least, questions open to philosophical answers. Philo's intense engagement with the Law of Moses makes it difficult to agree with Barclay's claim that "Philo's philosophy always leads *away* from Jewish particularity" (pp. 171–72; italics original).

Philo has in mind the patriarchs Abraham, Isaac and Jacob, his main "triad" of righteous persons, together with Joseph and the members of the lesser "triad" – Enosh, representing hope (7–16), Enoch, representing repentance (17–26), and Noah, representing perfection (27–47). By their exemplary merits, and by the fact that they have been set down in writing, these figures are themselves "laws", prescribing what is right and prohibiting what is wrong for all who read of them. In them, the laws take incarnate form. They are the archetypes of which the later written laws are the copies. In their life-stories, we encounter the "Thou shalt" and "Thou shalt not" of the divine command, the call to "go and do likewise". It follows that Genesis is no less a book of laws than the rest of the Pentateuch. The incarnate laws, however, are already written laws – no different in that respect from the explicit laws given at Mount Sinai. Yet their written form, in the text of Genesis, is secondary to the unwritten law which the patriarchs obeyed, prescribed not by merely human authorities but by nature itself. The specific laws delivered at Sinai have a twofold genealogy: they derive from the lives of the patriarchs, which themselves derive from the unwritten law of nature. Thus the Law of Moses shows itself to be grounded in the created order, and not in an arbitrary divine will. That is why the laws open not just with the patriarchal history but with an account of the world's own creation. Moses thereby shows

> that the world is in harmony with the law, and the law with the world, and that the law-observant man is truly a citizen of the world *[kosmopolitou]*, aligning his actions with the will of nature, through which the entire world is governed. (*Op.* 3)

> He considered that to begin his writing with the creation of a merely human city *[poleōs cheiropoiētou]* was beneath the dignity of the laws. Surveying the greatness and beauty of the entire legislation with great clarity of vision, and considering it too good and divine to be confined within any earthly limits, he told of the genesis of the World-City *[tēs megalopoleōs tēn genesin]*, regarding the laws as the most faithful image of the world's own polity. (*Mos.* ii.51)

Far from relativizing the significance of the explicit laws, Philo claims that these are grounded in the created order and its unwritten law, and appeals to the lives of the patriarchs as living proofs of this claim – mediating as they do between the original creation on the one hand and the Sinai revelation on the other.[31]

---

31. On the relation between Mosaic and cosmic laws, see P. Borgen, *Philo of Alexandria*, pp. 144–53. Borgen rightly argues (against Goodenough) that Philo does not assign a secondary status to the laws enacted through Moses (p. 148).

Philo shares with the author of *Jubilees* a desire to project the law into the patriarchal era, in response to the fact that, in the scriptural narrative, the Mosaic Law appears not to be foundational for the being and life of the elect people. The author of *Jubilees* minimizes the distinction between the pre-Mosaic and the Mosaic eras, in part by insisting that written texts were already an important feature of the earlier era – in the form of books inherited from the fathers, and the heavenly tablets on which laws are prescribed and recorded. In *Jubilees*, writing is associated with an arbitrary divine will: because it is arbitrary and cannot be read out of the natural order, this divine will must be revealed, and the revelation must be preserved in written form for future generations. The belatedness of the Sinai revelation has little or no inherent significance for the author of *Jubilees*. For Philo on the other hand, it is of the greatest significance. It makes it possible to dispel the appearance of arbitrariness by tracing the divine decrees back to earlier lives lived in conformity to an unwritten law inscribed in the created order itself. According to the full title of the treatise *On Abraham*, this work presents "The Life of the Wise man perfected by Teaching..." But there is also an additional, alternative title: "... or, On the Unwritten Laws, Book One: concerning Abraham". The unwritten laws, incarnated in Abraham and derived from nature, must necessarily precede the written ones. The Book of Genesis is not an anomaly within the Mosaic legislation, but rather its hermeneutical key.[32]

Philo and the author of *Jubilees* offer different solutions to the exegetical problem posed by the secondariness of the Sinai revelation. From a Pauline standpoint, however, these are different versions of the same solution. In both cases, Genesis is understood as a book of law. The two interpreters agree that "the holy laws" were "written in five books" rather than four (cf. *Abr.* 1). The laws revealed at Sinai were preceded by earlier articulations of those same laws; whether these were written or unwritten, the mode of divine discourse is fundamentally the same before Moses as through Moses. The fact that the God of Abraham, Isaac and Jacob does not only issue commands, or commend obedience to them, remains unacknowledged. Abraham and the other patriarchs are praiseworthy,

---

32. The difference between Philo and the author of *Jubilees* may thus be described in hermeneutical terms, and is not simply a question of the use made of Greek philosophical resources – a view which leads to the assumption that Philo's Judaism was less "pure" than that of his Palestinian counterparts. When E. R. Goodenough speaks of "the *problem* of Philo's relation to Judaism", it is assumed that what is "properly Jewish" in his work is ideally to be differentiated from "hellenistic influence", and is in principle quantifiable (*An Introduction to Philo Judaeus*, p. 75; italics added). Within this essentialist framework, Philo emerges as significantly "less Jewish" than (for example) the author of *Jubilees*, and the significance of his work is devalued accordingly. On this see the forthright comments of G. Boccaccini (*Middle Judaism*, pp. 189–91).

exemplary figures whose conformity to the written or unwritten will of God should inspire the reader to emulation. Yet neither writer intends to detract from the glory of God by glorifying these human figures. Indeed, their glory serves to enhance the divine glory, vindicating the assumption inherent in the command, that human beings are capable of an obedient response and are open to a dialogical relationship with God. In insisting that Genesis is a book of promise rather than law, Paul cannot appeal to any neutral criteria that might vindicate his own interpretation of the divine–human relationship as rendered in scripture, over against the alternative ones. It is simply that, for Paul but not for the other interpreters, God in Christ has acted definitively and decisively for the world's salvation – a divine act that seems to him to correspond closely to the unconditional promise which, according to Genesis, preceded the law given at Mount Sinai. If and only if this claim is true, Abraham must "give glory to God", and cannot retain any "grounds for boasting" before God (cf. Rom.4.2, 20).

The giftedness of the soul

For Paul, the promise to Abraham and his seed is "not through law", it is "by faith, so as to be according to grace" (Rom.4.13, 16). The characteristic prepositional phrases aim above all to establish an antithetical structure, in which terms such as "promise", "faith", "grace" and "gift" are set over against terms such as "law" and "works". The Pauline antitheses as developed in Romans 4 and Galatians 3–4 represent two opposing readings of the Abraham narrative: an "anthropocentric" reading, in which Abraham is a model of piety, and a "theocentric" one in which he is primarily the recipient of God's promise, the unconditional divine commitment to a saving action that ultimately encompasses the entire world. In their different ways, Philo and the author of *Jubilees* read the Genesis narrative along the lines that Paul rejects. Given the Pauline antithesis, it is possible to place their readings on one side and his on the other. To that extent, the two types of reading are incommensurable: what is affirmed by the one is denied or downplayed by the other. Yet the antithesis is not simply a given; it must be carefully adapted to individual cases. The terms "theocentric" and "anthropocentric" must be used flexibly, since they represent a hypothesis seeking not only confirmation but also clarification. They do not rule out the possibility that Philo, for example, may have much to say about a God of Abraham who is as such a God of grace. If for Paul it is one thing for God to command, another for God to be gracious, that is not necessarily the case for Philo.

As we have seen, Philo's two triads of patriarchs (Enosh, Enoch, Noah; Abraham, Isaac, Jacob) constitute a proof of the actuality and practicability of the unwritten law of nature, which is the ontological foundation of the written laws. Applied specifically to Abraham, Philo's theory takes the following form:

> He, then, being a zealot for piety *[eusebeias zēlōtēs]*, the highest and greatest of virtues, was quick to follow God and to be obedient to the things commanded by him, taking as commands not only those communicated by speech and writing, but also those manifested through nature with still clearer signs, and comprehended by the truest of the faculties, superior to the unreliability of hearing. For whoever beholds the order in nature *[tēn te phusei taxin]* and the indescribable excellence of the polity under which the world operates, is taught without any speaker to practise a law-abiding and peaceful life, seeking to conform himself to its beauties. *(Abr.* 60–61)

In this passage, Philo introduces Abraham as an individual figure characterized above all by his piety *(eusebeia)*. It is this quality – "the highest and greatest of virtues" – that he seeks to uncover in the various episodes from Abraham's life discussed in the main body of the treatise. Concerned as he is to trace the progress of Abraham's piety through the Genesis narrative, Philo devotes very little attention to the theme of the divine promise. Thus, his account of Abraham's "migration" from Chaldea has the divine command as its primary focus (Gen.12.1; *Abr.* 62–71), and ignores the promises that follow it (Gen.12.2–3).[33] Yet, in his own way, Philo does emphasize the theme of God the giver, since his God

---

33. The promises of Genesis 12.2–4 are, however, a central theme of another treatise, *On the Migration of Abraham* – although this is not part of the *Exposition*. Philo here finds in Genesis 12.1 an account of how "God, wishing to cleanse the human soul, first gives it the possibility of full salvation, in its removal from three locations: that is, body, sense, and speech. 'Land' is a symbol of body, 'kindred' of sense, 'the father's house' of speech" *(Migr.* 2). The promises that follow are presented as a series of enumerated "gifts": first, "the land I will show you", which speaks of "the disclosure and contemplation of things immortal *[epideixin kai theōrian tōn athanatōn]*" *(Migr.*53); second, "I will make you a great nation", where progress is promised in the innumerable principles of virtue (53); third, "I will bless you", where the blessing is excellence of reason and speech *[eu-logia]* (70); fourth, "I will magnify your name", where the gift consists in a merited reputation for virtue (86); fifth, "you will be blessed", referring to the being that must underlie the appearance indicated in the previous gift (106). These, then, are "the prizes which he gives to the one who is becoming wise *[tō genēsomenō sophō]*" (109). The two final promises are discussed but are not included in the series, since they are no longer addressed to the *sophos*. "I will bless those who bless you, and I will curse those who curse you" speaks of the praise due to the one whose praise of another is grounded in reality (109–10). "In you shall all the tribes of the earth be blessed" leads to reflection on the fact that "the righteous person is truly the foundation of the human race" (121), and on Abraham's intercession for Sodom (122–23). The hermeneutical premise of this interpretation is that Abraham's journey is religiously significant, and that this significance is universal.

is one who commands only so as to draw the soul out of the realm of the senses to its true home in himself. If Genesis is seen as the first of the five books of the laws, that is for Philo entirely compatible with the notion of divine grace.

For Philo, the divine command to Abraham represents a call to abandon the *astronomia* of the Chaldeans in order to seek the world's creator and origin beyond the realm of the visible. Abraham's arrival at Haran provides him with an all-important clue. "Haran" means "holes", an allusion to the bodily orifices associated with the senses, which are presided over by the invisible mind. The analogy of the mind's rule over the body enables us to infer (with Abraham) that the world itself is ruled by a single invisible mind, which we call "God" (*Abr.* 72–76). Abraham's "migration" is the passage from knowledge of the visible to knowledge of the invisible by way of self-knowledge. In this case, the literal interpretation relating to the historical individual and the allegorical interpretation applying to the soul are closely related. Abraham is "the man who, obeying the divine words, was drawn away from what had held him bound", and he is also "the mind" which

> did not remain standing in the realm of sense *[epi tēs aisthētēs ousias]*, as though for ever deceived, nor suppose that the visible cosmos was the great and primal God, but ran upwards by means of reason and gazed on another, intelligible nature, better than the visible one, and on the one who is maker and ruler of both alike. (*Abr.* 88)

The question at issue is how this human act of obedience relates to divine action. Is God's action confined to a bare command, or is there also a divine giving here? If Abraham "was drawn away from what had held him bound" and "ran upwards by means of reason", does this suggest that the human running is impelled by a divine drawing?

Philo assumes that Abraham receives the command to leave country and kindred while he is still in Chaldea (*Abr.* 66–67) – and not when he is already in Haran, as in Genesis and *Jubilees* (Gen.12.1, Jub.12.22–24). There is therefore a second migration, from Haran, which Philo here identifies with the journey "into the desert" referred to in Genesis 12.9 (*Abr.* 67, 85–87). Philo can treat the scriptural chronology with great freedom, however. Thus, in terms of its allegorical significance, the second migration is closely related to the first, and does not mark a distinct new stage in the soul's journey into God. Given this freedom from chronology, Philo can draw upon two further texts from Genesis to shed light on what is essentially a single "migration" *(apoikia)*. His interpretation of these texts helps to clarify his view of the divine action that corresponds to Abraham's action.

In Genesis 12.7, it is said that, on Abram's arrival in the land of Canaan, "the Lord appeared *[ōphthē]* to Abram" and promised that his descendants would inherit the land. Philo cites the opening words in the form "God appeared to Abraham", detaches them from their scriptural context, and uses them to shed further light on the initial *apoikia*. "God appeared to Abraham" shows, first, that God had not previously been manifest to him when he had practised Chaldean astronomy without a thought for the intelligible world beyond the world of sense (*Abr.* 77). It was when he turned away from Chaldean science that "God appeared to him". That is to say,

> God, out of love for humanity *[heneka philanthrōpias]*, did not remain aloof on the soul's arrival, but advancing to meet it revealed his own nature, so far as the beholder's power of sight permitted. Thus it is said not that the wise man saw God, but that "God appeared" to the wise man; for it is impossible for anyone of himself to comprehend the one who truly is, if he did not reveal and manifest himself. (*Abr.* 79–80)

The words, "God appeared to him" are here removed from their scriptural context and applied to Abraham's initial migration, so that Philo can emphasize that the knowledge of the true God can only be attained by way of divine revelation. God is not an inert object waiting to be found; God in love "advances to meet" the questing soul, like the father in Jesus' parable (cf. Lk.15.20).[34] Like the prodigal son, however, it seems that the soul must make the first move. God comes out to meet the soul that is already journeying towards him.

Philo claims that this point is confirmed by a second passage, the reference in Genesis 17.5 to Abraham's change of name (*Abr.* 81–84). By the addition of the single letter *alpha*, Abram becomes Abraam. "Abram" means "uplifted father", a reference to the astronomical activity of his Chaldean days. But the new name, "Abraam", means "chosen father of sound" – "father" signifying the ruling mind, "sound", spoken thought, and "chosen", his personal worth. This recalls the point that Philo has earlier extracted from "Haran": the ruling mind perceives in God its own likeness and archetype. While the change of name is again applied to the conversion accomplished in Abraham's "migration", it is not clear exactly what part God plays in bestowing the additional *alpha*. Does this make Abraham's conversion God's own act, or does the new name signify God's acknowledgment of what Abraham himself has accomplished? It is probable that Philo takes the latter view – in which case the initial movement signified in the change of name is achieved by Abraham himself. When the soul turns away from the world to God, God responds by turning towards the soul: divine action is contingent upon human action.

---

34. This invalidates S. Sandmel's claim that Philo simply replaces the biblical concept of divine revelation with the Platonic concept of the human ascent to deity (*Judaism and Christian Beginnings*, p. 297).

When God condescends to name himself as "the God of Abraham, Isaac and Jacob", he does so "because of the excellence of the virtues in which they lived their lives" (*Abr.* 50). Human virtue precedes, the divine acknowledgment follows.

If there is a sense in which, for Philo, divine grace precedes and enables human virtue, it is to be sought in the background of his eulogies to patriarchal excellence, rather than the foreground. If we ask how it was possible for the virtue of true piety to develop in Abram the Chaldean astronomer, the answer is to be found in the concept of the "soul". Abraham, Isaac and Jacob represent three types of soul, which "pursue the good one by teaching *[ek didaskalias]*, one by nature *[ek phuseōs]*, and one by practice *[ex askēseōs]*" (*Abr.* 52). Abraham pursues the good because his soul is instructed by nature – as, for example, when at Haran self-knowledge teaches him the limitations of Chaldean astronomy. Isaac represents the soul that conforms naturally to the dictates of nature, Jacob the soul that learns to do so by practice and self-discipline. The three endowments belong together, and each is dependent on the other two; but in each of the three patriarchs, one is predominant over the others. Abraham exemplifies the soul that is instructed by nature – but that also possesses an inherent conformity to nature which is further developed by practice (53). He is, then, the recipient of divine *gifts*: for instruction, conformity to nature, and practice form a triad of endowments of the soul

> which by another name people call, "Graces" *[Charitas]*, also three in number – whether because God has given *[kecharisthai ton theon]* our race the three capacities *[dunameis]* for the perfecting of life, or because they have given themselves *[dedōrēntai heautas]* to the rational soul, as a perfect and most excellent gift. (*Abr.* 54)

In this difficult but important passage, Philo apparently alludes to a piece of Stoic allegorical interpretation in the tradition of Chrysippus, in which the three *Charites* or Graces of Greek mythology – *Aglaia* the Radiant, *Euphrosyne*, Joy, and *Thaleia* the Flowering, daughters of Zeus from whom all good things proceed – were identified with precisely the endowments of the soul that Philo himself discovers in the three patriarchs. (For Philo, Isaac represents "Laughter" or Joy [*Praem.* 31–35], and so corresponds to Euphrosyne.) The Stoic allegorizer may have thought that the three capacities bestow themselves on the soul, or that they are given by God: in either case, they are nature's *gifts*. Whatever was meant, it is Philo's own view that "God has given to our race the three capacities for the perfecting of life".[35] Abraham's rational soul is

---

35. For another example of Philo's use of an allegorical interpretation of Greek mythology, see *On Noah's Work as a Planter*, 127–29 (the birth of the Muses); both

endowed with the God-given capacity to attend to nature's instruction, and to act upon it by turning from vain opinion and seeking the true God. In that sense, Abraham's migration is initiated by the divine grace, manifest in that endowment or giftedness of the soul that enables it to hear and respond to the voice of nature. In the gift of this capacity lies the potential for the knowledge of God that is the true goal of every human life. Conversely, the divine grace that intends the human knowledge of God is grounded in being itself. To attend to nature's demand that we leave the world of the senses and the passions, in quest of the true God, is to become aware of our own nature as divinely gifted with the capacity to receive this instruction and to attain the goal to which it directs us.

This point is underlined by Philo's interpretation of the divine name. God needs no name, but condescends to take a name to himself in order that human beings should find comfort in addressing him in prayer; and the "eternal name" taken by God is "the God of Abraham, the God of Isaac and the God of Jacob" (*Abr.* 51, cf. Ex.3.15). Thus, the word "God" is no longer an absolute noun *(to kathapax)* and has become relative to something else *(to pros ti)*, along with terms such as "father" and "king" (*Abr.* 51).[36] If this divine name is eternal, however, the names "Abraham", "Isaac" and "Jacob" cannot refer merely to mortal human beings but to incorruptible virtues: for "it is more reasonable for the eternal [name] to be referred to what is incorruptible rather than to what is mortal, since there is a kinship between incorruptibility *[aphtharsia]* and eternality *[aidiotēs]*" (55). God's gracious self-naming as the God of Abraham, Isaac and Jacob identifies him as the God of the virtues acquired through Teaching, Nature and Practice, the powers or capacities that enable human beings to attain to the highest vocation assigned to any creature, which is the knowledge of God. The divine self-naming identifies God as the God of the giftedness of the soul.

Philo uses the resources of Platonic and Stoic philosophy in order to present the piety or *eusebeia* of Abraham and other patriarchs as grounded in being itself.[37] So far as possible, he seeks to eliminate every

---

interpretations may be traced back to passages in Hesiod's *Theogony*. As Goodenough states, Philo's acceptance of philosophical allegory means that he "does not oppose the gods or the polytheistic poetry of the Greeks even as strongly as, at times, did Plato himself" (*Philo Judaeus*, p. 81).

36. Philo here employs the distinction between relative and absolute nouns employed by Greek and Latin grammarians: so F. H. Colson, in the Loeb Philo, 6.597; see also *On the Change of Names*, 27–29, where Philo is commenting on "I am your God" (Gen.17.1 LXX).

37. In contrast, S. Sandmel argues that philosophy is for Philo the *content* of scripture, not just the means of elucidating it: allegory is "the device by which Philo makes Scripture yield a

appearance of contingency from the scriptural record. He does not follow the author of *Jubilees* in deriving earthly contingencies from an arbitrary divine predestination whose decrees are inscribed on heavenly tablets. For Philo, it is inadequate to say that something should be done because God commands it to be done, or that something has taken place because God willed it to take place: postulating a heavenly contingency in explanation of an earthly one simply compounds the problem. To practise piety is not to obey arbitrary divine decrees. Rather, it is to be responsive to nature's instruction about God, the soul, and the conformity between the two; it is to recognize that the soul has been endowed with the capacity to turn away from the visible world to the invisible God, in whom it finds its true and inalienable good. Philo would claim to have learned all this not just from Plato or the Stoics but above all from Moses, who prefaces his laws with an account of the creation of the world precisely so as to demonstrate that the world and the laws are at one, deriving as they do from a single divine origin. Nature or the created order is not a mere neutral background, a stage on which various contingent interactions between deity and humanity can take place – as in the case of *Jubilees*. Moses' account of the creation or *kosmopoiia* implies "that the world is in harmony with the law, and the law with the world, and that the law-observant man *[tou nomimou andros]* is truly a citizen of the world, aligning his actions with the will of nature, through which the entire world is governed" (*Op.* 3). Abraham perfectly exemplifies this picture of the law-observant person as the one who acts out the uniquely privileged status bestowed on the human soul by a "nature" established by the will of the creator. In this reading, the patriarchal narratives are constantly referred back to the portrayal of God, the created order, and the human being in the divine image with which Genesis opens.

If Philo's concern with ontology were merely the product of his Greek philosophical training, then we would have to conclude that this concern is simply absent in Paul, who draws on philosophical conceptuality and vocabulary without any interest in its ontological presuppositions. But if Philo is first and foremost an interpreter of scripture, then his concern with ontology is motivated by the desire to grasp the fundamental coherence and rationale of the Genesis narrative – on the assumption that God's being and action as attested by scripture is in accordance with reason. Since there can be nothing irrational in scripture, the interpreter's task is to demonstrate the divine and scriptural reasonableness by tracing the

host of philosophical items culled primarily from Plato and the Stoics" (*Judaism and Christian Beginnings*, p. 285). Sandmel rightly states that "the allegorical meaning of Scripture is... the spiritual journey of every man" (p. 286), but fails to note that it is the scriptural story of Abraham that has given Philo (and ourselves) the concept of the "spiritual journey".

individual text back to first principles laid down in the beginning. For Paul, on the other hand, the centrality of the promise motif means that the coherence and the rationale of the Genesis narrative is to be found not in the beginning but in the eschatological end. To this end the promises point, and from it they derive. Abraham is "heir to the world", he is "father of many nations" (Rom.4.13–18), and in both cases he is defined in relation not to his primordial origin but to his eschatological destiny. The God in whom Abraham believed is the God "who calls non-beings into being", and the reference is not to the God who created in the beginning but to the one "who gives life to the dead" at the end. This end is realized in Jesus' resurrection, and is typologically foreshadowed in the birth of a son to the virtually "dead" Abraham and Sarah (cf. Rom.4.17–25).[38]

The queen of the virtues

Like Paul, Philo regards the statement about Abraham's faith in Genesis 15.6 as the key to his entire life. His treatise on the life of Abraham covers a number of selected episodes: his migration (*Abr.* 62–88), his sojourn in Egypt (89–106), his hospitality to the three visitors (107–67), his offering up of Isaac (167–207), his treatment of Lot (208–44), and his conduct on the death of Sarah (245–61). Yet Philo is not content simply to present these episodes one after the other, since he assumes that the life of Abraham is not just a series of contingent events and actions but a unitary phenomenon open to subsequent assessment. A "life" of Abraham must not only tell of what he did and what happened to him, it must also show what kind of person he was. For Philo, the definitive judgment has already been announced by Moses, who wrote of Abraham that he "believed in God" (Gen.15.6), thereby bestowing on him the highest possible accolade. Philo assumes that what Moses meant was not, "Abraham believed God...", referring back to a specific divine utterance to which Abraham gave credence, but rather, "Abraham believed in God", or "trusted in God" – a reference to the entire course of Abraham's life. The significance of this belief or trust in God becomes apparent if we contrast it with other, this-worldly things we might believe or trust in: political office, fame, honour, wealth, noble birth, health, strength, beauty, and so on (263–67). All of these external things are precarious and problematic, and do not provide a sure foundation on which to build our lives. In contrast,

> faith in God *[hē pros theon pistis]* is the only true and sure good; it is consolation of life, fullness of good hopes, scarcity of evils, harvest of goods, immunity from misery, knowledge of piety, heritage of

38. A closer analogy between Philo and Paul might be found by comparing Romans 4 with *On the Virtues*, 211–19, where Abraham becomes a model for all proselytes *(epēlutai)*.

happiness; it is the comprehensive improvement of the soul firmly stayed on the one who is the cause of all things and who can do all things, yet wills only the best. For just as those who walk on a treacherous path slip over and fall, whereas others on a dry road make their way without stumbling, so those who lead the soul by way of the bodily and the external merely accustom it to fall – for these things are slippery and utterly insecure – whereas those who press on towards God in accordance with the principles of virtue walk along a path safe and firm. So we can most truly say that the one who trusts in these things distrusts God, whereas the one who distrusts these things trusts in God *[ho men ekeinois pepisteukōs apistei theō, ho d' apistōn ekeinois pepisteuke theō]. (Abr.* 268–69)

Here, the greatness of faith or trust in God lies primarily in its object. In contrast to the unstable and illusory objects of trust within the sensory world, this object is utterly reliable, a firm foundation upon which to build, the source of all good. When the sacred oracles speak of Abraham's "faith in that which truly is" *(tēn pros to on pistin)*, it is this relation to true being that makes faith "the queen of the virtues" (270). On the other hand, Abraham himself merits the highest praise for his possession of this supreme virtue: the greatness of faith is to be found in its subject as well as its object. The reason for this is that the choice of the sure path rather than the slippery one requires a distrust of visible objects which, though entirely rational, will seem counter-intuitive to those still under the sway of the body and the passions.[39] The classic instance of Abraham's heroic and unwavering trust in the invisible and distrust for the visible is to be found in his offering of his son in obedience to the divine command, after which the promise was confirmed by a divine oath because God himself "marvelled at Abraham's faith in him" (273). Thus Moses' inspired statement about his faith (Gen.15.6) is "a written commendation" *(anagraptos epainos)* of Abraham himself *(Abr.* 262). To glorify Abraham is to enhance the glory of God, and not to detract from it.

In addition to the eulogy of Genesis 15.6, and in harmony with it, Moses also states that "this man performed the divine law and all the divine commands" (cf. Gen.26.5), referring not to written words but to the unwritten instruction of nature *(Abr.* 276).[40] Abraham's faith and his obedience to the law are of a piece, since faith itself is the supreme and primary act of obedience to the unwritten law taught by nature. For Paul, however, Moses meant nothing of the sort when he wrote the words

39. A similar reading of Genesis 15.6 occurs in *Who is the Heir?*, 90–95. In the *Questions and Answers on Genesis*, there is a lacuna between Genesis 10.8–9 and 15.7.

40. As P. Borgen notes *(Philo of Alexandria*, p. 69), Philo here corrects the view of Abraham represented by *Jubilees:* Abraham "obeyed the law, some will say, but rather, as our discourse has shown, he was himself a law and an unwritten statute" *(Abr.*276).

recorded in Genesis 15.6. There is a sharp disjunction between the fact that "Abraham believed God" and all the "works" of obedience that he may or may not have performed. Philo finds in Genesis 15.6 a general statement about Abraham's entire life: "Abraham believed in God", God was the object of his constant trust. But Paul claims that Genesis 15.6 speaks only of a single defining moment in Abraham's life, when he gave credence to the specific divine promise, "Thus shall your seed be" (v.5): it is this act of credence that constitutes Abraham's righteousness before God. Abraham, then, is simply the recipient of the promise, the beneficiary of future divine saving action, of which he can be absolutely sure because it has been promised, and because that promise is divine and therefore credible – in spite of its apparently incredible content. If we ask who Abraham is apart from the promise, Paul's answer is simply that he belongs to the company of the "ungodly", whom God justifies and whose sins are therefore forgiven (Rom.4.5–8). In opposition to all eloquent eulogizing of his virtues, Abraham is understood as an unremarkable figure, who becomes remarkable only as the object of a divine promise that insistently reshapes his life by setting it in the light of the world's eschatological future.[41]

The Founder of Religion and Science

For Philo, Abraham's lifelong pursuit of virtue is summed up in the statement that "Abraham believed in God". In contrast, Josephus simply omits this statement from his paraphrase of the Genesis narratives, moving directly from the divine promise of a posterity numerous as the stars in the sky to the sacrificial rites of the covenant (*Ant.* i.183–84). To respond to God's promise by offering a sacrifice is to demonstrate that one believes the promise, but Josephus regards Abraham's belief as too obvious to be worth mentioning. Since Abraham always believes God when God speaks to him, it is necessary to avoid the misleading impression that his belief in God was confined to one particular moment and to a single divine utterance. Thus Josephus and Philo are agreed that the statement of Genesis 15.6 is difficult to understand within its immediate scriptural context. Josephus eliminates this text from his exposition of its context, whereas Philo interprets it as a summary of Abraham's entire career – and both procedures tacitly acknowledge the same exegetical difficulty. The statement is in effect misplaced. Moses might have located it where Philo

---

41. In the treatise *On Abraham*, 178–83, Philo presents at some length the views of those (fellow-Jews?) who question the praiseworthiness of Abraham's action in offering up his son (for other similar cases, see John Barclay, *Jews in the Mediterranean Diaspora*, pp. 108–109, 169). It is possible, though entirely unprovable, that Paul may at some point have encountered some such Jewish willingness to criticize the great figures of scripture.

does, at the conclusion of the story of Abraham, where it would have served as a retrospective summary of his life. Or he might have located it at the beginning of the story, to underline the connection between Abraham's departure from Chaldea and the dawning of his faith in the one true God. For both Philo and Josephus, it is that initial event in Abraham's recorded career that determines his true significance, and that provides the basis for the outstanding "virtue" that marks his subsequent history.

The religious reformer

In Genesis 11.26–32, Abraham is introduced as the son of Terah, who emigrated with his family from Ur of the Chaldeans to Haran – although the original intention had been to go to the land of Canaan (v.31). The report of this emigration is succinct, providing little more than factual information about relationships, ages and places: only gradually does the Genesis narrator extricate himself from the genealogy of Shem (11.10–32) which serves to link Abraham back to Noah. Later, it will be said that YHWH brought Abraham from Ur of the Chaldeans (Gen.15.7), but the command and the promises of Genesis 12.1–3 are addressed to him after the move from Ur to Haran. The first emigration takes place without a divine command or promise, and indeed without any indication as to why it took place. In the narrative as it stands, the divine command and promises serve both to reinterpret the original plan to journey from Ur to Canaan as willed by YHWH, and to motivate Abraham to resume the journey, interrupted by the decision to settle in Haran. The retrospective reinterpretation of the initial departure from Ur as willed by YHWH is underlined by the later announcement that "I am YHWH who brought you from Ur of the Chaldeans..." (15.7). Whatever led Terah and his family to leave Ur of the Chaldeans to journey to Canaan, and whatever caused them to abandon that plan and to settle instead in Haran, the journey was part of the divine purpose, which Abraham must now assume.[42] In this narrative, Abraham only emerges as a character in his

---

42. The source critical solution to the problem of Abraham's call is to trace 11.28–30 to J and 11.31–32 to P. Thomas L. Thompson finds a variety of traditions underlying the sources: *(i)* the Sethite genealogy (11.10–26, P), which consists of "a collection of appelatives and names of cities and regions that can probably be located and identified with the Aramaean city-states in the region of Harran in North Mesopotamia" (*The Historicity of the Patriarchal Narratives*, p. 304); *(ii)* traditions known to both J (Gen.11.28, 15.7) and P (Gen.11.31) that place Abraham's origin in *'wr kśdym*, a city belonging to "the region of Southern Mesopotamia occupied by the Chaldaean Arameans from the beginning of the first millennium to the end of the sixth century B.C." (p. 303); *(iii)* a tradition that Abraham was 75 years old when he left Haran (12.4b, P); (4) a tradition that it was Terah, not Abraham who left Ur of the Chaldees to go to the land of Canaan (11.31a, P) (p. 309). Essentially there are two problems here: Ur/Haran and Terah/Abraham; P solves them by postulating a halt in

own right at the moment when he is addressed by YHWH. Unlike his
father Terah (11.31) he takes no independent initiative, but acts only on
the basis of an address that initiates him into the divine purpose and his
own central role in it. That divine purpose is summed up in the promise of
a "blessing" that extends from Abraham to encompass the whole world.
For the Genesis narrator, Abraham is who he is only as the addressee of
the divine command and promise.

Josephus reads the text differently. An explanation is given for the first
emigration, from Ur to Haran. The biblical text mentions that Terah's
third son, Haran, "died before his father Terah in the land of his birth, in
Ur of the Chaldeans" (Gen.11.28), and Josephus conjectures that Therros
(Terah) left Ur "because he hated Chaldea on account of his sorrow for
Aran" (*Ant.* i.152).[43] The second emigration is described as follows:

> Abram adopted Lot, the son of his brother Aran and brother of his wife
> Sarra, since he lacked a son of his own; and he left Chaldea, aged
> seventy-five, at the command of God *[tou theou keleusantos]*, in order
> to go to Canaan, where he settled and left the country to his
> descendants. (*Ant.* i.154)

This passage briefly summarizes the fuller narrative of Genesis:

> And Abram went, as YHWH told him, and Lot went with him. And
> Abram was seventy-five years old when he left Haran. And Abram took
> Sarah his wife and Lot his brother's son and all the possessions and
> persons they had acquired in Haran, and they set out to go to the land of
> Canaan. And they came to the land of Canaan, and Abram passed
> through the land to the place known as Shechem, to the oak of
> Moreh... And YHWH appeared to Abram and said: To your seed I
> will give this land... (Gen.12.4–7)

Josephus provides additional information about Abraham's relationship
to Lot, although the occasion for this is provided by the double reference
to Lot in the biblical text. The departure from Haran is presented as a
departure from Chaldea, although the first emigration was supposed to
have taken Terah and his family from Chaldea to Mesopotamia (*Ant.*
i.152); the discrepancy probably reflects a tendency to assimilate the two
emigrations. The allusion to the divine command is in agreement with
Genesis, together with the references to Abram's age and to the intended
goal. The biblical details about the places Abram visits (Gen.12.6–9) are

---

Haran and Terah's death there (p. 310). In the patriarchal narratives, "we are not so much
involved with the history of Israel as with the history of the development of Israel's literature"
(p. 314).

43. For Josephus, Abraham's place of origin is *Ourē tōn Chaldaiōn* (*Ant.* i.151), in spite of
the LXX's substitution of "the land of the Chaldeans" in Genesis 11.28, 31; 15.7.

replaced by a general reference to his "settling" in Canaan. Significantly, the divine appearance and the accompanying promise are omitted, and the impression is given that Abram bequeathed the land to his descendants on his own initiative; a divine promise is replaced by a human bequest. This substitution is in keeping with Josephus's complete suppression of the promises of blessing (Gen.12.2–3). The command (Gen.12.1) is likewise omitted, although Josephus does offer a paraphrase of, "... as YHWH told him" (Gen.12.4). In this rendering, then, Abraham is no longer introduced as the object of the divine address, in which the command is accompanied by the promise of universal blessing. And God is no longer presented as the God of the future who discloses that future to Abraham in the form of the promise. In this untheological, purely historical rendering of the Abraham story, the initial divine address that makes Abraham who he is has been virtually eliminated.[44]

The motivation for this is clear. Abraham is no longer the addressee of the divine promise because another role has been assigned to him: he is to be a religious reformer, the first great apostle of monotheism. No longer is he the one to whom God speaks – or rather, he is that only incidentally. Instead, he is the one who speaks about God. Having suppressed the divine address, and recounted the emigration to Canaan only briefly, Josephus becomes expansive as he begins to speak of Abraham's religious insights:

> He was a man skilful in understanding in all matters, persuasive to his hearers, unerring in his conclusions. For that reason he began to think about virtue more profoundly than others, and decided to reform *[kainisai]* and to alter the ideas generally held about God. He was the first courageously to proclaim that God, the creator of all things, is one, and that, if any other entity contributes to human well-being, it does so at God's command *[kata prostagēn tēn toutou]*, not by any inherent power of its own *[ou kat' oikeian ischun]*. (*Ant.* i.155)

Abraham's intellectual acumen enables him to perceive the falsehood of current polytheistic dogma, and his courage and persuasiveness enables him to expose and challenge it. He speaks not of himself as the addressee of a divine command, but of the various benevolent powers of the created order which operate as they do in obedience to God. His assertions are supported by rational arguments: he claims that the irregularities of the created order demonstrate its tendency to degenerate into anarchy if freed from the authority of the divine command. Thus, these irregularities reveal the powerful operation of that authority; the world around us displays an

---

44. Josephus' general tendency to avoid the promise motif is noted by P. Spilsbury, who refers especially to Josephus' treatment of Genesis 22 (*The Image of the Jew in Flavius Josephus' Paraphrase of the Bible*, p. 71). See also John Barclay, *Jews in the Mediterranean Diaspora*, p. 359, suggesting political motives for the playing down of the promise of land.

order imposed on chaos from above (i.156). If the world is providential for us, it is so not inherently but by divine appointment.[45] According to Josephus, these heterodox views were opposed by the Chaldeans and the other peoples of Mesopotamia, and it was this opposition that led Abraham to seek refuge in the land of Canaan (i.157). Abraham journeys to Canaan in accordance with the will of God, yet his emigration is also motivated by the desire to escape the religious persecution that his proclamation of the one true God has brought upon himself.

In substituting the God inferred from the created order for the God of the promise, Josephus further develops a trend also evident in *Jubilees* and Philo. All three authors see Abraham's emigration as motivated by his religious insights, opposed as they are to the views current in Chaldea. In *Jubilees*, Terah and his family are forced to leave Chaldea when Abraham burns down "the house of the idols", in spite of his father's plea that he should keep his views on idolatry to himself (Jub.12.1–15). In Haran, Abraham attains a further insight as he studies the stars so as to determine that year's rainfall: "And a thought struck him, and he said, All the signs of the stars and the signs of the moon and sun are in the hand of the Lord; why then should I enquire into them?" (12.17–18). For the Abraham of *Jubilees* the issue is the practice of astrology, whereas Josephus's Abraham is concerned with the self-sufficiency or otherwise of the providential order; yet common to both is the idea that this order is subject to God's command, whether this is attained by revelation or by rational argument. For Philo, Abraham perceives the folly of Chaldean divinizing of the creation by the self-knowledge represented by "Haran" (*Abr.* 72–76). The recognition that an invisible mind presides over the senses within the human frame gives him the model he needs in order to comprehend the world itself. In each case, and in different though overlapping ways, these three interpreters present Abraham as the originator of the monotheistic creed that differentiates the people descended from him from all other peoples. It is this religious insight that underlies the difference symbolized by the departure from Chaldea and the journey to Canaan. In *Jubilees*, the fundamental promises of Genesis 12.2–3 are still cited (Jub.12.22–24), whereas in Philo's life of Abraham and in Josephus they are absent. In all three cases, however, it is the religiously motivated departure from Chaldea that is the focus of the interpreter's interest. This event is not just the starting point for Abraham's career in and around the land of Canaan, as narrated in Genesis. Rather, it establishes Abraham's fundamental significance at the very outset of his story. No event – even the offering of

---

45.   L. H. Feldman sees here a distinctively Jewish argument for the divine freedom, over against a Stoicism in which God is a prisoner within his own system ("Abraham the Greek Philosopher in Josephus", pp. 146–47).

Isaac – is so central to his identity as this one. Abraham discovers the true God who presides over the operations of the natural order, and who is the God of the promise only incidentally and secondarily.

Abraham in Egypt

The story of Abraham's sojourn in Egypt (Gen.12.10–20) created difficulties for its ancient interpreters. The author of *Jubilees* finds here two of the ten tests to which Abraham was subjected: the Lord tested him through the famine in the land of Canaan which led him to seek refuge in Egypt, and through the abduction of his wife (Jub.17.17). In these as in all his other tests, Abraham was found faithful. Yet, for interpreters whose main concern is to celebrate Abraham's superlative virtue or obedience to the divine command, the problem is that the story as written seems to show Abraham as largely to blame for Sarah's abduction:

> And when he was about to enter Egypt, he said to Sarai his wife, Look, I know that you are a very beautiful woman; so when the Egyptians see you, they will say: This is his wife – and they will kill me, but you they will spare. Say that you are my sister, so that it may go well with me because of you, and my life may be spared on your account. (Gen.12.11–13)

No explanation is given of the anxieties that lead Abraham to adopt this desperate expedient, in which he effectively renounces his marriage and prostitutes his wife in order to preserve himself from dangers that the narrator does not trouble to make credible – incidentally deriving substantial material rewards from the transaction (cf. Gen.12.16). Far from justifying Abraham's conduct, the narrator allows Pharaoh to express an understandable sense of outrage:

> And Pharaoh called Abram and said: What is this that you have done to me? Why did you not tell me that she is your wife? Why did you say, She is my sister, so that I took her as my wife? Now then, here is your wife – take her, and go. (Gen.12.18–19; cf. also 20.1–13)

If the theme of the Abraham narrative is the divine promise, and if its God is the God who justifies the ungodly, then this story tells how the promise was jeopardized by human (especially male) folly and wickedness, and how it was safeguarded by the divine intervention. But if the theme is Abraham's virtue, then this story will have to be rewritten.

The author of *Jubilees* solves the problem by omitting all reference to Abraham's scheming. He and Sarah "lived in Egypt five years before his wife was torn away from him" (Jub.13.11). The abduction of Sarah is unanticipated, and Pharaoh has no cause for grievance against Abraham. Philo acknowledges that it requires some spiritual discernment to grasp the significance of Abraham's actions in this story. He adopts essentially the same solution as the author of *Jubilees*, exploiting the motif of the licentious monarch who preys upon the vulnerable, and emphasizing that Sarah's chastity was preserved (*Abr.* 89–98).[46] The divine protection was a reward for Abraham's preceding act of obedience in abandoning Chaldea and its creed: "God, then, approving the action just related, immediately rewards the worthy man with a great gift – for when his marriage was endangered by the designs of a powerful and dissolute man, God kept it safe and unharmed" (*Abr.* 90). In contrast to *Jubilees* and Philo, Josephus does mention Abraham's plan to pass Sarah off as his sister, but implies that his fears of "the Egyptians' frenzy for women" were well founded (*Ant.* i.162). Sarah's chastity is again preserved, and Pharaoh is concerned only to excuse his own conduct and not to criticize Abraham's (164–65). In the *Genesis Apocryphon*, Abraham's plan originates in a dream in which a cedar tree is to be felled in order to leave a palm-tree standing by itself (1QapGen xix.14–21); Sarah's beauty is extolled at length, and she saves Abraham's life by acknowledging him as her brother (xx.2–10). Her chastity is preserved throughout her two-year ordeal, after which the plagues suffered by Pharaoh's household are traced back to the wrong done to Abraham and Sarah, through the intervention of Lot (xx.16–26). In this context, Pharaoh's complaint about Abraham's conduct seems less than convincing. In each reading of the story, interpreters take pains to exclude the possibility that the Genesis narrator leaves open: that in this story Abraham's own conduct is blameworthy.

Josephus parts company with the other interpreters when he finds an additional role for Abraham in Egypt. Abraham is not only the wronged husband, he is also the emissary of Chaldean science and culture. His initial reason for visiting Egypt is twofold. He seeks

> both to benefit from their abundance and to hear what their priests said about the gods – intending, if he found their views preferable to his own, to conform to them, or else to convert them to a better mind if his own beliefs proved superior. (*Ant.* i.161)

This passage continues to develop the theme of Abraham as the religious reformer, who here adds open-mindedness to his other virtues. After the unfortunate misunderstanding relating to Sarah has been resolved, Abraham gains the admiration of the Egyptian intelligentsia by demonstrating that none of their various conflicting standpoints contains any truth (i.166). Of the two initial possibilities, that Egyptian views on the gods might be preferable to his, or that his might be superior to theirs, it is the second that proves to be correct. It is therefore to be

---

46. In the parallel stories in Genesis 20 and 26, the Genesis narrator himself shows a similar concern for matriarchal chastity (20.6, 26.10).

expected that Abraham will instigate a programme of religious reform in Egypt, and also that, as in Chaldea, this will prove to be unsuccessful – for it is common knowledge that Jewish monotheism is utterly opposed to the religious views of the Egyptians. "Our religion", as Josephus remarks elsewhere, "is as far removed from the one established among them as is the nature of God from that of irrational animals" (*c.Ap.* i.224).

Yet Josephus here takes a different tack. Abraham does not try to promote the views on deity that had proved so unpopular in Chaldea, but instead offers his Egyptian audience a course of instruction in Chaldean science.[47] The religious reformer becomes a cultural ambassador:

> Being admired by them... as a man of the greatest insight and ability, capable not only of understanding but also of speaking persuasively about any subject that he undertook to teach, he imparted to them the science of arithmetic and handed down to them the laws of astronomy. For before Abraham's arrival, the Egyptians were ignorant of these sciences, which passed in this way from the Chaldeans into Egypt, from where they came also to the Greeks. (*Ant.* i.168)

Abraham's conduct here seems at variance both with his earlier desire to speak with the Egyptian priests specifically about the nature of deity (i.161), and with his ideological breach with Chaldea (i.157). Josephus wishes to show Graeco-Roman readers that they have Abraham to thank for their scientific knowledge, and that his establishment of the characteristically Jewish form of monotheism does not exhaust his cultural significance. Yet the two sides of his presentation of Abraham are in tension with one another, and derive from different roots. The image of Abraham as religious reformer may be traced back to Philo and *Jubilees*; the image of the cultural ambassador stems from a tradition of Jewish apologetic that has survived only in fragmentary form. For our purposes, the most significant representative of this school of thought is Eupolemus, whose work dates from the mid-second century BCE and who is perhaps to be identified with the "Eupolemus son of John" whose leading role in a Jewish embassy to Rome is mentioned in 1 Maccabees 8.17.[48]

---

47. As P. Spilsbury notes, Josephus seems here to miss an opportunity to present Judaism as a "missionary religion" – which may suggest that he did not see it as such (*The Image of the Jew in Flavius Josephus' Paraphrase of the Bible*, p. 64).

48. The first of the excerpts attributed to Eupolemus is widely held to be the work of an anonymous Samaritan author, designated "Pseudo-Eupolemus"; it is this excerpt that is our concern here. In my view, the arguments of R. Doran against the pseudo-Eupolemus theory are compelling (*OTP* 2.873–76). Even if the theory is correct, there is no reason to attach the epithet "pseudo-" to one of the two Eupolemuses rather than the other.

In book nine of his *Praeparatio Evangelica*, Eusebius inserts a long excerpt from a treatise *On the Jews* by Cornelius Alexander of Miletus, generally known as Alexander Polyhistor – a historian active in Rome in the mid-first century BCE and also known to Josephus and to Clement of Alexandria.[49] Eusebius transcribes this material verbatim, and his own interventions are confined to insertions of supplementary material and indications of omissions. The value of this excerpt from Alexander Polyhistor is that it consists almost entirely of excerpts from earlier writers on Jewish history – most of whom appear to have been Jewish, in spite of their Greek names. These excerpts include full citations and summaries, and Alexander uses them to present an outline of Jewish history from Abraham onwards. Abraham himself is assigned to Eupolemus, Artapanus, an anonymous work, the anti-Jewish Molon, and the poet Philo; Alexander also adds an account of the sacrifice of Isaac, apparently in his own words (*Pr.Ev.* ix.17–20). There was also an excerpt from a history of the Jews by Cleodemus Malchus, which spoke of the sons of Abraham by Keturah (*Pr.Ev.* ix.20): Eusebius inserts this here as cited by Josephus (*Ant.* i.240–41), and it is not clear if this was its original place in Alexander's treatise. Returning to the direct citation of Alexander's work, the story of Jacob and his family is retold by Demetrius (*Pr.Ev.* ix.21); Theodotus contributes a poetic account of the destruction of Shechem, based on Genesis 34 (*Pr.Ev.* ix.22), Artapanus and Philo the poet add further material relating to Joseph (ix.23–24), and Aristeas tells the story of Job on the assumption that he is the son of Esau (ix.25). Moving on to Moses, a brief statement from Eupolemus about Moses' cultural significance (ix.26) is followed by a lengthy account of his life by Artapanus (ix.27), supplemented by excerpts from Ezekiel's tragedy on the exodus and from Demetrius (ix.28–29). Eupolemus contributes a brief survey of the history of the Jews from Moses to David, which leads to a fuller account of the construction of Solomon's temple based on 1 Kings 5–8, including a correspondence between Solomon and Vaphres king of Egypt and Suron king of Phoenicia (30–34). A brief reference to Theophilus is also inserted here (34). Eusebius's presentation of Alexander's material concludes with some descriptions of Jerusalem drawn from Timochares, an anonymous author, and Philo the poet (35–37), and an account of the fall of Jerusalem to the Babylonians (39).[50]

---

49. For the Greek text of this work, with English translation, see the edition of E. H. Gifford (1903). English translations of the fragments preserved by Eusebius are found in *OTP* 2.843–903; introductory material is also to be found in M. E. Stone (ed.), *Jewish Writings of the Second Temple Period*, pp. 160–71 (H. W. Attridge).

50. It is not clear that this last fragment should be ascribed to Eupolemus (as in *OTP* 2.871 and elsewhere).

Alexander's work was known also to Clement of Alexandria. Excerpts from accounts of the life of Moses by Eupolemus, Artapanus and Ezekiel the tragedian correspond to Eusebius's material, and are obviously drawn from Alexander Polyhistor (*Strom.* i.23.153–56). Alexander is explicitly mentioned in a reference to the correspondence between Solomon and Vaphres of Egypt (*Strom.* i.21.130). Eusebius breaks off his presentation of material from Alexander with the Babylonian destruction of Jerusalem, which might suggest that Alexander's account of Jewish history was confined to the scriptural period. However, Clement adds some valuable chronological information drawn from three of the authors cited by Alexander in the material preserved by Eusebius: Demetrius, Philo and Eupolemus. These citations bridge the gap between the biblical period and the present era, and they probably represent the original conclusion of Alexander's historical survey.

According to Clement (*Strom.* i.21.141–44), Demetrius states that three hundred and thirty-eight years and three months elapsed between the fall of Jerusalem and the accession of Ptolemy IV – during whose reign (*c.* 221–204 BCE) Demetrius's work was presumably written. Philo is merely said to have disagreed with Demetrius about the kings of Judah. Eupolemus is said to have computed the time from Adam and the exodus to "the fifth year of Demetrius, while Ptolemy was in his twelfth year as king of Egypt"; this makes it possible to date his work to 157 BCE.[51] It is presumably Alexander Polyhistor himself who updates these figures by noting the further one hundred and twenty years until "the consulship in Rome of Gnaius Dometianus and Asinius" – suggesting that his own work on the Jews is to be dated to *c.* 40 BCE. The fact that Clement gives this second, more recent date alongside the date of Eupolemus's work is a clear indication that his knowledge of that work is derived from a secondary source. Since time and place both agree with what is known of Alexander, and since Alexander cites Eupolemus and the other two authors elsewhere, it is probable that Clement's chronological information was derived from him.[52]

Josephus too had access to the work of Alexander Polyhistor. It is true that his vivid depiction of Moses as an Egyptian general who campaigns successfully against the Ethiopians (*Ant.* ii.238–57) is only distantly related to the parallel story that Alexander cites from Artapanus (*Pr.Ev.* ix.27). In book one of *Against Apion*, however, Josephus concludes his survey of non-Jewish references to Jews and Judaism by listing a number of figures he has not been able to discuss (Theophilus, Theodotus, Mnaseas,

---

51. So H. W. Attridge, "Historiography", in M. E. Stone (ed.), *Jewish Writings of the Second Temple Period*, pp. 157–84; pp. 162–63.
52. So F. Fallon, *OTP* 2.861–62.

Aristophanes, Hermogenes, Euhemerus, Conon, Zopyrion). Theophilus and Theodotus may be identical to the authors cited by Alexander Polyhistor (*Pr.Ev.* ix.22.1–12, ix.34). More significantly, Josephus continues:

> The majority of these writers have misrepresented the truth about our earliest history, because they have not read our sacred books. Yet they all agree in testifying to our antiquity... Indeed, Demetrius Phalereus, the earlier Philo and Eupolemus have not deviated greatly from the truth, and their errors deserve to be pardoned – for they were unable to follow the sense of our writings with the required accuracy. (*c.Ap.* i.217–18)

It is striking that the (supposedly) non-Jewish writers that Josephus singles out for praise are precisely the three with whom Alexander Polyhistor's account of Jewish history appears to have concluded.[53] Since Josephus cites Alexander explicitly as the source of a passage by Cleodemus Malchas (*Ant.* i.240–41), it is probable that he was also acquainted with Demetrius, Philo and Eupolemus through Alexander. And this brings us to the point of this excursion into Hellenistic Jewish literary history: Eupolemus's retelling of the story of Abraham in Egypt is probably the main source for Josephus's "cultural ambassador" theme.

As we have seen, Josephus follows Philo and *Jubilees* in taking Abraham's departure from Chaldea to signify his rejection of Chaldean science (*Ant.* i.157), but parts company with them when he portrays Abraham as communicating Chaldean science to the Egyptians (*Ant.* i.167–68). Precisely this view is found in the first three of Alexander Polyhistor's excerpts relating to Abraham, which seem to take the form of summaries rather than direct quotations. According to Artapanus,[54] Abraham

> came with all his household to Egypt, to Pharethothes king of the Egyptians,[55] and taught him astronomy *[astrologia]*; after remaining there for twenty years, he returned again into the regions of Syria. (*Pr.Ev.* ix.18.1)

53. N. Walter argues that Josephus and Clement cannot have obtained the chronological information of Demetrius, Philo and Eupolemus from Alexander Polyhistor, since otherwise Josephus could not have mistaken them for non-Jewish writers ("Zur Überlieferung einiger Reste früher jüdisch-hellenistischer Literatur bei Josephus, Clemens und Eusebius", pp. 314–20). However, Alexander gives no information about the authors he cites other than their names – which, with the exception of Ezekiel the tragedian, are all Greek. In arguing that Eupolemus was Josephus's source, I assume that Josephus knows of him from Alexander Polyhistor.

54. On Artapanus see especially J. Barclay, *Jews in the Mediterranean Diaspora*, pp. 127–32: in his positive attitude even towards Egyptian religion, Artapanus is an extreme instance of "cultural convergence".

55. Cf. *Pharaōthēs ho basileus tōn Aeguptiōn* (*Ant.* i.163).

This is confirmed by the anonymous work cited next,[56] which states that

> Abraham having been taught the science of astronomy *[tēn astrologikēn epistēmēn paideuthenta]* came first into Phoenicia and taught astronomy to the Phoenicians, and later passed on into Egypt. (*Pr.Ev.* ix.18.2)

The fullest statement of this view is ascribed to Eupolemus, the first author to be cited.[57] According to Alexander Polyhistor's summary, Eupolemus states that

> in the tenth generation, in the Babylonian city of Kamarina, which some identify with the city of Ourie (which may be translated, City of the Chaldeans), ... Abraham was born, surpassing everyone by his noble birth and his wisdom. He was the inventor of astronomy and Chaldean science *[Chaldaikē]*, and found favour with God on account of his zeal for piety *[eusebeia]*. This man came to dwell in Phoenicia by the command of God, and, teaching the Phoenicians the changes of the sun and the moon and all other matters, he found favour with the king. (*Pr.Ev.* ix.17.3–4)[58]

Although Abraham's emigration is here still commanded by God, it represents the exact opposite of the ideological conflict with the Chaldeans assumed by other interpreters. God's intention is not to separate Abraham from Chaldean science, but to use him to propagate it – first in Phoenicia, and later in Egypt. The journey to Egypt here takes place only after the military exploits of Genesis 14 (and not before, as in Genesis).[59] Apart from its positioning, however, the story of the abduction of Sarah is retold

---

56. In this context, the phrase *en de adespotois heuromen ton Abraam ktl* is most likely to refer to a single anonymous work.

57. Alexander Polyhistor distinguishes clearly between the anonymous work and the work of Eupolemus, whom he introduces here for the first time: "Eupolemus, in his work on the Jews..." It is not easy to see how or why a false attribution to Eupolemus could have occurred. On this material, see B. Z. Wacholder, "Pseudo-Eupolemus' Two Greek Fragments on the Life of Abraham", in his *Essays on Jewish Chronology and Chronography*, pp. 75–105.

58. The phrase *en triskaidekatē genea* ("in the thirteenth generation") is perhaps a gloss which seeks awkwardly to correct the preceding reference to the tenth generation (so M. Hengel, *Judaism and Hellenism*, 2.61n); it is therefore omitted here. R. Doran's rendering (*OTP* 2.880) has the disadvantage of undermining the equation of Camarina and Ur, which seems to be implied in the Greek.

59. As a result of his military success, "Abraham was treated as a guest by the city in the temple of Argarizin, which means 'Mountain of the Most High'" (*Pr.Ev.* ix.17.5). This identification of Salem, the city of Melchizedek, with "Argarizin" has been thought to indicate that the author must have been a Samaritan, and that he cannot have written the other fragments attributed to Eupolemus. This fragment has therefore been attributed to a "Pseudo-Eupolemus". R. Doran points out, however, that Eupolemus elsewhere derives the name "Jerusalem" not from Melchizedek's "Salem", but from *Hieron Solomōnos*, the Temple of Solomon (*Pr.Ev.* ix.34.13); and also that Salem is located in Samaria in Genesis 33.18 LXX,

in straightforward fashion. According to Alexander, Eupolemus explained at great length *(perissoteron historēsen)* how the sickness inflicted on Pharaoh and his household served to protect Sarah's chastity – a point that also concerns the *Genesis Apocryphon* (1QapGen xx.12–18), Philo *(Abr.* 95–98) and Josephus *(Ant.* i.164). Eupolemus states that the problem was correctly diagnosed by Pharaoh's diviners, who told him that the woman was not a widow – thereby indicating that Sarah was the wife of Abraham *(Pr.Ev.* ix.17.7). The diviners also appear in the *Genesis Apocryphon*, where they fail to reach a diagnosis (1QapGen xx.18–20), and, in the guise of priests, in Josephus, where they tell Pharaoh "that his calamity was due to the wrath of God, because he wished to outrage the stranger's wife" *(Ant.* i.164). Another point of contact between Eupolemus and Josephus is that (unlike Philo and the author of *Jubilees*) both writers acknowledge that Abraham claimed that Sarah was his sister *(Pr.Ev.* ix.17.6; *Ant.* i.162).

These parallels suggest that it is from Eupolemus that Josephus derives his claim that Abraham taught Chaldean science to the Egyptians. Alexander Polyhistor summarizes Eupolemus's rendering of this theme as follows:

> And Abraham, dwelling in Hieropolis with the Egyptian priests, taught them many things, introducing astronomy and the other sciences to them, claiming that the Babylonians and indeed he himself had discovered these things, but tracing back the first discovery to Enoch – and saying that he had first discovered astronomy, not the Egyptians... *(Pr.Ev.* ix.17.8)

Eupolemus and Josephus are agreed that Abraham's astronomical lectures to the Egyptians underlie the transmission of Chaldean science to the Greeks.[60] They also agree that the story of Abraham's role in the history of science is to be distinguished from the less happy story of his dealings with

---

where *šlm* is taken as a place-name and not as a verb: "And Jacob came to Salem the city of Shechem" *(OTP* 2.875). Mount Gerizim has a role in Jewish as well as Samaritan tradition (cf. Deut.11.29, 27.12; Josh.8.33).

60.   Compare Eupolemus's claim that the Phoenicians, from whom the Greeks received the alphabet, had received it from the Jews, who had been taught it by Moses *(Pr.Ev.* ix.26.1). In the light of this parallel, it is difficult to agree with Hengel's contrast between "the universalist breadth of the Abraham narrative in the anonymous Samaritan [i.e. the supposed "Pseudo-Eupolemus"] and the Judean nationalist narrowness of the fragments of Eupolemus, where even the international relationships of Solomon only serve the greater glory of the Jewish king and the sanctuary built by him" *(Judaism and Hellenism,* 1.95). The treatment of the Abraham narrative is exclusively concerned with the greater glory of the Jewish people, and represents the opposite extreme to the view that the Jews are "the least intelligent of the barbarians, and therefore the only people who have contributed no useful invention to civilization" (Apollonius Molon, as summarized in Josephus, *Against Apion,* ii.148; cf. ii.135, 182, which indicate that this was a widely held view).

Pharaoh. In contrast, Artapanus has Abraham initiating Pharaoh himself into the mysteries of astronomy (*Pr.Ev.* ix.18.1).

Surprisingly, there is a textual basis for this unlikely image of Abraham as astronomer. The text in question probably underlies the claims made by Eupolemus and Artapanus, and is explicitly cited by Josephus. At several points in his work, Josephus refers to Berosus, the author of a history of Babylon in three books and dedicated to Antiochus I (281–61 BCE).[61] Between his accounts of Abraham's departure from Chaldea and his journey to Egypt, Josephus inserts several supporting testimonies from non-Jewish writers, of whom Berosus is the first:

> Berosus mentions our father Abraham, although not by name, when he says this: "After the Flood, in the tenth generation, there lived among the Chaldeans a man righteous and great and expert in heavenly matters *[ta ourania empeiros]*." (*Ant.* i.158)

Elsewhere, Josephus provides information about the context of Berosus's statement. In book one of *Against Apion*, he quotes at length from Berosus's account of Nebuchadnezzar's military campaigns and other exploits, which – with its reference to Jewish prisoners being taken into exile in Babylon – provides him with valuable confirmation of the veracity of the scriptural record (*c.Ap.* i.132–41). For our purposes, it is Josephus's introductory remarks about Berosus's work that are significant:

> The witness to these matters is Berosus, a man of Chaldean birth but well known to educated people for publishing works on astronomy and Chaldean philosophy for Greek readers. This Berosus, following the most ancient records, tells of the Flood and the consequent destruction of the human race, just as Moses did, and of the ark in which Noah, the founder of our race, was saved when it landed on the summits of the Armenian mountains. Then he lists the descendants of Noah, together with their dates, and comes down to Nabopalassar, king of Babylon and Chaldea. (*c.Ap.* i.129–31)

Thus, Berosus's genealogy traced the ancestry of Nabopalassar and his son Nebuchadnezzar back to Noah – or rather, to Xisuthrus or Ziusudra, the hero of the Sumerian version of the flood legend. In the Babylonian legend unlike the scriptural one, the protagonist is a kingly figure, and this accounts for his genealogical significance for the Babylonian monarchy.

---

61. Elsewhere in the *Antiquities*, Josephus derives from Berosus a claim that parts of the ark still survive in the mountains of Armenia (*Ant.* i.93); confirmation of the longevity of the first generations of humans (i.106); references to Sennacherib, king of Assyria (x.20) and Baladan, king of Babylon (x.34); and an account of the reign of Nebuchadnezzar, taken from Berosus's third book (x.219–26 = *c.Ap.* i.132–41).

It is this genealogy that must have provided the context for Berosus's statement that, "after the Flood, in the tenth generation, there was among the Chaldeans a man righteous and great and expert in heavenly matters".[62] In the context of a genealogy from Xisuthrus to Nabopalassar, this figure could only have been identified with Abraham by Jews anxious to co-ordinate their own scriptural traditions with the traditions of other nations. If the enumeration begins from Noah's son Shem, then Abraham represents the tenth generation after the Flood, according to the genealogy of Genesis 11.10–26. For Jewish readers, then, Berosus's astronomical expert is to be identified with Abraham, and Abraham thereby becomes an astronomer – perhaps even the inventor of astronomy. Since the Jewish reader knows that the Xisuthrus of Berosus was actually called Noah, it is easy enough to correct or supply other names on the basis of the scriptural record.

As we have seen, Jewish interpreters view Abraham as an expert in Chaldean astronomy and science, whether he leaves Chaldea in order to propagate his scientific knowledge (Eupolemus, Artapanus, Josephus) or because he has renounced it (*Jubilees*, Philo). If this Jewish interpretation of Berosus's statement is indeed the basis for the image of Abraham as astronomer, then it long predates Josephus. It is significant that Berosus's exact phrase, "in the tenth generation" *(dekatē genea)* recurs at the beginning of Eupolemus's statements about Abraham (*Pr.Ev.* ix.17.3; cf. *Ant.* i.148, where Abraham is said to be "tenth in descent from Noah"). A process of assimilation has occurred in which Abraham fulfils the role of Berosus's righteous man of the tenth generation, expert in heavenly matters.[63] The identification of the city of Kamarina with the biblical Ur can also be explained in the same way.[64] From the standpoint of Eupolemus and Josephus, the image of Abraham as astronomer has a sound textual basis, if non-biblical material is allowed to fill out the biblical picture.[65]

---

62.   Berosus is said to have listed eighty-six kings from Xisuthrus to the overthrow of Babylon: they were recorded in full by Alexander Polyhistor, but few of the names are still extant (F. Jacoby, *Die Fragmente der griechischen Historiker*, IIIC, p. 384).

63.   For (Pseudo-)Eupolemus's relationship to Berosus, see M. Hengel, *Judaism and Hellenism*, 1.88, 2.59n, and the literature cited there.

64.   Compare the equation of Enoch and Atlas later in the same passage (*Pr.Ev.* ix.17.9). In this passage, Eupolemus's interest in what "the Chaldeans say..." as well as in what "the Greeks say..." is noteworthy: the concern is with the co-ordination of non-Jewish traditions with scripture. Eupolemus implies a euhemeristic account of pagan deities, in which "Belus, Kronos, Atlas and the Babylonian and Greek pantheons are none other than pagan names for the ancestors of Abraham" (B. Z. Wacholder, "Pseudo-Eupolemus' Two Greek Fragments on the Life of Abraham", p. 83).

65.   Other contributory factors may have been Genesis 15.5 (so S. Davis, *The Antithesis of the Ages*, p. 164), and the general cultural connection between Chaldea and astronomy/ astrology (cf. Matt.2.2).

There is no doubt a considerable gulf between those interpreters for whom Abraham renounced Chaldean astronomy and those for whom he introduced it to the wider world – in spite of Josephus's attempt to harmonize the two views. Yet this difference of opinion is not easy to assess. It does not correspond to the (often unhelpful) distinction between a "Palestinian" and a "Hellenistic" Judaism, since the Palestinian author of *Jubilees* and the Hellenistic Philo are ranged on the same side of it, in spite of their other differences. Indeed, an adequate typology for all the various appropriations of the figure of Abraham hardly seems possible, since there are too many variables involved. In its "chaldaizing" of Abraham, Eupolemus's work may express a syncretizing concern to play down Jewish distinctiveness, or a nationalistic claim to the honour due to the founder of the sciences, or an open-minded apologetic and missionary strategy; or, more plausibly, it might represent each of these things to different people with different standpoints. Josephus shares some of Eupolemus's concerns, and yet his fidelity to the text of scripture rivals that of *Jubilees* – although both betray a tendency towards legendary expansion that comes to fuller expression in the *Genesis Apocryphon*. *Jubilees*, Philo and Paul are all concerned to define Abraham's relationship to the law, whereas Josephus and the *Genesis Apocryphon* show no interest in this question. The attempt to sum up Abraham's exemplary significance in terms of his faith or faithfulness is likewise common to *Jubilees*, Philo and Paul. Abraham has become such a malleable figure that it is hard to limit the possibilities he represents to his interpreters.

Arguably, each of these interpretations is distinctive in relation to all the others. Eupolemus is distinctive for his thoroughgoing "chaldaizing" of Abraham; *Jubilees*, for its portrayal of Abraham as already observing the letter of the law; Philo, for his interpretation of Abraham as a symbol of the soul's progress towards God; Josephus, for his attempt to present Abraham within the generic conventions of Graeco-Roman historiography. It cannot be said that any of these images of Abraham – that of *Jubilees*, for example – is any more "authentically Jewish" than the others. Rather, they demonstrate that Jewish identity is a contested concept, in which even the main dividing lines that might structure the debate remain unclear. They represent a number of ways in which Jewish identity might be negotiated within a Graeco-Roman context – insofar as Jewish identity is bound up with the figure of "our father Abraham" (*Ant.* i.158, cf. Rom.4.1).

Paul's depiction of Abraham is clearly distinctive in its emphasis on the God of the promise who is also the God who justifies the ungodly. Although his reflections on Abraham are quite brief in comparison to the other interpreters, this is compensated for by the density of his argumentation and by his appeal to a range of instances of the Genesis promise motif. The question whether Paul is more distinctive in relation to other interpreters than, say, Philo rests on the doubtful assumption that neutral criteria are available through which distinctiveness might be quantified.

Yet it can be shown that, from a Pauline perspective, the other interpretations of Genesis are in the last resort surprisingly similar. All of them are concerned to present Abraham as an exemplary figure or role model for human conduct in relation to God. He was, says Josephus, "a man supreme in every virtue, who was duly honoured by God for his zeal on God's behalf" (*Ant.* i.256). For Eupolemus, Abraham "found favour with God on account of his zeal for piety" (*Pr.Ev*, ix.17.3). The author of *Jubilees* states that "in every test to which the Lord subjected him, he was found faithful" (Jub.17.18); and also that "Abraham was perfect with the Lord in all his works, and well-pleasing in righteousness all the days of his life" (Jub.23.10). For Philo, Abraham not only observed the unwritten law, but "is himself a law and an unwritten statute" (*Abr.* 276). Abraham's acts of obedience are heightened and celebrated, and actions about which questions might be raised are rewritten to ensure that such questions are *not* raised. In contrast to this eulogizing and hagiography, Paul sounds a very different note when he insists on taking Genesis 15.6 at face value: Abraham's righteousness is constituted merely by his acceptance of God's promise to act on his behalf.

Corresponding to this different construal of Abraham is a different understanding of the God of the Genesis narrative. Apart from Paul, Jewish interpreters regard the promise motif as secondary to a story whose primary aim is to celebrate Abraham's outstanding piety and virtue. In Genesis 15.1, for example, the Genesis narrator presents the divine reassurance to Abraham as originating simply in the unmotivated divine election:

> After these things the word of YHWH came to Abram in a vision, saying: Fear not, Abraham, I am your shield, your reward shall be very great.

In contrast, Josephus sees the divine reassurance as occasioned by the pious action that Abraham has just performed, in renouncing the spoils of his successful guerrilla raid on the invading Assyrian army (cf. Gen.14):

> Commending his virtue *[epainesas autou tēn aretēn]*, God said: "You shall not lose the rewards *[misthous]* that you are worthy to receive for such good deeds *[epi toiautais eupragiais]*." (*Ant.* i.183)

Similarly, in *Jubilees* the initial promises of Genesis 12.2–3 are occasioned by Abraham's renunciation of the idolatry and astronomy of Chaldea in his quest for the true God (Jub.12.1–24). The tendency to subordinate the divine promise to Abraham's piety comes to a head in passages where the promise motif is actually omitted from the opening of Abraham's story, to be replaced by a presentation in which Abraham makes his own way to the true God by inferences from the created order or from self-knowledge (*Ant.* i.154–55, 161; *Abr.* 61–88), or confines himself to the knowledge of the created order (*Pr.Ev.* ix.17.4, 8; *Ant.* i.166–68). It cannot be said that these interpreters systematically neglect the promises. Philo devotes the first half of his treatise *On the Migration of Abraham* to a detailed discussion of Genesis 12.2–3 (*Migr.* 1–126). The *Genesis Apocryphon* expands the divine reassurance of Genesis 15.1 into a reminder of all the material blessings that Abraham has received since he left Haran, and a promise that this divine generosity will continue (1QapGen xxii.27–32). In general, however, the motif of the divine promise is incidental in these texts. Here, God speaks primarily to command or to commend: and in either case it is Abraham's faithfulness, obedience, piety, virtue or intellect that takes centre stage.

In contrast, Paul consistently focuses on the promise motif whenever he speaks of Abraham. In this reading of Genesis, the overriding theme is the future divine saving action in its worldwide scope. Both God and Abraham are understood in terms of the universal future that is entailed in their relationship. Yet the Genesis narrative is primarily concerned with the God of that future. Abraham no longer holds the central position in his own story.

Part Three

The Wilderness

Chapter 6

Exodus

Fundamental to Pauline scriptural interpretation is the citation of specific texts. For Paul, the individual scriptural utterance is everything. He offers his readers no general discussion of the prophetic testimony to divine saving action; rather, he cites a tiny, six-word fragment of text from Habakkuk, finding in it the semantic resources for one of his most far-reaching theological arguments. Where scripture is in view, Paul will rarely if ever detach himself from its specific wording. Even a reference to an individual scriptural story must be made still more specific by quoting the words that best express its significance. Thus, the Golden Calf story is understood as a warning against idolatry, but its meaning for us must also be crystallized in the form of a citation: we are not to be idolators like the Israelites – "as it is written: 'The people sat to eat and drink, and rose to play'" (1 Cor.10.7; Ex.32.6). Even where Paul uses relatively abstract terms such as "promise" or "law", the individual scriptural text is not far away. The concept of "the promise" is derived from "the promises" that are to be found in individual texts in Genesis (cf. Gal.3.16–18). The significance of "the law" is articulated in individual texts drawn from Leviticus and Deuteronomy (cf. Gal.3.10–12). For Paul, it is the written words that matter: in that sense, the citation formula, "As it is written..." is the foundation stone of Pauline scriptural interpretation. His hermeneutical maxim is simply, "Not beyond what is written" (cf. 1 Cor.4.6).[1]

Paul's preoccupation with the particular scriptural utterance has led to serious misunderstanding. It is widely assumed that his engagement with scripture amounts to little more than an *ad hoc* citation of isolated texts, pressed into the service of whatever argument he happens to be pursuing at the time – usually in defiance of their plain sense. Where the argument in question relates to "the law", it is assumed that Paul propounds a dogmatic "view" of the law that is essentially independent

---

1. Paul appears here to be citing a well-known slogan, which itself alludes to his standard citation formula (*ha gegraptai* corresponding to *kathōs gegraptai*); see M. D. Hooker's helpful discussion, in her *From Adam to Christ*, pp. 106–12.

of the texts he cites in support of it. Paul's forced readings of his supposed "proof texts" about the law are said to confirm their secondary status within his discourse. So it is that debate about "Paul's view of the law" persistently overlooks the fact that the law is above all *a text that is read.*

"Paul's view of the law" is a scholarly construct that concerns itself with a narrow range of well-worn problems. For example, one may seek to identify the eschatological or christological beliefs that underlie Paul's remarkably "negative" statements about the law – in an attempt to see his view of the law as a logical corollary of his *a priori* dogmatic commitments.[2] If the intention is to present Paul as a good though idiosyncratic first-century Jew, one may choose to play down his more negative statements, emphasizing their situational character and contrasting them with the more "balanced" assertions supposedly found in less polemical contexts.[3] If, on the other hand, the preference is for a more radical, proto-Marcionite Paul, one will give the negative statements all possible emphasis – highlighting the fact that Paul at one point seems to downgrade the law to the production of angels.[4] The issue of coherence may also be addressed. Does Paul have a "consistent" view of the law, or does he make a number of contradictory statements which cannot be harmonized?[5] Does Paul's view of the law develop, especially between Galatians and Romans?[6] Does Paul believe that the law is not fully binding

---

2. See on this Albert Schweitzer, *The Mysticism of Paul the Apostle*, pp. 186–96. For Schweitzer, it is because "[t]he supernatural world already exists within the sphere of the corporeity of those who are in Christ, filled as it is with the death- and resurrection-producing forces" of the messianic era, that "the Law is no longer valid for those who are in Christ Jesus" (p. 188). In E. P. Sanders' position, Schweitzer's eschatological emphasis has receded somewhat. Sanders argues that Paul's varying statements about the law stem from the conviction that, "[i]f salvation is by Christ and is intended for Gentile as well as Jew, it is not by the Jewish law *in any case*, no matter how well it is done, and without regard to one's interior attitude" (*Paul, the Law, and the Jewish People*, p. 152; italics original). Schweitzer and Sanders both assume that Paul's view of the law is a secondary deduction from a primary dogmatic commitment.

3. Compare J. D. G. Dunn, *Theology of Paul the Apostle*, pp. 128–61.

4. According to J. L. Martyn, Paul in Galatians 3.19–20 does not intend "merely to establish the inferiority of the Sinaitic Law ... To speak of comparative inferiority is in this case to domesticate a radical picture" (*Galatians*, p. 368). Rather, Paul "compels the Gentiles ... to gaze for a moment into the abyss of a Law that is for them godless" (p. 370).

5. The claim of H. Räisänen, that "Paul's thought on the law is full of difficulties and inconsistencies" (*Paul and the Law*, p. 86), has been widely criticized. Yet assertions of coherence do not amount to convincing demonstrations. The tendency of the present reading is to find the most significant inconsistencies within the Torah itself, as Paul reads it.

6. As argued by H. Hübner, *Law in Paul's Thought*. Hübner believes that Paul wrote the more conciliatory Romans in response to criticism of Galatians emanating from James (pp. 63–64).

on Gentiles but is still in force for Jews?[7] And how are we to understand
the role of the law in the ongoing life of the Christian?[8] Most importantly
of all, perhaps: what part does the law play in the quarrel between Paul
and certain representatives of a "judaizing" version of the Christian
gospel? (And does the answer to that question bear any resemblance to the
answer that the sixteenth-century Reformers thought they had found?)[9]
Some of the traditional problems attach to specific texts. What did Paul
really mean when he described Christ as the *telos* of the law in Romans
10.4?[10] Who is the speaker who analyses the painful tensions of life under
the law in Romans 7?[11] These, then, are some of the items on the agenda of
the debate on "Paul's view of the law". Most of them have been on that
agenda for at least a century, and they will no doubt remain there for the
foreseeable future – a constellation of interrelated "problems" as fixed and
stable as the stars in the night sky.[12]

Since Paul's citations from the law are regarded as secondary, the fact
that "the law" is actually a *text* hardly seems to impinge on this endlessly
circulating debate. And yet it seems plausible that, when Paul speaks of
"the law", he has in mind the text known as "the Law of Moses", with a
particular emphasis on the four later books which are concerned with the
event at Mount Sinai and its aftermath. *Paul's "view of the law" is nothing
other than his reading of Exodus, Leviticus, Numbers and Deuteronomy.* He
speaks of the law not as a propounder of dogmatic assertions but as an
interpreter of texts.

Paul engages with these texts by way of representative narratives and
individual texts which are supposed to articulate the fundamental
dynamics of the Torah as a whole. From his reading of the Book of
Exodus, Paul knows of the complex event of the giving of the law at
Mount Sinai – an event crystallized in the scriptural rendering of Moses'
twofold descent from the mountain bearing the inscribed stone tablets
(Ex.32–34; 2 Cor.3). From the Book of Leviticus Paul learns that the

---

7.   Mark C. Nanos succinctly summarizes the concern here: "Where a Law-free gospel has
[traditionally] been presupposed, this reading has uncovered a Law-observant one for Jews
and a Law-respectful one for Gentiles" (*The Mystery of Romans*, p. 337).

8.   E. P. Sanders argues that, although "the Law is not an entrance requirement", it
remains the case that "the Law should be fulfilled" (the titles of chapters 1 and 3 of his *Paul,
the Law and the Jewish People*).

9.   The unbridgeable gulf between the real Paul and the Reformers' reading of him is the
fundamental dogma of the "new perspective on Paul" – as illustrated by the title of an early
article by N. T. Wright, "The Paul of History and the Apostle of Faith".

10.   R. Badenas devotes an entire monograph to this word (*Christ the End of the Law*).

11.   W.-G. Kümmel was once widely thought to have solved this old problem, arguing that
we have in this passage a description of the non-Christian from a Christian standpoint (*Römer
7 und die Bekehrung des Paulus*, p. 138).

12.   I draw this image from H.-G. Gadamer, *Truth and Method*, p. 340.

legislation that promotes the holiness of the people of Israel has their ultimate well-being as its goal: "The one who does these things will live by them" (Lev.18.5; Gal.3.12, Rom.10.5). In the Book of Numbers, Paul reads the disastrous history of the wilderness generation in the aftermath of the Sinai event, and concludes from it that the law is necessarily entangled with sin and death (Num.11–25; Rom.7, 1 Cor.10). From the Book of Deuteronomy Paul derives the theme of the law's curse, the threat that comes to the fore precisely as the book and the Torah as a whole draw to a close (Deut.27.26; Gal.3.10). In each case, the individual text plays a representative role, standing for a broad complex of scriptural material relating to the giving of the law, to its positive goal, or to its negative impact. These texts have not been wrenched from their context and forced into the service of an alien dogmatic argument; on the contrary, there are many indications that they bring their contexts with them. Additional texts are also brought into play. The tenth commandment plays an important role in Romans 7; in Romans 10 the Leviticus text is countered by a remarkable rewriting of material from Deuteronomy 30; the history of the wilderness generation is represented not only by the narratives of rebellion from Numbers but also by the story of the Golden Calf from Exodus; in Deuteronomy 32, the Song of Moses speaks of a future beyond the curse of the law.

When the Genesis "promise" texts are also taken into account, the contours of a Pauline reading of the whole Pentateuch begin to emerge. This reading survives only in fragments, and those fragments are often embedded in contexts shaped by situational factors. In 2 Corinthians 3, for example, it is Paul's critique of his opponents' letters of recommendation that occasions the focus on "writing" within the ministry of Moses. And yet, when the fragments are set alongside one another, the outline of a broadly coherent picture comes to light. In contrast to his relatively casual use of a text such as Deuteronomy 25.4 ("You shall not muzzle an ox ... " [cf. 1 Cor.9.9]), Paul lays the greatest emphasis on his primary texts from the Torah. For him, these texts articulate the significance of the whole Torah – its acknowledgment that its conditional promise of life was from the outset overtaken by the reality of sin and death, together with the indirect testimony to God's saving action in Christ that is hidden within this acknowledgment. In each case, we shall see that Paul's interpretations exploit the semantic potential of the scriptural text itself, especially in its internal tensions. That is not to say that Paul's reading can be shown to uncover the "real" meaning of these texts, from the standpoint of any neutral hermeneutical criteria. Yet the conventional scholarly view, which is that Paul reads his theology into the scriptural texts and not out of them, turns out to be demonstrably false.

One fundamental characteristic of Paul's reading of the Torah has already come to light in the preceding chapters. Paul is acutely aware of the tension between the unconditional Genesis promises and the conditional offer of "life" that derives from the law given at Mount Sinai. In the promise, God commits himself unconditionally to future saving action on behalf of Abraham and his seed – an action that will bring blessing to the entire world. In the law, "life" is now conditional on observance of the commandments. Other contemporary readers of the Torah share Paul's awareness of the potential disjunction between Genesis and Exodus, patriarchs and Sinai. The disjunction may be overcome by heightening the anticipations of the Sinai revelation already present in Genesis itself (as in *Jubilees*), or by presenting the exemplary lives of the patriarchs as foundational to everything that follows (as with Philo). Faced with the same interpretative problem, Paul insists that the disjunction is to be maintained. His gospel is correlated exclusively with the promise, since it announces the divine saving action in which the promise is fulfilled. The law as a way of salvation is compatible with the promise only because it ends in failure, its conditional offer of life unrealized. Nothing said at Mount Sinai can be allowed to alter the terms of the unconditional commitments that God undertook in the promises to Abraham. Thus, for Paul, utterances from Exodus, Leviticus and Deuteronomy are utterances of "the law" (Rom.7.7; 1 Cor.9.9; Gal.3.10, 12), whereas the promises of Genesis represent the gospel itself in anticipatory form (Gal.3.8).[13]

Having already established this disjunction from the perspective of the Genesis promise, we shall now see how it is confirmed by Paul's interpretation of the Sinai event and its aftermath, as rendered by Exodus-Deuteronomy. Here too, on this side of the disjunction, Paul's reading of this material is highly distinctive when compared to other contemporary readings. For him, the law that brings with it the conditional offer of life is overtaken by the realities of sin and death, so that those who are under law are under its curse. Paul makes this claim not because of his prior dogmatic commitments, but because he has read and noted the scriptural stories that tell of the law's disastrous impact on its first addressees, who rebel against it and who are doomed to die in the wilderness in consequence. Other interpreters appear to skirt around the fact that the post-Sinai history of Israel in the wilderness is a history of catastrophe. For Paul, this represents an act of interpretative repression. It is the narratives of the Torah itself that lead him to claim that "the letter kills" (2 Cor.3.6).

For Paul, the Book of Exodus is dominated by the event at Mount Sinai. The law, as a body of legislation, is closely tied to the event of its own

---

13. Only once, in Galatians 4.21, does Paul extend the term "law" to cover material from Genesis, and even that single case is rhetorically motivated.

origin; and it is especially the Book of Exodus that makes this connection clear. It is true that the encounter with YHWH at Sinai extends beyond Exodus into Leviticus and Numbers. Leviticus records "the statutes and ordinances and laws which YHWH made between himself and the people of Israel on Mount Sinai by the hand of Moses" (Lev.26.46); Numbers opens with YHWH speaking to Moses "in the wilderness of Sinai, in the tent of meeting" (Num.1.1), and records the people's departure from Sinai "in the second year, in the second month, on the twentieth day of the month" (10.11) – eleven months after their arrival there (Ex.19.1). Yet YHWH's voice is now associated primarily with the "tent of meeting" – the mobile shrine that ensures the continuing availability of that voice as the people leave Mount Sinai and continue on their journey. While Numbers opens with a reference both to Sinai and to the tent of meeting, only the tent is mentioned at the beginning of Leviticus. The specific geographical location is not entirely forgotten (cf. Lev.7.38; 25.1; 27.34), but it stands in the background even in the brief narrative sections of this book (Lev.10.1–7; 24.10–14). It is only in the central chapters of Exodus (ch.19–34) that the mountain is physically present as the site and symbol of the event in which the law was given. When Paul speaks of the law in connection with the specific event of its origin, he is primarily dependent on the narrative of Exodus.

Exodus does not only speak of the origin of the law. It speaks also of passover and unleavened bread, the crossing of the Red Sea, the manna and the rock in the wilderness; and what it says of these things has direct application within the Christian community (1 Cor.5.6–8, 10.1–4; 2 Cor.8.13–15). From Moses' intercession for the people and his conflict with Pharaoh in Egypt, Paul finds further confirmation of the free sovereignty of the divine election, beyond what he has already learned from Genesis (Ex.9.16, 33.19; Rom.9.14–18). Yet the giving of the law at Sinai is crucial for Paul. Exodus is not strictly necessary to a discourse about the divine sovereignty, or to ethical instruction. Exodus *is* strictly necessary, when Paul wishes to speak of the law – and specifically, of the event in which the law has its origin.

For Paul, the law has a historical origin, and is in no sense eternal or timeless. Thus, the time before Moses is described as a time without law (Rom.5.13–14). The law then "came in" (5.20), intervening in a situation from which it had previously been absent. This transition from a time without law to a time under law is re-enacted in the experience of the *ego* of Romans 7: "I was once alive without law, but with the coming of the commandment sin came to life and I died . . . " (vv.9–10). The moment of the law's coming can, indeed, be identified more precisely. In relation to the promise, this event took place "after four hundred and thirty years" (Gal.3.17). Paul draws this figure from the statement of Exodus 12.40 LXX, that the time in which the sons of Israel lived in the land of Egypt and in the land of Canaan was four hundred and thirty years. And it came to pass, when the four hundred and thirty years were complete, that all the hosts of the Lord went forth from the land of Egypt.

The MT lacks the phrase, "and in the land of Canaan", which is crucial for Paul's purposes – since Canaan is the place where the promises were made. In a move that indicates where his interpretative priorities lie, Paul uses the precise chronological information to date not the exodus but the giving of the law. This event has an exact location as well as an exact time: it took place at "Mount Sinai" – Sinai being "a mountain in Arabia", a region with which Paul himself is familiar (Gal.4.24–25; 1.17).[14] If the law is a text, it is also the event of the text's origin, as attested by the text – and especially by the Book of Exodus, which is for Paul the primary scriptural record of this event.

Paul draws on further material from Exodus in order to make his reference to this event still more precise. The law was "ordained through angels by the hand of a mediator" (Gal.3.19). The description of Moses (unnamed in Galatians) as a "mediator" derives from the aftermath of the decalogue:

And all the people perceived the voice and the lightnings and the sound of the trumpet and the mountain smoking; and all the people were afraid and stood at a distance. And they said to Moses, You speak to us, but let not God speak to us, lest we die... (Ex.20.18–19; cf. Deut.5.5, 22–31)

As the fuller account in Deuteronomy makes clear, Moses will in future act as a mediator between God and the people.[15] There will be no more direct divine utterance; from now on, it will all be channelled through Moses. It is therefore Moses the mediator to whom the next divine speech is addressed (Ex.20.21–23.33), who conveys the commandments to the people (24.3), who writes them in a book (24.4a), and who enacts a covenant between YHWH and Israel on the basis of the book and accompanying sacrifices (24.4b–8). This, then, is the "covenant" that is "from Mount Sinai" and that, Hagar-like, bears children for slavery (Gal.4.24). At each point, Paul is dependent on quite specific scriptural sources.[16]

14. Reading *to de Sina* in 4.25, with P[46] (cf‌ℵ C F G etc., where *gar* is substituted for *de*). Paul's statement is intended to strengthen the identification of Hagar with the Sinai covenant, and presupposes a known connection between Hagar and Arabia.

15. In Galatians 3.19–20, *[ho] mesitēs* refers to a quite specific role assigned to Moses in the scriptural texts – as in Philo, *On Dreams*, i.143, where Exodus 20.19 is cited.

16. In v.20a "the mediator" is still specifically Moses and "is not of one" refers to the angels (cf. v.19). Interpreters normally understand this as a general statement about the nature of mediation: Paul is supposedly saying either that a mediator implies the existence of two

For Paul, the mediator receives the law from a plurality (the angels) rather than directly from the one God (Gal.3.19–20). In contrast to the direct divine speech to Abraham, the law is doubly indirect divine address: it comes to us only from the hand of the mediator, who himself received it not directly from God but from angels. Paul may here simply exploit an established tradition about an angelic presence at Sinai – although the evidence for this tradition is less clear than is often thought.[17] Whatever the traditions at his disposal, Paul's hypothesis of the plurality of the law's angelic authors is probably motivated by his sense of the plurality and difference within the text itself.[18] In Galatians 3, he has already cited texts from Leviticus and Deuteronomy that seem to him both to affirm and to deny that law observance is the way to life (Gal.3.10–12). Later, he will differentiate between the law's requirement of circumcision, observance of which exposes the Galatians to condemnation, and the commandment to love one's neighbour in which the positive content of the law is summed up (Gal.5.3, 14; Lev.12.3, 19.28). It is the plurality of the angels that accounts for what Paul takes to be the confused state of the text.[19]

---

parties, in this case God and Israel (so Lightfoot, pp. 146–47; Burton, pp. 191–92; R. Longenecker, pp. 141–42); or that a mediator implies a plurality of persons on both sides of the transaction, in this case the angels and Israel (so Lietzmann, pp. 21–22; Martyn, pp. 365–66). Against this consensus, N. T. Wright rightly argues that v.20a speaks exclusively about Moses (*Climax of the Covenant*, pp. 169–70) – although his attempt to break the link between the mediator and the angels, so clear in the previous verse, is unconvincing (p. 172).

17.   To speak of "the association of angels in the giving of the law" as "a quite familiar motif... in Jewish thought of the time" (Dunn, *Galatians*, p. 191), or even as "the dominant tradition in Paul's day" (Longenecker, *Galatians*, p. 140), goes well beyond the available evidence. Other New Testament references to a plurality of angels (Acts 7.53; Heb.2.2) may be dependent on Paul, as the phraseology suggests. In Acts 7.38, "the angel who spoke to [Moses] at Mount Sinai" is the angel of the burning bush story (cf. v.30), identified with the guiding angel of Exodus 23.23; 32.34; 33.2. Philo (*Somn.* i.143) actually indicates that this writer does *not* know of a tradition associating angels with the giving of the law, since a general discussion of angelic mediation (arising from Genesis 28) here assigns the role of angelic mediator to Moses himself. In *Jubilees* 1.29–2.1, Moses is introduced to "the angel of the presence, who used to go before the camp of Israel", and who will dictate to him the remainder of this book. Josephus (*Ant.* xv.136) has Herod the Great asserting that "we learned from God the finest and most holy of the teaching of our laws *di' aggelōn*", which may refer to the scriptural writers rather than angels. The context is concerned with the inviolability of human heralds *(kērukes)*, and Josephus elsewhere uses *aggelos* with reference to a human messenger (*Ant.* xiv.451; *Vita* 89). There is no evidence that Deuteronomy 33.2 has exercised any influence.

18.   The widespread view that the angels here function to distance the law from God (e.g. Burton, p. 189; Betz, pp. 169–70) does not do justice to the plurality/unity contrast of Galatians 3.20.

19.   The later gnostic tendency to assign different parts of the scriptural texts to different angelic authors probably derives from the Pauline ascription of the law to a plurality of angels. In the "Sethite" system summarized by Irenaeus (*adv.haer.* i.30), the subordinate role

As we have argued, Paul likes to find major complexes of scriptural material concentrated in quite specific passages, which come to serve a representative function. This is true also of the giving of the law. If for Paul there is a single moment when the law is given, it is the moment of Moses' descent from the mountain bearing the inscribed stone tablets. Admittedly, this single moment is doubled: for Moses twice descends the mountain bearing stone tablets, the first time in deadly anger, the second time with a face transfigured by the divine radiance. We turn now to consider Paul's reflections on this dual event.

The Veiled Text

In 2 Corinthians 3, Paul presents a typological reading of the story of Moses' second descent from the mountain with the tablets of the law (Ex.34.29–35). According to this reading, the veil with which Moses later concealed his temporarily transfigured face is a type of the veil that now covers both the reading of the law and the hearts of those who hear it (2 Cor.3.14–15). This veil prevents them from perceiving the eclipse of the law's glory by "the surpassing glory" of the exalted Christ (3.10). Thus, a story about Moses and "the sons of Israel" is applied to the Law of Moses as read and heard within the Jewish community "to this day" (vv.14, 15). The Moses who veils himself becomes the Moses who is read (vv.13, 15). We who conduct ourselves with openness and freedom of speech are

> not like Moses, [who] used to place a veil upon his face so that the sons of Israel might not look upon the end of what was passing away. (But their hearts were hardened.) For until this day the same veil remains upon the reading of the old covenant, not removed because only in Christ does it pass away. But to this day, whenever Moses is read, a veil lies over their hearts... (2 Cor.3.13–15)

Here, the person and the text are one and the same; the story of Moses' veil is a parable of the reading of Moses in the synagogue. Paul exploits the fact that, at the start of this particular story, Moses descends the mountain bearing a text – stone tablets, written by the hand of God – that is

---

of the God of Jewish scripture is played by Ialdabaoth, who generates six further powers whose names are mostly derived from scriptural God-language (Iao, Sabaoth, Adonai, Eloi, Oreus, Astanpheus). Particular scriptural texts are assigned to each of these angelic powers; thus Ialdabaoth himself is associated with the books of Moses, Joshua, Amos and Habakkuk (i.30.11). The terminology used to describe these powers – *angelos, et archangelos, et virtutes, et potestates, et dominationes* (i.30.5) – clearly reflects Pauline influence. In gnostic texts, however, the gulf between the subordinate angelic powers and the supreme God is far wider than in Paul. On the importance of this "Sethite" myth in early gnostic development, see A. Logan, *Gnostic Truth and Christian Heresy*, pp. 29–69.

foundational for the larger text known as "the Law of Moses". In that sense, the story from Exodus is self-referential: it speaks not only of Moses as a historical individual but also of the entire text traditionally ascribed to him.[20] The present interpretation will focus on Paul's understanding of this story as a parable of the Torah – its deadly impact, its passing glory, and its veiling.

It is often supposed that in 2 Corinthians 3 Paul rewrites the Exodus story at two crucial points. In Exodus, it is said, Moses veils himself to conceal the glory; in Paul, Moses veils himself to conceal the *passing* of the glory. In addition, there is no basis in Exodus for Paul's assumption that Moses' ministry is a "ministry of death".[21] Indeed, the passage as a whole might be seen as decisive proof of the arbitrary and secondary nature of Paul's scriptural interpretation, determined as it is by extraneous dogmatic presuppositions. In what follows, we shall find reason to question this view, which stems from a series of misreadings both of the Exodus text and of Paul's interpretation of it. Once again, we must attend closely to the scriptural text itself, reread in the light of its Pauline reception.

The writing of God

The story from Exodus opens with Moses' descent from Mount Sinai, where he has communed with the Lord for forty days and forty nights without eating or drinking (Ex.34.28). He comes bearing two inscribed tablets in his hands (v.29), and the first task is to determine who wrote them and what they contain.

Moses was summoned by the Lord to climb Mount Sinai in order to receive on the people's behalf "the stone tablets, the law and the commandments which I wrote so as to legislate for them *[nomothetēsai autois]*" (Ex.24.12). This is the "legislation" *(nomothesia)* that Paul lists among the privileges of Israel in Romans 9.4.[22] Nothing further is said about the stone tablets until Exodus 31.18, following the detailed instructions relating to the tabernacle and its ministry (25.1–31.11). When these instructions are completed, the promised text is at last handed over, although there is still no indication as to exactly what it contains:

---

20. As Richard Hays argues, "a coherent reading of 2 Cor.3:12–18 is possible only if we recognize that in these verses a metaphorical fusion occurs in which Moses *becomes* the Torah" (*Echoes of Scripture*, p. 144; italics original). This crucial insight – extended to cover the whole of 2 Corinthians 3 – is fundamental to the reading that follows.

21. For both points, see V. P. Furnish, *II Corinthians*, pp. 226–27.

22. There are no other occurrences of the verb or its cognates in the Pentateuch – with the sole exception of Deuteronomy 17.10, where it is the Levitical priests who "legislate". The context in Romans 9.4 suggests that *nomothesia* here has a more restricted sense than in texts such as 2 Maccabees 6.23, where it refers to the law in its entirety.

> And he gave to Moses, when he ceased speaking with him on Mount
> Sinai, the two tablets of the testimony, stone tablets written by the finger
> of God *[plakas lithinas gegrammenas tō daktulō tou theou]*. (Ex.31.18)

As Moses descends the mountain to confront the people's idolatrous
revelling, a more detailed description of these tablets is given:

> And Moses turned and came down from the mountain, with the two
> tablets of the testimony in his hands, stone tablets written *[katage-
> grammenai]* on both sides, front and back they were written
> *[gegrammenai]*. And the tablets were the work of God, and the writing
> was the writing of God *[graphē theou]*, carved *[kekolammenē]* into the
> tablets. (Ex.32.16–17)

It is this divine production that is broken into pieces at the foot of Mount
Sinai, a violent act that initiates the destruction both of the Golden Calf
and of three thousand of the people (32.19–20, 28).

In place of the broken tablets, Moses must provide new tablets of his
own, on which the Lord will rewrite what was written on the first tablets
(34.1–4). In spite of the divine promise that "I will write upon the tablets
the words which were on the first tablets, which you broke" (34.1), the
tablets play as limited a part in this second period on the mountain top as
in the first. On the mountain top, Moses receives a new series of
commandments, which establish a covenant between the Lord and Israel
and which Moses is to write himself (34.27; cf. 24.4). It is then said that "he
[Moses? the Lord?] wrote these words upon the tablets of the covenant, the
ten words *[deka logous]*" (34.28). But what are these "ten words", and
what is their relation to the covenant that has just been enacted? And who
writes what?

A clearer picture emerges from Moses' later recollection of these events
during the long second speech that comprises the greater part of the book
of Deuteronomy (Deut.5–26). At the end of his life, and on the verge of the
promised land, Moses repeats the ten commandments and recalls the
circumstances in which they were given:

> These words the Lord spoke to all your congregation *[sunagōgēn]*, at
> the mountain, from the midst of the fire, the darkness, the gloom and
> the whirlwind, with a loud voice – and he added nothing. And he wrote
> them upon two stone tablets, and gave them to me. (Deut.5.22)

Here, there is no reference to Moses' writing the words of the covenant in
parallel to the divine writing, and the content of this divine writing is
clearly identified as the ten commandments. Later in Deuteronomy, the
handing over of the stone tablets is described more fully (Deut.9.6–10.5).
As in Exodus, they are written by the finger of God and subsequently
broken at the foot of the mountain; but it is clearer here that their content
is confined to the ten commandments, the only words that the Lord uttered

directly to the people (Deut.9.10, 17). In this version of the story, the second pair of tablets is unambiguously written by God, and the "ten words" *(tous deka logous)* that they contain are equally clearly identified with the ten commandments (10.1–5).[23] In Deuteronomy, Moses also recalls how he constructed a wooden ark on the mountain, and placed the stone tablets in it after his descent (10.1–5). Nothing is said about his appearance or his veiling himself.

Precritical readers wishing to harmonize Exodus with Deuteronomy would no doubt assume a change of subject in the Exodus passage:

> And the Lord said to Moses, Write for yourself these words – for with these words I establish my covenant with you and with Israel. And Moses was there before the Lord forty days and forty nights; he ate no bread and he drank no water. And he wrote these words upon the tablets of the covenant – the ten words. (Ex.34.27–28)[24]

Since Moses is commanded to write, it might appear that it is he who wrote on the tablets of the covenant, and that the "ten words" that he wrote represent the preceding instructions rather than the decalogue.[25] In the Deuteronomy parallel, however, it is clear that God fulfilled his promise to write the commandments himself, and that what God wrote was the ten commandments:

---

23.   In the light of Deuteronomy 4.13, 5.6–22, 9.9–11, and 10.4, it can hardly be claimed that "precisely what was written on them [the tablets] is nowhere said in the OT" (J. I. Durham, *Exodus*, p. 345).

24.   In v.28b, MT reads: *wyktb 'l hlht 't dbry hbryt 'śrt hdbrym*; LXX, *kai egrapsen ta rēmata tauta epi tōn plakōn tēs diathēkēs, tous deka logous*. For discussion of the textual problems, see J. W. Wevers, *Notes on the Greek Text of Exodus*, p. 569.

25.   On this reading, Exodus 34.10–26 (J) is held to contain a "cultic decalogue", in contrast to the "ethical decalogue" of Exodus 20 (E). This version of the decalogue would open, like the first, with the prohibition of (1) the worship of other gods (34.11–16) and (2) the production of an image (v.17), and proceed to commandments or prohibitions concerning (3) the feast of unleavened bread (v.18), (4) firstlings (vv.19–20), (5) the sabbath (v.21), (6) the three annual feasts (vv.23–24), (7) leaven in sacrifice (v.25a), (8) the consumption of the passover before morning (v.25b), (9) first fruits (v.26a), and (10) boiling a kid in its mother's milk (v.26b). M. Noth argues that the reference to "ten words" in v.28 is shown by its position to be a secondary gloss, that the glossator must have found "ten commandments" in the version of vv.14–26 that stood before him, but that the passage as it stands contains more than ten commandments (*Exodus*, p. 262). Although individual commandments may have been expanded, however, the basic enumeration seems to have been retained. According to Noth, the connection between this covenantal passage (cf. vv.10, 27, 28) and the theme of the new stone tablets (vv.1–4) is secondary (p. 260); that would explain the discrepancy between the promise of a divine writing in v.1 and Moses' writing in vv.27, 28. It is arguable, however, that in the present form of the text v.1 compels us to understand v.28b as referring to a divine writing whose content is distinct from what Moses is commanded to write (v.27).

And he [God] wrote on the tablets, in accordance with the first writing, the ten words which the Lord spoke to you at the mountain, from the midst of the fire... (Deut.10.4)

The Exodus passage can be harmonized with this if "he wrote these words upon the tablets..." is understood to refer not to Moses but to God, and if the "ten words" represent the decalogue.[26] If so, then the sequel (Ex.34.29–35) describes how, for the second time, Moses descends the mountain bearing two stone tablets, on which the ten commandments have been inscribed by the finger of God. In its canonical form within the Pentateuch, the complex Exodus presentation may be read in the light of the simple, coherent presentation in Deuteronomy.[27]

That is the interpretation of the Exodus material adopted by Josephus (although in the *Antiquities* the first, wrathful descent from the mountain and the shattering of the tablets is omitted). Josephus states that, when Moses returned to the people,

---

26.   If Exodus has been subjected to an extensive deuteronomic redaction, as argued by W. Johnstone, then a "harmonistic" reading may be preferred even on literary critical grounds. According to Johnstone, "The parallel in Deuteronomy makes it quite unambiguous that God himself wrote the Decalogue and that 'God' is the subject of the verb 'wrote' in Exod. 34.28b" (*Exodus*, p. 80). For the deuteronomic redactor, v.27 serves "to include the Book of the Covenant – the conclusion of which has just been cited – as part of the basis of the renewed covenant" (*ibid.*). This does not explain why the redactor did not distinguish more carefully between vv.27, 28b, but actually assimilated the two verses in describing what was written on the tablets as "the words of the covenant" and not just as "the ten words" (cf. Deut.10.4).

27.   This canonical reading would lose none of its validity if the origins of the traditions enshrined in these two texts suggested quite different relationships. According to E. Zenger, for example, the oldest stratum of Exodus 34 was originally linked with the theophany narrative (ch.19) and the Golden Calf narrative (ch.32) by advocates of a YHWH-alone programme associated with the reception of the book of Hosea in the southern kingdom following the fall of Samaria ("Wie und wozu die Torah zu Sinai kam", pp. 279–80). In the "Jerusalemer Geschichtsbuch" (*c.* 690 BCE), then, only sacral and cultic commandments were associated with Sinai (p. 284). It was only late in the editing of Deuteronomy that ethical commandments were transferred to Sinai, in the form of the second half of the decalogue of Deuteronomy 5 (p. 287). Exodus 20.1–17 would then represent a still later insertion into the text of Exodus, as would the "Book of the Covenant" (Ex.20.22–23.33). None of this affects the fact that, in the canonical Pentateuch, Deuteronomy frequently serves as commentary on preceding material – especially in Exodus and Numbers. In any case, Zenger's reconstruction is only one of a number of ways of making sense of the fragmentary and ambiguous evidence the texts provide about their own prehistory. Thus, it might be argued that Exodus 34 was composed in order to meet the needs of the postexilic community (so E. Blum, "Das sog. 'Privilegrecht' in Exodus 34,11–26"), that the "Book of the Covenant" is in fact dependent on Deuteronomy (so J. Van Seters, "Cultic Laws in the Covenant Code"), and so on. The canonical relationship between the pentateuchal texts is not affected by these various possibilities.

he showed them the two tablets on which were inscribed the ten words
[eggegrammenous echousas tous deka logous], five on each; and the hand
was in the writing of God *[cheir ēn epi tē graphē tou theou]*. (*Ant.* iii.101)

The reference to the divine handwriting derives from the description of the
(first) stone tablets that is given as Moses descends the mountain: "The
writing was the writing of God *[graphē theou]...*" (Ex.32.16). Also
derived from Exodus is the passive participle, *eggegramenous* (cf. Ex.31.18,
32.15 [× 2], 16; Deut.9.10). As in Deuteronomy, however, the "ten words"
are clearly the ten commandments, which Josephus has distributed equally
between the two tablets – following an older tradition.[28] A little later, a
further detail is added:

> In this [the ark] he set the two tablets, in which the ten words had been
> recorded *[sumgraphthai]*, five on each of them, with two and a half on
> either face. (*Ant.* iii.138)

The exactly equal distribution of the commandments between the *recto*
and the *verso* of the two stone tablets is suggested by the assertion in
Exodus that these were "written on both sides, front and back" (Ex.32.15).
Along with the equation of the ten words with the ten commandments,
however, the depiction of the ark as the container for the stone tablets is
drawn primarily from Deuteronomy (Deut.10.1–5; but cf. Ex.25.21, 40.20).
Consciously or otherwise, Josephus derives his presentation from both
Exodus and Deuteronomy. In the canonical form of the Pentateuch, the
simplified narratives of Deuteronomy 4–10 serve as authoritative
commentary on the more complex presentation of Exodus.

Paul too presumably believed that the tablets that Moses brought down
from the mountain contained the ten commandments, the "ten words"
(Ex.34.28; Deut.10.4). It is therefore the ten commandments that constitute
the sinister "ministry of death, carved in stone letters" (2 Cor.3.7).

Why the letter kills

The Exodus account of Moses' second descent with inscribed stone tablets
opens as follows:

> ... And he wrote these words on the tablets of the covenant – the "ten
> words". So Moses descended from the mountain, and the two tablets
> were in Moses' hands. As Moses descended from the mountain, he did
> not know that the appearance of the skin of his face was glorified
> *[dedoxastai hē opsis tou chrōtos tou prosōpou autou]*,[29] because he had

---

28. Also attested in Philo, *On the Decalogue*, 50 (on which see below).

29. Following A, as in v.30: "skin" *(chrōtos)* rather than "colour" *(chrōmatos)*. On this,
see J. W. Wevers, *Notes on the Greek Text of Exodus*, pp. 570–71.

been speaking with him [God]. And Aaron and all the sons of Israel *[hoi huioi Israel]*[30] saw Moses, and the appearance of the skin of his face was glorified *[dedoxasmenē]*, and they were afraid to draw near to him. (Ex.34.29–30)

As Paul reads this passage, the "glory" is associated not just with Moses' face but also and above all with the text that he bears in his hands. Here, Moses is already text as well as person:

If the ministry of death, carved in letters of stone *[en grammasin entetupōmenē (en) lithois]* came in glory, so that the sons of Israel were unable to look at Moses' face because of the glory of his face, passing though this was, how much more will the ministry of the Spirit be in glory? (2 Cor.3.7–8)

It is clear from the imbalance between the lengthy protasis ("If . . . ") and the brief apodosis ("how much more . . . ") that Paul is genuinely interested in the Exodus story, and is not simply exploiting it for his own ends.[31] It is also clear that he is primarily concerned with the text inscribed on the stone tablets, which is mentioned before Moses himself: the glory on Moses' face is the glory of the text. The effect of this immediate highlighting of the text is to heighten the story's significance. Far from being a mere isolated anecdote, it encapsulates the complex process of the giving of the law to the people of Israel, as narrated in the final four books of the Pentateuch. As we have seen, Paul associates the law with the event of its "coming" (Rom.5.13, 20; 7.9), and does not believe in its eternal validity. The significance of the Exodus story is that it tells how this "coming" of the law actually took place. The stone tablets, on which the ten commandments are inscribed, represent the entire ministry *(diakonia)* of Moses, the lawgiver.[32]

Paul speaks of that ministry as "carved in letters of stone" (2 Cor.3.7), that is, as "written on stone tablets" (v.3). For Paul as for Josephus, the

---

30. In v.30, A reads *huioi* rather than *presbuteroi*; 2 Corinthians 3.7 *(hōste mē atenisai tous huious Israēl)* appears to presuppose the A reading. See Wevers, *Notes on the Greek Text of Exodus*, p. 571.

31. Against Furnish, for whom the theme of vv.7–11 is "not Exod 34:29–34 as such but rather, with specific reference only to Exod 34:29–30, the meaning of the new covenant as a resplendent ministry of the Spirit and of righteousness" *(II Corinthians*, p. 230).

32. The possibility that Moses' transfigured face may be related to the inscribed tablets he bears is overlooked by recent interpreters, who argue that this story is primarily concerned to assert the authority that Moses possessed on the basis of his intimate relationship with YHWH (so George W. Coats, *The Moses Tradition*, pp. 70–71; Thomas B. Dozeman, "Masking Moses and Mosaic Authority in Torah", pp. 28, 35 – although it is also argued here that this authority is relativized by the final priestly redaction of Exodus [pp. 39–44]). If the stone tablets are left on the margins of this story, the deliberate contrast with the descent narrated in Exodus 32 (noted by J. I. Durham, *Exodus*, p. 466) will be missed.

primary source for this language is Exodus 32.15–16. There, the first "stone tablets" *(plakes lithinai)* are said to have been "written" *(gegrammenai)* or "carved" *(kekolammenē, a synonym for Paul's entetupōmenē)*; since what was written on them is "the writing of God", these passive participles must refer to God (cf. Ex.31.18). Paul assumes that what was said about the first pair of stone tablets can also be applied to their replacements, and therefore speaks of the second pair (Ex.34) in scriptural language that describes the first (Ex.32). The scriptural basis for that assumption is to be found not only in Deuteronomy but also in Exodus 34.1:

> And the Lord said to Moses, Cut for yourself two stone tablets like the first, and come up to me into the mountain, and I will write on the tablets the words that were on the first tablets, which you broke.

In spite of the later confusion about what was written and by whom (cf. Ex.34.27–28), there is scriptural warrant for the assumption that the second stone tablets corresponded exactly to the first.

Paul has also carried out a much more significant assimilation of the two accounts of Moses' descent from the mountain with stone tablets. While he must have believed that what was written on the tablets was the ten commandments, he does not actually say so. For Paul, what was "carved in stone letters" was "the ministry of death" (2 Cor.3.7). Succinctly expressed: "The letter kills" – or, as this should perhaps be translated, "The writing kills", referring not to writing in general but to the divine writing on the stone tablets (v.6).[33] The reference can only be to the story of Moses' first descent from the mountain: for Moses' advent with the first pair of stone tablets issues in the death of three thousand of the people of Israel, who had earlier flouted the divine prohibition of idolatry when they "sat to eat and drink and rose to play" (Ex.32.6; 1 Cor.10.7). After destroying the Golden Calf, Moses addresses the Levites:

> Thus says the Lord God of Israel, Let every man put his sword on his side, and go to and fro from gate to gate throughout the camp, and kill *[apokteinate]* every man his brother and every man his neighbour and

---

33. The *gramma* of v.6 is closely related to the *grammata* of v.7; compare the reduction of the multiple scriptural "promises" to a singular "promise" in Galatians 3.16–18. Interpretations of "the letter" in 2 Corinthians 3.6 tend to find its primary scriptural background not in Exodus but in Jeremiah and Ezekiel – as Scott Hafemann does when he claims that *gramma* "carries the nuance of the Law as being *merely* expressed in writing rather than being incorporated into one's heart by the Spirit" (*Paul, Moses, and the History of Israel*, p. 168; italics original). The Law killed "not because the Law was somehow deficient, but because, in God's sovereign purposes, Israel was granted the Law without the transforming work of the Spirit" (p. 284).

every man his friend. And the sons of Levi did as Moses told them, and
there fell of the people in that day three thousand men. (Ex.32.27–28)

Since Moses' action issues directly from the divine commandments
inscribed on the tablets, it demonstrates the truth of Paul's claim that
"the writing kills", and that what is "carved in tablets of stone" is a
"ministry of death".[34]

While there is no such disastrous outcome to Moses' return with the
second pair of tablets, Paul's reading appears to assimilate not only the
tablets but also the events associated with them. The two pairs of stone
tablets represent two sides of the single event of the giving of the law. The
second pair is associated with the glory of Moses' transfigured face, the
first with Moses' deadly vengeance on the idolatrous people: and, just as
the pairs of inscribed stone tablets are essentially the same, so the glory and
the killing belong together. It is because Paul has assimilated the two
stories that he can speak of a "ministry of death, carved in letters of
stone", which nevertheless "came in glory". Although he is primarily
concerned with Moses' second descent from the mountain and not the first,
the death that is the outcome of the first is carried over into Paul's
understanding of the second.[35] The divine writing that once killed is still a
writing that kills (cf. v.6).[36]

The motif of death is, however, subordinated to the glory motif that is
central to the second scriptural story. On this occasion, the bearer of the
law came not with a sword but with his appearance transfigured – "so that
the sons of Israel were unable to look at Moses' face because of the glory
of his face, temporary though this was" (2 Cor.3.7). As in the Exodus
narrative, the sons of Israel are unable to look at Moses simply because his
appearance is dazzling – and not because they cannot bear the thought that

---

34.   Contra Carol Stockhausen, who argues that Paul's characterization of Moses'
ministry as a "ministry of death" is "certainly contradictory to the view-point not only of
Exodus 34, but of the Book of Exodus as a whole" (*Moses' Veil and the Glory of the New
Covenant*, p. 113).

35.   This "killing" is therefore actual rather than hypothetical. According to Scott
Hafemann, Paul finds support for his view of Moses' "ministry of death" in the reference to
the Israelites' fear of his transfigured face in Exodus 34.30. Appealing especially to Exodus
33.5, 34.9, Hafemann argues that "the Israelites were not able to gaze intently at [Moses'] face,
since the result of the glory of God in the midst of a 'stiff-necked' people would be
destruction" (*Paul, Moses, and the History of Israel*, p. 283). Although Hafemann mentions
"the slaughter of the guilty by the sons of Levi in Exod. 32.27–29" (pp. 283–84), this does not
play a central part in his reading. Paul's ability to establish the connection between law and
death purely from Pentateuchal narrative will be confirmed in chapter 8.

36.   According to Furnish, the letter kills "because it enslaves one to the presumption that
righteousness inheres in one's doing of the law, when it is actually the case that true
righteousness comes only as a gift from God" (*II Corinthians*, p. 201). If "the letter kills" is an
allusion to the Exodus narrative, this type of explanation becomes superfluous.

the glory is only temporary. The fact that the glory is temporary is something that Paul knows but the sons of Israel do not. It is therefore misleading to translate: "... the sons of Israel were unable to look at Moses' face because of the passing glory of his face" – as though the diminution of the glory was perceptible from the start.[37] At this point, both in the original story and in Paul's rendering of it, there is no mention of a veil (Ex.34.29–32; 2 Cor.3.7–11). In the story, Aaron and the sons of Israel are afraid at the sight of the transfigured Moses (Ex.34.30); yet, rather than veiling himself at this stage, Moses calls the entire people to himself in order to communicate the divine commandments. Aaron and the rulers are the first to overcome their fear (v.31), and they are followed by "all the sons of Israel" (v.32). It is only after handing on to them "everything that the Lord spoke to him on Mount Sinai" that Moses conceals his face behind a veil (v.33). Paul's two statements about the Israelites' inability to look at Moses' face relate to quite different points in the story. The Israelites are initially unable to bear the brightness (Ex.34.30; 2 Cor.3.7); that problem is overcome when they draw near to hear the divine commandments; and Moses then veils himself, so that, according to Paul, "the sons of Israel might not look upon the end of that which was only temporary" (2 Cor.3.13). The Israelites are unable to look at Moses' face first because of the dazzling glory, and then because of the veil which conceals the fact that the glory is departing. The relation between Moses' veil and the temporary nature of the law will be the subject of the following section.

At the beginning of the Exodus story, Moses is the subject and the stone tablets are referred to only in a subordinate clause. In Paul's reading, the order is reversed. The subject is "the ministry of death carved in stone letters", which is illuminated by the radiance of Moses' transfigured face. As this focus on text rather than person indicates, Paul finds in the Exodus narrative both the definitive scriptural account of the origin of the law and the disclosure of its deadly impact on its addressees. Originating in the divine glory, the law nevertheless issues not in life but in death. Paul's statements derive not from a dogmatic "view of the law" but from his reading of the scriptural text. More specifically, they derive from his insistence that the law given at Sinai should not be abstracted from the narratives that recount its impact on its first addressees. The equivalence between Moses as character in the narrative and Moses as text enables Paul to find paradigmatic significance in the Exodus story. Here, perhaps uniquely, the Torah tells a story that is actually a parable about its own

---

37. Compare Furnish's translation: "Now if the ministry of death, chiseled in letters on stone, took place with such splendor that the Israelites could not bear to gaze at Moses' face – *because* the splendor of his face was being annulled ... " (*II Corinthians*, p. 201; italics added).

impact on those it addresses. The story that tells how the coming of the inscribed law brought death to the people of Israel continues to be re-enacted here and now, "to this day", as "Moses is read" (2 Cor.3.15). If we wish to know why "the letter kills", we are referred back to this story.

Paul is not here primarily concerned with the eschatological fate of the contemporary "sons of Israel" (vv.7, 13) – a topic on which he has positive things to say elsewhere (cf. Rom.11.25–32). He does claim that their regular encounter with Moses, who is read to them each sabbath in the synagogue, is fatal to them. His own experience is typical: "When the commandment came, sin sprang to life and I died . . . " (Rom.7.9–10). The claim about the fatal effects of the law is, of course, highly controversial. If Paul made a habit of promulgating his readings of the Torah in synagogues, it is unsurprising that, as he puts it, "from Jews I have five times received the forty lashes less one" (2 Cor.11.24).[38] Yet, though controversial, Paul's claim about the death-dealing law does not correspond to any of the genres of sectarian rhetoric that normally come into play in connection with the majority community or its leaders. In essence, it is a claim not about eschatological destiny but about hermeneutics. One reading of Torah reads it as indirect testimony to salvation. The other reading fails to recognize its own powerlessness in the face of the law's threatened vengeance on transgressors. The latter is not a straightforward misreading, however, of the kind that might be equally straightforwardly denounced. On the contrary, in the symbol of Moses' veil the Torah itself acknowledges its own complicity in this misreading. Those who misread are misled – and by Moses himself.

The deceptive veil

There is no reference to a veil in the first part either of the Exodus story (34.29–32) or of Paul's reading of it (2 Cor.3.7–11). After the initial reunion with the Israelites, however, Moses does indeed veil himself, and it becomes his custom to do so whenever he leaves the presence of the Lord in order to instruct the people:

> And when he had finished speaking to them, he placed a veil over his face. But whenever Moses went in before the Lord to speak with him, he removed the veil until he came out. And going out he spoke to all the sons of Israel whatever the Lord had commanded him. And the sons of Israel saw that the face of Moses was glorified, and Moses placed a veil over his face, until he went in to speak with him. (Ex.34.33–35)

---

38. "From the Jews" (Barrett, Furnish; still uncorrected in NRSV, REB) is seriously misleading as a translation of *hupo Ioudaiōn*.

The passage describes the origin of a custom. When the transfigured Moses descended from the mountain, he communicated the divine commandments and veiled the glory of his face – and he continued to act in the same way every time he finished communing with the Lord in the tabernacle.[39] Paul's use of the imperfect tense indicates that he is referring to Moses' customary practice, which originated in something he did when he returned from the mountain top: Moses "*used to* place a veil over his face" (2 Cor.3.13).[40] No explanation is given for Moses' practice. It does not seem to be connected to the fear that initially led the Israelites to keep their distance, since that problem was overcome without recourse to a veil (Ex.34.30–32). When the Israelites habitually behold Moses' glorified face as he leaves the tabernacle, it is not said that they are afraid – and yet Moses veils himself all the same (v.35). In other words, Moses' veiling appears to be relatively unmotivated: the veil enters the story at a point where it is too late for it to be useful. Indeed, both on the initial occasion of masking and in the subsequent custom, the use of the veil is exactly the opposite of what one would expect. One would expect Moses to wear his veil while communicating the divine instructions to the people, and to resume his normal appearance at all other times. If his face poses a threat at all, it is surely at those times when he has been in closest proximity to the divine presence, and when the people are gathered around him to hear the newly revealed words of God. As the text stands, however, the veil serves to conceal Moses' face only at those times when he is *not* fulfilling his role as mediator of God's commandments.[41] At the heart of Paul's reading is an attempt to provide a solution to a problem posed by the text itself.

---

39. The Exodus story "suggests that Israel's perception of Moses continued to be restricted to his shining skin during cultic revelation and his veil at all other times" (Thomas B. Dozeman, "Masking Moses", pp. 22–23).

40. In turning here to the theme of the veil, Paul is simply following the order of the Exodus story, which begins with Moses' transfiguration and the Israelites' fear (Ex.34.29–32; 2 Cor.3.7–11), and only subsequently introduces the veil motif (Ex.34.33–35; 2 Cor.3.13–18). There is therefore no problem in relating vv.13–18 to the preceding (against R. P. Martin, *2 Corinthians*, p. 65).

41. Although Brevard Childs argues (wrongly, in my view) that the veil is introduced in response to the Israelites' initial fear, he acknowledges that this is no longer the case when the use of the veil has become customary (Ex.34.34–35): "[T]he people continue to see the glow on Moses' face. The veil covers his face only in the period when he is not performing his office of receiving or communicating God's word ... Verse 35 makes it unequivocal that Moses came out from speaking with God and addressed the people, both times, without a mask. What function the mask has is then not fully clear" (*Exodus*, pp. 618–19). As Childs rightly argues in relation to Paul, "The fact that the text itself does not offer a motivation for the wearing of the veil would naturally evoke a midrashic interpretation" (*ibid.*, p. 623). See also the excellent discussion in D. Boyarin, *A Radical Jew*, pp. 102–103.

Why, then, did Moses put on a veil, although the sons of Israel had quickly overcome their initial reluctance to look at his transfigured face and had become accustomed to it? And why did he continue to do so, after leaving the tabernacle and communicating the divine commandments to the people? It is not that he simply wanted to avoid overwhelming the people with his radiant face – for, in the customary practice established at Sinai, veiling takes place only after the transfigured Moses has communicated the divine commandments. The people receive the commandments from one who visibly manifests the divine glory – in token that these commandments truly arise out of face-to-face communion with deity. There is no indication, however, that Moses' face remains permanently transfigured. If the glory is on each occasion manifested precisely as Moses leaves the tent and addresses the people, it is natural to suppose that the glory arises from the communion with deity that has just taken place. After communicating the latest divine instructions, Moses will presumably resume his normal appearance, until his next visit to the tent of meeting? One would expect the glory to fade with the passing of the immediate occasion of encounter with divinity – as in the later case of the transfigured Jesus. It is just this supposition that the veil makes it impossible to confirm: for the transfigured Moses places the veil over his face until his next encounter with deity, and only removes it again in the private space of the tent of meeting. From the standpoint of the people of Israel, Moses is only unveiled on those occasions when, with face transfigured, he communicates the commandments he has received within the tent. Otherwise he is permanently veiled. This makes it possible for the people of Israel to suppose that the glory must be his own permanent possession, and not the temporary after-effect of specific occasions of communion with the deity. Since the glory is manifest only on those specific occasions, it seems unlikely that it has actually become a permanent feature of Moses' appearance; and yet it is understandable that those who behold the subsequently veiled Moses draw an erroneous conclusion from his self-concealment. They believe that what is concealed is a permanent state of transfiguration; but what is actually concealed is the fading of the glory. In his dealings with the children of Israel, then, Moses displays something other than the "openness" *(parrēsia)* that characterizes Pauline speech (2 Cor.3.12–13). In keeping his transfigured face concealed behind a veil, Moses prevents the Israelites from beholding the gradual fading of the glory; he does not allow them to look upon "the end of that which was passing" *(to telos tou katargoumenou)* (3.13).[42] Contrary to almost

42. There are two interrrelated translation problems here. First, *telos* might mean "goal" rather than "end". Yet the correlation with *tou katargoumenou* suggests that "end" is more appropriate. In virtually all Pauline uses of *katargein*, the reference is to a (potentially violent)

unanimous exegetical opinion, Paul's interpretation is firmly grounded in the Exodus text.[43]

If this is correct, Paul reads the scriptural story much more acutely than those modern scholars who assume that he is here (yet again) practising eisegesis rather than exegesis. Yet he does not read it in a vacuum, but from the *a posteriori* standpoint of faith in Christ. In the end, it is the surpassing, unfading glory of the exalted Christ that teaches him that the glory on Moses' face cannot have been permanent, and that it was the fading of the glory that the veil concealed. This is stated quite explicitly in 2 Corinthians 3.10:

> For, in this case, that which was glorified *[to dedoxasmenon]* has been deprived of glory *[ou dedoxastai]*, on account of the glory that surpasses it *[tēn huperballousan doxan]*.

The neuter participle refers to Moses' face, and derives from the corresponding feminine participle in Exodus 34.30: "And the appearance of the skin of his face was glorified *[ēn dedoxasmenē]*". The verb *(ou dedoxastai)* is also derived from Exodus, where it is said that "the sons of Israel saw that the face of Moses was glorified *[dedoxastai]*" (34.35; cf. v.29, where the same verb form is used). Paul can negate this verb because he knows of a glory greater than that of Moses – the glory of the risen Christ. It is this knowledge that enables him to speak so confidently of the temporary nature of Moses' glory, resolving the interpretative dilemma

bringing-to-an-end, and never to a bringing-to-a-goal (cf. Rom.3.3, 31; 4.14; 6.16, 7.6; 1 Cor.1.28, 2.6; Gal.3.17, 5.4; 2 Thes.2.8). Particularly instructive is the correlation of *telos* and *katargein* in 1 Corinthians 15.24: "Then comes the end *[to telos]*, when he hands over the kingdom to the God and Father, when he has destroyed *[hotan katargēsē]* every rule and every authority and power." Second, *to katargoumenon* may be translated "that which is being set aside", in 2 Corinthians 3.13 as in vv.7, 11 (NRSV; cf. Barrett, Furnish *ad loc*; rightly criticized by L. Belleville, *Reflections of Glory*, pp. 204–205). This over-literal rendering of a present passive participle cannot account satisfactorily for the contrast in v.11 between *to katargoumenon* and *to menon* (cf. the similar antithesis in 4.18 between *proskaira* and *aiōnia*). While it is true that *katargein* does not in itself mean "fade", a "passing" glory is also a "fading" glory. Recent attempts to eliminate the idea of "fading" from this passage (e.g. R. Hays, *Echoes of Scripture*, pp. 133–34) fail to convince.

43.   On this point Margaret Thrall writes: "With some degree of ingenuity it is just possible to detect the idea [of the impermanence of the glory] in Exod 34.34–35: Moses removed the veil when he entered to speak with the Lord, his face shone when he emerged from the tent, and he then put on the veil until he entered the tent once more; hence, it would seem that contact with Yahweh renews the radiance, and one might deduce that it fades when the contact is broken. But the thought is implicit in the narrative only for those determined to see some disparaging element in it" (*II Corinthians*, 1.243). Yet it is only because the veil prevents us from confirming the fading of the glory that this is merely "implicit"; and it is only because the story gives no satisfactory explanation for Moses' recourse to the veil that the possibility of "disparagement" enters.

about the rationale of Moses' veil. If the Exodus story is read purely on its own terms, the reader might *suspect* that the veil conceals not the glory but the fading of the glory. But if the scriptural story is itself illuminated and transfigured by the light of the exalted Christ, then the reader can *know* that, behind the veil, the glory has departed.

Paul's explanation of the veil intends to speak not just of Moses' person but also and above all of the text, with which Moses is so closely associated throughout this passage (cf. vv.7, 15). The story of Moses' veil is the text speaking of itself: we have here a self-referential parable or allegory of the Torah. In the allegorical figure of the veiled Moses, the Law of Moses secretly acknowledges that it does not speak with complete openness, that it conceals the fact of its own transitoriness, and that its glory is destined to be eclipsed by a surpassing glory that endures for ever. Paul's understanding of Moses' veil is ultimately concerned not with matters of history or biography but with "Moses" as a text that is read, and with "the sons of Israel" as the (non-Christian) Jewish community of the present, gathered each sabbath to hear it being read. This shift from past to present occurs in vv.14–15, where it is underlined by the repeated use of the phrase, "to this day":

> But their minds were hardened. For to this very day the same veil remains upon the reading of the old covenant, unlifted *[anakaluptomenon]* because only in Christ is it removed.[44] But to this day whenever Moses is read, a veil lies over their heart.

Here, the veil covers both the text that is read and the hearts of those who hear. What it conceals is the fact that the glory of the law is a passing glory, destined to be eclipsed and extinguished by the glory of Christ (cf. vv.10–13). Those who attend to the reading of the Torah do so in the firm belief that its absolute divine authority endures for ever, and that obedience to the commandments inscribed in letters of stone must be the fundamental motivation of everyday living. Thus, *the veiling of Moses' face signifies the fact that, apart from Christ and its own indirect testimony to Christ, the Torah itself promotes a belief in its own enduring and unsurpassable authority.* For whatever reason, perhaps because of the Israelites' hardness of heart, Moses' text is less than completely open about itself. In its veiled form, it conceals the fact of its own transitoriness, thereby encouraging a belief in its permanence and a disbelief in the gospel's claim that God's definitive self-disclosure occurs not at Sinai but in the raising of Jesus.

After all it was Moses who, summarizing his entire ministry, exhorted his hearers to choose life rather than death, blessing rather than curse, by

---

44. The subject of this verb is probably the veil (RSV, NRSV, NIV, REB), not the old covenant (NEB).

following the way of the commandments; and it was Moses who wrote that
"the person who does them shall live by them" (Rom.10.5; Gal.3.11). Paul
uses the scriptural image of the veil to speak not just of some "Jewish
misunderstanding" but of a problematic feature of the scriptural text itself.
In the story of Moses' veil, the text acknowledges that it conceals the truth
about the revelation at Mount Sinai, which is also the event of the text's
own origin: and what it conceals is the fact that the definitive, unsurpassable
manifestation of the divine glory is to be found not at Mount Sinai but
elsewhere. Insofar as it implies that the Sinai revelation is definitive and
unsurpassable, the text casts a veil of seeming permanence over an event
whose significance was strictly limited. The text conceals the fact that it is
"the old covenant", destined to give way to the new (cf. 2 Cor.3.6, 14).[45]

The law's claim to an enduring glory is not subverted by Christ alone.
Rather, the glory of the risen Christ confirms and illuminates what is
hinted at in the scriptural text itself, in its self-referential depiction of
Moses veiled. The text itself raises the suspicion that Moses' veiling is
disingenuous, and that, seeming to conceal a permanent glory, it actually
conceals the passing of that glory.

Within the sanctuary

The text need not remain veiled. In Christ the veil is removed (v.15).
According to Paul, the Exodus story speaks not only of the veiling of
Moses but also of the unsurpassable glory of Christ. The term "glory",
which (with its cognate verb) occurs twelve times in 2 Corinthians 3.7–18,
is drawn here directly from the Exodus story: it is the account there of the
glory that attended the giving of the old covenant that enables Paul to
speak of the surpassing glory of the new (vv.7–11, 16–18). Despite the
antitheses of letter and Spirit, life and death, condemnation and
righteousness, the temporary and the permanent (vv.6–11), the relation
of the scriptural story to the new reality of Christ and Spirit is
fundamentally a positive one. The passage about the veil (vv.12–15) is a
kind of *apologia* for the fact that the text, on its own and apart from
Christ, conceals the impermanence of the revelation on which it is founded.
But Moses is not always veiled: his face is radiant as he descends the
mountain, and again as he communes with the Lord in the sanctuary. For
Paul, this radiance speaks of the radiance of Christ.[46] And so at the end of

45. The phrase "the old covenant" reflects the fact that the ten commandments are
inscribed on "the tablets of the covenant" (Ex.34.28; cf. vv.10, 27). Elsewhere Paul derives the
term "covenant" from Genesis 15.18 (Gal.3.17), and thus has quite specific scriptural sources
for his references to "two covenants" (Gal.4.24; cf. also Ex.19.5; 24.7, 8).

46. This "dialectical" character of Paul's argument in 2 Corinthians 3.12–18 is subtly
analysed by Richard Hays, *Echoes of Scripture*, pp. 140–53.

the chapter Paul returns to the theme of Moses' glory, following once again the unfolding of the Exodus story:

> But whenever Moses went in before the Lord *[henika d' an eiseporeueto Mōusēs enanti kurion]* to speak with him, he would remove the veil *[periēreito to kalumma]* until he went out... (Ex.34.34–35)

Paul alludes to this passage when he writes:

> Whenever he turns to the Lord *[hēnika de ean epitrepsē pros kurion]*, he removes the veil *[periaireitai to kalumma]*. (2 Cor.3.16)

Since Paul has just stated that "... whenever *[hēnika an]* Moses is read, a veil lies upon their hearts" (v.15), the third person singular verbs of the following verse must surely refer to Moses. Whenever Moses is read, the veil is in place; but whenever he turns to the Lord, he removes it. Both the syntax of this statement and its scriptural background make the reference to Moses unambiguously clear.[47] Within the sanctuary, which is the dwelling place of the Lord who is the Spirit, the unveiled Moses signifies the reality of Christian worship (vv.16–18). There, participants behold the glory of the Lord with unveiled face and are thereby transfigured, just as Moses was. Here too, the scriptural text testifies indirectly to the surpassing glory of the new reality inaugurated by Christ.[48]

This passage shares with other Pauline texts the view that the divine command embodied in the law leads only to death and condemnation, owing to the inescapable reality of human sin.[49] It also shares with other texts the view that the time of the law's supreme authority is limited by the coming of Christ and his Spirit.[50] In all such passages, Paul seeks to establish his position not just on the basis of prior dogmatic commitments, but also by way of an exegesis of selected texts from the law and the prophets which seem to him to show that his understanding of the law coincides with the law's own self-understanding – even if this self-understanding must be sought not on the surface of the texts but in their

---

47. So Hays, *Echoes of Scripture*, p. 147. According to Furnish, on the other hand, "the changes are too far-reaching to permit the conclusion that Paul is specifically citing" the Exodus text (*II Corinthians*, p. 211). If the text is translated as Furnish suggests ("Whenever anyone turns to the Lord, the veil is removed" [p. 202]), the changes – insertion of an indefinite pronoun, substitution of a passive for an active sense – are indeed far-reaching. But the changes have been introduced by Furnish, not by Paul. In discussing v.17, however, Furnish acknowledges that "the Lord is the Spirit" is "an exegetical gloss" (p. 212) – in which case v.16 must be a citation. S. Hafemann rightly points out that v.16 is "the most explicit reference to Exod. 32–34 in our passage" (*Paul, Moses, and the History of Israel*, p. 387).

48. For an analysis of the experiential dimension of 2 Corinthians 3.18, see Alan Segal, *Paul the Convert*, pp. 59–61.

49. Cf. Rom.3.9–20, 4.15, 7.7–25; Gal.3.10.

50. Cf. Rom.10.4–10; Gal.3.15–4.11.

anomalies and gaps. Paul demonstrates in 2 Corinthians 3 that, even where the scriptural text is the writing that kills, it also bears positive though indirect witness to an event that lies beyond its own horizons – the event in which the divine glory is unsurpassably manifested in the face of the risen Jesus and in the presence of his Spirit. This scriptural witness belongs within the sphere of the event; it is not extraneous to it but is constitutive of it, in the sense that the event would not be the event it actually is without the scriptural witness. From a Pauline perspective, it is of the nature of the Christ-event to make itself known, and to do so by way of scriptural texts and a proclamation that is nothing other than the authoritative exegesis of these texts. If it is true that for Paul "the scripture must be read in the light of Christ",[51] it is equally true that Christ must be read in the light of the scripture. This version of the hermeneutical circle has its own teleology, however; the relationship between Christ and scripture is not a symmetrical one, as though "Christ" and "scripture" were two independent objects that could mutually shed light on one another. Paul reads the scripture in the light of Christ only *in order* to read Christ in the light of scripture; scriptural interpretation *per se* is of no interest to him. And yet, in interpreting the Christ-event, it is genuinely scriptural interpretation that Paul practises – an interpretation that acknowledges the indirect and sometimes anomalous character of the scriptural testimony, as symbolized by Moses' veil.

The Glory of Moses

According to Paul, the narrative context of the Sinai revelation shows the law to be the bringer of death rather than life. It is this terrible paradox that calls forth the apologia for the law in Romans 7, where (as we shall see) Paul again reflects on the scriptural stories that tell of the catastrophic impact of the Sinai event. Yet within these stories hints are also to be found that the death sentence decreed by the law is not the final, irrevocable destiny of Israel or the human race. Behind the blank exterior of the veil, the law's glory fades; for the divine glory is not inherent to the law as such but shines on the text from beyond itself – from the exaltation of Jesus, whose glory the text reflects back whenever Moses turns to the

---

51. E. Käsemann, "The Spirit and the Letter", in his *Perspectives on Paul*, pp. 138–66; p. 155. The problem with Käsemann's formulation is that it tends to portray scripture as an inert object with no voice of its own. It is symptomatic of this problem that Käsemann can find in Romans 10.6–9 the paradigmatic instance of Pauline theological exegesis (pp. 155–66): for there, the voice of the scriptural author (in this case Moses) is displaced by a personified "Righteousness of faith", whose rendering of the scriptural text is actually a rewriting (on this, see chapters 7, 9, below). Precisely in the context of Romans 9–11, however, this displacement of the scriptural author is highly unusual.

Lord. These startling claims arise not only from Paul's knowledge of the glory of God in the face of Christ, but also from a careful reading of the Exodus text that does not gloss over its anomalies, but probes them until they yield up the meaning hidden behind Moses' veil. Underlying this reading is the straightforward hermeneutical assumption that the giving of the law should not be considered in abstraction from its reception. The giving and the reception are united above all in the narratives of Moses' twofold descent from Sinai bearing inscribed stone tablets.

If this is correct, then (from a Pauline standpoint) readings of Exodus that celebrate the advent of the law will be characterized by a certain evasiveness. They will tend to conceal the darker side of this event, in which the reception of the gift turns a blessing into a curse. They will effect this concealment by the simple expedient of detaching the gift from its reception – in spite of their oneness within the scriptural text. Philo's interpretation of the Sinai event illustrates the operation of such a hermeneutic. Philo treats the stories about Moses' descent from Mount Sinai quite separately from the giving of the law, which occurs through divine speech rather than divine writing (cf. Ex.20). While Philo's reading and Paul's are at crucial points diametrically opposed, there are no neutral hermeneutical criteria that could show one reading to be more faithful to the scriptural text than the other. Both readers can claim to be realizing the semantic potential of the text, or of the different parts of it that they have chosen to highlight. In the symbolism of the veil, however, Paul acknowledges that readings celebrating the glory of the law and the lawgiver are indeed validated by the scriptural text.

Moses' descent(s)

In the two books of Philo's *Life of Moses*, Moses is presented as "king" or leader of the nation (book 1) and as lawgiver, high priest and prophet (book 2).[52] His kingly or leadership role receives a straightforward narrative presentation based on Exodus 1–17 (*Mos.* i.5–219) and Numbers

---

52. Philo's *Vita Mosis* appears to be independent of the treatises comprising his *Exposition of the Law*. It does not form part of the series that begins with the creation, continues with lives of Abraham, Isaac (lost), Jacob (also lost) and Joseph, and concludes with treatises on the decalogue, the individual laws, virtues, and rewards and punishments, since the connective references to preceding treatises in the *Exposition* (*Abr.* 2–3; *Jos.* 1; *Dec.* 1; *Spec.Leg.* i.1; *Virt.* 1) are lacking here. In the *Vita Mosis*, the introductory material implies that this is to be a freestanding work (*Mos.* i.1–4, ii.1–3), and references to it towards the end of the *Exposition* (*Virt.* 52; *Praem.* 53) appear to confirm its independent character. A passage in the *Life of Moses* has been understood as an announcement of the forthcoming *Exposition* (so E. R. Goodenough, *Introduction to Philo Judaeus*, pp. 34–35), but is more likely to refer to the discussion that immediately follows (ii.47–65, at which point there appears to be a lacuna). See the discussion in E. Schürer, *History of the Jewish People in the Age of Jesus Christ*, II.2, pp. 854–55.

13–14, 20–25 and 31–32 (i.220–333). Material relating to Sinai is absent here. In book 2, the opening discussion of Moses' role as lawgiver is confined to generalities about the excellence of his laws, their immutability, their availability to non-Jews, and their relation to the Genesis narrative that precedes them (ii.8–65). As for his high priesthood, Moses exercises this by setting up the system of worship, in accordance with the instructions received on the mountain (ii.66–158; Ex.25–31, Lev.8–9), and by appointing the Levites and the sons of Aaron to carry out the work of the sanctuary (ii.159–186; Ex.32, Num.16–17). As prophet, Moses receives divine answers to questions he has put to God, and also declares words from God received under divine inspiration (ii.187–291). Here, Philo draws eclectically from Exodus, Leviticus and Numbers, and finds crowning examples of prophetic inspiration in Moses' blessing of the twelve tribes and in his anticipatory account of his own death (Deut.33–34). It is, however, in his presentation of Moses' high priesthood that Philo reflects on the Sinai event, as narrated in Exodus.

Moses' high priesthood consists not only in his institution of the system of worship but also and most fundamentally in his own personal relationship with the deity. On the mountain, he receives the necessary instructions for establishing the sanctuary, but above all he communes with God. Philo therefore opens his account of Moses' high priesthood by emphasizing the personal relationship with deity that lay at its heart, and finds the scriptural resources he needs in the Sinai narrative. Moses ascends the mountain in order to commune with the Lord who has taken up residence on its hidden summit; there, he practises an extreme ascetic discipline, renouncing all food and drink for forty days; and afterwards he returns to the people with his face transfigured. From these scriptural motifs Philo creates an account of Moses' contemplation of deity that glows with platonizing enthusiasm:

> Thus, as few others, he came to love God and to be loved by God, inspired by heavenly love and worthily honouring the Ruler of all ... As for eating and drinking, he thought nothing of them for forty whole days, obviously because he possessed a better food, that of contemplation *[theōria]*. By this means, inspired from heaven above, he progressed first in mind and then in body through the soul, in both so increasing in strength and well-being that those who later saw him could not believe it. For, ascending by divine command the highest and holiest mountain of that region, inaccessible and pathless as it was, it is said that he remained there for the time stated, taking no food for his subsistence. Then, forty days later, he descended with a countenance *[opsin]* far more beautiful than when he ascended, so that those who saw him were filled with awe and amazement; nor could their eyes endure for long the brightness that flashed from him like rays of the sun. (*Mos.* ii.67, 69–70)

For Philo, Moses' transfiguration is unrelated to the stone tablets of the law, which are not mentioned here (cf. 2 Cor.3.7). It derives instead from Moses' ascetic communion with God, through which he comes to participate in the divine radiance. His transfiguration is a mark of the exceptional, perhaps unique, love that existed between Moses and God, radiating outwards from his soul until even his bodily appearance was visibly illuminated. Moses' visible glory is the vestige of the vision of God he experienced on the mountain top.[53]

Philo is here concerned with the ineffable event that takes place between Moses and God, and he reads the scriptural reference to Moses' transfigured face as evidence of what had previously taken place up above. He draws on the scriptural reference to the forty-day fast (Ex.34.28), and must also have in mind the moment when Moses receives the revelation of the divine name (Ex.34.5–8), understood as the fulfilment of the earlier promise of an encounter with the divine glory (Ex.33.18–23). Most significantly, there is for Philo just one period of forty days on the mountain, rather than two, as in Exodus (Ex.24.18, 34.28). There is therefore only one descent from the mountain. Philo is deeply interested in the instructions about the tabernacle that Moses receives during the first period of forty days, summarizing and interpreting them at length (Ex.25–31; *Mos.* ii.71–140). Yet, omitting all reference to the Golden Calf or the shattering of the stone tablets, he proceeds straight to the descent from the mountain with transfigured face. Moses ascends the mountain at the divine command, and remains on its hidden summit for forty days, communing with deity; he beholds the heavenly patterns that must be reproduced in the earthly tabernacle; and he returns with traces of the divine glory still visible in his countenance. In the scriptural account of the first descent, the gift of the law becomes entangled in sin and death; but in Philo's reading, this is eclipsed and concealed by the radiance that attended the second descent. In contrast to the Pauline fusion of the two descents, we have here an elimination of the first.[54] Nothing is said here about Moses' veil, but Philo

53. There is no evidence that Paul's opponents at Corinth held a similar understanding of the Sinai narrative to Philo's (against D. Georgi, *The Opponents of Paul in Second Corinthians*, p. 254). Georgi's attempt to reconstruct a *Vorlage* for 2 Corinthians 3 written by the opponents themselves (pp. 264–71) is unconvincing.

54. A parallel to the Pauline fusion of the descents is found in Pseudo-Philo's *Liber Antiquitatum Biblicarum*, where an extensive and free rendering of the Golden Calf story is preceded by Moses' descent from the mountain with "the light of his face surpass[ing] the splendour of the sun and the moon" (*LAB* 12.1). When Moses realized that his face had been (permanently?) transfigured, "he made a veil for himself with which to cover his face" (*ibid.*) – after which, on discovering the golden calf, "he looked at the tablets and saw that the writing was gone, and he hurried to break them" (12.5; cf. 19.7). The new stone tablets are to be rewritten by Moses himself (12.10). This fusion of the two descents would be more significant for Pauline interpretation if an early date for Pseudo-Philo could be established. The apparent

may have concluded from it that the radiant glory on Moses' face was enduring.[55]

Unlike Josephus, however, Philo does not simply suppress the Golden Calf story.[56] More subtle means are adopted in order to defuse the nexus of law and death so starkly represented here. Towards the end of his presentation of Moses' high priestly office, Philo does retell this story – but in a form that is intended to glorify Moses himself. In Philo's view, Moses' high priestly role is evident mainly in the instructions for the tabernacle and its worship that are communicated through him. After summarizing the scriptural depiction of the tabernacle (Ex.25–31) and of the consecration of Aaron and his sons to minister in it (Lev.8–9), Philo proceeds, logically enough, to discuss the role of the Levites (cf. Num.3–4, 7–8). At this point, the Golden Calf story is retold in order to account for the Levites' privileged status (*Mos.* ii.159–73) – again, logically enough, as the story lends itself to being understood in this way. The Levites receive a privileged status as ministers in the tabernacle because it was "all the sons of Levi" who had previously heeded Moses' call to take the Lord's side and to pass through the camp killing the idolators (cf. Ex.32.25–29). Moses

reference to "740 years" of worship in the temple in Jerusalem as an era belonging to the past (19.7) makes an early dating difficult – in spite of the arguments summarized by D. J. Harrington (*OTP* 2.298–99). The lateness of the manuscript tradition (11th–15th century) is also a reason to be cautious about an early dating. Issues of dating also affect L. Belleville's supposed "Moses-*Doxa* tradition", on which it is claimed that Paul could have drawn (*Reflections of Glory*, pp. 24–79). For a detailed analysis of Pseudo-Philo's reading of the Golden Calf story, see C. T. Begg, "The Golden Calf Episode according to Pseudo-Philo".

55. So S. Hafemann, *Paul, Moses, and the History of Israel*, p. 295, arguing against L. Belleville, *Reflections of Glory*, p. 35.

56. In Josephus's presentation of the Sinai event, Moses ascends the mountain after instructing the Hebrews to camp at its foot to await his return (*Ant.* iii.75–78; Ex.19.2b–3a, 14–15). Cloud, thunder, lightning and rain (cf. Ex.19.16) herald the "advent of God" *(parousia tou theou)*, and the people fear that Moses has perished (*Ant.* ii.79–82). This latter motif contrasts with Exodus 19.17, where Moses is still present with the people, and is drawn from the opening of the Golden Calf story (Ex.32.1, 23). Moses suddenly returns, however, "exultant and high-spirited" *(gauros te kai mega phronōn)*, and his reappearance allays the people's fears (iii.83). Gathering them together, Moses insists that his words be received as the words of God (iii.84–88; cf. Ex.19.7). In the first instance, however, it is God who speaks: a voice is heard from on high, uttering the ten commandments "which Moses has left inscribed on the two tablets *[en tais duo plaxi gegrammenous]*" (iii.89–92; cf. Ex.20.1–17). At the people's request (cf. Ex.20.18–19), Moses ascends the mountain a second time and remains fasting on its summit for forty days (cf. Ex.24.18; 34.28), reawakening the people's fears for his safety (iii.95–98). On his reappearance, Moses passes on the divine instructions regarding the tabernacle (iii.99–101), which the people proceed to construct (iii.102–203; cf. Ex.35–40). Thus, Josephus's omission of the Golden Calf incident should be set in the context of his wholesale recasting of the entire narrative framework of Exodus 19–40 – occasioned no doubt by the complexities and confusions of the scriptural text, as well as the particular offensiveness of Exodus 32.

thus "selected and appointed one of the twelve tribes for its special merit, giving them the office as the prize and reward of a deed pleasing to God" (*Mos.* ii.160). In the story of that meritorious deed, Moses' conduct too is, as always, entirely admirable. On the mountain top, his communion with deity is interrupted by the distant sound of debauchery below. What is he to do? Moses

> was in a dilemma, as one beloved of God who was also a lover of humanity. He could not bear either to leave his communing with God, in which he spoke with him one to one and in private, or to ignore the multitudes, filled as they were with the evils that stem from anarchy... So, pulled one way and then the other by each side of his character, he did not know what he should do. (*Mos.* ii.163, 165)

Philo is familiar with Moses' dilemma from his own personal experience. In a later autobiographical passage, he speaks at length of his own mountain-top experiences of contemplation, and of how they were rudely brought to an end as he was dragged downwards into the turbulent realm of political affairs (*On the Special Laws*, iii.1–6).[57] Precisely this tension between philosophy and politics is projected onto Moses on the mountain top. No less admirable is Moses' conduct at the foot of the mountain. His cry, "If anyone is on the Lord's side let him come to me" is intended to distinguish between incurable apostates and those who remain faithful, or who have repented of their former actions (*Mos.* ii.167–68). The mass slaughter that follows enables the survivors to "learn wisdom from fear" (ii.172). There is no shattering of the stone tablets of the law, and no acknowledgment of the anomaly of a law that intends human well-being and yet results in death. Like miscreants everywhere, the apostates deserved to die – and that is the end of the matter. It was fitting that those who took up arms for the honour of God should be rewarded with a part in the service of God's sanctuary (ii.173).

Although Moses' first descent from the mountain is initially eclipsed by the second, Philo is evidently unembarrassed by the Golden Calf story. If the story shows the depraved state of a people who could be guilty of apostasy even at the foot of Mount Sinai, it also speaks of a praiseworthy zeal for the honour of God that is prepared to slaughter even relatives or neighbours to avenge the insult of idolatry. Later, having turned to his final topic, Moses' prophetic office, Philo recounts the story of the Golden Calf for a second time.[58] Here Moses' appeal to those who were on the

---

57. For a study of this passage as an autobiographical ascent narrative, see P. Borgen, *Early Christianity and Hellenistic Judaism*, Edinburgh: T. & T. Clark, 1996, pp. 309–20; on Moses' ascent, see *ibid.*, pp. 303–305.

58. Other repetitions in this work include the stories of the Red Sea (i.163–80; ii.246–57) and of the manna (i.191–213; ii.258–69).

Lord's side is presented as one of his many divinely inspired utterances. On seeing the Golden Calf,

> Moses was distressed that, in the first place, the whole people had suddenly become blind, who shortly before had been the most clear-sighted of all nations; and that, in the second place, a fable falsely invented could quench such radiance of truth, which neither the sun can eclipse nor the whole choir of the stars can overshadow – for it is illuminated by its own light, intelligible and incorporeal, in comparison with which the light of the senses would seem to be as night to day. For that reason, he no longer remained the same man, both his countenance and his mind were changed, and, divinely inspired, he said: "Who is there who has no part in this error, and has not addressed as lords those who are no lords? Let all such come to me!" (*Mos.* ii.271–72)

While the first retelling of this story serves to explain the role of the Levites, the second finds here an instance of divinely inspired utterance; and in both cases what is highlighted is a heroic zeal for God's honour. The act of apostasy becomes an occasion to praise the divine truth that is incomprehensibly rejected, and the human steadfastness of the few who remain loyal to it. In Philo's readings, it is zeal rather than apostasy that lies at the heart of this story. In the statement about Moses' divinely inspired utterance, the motif of the transformed appearance is apparently borrowed from the transfiguration story of Exodus 34. It seems that Philo can account for everything he reads in the stories of Israel at Sinai.

Or rather: almost everything. In both renderings of the Golden Calf story, as in the earlier retelling of the transfiguration story, the inscribed stone tablets are missing. This is not a minor or accidental omission. In Exodus, Moses twice ascends the mountain precisely in order to receive the stone tablets and to convey them to the people. In the divine inscription on the stone tablets, the voice that initially uttered the ten commandments is preserved and enshrined for all time, in the most durable medium available (a durability subject, of course, to normal use). The shattering of the first stone tablets signifies and dramatizes the breach of the first and second commandments that is occurring before Moses' eyes; it also expresses a human anger embodying the divine anger, which will shortly issue in the mass slaughter of the idolators. Here as in the transfiguration story, Moses is closely identified with the inscribed stone tablets: as Paul points out, he is both person and text. If, however, the person of Moses is already identified with the text, the Sinai stories are not just edifying anecdotes from the life of Moses. They are stories about the law itself, in which the divine voice that spoke at Sinai is transformed into the quasi-permanence of a writing inscribed in stone – with immediate and disastrous consequences for an apostate people. Thus the inscribed tablets can be associated both with glory and death: although originating in the divine glory, "the letter kills".

For Philo, the inscribed tablets play no part in the narrative, which speaks instead of the traces of Moses' intimate communion with deity, and of his holy zeal for the divine honour. The stories are read as edifying biographical anecdotes from the life of Moses. From a Pauline perspective, this is to evade the unpalatable truths they seek to communicate – that the text kills, and that it conceals the fading of its own glory.

The divine speech

The story of Moses' twofold descent from Sinai is significant for Paul as marking the occasion of the giving of the law. The inscribed stone tablets represent the entire written text which Paul can describe as "the old covenant" or simply as "Moses". According to Paul, what is given at Sinai is above all a written text. In that sense, his reading of the story of Moses' second return to the people of Israel is not strictly comparable with Philo's, where Moses' transfiguration represents the intimacy of his communion with deity but is unrelated to his role as lawgiver. If, for Philo, there is a single event in which the law is given, this occurs above all in the divine proclamation of the ten commandments in the hearing of the people (Ex.19.16–20.20). This event is passed over in Philo's treatise on the life of Moses, owing to his primary focus there on the person of the lawgiver. Elsewhere, however, he presents an eloquent and compelling interpretation of the decalogue, in a treatise belonging to the series known as *The Exposition of the Law*.[59]

In this treatise *On the Decalogue*, Philo offers an interpretation both of the commandments themselves and of their narrative context in Exodus 19–20. There is no interest in the circuitous route from the audible proclamation of the decalogue to its final written form. The stone tablets are mentioned only because there were two of them, enabling Philo to divide the commandments into two sets of five (*dec.* 50). Here, the giving of the law takes place when the ten commandments are declared to the people by the divine voice. Philo's emphasis on the eternal and universal validity of a law based on the "ten words" may serve as a foil for Paul's insistence on the law's transitoriness.[60]

According to Philo, "the ten words or oracles *[tous deka logous ē chrēsmous]*, which are in reality laws or statutes, the Father of all declared

---

59. For a survey of this series, see Peder Borgen, "Philo of Alexandria", in M. E. Stone (ed.), *Jewish Writings of the Second Temple Period*, pp. 233–41.

60. In 2 Corinthians 3, the Pauline relativizing of "the letter" has been plausibly linked to the speech/writing antithesis, a Hellenistic philosophical *topos* originating in Plato's *Phaedrus* (so Windisch, p.111; Furnish, p.195). The same *topos* accounts for Philo's privileging of the divine speech over the divine writing.

when the nation, men and women alike, were gathered together in assembly *[eis ekklēsian]*" *(dec.* 32).[61] We are not to imagine that God actually spoke in an audible voice. Rather, God must have engineered a technological miracle, creating in the air a speech that was equally audible to every member of the vast congregation *(dec.* 32–35). It is striking that this miraculous speech is addressed not to the congregation as a whole but to each of its individual members. God

> saw fit to declare each of the ten words not as to many but as to one, saying: Thou shalt not commit adultery, Thou shalt not kill, Thou shalt not steal, and the other commandments similarly. *(dec.* 36)

One possible explanation for this singular address is that a single law-abiding person is worth a whole nation (37–38). Another explanation is that direct second person singular address makes it impossible to hide oneself away in the crowd (39). A third possibility is that this mode of address was intended to check the presumption of the arrogant by showing how the eternal God "could not bear to overlook even the most humble, but saw fit to feast him on sacred words and statutes, as though he were the only guest..." (41). Human arrogance should learn to imitate the divine humility (41–43).

When the miraculous speech sounded forth out of the fire, the ten commandments simply followed one after another, without a break. When inscribed on stone tablets, however, they were divided into two sets of five, one for each tablet. In its original written form the decalogue is distributed between two divine texts with a different subject matter:

> Both are excellent and profitable for life, opening up broad pathways and thoroughfares that terminate in a single goal, providing an easy journey for the soul that always desires the best. The primary set of five is concerned with the following: the sole rule *[monarchia]* to which the world is subject; wood-carvings and sculptures and any other image made by human hands; not addressing God in vain; observing the seventh day as befits its holiness; and the honour due to parents, both individually and together. Thus one of the two writings takes its beginning from God the father and maker of all, and ends with parents, who imitate the divine nature by producing further individuals. The other set of five contains all the prohibitions, of adultery, murder, stealing, false witness, and evil desires. *(dec.* 50–51)

---

61. The explicit inclusion of women among the addressees at Sinai is striking in the light of Exodus 19.15, which appears to presuppose a purely male audience for the divine address (cf. 20.17). On this point see Athalya Brenner, "An Afterword: The Decalogue – Am I an Addressee?" Philo's "men and women alike" is perhaps intended to exclude a "masculinist" reading of Exodus.

Thus, the commandments of the first tablet speak of the human relation to God; the commandments of the second tablet speak of the relation to the fellow-human.

The first two commandments enable Philo to make fundamental claims about the divine nature, in opposition first to the polytheistic deification of various created entities of heaven or earth (52–65), and second to the worship of the products of human workmanship – an even worse error (66–81). The commandments begin from God because God is "the ultimate source of all that is, as piety is of the virtues" (52). In opposition to all ascriptions of ultimacy to the cosmos, the first commandment tells us that the world

> has come into being, its origination being the basis for its dissolution
> *[genesis de phthoras archē]*, even if by the providence of its Maker it
> should become immortal. Thus, there was a time when it was not *[ēn*
> *pote chronos hote ouk ēn]*. But to speak of *God* as formerly not being,
> and as coming into being at a particular time rather than existing
> eternally, is not permissible. (*dec.* 58)

As elsewhere in Philo, the fundamental analogy for the relation of the invisible God to the visible universe is the relation of the human soul to the body (60). Yet the first commandment requires us not only to believe in the existence of this God, but above all to honour and acknowledge him as God. The all-sufficient God does not need this honour and acknowledgment from us, but requires it from us for our own sake –

> wishing to lead the human race, straying in pathless wastes, to a way
> from which there is no straying, so that by following nature it might
> attain the highest goal, knowledge of the One who truly is *[tou ontōs*
> *ontos]*, the original and most perfect good from whom, as from a
> fountain, there flows forth to the world and its inhabitants every
> particular good. (*dec.* 81)

Here there comes to light a new aspect of the principle that the one who does these things shall live by them. In these commandments that form the basis of the divine–human relation, the way is integrally related to the goal: "life" is not simply an external reward for miscellaneous instructions duly carried out. As elsewhere, Philo here strives for an ontological interpretation of the divine–human relation established by the commandment.

The third commandment concerns the proper use of the word "God", after the first two have spoken of the reality that the word denominates (82–83). The fourth commandment makes practical provision for the worship and contemplation of the true God that is theoretically safeguarded by the first two (98). The fifth commandment forms a link between the two series of commandments. On the one hand, it is related to the second series in its concern for the duties human beings owe each other;

on the other hand, its place within the first series reflects the fact that it is in parenthood that human beings approximate most closely to the relationship of creator to creation (107). On this boundary between the two series, we may note the importance of balancing the love of God with the love of our fellow-humans, not neglecting one for the sake of the other (108–10). We may also note the order and lucidity with which the interconnected commandments are arranged. Precisely here, where we are dealing with the foundations of all the various "special laws" that are to come, it is evident that the Law of Moses is anything but a miscellaneous collection of arbitrary instructions.

The commandments of the second series are numbered from one to five (not from six to ten) – obviously under the influence of the tradition of the two tablets. As in some Septuagint manuscripts, the prohibition of adultery precedes the prohibition of murder.[62] In Philo's discussion, adultery, murder, theft, false witness and evil desire are shown to be incompatible with human well-being; it is not simply that God happens to disapprove of them. For Philo, the second series of commandments is the product of an enlightened religious humanism; there is a marked emphasis on the social and political effects of the sins in question. Thus, the prohibition of theft is here seen as directed not just against petty criminals but also against the powerful, who "perpetrate acts of theft on a grand scale yet conceal the reality of robbery under the high-sounding names of government and leadership" (136). The prohibited "desire" *(epithumia)* is the source of "all the wars of Greeks and barbarians between themselves or against each other", which "bring disaster to the human race" (153).

In the final part of his treatise, Philo outlines his understanding of the ten commandments as "summaries of the specific laws that occur throughout the legislation as recorded in the sacred texts" (154). This is the view that will determine his presentation of these laws in the four books of the work that follows, *On the Special Laws* – thereby enabling Philo to create relative order out of apparent chaos. Thus, the fourth commandment of the first series "is to be regarded as nothing other than a summary of the feasts, and of the purifications prescribed for each of them" (158). The fifth commandment points towards the "many necessary laws enacted in order to regulate the relations of old and young, rulers and subjects, benefactors and recipients, slaves and masters" (165). This distinction in kind between the ten commandments and the "special laws" is related to

---

62. In Exodus 20.13–15 and Deuteronomy 5.17–19 LXX, the MT order (killing, adultery, stealing) is attested in A and the majority. B and ℵ give the order as adultery, stealing and killing in Exodus 20.13–15, and as adultery, killing and stealing in Deuteronomy 5.17–19; the latter is attested both by Philo and by Paul in Romans 13.9. In Josephus, *Ant*. iii.91–92, the enumeration runs from one to ten, and the order is: murder, adultery, stealing (as in MT).

the fact that in the former we are addressed directly by God, whereas in the latter we are addressed only through the mediation of Moses:

> For it was in accordance with [God's] nature to declare the summaries of the specific laws in his own person *[autoprosōpōs]*, but the particular laws through the most perfect of prophets, whom, selecting him for his merits and filling him with the divine spirit, he chose to be the interpreter of the divine utterances *[hermenea tōn chresmōdoumenōn]*. (*dec.* 175)

Here, Philo reflects on the scriptural distinction between divine words addressed directly to the people (the decalogue) and those communicated through Moses (everything other than the decalogue). The distinction arises from the people's request to Moses, after they have heard the ten commandments directly from God: "You speak to us, and we will hear; but let not God speak to us, lest we die" (Ex.20.19, cf. Deut.5.22–31). For Philo, this implies that Moses plays an active part in the formulation of the specific laws, and is not simply a mouthpiece of deity – a view which shows the influence of Deuteronomy, which lacks the divine instructions in direct speech that pervade Exodus, Leviticus and Numbers.[63] On the basis of this distinction between direct divine utterances and Moses' role as interpreter, Philo would not have accepted the Pauline claim that the entire law is mediated through Moses (Gal.3.19), and that there is no essential difference between the commandments inscribed on stone tablets and the rest of the law (cf. 2 Cor.3.7). For Philo, Moses is the interpreter of divine words that are still available to us in their uninterpreted form. He is commonly regarded as "the lawgiver of the Jews", but he may also be described as "the interpreter of the holy laws *[hermeneus nomōn hierōn]*" (*Mos.* i.1). The holy laws are "the ten words", and all else is interpretation.

Both the ten divine words and their inspired interpretation are to be found within Moses' sacred books, and these books are to be regarded as God's gift not just to Israel but also to the world. Philo finds evidence for this at two points: first, in the widespread tendency for non-Jews to "honour our laws" and to imitate Jewish practices such as the weekly day of rest (*Mos.* ii.17–24); and second, in the public availability of these laws in the form of the inspired Septuagint translation, an achievement which is

---

63. In Exodus-Numbers, YHWH's *ipsissima verba* are to be passed on by Moses to the people; in Deuteronomy, Moses speaks in his own voice, although his words are sanctioned by YHWH (occasional exceptions, in 7.4a, 11.13–15, 28.20, 29.5–6, are of no real significance: so von Rad, *Deuteronomy*, p. 22n). The result is a sharp distinction between the decalogue and the rest of Deuteronomy. As R. D. Nelson notes, the statement that YHWH "added nothing more" (Deut.5.22) "helps segregate the limited content of Horeb from what Moses would speak in Moab and also highlights the special, 'canonical' authority of the Decalogue" (*Deuteronomy*, p. 84). Philo's view of Moses as the interpreter of the ten primary divine utterances is derived from Deuteronomy.

still celebrated in Alexandria in an annual ceremony (ii.25–42). In that ceremony, non-Jews as well as Jews gather on the island of Pharos, "both to honour the place in which that translation first shone forth, and to give thanks to God for that old yet ever new gift" (ii.41).[64] Thus, in the decalogue and its broad interpretative framework, God addresses not Israel alone but also the world. To be human is to be addressed as "thou" by the divine commandment, which thereby opens up the way to our highest good.

The old and the new

In sharp contrast to this generous universalism, Paul claims that Moses represents not the gift of life but a sentence of death (2 Cor.3.7). Since this is a claim about Moses himself, and not just about his contemporary interpreters, it is comprehensive enough to encompass not only the sectarian nomism of Qumran but also the universalizing nomism represented by Philo. Paul shows that he is aware of this universalizing possibility when he addresses himself to a fictive Jewish teacher of the law, who sees himself as a light to those who are in darkness and who expounds the law as the embodiment of all knowledge and truth (cf. Rom.2.17–20). Quite apart from the specific vices that Paul ascribes to this figure (Rom.2.21–24), such a proclamation of the law to the world would still represent death and not life, condemnation rather than righteousness (cf. 2 Cor.3.6–9). Even as expounded by a figure such as Philo, it remains the case that "the writing kills" – that is, Moses' writing of the divine writing inscribed on the stone tablets.

As we have seen, this Pauline claim derives from a specific interpretation of the Exodus narrative, and is not a general statement of dogmatic principle. Yet Paul's scriptural interpretation cannot be abstracted from his gospel, with its announcement of God's saving action in Jesus Christ. While Paul genuinely reads the scriptural texts, this is a reading guided by the claims of the gospel, not one carried out from a position of disinterested neutrality. When Paul draws radical conclusions from the narrative context in which the decalogue is set, those conclusions are generated neither by the text alone nor by Paul's gospel alone, but by the conjunction of the two. Neither of these two entities straightforwardly precedes or grounds the other. The gospel that is brought to the text is also articulated through the text: indeed, that is the only reason why scriptural interpretation is worth practising at all. In focusing primarily on Paul as reader and interpreter, it must not be forgotten that Paul reads and

64. As P. Borgen notes, Philo sees the production of the Septuagint as "a decisive event in revelatory history" (*Philo of Alexandria*, p. 143).

interprets precisely as an apostle with a gospel to proclaim and communities to build. Thus the evangelical logic of Paul's reading of Exodus requires some further clarification. In particular, his claim that what was disclosed at Sinai was only "temporary", and that it is only the deceptive veil over Moses' face that makes it look permanent, cries out for explanation. Even if he can appeal to genuine anomalies in the Exodus text, it is not yet clear why he would *want* to read the text in this way.

Paul may have been aware of the tradition represented by Philo, according to which the law as a whole is no more than commentary on the ten commandments. If so, he takes this one stage further when he claims that the second table of the decalogue is itself commentary on the single commandment of love for the neighbour:

> Owe no one anything, except to love one another. For the one who loves has fulfilled the rest of the law. For the commandments, You shall not commit adultery, you shall not kill, you shall not steal, you shall not desire, and any other commandment, are summed up in this single utterance: You shall love your neighbour as yourself. Love does no harm to the neighbour. And so the fulfilment of the law is love. (Rom.13.8–10)

If, like Philo and Josephus, Paul envisages a division of the decalogue into two series of commandments, this passage would summarize the content of the second of the divinely inscribed tablets. As in Philo and the majority LXX reading, the series opens with the prohibition of adultery and continues with the prohibitions of murder and theft (in MT the order is murder, adultery, theft). Paul omits the fourth commandment of the second series (the prohibition of false testimony), and repeats the abbreviated version of the final commandment introduced in Romans 7.7. The omission of the fourth commandment in this series is covered by the surprisingly indefinite reference to "any other commandment", which may indicate that Paul, unlike Philo, does not envisage any fundamental difference between the decalogue and the other commandments of the Torah. The commandments of the decalogue are representative of "the rest of the law" (i.e. the whole law apart from the commandment to love the neighbour), but there may also be other commandments outside the decalogue that give concrete expression to the requirement to love our neighbour as ourselves. Yet there is no indication that readers of Romans should turn to the text of the Torah in order to discover what those other expressions of love for the neighbour might be. On the contrary, the single commandment is sufficient – not just because of its status within the Torah but because it conforms to the distinctively Christian imperative that we are to "love one another". In Romans, this love is grounded in and defined by the love of God set forth in the death of Christ and the outpouring of the Holy Spirit (cf. 5.5–8; 8.35–39).

In its subordinate, illustrative role within the new order defined by the act of God's love, the second tablet of the decalogue no longer represents a "ministry of death" or of "condemnation". As the veil is removed, the face of the text is illuminated by a glory originating outside itself, in the risen Christ. Why, then, does Paul insist on portraying Moses as the bringer of death, and as disingenuously claiming to possess an enduring glory of his own? It is true, and central to the present argument, that Paul does so because he feels constrained to do so by the scriptural texts he seeks to interpret. (Thus 2 Corinthians 3 preserves the original narrative context of the decalogue in a way that Romans 13 does not.) Yet it still remains to be seen how Paul's *gospel* impacts on his reading of the Exodus text. Paul is a minister of the "new covenant", Moses of the "old covenant" (2 Cor.3.6, 15): but what exactly is the reality that constitutes the newness of the new and the oldness of the old?

The new order is variously characterized here. It is the order established by the life-giving Spirit of the living God, who writes in fleshly hearts a letter of recommendation for the apostle that is also Christ's message to the world – Christ addressing the world by way of the Spirit-filled community. This new order endures for ever; it is final and definitive, and will not be superseded by any still newer order. In it, the "righteousness" and "life" which constitute true human fulfilment are finally established. Its surpassing glory is its own and does not fade; and this is the transforming glory of the risen Christ. It is *this* glory that eclipses the temporary, borrowed glory that shone at Sinai. Still the question persists, however: what is the underlying logic of the antithesis between new and old? The task is not simply to describe the antithesis, paraphrasing Paul's language. We wish to make sense of it.

For Paul, the old and the new are characterized by two different accounts of divine agency. Fundamental to the old is the divine act of *inscription*. What is inscribed, however, is *prescription*: a series (or two series) of demands, formulated either positively or negatively. The addressee of these demands is directed towards his or her future conduct, which must either conform to them or transgress them. No third option is available. What Paul describes as "the old covenant" is characterized by the invitation to reshape and reform human conduct in the light of what is inscribed and prescribed on the stone tablets. As Philo already shows, this divine writing constitutes a framework capable of comprehending human life in its entirety – ranging as it does from the foundational principles of true religion to the most trivial instances of the desire or envy that can disrupt the relationship of one person to another. It is not unreasonable for Philo to imagine that the decalogue could in principle generate a universal consensus.

The new is characterized by a quite different divine action: the raising of Jesus from the dead and the outpouring of the Holy Spirit. Human well-being ("life", or "righteousness") is brought about by a divine fiat no less unilateral than the one that originally called forth light out of darkness: for "it is the God who said, Let light shine out of darkness, who has shone in our hearts with the light of the knowledge of God's glory in the face of Jesus Christ" (2 Cor.4.6). This identity description of the true God is itself a paraphrase of a simpler identity description, according to which God is "the one who raised the Lord Jesus" (4.14). "God", then, is defined by way of this singular though complex act of life-giving or light-creation; and the same is true of human beings, who are now redefined as the objects and beneficiaries of that divine action.[65] In place of prescription there is creation: not the outline of a required though hypothetical human praxis, but the realization of light and life as the true goal of human existence. The divine writing issues a series of demands, whereas the gospel announces the dawning of the saving action of God. That is the fundamental contrast between the old and the new.

No doubt it is possible to reject the new on the grounds that "the old is better". Philo's enlightened humanism may well seem more attractive than Pauline paradox. Indeed, if the dawning of the light is a divine work, then so too is the creation of eyes with which to see it. In the absence of such illumination from above, the old may very well seem to point the way to true human well-being or "salvation". Yet there are indications in the scriptural text that all is not well even at Mount Sinai. Originating in the divine glory and inscribed by the divine hand, the stone tablets bring death rather than life to those for whom they were intended. The self-veiling of the text makes it impossible to be sure that its glory is enduring. At moments such as these, the Book of Exodus appears to subvert its own proclamation of the divine commandment, and to create space for a "new covenant, not of the letter but of the Spirit".

---

65. On this point, see my article on "The Triune Divine Identity: Reflections on Pauline God-language in disagreement with J. D. G. Dunn".

Chapter 7

Leviticus

In his extant letters Paul cites just two texts from Leviticus.[1] Like Numbers, but in contrast to Genesis, Exodus and Deuteronomy, Leviticus makes only a limited contribution to the fragmentary Pauline reading of the Torah that we are attempting to reconstruct. Yet Paul's two Leviticus texts carry very great weight. Cited both in Romans and in Galatians, they are said to encapsulate the very essence of the law, summing up the law's entire rationale and content in a single lapidary utterance. But what is said about the one seems in tension with what is said about the other.

In Leviticus 19.17–19a (LXX) we read:

> You shall not hate your brother in your heart, but with reproof you shall reprove your neighbour, and you shall not incur sin on his account. And your hand shall not take vengeance, and you shall not bear a grudge against the sons of your people; and you shall love your neighbour as yourself. I am the Lord; my law you shall keep *[ton nomon mou phulaxesthe]*.

In its original context, the commandment about love of neighbour seeks to exclude both the harbouring of secret hostility and its expression in the form of revenge. Points of disagreement are to be raised, but in a form that is consistent with the neighbour's well-being as well as one's own. In the Septuagint, the reference to love of neighbour is followed by a reference to "my law" – in contrast to the Masoretic text's "my statutes" *('t-ḥqty)*. This may have contributed to the Pauline assumption that the whole law is summed up in the single commandment about love of neighbour. For Paul, all of the divine commandments, and especially those of the second table of the decalogue, are here traced back to their source (cf. Rom.13.8–10; Gal.5.14). At this point the law is in harmony with the Holy Spirit, the first fruit of whose activity is love (cf. Gal.5.22).

---

1. Lev.18.5; 19.18. (I omit the conflation of Leviticus 26.11 with Ezekiel 37.26 in 2 Corinthians 6.16, on which see M. E. Thrall, *II Corinthians*, 1.477.) The significance of both texts for Paul indicates that the relative importance of the various scriptural books cannot be established simply by counting citations – as D.-A. Koch assumes (*Die Schrift als Zeuge des Evangeliums*, p. 47).

Still more significant for Paul is a statement of Leviticus that concerns the law's goal and rationale. In its Pauline form, extracted from its context and converted into a freestanding utterance, this reads: "The person who does these things will live by them" (Lev.18.5). The way to ultimate human well-being is the way of the commandments: or so it is written in Leviticus. Remarkably, Paul twice cites this text only to state that what it says is in reality not the case (Gal.3.12; Rom.10.5). It is "faith", the acknowledgment of God's definitive saving action, that is the divinely ordained way to ultimate human well-being – as the prophet Habakkuk recognized in a statement that seems deliberately to counter the Leviticus one, and as even Moses saw so clearly when he wrote of Abraham's response to the divine promises. The Leviticus statement encapsulates the fundamental disjunction Paul sees within the Pentateuch – thereby sharply differentiating himself from other contemporary readers of these texts.

This text from Leviticus is the central focus of the present chapter. We must ask how it is to be understood within Leviticus itself, and how it was creatively reinterpreted both by Paul and by another Jewish writer who shared Paul's Pharisaic background: Josephus.

The Law of Life

The way of the commandments

The words cited by Paul conclude a paragraph of general exhortation which introduces a series of prohibitions relating to sexuality (Lev.18.6–23). Together with the exhortation at the end of this divine speech (18.24–30), the introduction sets the prohibited practices in the general context of a warning against the practices of the inhabitants of Egypt and of Canaan.[2] To observe the commandments of the Lord is to be different from the surrounding nations, and to be vigilant in maintaining this difference. In order to bring out lexical features relevant to Pauline usage, we shall for the moment follow the Septuagint:

> And the Lord spoke to Moses saying: Speak to the sons of Israel, and you shall say to them, I am the Lord your God. According to the customs of the land of Egypt, in which you dwelt, you shall not do *[ou poiēsete]*, and according to the customs of the land of Canaan, into which I am bringing you, you shall not do and in their observances you

2. As Martin Noth points out, the reference to Egypt in addition to Canaan is unusual (it is omitted from later references to Canaanite practices in Leviticus 18.24–30; 20.23). It may reflect the fact "that the Israelites, here in their supposed position at Sinai, could not yet have knowledge of the Canaanites as a warning example, but only of the Egyptians, whose way of life is here equated with that of the Canaanites" (*Leviticus*, p. 134).

shall not walk *[ou poreusesthe]*. My judgments you shall do and my decrees you shall keep, to walk in them. I am the Lord your God. And you shall keep all my decrees and all my judgments and you shall do them *[poiēsete auta]*, doing which a person shall live by them *[ha poiēsas anthrōpos zēsetai en autois]*. I am the Lord your God. (Lev.18.1–5 LXX)[3]

The opening reference to "the sons of Israel" is characteristic of a number of the divine speeches in Leviticus (1.1–2; 4.1–2; 11.1–2; 12.1–2; 15.1–2; 17.1–2), but differs from the immediately preceding speeches by omitting all reference to Aaron as co-addressee either of Moses (11.1; 13.1; 14.33; 15.1; cf. 16.2) or of the people (17.2). With the exception of a series of speeches in Leviticus 21–22, it is only the people of Israel whom Moses is commanded to address in the concluding section of the book (chapters 18–27), and this corresponds to a primary focus on concerns that are no longer specifically priestly. The theme of these chapters is the distinctive way of life of the people of Israel, summarized in the call to be holy as God is holy (19.2). It is the function of the opening exhortation of Leviticus 18 to mark this shift in subject-matter, and not just to introduce the series of prohibitions that immediately follows.[4] Indeed, if Leviticus 27 is regarded

---

3.   LXX and MT diverge here at five main points. First, the translation of *m'śh* (doing, work) as *epitēdeumata* (customs) in v.3 fails to reproduce the verbal link with "you shall not do". Second, MT lacks the double "all" in v.5a, which the translator may have inserted for greater emphasis (as also in 18.26; cf. 19.37, 20.22 MT). Third, LXX inserts, "... and you shall do them". Fourth, LXX converts *'śr y'śh 'tm h'dm* into the participial clause, *ha poiēsas anthrōpos* (we shall return to this point below). Fifth, *'ny yhwh* is expanded into, *egō kurios ho theos humōn*.

4.   The claim that Leviticus 18 marks the opening of a new section is in some tension with the older critical hypothesis that the concluding chapters of Leviticus derive from a prior source (the "Holiness Code") which opened with chapter 17. A *Heiligkeitsgesetz* comprising Leviticus 17–26 would resemble other early law codes (Ex.20–23, Deut.12–28) in opening with instructions relating to the place of sacrifice and closing with exhortations and warnings (so S. R. Driver, *Introduction*, p. 48). More recently, the hypothesis of a prior Holiness Code has been challenged – for example, by V. Wagner, who argues that the literary structure of Exodus 25-Leviticus 26 cuts across the material assigned to "H" ("Zur Existenz des sogenannten 'Heiligkeitsgesetzes'", pp. 312–15). (For a different, more speculative analysis of the literary structure of Leviticus as a whole, see Mary Douglas, *Leviticus as Literature*, pp. 195–251.) If the hypothesis of a prior source is abandoned, then it becomes clear that Leviticus 17 is more closely related to chapters 1–16 than to chapters 18–26. Thus, "camp" (17.3) occurs 13 times in ch.1–16, but elsewhere only in the narrative of 24.10–23 (x 3). "Tent of meeting" (17.4, 5, 6, 9) occurs 37 times in chapters 1–16, but elsewhere only in 19.21 and 24.3. On the other hand, distinctive features of chapters 18–25 are absent from chapter 17: for example, the formula *'ny yhwh*, which occurs 50 times in various forms in chapters 18–26 but elsewhere only in 11.44, 45. In citing 18.5, Paul draws from a passage (18.1–5) whose position in the structure of Leviticus lends it considerable rhetorical weight.

as an appendix, a connection might be made between the opening of chapter 18 and the summary statement that concludes chapter 26:

> These are the judgments and the decrees and the law *[ho nomos]*, which the Lord gave *[edōken]* between himself and the sons of Israel at Mount Sinai by the hand *[en cheiri]* of Moses. (Lev.26.46)

This passage echoes the opening exhortation to "the sons of Israel" to "perform the Lord's judgments and decrees" (18.1–5). The unusual reference to the "giving" of "the law" (note the singular) "by the hand" of Moses, is taken up by Paul in Galatians 3.19–21. The allusion to Leviticus 18.5 in Galatians 3.21 ("If a law *was given* that was able to make alive...") suggests that Paul himself may have linked the two Leviticus passages.[5] The two passages are also connected by a chain of general exhortations that use similar terminology:

> And you shall keep all my laws *[panta ta nomima mou]* and all my decrees and you shall not do any of these abominations, either the native-born or the proselyte who dwells among you. (18.26)

> And you shall keep my decrees, so as to avoid the abominable customs which were practised before you: you shall not defile yourself by them. I am the Lord your God. (18.30)

> You shall keep my law *[ton nomon mou]*. (19.19)

> And you shall keep all my law *[panta ton nomon mou]* and all my decrees and you shall do them. I am the Lord your God. (19.37)

> And you shall keep my decrees and you shall do them. I am the Lord, who sanctifies you. (20.8)

> And you shall keep all my decrees and my judgments and you shall do them, so that the land may not be angry with you, into which I bring you to dwell upon it. (20.22)

The pairing of "you shall keep" and "you shall do" is established in Leviticus 18.5 and repeated in three of these subsequent passages (19.37; 20.8, 22). By means of these and other verbal links, a chain is created that

---

5. Only in Leviticus 26.46 is the phrase "by the hand of Moses" found in conjunction with "the law" (cf. Gal.3.19). The closest parallels are in Numbers 15.23 ("all these commandments... as the Lord commanded you by the hand of Moses") and 36.13 ("These are the commandments and the ordinances and the judgments which the Lord commanded by the hand of Moses"). Other occurrences of this phrase refer to specific commandments relating to the census of the Levites (Num.4.37, 41, 45, 49; cf. 17.5) or to the journey through the wilderness (Num.9.23, 10.13; cf. 33.1).

connects the opening exhortation (18.1–5) with the concluding summary (26.46).[6] Also noteworthy are the repeated references to "my law" (19.19, 37) or "the law" (26.46), where the Septuagint's singular nouns diverge from the plurals of the Masoretic text.[7] The passage from which Paul draws the crucial statement that "the person who does them shall live by them" (Gal.3.12, Rom.10.5) has an important function in the book of Leviticus as a whole.

In Leviticus 18.1–5, the "doing" of the commandments of God is a matter of exclusive loyalty to the one who announces himself at the beginning and the end with the words, "I am the Lord your God" (Lev.18.2, 5) – a repeated refrain in the chapters that follow, which serves to direct attention back from the specific content of the individual commandments to the identity of the one who commands.[8] The fulfilling (*'śh, poiein*) of these commandments entails a non-fulfilling of the practices of the Gentiles out of loyalty to one who identifies certain actions or abstentions as "*my* judgments and *my* decrees" (vv.4, 5). To "do" (or fulfil, practise or perform) these judgments and decrees is also, in more metaphorical language, to "keep" or "guard" them and to "go" or "walk" in them. If one metaphor emphasizes the need for vigilance, the other characterizes the practice of the law as a lifelong journey. And the intended outcome and goal of this vigilant, ongoing practice of the commandments is that "a person shall live by them" (v.5). Paul, as a former Pharisee, understands this as a reference to the eschatological life of the resurrection.[9] In its original context in Leviticus, however, this cryptic statement may be seen as anticipating the fuller account of the blessings of obedience given in chapter 26, where the "doing" of the commandments is again supplemented with the metaphors of "walking" and "keeping":

> If you walk in my decrees and keep my commandments and do them
> *[kai poiēsete autas]*, I shall give you the rain in its season, and the earth
> will give her produce, and the trees of the fields will give their fruit. And
> your threshing will overtake the vintage, and the vintage will overtake
> the sowing, and you shall eat your bread in abundance and dwell with

6. Links between these passages are noted by J. Milgrom, *Leviticus*, pp. 1581, 1709–10, 2342.

7. Replacement of Hebrew plurals (*ḥqty*, Lev.19.19, 37; *twrt*, 26.46) by the singular *ho nomos* also occurs in Exodus16.28[?]; 18.16 *(twrtyw)*, 20 *(twrt)*. In the MT, the singular occurs in relation to specific laws (e.g. Lev.6.1, 7, 18; 7.1, 11, 37), and, with a comprehensive reference, in Exodus 13.9, 16.4 and frequently in Deuteronomy.

8. Milgrom argues on the basis of Numbers 14.35 and parallel passages in Ezekiel that *'ny yhwh* is an abbreviation of the longer formula, "I YHWH have spoken" (*Leviticus 17–22*, p. 1518).

9. Compare the interpretation of a parallel text (Deut.30.19) in 4 Ezra and 2 Baruch, discussed by Shannon Burkes, "'Life' Redefined". On this see also chapter 10 below.

security in your land. And war shall not pass through your land, and I
will give peace in your land, and you shall sleep and no-one shall make
you afraid... (Lev.26.3–6)

The "life" that the commandments intend is a life of abundance and
security within the land.[10] This passage also makes explicit the conditional
nature of the earlier offer of "life" to the one who observes the
commandments. "*If* you walk in my decrees and keep my commandments
and do them", there will be one outcome, but there will be quite another
outcome "if you will not obey me, and will not do *[mēde poiēsete]* these
my decrees..." (26.14). The law's offer of life stands on one side of the
dual hypothesis represented by this *if* and *if not*. On both sides, divine
action is contingent on human action, and the prior human action is
oriented towards subsequent divine action. The promise that "the person
who does these things will live by them" ascribes a conditional saving
efficacy to human action.

There are, however, two problems of translation in Leviticus 18.5. A
word-for-word translation of the Masoretic text would run: "And you
shall keep my statutes and my decrees, which a person *[h'dm]* shall do
them, and shall live by/in them *[bhm]*". The first question relates to the
redundant "them" in the relative clause; the second to the translation of
the preposition *b-*: "by them", or "in them"? Both questions are relevant
to the Pauline interpretation of this text, and the second is crucially
important.

The syntactically awkward, "... which a man shall do them" probably
reflects the semantic indeterminacy of the Hebrew connective *'šr*.[11] The
pronoun "them" is inserted simply to indicate that *'šr* here functions as a
relative pronoun, and it should therefore be omitted in translation: "...
which a person shall do, and shall live by/in them". The Septuagint
resolves the syntactical problem by converting the first phrase into a
participial clause subordinated to the second: "... which a person doing
[ha anthrōpos poiēsas] shall live by/in them". In the Hebrew, however, the
redundant pronoun makes it possible to convert a dependent statement
into a freestanding one: "A person shall do *them*, and shall live by/in
them." Although there is some doubt about the precise wording of Paul's
citations of this text, it is clear that he exploited this possibility while
retaining the Greek participial clause: "The one doing them *[ho poiēsas
auta]* shall live by/in them" (Gal.3.12).

10. The link between obedience, life and possession of the land is clear in parallel texts in
Deuteronomy (4.1; 5.33; 8.1; 16.20; 30.15–20); cf. Ex.20.12 = Deut.5.16. On this point, see
further below.
11. As BDB notes, *'šr* is a mere connecting link, and requires to be supplemented by
another word in order to define the nature of the relation more precisely (p. 81).

Much more significant is the second issue. The text may be translated: "... which a person shall do, and shall live *by* them". But it might equally be translated: "... which a person shall do, and shall live *in* them". "By them" *(bhm, en autois)* suggests an instrumental understanding of the Hebrew or Greek preposition: the divine commandments are the means to an end, which is life. But "in them" is also a possible translation, and it would support the interpretation of the whole statement offered by J. D. G. Dunn. Dunn argues that

> Moses did *not* say, and Paul does not understand him to say, that keeping the law was a means of earning or gaining life (in the future ...). Rather the law prescribes the life which is to be lived by the covenant people.[12]

In other words, "the person who does these things will live in them" means that those who observe the commandments will find in them the necessary orientation for their lives. Leviticus 18.5 speaks of "a way of life, and not of a life yet to be achieved or attained".[13] In that case, to "live in them" (i.e. in the commandments) would simply be synonymous with to "walk in them":

> My decrees you shall do *[t'św]* and my statutes you shall keep, to walk in them *[llkt bhm]* (18.4)

> And you shall keep my statutes and my decrees, which a person shall do *[y'śh]*, and shall live in them *[why bhm]*. (18.5)

If to "do" God's commandments is "to walk in them", so, arguably, it is also to "live in them". That would make 18.5b ("and shall live in them") parallel to the preceding statement, rather than being a final clause indicating the goal or reward of law observance ("... so as to live in/by them"). On this view, neither Moses nor Paul speaks of any such thing.

This is a serious exegetical possibility, but it is probably wrong in relation both to the original Hebrew text and to its later interpretation.[14] There is abundant evidence that "life" could be seen as the goal of law observance, not as a synonym for it.

---

12. *Romans 9–16*, p. 612, italics original; compare *The Theology of Paul the Apostle*, pp. 152–53. Dunn does not reach a clear decision on the translation issue, but a non-instrumental interpretation of *bhm/en autois* would offer strong support for his view.

13. *The Theology of Paul the Apostle*, pp. 152–53.

14. See S. J. Gathercole's detailed rebuttal of Dunn and N. T. Wright ("Torah, Life, and Salvation: Leviticus 18:5 in Early Judaism and the New Testament"), which brings together a range of later passages that reflect the influence of the Leviticus text. Gathercole argues that "Paul is in dialogue with a Judaism that thought in terms of obedience, final judgment, and eternal life, not a Judaism merely organized around sin-repentance-forgiveness or sin-exile-restoration" (p. 150).

(1) While there is no parallel in Leviticus to this conjunction of "doing" and "living", there are clear parallels in Deuteronomy. Here, "life" is the *goal* of "doing":

> And now, Israel, listen to the statues and to the decrees which I am teaching you to do *[l'śwt]*, so that you may live *[lm'n tḥyw]* and go and possess the land which YHWH the God of your fathers is giving you. (Deut.4.1)

> All the commandments which I command you this day you shall be careful to do *[l'śwt]*, so that you may live *[lm'n tḥywn]* and go and possess the land which YHWH promises to your fathers. (Deut.8.1)

Here, doing the commandments leads to life as the way leads to its goal.[15] This "life" is not the way of life appropriate to the covenant, but is rather the covenantal blessing promised to those who observe the commandments (cf. Deut.28; Lev.26).

(2) There are allusions to Leviticus 18.5b in Ezekiel 20.11, 13, 21, in the context of an account of Israel's long history of apostasy (cf. also Neh.9.29). In the wilderness,

> I gave them my statutes, and my decrees I revealed to them, *which a person shall do and shall live by/in them*... And the house of Israel rebelled against me in the wilderness. They did not walk in my statutes, and they rejected my decrees, *which a person shall do and shall live by/in them*... (Ezek.20.11, 13)

In Ezekiel as in Leviticus, the italicized statement may mean simply that people are to "do" YHWH's commandments, that is, to "live" or to "walk" in them. Yet the repeated and precise allusion implies that the statement has dogmatic import – compare Deuteronomy 8.3, where the subject is also *h'dm* ("Man shall not live by bread alone..."). The perverseness of Israel's rebellion is heightened if what is rejected is not just the commandments as such, but also the covenant blessing of "life" which is their goal. This interpretation is confirmed by the parallel in Ezekiel 18, where "he shall live by/in them" is abbreviated to "he shall live":

> If a person is righteous, and does justice and righteousness, and does not eat upon the mountains or lift up his eyes to the idols of the house of Israel... and walks in my statutes and has kept my decrees, acting with integrity: he is righteous, he shall surely live *[ḥyh yḥyh]*, says the Lord YHWH. (Ezek.18.5–9)

---

15. LXX: ... *hosa egō didaskō humas sēmeron poiein, hina zēte*... (Deut.4.1); *pasas tas entolas, has egō entellomai humin sēmeron, phulaxesthe poiein, hina zēte*... (Deut.8.1).

Here, omission of the prepositional phrase, "by/in them" means that the potential ambiguity of the reference to life is dispelled. To live is the covenantal blessing promised to those who observe the commandments, and is not a synonym for "walking in my statutes". Ezekiel 18 as a whole should indeed be seen as a commentary on Leviticus 18.5, and the understanding of "life" here should be extended to the explicit Leviticus allusions in Ezekiel 20.[16]

(3) The possibility that the two parts of Leviticus 18.5b might be parallel to one another was also overlooked by a second commentator on this text, the Septuagint translator. In the Septuagint, as we have seen, the first phrase – literally, "which a person shall do them" – is rendered with a participial clause, thus subordinating the first phrase to the second: "... which a person doing *[ha poiēsas anthrōpos]* shall live by/in them". The implication is that doing and living are not synonymous: "The person who does them shall live in them" would be pure tautology, and readers of the Septuagint such as Philo and Paul do not appear to have taken the text in that way. Philo cites the whole of Leviticus 18.1–5 in a form closely resembling the Septuagint, and adds an interpretative gloss specifically to the statement about "life":

> "... And you shall keep all my decrees and judgments, and you shall do them. The one who does them *[ho poiēsas anthrōpos]* shall live by them." So, then, the true life *[hē pros alētheian zōē]* is that of the one who walks in the judgments and decrees of God... (*de cong.* 86–87)

"True life", life in communion with the deity, arises from the practice of the divine commandments but is not synonymous with that practice.[17] In the case of Paul himself, evidence that he regarded "life" as the goal of the law may be seen in statements alluding to Leviticus which say exactly that (cf. Gal.3.21; Rom.7.10).

Leviticus 18.5 is most plausibly to be understood as a conditional promise of "life" – that is, the totality of the covenant blessings – for those who observe the divine commandments. On this interpretation, this brief dogmatic statement anticipates the full description of the covenant blessings in chapter 26. Its claim that "doing" the commandments is the

---

16. According to W. Zimmerli, "life" in these Ezekiel passages is "the gift given in the sphere of the sanctuary as the place of God's presence" (*Ezekiel*, 1.376). Zimmerli cites Amos 5.4–5 as a parallel, and finds here a reference to the sacral law proclaimed at the temple gate, observance of which was a condition of entry (*ibid.*). While Zimmerli under-emphasizes the intertextual link with Leviticus, the view of law observance as a precondition of entry into life is clear.

17. The passages from Ezekiel and Philo are briefly and inadequately discussed by Dunn himself (*The Theology of Paul the Apostle*, pp. 152–53).

way to "life" is paralleled both in Deuteronomy and in its own early commentators, from Ezekiel and the Septuagint translator to Philo and Paul.

Some false dichotomies

Since the work of Sanders, a veto has been imposed on the supposition that the commandments could have been understood as the way to life in Second Temple Judaism. It is assumed that such an understanding of human action is incompatible, first, with God's covenant with Israel; second, with the divine mercy and forgiveness; and third, with the role of the commandments as marking out the boundary between the elect people and the Gentiles. As regards Leviticus itself, these are all false dichotomies.

(1) The mode of human action that leads to life occurs only in the context of the covenant between God and Israel. The Book of Leviticus promulgates not an abstract "legalism" (or "ritualism") but a "covenantal nomism" in which the divine election of Israel issues in the divine call for specific forms of human responsive action. The commandments cannot be detached from the one who speaks in them, and who repeatedly announces himself as "the Lord your God" (18.2, 4). And yet these commandments are no mere secondary addition to a prior covenant of pure grace. On the contrary, covenant and commandment are inseparable: the commandments are the fulfilment and completion of the covenant whose roots go back to the patriarchal era. In Leviticus, the term "covenant" *(bryt, diathēkē)* occurs almost exclusively in chapter 26, at precisely the point in the book where the conditional nature of the divine blessing is so strongly underlined. The promise that "I will confirm my covenant with you" (26.9) is dependent on the prior condition that "you walk in my decrees and keep my commandments and do them" (v.3). In the long conditional clause that opens the series of divine threats (vv.14–39), to disobey God's decrees and to fail to perform his commandments is "to break my covenant" (vv.14–15). Where the commandments are broken, there follows a "sword enacting the vengeance of the covenant" (v.25). The divine threats culminate in the loss of the land (vv.33–39), and at this point the origin of the covenant concept comes into view:

> And they shall confess their sins and the sins of their fathers, that they transgressed and disregarded me, and that they walked contrary to me, and I walked contrary to them, and in wrath, and I destroyed them in the land of their enemies. Then their uncircumcised heart shall be ashamed, and then they shall make good their sins. And I shall remember the covenant of Jacob and the covenant of Isaac and the

covenant of Abraham I shall remember, and I shall remember the land.
(26.40–42 LXX)

At this point in the chapter, the conditional character of the argument –
indicated by the repeated "if"-clauses (vv.3, 14, 21, 23, 27) – gives way to a
prophetic announcement of a foreordained or foreseen future event of
confession and repentance, to which the Lord will respond by remember-
ing the covenant(s) with the patriarchs.[18] Even here, it is the human action
that is the precondition of the divine. The covenant is also rooted in the
exodus:

> And when they were in the land of their enemies, I did not abandon
> them, nor was I so angry with them as to destroy them and to break my
> covenant with them; for I am the Lord their God. And I shall remember
> their first covenant *[autōn tēs diathēkēs tēs proteras]*, when I led them
> out of the land of Egypt, from the house of slavery, before the Gentiles,
> to be their God. I am the Lord. (26.44–45)

On the basis of the deliverance of the forefathers from Egypt, it is said that
no amount of disobedience will ever lead God to cancel the covenant.
There will always be a way out of the land of exile; life under the enduring
wrath of God will never be Israel's only option. And yet (in the light of
vv.40–42), there is no way out that bypasses confession and repentance.[19]
The covenant with the patriarchs and the exodus generation simply keeps
open the conditional promise of blessing announced at Sinai (cf. 26.3–13),
but it does not guarantee it. It demonstrates that even exile does not bring
the covenant relationship to an end, but it does not affect the conditional
nature of the divine blessing. The whole chapter explores the logic of a
covenant in which future divine blessing is contingent on human obedience
to its terms. This is also the logic of the conditional promise of Leviticus
18.5: that the person who does these things will live by them.

In Leviticus, the covenant with the patriarchs and the exodus generation
is completed by the commandments revealed at Sinai together with the
conditional promise attached to them. In the event of obedience, the Lord
will confirm this covenant (26.9); but if the covenant is broken from the
human side, this will issue in "the vengeance of the covenant" (vv.15, 25).
The covenant is characterized by *mutual obligation*, and both sides of it are
equally fundamental; the Sinai revelation serves to redress the apparent
one-sidedness of the earlier, unilateral covenant with the patriarchs and the

---

18. In v.40, there is no equivalent to the conditional *if* (*'m, ean*) in the five earlier instances.
The apparent reference in v.42 to covenants with each patriarch probably refers to a single
covenant given in threefold repetition. For a possible explanation of the unusual order, see J.
Van Seters, *The Yahwist as Historian*, pp. 236–37.

19. So Milgrom, *Leviticus 22–27*, p. 2340: "[A]s explicated in vv.40–41, the divine
willingness to fulfill the covenant is dependent on Israel's penitence."

exodus generation. Whereas Paul argues that the covenant of Genesis 15 is already definitive, and that it *cannot* be altered by what followed centuries later at Sinai (Gal.3.15–18), Leviticus assumes that everything that preceded the Sinai disclosure comes to fruition in it. It could be argued that only so does the divine–human relationship become truly mutual – without, of course, losing its asymmetry.[20]

It is worth comparing this scriptural understanding of the covenant with E. P. Sanders' account of "the overall pattern of Rabbinic religion". Sanders writes:

> God has chosen Israel and Israel has accepted the election. In his role as King, God gave Israel commandments which they are to obey as best they can. Obedience is rewarded and disobedience punished. In case of failure to obey, however, man has recourse to divinely ordained means of atonement, in all of which repentance is required. As long as he maintains his desire to stay in the covenant, he has a share in God's covenantal promises, including life in the world to come. The intention and effort to be obedient constitute the *condition for remaining in the covenant*, but they do not *earn* it.[21]

Applied to Leviticus, this description would be seriously deficient at several points. First, it implies a (remarkably Pauline) distinction between an election that is primary and commandments that are secondary.[22] In Leviticus, the divine commandments belong to the primary form of the covenant, which they bring to completion. Second, there is no place in Leviticus for Sanders' language about desiring to stay in the covenant, intending and striving to be obedient – language oddly reminiscent of

---

20. W. Eichrodt claims that, for the Priestly writer, "the solemn conclusion of Yahweh's covenant with Israel takes place at the Abraham covenant only, and the events of Sinai are not given the status of an independent covenant-making, but only of a renewal and refashioning of the earlier one with Abraham" (*Theology of the Old Testament*, 1.56). This assessment is unduly influenced by traditional concerns about "grace" and "obedience", and fails to note the radical nature of the "refashioning" that occurs in Leviticus 26.

21. *Paul and Palestinian Judaism*, p. 180; italics original.

22. Sanders begins his important section on "the election and the covenant" (*ibid.*, pp. 84–107) by discussing rabbinic passages indicating "that entrance into the covenant was prior to the fulfilment of commandments" (p. 85). These show "that the view that God had first chosen Israel and *only then* given commandments to be obeyed is not lacking in Rabbinic literature" (p. 87; italics added). A view that is initially, and realistically, described as "not lacking" is ultimately elevated to full dogmatic status: "The universally held view was [that] those who accept the covenant, which carries with it God's promise of salvation, *accept also* the obligation to obey the commandments given by God in connection with the covenant" (p. 204; italics added). Crucial for Sanders' construction of this "universally held view" are some specific rabbinic comments on scriptural passages (Ex.20.2; Lev.18.1–3) where the statement "I am the Lord your God" precedes and grounds the commandments which follow (pp. 85–86).

Romans 7. Leviticus is concerned with concrete acts of obedience to specific divine commandments: there is no sense that the commandments are problematic, and that in relation to them one can only desire, intend and strive. On the contrary: "You shall *do* my ordinances and *keep* my statutes and *walk* in them" (Lev.18.4). Third, in Leviticus one does not merely remain within a covenant that already has a "covenantal promise" of "life" attached to it. Since covenant and commandment are inseparable, the relation between obedience and life is more straightforward and less circuitous than Sanders implies. While the over-worked term "earn" is inappropriate in that it turns the covenant into a relationship between employer and employee, "condition for remaining in the covenant" simply introduces new confusions. According to Leviticus, obedience to the commandments is the way to the covenant blessings.[23]

(2) It is often assumed that, at least in its Pauline usage, Leviticus 18.5 implies a "perfectionist" account of a Torah observance that has no need of the divine mercy or forgiveness. "Life" would then be promised to the one who has practised a lifelong, sinless observance of all the divine commandments, without even a single minor lapse. Yet Paul says nothing of this. Both in Galatians and in Romans, the Leviticus text is set in opposition to texts which for Paul speak of the divine saving action and its human acknowledgment (Habakkuk 2.4 and Deuteronomy 30.12–14, respectively). In contrast, Leviticus speaks of a human salvific action and its divine acknowledgment. This broad contrast does not require that the human action that leads to salvation or "life" must be perfect or sinless; such an assumption is irrelevant to Paul's argument, and contradicts Leviticus itself.[24]

Admittedly there is in Leviticus a certain class of transgression for which no atonement is possible, since it is punishable by death. Offences in this category include the offering of children to Molech (Lev.20.2, 4), cursing one's parents (20.9), adultery and other sexual sins (20.10–16), blasphemy (24.13–16) and murder (24.17, 21).[25] In a related class of offences, the offender is to be "cut off from among his people": that is, God himself will take responsibility for inflicting the death penalty (cf. Lev.20.4–5). These

---

23. In the Pentateuch as a whole, the term "covenant" is used in connection both with Abraham (Gen.15.18; 17.2, 4, 7, and *passim*; Ex.2.24; 6.4, 5; Deut.7.12; 8.18) and with Sinai/Horeb (Ex.19.5; 24.7, 8; 34.10, 27, 28; Deut.4.13, 23, 31; 5.2, 3; 9.9, 11, 15; 28.68; 31.16, 20). The priestly stratum seeks to integrate the two by seeing the Sinai legislation not as a new covenant but as the full realization of the covenant with Abraham.

24. It is widely assumed that, for Paul, the law requires perfect obedience and fails to deliver the life it promises only because perfect obedience is never forthcoming (see, for example, S. Westerholm, *Israel's Law and the Church's Faith*, p. 142).

25. For discussion, see Milgrom, *Leviticus 1–16*, pp. 457–60.

offences include eating a sacrifice beyond the permitted time (7.18, 19.8) or in a state of impurity (7.20–21); consuming blood (7.27; 17.10, 14) or suet (7.25); slaughtering or sacrificing animals away from the sanctuary (17.3–4, 8–9); offering children to Molech – for which a death penalty is also specified (20.3–5); consulting the dead (20.6); and failing to fast or working on the Day of Atonement (23.29-30). If observing the commandments is the way to life, then a special importance obviously attaches to those commandments whose transgression entails death at divine or human hands.[26] For such offences there is no expiation. The death penalty is not the norm, however; transgression does not necessarily entail death, Unconscious offences can be expiated through sin offerings or guilt offerings (4.1–35; 5.14–19). Conscious offences also require the confession of the transgressor (5.5), or of the high priest on the Day of Atonement (16.21). Indeed, in the circumstances of exile confession can even bring about atonement in the absence of sacrifice (26.40–42). This provision for expiation does not represent an exception or qualification of the principle that "the one who does these things will live by them", since the sacrificial system itself consists in commandments that must be obeyed – in the form of prescriptions for the sin- or guilt-offering, or for participation in the rites of the Day of Atonement through fasting and abstention from work (23.26–32). In that sense, "doing these things" is compatible with transgression, since "these things" include prescriptions for dealing with transgression. We may conclude from this that the commandments both assume a measure of human responsibility and recognize the reality of human weakness. They thereby reflect the character of a deity characterized not only by holiness – "You shall be holy, for I the Lord your God am holy" (19.2) – but also by mercy (cf. Ex.33.19; 34.5–7). There is no contradiction or tension between the divine mercy and the proposition that Torah observance is the way to life – even if this mercy is something other than what Paul means by the term "grace".

Sanders' analysis of the rabbinic "pattern of religion" implies that there is something logically odd about statements about God's mercy in relation to statements about God's justice:

> If one asks how the idea that God is just and pays to each his due is to be reconciled into a doctrinal unity with the statement that God's mercy predominates over his justice, the answer is... that this is not a doctrinal system in which every statement has a logical place. One thing or the other would be said depending on the particular needs of the instance. But there should be no doubt that the latter type of statement –

---

26. Paul himself alludes to this aspect of the Torah when he lists the transgressors excluded from the kingdom of God (1 Cor.6.9–10, cf. Gal.5.19–21).

that mercy outweighs justice – reflects the Rabbinic attitude towards God at its most basic level.[27]

Whether or not this is an accurate summary of the Tannaitic literature surveyed by Sanders, it does not apply to Leviticus. In Leviticus, the fundamental concern is with the creation of a human holiness that corresponds to the divine. In the light of this divine holiness, two types of transgression may be identified. For one type, there is no expiation; for another, expiation is provided. Those who transgress remain subject to divine commandments that stipulate either their death or the means to their purification. There is no logical oddity here, and no problem in allowing scope for the divine mercy within a primary concern with human conduct.

(3) The calling to be holy and to observe the divine commandments has the effect of demarcating the people of Israel from the surrounding nations. To do what is commanded is to refrain from doing what is done in the land of Egypt or of Canaan (18.3). Indeed, some commandments have the specific role of signifying the difference:

> I am the Lord your God, who separated you from all the Gentiles *[apo pantōn tōn ethnōn]*. You shall therefore distinguish between the clean and the unclean animals, and between the clean and the unclean birds, and you shall not profane your souls with the animals, birds or reptiles of the earth which I have separated from you in uncleanness. And you shall be holy, for I the Lord your God am holy, who separated you from all the Gentiles to be mine. (20.24b–26)

Here, the Jew/Gentile distinction is projected onto the animal world, from where it is reflected back. Whereas other commandments *enact* that distinction (cf. 18.24–30; 20.22–23), the commandment distinguishing clean from unclean creatures *signifies* it. As presented here, this is a second-order commandment that represents the distinction enacted in the first-order commandments. To be holy is to live on the basis of a distinction and of its representation, and in Leviticus it is the dietary code that fulfils that representational role – and not, for example, circumcision or the sabbath (cf. 12.3; 23.3; 26.2).

According to J. D. G. Dunn, Paul's claim is that unbelieving Israel has converted the divine gift of the Torah into an exclusive privilege. The law

> came to reinforce the sense of *Israel's privilege*, the law as marking out this people in its set-apartness to God. As God's choice of Israel drew the corollary that God's saving righteouness was restricted to Israel, so

27. *Paul and Palestinian Judaism*, p. 124.

> the law's role in defining Israel's holiness to God became also its role in *separating Israel from the nations.*[28]

In fact, as Leviticus shows, holiness and separation belong together from the start. The idea that the emphasis on separation is a secondary corruption of the original concept of holiness is clearly wrong. More significantly, Dunn assumes that his own emphasis on the social function of the law in establishing Israel's separation represents a straightforward alternative to the old view of the law as a supposed way to salvation – a view now stigmatized as "Lutheran". Thus, interpreting the Leviticus citation in Galatians 3.12, Dunn correctly notes that "in context Lev. xviii.2–5 emphasizes the distinctiveness of Israel's way of life from that of the surrounding nations", but also asserts, without the slightest foundation in the text, that "the thought is badly skewed if the emphasis is placed upon 'doing' the law".[29] This is a false dichotomy, however. How could one cite Leviticus 18.5 *without* putting emphasis on doing the law? Leviticus 18.1–5 speaks of a praxis that both differs from that of other nations and leads to "life".

The Leviticus text makes life conditional on law observance. This is fully compatible with assumptions about the covenant, the divine mercy, and Israel's separation from the nations that come to expression elsewhere in the book. The dichotomies that have been set up in this area should be dismantled.

Moses rewritten

As we have seen, Paul and Philo are agreed in citing Leviticus 18.5 as a self-contained statement rather than a relative clause: "The one who does these things shall live by them." The introduction of "these things" *(auta)* may be influenced not directly by the Hebrew but by the Septuagintal rendering of passages alluding to the Leviticus text (cf. Ezek.20.11, 13; Neh.9.29 = Esdr.B 19.29). In Galatians 3.12 as in Philo, *anthrōpos* was probably omitted; in Romans 10.5, it was probably included.[30] In Galatians, the Leviticus passage is cited in order to demonstrate the proposition that "the law is not of faith". Here, the phrase translated "of faith" is the *ek pisteōs* of the Habakkuk citation of the previous verse:

28. *Theology of Paul the Apostle*, p. 355; italics original, cross references omitted.
29. *Galatians*, p. 176.
30. Although the majority of manuscripts include *anthrōpos* in Galatians 3.12, it is omitted in P[46] and ℵ. The earliest manuscripts include it in Romans 10.5. C. D. Stanley convincingly argues that the word was deliberately omitted in Galatians 3.12 in order "to create a near-perfect verbal parallel between this verse and the quotation from Hab 2.4 in v.11" (*Paul and the Language of Scripture*, pp. 244–45).

"The one who is righteous by faith will live" (Hab.2.4; Gal.3.11). According to Paul, the texts from Habakkuk and Leviticus assert a fundamentally different understanding of the divine–human relationship; the theology of righteousness by faith that he develops in Galatians is nothing other than the attempt to establish this difference and to uncover its rationale.[31] Paul here creates a hermeneutical framework for the right interpretation of scripture as a whole, in its differentiated though ultimately convergent testimony to God's saving action in Christ. The unity and harmony of this scriptural testimony can only be grasped if one understands the inner-scriptural antithesis which Paul's oppositional terminology seeks to identify.[32]

In Romans 10 as in Galatians 3, the Leviticus text represents one side of this inner-scriptural antithesis, which Paul here characterizes as "the righteousness which is by the law", which Moses "writes" (Rom.10.5).[33] The other side is here represented by a text that derives not from the prophets, as in Galatians, but from within the Torah itself (Deuteronomy 30.12–14). This is here attributed not to Moses, as in the case of the Leviticus text, but to a personified "Righteousness of faith". What Moses writes is contrasted with what the Righteousness of faith says:

31.   The common ground on which the antithesis stands is represented by the term "life", which occurs in both the Habakkuk and the Leviticus citations. There are "functional equivalents in early Judaism to Paul's concept of final salvation" (S. J. Gathercole, *Where is Boasting?*, p. 22), and this equivalence is tacitly acknowledged by Paul himself.

32.   According to Alan Segal, it is not the biblical text that generates the antithesis between Leviticus and Habakkuk: rather, it is Paul's "conversion from Pharisaism to Christianity and his subsequent experience of dealing with gentile and Jewish Christians" that cause him to see faith and law as "two different paths" (*Paul the Convert*, p. 122). The present attempt to understand Pauline antithesis in hermeneutical terms does not deny that the antithesis is determined in part by Paul's experience of Gentile mission. Indeed, Segal's claim that "Paul's… opposition of faith and law is a social and political justification for a new variety of community" (p. 122) parallels the central thesis of my own *Paul, Judaism and the Gentiles*. In the present context, however, I am more interested in the interaction between text and reader than in the external conditioning of the act of reading. According to Segal, "The text itself does not support Paul's distinction" (p. 122). But is it *only* the experience of living among Gentiles that leads Paul to distinguish between the soteriologies of Leviticus and Habakkuk?

33.   According to P[46] and the majority, the text of Romans 10.5 should read: "Moses writes the righteousness of the law, that the person who does them will live by them". In ℵ, A and other manuscripts, the text reads: "Moses writes that the person who does the righteousness of the law will live by it." It can be argued that the former reading represents an assimilation to the text of Leviticus 18.5 LXX (so Sanday and Headlam, Cranfield, Käsemann, Wilckens). These scholars fail to note the awkwardness of "Moses writes the righteousness which is by the law…", which thus qualifies as the harder reading. The secondary reading is a fairly successful attempt to create an easier text, although this results in an odd word order (the object before the subject) and the conversion of the quotation into a paraphrase. A "righteousness by the law" that is written is no more surprising than a "righteousness of faith" that speaks (cf. Rom.10.6).

> For Moses writes the righteousness which is by the law, that "the person who does these things will live by them". But the Righteousness of faith speaks like this: "Do not say in your heart, Who will ascend into heaven?" (that is, to bring Christ down), or, "Who will descend into the abyss?" (that is, to bring Christ up from the dead). But what does it say? "The word is near you, in your mouth and in your heart" (that is, "the word" of faith which we preach; for if you confess "in your mouth" that Jesus is Lord and believe "in your heart" that God raised him from the dead, you will be saved ...). (Rom.10.5–9)

Paul aims here to show that, despite the impressive clarity of the Leviticus text, the soteriology of the Torah is not a singular, monolithic entity. Beneath the surface of Moses' text, a second, very different voice may be discerned.[34] There is here a genuine antithesis: the distinction between the two texts (as understood by Paul) should not be downplayed.[35] And it is, more precisely, an inner-scriptural antithesis that is here asserted. It should not be assumed that Paul is opposing the teaching of Leviticus with a freestanding doctrine of righteousness by faith that only incidentally avails itself of phraseology adapted from Deuteronomy.[36] Here too, it is essential to note the hermeneutical orientation of Paul's righteousness language.

In order to understand Paul's citation of the Leviticus passage, it must be set alongside the references to the law in two preceding passages. These are, indeed, the only references to the law in the whole of Romans 9–11:

34. There is no antithesis here between "writing" and "saying" – so correctly U. Wilckens, *Römer*, 2.226, who draws attention to the interchangeability of "writing" and "speaking" throughout the citations in Romans 9–10 (cf. 9.15, 17, 33; 10.1, 15, 16, 19, 20, 21).

35. As it is by Cranfield, who argues that Paul interprets Leviticus 18.5 christologically: "Christ has – alone among men – obeyed perfectly and so earned a righteous status and eternal life for Himself, but also (vv. 6–13) for all those who will believe in Him" (*Romans*, 2.522). This interpretation overlooks the evident contrast between what "Moses writes" (Rom.10.5) and what "the Righteousness of faith says" (v.6), and is seemingly motivated by Cranfield's justified opposition to the hypothesis of a proto-Marcionite Paul, capable even of disparaging the holy Law of God (on which point see his earlier article, "St Paul and the Law"). Yet the fact that the law's project (summarized in Leviticus 18.5) results in failure is integral to its indirect witness to the divine saving action in Christ; there is no question of any "disparagement". For other attempts to remove the antithesis from Romans 10.5–6, see R. Hays, *Echoes of Scripture*, p. 76, warning of "disastrous consequences for Christian theology"; and Ross Wagner, *Heralds of the Good News*, p. 160. If, as Wagner argues, Paul here "*redefines* 'doing' as 'believing/trusting in what God has done in Christ'" (*ibid.*; italics original), it is hard to see why the Leviticus quotation is introduced as a statement of "the righteousness which is of the law" (Rom.10.5).

36. The view of F. A. Philippi (1878), for whom, in the course of an "independent dogmatic argument", there occurs "a free employment of the words of Moses, which the apostle uses as an apt substratum for his own course of thought" (cited by J. Murray, *Romans*, 2.52).

For Moses writes the righteousness which is by the law *[ek (tou) nomou]*, that "the person who does these things will live by them". (Rom.10.5)

For Christ is the end of the law *[telos nomou]*, for righteousness for everyone who believes. (10.4)

... but Israel, pursuing the law of righteousness *[nomon dikaiosunēs]*, did not attain to the law *[eis nomon]*. Why? Because not by faith but as if by works... (9.31–32)

As we have seen, Paul draws a contrast between what Moses writes and what the Righteousness of faith says (10.5–9), and this entails the setting aside of the soteriological possibility summarized in Leviticus 18.5. In the realm of the Righteousness of faith, it is not the case that "the person who does these things will live by them" – for it is that other righteousness, the righteousness of the law, that comes to expression in the scriptural text. The initial function of the Leviticus citation, however, is to confirm the assertion of the previous verse, that "Christ is the end of the law" (10.4). Since the regime represented by the Leviticus text has been terminated by the righteousness of faith, the contested term *telos* should be translated "end", not "goal". There is for Paul a clear boundary between "the righteousness which is by the law" and "the righteousness of faith" (10.5–6), and between "works" and "faith" (9.32). The antithetical structure of Paul's language appears to rule out the possibility that the one could develop into the other in some kind of linear process. While it is true that believing Gentiles have attained precisely the goal that Israel sought by way of the law (9.30–31), that of righteousness, the passage as a whole emphasizes the disjunction between the two righteousnesses.[37] There is a righteousness by faith and a law of righteousness (9.30–31), a righteousness of God and a righteousness of one's own (10.3), and the form of righteousness that Paul rejects is identical to "the righteousness that is by the law", articulated in the Leviticus citation (10.5). In its proclamation that "the person who does these things will live by them", the law promotes the pursuit of a righteousness of one's own, arising from an uninformed zeal for God that is ignorant of God's saving action in Christ (cf. 10.2–3). In this context and in this sense, the law is brought to an end by Christ. This assertion is supported, and indeed determined, by the claim that Leviticus articulates something other than the righteousness of faith; it

37. The relevance of 9.30–31 is emphasized by J. Fitzmyer, in support of translating *telos* as "goal" (*Romans*, p. 584). The arguments of H. Räisänen in favour of "end" (*Paul and the Law*, pp. 53–56) seem to me to be compelling. In the present discussion, the question of what *telos* means in Romans 10.4 is subordinate to the question how Leviticus 18.5 is used in the following verse.

is a serious methodological mistake to detach the *telos nomou* statement from its sequel.[38] The law that is brought to an end in Christ is the law whose soteriological rationale is summed up in the Leviticus citation.

In Romans 10.5, Paul's gloss on Leviticus 18.5 states that the theme of this text is "the righteousness which is by the law". "Law" and "righteousness" are also correlated in Romans 9.31–32, where is said that "Israel, pursuing the law of righteousness *[nomon dikaiosunēs]*, did not attain to the law" – pursuing it "not by faith but as if by works". Here, "righteousness" is evidently the goal intended in the practice of the law; it corresponds to the "life" promised in the Leviticus text. Both references to the law in 9.31 are problematic, since they appear to intrude upon the otherwise clear contrast between Israel and the Gentiles:

> What then shall we say? That Gentiles who did not pursue righteousness gained *[katelaben]* righteousness, the righteousness that is by faith; but Israel, which pursued the law of righteousness, did not attain to *[ouk ephthasen]* the law. (9.30–31)

The contrast between pursuing and not pursuing, gaining and not attaining, would have been still clearer had Paul written: "... but Israel, which did pursue righteousness, did not attain to righteousness". That is, indeed, part of what he means here. Yet the double intrusion of the term "law", supplementing the first occurrence of "righteousness" and supplanting the (anticipated) second one, is not without reason. The difference between Israel's action and the Gentiles' inaction is mediated through a *text*, "the law", whose message is succinctly summarized in the statement that "the person who does these things will live by them". This same text is also implicated in the failure of Israel's quest, in its contrast to the Gentiles' unmerited success: Israel "did not attain to the law", in the sense that it did not arrive at the goal of "righteousness" or "life" that the law intends.[39] Why? Because it sought the law's goal of righteousness or life "by works" (9.32). This expression too, which is as sharply contested as the term *telos* in 10.4, must be understood in the light of the Leviticus citation. For Paul, "works" are simply the actions performed by "the person who does these things". The term arises straightforwardly out of the language of scripture.

---

38. Commentators tend to assume a break between Romans 10.4 and 5, and to divide 9.30–10.21 into three paragraphs of approximately equal length (9.30–10.4; 10.5–13; 10.14–21). But these distinctions are merely a matter of presentational convenience. Even 9.30 does not mark a sharp break in the argument.

39. I do not find here an attempt to isolate "law" from "works", as Ross Wagner does (*Heralds of the Good News*, pp. 157–59). In the wisdom of the divine predestination, Israel has (temporarily) been misled by the law and the "works" or actions it prescribes as the way to righteousness and life.

That this correlation between "works" and "doing" was available to Paul is clear from Exodus 18.20 LXX, words of advice addressed to Moses by his father-in-law:

> And you shall proclaim to them the decrees of God and his law *[kai ton nomon autou]*, and you shall show them the ways in which they shall walk, and the works which they shall do *[ta erga ha poiēsousin]*.

It is only a short step from this scriptural reference to God's "law" and the "works" it prescribes to the Pauline "works of law"; and it is equally a short step from "doing" to "works". Indeed, the relationship between the two terms is still closer than this Septuagintal text suggests. The non-cognate noun (*erga*, "works") and verb (*poiein*, "do") conceal the fact that in the underlying Hebrew noun and verb derive from the same root *('śh)*. The equation of "doing" and "works" is therefore already implicit in Paul's text from Leviticus: "the person who does them" (cf. *y'śh 'tm h'dm)* is the person who practises "works of law" *(m'śy htwrh)*.[40] When it is said that "you shall keep all my decrees and all my judgments and you shall do them, doing which a person shall live by them" (Lev.18.5), it is nothing other than "works of the law" that are enjoined. "Works of law", then, is a comprehensive expression that refers to the entirety of the actions and abstentions prescribed by the law. It does not refer only or primarily to so-called "identity markers" that differentiate Israel from the Gentiles, for the Pauline Israel is differentiated from the Gentiles not by individual observances such as circumcision *per se*, but by the attempt to practise the law's requirements in their entirety.[41] When Paul speaks of a pursuit of

40.   A point rightly emphasized by Simon Gathercole, *Where is Boasting?*, pp. 92–93.

41.   In his *Theology of Paul the Apostle*, J. D. G. Dunn acknowledges the comprehensive sense of the Pauline phrase, but continues to maintain the primacy of his "identity markers". He writes: "[T]he phrase 'the works of the law,' does, of course, refer to all or whatever the law requires, covenantal nomism as a whole. But in a context where the relationship of Israel with other nations is at issue, certain laws would naturally come more into focus than others. We have instanced circumcision and food laws in particular" (p. 358). In a footnote, Dunn complains of "repeated misunderstanding" of his seminal "New Perspective" essay of 1982, asserting that "I do not (and never did!) claim that 'works of the law' denote only circumcision, food laws and Sabbath", and that "a careful reading" of the essay in question "should have made [this] clear" (p. 358n). In the 1982 essay, however, Dunn does in fact lay himself open to the reading that he later characterizes as a "misunderstanding" (not omitting to name and shame two of the culprits). "The phrase 'works of the law' in Galatians 2.16 is", he then wrote, "a fairly restricted one: it refers precisely to these same identity markers described above, *covenant* works... To be a Jew was to be a member of the covenant, was to observe circumcision, food laws and sabbath" ("The New Perspective on Paul", repr. in *Jesus, Paul and the Law*, p. 194). "Once again we must observe the limited target that [Paul] has in his sights. It is works which betoken racial prerogative to which he objects..." (p. 200). Sanders is sharply criticized for equating "works of law" with "doing the law" (pp. 201–202). In Romans 9.30–10.5, however, this equation is fully justified. The remarkably select trio of

righteousness by works of law, he is simply paraphrasing Leviticus 18.5. His cryptic claim that Israel, "pursuing a law of righteousness, did not attain the law" (Rom.9.31) means that the practice of "works of law" did not lead to the "righteousness" or "life" promised to "the person who does them". What Israel pursues, then, is the programme laid down by Moses, that "the person who does these things will live by them". For Paul, the scriptural text summarizes the actual practice of his non-Christian Jewish contemporaries, together with its underlying hermeneutical rationale.

Paul's disagreement with his own people is that they strive to live out the programme summarized in Leviticus 18.5, literally understood. They have failed to recognize that the law's project has now been brought to an end by the divine saving action in Christ. The continuing practice of the law as the way to righteousness and life presupposes that God has *not* acted in Christ, in his descent from heaven to take human form and in his resurrection from the dead (cf. Rom.10.6–9). But in fact, God *has* so acted, and his action intends its own acknowledgment in human mouths and hearts. In that sense, "Christ is the end of the law ... " (Rom.10.4). If the divine–human relationship was ever based on Moses' principle that "the person who does these things will live by them", it is so no longer. Moses' statement places a specific human praxis in the foreground, whereas faith speaks exclusively of the divine praxis that has established Jesus as Lord. Paul proceeds to underline the universal scope of Jesus' lordship (Rom.10.11–13), but the contrast between the utterances of the Righteousness of faith and of Moses does not lie in the universal scope of the one and the limited, particularistic scope of the other. Although addressed to "the sons of Israel", Moses' statement concerns universal human destiny – as the use of *anthrōpos* indicates.[42] There is no reason in principle why the nations should not subject themselves to the Law of Moses, and – from the standpoint of a non-Pauline Judaism – every reason why they should (cf. 2.17–20). It is the contrast between human and divine saving initiative that underlies the statement that "the law is not of faith"

"identity markers" is absent here, as indeed it is from all of Romans apart from 2.25–29, 4.9–12, and 14.1–23. I may be permitted to note that I too criticized Dunn's earlier restrictive understanding of "works", in my *Paul, Judaism and the Gentiles*, pp. 198 n.79, 199 n.90. The claim that "the term 'works of the law' refers not to morality in general but to the practice of the law within the Jewish community" (p. 64) still seems to me to be correct, and indeed important.

42. Noting the shift in Leviticus 18.5b from the second plural address to "the sons of Israel" in vv.2–5a, Milgrom explains the third person reference to *h'dm* as intended to include the "sojourner" within the scope of the commandments; cf. 18.26 (*Leviticus 17–22*, p. 1522). Since Leviticus normally extends the commandments to "the sojourner" by means of an explicit reference, this would not adequately explain the striking use of the universal term in 18.5.

(Galatians 3.12, elaborated in Romans 10), and not the contrast between Jewish exclusiveness and Pauline universalism.

Paul opposes the righteousness of the law not simply in his own language but in the language of the law itself (Rom.10.6–9) – drawing selectively on phraseology derived mainly from Deuteronomy 30.12–14, supplemented by his own interpretative glosses. Once again it is evident that Paul develops his theology of righteousness as an exercise in scriptural interpretation. The apostle of "justification by faith" is, as such, an interpreter of scripture. Romans 10.6–9 may be analysed as follows:

A^1 But the Righteousness of faith speaks thus:
B^1 Do not say in your heart, "Who will ascend into heaven?",
C^1 that is, so as to bring Christ down,
B^2 or, "Who will descend into the abyss?",
C^2 that is, so as to bring Christ up from the dead.

A^2 But what does it say?

B^3 "The word is near you, in your mouth and in your heart",
C^3 that is, "the word" of faith which we preach: for if you confess "in your mouth" that Jesus is Lord and believe "in your heart" that God raised him from the dead, you will be saved...

Here, A represents the introduction to the Righteousness of faith's speech, in the form of a two-part citation formula. The formulation of the second part (A^2) is slightly confusing, implying a preceding negative reference to what the Righteousness of faith does *not* say. A^1 is affirmative, however, and the negative, "Do not say in your heart" occurs only at B^1, as part of the speech. At A^2, Paul marks the point where the speaker turns from prohibition to affirmation. Having ruled out certain proposals that its addressee might wish to make, the Righteousness of faith is now invited to speak directly about its own positive content.

B represents the speech itself. In B^1 and B^2, the negative part of the speech serves to eliminate two anticipated proposals. Although not explicitly attributed to a scriptural author, $B^{1,2}$ consists in scriptural language derived initially from Deuteronomy 8.17, 9.4 ("Do not say in your heart...") but primarily from 30.12–13. B^3 is the positive counterpart to $B^{1,2}$, and cites Deuteronomy 30.14 at greater length – in contrast to the preceding highly selective quotations.

C represents the three interpretative glosses that comment on the respective scriptural utterances that precede them. In C^3, the phrase, "... which we preach" indicates that the speaker in these glosses is Paul himself, and that the speech of the Righteousness of faith is confined to the scriptural material *(B)*. Although they are all introduced by the same formula, "that is, ...", the first two glosses function differently from the third. The third (C^3) offers a paraphrase of three expressions in the scriptural citation ("the word", "in your mouth", and "in your heart"). In contrast, the first two glosses (C^1, C^2) explain the rationale for the hypothetical (and forbidden) journeys up into heaven (B^1) and down into the abyss (B^2), referred to in the scriptural text. According to the glosses, the point of the one journey would be to bring Christ down from heaven, the point of the other would be to bring him up from the realm of the dead: the journeys are thus characterized as *quests*, arduous endeavours to acquire a remote and valuable object.

The relation between this passage and its scriptural exemplar becomes clear if we subject the Deuteronomy text to a corresponding analysis:

a   For this commandment, which I command you this day, is not too exalted, nor is it far from you.

b^1 It is not in heaven above, saying, "Who shall ascend for us into heaven,

c^1 and bring it to us, so that hearing it we may do it?"

b^2 Nor is it beyond the sea, saying, "Who will cross the sea for us,

c^2 and bring it to us, and enable us to hear it so that we may do it?"

b^3 The word is very near you, in your mouth and in your heart, and in your hands,

c^3 so as to do it. (Deut.30.11–14)

The correspondences between Romans and Deuteronomy are only approximate, although still significant (hence the differentiation between upper and lower case). In the Deuteronomy passage, *a* introduces not a speaker (as in *A*) but a theme: the accessibility of the commandment. In *A*, however, the theme of the passage is already alluded to in the name that is assigned to the speaker. Although $c^{1,2}$ are not interpretative glosses on $b^{1,2}$, they resemble $C^{1,2}$ in providing a rationale for the proposed journeys – a rationale that is, once again, that of the quest. The heroic agent of the quest is to climb up to heaven or to cross the primeval ocean, so as to acquire the remote and valuable object – here, the commandment – that is needed for the people's well-being. There is no direct correspondence between c^3 and the paraphrastic gloss in C^3. Instead, c^3 returns to the emphasis on the "doing" of the commandment that is already evident in $c^{1,2}$. The point of the hypothetical quests was that the hero should bring back the commandment so that, hearing it, we might do it. In reality, there is no need for any such quest: for the commandment is already intimately present among us, for us to hear and do.

In Romans, the Deuteronomy passage is comprehensively rewritten. The transitions from *a* to *A*, from *b* to *B* and from *c* to *C* all require close attention.

a/A According to *a*, the commandment is easily accessible: the whole passage elaborates its claim that "this commandment, which I command you this day, is not too exalted, nor is it far from you" (Deut.30.11). The two preconditions for the performance of the commandment are that it should be knowable and that it should be practicable, and both of them have been met. Paul, however, suppresses the theme of the knowability and practicability of the commandment: the passage in its original form would be the utterance not of "the Righteousness of faith" but of the "righteousness which is by the law", of which Moses writes in Leviticus 18.5. The attribution of a scriptural text to a personified theological concept is, of course, highly unusual, and contrasts strikingly with the widespread tendency in Romans 9–11 to name the scriptural authors whose texts are cited.[43] Moses is not named in connection with Deuteronomy 30 because Paul has no intention of citing this text in the form in which Moses wrote it.[44] In its original form, the text offers eloquent support for the law's programme as summarized in Leviticus 18.5. The way of the commandments is the way to life; these commandments have been fully made known, and they are easy to perform. The key terms in the Leviticus text – "doing" and "life" – are both present in Deuteronomy 30. The nearness of the word means that "you can do it", and the decision whether or not to obey it is essentially a choice between "life and good" on the one hand, and "death and evil" on the other (30.14–15, cf. v.19). It is this focus on "the commandment" that Paul suppresses at the outset. The Deuteronomy text must be rewritten so that it testifies to the righteousness of faith, and *against* the righteousness of the law as articulated in the Leviticus citation.

b/B In order to suppress the reference to the commandment in *a* and *b¹*, Paul must provide his quotation with a new opening, and finds what he needs in two earlier passages:

> Do not say in your heart, My strength and the might of my hand have brought me this great power. (Deut.8.17 LXX)

---

43.   Moses in 10.5, 19, cf. 9.15; Isaiah in 9.27, 29; 10.16, 20–21; Hosea in 9.25; David in 11.9.

44.   According to Ross Wagner, "Paul's refusal to collapse the two quotations from Moses' writings into one voice creates the rhetorical effect of having two witnesses to substantiate his point" (*Heralds of the Good News*, p. 160n). But that is to underestimate the significance and scope of Paul's rewriting of the Deuteronomy text.

> Do not say in your heart, when the Lord your God drives out the
> nations before your face: Because of my deeds of righteousness *[tas
> dikaiosunas mou]* the Lord brought me in to inherit this good land.
> (Deut.9.4 LXX)

Paul attaches the phrase, "Do not say in your heart" to his quotation from
Deuteronomy 30 in order to conceal the fact that, in its literal sense, it
speaks unambiguously of the righteousness of the law. It is possible that he
also intends to evoke the attack on "one's own righteousness" in
Deuteronomy 9.4, and so to suggest that this book on occasion testifies
to something other than the righteousness that is by the law.[45]

In $B^{1,2}$, Paul omits the phrase "for us" that indicates the altruistic nature
of the proposed journeys in $b^{1,2}$. More significantly, Deuteronomy's
perilous sea-crossing (reminiscent of Gilgamesh's quest for eternal life)[46] is
replaced by a descent into the depths in quest (as will emerge in C^2) of the
dead Christ (b^2, B^2). B^3 reproduces the corresponding Deuteronomy
material more fully and exactly than in the other two cases.

c/C As noted above, the first two Pauline glosses $(C^{1,2})$ correspond to $c^{1,2}$
in providing a rationale for the hypothetical quests. Here too, a
substitution has taken place: the scriptural quests have as their goal the
hearing and doing of God's commandment, the Pauline ones the presence
of Christ. Indeed, all three references to the "doing" of the commandment
in Deuteronomy 30.12–14 are systematically eliminated by the Pauline
glosses:

b^1, c^1 Who will ascend for us into heaven and bring it to us, so that hearing
it we may do it *[kai akousantes autēn poiēsomen]*?
B^1, C^1 Who will ascend into heaven (that is, to bring Christ down)?
b^2, c^2 Who will cross the sea for us, and bring it to us, and enable us to hear
it so that we may do it *[kai akoustēn hēmin poiēsei autēn, kai poiēsomen]*?
B^2, C^2 Who will descend into the abyss (that is, to bring Christ up from the
dead)?
b^3, c^3 The word is very near you, in your mouth and in your heart, and in
your hands, so as to do it *[kai en tais chersin sou auto poiein]*.
B^3, C^3 The word is near you, in your mouth and in your heart (that is, the
word of faith that we preach...)

---

45. According to Richard Hays, Paul "has deftly chosen the words, 'Do not say in your
heart' to introduce the discourse of The Righteousness from Faith because these words evoke
an earlier word of God to Israel, in which the Lord God warns them against the presumption
of their own righteousness" (*Echoes*, p. 79). Hays argues that, through such intertextual
echoes, "a historically outrageous reading gains poetic plausibility" (p. 82).
46. So R. D. Nelson, *Deuteronomy*, p. 349.

The Pauline glosses are not the straightforward interpretative additions that they appear to be. Like other glosses, they expand the text through explanation and paraphrase; unlike other glosses, they also *rewrite* the text, filling the spaces left blank by erasures from the primary text. The one common element in these erasures is the verb, "to do" (*poiein*) – the key term in the Leviticus summary of the righteousness that is by the law. Where Deuteronomy speaks of the doing of the commandment, Paul rewrites it so that it will speak of Christ and of faith.[47]

In rewriting Deuteronomy from the perspective of the righteousness of faith, Paul is addressing himself to the Leviticus text, with its articulation of the righteousness that is by the law. At this point, it becomes possible to answer another of the many questions raised by this enigmatic passage: the question why Paul is interested in the "prohibited quest motif" (Rom.10.6–7), and why he does not confine himself to the statement about the nearness of the word (10.8–10). According to Paul's rewriting of Deuteronomy, we are not to undertake a self-directed quest for Christ, seen as a passive object resident either in heaven or in the underworld – it hardly matters which. We are not to undertake any such quest because the inert Christ who must be brought to us by human initiative simply does not exist. The incarnate and risen Christ is already present among us as the result of a divine saving initiative that we can only acknowledge and confess, thereby attaining the righteous standing before God that the divine saving initiative itself intends.[48] The motif of the impossible quest for Christ serves as a foil for Paul's subsequent statements about the actuality of God's saving action.

It may also do more than that. We may ask who is the addressee of the second person singular address of the Righteousness of faith, opening with the exhortation, "Do not say in your heart . . . " The most probable answer is that this is addressed to the *anthrōpos* of Leviticus 18.5, who embodies "Israel", in its pursuit of "the law of righteousness" (Rom.9.31, 10.5). The unreal Christ of vv.6–7 is presumably the embodiment of "salvation",

47. According to D.-A. Koch, Paul here "füllt . . . die Lücken, die durch die konsequente Loslösung des Zitats vom Thema des Gesetzes entstanden sind" (*Die Schrift als Zeuge des Evangeliums*, p. 131). But Paul's glosses actively suppress the wording of the scriptural text, rather than simply filling gaps.

48. In itself, the hypothetical bringing down of Christ from heaven might allude either to his pre-existent or to his exalted state. J. D. G. Dunn advocates the latter possibility, on the grounds that the order of the questions in vv.6–7 would then match the order of v.9, where the reference to the Lordship of Jesus precedes the reference to his resurrection (*Christology in the Making*, p. 187). Against this, C. E. B. Cranfield rightly argues that the order of vv.6, 7 is decisive and that, if v.7 alludes to a realized divine action (the resurrection), then so too must v.6 (*On Romans*, pp. 59–60).

"righteousness" or "life" – which is why the quest for him seems so important. It is "the righteousness that is by the law", the law's proclamation that the person who does these things will live by them, that articulates the quest to which Paul now calls a halt in the light of the reality of God's saving action in Christ. The person who does these things in the hope of acquiring life by them is like the would-be hero who sets off into the unknown in order to acquire the infinitely valuable object that is, in fact, already present and accessible. To practise the law as the pathway to life is to live as though the sending and raising of Christ had never taken place. There is a genuine zeal for God in this heroism – but it is thoroughly misplaced (cf. 10.2). However impressive and deserving of respect, this kind of human religious endeavour is now, *post Christum*, simply outdated.

Paul, then, employs the "prohibited quest motif" of Deuteronomy 30 in criticism of the righteousness by the law that is articulated in the Leviticus text. The fact that Israel is said to "pursue" the righteousness intended in the law is a further indication that this is the quest that Paul declares to be at an end. Paul himself, in a quite different context, twice uses the same verb *(diōkein)* to describe his manner of life even as a Christian – forgetting what lies behind and pressing on to what lies ahead, which is "the goal of the upward calling of God in Christ Jesus" (Phil.3.12–14). In Paul's case, the hope of "apprehending" *(katalambanein*, cf. Rom.9.30) derives from the fact that he has already been "apprehended by Christ Jesus" (Phil.3.12). In the sphere of the righteousness that is by the law, however, the pursuit of the goal is essentially self-initiated and self-directed. In the mouth of the Righteousness of faith, the words of Deuteronomy become a witness against the Leviticus text in its literal sense. Those who zealously practise the law as the divinely appointed way to life, as instructed by Leviticus, are bluntly exhorted to desist by a strange new voice that avails itself of the words of Deuteronomy.

How can this be? How can Paul presume to rewrite Deuteronomy in order to criticize Leviticus? It seems that Paul heard two voices in the Deuteronomy passage, contending with one another like Esau and Jacob in their mother's womb. One was the voice of Moses, speaking eloquently of "the commandment" as the way to life in precisely the manner of Leviticus. The other was the voice of the Righteousness of faith. At one point, for example, we read no longer of "the commandment" but of "the word", a saving message that can be heard and internalized and communicated to others. In the preceding verses, we learn the folly of every quest for salvation by human initiative that somehow bypasses the reality of God's own saving initiative.

Moses ostensibly addresses a situation in which the divine commandment leaves its human recipients with the free choice to obey or not to obey. Yet, in and through his words, there may also be discerned a voice from a future in which radical divine saving initiative has become a reality.

Law and Immortality

We have seen that, in Paul's view, the law's goal is most clearly and succinctly summed up in the statement that the person who observes its commandments will live thereby. In this statement, Moses sanctions and underwrites Israel's pursuit of righteousness by works of law. On the assumption that the law's authority remains intact, an interpretation of the law along these lines will naturally result in an affirmative, optimistic account of the law's viability as the God-given way to the fullness of the divine blessings.

In his *Against Apion*, Josephus seeks to refute those who deny or question the antiquity of the Jewish people – and who thereby throw into question the reliability of his own historical work. It is, Josephus argues, the Greeks and not the Jews who are a relatively recent nation. They have no literature predating the Homeric writings, which were themselves originally oral. Historical writing in Greece does not long predate the Persian invasion, and there is no basis for the assumption that Greek historiography is uniquely reliable. Genuinely ancient nations, such as the Egyptians, the Chaldeans, the Phoenicians, and especially the Jews, have taken far more care than the Greeks to keep a reliable record of their own history – in the case of the Jews, in the form of the twenty-two sacred books. If it is claimed that the absence of the Jewish people from Greek histories proves that it cannot be genuinely ancient, the answer is that evidence of that people's existence can be found in a wide range of writers, both Greek and non-Greek.

Josephus also seeks to refute hostile criticism of his nation, as found in the work of a group of Egyptian writers, most notably Apion. Building on the work of his predecessors, Apion gives a defamatory account of the exodus events, according to which the Jewish people were originally a group of Egyptians who suffered from various diseases and were consequently expelled from their native country. He attacks the Jews of Alexandria, who he claims have no right to Alexandrian citizenship, and pours scorn on Jewish worship and customs. In response to this man and other critics, who regard Moses as a charlatan and an imposter, Josephus concludes his work with an eloquent defence of the law (ii.145–296). For our purposes, it is this conclusion that is of particular importance.

Of all the legislators who founded their people's constitutions, Moses is the most ancient (*c.Ap.* ii.154). The constitution he provided for the Jewish people is, says Josephus, a "theocracy" *(theokratia)*, all authority *(kratos)* being placed in the hands of God (165). This is the God who is one, uncreated and unchanging, made known to us in works of power although his true being surpasses knowledge (167). In this legislation, piety *(eusebeia)* is not one virtue among many, it is the sum of all the virtues, governing our actions and our speech in their entirety (170–71). The legislator took care to ensure that the laws should both be practised in daily life, and also known and understood. To ensure that they would be taught to the entire community, he set aside the sabbath, on which day people leave their other occupations and assemble to hear and study the Law (175). Thus, uniquely, all members of our nation are thoroughly familiar with their own laws, which are as it were engraved on our souls *(en tais psuchais hōsper enkecharagmenous)* (178). This is true even of our wives and servants (181). A number of selected examples illustrate variously the wisdom, the severity and the humanity of the laws (190–214). We are, says Josephus, unique in our faithful observance of our own laws, although they are far more demanding than other law-codes (228). Our lifelong training in obedience makes us willing to endure even death for the sake of the laws (232–35). We can bear to be deprived of our wealth, our cities, and all other worldly goods, for our law remains immortal *(ho nomos hēmin athanatos diamenei)*, and it alone merits our unqualified loyalty (277–78). Other nations too have acknowledged its excellence: the philosophers have learned their doctrine of God from Moses, and the masses increasingly practise our customs (279–86). They too join with us in refuting those who disparage our lawgiver (290). All who look into these laws will find that they promote not impiety but true piety *(ouk asebeian men eusebeian d' alēthestatēn)*, not misanthropy but humanity; that they are enemies of all injustice and are scrupulous for justice *(dikaiosunēn epimeleis)*; that they teach people to be self-sufficient and hard-working, and that their excellence is confirmed above all by the actions they engender *(tois ergois aei bebaioumenoi)* (291–92).

The law prescribes punishments for those who transgress, but it also rewards those who live by it. For most offences, in sexual matters for example, the penalty is death (215–17). But the reward the law promises is nothing less than eternal life:

> To those, indeed, who live lawfully *[nomimōs biousi]* the prize is not silver or gold or a crown of wild olive or of parsley or any such sign of distinction. Yet every one of them, his conscience bearing witness, has believed *[pepisteuken]* that, as the lawgiver has prophesied and as God's sure testimony has confirmed, to those who keep the laws, and, if it is necessary to die for them, die willingly, God grants to become again *[dedōken ho theos genesthai te palin]* and to receive a better life in the revolution of ages. (*c.Ap.* ii.217–18)

The law punishes transgression with death, but those who observe it – to the point of laying down their lives for it if necessary – will find it to be the way to eternal life. Furthermore, those who observe the law do so in the *belief* – based on the lawgiver's own prophetic utterance and its divine confirmation – that the law is the way to eternal life. At this point

Josephus's Pharisaic leanings are evident.[49] In his reference to the divine confirmation of Moses' prophetic utterance, Josephus may have in mind the sum of all his arguments against the view of Apion and the other critics that Moses was a charlatan and an imposter. As for the prophetic utterance itself, it is possible that Josephus has a specific passage such as Leviticus 18.5 in mind, but more likely that he has at his disposal a collection of Pharisaic proof-texts intended to refute the Sadducean claim that resurrection is not taught in the Torah.[50] Other such texts might include Deuteronomy 30.19 ("Choose for yourself life, that you may live!", as cited in 4 Ezra 7.129); Deuteronomy 32.39 ("I kill and I make alive", cited in 4 Maccabees 18.19); and perhaps Exodus 3.6 ("I am the God of Abraham, the God of Isaac, and the God of Jacob", cited in Mark 12.26 and parallels). The fact that Paul (a fellow-Pharisee) twice cites Leviticus 18.5 in this sense suggests that this text too was understood as part of Moses' testimony to the eternal life that awaits those who observe the laws. In any case, Josephus's statement about the goal and rationale of law observance closely resembles Paul's understanding of "righteousness by the law" as articulated in the Leviticus text (Rom.10.5; Gal.3.12).

There are two points in Josephus's presentation that suggest a comparison with Paul, and specifically with Romans 2 – a passage in which the logic of Leviticus 18.5 is extended to the whole of humanity. For example, when it is stated that "the doers of the law shall be justified", the statement is illustrated with a reference to Gentiles who lack the law but who nevertheless do what the law requires and may therefore hope for salvation (2.13–16). As with the statement about righteousness through the law in Romans 10.5, it will emerge from what follows it that Romans 2 does not adequately represent Paul's positive soteriological convictions. Nevertheless, the comparison with Josephus is revealing.

---

49.   Josephus claims allegiance to the Pharisees in *Vita* 12 (cf. *Ant.* xvii.398; xvii.354). For a brief account of recent scholarly debate on Josephus's relation to the Pharisees, see *EDSS*, 2.660–61.

50.   Josephus's two major presentations of Pharisaic and Sadducean positions state that they diverged over the scope of free will and the destiny of the soul after death (*BJ* ii.162–65; *Ant.* xviii.12–17). The later passage also refers to the issue of scripture and tradition (cf. also *Ant.* xiii.297–98, xvii.41; in *Ant.* xiii.171–73, only the issue of free will is mentioned). That the destiny of the soul was a matter of active disagreement between the two parties is confirmed by Mark 12.18–27 and Acts 23.6–9. Differences of opinion on free will and on life beyond death can be traced back to Ben Sira on the one hand and the Enochic tradition on the other (see G. Boccaccini, *Middle Judaism*, pp. 105–25).

The ideal community

According to Josephus, this law observance that leads to eternal life is faithfully practised by virtually the entire Jewish community. He would presumably have had little sympathy with the claim that, precisely when one desires to do the good that is prescribed in the law, evil lies close at hand (Rom.7.21). The law for Josephus is a constitution *(politeia)* which, like any other, regulates and shapes the distinctive life of a specific community. Its requirements are generally highly specific, and, since they are inculcated by practice and by constant instruction from early childhood onwards, there is no reason why they should not be consistently observed. Josephus's case for the superiority of Moses' legislation requires him to argue not only that it is better in itself than all other legislations, but also that it is more rigorously practised by the community for which it was intended. If among other nations disregard for their own laws is now commonplace, that is not the case with the Jewish nation (*c.Ap.* ii.276–77). An idealizing account of Jewish practice of the law is a necessary element in the case for the superiority of Jewish culture over Greek. Within the Jewish community, "no difference will be seen in the way we conduct our lives, but all participate in common actions *[koina men erga pantōn]* ..." (181). The law, it seems, is uniformly and perfectly observed.

In an earlier and fuller account of the contents of the Law of Moses, Josephus can claim that the laws

> have in every age been steadfastly observed *[bebaiōs phulachthēnai]*, since they are held to be a gift of God *[dōrean tou theou]*, so that neither in peace, through luxury, nor in war, through compulsion, have Hebrews transgressed any of them. (*Ant.* iii.223)

Yet, shortly after this statement, Josephus gives an account of the legislation in Leviticus that concerns sacrifices for sins. These are brought either by a person who has fallen into sin through ignorance *[kata agnoian]*, and who has been informed of this by another, or by a person "conscious in himself of being a sinner, and having no-one else to reprove him" (*Ant.* iii.231–32). Rulers and people alike bring offerings for sin, and on the Day of Atonement provision is made for the sins of the whole people to be removed (iii.241). Josephus here acknowledges that the law itself makes provision at least for relatively minor infringements to be dealt with. If so, the law does not require lifelong, sinless observance if it is to lead to eternal life. To live by the law, in hope of eternal life, is also to benefit from the law's provision for the removal of sin. Although the law sets the highest standards for human conduct, and, to a considerable extent, enables the community to achieve them, it is not unaware of the realities of human ignorance and weakness, and deals mercifully with them. For Josephus as for Paul, the Jewish belief that law observance leads to eternal life is fully compatible with the law's provision of means of atonement for sins. Both writers ascribe to the Jewish community an optimistic assessment of human capacity for law observance, but not a perfectionist one.

Yet Josephus does employ a perfectionist rhetoric, at least in the work *Against Apion*, and this leads him to minimize all indications that the law takes account of human weakness. For him, the law's own perfection is dependent on its ability to create and sustain a community which itself approximates as closely as possible to perfection. It is not his view that only a proportion of the community will through law observance attain eternal life. Since its loyalty to the laws is so unswerving and so uniform, the community as a whole will presumably do so – with the exception only of the insignificant minority who transgress, who are in any case quickly removed from the scene by the law's sentence of death (*c.Ap.* ii.215–17). Josephus does not dwell on the prospect of eternal life, since his primary concern is not to develop a soteriology but to demonstrate the excellence of the laws and of the community's devotion to them. The law is not simply a means to the end of eternal life, it is above all an ideal constitution *(politeia)*, far superior to others, whether real, as in the case of Sparta, or imaginary, as in the case of Plato's *Republic* (ii.220–35). Other nations and individuals should learn to respect it and to adapt themselves to it. Yet it is important for Josephus to maintain that those who observe the law will be vindicated eschatologically, since this reinforces the claim that the ideal constitution derives not just from a human lawgiver but from God.

Josephus's account of the law self-consciously locates itself within Graeco-Roman political discourse, and it is therefore not easy to compare it with the view of the law that Paul ascribes to his Jewish contemporaries, influenced as this is by his own soteriological convictions. In one sense, Josephus and Paul on the law are simply incommensurable. As is often the case when a non-Christian text is used to provide a "background" to a text from the New Testament, the two writers are not simply giving different answers to the same question, they are answering different questions. On the other hand, there is in this case a common subject-matter – the Law of Moses – and a shared acknowledgment that Moses teaches the commandments as the way to "life", the eschatological endorsement of the life that accords with them in the present. If Pauline discussion of this topic has any cogency at all, it should be possible to bring it into dialogue with Josephus.

In Romans 2, Paul presents a portrait or caricature of the Jewish teacher of the law who is in fact a transgressor of the law:

> But if you call yourself a Jew, and rely on the law, and boast in God, and know his will, and approve the things that really matter, being instructed by the law, regarding yourself as a guide to the blind, a light

to those in darkness, an instructor of the ignorant, a teacher of children, possessing in the law the embodiment of knowledge and truth – you who teach another, will you not teach yourself? You denounce stealing, but do you yourself steal? You denounce adultery, but do you yourself commit adultery? You abominate idols, but do you rob their temples? You boast in the law, but do you dishonour God by transgressing the law? For "because of you the name of God is blasphemed among the Gentiles", as it is written. (Rom.2.17–24)

In his pride in the law, his conviction that all the guidance, instruction, knowledge and truth that humankind requires and seeks is to be found in Moses' sacred writings, Paul's fictional Jewish teacher bears at least a passing resemblance to Josephus. He bears a still closer resemblance to Josephus's depiction of an unnamed Jewish teacher in the time of Tiberius, whose conduct is said to have caused the expulsion of the entire Jewish community from Rome (19 CE):

There was a man who was a Jew *[anēr Ioudaios]*, who had fled his homeland because he was accused of transgressing certain laws and feared punishment for that reason – a person of utter depravity. At this time he was living in Rome, and pretended to expound the wisdom of the laws of Moses *[exegeisthai sophian nomōn tōn Mōuseōs]*, after gaining the support of three men of similar character to himself. When Fulvia, who was among the women of high rank, began to meet with them and became a convert to the Jewish laws *[kai nomimois proseleluthuian tois Ioudaikois]*, they persuaded her to send purple and gold to the temple in Jerusalem – and used them for their own personal expenses, as had been their intention all along. (*Ant.* xviii.81–82)

In asking his fictional Jewish teacher of the law whether he practises what he preaches, Paul may have in mind actual instances such as this one, in which the conduct of particular Jewish teachers became a matter of public scandal. Eloquent and persuasive instruction in the Law of Moses has been accompanied by gross misconduct, so that the God of Israel is dishonoured among the Gentiles.

All this is highly relevant to Josephus's *apologia* for the Law of Moses (although not because of his own personal conduct). Like Paul's fictional teacher, Josephus paints an idealized picture of the law and the benefits it has to offer to the human race. Reading him, one would imagine that the community of the law is a community of saints or angels, living in total harmony with one another and in unwavering fidelity to the law, untouched by ordinary human passions or by the vicissitudes of history. Paul's caricature is an expression of scepticism about any such idealizing of the Jewish community and its manner of life. All too often, he implies, there is an embarrassing gulf between what is taught and what is actually practised. Word and deed are at odds with one another, so obviously that the Gentiles find here not the embodiment of all knowledge and truth but a welcome pretext to disparage not only Israel but also Israel's God. For Paul, the world's indifference or hostility towards Israel's Law cannot simply be attributed to the malicious distortions of Apion or Manetho and their kind. It is also occasioned by the gulf between preaching and practice within the Jewish community itself. The credibility of the law itself is thereby undermined, along with the exaggerated, idealizing claims of its apologists.[51]

In itself and in isolation from its wider context, Paul's caricature might seem to be no more than a piece of *ad hoc* polemic, no less exaggerated and one-sided than Josephus's idealizing. It would be easy to suppose that the truth of the matter must lie between the two extremes of idealization on the one hand and scepticism on the other. Yet Paul's portrayal of the gulf between preaching and practice is already an expression of a fundamentally different view of the law to Josephus's. According to Paul, the law's project – which is to promote observance of its commandments as the way to life – turns out to be a dead-end and a failure. Indeed, the law itself acknowledges this. The public scandal caused by the occasional erring teacher of the law is symptomatic of a deeper problem that goes to the heart of the communal life founded upon the Law of Moses. The problem is that the communal practice of the law takes place in a context already permeated by unrighteous speech and conduct; a context which the law is powerless to overcome (Rom.3.9–20; cf. 7.7–25). Precisely in the sphere of the law, it remains the case that "there is no-one who is righteous, not even one", that "all have turned aside", that "with their tongues they deceive", and that "venom of asps is under their lips". Life under the law is on a continuum with life apart from the law. The law is unable to transform human life into the life intended by God, because it places ultimate responsibility for that transformation in human hands. Or so Paul would argue, in response to Josephus.

Inclusive eschatologies

We recall that (according to Josephus) Moses' prophetic utterances indicate that "to those who keep the laws... God grants to become again and to receive a better life in the revolution of ages" (*c.Ap.* ii.218). Although it is not clear exactly where Josephus supposes Moses to have spoken about the future life, it is possible that, like Paul, he finds evidence of this in the conditional promise of Leviticus 18.5. What is more

---

51. Paul is not concerned in Romans 2.17–29 just with an individual, as the plurals of 2.24 indicate (against S. Stowers, *A Rereading of Romans*, p. 144). In 2.25–29, Paul's addressee is simply a Jew, and no longer specifically a teacher.

significant is the fact that both writers agree – against the Sadducees, and in accordance with their common pharisaic background – that Moses teaches the doctrine of the life to come.[52]

There are two further points of agreement. First, it is probable that Josephus like Paul understands the life to come in terms of resurrection. Elsewhere, in a brief account of the teaching of the Pharisees (with whom he probably aligns himself), Josephus states that for them "every soul is immortal, but the soul of the good alone passes into another body *[psuchēn te pasan men aphtharton, metabainein de eis heteron sōma tēn ton agathon monēn]...*" (*BJ* ii.163; cf. iii.374). Although his language is reminiscent of the Platonic doctrine of reincarnation, rather than resurrection, the fact that re-embodiment is the destiny of the good alone clearly implies resurrection; in Plato, reincarnation is the fate only of the wicked.[53] When, in the passage from *Against Apion*, Josephus speaks about a renewed life for those who observe the laws, he glosses over the distinction between bodily resurrection and the immortality of the soul, perhaps with potential non-Jewish readers in mind.[54] But he himself probably shared Paul's belief that, in the fullness of time, God will give life even to our mortal bodies (Rom.8.11). Paul too can speak of "eternal life" without explicitly mentioning resurrection (Rom.2.7). He and Josephus agree that, when Moses promises "life" to the one who observes the commandments, he is speaking of the life of the resurrection.

Second, both writers tend to detach the life to come from the "national eschatology" familiar from other contemporary Jewish texts, concerned as this is with the fulfilment of prophetic promises typically addressed to Israel or Jerusalem, but rarely if ever to the individual. Paul proclaims a very different fulfilment of the prophetic promises, while Josephus, with rare exceptions, tends to avoid the whole subject.[55] For both, eternal life is the intended destiny of human existence as such, and not just of Israel's national existence. Although Josephus is otherwise so concerned to present an image of a law-observant community, his statements about the life to come are couched in purely individual terms.

---

52. For a useful survey of Josephus's various statements on the next life, see S. Gathercole, *Where is Boasting?*, pp. 142–49. Gathercole points out that "Josephus's understanding of eschatology... is highly problematic for a covenantal-nomist model of Jewish religion" (p. 149).

53. On this, see the *Timaeus*, 42B–D, 90E–92C; *Phaedo*, 81D–82B; *Phaedrus*, 248C–249B; cf. *Republic* 614A–621B.

54. So N. T. Wright, *The Resurrection of the Son of God*, pp. 177–78.

55. See, however, Josephus's discussion of the Book of Daniel (*Ant.* x.266–81; cf. x.208–10, xi.337, xii.322). For a possible link with the scriptural prophecy referred to in *Jewish War*, vi.312–15 as the cause of the revolt against Rome, see N. T. Wright, *The New Testament and the People of God*, pp. 312–14. In general, Josephus understands prophets as foretelling specific future historical events rather than eschatological ones.

The parallel between the two writers can be extended further. An extreme expression of Josephus's tendency to gloss over the difference between bodily resurrection and the immortality of the soul occurs in the context of an idealized account of Essene practice and belief (*BJ* ii.119–61). When tortured by the Romans, we are told, the Essenes "gladly gave up their souls, confident of receiving them back again *[euthumoi tas psuchas hēphiesan hōs palin komioumenoi]*" (*BJ* ii.153). In what follows, however, Essene belief in immortality is assimilated to Greek. The Essenes are said to teach that the soul descends from above and becomes entangled in the prison-house of the body, from which death liberates it to return to the ethereal regions in which it originated – unless, of course, it has been so corrupted by its residence in the body as to be fit only for endless punishment (*BJ* ii.154). In a description of the respective abodes of just and unjust souls, Josephus makes explicit his parallel between Essenes and Greeks:

> And to the good *[kai tais men agathais]*, they maintain, sharing the opinion of the children of the Greeks, that there is prepared a home beyond the ocean, a place oppressed neither with rain nor snow nor heat, but which a gentle west wind, always blowing from the ocean, refreshes; whereas to the wicked *[tais de phaulais]* they assign a place of gloom and cold, full of unending punishments. (*BJ* ii.155)

The Greeks sought to establish immortality so as to promote virtue and restrain vice, in the belief that hope of a reward after death makes the good better, whereas fear of punishment restrains the passions of the wicked. The Essenes would seem to have reached the same conclusions independently (*BJ* ii.156–57).

Josephus's tendency to clothe Jewish thought in Greek dress is evident throughout his depictions of the three (or four) Jewish "philosophies", and this is obviously another instance of that tendency. What is most significant for our purposes is the conjunction between this passage, with its leanings towards a Greek view of immortality, and the passage from *Against Apion*, with its promise of life to come for those who practise the Law of Moses. In both cases, eternal life is the reward for righteous actions, and punishment here or hereafter is the fate of those who transgress. In one case, however, righteous action is defined as action that conforms to Moses' laws, many of which are explicitly stated; in the other case, it is assumed that a knowledge of righteous action is universally accessible, even if it is not always acted upon. Within the Jewish community, it is conduct conforming to the law that leads to eternal life; outside the Jewish community and apart from the law, there is still sufficient knowledge of good and evil to guide the soul on its way to eternal life. This composite picture sheds considerable light on the nature of Paul's argument in Romans 2.

In this chapter, Paul argues that God judges all people impartially on the basis of their works, and that the divine judgment will issue in one of two possible outcomes:

> To those who by patience in good work seek glory and honour and immortality, eternal life; but to those who rebel and disobey the truth and obey wickedness, wrath and fury. There will be suffering and distress for every human soul which does evil, the Jew first and also the Greek, but glory and honour and peace to everyone who does the good, the Jew first and also the Greek. (Rom.2.7–10)

In this chiastic passage, a statement about the two possible outcomes of judgment is repeated, with the initial order (salvation/punishment, conduct/outcome [vv.7–8]) reversed in the repetition (vv.9–10). In the repetition, it is emphasized that both forms of conduct and outcome are a universal possibility. In form as well as content, the initial statement corresponds especially closely to Josephus's summary of Essene (and Greek) belief: "And to the good ... they maintain that there is prepared a home beyond the ocean ..., whereas to the wicked they assign a place of gloom and cold, full of unending punishments" (*BJ* ii.155). Since for Josephus the Essenes are at this point representative of Jewish belief in general (the Sadducean denial of immortality being a minority position), his view is that a belief in reward and punishment hereafter is held by both Jew and Greek. Paul's not dissimilar view is that reward and punishment hereafter will be *experienced* by both Jew and Greek.

Like Josephus, however, Paul also believes that there is a difference between Jew and Greek: "Those who sinned without law [*anomōs*] will be judged without law, and those who sinned under the law [*en nomō*] will be judged by the law [*dia nomou*]" (Rom.2.12). The same process of judgment, in which righteous conduct is rewarded and wickedness is punished, will take account of the difference between the full knowledge of God's will accessible to the Jew and the more rudimentary knowledge accessible to the Greek. But what is emphasized is that this difference occurs only within a single, impartial process, and that in some cases Gentiles may well emerge with more credit than Jews. The figure of the Jewish teacher who transgresses the law (2.17–24) is thus contrasted with Gentiles who, totally lacking in the Jew's expert knowledge of the law, nevertheless do what the law requires more successfully than he does, and perhaps attain to salvation thereby (2.14–16).[56] In Josephus and in Paul, the prospect of reward or punishment hereafter for those who observe or

---

56. According to Stowers, Paul's arguments in Romans 1–2 "seek to establish that God will accept gentiles, provided they behave toward God and neighbor as the law requires, even if they do not become Jews or live as some sort of God-fearing gentile community that possess the law" (*A Rereading of Romans*, p. 141). This overlooks the specific role of the references to

who transgress the law is extended into the realm of the Gentiles, where, even apart from the Law of Moses, there is sufficient knowledge of good and evil for a single judgment to apply impartially to all. Josephus, however, lacks the Pauline claim that the actuality of Gentile obedience will contribute to the condemnation of Jewish transgression (cf. Rom.2.27).

In Paul as in Josephus, this universal doctrine of reward and punishment is an extrapolation from the law. It is the principle that "the person who does them will live by them" (Lev.18.5), extended to cover the whole of humanity. The claim that the logic of the law is impartial and universal marks an important step in Paul's unfolding argument. In Romans 2–3 as in chapter 10, he prefaces his articulation of the righteousness of faith with a statement of the Mosaic doctrine of salvation through human fulfilment of the law (cf. Rom.10.5–13). In both passages, the law's soteriology is superseded by the gospel's claim that salvation takes place solely by God's action in the death and resurrection of Jesus, which intends its own acknowledgment. In Romans 3.9–20, the law itself bears indirect witness to the gospel's claim in its acknowledgment of the failure of its own project: "By works of law shall no flesh be justified before him, for through law comes knowledge of sin" (3.20). The principle that "the person who does them will live by them" is first shown to be impartial, and to imply no privileged access to salvation for Jews (chapter 2), and is subsequently shown to lead into a dead-end in which, as the law itself says, "There is no-one who is righteous, not even one" (3.10). In that way, the law prepares and attests the gospel's announcement of the righteousness of God through faith of Jesus Christ (3.21).[57]

Gentiles, which is simply to suggest the extent of Jewish alienation from God (so U. Wilckens, *Römer*, 1.160). Stowers' attempt to eliminate from this chapter every trace of "polemic against Judaism" (p. 143) is hardly successful.

57.   On this account, Romans 2 is related to Romans 3 much as Romans 10.5 is related to 10.6–10: a statement of the righteousness that is by the law is followed and superseded by a statement of a righteousness by faith that is also in some sense attested by the law. That would appear to be the best resolution of the tension between Romans 2.13 ("the doers of the law will be justified") and 3.20 ("by works of the law shall no flesh be justified"). The motif of the "obedient Gentiles" serves in Romans 2 to establish divine impartiality, in opposition to the assumption that Jews will receive favourable treatment at the judgment (cf. Jub.5.10–18). In chapter 3, on the other hand, these obedient Gentiles retrospectively turn out to be an unreal hypothesis. For a recent defence of the view that the Gentiles of Romans 2 are Gentile Christians (a view that I earlier advocated; see *Paul, Judaism and the Gentiles*, pp. 115–22), see S. J. Gathercole, "A Law unto Themselves". Readings of this kind typically (1) overlook the rhetorical function of the references to Gentiles in an argument directed (at least ostensibly) to Jews; (2) underestimate the problem of the *prima facie* contradiction between Romans 2.13 and 3.20. Admittedly, there are difficulties in any attempt to interpret Romans 2 consistently. On the "rhetorical" reading I am proposing, in which Romans 3.1–20 show the "real" situation to be different to what chapter 2 has led us to believe, the distinctively Christian

If Josephus had ever read what Paul wrote in Romans 2, he might have agreed in principle with much of what is said there. He would no doubt be prepared to entertain the hope that wicked Jews such as the man who stole gifts intended for the temple would be punished in the world to come, whereas virtuous Gentiles such as his patron Epaphroditus would receive their due reward.[58] After all, a relationship between the law and the virtues and vices acknowledged by Gentiles is undeniable, and is only to be expected if the God of Israel is truly the God and creator of all humanity. In the following chapter of Romans, however, in which the law's project is superseded by the definitive saving act of God, Paul and Josephus would have to part company. Josephus's Jesus may perhaps have been a wise man who performed miracles, who was known as "the Christ", and who appeared in visions to his followers after his death (cf. *Ant.* xviii.63–64); but to Josephus the Pauline claim that this Christ is the end of the law would have seemed insanity and blasphemy. The law does not come to an end. In the Leviticus text and elsewhere, it continues to hold out the promise that the one who observes its commandments will live eternally.

terminology in 2.27–29 is a difficulty (cf. Käsemann, *Romans*, p. 75). Is Paul describing his anonymous righteous Gentiles as though they were Christians? Within Romans 2 itself, he certainly wishes them to sound like real people.

58.   Epaphroditus is commended for his devotion to virtue in *Antiquities*, i.8 (cf. *Vita* 430; *c.Ap.* i.1; ii.1, 296). Josephus's acceptance of the concept of a common standard of morality is illustrated by an important passage in *Antiquities*, xvi.175–78, discussed by John Barclay (*Jews in the Mediterranean Diaspora*, pp. 360–61).

Chapter 8

Numbers

Of the books of the Pentateuch, it is Leviticus that most nearly lacks any kind of narrative framework. In relative abstraction from the history of Israel, the legislation of Leviticus acquires an ideal, timeless quality, so that it here seems entirely plausible that the commandments truly represent the divinely ordained way to life. In the other Sinai-related books of the Pentateuch, that is not the case: for in Exodus, Numbers and Deuteronomy, the narrative framework serves only to problematize the conditional promise of life classically articulated in Leviticus 18.5 (and echoed in Deuteronomy 30.19). As narrated in these books, the history of Israel's first encounter with the law is characterized by death rather than by life. If there is a "contradiction" implied in, for example, Paul's citation of the Leviticus promise of life in the same context as the Deuteronomic "curse of the law" (Gal.3.10, 12), the contradiction lies not so much in Paul as in the scriptural texts themselves.[1] The Pauline reading of the Pentateuch is distinctive in the way that it highlights and exploits such inner-scriptural anomalies. It does so not because anomalies are of any interest in themselves, but in order to clarify the fundamental dynamics of the scriptural testimony to unconditional divine saving action.

For Paul, each of the books of the Torah has its own crucial contribution to make. None of them is superfluous. Paul is dependent on Exodus for his insistence that the law originates in a specific event, and on Leviticus for his understanding of the soteriology implied in the commandments of the law. The specific contribution of the Book of Numbers is to recount the immediate aftermath of the Sinai event: the book opens with an account of the preparations for leaving Sinai (Num.1.1–10.10), and continues by telling of a wilderness journey in which the comforting divine presence in the cloud and the fire (cf. 9.15–23; 10.11–12, 34) is much less prominent than the repeated cycle of rebellion

---

1. H. Räisänen traces this anomaly to Paul's own thought: statements implying that the law "was designed to lead men to life" run counter to "Paul's assertions of an exclusively negative purpose for the law" (*Paul and the Law*, p. 200). According to Paul, it is scripture itself that presents this anomaly.

and retribution. The journey is framed by two censuses, in which males eligible for military service in the conquest of the land are numbered tribe by tribe; the first census occurs "in the wilderness of Sinai" (1.1, cf. 26.63), the second "in the plains of Moab, by the Jordan at Jericho" (26.3, 64). At the conclusion of the second census, it becomes clear that the entire generation of those numbered at Sinai has perished:

> These were those numbered by Moses and Eleazar the priest, who numbered the sons of Israel in the plains of Moab by the Jordan at Jericho. But among these was not a man of those numbered by Moses and Aaron the priest, who had numbered the sons of Israel in the wilderness of Sinai. For YHWH had said of them, They shall surely die in the wilderness. There was not left a man of them (except Caleb the son of Jephunneh and Joshua the son of Nun). (Num.26.63–65)

The first census turns out to be an enumeration not for military service but for slaughter. At Sinai, the entire adult congregation (as represented by its adult males) is marked out for death. All those who were numbered became subject to the divine decree: "They shall surely die in the wilderness" (cf. 14.28–30).[2]

In moving from Leviticus to Numbers, then, we find that the law's conditional promise of life is overtaken by the reality of death – the destruction of the entire generation that stood before YHWH at Sinai. In the narrative of Numbers 11–25, the slaughter that followed the Golden Calf incident in Exodus 32 becomes an established pattern. Therein lies its significance, at least from a Pauline perspective. For Paul, the Book of Numbers shows how, in the aftermath of the Sinai event, the law represented a sentence of death for virtually all its original addressees. Numbers rules out the possibility that the earlier incidents of the Golden Calf, or of Nadab and Abihu or the man who blasphemed (Lev.10.1–7; 24.10–23), are mere isolated occurrences. In each of these events, which occur at Mount Sinai itself, transgression of the law leads to death by human or divine agency. In Numbers, further episodes of rebellion and death occur in the context of a death sentence pronounced upon an entire generation. On its own, the Golden Calf incident might not justify the conclusion that "the letter kills". Read in the light of the universal death sentence pronounced in the Book of Numbers, this and the other incidents acquire paradigmatic significance. As we shall argue, this material from Numbers represents the primary scriptural background for the first person narrative of Romans 7.7–12, where it is recounted how an initial encounter with the law proved to be the occasion not of life but of death.

---

2. The structural significance of the two census lists is rightly emphasized by D. T. Olson, *The Death of the Old and the Birth of the New*, pp. 83–118; see also T. Fretheim, "Numbers", p. 111.

Paul's most explicit use of material derived from Numbers occurs not in Romans 7 but in 1 Corinthians 10.1–13. Warning his readers of the perils of idolatry, immorality and other vices, Paul appeals to the scriptural narratives of Israel's experiences in the wilderness, citing the Golden Calf story from Exodus and several equally disastrous episodes from the Book of Numbers: the glut of quails (Num.11), Korah's rebellion (Num.16), the plague of snakes (Num.21), and the seduction by the daughters of Midian (Num.25). Like the Golden Calf episode, each of these cases involves mass death – in fulfilment of the divine judgment addressed to the exodus generation, that "your dead bodies shall fall in this wilderness", and that there "this wicked generation... shall come to a full end, and there they shall die" (Num.14.29–35). Paul repeatedly underlines the deadly consequences of the people's rebellious actions (1 Cor.10.5–10), and the references to individual incidents are prefaced by the general statement that "with the majority of them God was not pleased, for they were destroyed in the desert" (v.5). Although the law is not mentioned in 1 Corinthians 10, it will be argued in this chapter that the stories from Numbers inform Paul's claim in Romans 7 that the coming of the law leads to death and condemnation. The episodes of death in the desert recounted in the Book of Numbers are further confirmation that "the letter kills". In Romans 7 as in 2 Corinthians 3, Paul's crucial hermeneutical move is to read the Sinai legislation in the light of scriptural narratives that recount its impact on its first addressees.

Death in the Desert

Scriptural interpretation plays a less central role in Romans 5–8 than in chapters 1–4 (or 9–11). There are only two explicit citations in the entire section (Rom.7.7, citing Ex.20.17; Rom.8.36, citing Ps.43.23).[3] The second of these is purely parenthetical, and makes little direct contribution to Paul's argument: thus, "in all these things" in Romans 8.37 refers back to the trials and tribulations listed in v.35, ignoring the intervening passage from scripture.[4] In contrast, the Exodus citation plays a significant role in Paul's analysis of life under the law (Rom.7.7–25). Here at least, Paul does engage at length with crucial issues of scriptural interpretation. Also to be noted is the scriptural basis for the christological argument in 5.12–21. In general, however, Romans 5–8 would pose problems for any claim that Pauline theology as a whole is fundamentally hermeneutical in character.

---

3. Paul may, however, make constant allusions to the exodus tradition in Romans 8 (as argued by S. C. Keesmaat, *Paul and his Story*, pp. 54–154).

4. On this citation and its role in Paul's broader argument, see R. Hays, *Echoes of Scripture*, pp. 57–61.

The more modest argument here is simply that Pauline theology includes a highly significant hermeneutical and interpretative component, which comes to the fore especially in contexts where the talk is of "righteousness by faith", "law", "promise", and related matters.

Why are matters of scriptural interpretation so much less prominent in Romans 5–8 than in the surrounding sections (chapters 1–4, 9–11)? It is striking that, in Romans 1.16–11.36 as a whole, chapters 5–8 contain the overwhelming majority of direct references to the figure of "Christ" (or "Christ Jesus", "Jesus Christ our Lord", God's "Son", or other appelations).[5] Explicit scriptural material is in inverse proportion to references to Christ: when Paul cites scripture he tends not to speak explicitly of Christ, and when he refers to Christ he tends not to cite scripture.

It is important not to misinterpret this finding. It does not mean that Paul has abandoned his opening assertion that the gospel of God's Son was promised through the prophets in the holy scriptures (Rom.1.1–3), using scripture instead to support his "ecclesiological" claims about the Christian community in its relation to Israel. Scripture for Paul is most fundamentally the divine *promise*, in which God announces an unconditional saving action, universal in its scope, that lies beyond the horizon of the scriptural writers themselves. This promise is the true content of scripture as a whole, and is not just one theme among many: God "promised [the gospel] through his prophets in the holy scriptures" (Rom.1.2). The prophetic authors of scripture do not know of a "Christ" whose name is "Jesus", but they do know the God of the promise. When Paul speaks directly of the comprehensive divine act in which the promise is fulfilled, he must speak of "Jesus Christ"; but he does so on the basis of an *a posteriori* knowledge that was not accessible to the scriptural writers. It is this *a posteriori*, retrospective knowledge that predominates in Romans 5–8 – in contrast to chapters 1–4, where the assertion of the scriptural *a priori* entails a degree of abstraction from the actuality of divine saving action in Christ.[6]

Where Paul speaks of "the law", however, he is engaging in scriptural interpretation. If scriptural interpretation is of secondary importance elsewhere in Romans 5–8, this cannot be said of chapter 7. Many of the

---

5. Five occurrences in Romans 1.16–4.25 (2.16; 3.22, 24, 26; 4.24–25); eight in 9.1–11.36, mostly in chapter 10 (9.3, 5; 10.4, 7 *[bis]*, 9, 12, 17); and twenty-nine in 5.1–8.39, distributed fairly evenly (5.1, 6, 8, 10, 11, 15, 17, 21 [× 8]; 6.3, 4, 8, 9, 11, 23 [× 6]; 7.4, 25 [× 2]; 8.1, 2, 3, 9, 10, 11 *[bis]*, 17, 29, 32, 34, 35, 39 [× 13]).

6. This is the case especially in Romans 4, where a transition from the scriptural *a priori* to its Christian realization occurs only in vv.23–25. In Romans 3, the emphatic *nuni de* of v.21 results in a somewhat different balance between the gospel and its scriptural anticipation.

well-known problems of this chapter are resolved when it is understood as a highly distinctive reading of scriptural texts.

In developing the claim of Romans 7.1–6, that we have been freed from the law in order to belong to Christ, Paul takes his readers back onto scriptural terrain – a transition signalled by the threefold reference to "the law" in v.7, together with the citation of the tenth commandment (Ex.20.17). As in chapters 4 and 9, explicit christological references are at best marginal (cf. 7.25a). Like 3.1–20 but unlike chapters 4 and 9, the focus in 7.7–25 is on the law rather than the promise – with the result that the indirectness of the scriptural testimony to God's saving action in Christ is still more evident. If the promise speaks directly of God's unconditional future saving action, although without naming Christ, the law speaks of this divine saving action only by the highly indirect route of showing that salvation cannot be attained through human agency. The promise's affirmation is confirmed by the law's negation. Within Romans 7–8, indeed, it is the actuality of God's saving action in Christ and the Spirit that is indirectly confirmed by the law, and by the negative experience of life under the law. As we shall see, the "experience" described here has been shaped by Israel's initial encounter with the law as depicted in the scriptural narrative.

Paul's reflection on life under law opens by recounting an event in which an encounter with the law led to disaster:

> What shall we say then? Is the law sin? By no means! Yet I would not have known sin apart from the law. I would not have known desire [*tēn epithumian*] if the law had not said, You shall not desire [*ouk epithumēseis*]. But sin, seeing its opportunity in the commandment, created in me every kind of desire. For without law sin is dead. I was once alive apart from the law, but when the commandment came sin sprang to life, and I died; and the commandment supposed to lead to life led in my experience [*heurethē moi*] only to death. For sin, seeing its opportunity in the commandment, deceived me and by it killed me. (Rom.7.7–11)

The passage opens with a statement of what would have been the case without the law, or, more specifically, without the tenth commandment. In that case, the concepts of sin or illicit desire would have been meaningless. "Sin" refers to a category of human action which is created by the law, so that "where there is no law there is no transgression" (4.15).[7] Yet the knowledge spoken of in v.7 is not just an understanding of the word "sin"

---

7. Paul is not entirely consistent at this point. In Romans 7.7–8, "sin" is secondary to "law", and is synonymous with "transgression" *(parabasis)* in 4.15. This contrasts with the assertion of 5.13 that "sin was in the world before the law" – although that sin was admittedly "not reckoned".

and of its application: rather, it is the experience of finding oneself the victim of a malevolent power unexpectedly unleashed by the law – the power of "sin that dwells within me" (cf. 7.17, 20), which draws its power from the commandment itself and creates precisely the desires that the commandment prohibits (v.8a).[8] Without the commandment sin is dead while I live, but with the coming of the commandment a sinister exchange takes place: sin misappropriates the life that the commandment intended for *me*, whereas I succumb to its own former deadness (vv.8b–11). Less paradoxically expressed, the commandment has awakened in its addressee a resistance to its own authority. Since it claims authority not only over the outer world of actions but also over the inner world of desire, the commandment evokes a resistance initially manifested in an intense desire for every kind of prohibited object – a desire that already flouts the prohibition of desire itself, even if it does not lead to corresponding action in the external world (cf. Mt.5.27–28). Addressed by the law, "I" prove not to be the receptive, compliant hearer that the law's address intended.

Paul's mythic scenario has a scriptural background. For many interpreters, the event narrated here recalls the story told in Genesis 2–3.[9] There too, a commandment of God provides an opportunity for a power hostile to God to provoke disobedience and death. The claim that sin "deceived me" (*exēpatēsen me*, v.11) recalls Eve's explanation that "the serpent deceived me *[ēpatēsen me]*" (Gen.3.13): indeed, when Paul refers elsewhere to the deception of Eve, he uses precisely the same verbal form as in Romans 7.11 ("as the serpent deceived *[exēpatēsen]* Eve with his cunning..." [2 Cor.11.3]). Yet the paragraph in Romans 7 is not primarily a retelling of the story of paradise lost. The topic here is not the fall but the coming of the law, and the commandment, "You shall not desire" (v.7) is drawn not from Genesis but from the decalogue (Ex.20.17). The description of the commandment as leading to life (*eis zōēn*, Rom.7.10) is a clear allusion to Leviticus 18.5, which Paul will later quote:

8. This interpretation assumes a balance between "I would not have known sin/desire..." (v.7) and "sin... worked in me every kind of desire" (v.8). "Know" here must refer to a knowledge by first-hand experience, made possible through the law (cf. also v.5). The point is not simply that "the law brings it about that sin is unmasked as a transgression of the will of God" (against J. Fitzmyer, *Romans*, p. 466).

9. According to E. Käsemann, "The event depicted can strictly refer only to Adam" (*Romans*, p. 196). Possible correspondences with Genesis 2–3 are set out in my *Paul, Judaism and the Gentiles*, p. 152. As N. T. Wright notes, however, "The primary emphasis of the argument is on Israel, not Adam: what is being asserted is that when the Torah arrived it had the same effect on her as God's commandment in the Garden had on Adam" (*The Climax of the Covenant*, p. 197). Otherwise expressed, Paul here speaks of Israel's experience in the wilderness in language and conceptuality partially derived from Genesis 2–3 – in particular, the motif of deception and the personifying of sin.

> Moses writes concerning the righteousness that is by the law, that "the
> person who does these things shall live by them". (Rom.10.5)

The Genesis commandment not to eat neither prohibits desire nor
promises life: the texts in question are drawn instead from Exodus and
Leviticus. In telling of an encounter with these texts, Paul uses motifs
drawn from Genesis to speak of the event at Sinai and its aftermath, as re-
enacted in individual experience.[10]

Forbidden desire

In Romans 7, Paul identifies the law with the single commandment, "You
shall not desire". "Law" and "commandment" are interchangeable here. It
is "the law" that said, "You shall not desire", but it is "the
commandment" that sin used to elicit the prohibited desire (vv.7–8). The
speaker was once alive "without law", but died with the coming of "the
commandment" (vv.9–10). Just as "the law is holy", so "the commandment is holy and just and good" (v.12). The tenth commandment of the
Decalogue is first abbreviated and then cited as summarizing the content of
the law as a whole – just as Leviticus 18.5 summarizes its intended goal,
and Deuteronomy 27.26 its actual outcome (cf. Gal.3.10). In Romans 7,
the texts from Exodus and Leviticus are understood by Paul as speaking of
and for the law as a whole. How, then, is the law to be read in the light of
these texts? As we shall see, we must read on from Exodus and Leviticus
into the Book of Numbers in order to answer that question.[11]

In its full form, the tenth commandment specifies the desires that it
prohibits:

> You shall not desire *[ouk epithumēseis]* your neighbour's wife. You
> shall not desire your neighbour's house, nor his field, nor his male or
> female servant nor his ox nor his ass, nor any other of his animals, nor
> anything that belong to your neighbour. (Ex.20.17 LXX)

In the Septuagint, the Exodus version of this commandment is identical to
the Deuteronomy one (Deut.5.21). In the Masoretic text, however, the two
versions of this commandment differ significantly:

---

10. D. Moo rightly argues that *nomos* and *entolē* in Romans 7.7–12 refer to "that body of
divine revelation which had its origin with Moses", and that this "effectively rules out the
(purely) Adamic view" ("Israel and Paul in Romans 7.7–12", pp. 124–25). I am less convinced
by the suggestion that the *ego* here is "corporate" (p. 129), and that what is described here (in
first person narrative) is simply "the promulgation of the Sinaitic revelation" (p. 127). Rather,
the *ego* here is the individual "I" shaped by the internalizing of the scriptural narrative of
Israel's history.

11. Some of the material for the discussion that follows is derived from my *Agape, Eros,
Gender*, pp. 152–68.

You shall not desire *[l' thmd]* your neighbour's house. You shall not desire your neighbour's wife, or his male or female servant, or his ox or his ass, or anything that belongs to your neighbour. (Ex.20.17)

And you shall not desire *[l' thmd]* your neighbour's wife. And you shall not crave *[wl' tt'wh]* your neighbour's house, his field, or his male or female servant, his ox or his ass or anything that belongs to your neighbour. (Deut.5.21)

The two Hebrew versions of the tenth commandment differ in their use of the connective, and the Deuteronomy one adds a reference to the neighbour's field and introduces a different verb in the second part of the prohibition. Most significantly, the first part of the prohibition concerns the neighbour's house in Exodus and the neighbour's wife in Deuteronomy; correspondingly, the second part of the prohibition opens with a reference to the neighbour's wife in Exodus and to his house in Deuteronomy. In Exodus, the reference to the wife is simply one instance among others of a prohibited desire for the (male) neighbour's property. In Deuteronomy, desire for the neighbour's wife is different in kind to the other prohibited desires, and this difference in kind is marked by the new verb. In contrast, the repetition of the verb serves no obvious purpose in the Exodus passage.[12]

In the Septuagint, verbal differences between the two forms of the tenth commandment are eliminated. There is a slight tendency towards expansion: the phrase "nor any other of his animals" has no equivalent in MT, and the reference to the neighbour's field (Deut.5.18 MT) is incorporated into the Exodus version. More significantly, the same verb is employed in both parts of the prohibition (as in Ex.20.17 MT) and the first part of the prohibition concerns the neighbour's wife and not his house (as in Deut.5.18 MT). The effect is both to differentiate sexual desire for an illicit object from the other prohibited desires, and to present it as paradigmatic of all such prohibited desires. More successfully than either of the two Hebrew versions, the Septuagint rendering presents the tenth commandment as a differentiated unity, thereby making coherent sense of its bipartite form. The translation invites reflection on the problematic nature of "desire" as such, tacitly drawing upon the often negative connotations of the corresponding Greek noun, *epithumia*.[13] Paul can therefore cite the tenth commandment in an abbreviated form in which

12. In the LXX, the verb clearly refers to an inclination that leads to certain forms of action, not to the actions themselves. The distinction may be less clear in the Hebrew – on which see the discussion in B. Childs, *Exodus*, pp. 425–28. A possible problem with this emphasis on external action is that the tenth commandment would then overlap with the seventh and the eighth.

13. On this see *TDNT* 3.168–71.

"desire" itself is prohibited, without reference to specific objects.[14] He thereby understands the specific objects mentioned in the full text as exemplary of a much wider range of desires for forbidden objects. Abbreviation has the effect of widening the scope of the commandment.[15]

For Paul, the law's utterance of the words "You shall not desire" is an *event*, which separates the time that preceded it from the time that followed. In the time before the event, I was alive and sin lay dead (7.8b–9a), but, with the coming of the commandment, the situation was reversed: sin sprang to life and I died (vv.9b–10). Since "law" and "commandment" are used interchangeably in this passage, the reference must be to the giving of the law through Moses at Mount Sinai, re-enacted in individual experience. The reference to the Sinai event is confirmed by the earlier contrast between the period from Adam to Moses, when law was not (5.13), and the moment when "law came in", and previously unreckoned sin became transgression (5.20). Here and elsewhere, "the law" represents an event in the history of Israel and the world, attested in Israel's scriptures. The question is how Paul can claim, on the basis of those same scriptures, that the coming of the law, and specifically the commandment prohibiting desire, provided an opening for the very desire that was to be excluded – and so led not to life but to death. And the answer is that Paul's first person narration in Romans 7.7–11 arises out of the scriptural narratives of Israel's post-Sinai experience in the wilderness – in which a series of rebellions against Moses and the God of Sinai begin with desire and end in death. The speaker, who, like his readers, "knows the law" (v.1), has internalized the scriptural narrative of the law's reception, making Israel's story his own.

---

14. In *4 Maccabees* 2.5–6, the abbreviation of the tenth commandment occurs in two stages. The author initially cites it in the shortened form, "You shall not desire the wife of your neighbour, or anything that belongs to your neighbour". He then abbreviates further as he attempts to show that the commandment is the source of his thesis that reason is master of the passions: "And since the law has told us not to desire, I could prove to you all the more that reason is able to control desires." Philo's discussion of the tenth commandment is exclusively concerned with desire as such (*dec.* 142–53).

15. Paul probably takes over from the LXX rendering the assumption that sexual desire for an illicit object is paradigmatic of all prohibited desire. This scriptural background makes it unnecessary to find here a reference to Adam, as in D. Boyarin's fanciful haggadic reading. According to Boyarin, "the Torah has exacerbated the plight of Adamic humanity because of one provision it contains", that is, "the command to procreate, and the desire it produces in the members" (*A Radical Jew*, p. 159). This is the Pauline "other law", the "law of sin that is in my members" (Rom.7.23), over against which stands the prohibition of the forbidden fruit (Gen.2.17), understood as a prohibition of sexual desire (Rom.7.7): "Adam's double bind, commanded on the one hand to procreate and on the other to avoid eating of the fruit of the tree of (carnal) knowledge, is the type of Jewish humanity under the flesh, commanded to procreate but also not to have lustful desires, let alone act on them" (p. 165).

The tombs of desire

In Romans 7.7, on the basis of the tenth commandment, sin is seen to originate in illicit, prohibited desire. There is a close parallel in 1 Corinthians 10.6, where, in the course of applying the experiences of Israel in the wilderness to the Corinthian church, Paul states that "we are not to be desirers of evil things, as they desired", and proceeds to summarize a number of incidents from the scriptural narrative in which this illicit desire came to expression. In both passages, illicit desire leads directly to death. The warning against desire for evil things follows the statement that "with most of them God was not pleased, for they were destroyed in the desert" (1 Cor.10.5); and in three of the four specific incidents referred to, the destructive consequences of illicit desire are underlined (vv.8, 9, 10). In Romans 7 likewise, this correlation of desire and death derives not from Genesis but from Numbers.

According to Psalm 105.14–15, "They desired [with] desire *[epethumēsan epithumian]* in the wilderness, and they tested God in the desert. And he gave them what they asked, and sent fullness into their souls." The psalmist here echoes the narrative of Numbers 11, where it is said that

> the rabble that was among them desired [with] desire *[epethumēsan epithumian]*, and seating themselves the sons of Israel wept and said, Who will give us meat to eat? We remember the fish that we ate in Egypt for nothing, and the cucumbers. melons, leeks. onions and garlic; but now our soul is dried up, and there is nothing but manna before our eyes. (Num.11.4–6)

In response, the Lord promises to provide the people with meat every day for a month, until they are sick of it – "because you disobeyed the Lord who is among you" (vv.18–20). A wind from the Lord brings a glut of quails, which the people gather (vv.31–32). But

> while the meat was still between their teeth, before it was consumed, the Lord was angry with the people and the Lord smote the people with a very great plague. And the name of that place was called Tombs-of-Desire *[Mnēmata tēs epithumias]*, because there they buried the people who had desired *[ton laon ton epithumētēn]*. From Tombs-of-Desire the people journeyed to Aseroth, and the people were in Aseroth. (Num.11.33–35)

The memorials of desire are mentioned again in Numbers 33.16–17, in the context of an itinerary that takes the people of Israel from Egypt to the plains of Moab (vv.1–49), and in Deuteronomy 9.22, where Moses reminds the people how "at Conflagration *[en tō Empurismō]* and at Testing *[en tō*

Peirasmō] and at Tombs-of-Desire you angered the Lord your God".[16] This reference to these ill-fated places occurs in the context of the claim that the people will inherit the promised land not on account of their righteousness but in spite of their stubborn and rebellious heart (Deut.9.1–10.11); the incident of the Golden Calf is narrated here at length. Thus "desire" takes its place in a narrative of rebellion against God that is also characterized by idolatry and by testing. As in Romans 7.9–11, desire leads to death – a fact commemorated in the place-name, "Tombs-of-Desire". The people who desired remembered the rich food of Egypt, but they themselves were remembered only in the form of the warning embedded in the place-name.

The link between desire and death is especially clear in Psalm 77.26–31:

> He caused an east wind to blow from heaven, and led out the south wind by his power. And he rained upon them flesh like dust, winged birds like the sand of the seas, and made them fall in the midst of their camp, around their tents. And they ate and were well satisfied, for he brought them their desire *[tēn epithumian autōn]*. They were not rid of their desire *[apo tēs epithumias autōn]*, their food was still in their mouths, when the wrath of God *[orgē tou theou]* fell upon them. He killed *[apekteinen]* as they drank, as the elect of Israel danced together.

Even for the elect of Israel, desire leads to death. The psalmist finds in the traditional story a warning for his own contemporaries, just as Paul later does for his addressees at Corinth.

In 1 Corinthians 10.6–11, "desire" is no longer tied to the single story about the Israelites' desire for a more varied diet. A number of incidents of rebellion and death in the wilderness are here invoked in order to substantiate the warning that we are not to be "desirers of evil things *[epithumētas kakōn]*, as they desired *[epethumēsan]*" (v.6). "Desire" is now seen as the root of Israel's problems in the wilderness.

Having spoken of the experiences of divine favour enjoyed by "our fathers" at the time of the exodus (1 Cor.10.1–4), Paul proceeds to underline their negative outcome and to draw out appropriate lessons for his readers:

> But with the majority of them God was not pleased, for they were killed in the desert. And these things are examples to us, so that we should not

16. "Conflagration" is "Taberah", so called because there "a fire from the Lord" burned among the people (Num.11.3). "Testing" (cf. Deut.6.16) is "Massah", where the people of Israel put the Lord to the test by demanding water; its full name is Testing-and-Abuse (*Peirasmos kai Loidorēsis*), "because of the abuse *[loidorian]* of the sons of Israel and because they tested the Lord *[dia to peirazein kurion]*, saying, Is the Lord among us or not?" (Ex.17.7).

be desirers of evil things, as they desired. And do not be idolators, as were some of them – as it is written: The people sat to eat and drink and rose to play. (1 Cor.10.5–7)

The reference to desire in v.6 is clearly an allusion to Numbers 11, just as the warning against idolatry in v.7 is explicitly based on the Golden Calf incident of Exodus 32. It is possible, then, that "desire" is simply the first in a series of vices illustrated by specific incidents – and not the key to a series that begins with the reference to idolatry. Paul is saying either that Israel's conduct in the wilderness was characterized at various times by evil desire, idolatry, *porneia*, and so on; or that it was characterized solely by evil desire, expressed in acts of idolatry, *porneia*, and so on. Paul's syntax allows for either possibility, and the link between "desire" and the specific incident in Numbers 11 may seem to make the first more likely. The decisive argument against this interpretation is provided by the generalizing reference to the Israelites as "desirers of evil things" (1 Cor.10.6). If Paul had wished to extract a specific moral application from Numbers 11, he could have found in it a timely warning against gluttony. In the story, the Israelites' "desire" is specifically for meat, as a change from the monotonous wilderness diet of manna; Paul might have chosen to exploit this point in opposition to those at Corinth who longed to eat meat at "the table of demons" (cf. 1 Cor.8.10–13, 10.21). He does not do so, however, choosing instead to draw from the story a generalized warning against being "desirers of evil things" – thereby introducing the specific evils that follow, and tracing them back to an origin in "desire".[17]

Desire issues first in idolatry, the making of the Golden Calf together with the revelry that accompanied it: "The people sat to eat and drink and rose to play" (1 Cor.10.7, quoting Ex.32.6). Paul's selection of this brief quotation from Exodus 32 serves to emphasize that what he and his fellow-Jews call "idolatry" is associated not just with specifically cultic actions but also with feasting, singing and dancing – that is, with communal celebration. That is why its allure is so powerful.[18]

---

17. The comprehensive sense of *epithumein* here is rightly accepted by H. Conzelmann, who points to the general term *kakōn* and to the generalizing use of *epithumia* in Romans 7.7–12 (*1 Corinthians*, p. 167). Conzelmann does not see the potential problem for this interpretation posed by the specific scriptural background (Num.11.4–6, 34; Pss.77.29–30, 105.14).

18. As Richard Hays notes, the citation does not explicitly mention idolatry, and requires a reader who will recognize its source (*First Corinthians*, p. 163). The apparent mismatch between warning and citation is already noted by Calvin, who explains it with reference to the Corinthians: "For it is not likely that they were in the habit of attending the gatherings of unbelievers in order to prostrate themselves before the idols, but they used to share in the feasts which the unbelievers held in honour of their gods, and did not keep away from the debased rites which were the mark of idolatry" (*1 Corinthians*, p. 208).

Desire issues, second, in *porneia*. "We must not commit fornication, as some of them committed fornication, and twenty-three thousand fell in one day" (v.8). The reference is to another instance of idolatry, when

> the people profaned themselves by committing fornication *[ekporneu-sai]* with the daughters of Moab. They invited them to the sacrifices of their idols, and the people ate of their sacrifices and worshipped their idols. (Num.25.1–2)

Twenty-four thousand people died in the ensuing plague (v.9), which was halted by the zeal of Phinehas, who pierced an Israelite man and a Moabite woman through the body with a single thrust of his spear (vv.6–8).[19]

Desire issues, third, in "putting the Lord [or, the Christ] to the test, as some of them put him to the test and were destroyed by snakes" (1 Cor.10.9). On this occasion, "the people spoke against God and against Moses, saying, Why did you bring us out from Egypt, to kill us in the wilderness? For there is no bread or water, and our soul is tired of this worthless food" (Num.21.5). The plague of snakes that followed was halted by the setting up of a bronze snake on a pole, which brought healing to those who looked upon it (v.9). It is not explicitly said here that those who spoke against God and Moses "put the Lord to the test". But in Numbers 14.22 it is said that the people "have put me to the test these ten times, and have not listened to my voice" – indicating that "putting the Lord to the test" by making demands of him is a constant theme of these narratives. "They tested him again and again, and provoked the Holy One of Israel" (Ps.77.4).

Finally, desire issues in complaining: "Do not complain *[mēde gogguzete]*, as some of them complained and were destroyed by the destroyer" (1 Cor.10.10). Shortly after their deliverance at the Red Sea, the people begin to "complain" about their lot (Ex.15.24; 16.7–12); Exodus 17.2–3 indicates that "complaining" against Moses cannot be sharply distinguished from "putting the Lord to the test". But it is only after the giving of the law at Sinai that this tendency to complain has destructive consequences. In Numbers 14, the complaints that follow the report of the spies (*diegogguzon*, v.2) lead to the punitive divine decree that the present generation of Israelites will perish in the wilderness (vv.20–35). In Numbers 16, the Levites' complaints against Aaron's priestly prerogatives (*diagogguzete*, v.11) result in the destruction of Korah, Dathan and Abiram and their company. In 1 Corinthians 10.10, Paul's specific reference is to the scriptural account of the immediate aftermath of Korah's rebellion, where it is said:

---

19. Paul's accidental substitution of 23,000 for 24,000 (MT, LXX) may have been influenced by Exodus 32.28, which speaks of the 3000 killed by the Levites in the aftermath of the Golden Calf incident (so C. K. Barrett, *1 Corinthians*, p. 225). Paul has just referred to this incident, although without mentioning the deaths to which it led (1 Cor.10.7).

> And on the next day the sons of Israel complained *[egoggusan]* against
> Moses and Aaron, saying: You have killed the people of the Lord *[ton
> laon kuriou]*. (Num.17.6)

As a result, the killing resumes as a plague destroys still more of them –
until it is brought to an end through Aaron's atoning intervention (17.11–
13 [16.46–48]). It is Paul's reference to "the destroyer" that makes it certain
that he has this passage in mind: those who complained "were destroyed
by the destroyer" (1 Cor.10.10). This "destroyer" *(olothreutēs)* is the
"angel of death" of the passover story *(ton olethreuonta*, Ex.12.23), and the
link between this figure and the Korah story is established by *Wisdom of
Solomon* 18.20–25, where Aaron's saving intervention is presented as a
heroic victory over "the destroyer" *(ho olethreuōn*, v.25). This passage tells
how,

> when the dead had already fallen on one another in heaps, he [Aaron]
> intervened and held back the wrath, and cut off its way to the living. For
> upon his long robe was the whole world depicted, and the glories of the
> fathers were engraved on the four rows of stones, and your majesty on
> the diadem upon his head. To these the destroyer *[ho olethreuōn]*
> yielded, these he feared; for it was sufficient only to test the wrath.
> (Wis.18.23–25)

The similar reference to "the destroyer" in 1 Corinthians 10.10 indicates
that Paul too has the story of Korah's rebellion in mind.[20] Characteristically, Paul emphasizes the reality of the destruction, whereas the author
of *Wisdom* highlights Aaron's saving intervention.

In each of these incidents of idolatry, immorality, testing and
complaining, the people of Israel show themselves to be "desirers of
evil" (1 Cor.10.6). These narratives are all "memorials of desire"
(mnēmata tēs epithumias), warning their readers not to desire the evils
that the Israelites once desired. In three of the four cases he cites, Paul
emphasizes that the outcome of the Israelites' desire was death. Twenty-
three thousand fell when the people of Israel committed fornication with
the daughters of Moab. When they put the Lord to the test, they were
destroyed by snakes. When they complained, they were destroyed by the
destroyer. Although Paul himself does not mention this, we also recall the
three thousand idolators massacred by the sons of Levi in punishment for
the Golden Calf incident, together with the unnumbered victims of the
plague that followed (Ex.32.25–28, 35). In introducing his series of

20. So C. Wolff, *I Korinther*, 2.45. Gordon Fee wrongly states that the complaining motif
is insignificant in the Korah story, and that Paul's reference is more probably to Numbers 14
(*1 Corinthians*, pp. 457–58). Paul is referring to the specific point in the Korah story where
complaining leads directly to plague and destruction (Num.17.6–15 LXX). The belief that the
plague was the work of an angelic agent is also attested in *4 Maccabees* 7.11.

warnings based on specific incidents, Paul recalls the death in the desert of almost the entire exodus generation: "Yet with most of them God was not pleased, for they were killed *[katestrōthēsan]* in the wilderness" (1 Cor.10.5; cf. Num.14.16). The specific events are instances of a divine displeasure that engulfs virtually the entire people of Israel, so that the wilderness becomes their burial ground.

In the desert, desire leads to death: that, for Paul, is the theme of the stories recounted in the Book of Numbers. These stories are also the primary scriptural background to the first person narrative of Romans 7.7–11. The speaker tells how the Israelites' experience in the wilderness has been re-enacted in his own life.[21]

According to Romans 7.7–9, "I was once alive apart from the commandment". At that time, "sin lay dead". But then "the commandment came" – the commandment, "You shall not desire" – with the result that "sin, taking opportunity through the commandment, worked in me every kind of desire". Initially, I was alive and sin was dead; but then, through the law, sin came to life and I died. We have seen that in 1 Corinthians 10 Paul presents Israel's experience in the wilderness as a history of desire and death – extending a theme that in the Pentateuch is confined to the single incident in Numbers 11. In Romans 7.7, his reduction of the tenth commandment to a general prohibition of desire creates a link with his earlier reading of the wilderness narratives as a history of desire – a desire whose origin is now seen to lie in the very commandment that prohibited it. His selected examples of idolatry, immorality, testing and complaining all *follow* the giving of the law, for in the pentateuchal narrative it is only from Sinai onwards that Israel's rebellious actions have the deadly consequences that Paul underlines. In these events, "the letter kills"; the ministry of Moses turns out to be a "ministry of death" (2 Cor.3.6–7). But the law does not kill of itself. "It was sin, working death in me through what was good..." (Rom.7.13). "Sin, finding opportunity in the commandment, deceived me and by it killed me" (Rom.7.11). A latent tendency to sin, hardly a significant factor prior to the revelation at Sinai, expresses itself immediately afterwards in actions that wilfully transgress the commandments. In Paul's reading of this history, the divine prohibition has the effect of making the forbidden objects *desirable*.[22] In these acts, a latent resistance to the God of the covenant becomes manifest and visible in explicit acts of rebellion,

---

21. The link between Romans 7 and Numbers 11 is noted by Alan Segal, *Paul the Convert*, p. 243. Segal does not exploit this connection, however, arguing that Paul here is primarily concerned with the temptation to practise "the ceremonial Torah" (pp. 243–44).

22. This distinction between latent and realized sin corresponds more closely to Paul's language than T. Engberg-Pedersen's suggestion that the law increases and generates sin, "not

stemming from the "desire" that the commandment both prohibited and unwittingly enabled.

Resisting the God of Sinai

In Romans 7, unlike 1 Corinthians 10, Paul emphasizes the role of the law in Israel's disastrous history in the wilderness. It is striking that even in 1 Corinthians 10 Paul refers mainly to scriptural stories where the object of the rebellion is the God of Sinai, rather than simply the God of the exodus. This distinction provides the key to the rereading of the wilderness stories that underlies Romans 7 – and, specifically, to Paul's claim that the law is instrumental in the genesis of sin. Once again, Paul responds to cues provided by the texts themselves, and is engaging in a genuine act of scriptural interpretation.

In the wilderness narratives, acts of rebellion are often directed against the God of the exodus, and against Moses as his earthly representative. That is the case in the stories about food and drink, where the desire to be back in a now idealized Egypt, and so to undo the exodus, is a common motif. This motif first occurs at the beginning of the manna story:

> And the whole congregation of the sons of Israel murmured against Moses and Aaron in the wilderness. And the sons of Israel said to them, If only we had died at YHWH's hand in the land of Egypt, where we sat by the flesh pots and ate bread to the full. For you have brought us out into this wilderness to kill this whole assembly with hunger. (Ex.16.2–3)

Similarly, in the following chapter Moses is asked: "Why did you bring us out of the land of Egypt, to kill us and our children and our cattle with thirst?" (Ex.17.3). The story of the quails opens with the people of Israel recalling the rich and varied diet they enjoyed in Egypt, and contrasting it with the monotony of the manna (Num.11.4–6). This motif of the rejection of the exodus recurs again in a second story about the lack of water in the wilderness (Num.20.4–5), and in the complaint that leads to the plague of snakes (Num.21.5). In addition to these stories of hunger and thirst, the motif occurs in the account of the initial failure to enter the promised land, where the people, terrified by the spies' report, go so far as to seek to appoint a new leader who will take them back to Egypt (Num.14.1–4). In the story of Korah's rebellion, two rebel leaders from the tribe of Reuben even identify Egypt itself with the land flowing with milk and honey:

by making anybody sin *more*, but by making him now *sin* as opposed to doing what earlier did not *count* as sin" (*Paul and the Stoics*, p. 142; italics original). That would not explain Paul's emphasis here on sin's agency.

And Moses sent to call Dathan and Abiram, sons of Eliab. And they said: We will not come up. Is it not enough that you have brought us up from a land flowing with milk and honey, to kill us in the wilderness, that you also have to lord it over us? You have failed to bring us to a land flowing with milk and honey, or to give us an inheritance of fields and vineyards... (Num.16.12–14)

In these stories, Moses represents the God of the exodus and of the promise. Like his God, Moses himself is the deliverer from Egypt rather than the lawgiver of Sinai. In their acts of rebellion, the people of Israel reject the divine plan for their history, in which the event of the exodus occurs under the overarching promise of land, once given to the fathers. Since these complaints are unrelated to the law, they can occur before the giving of the law at Sinai as well as after it.[23]

In the four specific scriptural examples cited in 1 Corinthians 10.7–10, Paul makes little use of stories containing the motif of the rejection of the exodus. This motif plays only a subsidiary role in the account of Korah's rebellion, where Dathan and Abiram are minor characters in a story whose centre of gravity lies in Korah's challenge to the law as delivered by Moses.[24] The "murmuring" or complaining highlighted by Paul (v.10) is here unrelated to the anti-exodus motif:[25] the rebels' "murmuring" is motivated by Aaron's exclusive claim to the priestly office (Num.16.11), and, later, by the deaths of Korah and his company (Num.17.6 LXX). There is no trace of this motif in the stories of the Golden Calf and of the Moabite women (Ex.32, Num.25; 1 Cor.10.7–8). In the former, the exodus itself is celebrated, although it is now ascribed to deities other than YHWH (Ex.32.4, 8). Of the passages that Paul cites, it is only the story of the plague of snakes that contains this motif (Num.21.5; 1 Cor.10.9). As we have seen, Paul's statement about "desire" (1 Cor.10.6) derives from the story of the quails, where the motif does occur (Num.11.4–5), but he severs its links with that story in order to introduce all the incidents that follow as instances of illicit "desire". Most significantly of all, Paul implies that the destruction of the entire exodus generation was occasioned not by the refusal to enter the promised land (as in Numbers 14.20–35), but by the cases of idolatry, *porneia* and so forth that he proceeds to mention. Having described the liberation of "our fathers" from Egypt (1 Cor.10.1–4), Paul states that "with most of them God was not pleased, for they were killed in the desert" (v.5); and in three of the cases cited (the Golden Calf, the Moabite women, Korah's rebellion) the occasion for this mass death in the

---

23. In Exodus 16 and most of the other "murmuring" passages, "the substance of the rebellion is in fact the problem of the Exodus" (G. W. Coats, *Rebellion in the Wilderness*, p. 96).

24. So G. W. Coats, *ibid.*, p. 178.

25. In contrast to Exodus 16.7–12, 17.3; Numbers 14.2, 26–30.

desert is the people's disregard for the law. For Paul, *the exodus generation died not simply because it rejected the promise, but above all because it transgressed the law.*[26] With the exception of the story of the snakes, the stories Paul cites are all concerned with the law. Their presupposition is not the exodus but the event at Sinai. In 1 Corinthians 10 as in Romans 7, the experience of Israel in the wilderness is that the law leads to desire, desire to transgression, and transgression to death.[27]

The link between law, desire, sin and death is especially clear in the account of the "murmuring" or complaining that occurred at the time of Korah's rebellion (referred to, as we have seen, in 1 Corinthians 10.10).[28] At the beginning of the story, Korah the Levite assembles a formidable number of leaders of the people in support of his revolt against the authority of Moses and Aaron. Their objection is that:

> You claim too much for yourselves! For all the congregation are holy.
> every one of them. Why then do you exalt yourselves above the
> assembly of YHWH? (Num.16.3)

The war of words continues with a speech in which Moses attributes this challenge to the Levites' desire for the priestly prerogatives, assigned exclusively to Aaron and his sons:

---

26.   Thus Paul does not refer to the story of the people's failure to occupy the land in Numbers 13–14 – a story whose crucial role in the Book of Numbers is reflected in Hebrews 3.7–4.13, where, under the influence also of Psalm 95, it is unbelief that causes the destruction of the wilderness generation (*n.b.* Heb.3.17–19; 4.2). In Paul's somewhat schematic view of the history of Israel, the wilderness is the place solely of the encounter with the law.

27.   This scriptural link between law and death is also noted by J. Milgrom, in connection with the duplication of narratives about water from the rock (Ex.17.1–7; Num.20.2–13), the manna and the quails (Ex.16.1–15; Num.11.4–8, 31–34), and the initial stage of the journey (Ex.15.22–26; Num.10.33–11.3). Milgrom points out that "[i]n Exodus, God does not punish Israel for its murmuring; in Numbers, He does so consistently" (*Numbers*, p. xvi). The explanation is that "[t]he Exodus incidents are pre-Sinai; those of Numbers are post-Sinai... It can be postulated that for a number of wilderness narratives two traditions were reported, the one involving punishment, and the other, not. The redactor, then, with Mount Sinai as his great divide, dutifully recorded both, as either pre- or post-Sinai... Sinai, then, is the watershed in Israel's wilderness experience. Indeed, it is the pivot as well as the summit for the Torah books as a whole" (*ibid.*).

28.   In the final form of this story, Korah the Levite is singled out as the main opponent of Moses and Aaron (16.5, 6, 8, 16, 19, 32; 17.5, 14), rather than the lay rebels Dathan and Abiram (16.1, 12–14, 25–34). According to one recent analysis, the story has developed out of the following components: *(i)* a story concerning Dathan and Abiram, fragments of which have been incorporated into *(ii)* an account of the rebellion of 250 elders, who wish for the privilege of offering incense before the Lord); *(iii)* the priestly story of Aaron's rod; *(iv)* a final redaction in which the motif of a Levitical rebellion led by Korah comes to the fore (H. Seebass, *Numeri*, pp. 174–89). The effect of the synthesis is to represent all Israel as implicated in Korah's rebellion.

> Hear now, sons of Levi! Does it seem to you a small thing that the God
> of Israel has separated you from the congregation of Israel, to bring you
> near to himself, to perform the service of the tabernacle of YHWH, to
> stand before the congregation to minister to them? And he has brought
> you [Korah] near, and all your brothers the sons of Levi with you: and
> do you also seek the priesthood? Therefore you and all your company
> are gathered together against YHWH. And Aaron, what is he that you
> murmur against him? (16.9–11)

According to the narrator, the rebellion is directed against Moses as well as
Aaron (v.3); on the other hand, Moses himself assumes that Aaron is its
object, and that underlying the attack on Aaron is an act of rebellion
against YHWH himself. For our purposes, what is significant here is that
Korah is in revolt against the law.[29] More specifically, he is in revolt
against the divine decree that assigns priestly office to Aaron and his sons,
and only menial roles to other members of the tribe of Levi. YHWH's
word to Moses insists that a rigid distinction should be maintained at this
point:

> And YHWH said to Moses, Bring near the tribe of Levi, and set them
> before Aaron the priest, that they may minister to him. They shall
> perform duties for him and for the whole congregation before the tent of
> meeting, as they minister at the tabernacle. They shall have charge of all
> the furnishings of the tent of meeting, and attend to the duties for the
> people of Israel as they minister at the tabernacle. And you shall give the
> Levites to Aaron and his sons; they are wholly given to him from among
> the people of Israel. And you shall appoint Aaron and his sons, and they
> shall attend to their priesthood; but if anyone else comes near, he shall
> be put to death. (Num.3.5–10)

The Levites are descended from Levi's three sons, Gershon, Kohath and
Merari, and they are therefore divided into three orders entrusted with
different tasks. Korah is among the descendants of Kohath, whose role is
to bear the furniture of the tabernacle as the people of Israel wander in the
wilderness (cf. Num.3.31; 4.1–20). Unlike the sons of Gershon and Merari,
who are provided with wagons to transport the tabernacle, the court and
their accessories, the sons of Kohath must carry the tabernacle furniture
on their shoulders (7.1–9). They are under the supervision of Aaron's

---

29. Admittedly, a distinction may be drawn between Korah's initial assertion of the
holiness of the entire people (Num.16.3) and the assertion of the Levitical right to the
priesthood attributed to him by Moses (vv.8–11); the distinction is conventionally explained
along tradition-historical lines (so M. Noth, *Numbers*, pp. 120–22). Yet, in the canonical text,
the function of Moses' address to the "sons of Levi" (vv.8–11) is to expose the self-seeking
motivation of Korah's apparently selfless intervention on behalf of the people. At this point,
Moses chooses to ignore the lay element in the revolt.

eldest surviving son, Eleazar (3.32). The priests must take particular care to cover the sacred furniture, in case the Kohathites see what it is that they are carrying, and die as a result (4.1–20). Defining the distinctive role of the Levites is a major concern of the final section of the long Sinai pericope that begins at Exodus 19, continues throughout the book of Leviticus, and concludes at Numbers 10.10 (at which point the cloud rises up from the tabernacle, and the people of Israel resume their journey). In objecting to the Levites' subordination to Aaron, Korah challenges a fundamental element in the framework of legislation laboriously constructed at Sinai. In doing so, he challenges not only Aaron and Moses (cf. 16.3) but also God, God's law – and indeed the Book of Numbers itself, in which that law is enshrined for all time.[30] In his case, the law has generated an illicit desire (the desire for the priesthood) that causes him to challenge the law. The Book of Numbers here acknowledges and warns against the hostility that its own legislation may arouse. Death is the inevitable outcome of such hostility – the death not only of Korah, but also of the lay rebels Dathan and Abiram, their families, their followers, and ultimately many thousands of their sympathizers among the people of Israel (16.20–50). This, then, is the fate of those who resist Moses' account of the divine ordering that YHWH revealed to him at Mount Sinai. As in the stories of the Golden Calf and the Moabite women, the law is actually the precondition of such a sin: "Without law sin is dead . . . , but when the commandment came sin sprang to life, and I died" (Rom.7.8–10).

In 1 Corinthians 10, Paul partially identifies himself with the Israelites of the exodus generation when he speaks of them as "our fathers" (v.1). The disasters that befell them are warnings to us – but they remain "our fathers", and, as we read of their fate, we cannot be indifferent to it. In Romans 7, the identification with "our fathers" in the wilderness has gone much further. The speaker is again Paul himself, but in an unfamiliar role as "an Israelite, of the seed of Abraham . . . " (cf. Rom.11.1) rather than an apostle of Jesus Christ. This speaker addresses those who "know the law" and are familiar with its narratives and legislation, as one who himself knows the law (v.1). When "the law" is referred to here, it is its textual embodiment in the form of the Pentateuch, the Law of Moses, that is

---

30. In relating Numbers 16–17 to the concern with the role of the Levites elsewhere in the book, the aim is to substantiate Brevard Childs' claim that "the canonical process at work in the shape of Numbers incorporated much diverse material within the framework of an overarching theological construct" (*Introduction to the Old Testament as Scripture*, p. 200). Such an approach contrasts sharply with the view of Martin Noth, who can only see a "confusion and lack of order in its contents" (*Numbers*, p. 4). Noth can even claim that "Numbers participates only marginally in the great themes of the Pentateuchal tradition" (p. 5).

meant. The speaker numbers himself among the people of Israel who are the intended addressees of the instructions that YHWH communicated to Moses, and stands alongside his fathers at Sinai as he hears the legislation and the accompanying narratives being read and reread. Since he delights in the law and acknowledges its holiness and goodness (Rom.7.12, 16, 23), he utterly dissociates himself from those who committed idolatry with the women of Moab, and from those who murmured against the rightful authority of Aaron and Moses. He is inspired by the zeal of the sons of Levi and of Phinehas, whose response to the allure of idolatry was to slaughter those seduced by it (Ex.32.25–29; Num.25.6–13). And yet, on the basis of his own scripturally-shaped experience, he has come to recognize that the catastrophe that befell the law's first addressees is paradigmatic of life under the law in general. It is, then, not simply "our fathers" who were alive once, prior to the Sinai revelation and its aftermath, who received the law and discovered that it was an occasion for sin, and who died in consequence. It is "I", the hearer and reader of their disastrous story, of whom all this is true: for in "me" that story has been re-enacted. "My" encounter with the law is essentially the same as theirs. The speaker can understand the conflicting "desires" aroused by the law, which led some into forbidden acts of idolatry and *porneia*, and others to aspire to a priestly office that was equally forbidden to them: for he himself experiences just such desires as these. He may not have acted out his desires with the recklessness of the exodus generation, but he has still acted them out inwardly and in secret. His identification with "our fathers" becomes total and irrevocable when he recognizes that even to desire what they desired is already to transgress: for the tenth commandment prohibits not simply the act but even the desire in which the initial movement towards the act takes place. The law promises that the person who observes its commandments will live by them, but this is impossible where the person in question is pulled in every direction by a mass of conflicting and illicit desires.

A living death

In Romans 7.7–10, Paul sees the whole law as summarized in the tenth commandment, which he cites in abbreviated form. When he proceeds to state that "the commandment was unto life" (v.10a), he links his primary text (Ex.20.17) to a secondary one: for Paul alludes here to the succinct statement of the law's intention that he finds in Leviticus 18.5, according to which "the person who does these things will live by them" (cf. Rom.10.5). The promise of life is now attached specifically to the (abbreviated) tenth commandment, and is immediately subverted as the coming of the commandment generates illicit desire and so death. All this refers to an event that lies in the past, as the past tenses of vv.7–11 indicate: an event in the speaker's past in which an event in Israel's past is re-enacted.

In the light of this ill-fated conjunction of texts (Exodus 20.17 and Leviticus 18.5), Romans 7.13–25 may be understood as an analysis of the doomed attempt to live out the law's project, in which the "doing" *(poiein)* prescribed by the law is constantly frustrated by the very different actions that originate in the "desire" evoked by the tenth commandment. Whereas vv.7–12 describe a past event, vv.13–25 tell how that event continues to determine the present.[31]

The transition from a narrative about a past event to an analysis of present experience is visible in v.13, where the initial question – "Did what was good bring about my death?" – refers back to a single past event, while the answer speaks of this death as an ongoing reality, that of sin "working death in me through what is good". The present participle corresponds to the present tense usage of the same verb in the passage that follows (cf. vv.17, 20, where "sin that dwells within me" is again – by implication – the subject of *katergazesthai*).[32] The reference to death as ongoing reality is repeated in the plea for deliverance from "this body of death" (v.24), and alluded to again in the description of the "law of sin" (vv.23, 25) as a "law of sin and death" (8.2). The double reference in v.13 to the law as "the good" is a recurring motif in the following verses (cf. vv.16, 18, 19, 21, with slight variations of terminology). These connections suggest that the new section begins not with v.14 but with v.13, and that it seeks to analyse the present reality of the state of "death" spoken of in v.13.[33] The law promises life to the one who observes its commandment, which is holy and just and good. Yet sin's intervention ensures that what is done is the evil the law prohibits, not the good it demands, and that the outcome is not life but death.

The person who does what the law requires will live. It is the argument of Romans 7.13–25 that this "doing" is in practice impossible, since it is constantly subverted into its opposite by "sin that dwells within me". The riddle of this distorted "doing" is announced at the outset in v.15, which introduces the three synonymous terms that will bear the weight of the argument in vv.16–21:

31. Here Paul describes "den Zustand, der durch das Geschehen der Machtergreifung der Sünde nunmehr in mir besteht" (U. Wilckens, *Römer* 2.85).

32. Although 7.13 is normally translated, "sin ... *was* working death in me", "was" is absent in the Greek. Even if the reference is to the past, the participle would imply an ongoing process, in contrast to the punctiliar *apekteinen* of v. 11.

33. Most commentators connect v.13 with vv.7–12, although Paul's rhetorical questions normally signal the beginning of a new section (cf. 3.1; 4.1; 6.1, 15; 7.7). U. Wilckens is an exception (*Römer*, 2.85).

> For what I accomplish *[katergazomai]* I do not understand. For not
> what I want do I practise *[prassō]* but what I hate I do *[poiō]*.

Of the three synonyms, *poiein* is employed five times in this passage (vv.15,
16, 19, 20, 21), *katergazesthai* four times (vv.15, 17, 18, 20; cf. vv.8, 13),
and *prassein* twice (vv.15, 19). While *poiein* is the key scriptural term for
the practice of the law, the other two lack this scriptural background. Paul
chooses them in preference to scriptural synonyms for "do" such as
"keep", "obey" and "walk", because the "doing" he seeks to analyse is
one that intends the good, as prescribed in the law, but achieves only evil.
This is not simply a personal, psychological problem; it is above all a
problem with the law itself. The law promised life, and yet the speaker,
who delights in the law and constantly underlines its goodness and
holiness, is nevertheless held fast in the grip of the "death" whose origin he
has previously narrated.

Why does the law not enable him to break free? The initial answer is
to identify in his own self a second centre of action, in addition to the
mind that delights in God's law. That centre of action is described as
"sin that dwells in me" (vv.17, 20), and, more expansively, as "another
law in my members, fighting against the law of my mind and taking me
captive to the law of sin that is in my members" (v.23).[34] Common to
these expressions is the single word, "in" (in me, in my members), which
also occurs earlier in the statement that "sin, finding opportunity through
the commandment, worked *in* me every desire" (v.8). The sin that dwells
within me is the root cause of the sin that I practise in the external world,
and it is identical to the "desire" that the commandment unwittingly
aroused in the very act of prohibiting it. In Romans 7.13–25, then, it is
not simply that the law is powerless to enable its own fulfilment and so
to bring its promise of life to fruition.[35] Rather, the initial encounter with
the law continues to produce the prohibited "desire" that is already
transgression of the law, even before it issues in specific actions in the

34.   Here, the "other law" or "law of sin" is to be understood neither as a "principle" (the
older interpretation, still maintained by Fitzmyer, *Romans*, p. 476) nor as the Torah under the
dominion of sin (a more recent suggestion, represented by Dunn, *Romans 1–8*, pp. 409–10). In
both phrases, "law" is used *metaphorically*, thereby making the point that "sin which dwells
within me" claims an authority over me analogous to that which is claimed by the law of God.
Although Paul might here have ascribed to the Torah "a strange double role" (so N. T.
Wright, *The Climax of the Covenant*, p. 198), it is not clear that he actually does so: for the
phrases, "another law in my members" and "the law of sin which is in my members" (v.23, cf.
v.25) are modelled on "sin which dwells within me" in vv.17, 20, and are clearly identified as
other than the law of God. Even when the law of God plays an unwitting part in the genesis of
sin and death (vv.5–12), it does not cease to be itself. I regret that one of my own
undergraduate essays continues to mislead my former tutor (see *ibid.*, p. 198n).

35.   Romans 7.13–25 thus describes the ongoing effects of the event described in vv.7–12,
in which sin installed itself in the human person and cut it off from all possibility of life. It is

external world. "Sin that dwells within me" is not a general bias towards evil that is unfortunately integral to being human. It has an origin and a history, arising as it does from the disastrous encounter with the law narrated in vv.7–12, and manifested in an ongoing subjection to "every kind of desire" (v.8). What should have been a life-giving and life-enhancing event has in fact ended in catastrophe – for the Israelites in the desert but also for those who read or hear their story and discover its re-enactment in their own lives.

In this reading of Romans 7, the speaker is Paul himself – but speaking not primarily as an apostle (cf. 1.1) but rather as an "Israelite" (cf. 11.1, 9.1–5), and as one who, like his implied readers, "knows the law" from personal experience (cf. 7.1).[36] In formal terms, his first person narrative in 7.7–25 is undeniably autobiographical, speaking as it does of realities past and present from the standpoint of individual experience[37]. Autobiography, however, is never simply a neutral chronicle of an individual life-story, but is always shaped by particular argumentative strategies which may differ widely. At one point, it suits Paul to present his own past as that of an exceptional Jew, a Pharisee who practised the righteousness required by the law with extraordinary diligence (Phil.3.4–6, cf. Gal.1.13–14). At another point, Paul presents his own experience as characteristic of life under the law in general, and as determined by Israel's disastrous encounter with the law at and after Sinai. Within the formal conventions of autobiographical writing, there is scope both for the highly individualized "I" of Philippians 3 and for the more representative "I" of Romans 7, just as there is scope for the more optimistic self-presentation of the first and the more pessimistic self-presentation of the second. The claim that Romans 7 cannot be autobiographical, since it would then conflict with Philippians 3, rests

unnecessary to find in vv.14–25 a distinct line of thought that dispenses with the linkage of sin and law established in vv.7–13 (against E. P. Sanders, *Paul, the Law, and the Jewish People*, pp. 72–81).

36.   Contrast the claim of S. Stowers that Paul here adopts the persona of a Gentile, who is as such constitutionally unable to keep the law; Paul here adapts a Hellenistic commonplace about the lack of self-control of the "barbarian" or uneducated other, and has nothing to say here about any distinctively Jewish experience of the law (*A Rereading of Romans*, pp. 258–84). Stowers does not explain how his Gentile speaker can have experienced the quintessentially Jewish event of the coming of the law (7.7–12; cf. 5.13, 20). His argument depends heavily on an undifferentiated and uninformed caricature of "the Western reading of Romans".

37.   For a persuasive critique of W. G. Kümmel's claim that the "I" here is purely fictitious (*Römer 7 und die Bekehrung des Paulus*, pp. 67–90, 118–32), see G. Theissen, *Psychological Aspects of Pauline Theology*, pp. 190–201.

on the naive assumption that there can only be one way of telling one's own story.[38]

Also present in Romans 7 but absent from Philippians 3 is a schema in which the innocence of early childhood is contrasted with the growing domination of the passions that occurs in later childhood and adolescence.[39] A version of this schema is found in Philo's treatise, *Who is the Heir of Divine Things?*, in connection with the statement of Genesis 15.16 that "in the fourth generation they shall come back here". Taking this as a reference to the full restoration of the soul only at the fourth stage of its life, Philo speaks as follows of the first and second stages or "generations":

> The newborn infant, for the first seven years which are the time of its childhood, is assigned a pure soul *[psuchēs akraiphnous memoiratai]* closely resembling smooth wax and not yet imprinted with the marks of good and evil *[tois agathōn kai kakōn charaktērsi]* ... This is, as it were, the first generation of the soul. The second is that which, after the age of childhood, begins to associate with evils, both those that the soul engenders out of itself and those that it willingly accepts from others. For there are many teachers of sin – nurses and instructors *[paidagōgous]* and parents and the written and unwritten laws of cities... For Moses says, "The human mind is intent on evils from youth." This is the most accursed "generation", in figurative language, or "age" in literal, when the body blooms and the soul is inflated, when smouldering passions are aroused and consume "threshing-floor and corn and fields" [cf. Ex.22.5] and whatever else they may encounter. (*Quis heres*, 294–96)

The first and second "generations" represent the initial fall from innocence, the third and fourth the healing and health bestowed by philosophy. Philo claims to derive this schema not from Hellenistic sources but from Moses, citing a text that dates the onset of sin to "youth" rather than to childhood (Gen.8.21).

A comparable account of a transition from childish innocence to youthful guilt occurs in Paul's first person narrative in Romans 7. The

---

38. Paul's reference to his "blamelessness under the law" (Phil.3.6) is one of the central points in Kümmel's influential opposition to autobiographical readings of Romans 7 (*Römer 7*, pp. 111–17). G. Theissen attempts to resolve the discrepancy by arguing that Philippians 3.6 tells of Paul's conscious experience, Romans 7.7–25 of an unconscious experience brought to light only by Christ (*Psychological Aspects*, pp. 234–43). Such an interpretation continues to assume that autobiographical writing represents a direct transcript of experience, and overlooks its rhetorical dimension.

39. In conjunction with the scriptural narrative of Israel prior to Sinai, this schema makes possible an autobiographical interpretation of Paul's statement that "I was alive once apart from law" (Rom.7.9). Kümmel's claim that such a view would be impossible for Paul (*Römer 7*, pp. 78–84) seems to ascribe to the apostle a fully fledged doctrine of original sin.

presence here of a pre-existing schema shows this to be an exercise in "representative autobiography": Paul chooses to develop his version of the schema by way of the autobiographical "I" whereas Philo does not, but the difference is one of degree and not of kind.[40] More significantly, in the Pauline account the emphasis lies on the encounter with "the law", in the form of the tenth commandment. It is Jewish, not universal human, experience that is rendered here. All humans succumb to the "fall" described by Philo, but the Pauline encounter with the law represents a distinctively Jewish version of that universal experience. The command-ment, "You shall not desire" is the occasion for a previously quiescent "sin"or sinful tendency to generate precisely the desires or passions that the commandment prohibits. The outcome is "death" – the living death of a life under the dominion of illicit desire, characterized as "death" because it represents the negation of the law's conditional promise of life to the one who performs what it prescribes. The introduction of the Law of Moses into the traditional schema means that the history of the individual's subjection to sin is now shaped by the scriptural material drawn from Exodus, Leviticus and Numbers.

There is no indication that the transition from a past event (Rom.7.7–12) to ongoing, present reality (vv.13–25) is a transition from a Jewish past to a specifically Christian present – in spite of the interjected thanksgiving of v.25a. On the other hand, the present tenses of the latter part of the chapter should be taken seriously. Paul is indeed speaking (representa-tively) of his own present reality, rooted as it is in the past event of the initial encounter with the commandment. Yet there is a crucial fictive element here: present reality is described *as if* it were still under the dominion of the law – which, according to Romans 7.1–6, it is not. This is present reality *as it would be* if the law were still in force as the definitive, divinely ordained way to salvation or "life". Exposed to the law's scrutiny, the speaker's life is still subject to the prohibited desire to which he succumbed when he first encountered the commandment. He is thereby shown to be in need of a salvation that is unavailable through the law, but that has (thankfully) already been realized through Jesus Christ (cf. v.25a).

The "fictive" element in Romans 7 is illuminated by 1 Corinthians 9.20, where Paul tells how "to those under law I became as one under the law *[hōs hupo nomon]*, while not actually being under law, so that I might win those who are under law". In Romans 7, Paul speaks representatively of his own experience as one who was once under law, and *as if* he still is.

---

40. Kümmel's continuing influence even on scholars aware of the rhetorical dimension of Pauline discourse is illustrated by Brian Dodd's remarkably cautious statement that "[i]t is probably an overstatement... that the 'I' of Romans 7 *cannot* include Paul..." (*Paul's Paradigmatic 'I'*, p. 224; italics original).

Paul's conclusions about the law naturally correspond to his belief that salvation is in Jesus Christ alone, as expressed in the interjected thanksgiving of v.25a. But it is not the case that his account of life under the law is derived exclusively from his christological beliefs. It is derived from his hearing and reading of the Law of Moses: its self-subverting presentation of the relationship between the divine commandment and Israel's response, its prohibition even of the first, purely inward movement towards the forbidden action, its capacity to shape and inform the experience of those who hear and read it. Exodus recounts the coming of the commandment, Leviticus promises that obedience to it will issue in life, but Numbers tells how the Israelites after Sinai succumbed to desire and death. The general schema of the fall from innocence has been recreated on the basis of these texts.

Narratives of Judgment and Salvation

In Paul's reading of Numbers the emphasis falls on the dire fate of the law's original addressees, which is paradigmatic for the experience of all who subsequently find themselves addressed by the law – including Paul himself, apart from his relation to Christ. As he elsewhere shows in his reading of the Exodus account of the Sinai event (2 Cor.3), Paul can move seamlessly from the scriptural "sons of Israel" to the Jewish community of the present (vv.13–15). It is just this typological move that also occurs in Romans 7 – although Paul here dispenses with the usual presentation of the scriptural story as the basis for the analogy, which is why it was necessary to draw so extensively on 1 Corinthians 10. Paul's reading of Numbers as of Exodus is, however, the reading of one for whom the veil of permanence and finality has been removed from the face of the text. The Book of Numbers will be differently understood by readers unaffected by the Pauline premise of the eclipse of the law's glory in the glory of Christ. For such readers, the Book of Numbers will contribute to the definitive Mosaic portrayal of the ongoing privileges and responsibilities of the people of Israel.

The exodus paradigm

As we have seen, Paul's first person narration in Romans 7 is informed by the reading of narrative material from Exodus and Numbers that is attested in 1 Corinthians 10. In contrast, the author of the *Wisdom of Solomon* appeals to much the same scriptural material to demonstrate the ongoing divine care for the elect people. In this text the motif of death in the desert is played down, and there can be no question of the Pauline claim that it is "the letter" – the law itself, in its written form – that "kills", having been subverted by "sin". In *Wisdom*, punishment is what happens not to Israel but to Israel's enemies – notably the Egyptians.[41] The main point that Paul and the author of *Wisdom* have in common is simply that they have reflected on some of the same scriptural texts.

(i) Numbers 11.1–34 Paul derives from the story of the quails the motif of illicit "desire", which he takes as the key to all the post-Sinai episodes of rebellion in the desert (1 Cor.10.6). This desire was evoked by the law's prohibition, and issued in death (Rom.7.7–11). For the author of *Wisdom*, the quails represent the overwhelmingly generous divine response to the people's desire for a more varied diet – in sharp contrast to God's employment of other forms of animal life to punish the Egyptians with loss of appetite (Wis.16.1–4). The author also draws on the statement that the wind of the Lord brought the quails "from the sea" (Num.11.31), to support his claim that "the whole creation in its own nature was fashioned anew, ministering to your commands" (Wis.19.6). Quails from the sea are "a new kind of bird", and so the people's demand for better food occasioned a remarkable disclosure of the divine power over nature (Wis.19.11–12).

(ii) Numbers 21.4–9 The story of the plague of snakes provides Paul with the third of his four scriptural cases in which illicit desire leads to death. The first two are used to warn against idolatry and *porneia* (1 Cor.10.7–8; cf. Ex.32, Num.25), and this one warns against putting the Lord (or Christ) to the test. When "some of them" committed this sin, by complaining about the lack of adequate food and water, "they were destroyed by the snakes" (1 Cor.10.9) – that is, by the "killer snakes" *(tous opheis tous thanatountas)* which the Lord sent among the people, so that "many people of the sons of Israel died" (Num.21.6). The author of *Wisdom* claims that this plague was short lived, that a means of deliverance was provided, that the whole event took place as a reminder of the divine commandments, and that all who were bitten were healed – in contrast to the just punishment of those Egyptians who were killed by the bites of locusts and flies (Wis.16.5–14). Of the two interpretations, one seeks to maximize the horror of this event, the other to minimize it. For one, the

41. The author's hostility towards the scriptural Egyptians implies a hostility to his own Egyptian contemporaries (cf. Wis.11.15; 12.24; 15.14; 19.13–16), and so a possible Alexandrian provenance. On the animosity between Jews and Egyptians, see Josephus, *Against Apion*, i.223–26. In contrast, D. Georgi argues that the (alleged) lack of contact between *Wisdom* and *Ben Sira* on the one hand and Philo on the other makes an Alexandrian provenance unlikely (*Jüdische Schriften aus hellenistisch-römischer Zeit*, III.4, pp. 395–96). Georgi's chronological placement of *Wisdom* between *Ben Sira* and Philo is convincing (*ibid.*, pp. 396–97), although his claim that the three are independent of one another is not.

382 Paul and the Hermeneutics of Faith

story testifies to the threatening reality of the divine judgment; for the other, to the saving power of the divine word.

(iii) Numbers 16.1–17.15 The author of *Wisdom* reads the stories of the quails and the snakes as testimony to a divine power exercised for the well-being of the people of Israel. The scriptural death motif (Num.11.33–34; 21.6) is eliminated – or rather, it is displaced onto the Egyptians (Wis.16.9). In his treatment of Korah's rebellion, however, the author does concede that "the experience of death also touched the righteous", and that this experience was not confined to the Egyptians as they bewailed the loss of their first-born (Wis.18.20). Here too, the primary interest is in the divine means of deliverance: no longer merely a "symbol" *(sumbolon)*, as in the case of the plague of snakes (16.6), but a human figure, the high priest Aaron who heroically stayed the hand of the angel of death (18.21–25; Num.17.6–14). In contrast, Paul is interested only in the punishment meted out to those who "complained", and he does not mention Aaron's action (1 Cor.10.10).

Unlike Paul, the author of *Wisdom* does not refer to the judgment following the unbelieving response to the spies' report (Num.14.1–38; 1 Cor.10.5), or to the seduction by the Midianites (Num.25.1–9; 1 Cor.10.8).[42]

The difference between the two readings of the wilderness traditions is also illustrated by their treatment of the Exodus stories of the miracle at

42. The post-Sinai narrative of Numbers 11–25 is also treated in Josephus, *Antiquities* iii.295–iv.15. Here, the scriptural stories are retold as accounts of rebellion against Moses' rightful leadership, but with little acknowledgment of the death motif (cf. also Ps.-Philo, *Liber Antiquitatum Biblicarum* 14–17). Josephus highlights the popular hostility to Moses expressed in the quail story, and the concluding reference to the plague and to the "tombs of desire" is simply a postscript (iii.295–99). The story of the spies is paraphrased at length (iii.300–16; iv.1–10), with a softening of the death sentence for the whole wilderness generation (iii.313–14) and a renewed emphasis on popular hostility towards Moses (iv.3–6). The latter theme is also prominent in an extended treatment of the Korah story (iv.11–66), which omits the scriptural account of the plague and of Aaron's intervention: at iv.50–66 Josephus moves directly from Numbers 17.6 (=16.41, the people's complaint) to 17.16–26 (Aaron's rod). Thus the destructive consequences of rebellion are toned down; indeed, God delivered the people "from those terrible consequences which would have followed from their rebellion but for Moses' watchful care" (iv.13). The story of the snakes is omitted: at iv.85 Josephus's paraphrase moves directly from the mourning over the death of Aaron (Num.20.29) to the arrival at the river Arnon (Num.21.13). Only in the story of the seduction by the Midianites (iv.126–55) is there a frank recognition of the scriptural "death in the desert" motif – although even here the number who perish is substantially reduced (iv.155). Josephus uses these narratives to develop his *apologia* for Moses' leadership, which mass death in the wilderness might serve to undermine. On the other hand, his emphasis on the hostility Moses endured serves "to increase the stature of Moses as an able politician who overcomes even the gravest

the Red Sea (Ex.14.1–15.21; Wis.10.17–21, 19.1–9; 1 Cor.10.1–2), and the provision of the manna (Ex.16.1–36; Wis.16.20–29; 1 Cor.10.3) and of water from the rock (Ex.17.1–7; Wis.11.4–10; 1 Cor.10.4). Paul and the author of *Wisdom* both read these stories as testimony to God's saving action on behalf of the people of Israel – "our fathers" (1 Cor.10.1). Paul reads them christologically, in order to emphasize the typological application to his Christian readers, whereas the author of *Wisdom* uses them to further his antithesis between the divine judgment inflicted on Egypt and the saving goodness experienced by Israel; but for both interpreters these are stories about salvation that remain paradigmatic for their own readers. Where the two interpreters diverge is in their construal of the overall shape of the wilderness traditions. For the author of *Wisdom*, the stories cited from Exodus 14–17 are of a piece with the stories from Numbers 11–21: God's saving goodness towards the people of Israel is manifested in the crossing of the Red Sea, in the gifts of bread from heaven, water from the rock and quails from the sea, and in the timely provision of means of deliverance from the snakes and from the destroying angel. In each case, a contrast is drawn with the sufferings endured by the Egyptians, so that every experience of salvation is paired with a corresponding experience of judgment. Thus, the Egyptians were unexpectedly deprived of water when the Nile was turned into blood; the Israelites were unexpectedly provided with water from a rock in the desert (Wis.11.4–14). For Paul, on the other hand, the contrast between salvation and judgment is to be located within the wilderness traditions themselves. It corresponds to the difference between the books of Exodus and Numbers – or, more exactly, to the difference between a time "without law" (Rom.7.9; cf. 4.15) and the time that began with the law's advent (Rom.7.9; cf. 5.20). The dividing-line between salvation and judgment is marked not by the exodus but by the giving of the law at Sinai – an event which the author of *Wisdom* hardly mentions.

In itself, the difference between the two interpretations of the stories from Numbers might amount to nothing more than a difference of homiletical strategy. Paul wishes to warn, the author of *Wisdom* to encourage, and the scriptural narrative provides resources for both purposes. This dual homiletical possibility is already acknowledged in the canonical juxtaposition of Psalms 105 and 106 (104 and 105 LXX). Psalm 105 celebrates the divine saving actions from the patriarchal era to the conquest of the land: the cloud, the fire, the quails, the manna and the water from the rock are all duly noted (Ps.105.39–41), as are the plagues of Egypt (vv.26–36). On the other

---

opposition", and also "strengthens his argument for the value of social harmony" (P. Spilsbury, *The Image of the Jew in Flavius Josephus' Paraphrase of the Bible*, p. 135). On these stories as a whole, see *ibid.*, pp. 127–46.

hand, Psalm 106 highlights the people's rebellious actions, already at the Red
Sea (v.7), and later in the illicit "desire" of the story of the quails (vv.13–15),
in the rebellion of Dathan and Abiram (vv.16–18), the Golden Calf incident
(vv.19–23), the failure to occupy the land (vv.24–27), the idolatry with the
Baal of Peor (vv.28–31), and the incident at Meribah (vv.32–33). Psalm 105 is
a hymn of thanksgiving, Psalm 106 a communal confession of sin. Their
canonical juxtaposition indicates that the scriptural narratives can
legitimately be read in both of these fundamentally different ways: as
testimony to the divine goodness, and as a dire warning of the consequences
of sin. The author of *Wisdom* stands closer to Psalm 105, Paul to Psalm 106:
but there is – arguably – no reason why the two later interpretations should
not peacefully coexist and indeed complement one another, just as the two
earlier ones do.

That might be a possible conclusion from the scriptural exegesis of 1
Corinthians 10 if considered in isolation. Yet, as we have seen, there are
clear indications here that Paul's exegesis reflects his understanding of the
Sinai event as the great dividing-line within the scriptural narrative.
"Desire" leads here to "death" (vv.5–10), just as in the first person
narrative of Romans 7.7–11. Although, in 1 Corinthians unlike Romans,
this train of events is not explicitly connected to the law, it is notable that
Paul's warnings are all derived from incidents that presuppose the coming
of the law, and, in the majority of cases, tell of transgression of the law.
The gap between the last of the "positive" events cited by Paul (water from
the rock: Ex.17.1–7, 1 Cor.10.4) and the first of the "negative" ones (the
making of the Golden Calf: Ex.32, 1 Cor.10.7) is occupied in Exodus by
the opening section of the Sinai pericope. Paul's reading of the stories from
Numbers is to be integrated into his reading of the Torah as a whole. And
the same is true of the author of *Wisdom*, who reads his selected stories
from Numbers in the closest connection to Exodus and (as we shall see) to
Genesis. In both cases, the reading of an individual text occurs only within
a particular construal of scripture as a whole.

Paul and the author of *Wisdom* agree that the pentateuchal narrative is
to be read soteriologically. For both, scriptural narrative discloses the
complex dynamics of a divine saving action that transcends its own
boundaries and that is to be realized definitively only in the eschaton. For
the author of *Wisdom*, the narrative articulates the salvation of the
righteous and the condemnation of the ungodly. This "paradox of
salvation" (Wis.5.2) is proclaimed as a (counter-intuitive) future hope in
chapters 1–5, and is shown in the second half of the book to be firmly
grounded in the primary scriptural narratives (chapters 10–19).[43] The

43. The close relationship between the eschatological scenario of Wisdom 1–5 and the
rereading of scriptural narrative in Wisdom 10–19 is rightly emphasized by N. T. Wright, *The*

paradigmatic story of salvation and judgment is that of the exodus event at the Red Sea, but analogous events of salvation and judgment are discovered in the traditions of the plagues of Egypt and of the wilderness wanderings, and in the detailed correspondences and contrasts between the two (Wis.11, 16–19). The exodus paradigm is also projected back into Genesis, in connection with the figure of "Wisdom" (Wis.10). At the heart of the scriptural narrative stands the event of the exodus: the pattern of divine action disclosed here is to be found throughout the narrative, and the Sinai event is notable by its absence. For the author of *Wisdom*, the narrative sequence from Genesis to Numbers consists in a homogeneous series of anticipations and repetitions of the exodus paradigm of salvation for the righteous and judgment for the unrighteous. This construal of the scriptural narrative contrasts with the Pauline disjunction between Genesis, which speaks of promise, righteousness and life (Rom.4), and Exodus-Numbers, which speak of law, sin and death (Rom.7).

If, simplifying slightly, we identify the narrative of Exodus 1–15 as "Exodus" and the main wilderness stories cited in *Wisdom* as "Numbers", the author's scriptural interpretation turns out to centre upon a dual relationship: Exodus-Genesis on the one hand, Exodus-Numbers on the other. This work offers an opportunity to compare two contrasting readings of the pentateuchal narrative as a whole. As we shall see, the key to the contrast lies in the treatment of Numbers.

A harmony of Exodus and Genesis

In *Wisdom of Solomon* 10–19, the author reflects extensively on the understanding of divine agency implied in the scriptural narratives of Genesis, Exodus and Numbers.[44] In the Genesis-related material in chapter 10, the author focuses on the agency of Wisdom in the lives of the righteous, from Adam to Joseph. This leads into a description of her role in the events of the exodus, where she is identified as the source of Moses' empowerment in his struggles with Pharaoh, as the enabler of the despoiling of the Egyptians, as the pillar of cloud and fire that aided the crossing of the Red Sea, and as the inspirer of the hymn of triumph that celebrated the saving event (Wis.10.15–21). This passage on the exodus represents a link between the Genesis material (10.1–14) and the extensive

---

Resurrection of the Son of God, pp. 165, 173. Points of contact with chapters 1–5 may be found especially in 11.14 (the vindication of Moses, cf. 5.1–5); 12.26; 14.11 (eschatological judgment, cf. 3.7, 4.20); 16.24, 19.6–21 (the co-operation of creation in salvation and judgment, cf. 6.20–23); 18.13 (the acknowledgment of Israel as God's son, cf. 2.13–18; 5.5).

44. In preparing this and the following sections, I regret not having had access to Udo Schwenk-Bressler's monograph on *Sapientia Salomonis als ein Beispiel frühjüdischer Textauslegung*.

reflections on the plague and wilderness stories that follow (11.1–18.25). In conjunction with chapter 19, where a more extensive account of the crossing of the Red Sea is given, it also constitutes an *inclusio*. More precisely, the two exodus passages represent a line of demarcation between divine acts of judgment (the plague traditions) and of mercy (the wilderness traditions). For the present, however, we are concerned with the relationship between Exodus and Genesis, and with the means the author uses to ensure that what is told is a single, harmonious story. Essentially, he does two things with these narratives. He finds evidence of Wisdom's initiatives throughout the story from Adam to Moses, and he reads the Genesis stories in the light of the exodus paradigm of deliverance from the ungodly. Wisdom belongs only within the Exodus-Genesis relationship (ch.10), and does not feature in the Exodus-Numbers material that follows (ch.11–19).

In this reading of the Genesis narrative, the main protagonist is the figure of Wisdom (Wis.10.1–14). She it was who protected Adam, delivered him from his sin, and enabled him to establish his rule over all things (vv.1–2).[45] She it was who steered Noah safely through the deluge (v.4), who recognized and preserved the righteousness of Abraham (v.5), and who rescued Lot from the destruction of Sodom (v.6). When Jacob fled from his brother, she accompanied him and came to his aid (vv.10–12) – as she did later in the case of Joseph (vv.13–14). Wisdom "delivers" (*exeilato*, v.1), "saves" (*esōsen*, v.4) or "rescues" (*errusato*, vv.6, 9, 13) the righteous person (*[ton] dikaion*, vv.4, 5, 6, 10, 13) from whatever threatens him: Adam from his transgression (v.1),[46] Noah and Lot from the punishments that befell the ungodly (vv.4, 6), Jacob and Joseph from the hostility of their brothers and, respectively, from the machinations of Laban and of Potiphar's wife. Wisdom also "guards" (*diaphulaxen, ephulaxen*, vv.1, 5, 12) or "keeps" (*etērēsen*, v.5) her servants. In many and various ways, she acts on their behalf as a beneficent providence – a point that is illustrated especially by the careers of Jacob (vv.9–12) and of Joseph (vv.13–14).

In this interpretation of Genesis, the acts of Wisdom are not identical to the acts ascribed to God in the Genesis text itself. Wisdom is not simply a surrogate for God. In several cases, her actions presuppose prior divine actions, indirectly referred to in a series of passive participles: the creation of Adam (v.1), the engulfing of the world in a flood (v.4), and the destruction of

---

45. Enoch is no doubt omitted because he is already referred to in 4.10–15. D. Georgi claims that this passage has been displaced from an earlier "hymn" underlying chapter 10 (*Jüdische Schriften aus hellenistich-römischer* Zeit, p. 436). The lack of reference to the agency of Wisdom makes this unlikely.

46. In the contrast with the unrighteous Cain, Adam functions as one of the "righteous", although this term is not explicitly applied to him (so H. Engel, *Das Buch der Weisheit*, p. 169).

the tower of Babel (v.5) and of Sodom (v.6). Indeed, Wisdom's actions are usually inferred from the scriptural text, and do not coincide with any divine or human actions that are explicit in the text. Wisdom, we are told, "preserved the first-formed father of the world... and delivered him from his transgression, and gave him strength to rule all things" (vv.1–2). In Genesis itself, no-one is said to deliver Adam from his transgression, or to give him strength to rule the world in accordance with his original commission (Gen.1.26–28). Similarly, Genesis knows of no supernatural aid that enabled Noah to steer the ark to safety (Wis.10.4), or that preserved Abraham's faithfulness under the severest test of all (v.5), or that gave Jacob victory over adversaries human and divine (vv.11–12). Yet, while Wisdom is not identified with the God of the Genesis narrative, she is at no point merely a personified human character trait. It is one thing for Noah or Abraham to be "righteous" (vv.4, 5), quite another for them to be assisted by Wisdom. In the *Wisdom of Solomon* particular people are described as "righteous" on twenty-four occasions,[47] but on only three as "wise".[48] Goodness or righteousness may be regarded as a kind of natural endowment (cf. 8.19–20), but Wisdom is always an additional gift of God, bestowed again and again – typically, in answer to prayer. The exemplary case of the human relation to Wisdom is Solomon himself, the implied author of this text whose prayer for wisdom (1 Kgs.3.1–15) is twice treated to extensive paraphrase (Wis.7.1–14; 8.17–9.18).[49] As these prayers indicate, wisdom is always a gift rather than a possession (cf. 7.7, 9.4): thus, "even if one is perfect among the sons of men, without the wisdom coming from you he will be reckoned as nothing" (9.6). Above all, however, Wisdom is a personal divine power, breathed out by God and pervading the whole world, entering especially into the souls of the righteous (cf. 7.25–27). The personal agency ascribed to her in the Genesis material in chapter 10 is to be taken seriously. Like the Pauline "Holy Spirit", she has her dwelling in the soul or heart of the individual without detriment to her own transcendent identity.[50] She is,

47. Wis.2.10, 12, 16, 18; 3.1, 10; 4.7, 16; 5.1, 15; 10.4, 5, 6, 10, 13, 20; 11.14; 12.9, 19; 16.17, 23; 18.7, 20; 19.17. The term is predominantly singular in chapters 1–10 (13 out of 16 occurrences), plural in chapters 11–19 (7 out of 8 occurrences).

48. Wis.4.17, 6.24, 7.15; contrast Proverbs and *Ben Sira*, where references to the wise are frequent.

49. In this text, first person singular usage is confined to 6.22–9.12. The speaker is identifiable as Solomon especially clearly in 9.7–12, where the speaker is not only "king over your people" (v.7) but has also been commanded to build the temple (v.8). The conception of Solomon as imparting his wisdom to his fellow-monarchs (cf. 1.1; 6.1–11, 21–25) is inspired by 1 Kings 5.14 (cf. 10.1–10, 24), where "the kings of the earth" acclaim "the wisdom of Solomon". In both paraphrases of Solomon's prayer, the author takes literally the king's reference to himself as "a little child" (1 Kgs.3.7; Wis.7.1–7, 8.19–21).

50. Wisdom is identified as "the Spirit of the Lord (1.6–8), as "the fashioner [*technitis*] of all things" (7.22), as the one who "orders all things well" (8.1), and as "your holy spirit"

then, neither a synonym for God nor a personified human characteristic, but a distinct hypostasis.[51] The actions ascribed to her in *Wisdom* 10 represent a secondary level of divine agency, in addition to the primary level that is explicit in the text of Genesis. The effect is to uncover a secret divine agency – that is, the agency of Wisdom – at points where Genesis knows only of human agency. The actions which demonstrate Abraham's faithfulness, Jacob's combative prowess and Joseph's chastity are not the actions of Abraham, Jacob and Joseph alone, but actions inspired by Wisdom who, it seems, co-operates with the righteous to bring their righteousness to fruition. Thus Wisdom is continually operative both in a life marked by frequent divine interventions (Jacob) and in a life lacking in such interventions (Joseph). The unfolding of Jacob's life-story and of Joseph's is Wisdom's doing.

In writing Wisdom into the text of Genesis, the author introduces a secondary level of divine agency into the narrative – a hidden agency operating from below rather than from above. This is particularly striking in the case of Adam. Wisdom

> guarded the first-formed *[prōtoplaston]* father of the world, when he alone had been created *[monon ktisthenta]*, and delivered him from his transgression, and gave him strength to rule over all things. (10.1–2)

Here, "first-formed" and "alone" allude to Genesis 2.7, 15 *(eplasen)* and 2.18, where it is acknowledged that it is not good that the man should be alone *(monon)*.[52] In *Wisdom*, the man is never entirely alone. As the Lord God prepares the Garden and the rivers that flow from it, the first, vulnerable human being is under the constant care of Wisdom – a maternal role that corresponds to the fact that Wisdom is "the fashioner of all things" (7.22) and that God made man by his wisdom (9.2). This maternal care continues even beyond the disaster of Adam's transgression, which, in some unspecified way, she helps to rectify – unlike the deity of Genesis, who has no further contact with Adam after the expulsion from the Garden.[53]

(9.17); compare also the list of her divine attributes in 7.22–27. For reflection on this identification of Wisdom and the Holy Spirit, in the context of feminist theological issues, see my *Text, Church and World: Biblical Interpretation in Theological Perspective*, pp. 198–200, 204–205, 216–17.

51. Against J. D. G. Dunn, *Christology in the Making*, pp. 172–73, where it is argued that "Wisdom" simply represents God's wise ordering of creation and action on behalf of his people.

52. Compare the still clearer allusion to Genesis 2.7 in *Wisdom* 7.1, where Adam is the "earth-born first-formed" *(gēgenous prōtoplastou)*.

53. The author of *Wisdom* may here show a knowledge of traditions about Adam's repentance, attested in the *Life of Adam and Eve* and the so-called *Apocalypse of Moses*. These are Latin and Greek texts respectively, which run in parallel for about two-thirds of their

At other points, the author reassigns to Wisdom actions ascribed in Genesis to another agent. When it is said of Abraham that Wisdom "recognized the righteous man" (Wis.10.5), the reference is probably to the recognition implied in the initial divine call (Gen.12.1–3). When Wisdom is said to have rescued Lot from the destruction of Sodom, she takes on the role of the two angels of Genesis 19. The account of her relationship to Jacob (Wis.10.9–12) recalls the dying patriarch's reference to "the angel who delivers me from all evil" – a figure parallel to, but apparently distinct from, "the God who has cared for me from my youth until this day" (Gen.48.15–16).[54] Later, she will also be identified with the pillar of cloud and fire in the exodus narrative (Wis.10.17b; Ex.13.21–22). In general, however, the tendency is to assign to Wisdom an agency independent of, and supplementary to, the various types of agency described in the Genesis and Exodus texts. When the exodus song of triumph is traced back to Wisdom's inspiration (Wis.10.20–21), there is no question of her merely assuming a pre-existing role.[55]

For the author as for the biblical narrator, the exodus is simultaneously an event of salvation and of judgment: the righteous were led through the deep waters in which the ungodly were drowned (Wis.10.18–20; 19.1–12). The author ensures the coherence of Genesis-Exodus not only by tracing the agency of Wisdom through the narrative, but also by projecting the exodus paradigm of salvation and judgment back into Genesis. If the Israelites and the Egyptians represent the primary objects of salvation and judgment respectively, the same pattern may be seen in Genesis in the pairing of Adam and Cain (10.1–4), Abraham and the builders of the tower of Babel (10.5), and Lot and the inhabitants of the Five Cities

---

content, and which appear to be Jewish rather than Christian in origin. In the *Apocalypse*, the angels who are carrying out the expulsion from the Garden allow Adam to offer a prayer of penitence. Although their intercession proves unsuccessful, they do secure divine permission for him to bring fragrant incenses with him, with a view to a future sacrificial offering (*Ap.Mos.* 27.1–29.6). In the *Vita*, Adam stands for forty days in the river Jordan as a mark of his penitence, while Eve undertakes a similar feat in the river Tigris – only to be deceived again by the devil, disguised as a radiant angel (*Vita* 4.3–10.4). Both texts end with an assurance of Adam's salvation (*Ap.Mos.* 33.1–41.3; *Vita* 46.1–47.3), and the *Apocalypse* emphasizes that this was made possible only by the intercession of angels (*Ap.Mos.* 33.5; 35.2–37.2). That the traditions attested in these texts were already extant at the turn of the eras is suggested by *Jubilees* 3.27 (cf. *Ap.Mos.* 27.1–29.6); 2 Corinthians 11.3, 14; 12.3 (cf. *Ap.Mos.* 16.1–21.6; *Vita* 9.1; *Ap.Mos.* 37.5); and Josephus, *Antiquities* i.70–71 (cf. *Vita* 49.2–50.2; also 2 *Enoch* 33.8–12). In *Wisdom* 10.1–2, Wisdom's role is comparable to the angels' in the *Apocalypse*.

54. The Genesis reference to *ho aggelos ho ruomenos me ek pantōn tōn kakōn* (Gen.48.16) may underlie the introduction to the Jacob material in *Wisdom* 10, which states that "Wisdom delivered *[errusato]* her servants from troubles *[ek ponōn]*" (10.9).

55. It is therefore incorrect to claim that, in this text, "God's saving deeds in and for Israel are retold, with the name of Sophia taking the place of the traditional name of God" (S. Schroer, "The Book of Sophia", p. 25).

(10.6–8).[56] While the author does not maintain this pattern in the cases of Jacob (vv.9–12) and of Joseph (vv.13–14), he does emphasize that Wisdom's interventions on their behalf were occasioned by the threat posed by their enemies. Wisdom is associated almost exclusively with salvation or deliverance, and is not herself directly involved in the fate of Cain and the other objects of divine displeasure. In this respect, the Egyptians are an exception: for Wisdom not only led the people of Israel through the waters, she also "drowned their enemies, and cast them up from the depths of the abyss" (10.19). In the Genesis examples, the ungodly go to their doom because they have apostatized from Wisdom:

> When an unrighteous man departed from her *[apostas ep' autēs]* in his
> anger, he too perished in his fratricidal fury. (10.3)

> For, passing Wisdom by *[sophian gar parodeusantes]*,
>   they [Lot's contemporaries] were not only prevented from knowing
>   the good *[ta kala]*,
>   they also left behind a memorial of folly for the future,
>   so that the causes of their overthrow could never be forgotten. (10.8)

To turn away from Wisdom is to set out on a way that ends inevitably in destruction, whether in the form of the spiritual death of Cain's exile from the earth, or of the "smoking wasteland" that still marks the site of Sodom and Gomorrah (10.7). Wisdom herself is a beneficent power, however, and it is not she who destroyed the Cities of the Plain or the other objects of the divine wrath. Events of divine judgment and salvation – the Flood, the tower of Babel, the destruction of Sodom – manifest the justice of God and the goodness of Wisdom. This may be compared with Philo's claim that, in the Sodom narrative, the supreme God preserves his own goodness intact by entrusting the tasks of punishment and of deliverance to two subordinate angelic powers, one punitive and the other beneficent (*Abr.* 142–46). For the author of *Wisdom*, the beneficent power is Wisdom, and the agent of destruction is not explicitly identified.

The importance of the exodus paradigm of judgment as well as salvation is underlined both by the linkages between Adam and Cain, Abraham and the tower of Babel (10.1–5), and by the graphic description of the enduring evidence of Sodom's overthrow (10.7–8). The Genesis events of judgment

---

56. The cities of this *pentapolis* are listed in Genesis 14.2, 8–9 as Sodom, Gomorrah, Admah, Zeboim and Bela/Zoar (cf. 10.19). In Genesis, it is only Sodom and Gomorrah that are destroyed (Gen.19.24–25); Zoar is so named as a place of refuge (19.19–23). Philo assumes that four out of the five cities were destroyed, finding in the sparing of Zoar a veiled reference to the supremacy of sight among the five senses (*Abr.* 147–66). Like the author of *Wisdom*, Philo claims that the smoke of the destruction continues to rise to this day (*Abr.* 141; cf. Wis.10.7).

and deliverance are types looking ahead to the supreme event narrated in Exodus. The exodus is the definitive fulfilment of the pattern established in Genesis.

After the exodus, it seems that Wisdom continues her beneficent work into the wilderness period. It is said that "she caused their works to prosper by the hand of a holy prophet" (11.1) – the prophet who was also the "servant of the Lord" in whose soul she had earlier taken up residence (10.16).[57] At this point, however, direct address to the deity is resumed (11.4; cf. 9.17–18), so that God rather than Wisdom is now the giver of the benefits bestowed on the people. "She gave" (10.2, 10, 14) is replaced by "you gave" (11.7).[58] The term *sophia* occurs 28 times in chapters 1–10, but only twice in the rest of the book (14.2, 5),[59] and the loss of the term entails the loss of a literary character. It seems that Wisdom's role is confined to the Exodus-Genesis axis, and that the Exodus-Numbers axis operates on a different basis. But why is this?

The suggestion that *Wisdom* 11.2–19.22 was originally a separate composition is ruled out by the seamless continuity between the first two verses of chapter 11, and by the *inclusio* formed by the two exodus passages (10.16–21; 19.1–12).[60] The explanation for Wisdom's disappearance lies instead in the rhetorical context of her rise to prominence within this work. Wisdom is introduced in chapters 1 and 6 in the context of an address to "those who rule the earth" (1.1), the "kings" or "judges of the ends of the earth" (6.1):

> To you, then, O monarchs *[turannoi]*, are my words addressed,
> so that you may learn wisdom and not transgress. (6.9)

---

57. Winston offers the translation, "Their works prospered at the hand of a holy prophet", eliminating the reference to Wisdom on the grounds that, "[a]fter introducing Wisdom six times with the emphatic *hautē*, our author would hardly abandon this rhetorical device at the climax" (*Wisdom*, p. 226). In fact, the emphatic *hautē* is always used to introduce a new beneficiary of Wisdom's action (10.1, 5, 6, 10, 13, 15). In 11.1, the beneficiary is the same as in 10.15–21. In addition, Wisdom has been named in 10.21 (as in 10.4, 8, 9), and is as clearly the subject of *euodōsen* (11.1) as of *ēnoixen* and *ethēken* (10.21).

58. Direct address to God occupies much of the second half of the book (9.1–12, 17–18; 11.4–12.25; 14.3–7; 15.1–3, 14, 18; 16.2–16; 16.20–17.1; 18.1–8, 13–16, 24; 19.5–9, 22). The meditation on the scriptural testimony to God's goodness to his people is really an extension of Solomon's prayer (chapter 9): so W. Horbury, "The Wisdom of Solomon", p. 660 – although Horbury also believes that 10.1–11.1 and 11.2–19.18 are later additions.

59. The parallel should be noted between 14.2, 5 and 10.4. The terminological differentiation of chapters 1–10 and 11–19 becomes less clear-cut when one notes that, of the 28 occurrences of *sophia* in chapters 1–10, only three are in chapters 1–5.

60. Separation of 1.1–11.1 from 11.2–19.22 is strongly advocated by S. Holmes, "The Wisdom of Solomon", in *APOT* 1.518, 521–24 (with details of older source-critical theories).

> If then you delight in thrones and sceptres, O monarchs of the peoples,
> 　　honour wisdom, so that you may reign for ever.
> What wisdom is, and how she came to me, I will tell,
> 　　and I will conceal no secrets from you,
> 　　but from the beginning of creation I will trace her course
> 　　and make the knowledge of her clear . . .
> Therefore be instructed by my words, and you will profit. (6.21–22, 25)

The appeal to the kings of the earth to receive instruction is followed by an "autobiographical" account of Solomon's quest for wisdom and its outcome (7.1–14). This is one king speaking to other kings, a conception inspired by the scriptural claim that

> all the peoples came to hear the wisdom of Solomon, and he received
> gifts from all the kings of the earth, who heard of his wisdom.
> (1 Kgs.5.14)

Solomon's wisdom is said to have surpassed the wisdom of the men of old, and the wisdom of the Egyptians and of celebrated individual sages (1 Kgs.5.9–11). "Wisdom" thus represents an international tradition, and is a universal concept: both for the biblical narrator and for the author of *Wisdom*, the fact that Solomon is a Jew addressing Gentiles is irrelevant.[61] In the later text, Wisdom is that immanent aspect of deity that is disclosed to humanity as such, quite apart from any special relationship to a particular people.[62] Solomon speaks not as a Jew but simply as a human:

> I too am a mortal human, the same as everyone,
> 　　a descendant of the first-formed child of earth,
> 　　and in the womb of my mother my flesh was formed . . .
> For no king has a different beginning of existence,
> 　　and there is one entrance into life and one exit, for all alike. (7.1, 5)

---

61. The author's view of the relationship between Wisdom and the law is unclear. On this, see E. J. Schnabel, *Law and Wisdom from Ben Sira to Paul*, pp. 129–34.

62. In the earlier tradition represented above all by Proverbs 1–9, the call of Wisdom is the call of an order immanent within creation; a "doctrine of the self-revelation of creation" comes to expression here (so G. von Rad, *Wisdom in Israel*, p. 169). Thus, "the addressee of this revelation is not . . . an Israel summoned to Yahweh by means of a covenant relationship – Israel is never discernible here as a theological entity – but the human being as such" (*ibid.*, p. 175). According to von Rad, there occurs in the *Wisdom of Solomon* "a decisive step along the road to a mythical, speculative deification of wisdom", and thus "a definitive abandonment of the tradition" (p. 170). The doctrine of the self-revelation of creation becomes a doctrine of the self-revelation of deity immanent within creation. Yet this may represent a development rather than an abandonment of the tradition. Von Rad himself notes that, even in the older tradition of Proverbs 1–9, the call of the world-order to humans "bears all the marks of a divine address" (p. 163).

As in the scriptural narrative, Solomon's wisdom is both practical and theoretical, giving him not only the ability to live and rule well (Wis.9.1–12; cf. 1 Kgs.3.3–28) but also "an unerring knowledge of what exists" (Wis.7.17; cf. 1 Kgs.4.33). This is the wisdom that Solomon offers to impart to the kings of the earth.

In *Wisdom* 10, the attempt to trace the activity of Wisdom in the narratives of Genesis belongs to this instruction in practical wisdom. The experiences of the righteous from Adam to Joseph are exemplary for the kings of the earth: for Wisdom gave Adam "strength to rule all things" (10.2, cf. 9.1–3), and bestowed on Joseph "the sceptre of a kingdom" (10.14). At such points as these, the fiction of an address by a king to other kings is maintained. As presented here, the Genesis story is not a Jewish story at all, but a story with universal exemplary significance. Thus, all personal names are suppressed, and the individuals aided by Wisdom are simply introduced as "righteous" (10.4, 5, 6, 10, 13).[63] Other equally anonymous figures serve to exemplify the fate of those who forsake Wisdom and her ways. The Genesis narrative is a message of hope and warning for the world and its rulers. In the backward projection of the exodus paradigm of salvation and judgment, that paradigm has been universalized.

In *Wisdom* 11.2–19.22, on the other hand, the meditation on the narratives of Exodus and Numbers is addressed not to the kings of the earth but to God. More significantly, God is here addressed not as the giver of wisdom, as in Solomon's earlier prayer (Wis.9.1–12), but as the God of Israel. If Genesis speaks of that aspect of deity that is manifest to all alike, Exodus and Numbers speak of a deity who uses the created order for the benefit of the holy people and for the overthrow of their enemies. In spite of this difference in the scope of the respective narratives, the same pattern of divine action may be seen throughout – a pattern characterized by the salvation of the righteous and the destruction of the unrighteous. Yet the author's more extensive reflections on the narratives of Exodus and Numbers require him to abandon the figure of Wisdom, since in these narratives deity is most characteristically manifest under another aspect – as a God who is bound to a particular people.[64] The problem of the transition from chapter 10 to chapter 11 is to be solved not by source criticism but by closer attention to the author's scriptural hermeneutics. The Genesis material in chapter 10 plays a dual role, as the continuation of the appeal to pursue wisdom, and as the beginning of the author's

---

63. The link between anonymity and universality is noted by S. Schroer, "The Book of Wisdom", p. 25.

64. Wisdom does not disappear in chapters 11–19 merely to show that "die das Heil wirkende Weisheit wirkt kein anderes Wirken als das Wirken Gottes" (H. Hübner, *Die Weisheit Salomons*, p. 147).

engagement with the fundamental scriptural narratives of Genesis, Exodus and Numbers.

A harmony of Exodus and Numbers

In *Wisdom* 10, Exodus is harmonized with Genesis by projecting the exodus paradigm of salvation and judgment back into Genesis, and by tracing the agency of Wisdom through Genesis into Exodus. We turn now to a fuller consideration of the Exodus-Numbers axis elaborated in chapters 11–19. Exodus comprises the fundamental exodus story (retellings of which bracket the whole lengthy section [10.15–21, 19.1–12]), together with the preceding plague stories. Numbers comprises the wilderness traditions, in which – according to the author – the means of the Egyptians' punishment prove to be the means of Israel's salvation. Of course, wilderness stories are found in Exodus as well as Numbers. Yet, as we shall see, it is material from Numbers that creates particular problems for the author's attempts at harmonization.

In Wisdom 11–18, the basic order is that of the ten plagues of Exodus 7– 12, two of which are omitted[65] and four of which are grouped together. The first plague (water into blood: Ex.7.14–24) is paired with the story of water from the rock (Ex.17.1–7), which is presented first:

> They thirsted and called upon you,
>> and there was given them water from sheer rock,[66]
>> and quenching of thirst from hard stone.
> For through the things whereby their enemies were punished,
>> through these same things they in their need received benefit
>> [*euergetēthēsan*].
> Instead of the spring of an ever-flowing river,
>> stirred up with defiling blood in reproof of the child-killing decree,
>> you gave them plentiful water unexpectedly [*anelpistōs*],
>> showing through the thirst they then endured how you punished their enemies.
> For when they were tested, although they were disciplined in mercy [*en eleei*],
>> they learned how the ungodly were tormented when judged with wrath [*met' orgēs*].

(Wis.11.4–9)

65. The author does not comment on the fifth and sixth plagues (cattle disease, boils: Ex.9.1–12).

66. Greek *ek petras akrotomou*, an allusion to Deuteronomy 8.15 LXX (*tou exagagontos soi ek petras akrotomou pēgēn hudatos*); MT here has *mṣwr hḥlmyš* ("from the rock of flint"), which accounts for RSV's incorrect "out of flinty rock" in *Wisdom* 11.4.

Here, the exodus represents the line of demarcation between an act of divine wrath and a corresponding act of divine mercy. Both of these involve thirst and water, and display the creator's sovereign power over the creatures. An explanation for the transformation of the river water into blood is found in Pharaoh's earlier decree that every male Israelite child should be drowned in this same river; for this author, divine agency is supremely rational in its workings. The author omits to mention the people of Israel's vociferous complaints about the lack of water (cf. Ex.17.1–7), and claims that they trustingly "called upon you" (cf. Ps.106.4–6) when subjected to divine disciplining.

The author turns next to the series of plagues involving animal or insect life: the plagues of frogs, fleas, dogflies and locusts (Ex.7.26–8.28 LXX; 10.1–20). The initial concern with these events is to show that – like the first plague – the punishment fits the crime, in this case the notorious Egyptian worship of animals.[67] The argument is facilitated by the breadth of the term *herpeta* ("creeping things"), which is comprehensive enough to include not only the frogs and insects of the plagues but also snakes, other reptiles, and smaller mammals.[68] The second, third, fourth and eighth plagues taught the Egyptians that "through the things whereby one sins, through these same things one is punished" (11.16). The symmetry between crime and punishment was a subordinate motif in the passage on the first plague (cf. 11.6–7), where the main point was to demonstrate a different symmetry – thirst and water as means both of punishment and of mercy. Here it comes to the fore, and it leads the author on to a new point. Although the animal plagues were in one sense a fitting punishment for the worship of animals, it might seem that they were far too lenient: for in them, God acted by way of small and irritating animals rather than large, terrifying and deadly ones. An omnipotent creator God could surely have summoned bears or lions, or, better still, fire-breathing dragons created specially for the purpose of literally frightening the Egyptians to death (cf. 11.16–19). There follows a long digression on the divine exercise of mercy or restraint even in punishment (11.21–12.22), taking in the parallel case of the Canaanites – whose frightful crimes were punished merely by wasps (12.3–11; cf. Ex.23.28–30). It seems that God gives even the most hardened

---

67. The Egyptians "have put their trust in beasts and most creeping creatures and animals *[herpetōn kai knōdalōn]*, they worship them and sacrifice to them both while alive and dead" *(Ep. Arist.* 138). The terminology of *Wisdom* 11.15 is similar.

68. According to *Wisdom* 11.15, the Egyptians worshipped *aloga herpeta*. In Genesis 1.20, 24, *herpeta* (from *herp[uz]ō*, to creep or crawl) covers all sea creatures and all land creatures except domesticated and wild animals – thus, insects as well as reptiles. In Leviticus, the term includes winged insects with four feet (Lev.11.20–23), but also reptiles and smaller mammals (11.41–45); compare the fivefold classification of the living world into humans, animals, birds, *herpeta* and fish (Deut.4.17–18).

sinners time and opportunity to repent. The ungodly must suffer various forms of unpleasantness, but they are not simply wiped out as they deserve to be. And if God is lenient in punishing our enemies, God will surely be all the more lenient in disciplining us (12.20–22). Underlying the argument is the anxiety that, in reality, God treats his own people *worse* than he treats his and their enemies. Given a choice between the Egyptians' experience with the frogs and the Israelites' fatal encounter with deadly snakes (cf. Num.21.5–9), one might well opt for the frogs – just as one might prefer the fleshpots of Egypt to a diet of manna and occasional quails. The author of *Wisdom* will shortly address just these problems, but he defers them for the moment in order to indulge in a second and a third assault on Egyptian animal worship and idolatry (12.23–27; 15.14–16.1), passages that enclose a broader analysis of the various religious errors of the Gentiles (13.1–15.13).

As the divine judgment on animal worship, the "animal plagues" have led the writer to address two broader issues: first, the comparative leniency of the divine punishment of the ungodly (11.17–12.27), and second, the root causes of the various religious errors, of which the worship of animals is the worst (13.1–15.13). The excursuses on these topics are framed by depictions of the Egyptians' folly (11.15–16; 12.23–27; 15.14–16.1): the author's interest in the symmetries of divine action is matched by the careful structuring of his own exegetical and theological argument.[69] Following the excursuses, the author returns to the format adopted in 11.4–14, where plague and wilderness traditions are compared and contrasted – in the earlier case, the turning of water into blood and the provision of water from a rock. As we shall see, the resumption of this format in 16.2 marks the beginning of an engagement with the narrative of Numbers which puts the author's entire argument under severe strain. The animal plagues are paired with the incidents of the quails (Wis.16.1–4; Num.11.4–35) and the deadly snakes (Wis.16.5–14; Num.21.5–9); the final plague, the destruction of the first-born, is paired with the story of Korah's rebellion (Wis.18.5–25; Num.16.1–17.15). The problem for the author is

---

69. The structure of the whole of *Wisdom* 11–19 is based on the plague and exodus stories of Exodus 7–15: (1) water into blood (Ex.7.14–24; Wis.11.1–14), (2) the animal plagues (Ex.8.1–32, 10.1–20; Wis.11.15–16.14), (3) the fiery hail (Ex.9.13–35; Wis.16.15–29), (4) darkness (Ex.10.21–29; Wis.17.1–18.4), (5) the firstborn (Ex.11.1–23.36; Wis.18.5–25), (6) the exodus (Ex.12.37–15.21; Wis.19.1–9; 19.10–22 is a summary). Exodus 7–15 provides the basic framework into which additional material from Exodus and Numbers is incorporated (even where the additional material is cited first, as in the case of 11.1–14). The usual view, which finds in *Wisdom* 11–19 "an elaborate *syncresis* employing seven antitheses", together with loosely related excursuses on the divine mercy and idolatry (D. Winston, *The Wisdom of Solomon*, p. 11), is therefore misleading. In 11.15–16.14, the excursuses and two of the antitheses all occur within a single discussion of the animal plagues.

that, in the stories from Numbers, *Israel in the desert is subjected to greater divine severity than Egypt has been through the plagues*. These are, we recall, stories of mass death in the desert which illustrate the fate of the entire exodus generation in the aftermath of the Sinai event. In order to maintain his contrast between God's judgment on Egypt and beneficence towards Israel, the author strives to eradicate the motif of death from these stories. In retelling the story of the quails, he simply overlooks this motif (16.1–4). In the story of the serpents, he displaces it onto the Egyptians (16.5–14). In the Korah story, the parallel with the death of the Egyptian first-born forces him to acknowledge it – but only in passing (18.20–25).

The author's problem is specifically with the Book of Numbers. Exodus causes him no comparable difficulties. Exodus includes wilderness as well as plague traditions; in the first of his comparisons, the author has already drawn from Exodus the motif of water from the rock, contrasting this with the first plague (Wis.11.1–14). When he finally completes his extended reflections on the animal plagues and their wider implications (11.15–16.14), the author constructs another Exodus-based analogy between the destruction of the Egyptians' crops by hail and fire (Ex.9.22–35) and the provision of manna to the Israelites (Wis.16.15–29; cf. 19.21). The author is particularly interested in the miraculous imperviousness of ice to fire in the seventh plague (Ex.9.23–24), and finds a parallel in the ice-like manna, which lay "like frost upon the ground" (Ex.16.14) but could still be cooked (Num.11.8) – although it melted in the sun's heat if left to lie upon the ground (Ex.16.21).[70] The author also claims that the taste of the manna was changed to suit everyone's liking (16.20–21, 25), and reflects on the spiritual significance of its arrival early each morning (16.27–29). Following this, the ninth plague – the darkness – is described in vivid detail, with only a brief reference to the pillar of fire that illuminated the night for Israel (17.1–18.4). The author thus draws from the Exodus wilderness traditions the motifs of water from the rock, manna, and the pillar of fire – finding in them a clear demonstration of God's beneficence towards Israel, in contrast to the corresponding divine severity manifested in the first, seventh and ninth plagues. The author can legitimately claim the support of Exodus for his main point – which is that "the creation, serving you its maker, exerts itself for the punishment of the unrighteous, but relaxes into beneficence *[eis euergesian]* towards those who trust in you" (16.24). But whether the Numbers stories of the deluge of quails, the deadly snakes and the devastating plague can be conscripted into the service of such an argument is another matter. The starkly negative Pauline reading seems more in keeping with the tendency of the canonical text.

---

70. For an attempt to make sense of a complex and perhaps confused argument, see S. Cheon, *The Exodus Story in the Wisdom of Solomon*, pp. 56–67.

For the author of *Wisdom*, it is the exodus and not Sinai that marks a dividing-line between judgment and salvation; and those who were judged were not the Israelites but the Egyptians. Stories from Numbers must be compelled to attest the same beneficent divine saving activity as the Exodus stories of the manna and the water from the rock.

In Numbers, the story of the quails can be read as a savage parody of the earlier story of the manna. The quails are to be provided in overwhelming quantities, so that the people will be compelled to eat without respite for an entire month (Num.11.18–20). When this promise or threat is fulfilled, the camp is surrounded by quails to a depth of two cubits, and for a day's journey all round (v.31). Are these quails really a gift, or are they a plague, like the frogs in Egypt? The feasting is cut short by a literal plague which strikes so suddenly that people die with the food still in their mouths (v.33). It is these deaths that are remembered in the place name, Tombs-of-Desire, and not the doubtful gift of the quails (v.34).

In *Wisdom* 16.1–4 the quails are most definitely a divine gift, the exact opposite of the frogs and other creatures that tormented the Egyptians. The frogs were to be found everywhere, even in bedrooms, ovens, kneading bowls and on one's own person (Ex.8.3–4) – from which details the author of *Wisdom* deduces that the Egyptians must have lost their appetites, almost to the point of starvation (Wis.16.3–4).[71] The Israelites on the other hand received an abundance of delicious food, so as to satisfy their appetite; their previous hunger gave them an insight into the far greater suffering of their enemies (vv.2–4). One might suppose that the author draws here not on the Numbers story but on the brief and positive reference to the gift of quails in the Exodus account of the giving of the manna (Ex.16.8, 12–13).[72] That is not the case, however. The later claim that "quails came up from the sea" (Wis.19.12) can only come from the Numbers version of the story (Num.11.31). More importantly, the author has derived from Numbers 11 the motif of "desire" *(epithumia)*, and transformed it. The Israelites' experience of animals from the hand of deity was, he argues, quite different from that of the Egyptians, who were justly punished by the animals they worshipped:

> Instead of such punishment you showed kindness *[euergetēsas]* to your people:

---

71. As in 11.15 and 12.27, the author treats the "animal plagues" as a single entity in 16.1 and is not referring exclusively to the frogs. On this, see S. Cheon, *The Exodus Story in the Wisdom of Solomon*, pp. 42–43. The parallel with Egyptian animal worship requires the scope of the animal plagues to be as broad as possible.

72. The view of M. McGlynn, *Divine Judgment and Divine Benevolence in the Book of Wisdom*, pp. 191–92.

a rare delicacy for appetite's desire *[eis epithumian orexeōs]*,
you prepared quails for food;
so that those [the Egyptians], desiring food *[epithumountes trophēn]*
yet disgusted by the creatures sent to them,
might lose even the necessary appetite *[tēn anagkaian orexin]*,
while these [the Israelites], having briefly suffered want,
might partake even of a rare delicacy.
For inexorable want had to come upon those who oppressed them,
and for them simply to be shown how their enemies were tormented.

(Wis.16.2–4)

In the contrasts here between plain and exotic foods, necessary appetite and desire for delicacies, the author alludes to the scriptural account of the people's demand for a richer diet, and to the immoderate desire that occasioned it (Num.11.4: *epethumēsan epithumian*). At the same time, he makes desire morally neutral, and places the emphasis on the gracious divine initiative that the quails are supposed to represent. In the scriptural narrative, the punitive dimension of the gift is present at the outset, in the motif of eating to the point of nausea (Num.11.19–20), and at the conclusion, where "the people who desired" *(ton laon ton epithumēton)* are struck down as they gorge themselves (11.33–34). In *Wisdom*, this punitive dimension is completely suppressed – or rather, it is displaced onto the Egyptians. The author has noted in the scriptural story the motifs of desire for food, creatures manifesting the divine anger, disgust at these creatures, and death by plague; and he has removed them from a story about the Israelites and transplanted them into a story of the plagues of Egypt, making some necessary adjustments along the way. Thus desire becomes loss of desire, and the punitive creatures are now a deterrent to eating rather than being themselves edible. Death becomes "inexorable want": while the author cannot quite say that the Egyptians starved to death, he places extraordinary emphasis on the suffering caused by their inability to eat. The motif of disgust may also be traced back to Numbers, where – in a divine announcement that remains unfulfilled – it is said that the sated people will find their food loathsome (11.20). Once the offending motifs have been evicted from their original context and rehoused elsewhere, what is left is a story of pure divine beneficence, displaying a wonderful blend of creatorly power and paternal goodness. At the same time, we should note that the new accommodation provided for the displaced motifs is not entirely suitable for them. It is frankly implausible that the Egyptians, plagued by frogs and insects, suffered most from a near-starvation induced by loss of appetite, or that this was the intended point of these plagues.

It seems that the scriptural text has to be substantially rewritten if the narrative of Numbers is to conform to the Exodus paradigm of salvation for God's people and destruction for their enemies. The technique of displacement is especially clear in the author's retelling of the story of the deadly snakes (Num.21.5–9), to which he now turns as he strives to differentiate the punitive from the salvific uses of living creatures.

Unlike the quails, the snakes would seem to be unambiguously punitive. This story has come to mind in the course of the author's extended reflections on the second, third, fourth and eighth plagues, in which God used living creatures to punish the Egyptians (Wis.11.15–16.14). As read by the author, the quail story provides an example of the exact opposite, God using living creatures to benefit the people of Israel. In the story of the snakes, the aim is to show that the punitive element belongs within a broader divine strategy of beneficence towards the holy people, and that this manifestation of divine wrath is fundamentally different to what the Egyptians suffered. The author's initial interpretative move is to connect the onset of the snakes as closely as possible to the divinely ordained means of healing, both being planned in advance with a single goal in mind:

> For when the fearful fury of beasts came upon them,
>   and they were being destroyed by the bites of twisting snakes,
>   your wrath did not continue to the end.
> As a warning *[eis nouthesian]* they were troubled for a short time,
>   having a symbol of salvation as a reminder of your law's command.
> For the one who turned to it was not saved by the visible object,
>   but by you, the Saviour of all. (Wis.16.5–7)

The "warning" constituted by the deadly snakes is assimilated to the "reminder of your law's command" constituted by the "symbol of salvation". The plague of snakes and the divine deliverance represent a *single* event that is both warning and reminder, with the result that judgment is subordinated to salvation and God is manifested as "the Saviour of all".

In the Numbers story, it is said that "many people of the children of Israel died" as a result of the snake bites. Following his intercession on their behalf, Moses is instructed to set up the bronze snake so that "every bitten person seeing it will live" (Num.21.6, 8). For those who have already died, it would seem to be too late. Yet it is just this that the author of *Wisdom* cannot accept. As in the biblical exemplar, there is a shift from plural ("they were troubled") to singular ("the one who turned to it"); but there is also a strong implication that the "symbol of salvation" was available to *all* those who were "troubled", and who were indeed "being destroyed", and that the singular and the plural subjects are coextensive. This interpretation is confirmed by v.11, where it is said that "to remind them of your words they were bitten and swiftly delivered" – once again, a single divine action with a single purpose, and the implication that all who were bitten were healed by God's word which "heals all" (v.12). In order to read the text this way, the author suppresses the scriptural statement that "many people of the sons of Israel died" (Num.21.6), rightly noting that it is not strictly necessary for the coherence of the narrative. Those who were bitten were "being destroyed", they were "troubled", they found themselves at the very "gates of Hades", they were delivered by the God who has "authority over life and death", but they did not literally die. As the motif of the divine wrath has been excised from the quail story, so the motif of death is excised from the story of the snakes.[73]

In the quail story, material that the author found unacceptable was displaced onto the Egyptians: notably the correlation of appetite (or its lack) with living creatures as emissaries of divine judgment, together with the motifs of disgust and of death (which becomes near-death by starvation). A similar but much simpler displacement takes place in the author's rendering of the story of the snakes. It was not the Israelites who died when they were bitten, it was the Egyptians:

> By this means [i.e. the healing miracle] you convinced your enemies
>   that you are the one who delivers from every evil.
> For them the bites of locusts and dogflies killed,
>   and there was found no healing for their soul,
>   since they deserved to be punished by such things;
> But your sons even the teeth of poisonous serpents could not conquer,
>   for your mercy helped and healed them. (Wis.16.8–10)

In the scriptural account of the eighth and the fourth plagues (Ex.10.12–20; 8.16–28 LXX), the Egyptians are neither bitten nor killed by the locusts or the dogflies. The locusts devour the produce of the land, and are described by Pharaoh as "this death" (Ex.10.15–17); the dogflies invade the Egyptians' homes and cover their persons, but do not otherwise harm them. Yet the author of *Wisdom* needs to find a place for the scriptural motif of the fatal bite, and chooses to attach it to the scriptural locusts – perhaps on the basis of Pharaoh's comment – and, more plausibly, to the dogflies. (The frogs were obviously unsuitable for this purpose, but it is curious that the author overlooked the *skniphes* – fleas, ants, gnats? – of the third plague [Ex.8.12–15].)[74]

By transplanting offending material from one context to another, the author solves the fundamental problem posed by the scriptural narrative – which is that the punishment endured by the people of Israel is far more severe than the equivalent punishment of the Egyptians. The issue has already been addressed at a more theoretical level in the earlier discussion of the divine leniency, which also arises out of reflection on the animal plagues (Wis.11.17–12.27). If scripture seems to contradict the principle

---

73. In Philo's two treatments of this story, the scriptural reference to death is acknowledged in one (*Leg.All.* ii.77–87) and overlooked in the other (*Agr.* 95–99). In the latter passage as in *Wisdom*, it is implied that all who were bitten looked at the bronze serpent and lived.

74. The frogs and the insects make an appearance at 19.10, however.

that "while disciplining us you scourge our enemies ten-thousandfold" (12.22), then scripture must be rewritten. Deviations from the Exodus paradigm – salvation for us, punishment for our enemies – are found especially in the Book of Numbers, and the technique of displacement is reserved exclusively for these stories.[75]

The Book of Exodus has already provided a straightforward contrast between the turning of the Nile to blood and the gift of water from the rock, demonstrating that "through the very things whereby their enemies were punished, they themselves received benefit in their need" (Wis.11.5). After the prolonged meditation on the "animal plagues" (11.15–16.14), the author confines himself to Exodus as he constructs a contrast between the seventh plague (hail, mingled with fire) and the gift of manna (16.15–29). In the case of the ninth plague (darkness), the author is primarily interested in the plague itself (17.1–21), but finds the desired contrasts with this in the light enjoyed by the holy nation in the land of Goshen, in the pillar of fire, and in the "imperishable light of the law" (18.1–4). None of this material creates serious difficulties for the author, for the exodus paradigm of judgment and salvation lies at the heart of the Book of Exodus (with the exception of the Golden Calf episode, which is not mentioned here). In his Exodus-related material, the author expands and develops but does not engage in any fundamental rewriting.

There is, however, a third and final story from Numbers to be negotiated. The death of the Egyptian firstborn leads the author to acknowledge that the Israelites did indeed undergo an analogous experience, in the form of the plague that followed Korah's rebellion and killed 14,700 people before it was brought to an end by Aaron's saving intervention (Num.17.6–15 LXX; Wis.18.20–25). As with the story of the snakes, the author hastens from the manifestation of divine wrath to the manifestation of divine saving power:

> Experience of death also touched the righteous,
> > and destruction came upon the multitude in the desert;
> > but the wrath did not endure for long.
> For a blameless man was swift to fight on their behalf,
> > taking the shield of his ministry,
> > prayer and incense for propitiation;
> > he resisted the anger and put an end to the disaster,
> > showing that he was your servant.
>
> (Wis.18.20–21)

---

75. S. Cheon rightly observes that the motif of death has been eliminated from the story of the snakes and that the death of the Egyptians from insect bites is non-scriptural, but does not explain the connection between the two (*The Exodus Story in the Wisdom of Solomon*, pp. 51–56).

In Numbers too, the narrator describes in vivid terms how "wrath went forth from before the Lord and began to destroy the people" (17.11 LXX), and how Aaron, armed with atoning incense, "stood between the dead and the living, and the destruction ceased" (17.13; cf. Wis.18.23). The author of *Wisdom* finds the source of Aaron's victory not simply in the prayer and incense, but also in his vestments, in which were symbolized the entire created order, "the glories of the fathers", and the majesty of God (18.24). More significantly for our purposes, the author transforms the impersonal "wrath" *(orgē)* or "destruction" *(thrausis)* of the Numbers narrative into a personal being against whom Aaron contends in one-to-one combat. While the author of *Wisdom* continues to use the impersonal scriptural language (Wis.18.20, 23), the image of single combat produces a counterpart for Aaron in the form of "the punisher" *(ton kolazonta,* v.22) or "the destroyer" *(ho olethreuōn,* v.25). To Aaron's spiritual weapons "the destroyer yielded, these things he feared" (v.25). "The destroyer" is none other than the angel of death, familiar from the passover narrative (cf. Ex.12.23). This "destroyer" is the sinister power against whom Aaron contends in the retelling of the story from Numbers. In other words, another displacement has occurred – but in the opposite direction to the earlier ones, from Exodus to Numbers rather than from Numbers to Exodus.

Why has the angel of death been transferred from the one book to the other? There appear to be two interrelated reasons for this. First, in the Exodus text "the destroyer" is sharply differentiated from the Lord himself. This means that Aaron can engage him in single combat on the Lord's behalf, and that the Lord is thereby distanced from the activities of the sinister destructive power. Second, the author of *Wisdom* associates the slaughter of the Egyptian firstborn not with "the destroyer" or with the Lord himself, but with the omnipotent divine Logos:

> For while gentle silence enveloped all things,
>   and night in its swift course was half gone,
> Your all-powerful Word leaped from heaven, from the royal throne,
>   a stern warrior, into the midst of the land doomed to destruction,
>   bearing the sharp sword of your authentic command.
> And he stood and filled all things with death,
>   and he touched heaven while standing on earth.

(Wis.18.14–16)

The shadowy "destroyer" (Ex.12.23) here gives way to a terrifying divine emissary who participates in God's own omnipotence.[76] Alternative

---

76. M. McGlynn suggests that the Logos is to be identified with Wisdom (*Divine Judgment and Divine Benevolence in the Book of Wisdom*, p. 209). Wisdom and the Word both proceed from God (7.25, 9.10; 18.15). If the Logos slaughters the Egyptian first-born (18.16)

employment is found for the destroyer in the Korah story. Yet, in the retelling of that story, it is the figure of Aaron who stands out as the true counterpart of the all-powerful Word of the passover retelling. Between them, these two great warrior figures embody God's punishment of his enemies and his saving action on behalf of his people. In other words, they re-enact the exodus paradigm. The technique of displacement is again used to ensure that juxtaposed material from Exodus and Numbers displays that paradigm as clearly as possible.

By such means as this, the author ensures that the books of Exodus and Numbers harmonize with each other. At the back of his mind is perhaps the sceptical objection that, according to the scriptural narrative, God treats his own people worse than he treats their enemies. As the author observes at one point: "Great are your judgments, and hard to explain, so that uninstructed souls have erred" (17.1). It does not occur to him, as it did to Paul, that Exodus and Numbers divide at the Sinai event, the culmination of the one text and the starting-point of the other, and that the situation after that event differed from the situation before it. From his own standpoint, such a reading would have given credence to the age-old (if hypothetical) Egyptian taunt, that the Lord led his people out of Egypt "with evil intent, to slay them in the mountains and to consume them from the face of the earth" (Ex.32.12).

The question that remains is this: what is at stake in the divergence between these two readings of the same narrative texts? Paul exploits the fact that the history of Israel in the aftermath of Sinai is a history of disaster, whereas the author of *Wisdom* does his utmost to conceal this fact. But the two interpreters engage with these scriptural texts because of the contribution they expect them to make to their wider theological projects. How, then, do the respective readings serve their authors' work of theological construction? And at what point do they part company with each other?

The demise of the holy nation

In their readings in the books of Exodus and Numbers, there is at least one small matter about which Paul and the author of *Wisdom* are in agreement. As we have seen, the author of *Wisdom* transfers the figure of "the destroyer" from the passover narrative to the story of Korah's rebellion and the plague that followed it (Wis.18.25). In 1 Corinthians 10.10, Paul repeats this interpretative move when he tells how the people who "complained" (cf. Num.17.6 LXX) were "destroyed by the destroyer". It is unlikely that both interpreters of Numbers inserted this figure into the text independently of each other, and it is at least possible that Paul is here dependent on *Wisdom*. Yet, in 1 Corinthians 10 in conjunction with

Romans 7, Paul exploits the very feature of the Numbers stories that so concerns the author of *Wisdom*: the fact that, according to Numbers, the sequel to the Sinai event is the destruction of all who had stood before the Lord at the mountain and received the law from the hand of Moses. It is just this aspect of Numbers that the author of *Wisdom* seeks to eliminate by means of his technique of displacement. This radical difference of reading perspective cannot be explained merely in terms of Paul's greater fidelity to the scriptural text. Even if such an explanation were partially justified, it would not answer the question *how* one reader can read the text with greater fidelity than another – granted that both are engaged in constructing the sense of the text, and not just reproducing it. The problem, then, is to identify the theological logic underlying the two readings, and, in particular, to identify where it is that they diverge. And at this point, the old issue of Pauline "dependence" on *Wisdom* turns out to be unexpectedly relevant.

Debate on this issue has tended to focus especially on Romans 1 in relation to *Wisdom* 13–14. In the following discussion, the intention is to plot the argument of Romans 1.18–2.5 against the parallel argument in *Wisdom* 13.1–15.6, with particular attention to the point at which they part company. We shall see that it is more appropriate to speak of a Pauline *engagement* with the earlier text rather than of "dependence".[77] Even if Paul's engagement were actually with a shared tradition rather than a specific text, the analysis would still be valid.[78] Yet the cumulative force of the parallels is such that the hypothesis of a shared tradition seems inadequate. There seems no good reason to doubt that Paul is consciously basing his argument on the template provided by *Wisdom*.[79]

The argument of Romans 1.18–32 develops in parallel to *Wisdom* 13.1– 14.31. Although the Pauline passage is only about a quarter of the length of its predecessor, the two passages make a series of similar points in a similar order. Both of them offer an analysis of the Gentile world, and speak of the wasted opportunity of knowing God through the created

77. Richard Bell argues that Paul "was to some extent influenced by Wisdom, but there are some significant differences" (*No one seeks for God*, p. 76). This statement implies that "influence" and "differences" are mutually limiting – a presupposition that also underlies G. Bornkamm's discussion (*Das Ende des Gesetzes*, pp. 18–21), resulting in a static confrontation of polarized positions. In fact, as the following analysis will show, the depth of Paul's engagement with this text is evident precisely at points where he also differs from it.

78. According to Brendan Byrne, Paul here "argues out of a defined tradition in Hellenistic Judaism", so as to "beguil[e] the implied reader with a conventional polemic against the Gentile world and its idolatry" (*Romans*, p. 65; texts illustrative of this tradition include *Ep.Arist.* 132–38, *Sib.Or.* iii.8–45, Josephus *c.Ap.* ii.236–54). Byrne acknowledges that the parallels with *Wisdom* are particularly striking, but does not assume any direct relationship.

79. As is rightly argued by Wilckens, *Römer*, 1.96–97; Dunn, *Romans 1–8*, p. 72.

order, the origins of idolatry and its disastrous social consequences, and
the impending divine judgment on this state of affairs. Naturally there are
differences in the way these themes are treated, and in another context a
full investigation of them would be rewarding. At present, however, the
concern is to trace what the two texts have in common, in order to
highlight their sudden and crucial divergence when they come to speak of
the people of Israel in relation to the Gentile world (Rom.2; Wis.15). This
is the point that will account for the divergence in scriptural hermeneutics.

(i) The true God might have been known by way of the created order, but
the opportunity has been wasted. As we have seen, the author of *Wisdom*
understands the "animal plagues" as the divine punishment for Egyptian
animal worship (11.15–16; 12.23–27), and finds an opportunity here for
broader consideration of Gentile religious errors and their consequences
(13.1–14.31). The first of these is the error of those who fail to "recognize
the craftsman while paying heed to his works" (13.1). Such people were
"worthless" *(mataioi,* 13.1) – or, as Paul puts it, "they became worthless
[emataiōthēsan] in their thinking" (Rom.1.21). God's invisible attributes
are "perceived" *(kathoratai)* in the things God has made (Rom.1.20); that
is to say, "from the greatness and beauty of the creatures their creator is
correspondingly seen *[analogōs theōreitai]*" (Wis.13.5). The syntactic,
semantic and grammatical correlation between the two verbs of seeing is
especially notable, as is the shared use of "knowing" terminology. People
"were unable to know the one who is *[eidenai ton onta]*" (Wis.13.1), and
should perceive *(noēsatōsan)* the creator in the creatures (Wis.13.4). Or
rather, people did know God *(to gnōston tou theou,* Rom.1.19; *gnontes ton
theon,* 1.21, cf. 1.28), but suppressed that knowledge. In both texts, seeing,
perceiving, knowing and recognizing are virtually synonymous. The
creator known through the created order is characterized above all by
his divine "power" (Rom.1.20; Wis.13.4). Those who fail to see this are
"without excuse" (Rom.1.20), "they are not to be excused" (Wis.13.8).
Both authors assert that the creator is manifest in his works, but they do
not reproduce the conventional Stoic argument for the existence of deity,
which sets up an analogy between the world and the products of human
craftsmanship.[80] One reason for this omission may be that, in both cases,

---

80. Cicero puts this argument into the mouth of the Stoic Quintus Lucilius Balbus in the
following terms: "If the works of nature are more perfect than the works of art, then as art
achieves nothing without a conscious purpose, nature itself cannot be thought to be devoid of
such a purpose. When you look at a picture or a statue, you recognize that it is a work of
art... How then can you imagine that the universe as a whole is devoid of purpose and
intelligence, when it embraces everything, including those artefacts themselves and their
artificers?" *(de nat.deo.* ii.87). Paul and the author of *Wisdom* are unlikely to have been so
sanguine about the evidential value of pictures and statues.

certain products of human craftsmanship are about to be severely criticized. *Wisdom* speaks of ignorance and of a possible search for God, whereas Paul speaks of a suppressed knowledge of God stemming from revelation (Wis.13.1, 6–7; Rom.1.18–19, 21, 28); *Wisdom* holds that the way from the creation to God is still open, whereas Paul does not. Nevertheless, the parallels are striking.

(ii) The most fundamental religious error is the manufacture and worship of idols.[81] People turn from the immortal God "to the image of a mortal human or of birds or of four-footed or creeping animals *[tetrapodōn kai herpetōn]*" (Rom.1.23). The author of *Wisdom* also notes that images may represent either humans or animals. The craftsman takes a piece of cast-off wood and "shapes it to the image of a human, or makes it like some worthless animal" (Wis.13.13–14). The animal worshippers do not even select the most beautiful animals for their use, but prefer those that have somehow evaded the divine blessing (Wis.15.18–19). These include the *herpeta*, or "creeping animals" (Wis.11.15). Paul follows *Wisdom* in this special focus on animal images, which stems from the author's anti-Egyptian polemics. The prohibition of animal as well as human images is scriptural (cf. Deut.4.16–18), but the scriptural polemics that underlie *Wisdom* 13.10–15.19 assume that actual functioning images will be human in form. These passages either focus on the figure of the craftsman and the process of manufacture (cf. Wis.13.10–19; 15.7–13), or emphasize the impotence of the idols, with their non-functioning eyes, ears, hands and feet (cf. Wis.15.15). The craftsman motif derives from Isaiah 44.9–20, where the craftsman is said to shape "the figure of a man" (Is.44.13), and the impotence motif derives from Psalm 115.5–7, where the idols have "hands" and are clearly human. The interest in animal images is therefore distinctive to *Wisdom*, and it is also reflected in the Pauline statement. It is striking, however, that Paul interprets idolatry without recourse to either of the scriptural motifs, finding in it a service of the creature rather than the creator (Rom.1.25). Paul thereby conflates the worship of divine and of human artefacts, carefully distinguished by the author of *Wisdom* (Wis.13.1–9, 10–19). Pauline dependence on *Wisdom* also expresses a degree of independence.[82]

81. The distinction in *Wisdom* 13 between the worship of created beings and of idols is also drawn by Philo (*dec.* 66; *spec.leg.* i.13–22) – although Philo connects this distinction to the first two commandments of the decalogue, and is prepared to accept that the heavenly bodies may be described as "gods" in a secondary sense.

82. On the other hand, John Barclay suggests that the polemic against idolatry in *Wisdom* displays greater subtlety than Paul's "in noting different forms of non-Jewish cult" (*Jews in the Mediterranean Diaspora*, p. 392). The Pauline conflation might be regarded either as a crude misunderstanding or as a sign of theological sophistication.

(iii) Idolatry is the root of all other evils. In Romans, this is because God "gave up" the idolators first to sexual sins (1.24–25, 26–27) and then to all kinds of social disorder (1.28–31). While the author of *Wisdom* does not find any divine involvement here, he too believes that "the idea of making idols is the beginning of fornication, and their invention the corruption of life" (Wis.14.12), and that "the worship of unmentionable idols is the beginning and cause and end of every evil" (Wis.14.27). Both authors illustrate this point with a list of typical vices (Wis.14.25–26; Rom.1.29–31). The general tenor of these lists is similar, although only two words ("murder" and "deceit") occur in both. In the *Wisdom* vice list, sexual and non-sexual vices are listed together, whereas Paul sets sexual vices apart for separate treatment (Rom.1.24–27). His view of homosexual practice as a corruption of the male/female relationship given in creation may reflect *Wisdom*'s reference to "sexual perversion *[geneseōs enallagē]*, disorder in marriage" (Wis.14.26). The apparent echo of the earlier author's "exchange" terminology is to be noted (*metēllaxan*, Rom.1.26).

(iv) Those who commit such sins are subject to the divine punishment. For Paul, these people are aware of the divine decree "that those who do such things are worthy of death" (Rom.1.32) – and yet they continue to do and to approve them. *Wisdom* claims that they are subject to "just penalties" *(ta dikaia)* for their errors about deity and for their false oaths (Wis.14.30). When they suffer after swearing falsely, that is a manifestation not of the anger of their non-existent gods but of "justice for those who have sinned", which "always overtakes the transgression of the unrighteous" (Wis.14.31). The author also hints at a general eschatological judgment of the idols (Wis.14.11).

As this analysis shows, Romans 1.18–32 follows *Wisdom* 13–14 not just at individual points but in the whole construction of the argument. Both writers argue that the true God might have been known by way of the created order, but that the opportunity has been wasted; that the most fundamental religious error is the manufacture and worship of idols; that idolatry is the root of all other evils; and that those who commit such sins are subject to the divine punishment. While the differences are real and important, there appears to be little or nothing in either text with which the author of the other would have disagreed.

This close relationship between the two texts has major implications for the interpretation of Romans 2, and especially for the opening of the chapter. In a startling rhetorical move, Paul singles out an individual who appears to agree with his own analysis of the depravity of the Gentiles, and accuses him of the very vices that he condemns:

> You have no defence, then, you who sit in judgment, whoever you may
> be – for when you judge another you pass judgment on yourself, since
> you the judge are guilty of the same things. (Rom.2.1)

The judge is not explicitly addressed as a Jew (cf. 2.17), but there are good
grounds for concluding that Paul has a fellow-Jew in mind from the
beginning of the chapter.[83] If so, however, Paul addresses him anonymously – as one who believes himself to have escaped the nexus of human
sin and guilt, and to have found a secure place from which to observe,
criticize and deplore. What is opposed here is the idea that certain people
stand outside and apart from the scene described in the previous chapter,
occupying some place of safety untouched by idolatry, sexual sin, and
violence. For the critic, the place of safety is founded and guaranteed by
"the wealth of [God's] kindness and forbearance and patience" (cf. 2.4),
which ensures immunity from the divine wrath that is coming upon the
entire world. Paul's address aims to show that this place of safety is a
house built upon sand.

This unexpected attack on the critic occurs at the very point where, in
the parallel text, the author of *Wisdom* turns from the depravity of the
Gentiles in order to meditate on the divine kindness and patience as
experienced by God's own people:

> But you, our God, are kind *[chrēstos]* and true, patient *[makrothumos]*
>   and ruling all things in mercy.
> For if we sin we remain yours, knowing your power;
>   but we will not sin, knowing that we are reckoned as yours.
> For to know you is perfect righteousness, and to acknowledge your
>   power is the root of immortality.
> For neither has the wicked purpose of human art deceived us, nor the
>   fruitless labour of painters...
>
> (Wis.15.1–4)

It is just such a position as this that Paul caricatures in Romans 2.[84] Here,
God is addressed as "our God" – not just as the creator whom the idol-
worshippers have failed to recognize, but as the God of Israel. Thus, those
who speak here in the first person plural are twice characterized as "yours"

---

83. See my *Paul, Judaism and the Gentiles*, pp. 109–10; S. J. Gathercole, *Where is
Boasting?*, pp. 197–200.

84. The relevance of *Wisdom* 15 for the interpretation of Romans 2 is pointed out by,
among others, C. H. Dodd, *Romans*, p. 58. In the *Wisdom* passage, the appeal to the kindness
and patience of God is rooted in Exodus 34.6, as H. Hübner emphasizes (*Die Weisheit
Salomons*, pp. 183–84). The fact that Paul attacks the mentality expressed here does not make
it "unscriptural" – rather, it is an indication that what is or is not "scriptural" is always
contested. Paul's caricature already reflects his own interpretation of the scriptural verdict on
the chosen people (cf. Rom.3.9–20).

(Wis.15.2). They are "your people" (12.19; 15.14; 16.2, 20; 19.5, 22), "your sons, whom you loved" (16.26; cf. 12.19, 18.4), "your holy ones" (18.1, 5), "the children of God" (12.7). They are "a holy people and a blameless race" (10.15), "the holy nation" (17.2), "the righteous" (10.20; 12.9; 18.20). Their "righteousness" is found in the knowledge of a God who is kind, patient and merciful (15.1–3), who can therefore deal gently with them in their human weakness (cf. 12.8a). While their righteousness may not take the form of a sinless perfection, they have at least renounced the cardinal sin of idolatry, the root cause of all other sins, and they feel nothing but contempt for those who practise it. This contempt comes to expression in the author's extended polemics, the aim of which is to assert the non-negotiable *difference* between the righteous and the unrighteous. The knowledge of God as "our God" is of a piece with the recognition that the rest of humanity is utterly alienated from this God. The dire consequences of this alienation from God are vividly depicted in the Exodus narrative, and the positive content of this same narrative can be summed up as follows:

> For in everything, Lord, you have exalted and glorified your people, and you have not failed to help them at all times and in all places. (Wis.19.22)

Here the book concludes, linking the divine goodness indissolubly to the well-being of the holy nation.[85]

While Paul can still speak of the "advantage" of the Jewish people (Rom.3.1), he does not believe that the difference between Jew and Gentile is the difference between the righteous and the unrighteous. There is, he claims, no place at which one might set oneself up as judge and critic, for one is already deeply implicated in precisely the vices one is most eager to denounce in others. Thus, having shadowed the author of *Wisdom* so closely in Romans 1, Paul now turns to him and denounces him – or rather, he denounces the outlook that the earlier author represents. Indeed, Paul appears consciously to use the language of the other text against it. *Wisdom* appeals to the kindness and patience of God (Wis.15.1), and Paul accuses his addressee of presuming on precisely those divine attributes (Rom.2.4a). When Paul reminds his interlocutor that "the kindness of God leads you to repentance *[eis metanoian]*" (Rom.2.4b), he is dependent on the teaching of *Wisdom* itself, that the divine mercy "overlook[s] the sins of humans for the sake of repentance *[eis metanoian]*" (Wis.12.23).

---

85. As John Barclay notes, "the conflictual tone of the Exodus stories both matches and shapes [the author's] perception of social relations between Jews and Gentiles" (*Jews in the Mediterranean Diaspora*, p. 189).

As for the claim to be untainted by idolatry, Paul has already alluded to the Golden Calf story as a preliminary indication that the scene described in Romans 1 really does include everyone. The allusion is unmistakable:

> *And they exchanged the glory* of the immortal God *for the likeness* of the image of a mortal human or of birds or four-footed or creeping animals. (Rom.1.23)

> *And they exchanged the glory* that was theirs *for the likeness* of a grass-eating calf.
>
> (Ps.105.20)

Here, Paul faces the fact that the author of *Wisdom* strives to suppress: that the holy nation is itself deeply complicit in the idolatry and ungodliness that it prefers to ascribe to the Gentiles. When the author of *Wisdom* denies any involvement in the worship of images and castigates the Egyptians for their worship of animals, this is just another example of his technique of displacement. The earlier author fails to mention the Golden Calf, preferring to maintain the righteousness of the holy people by projecting their unrighteousness onto the Gentiles. That for Paul is to pervert the truth of God and the sacred scriptures.

Paul and the author of *Wisdom* are agreed that the scriptural narrative of Exodus and Numbers bears paradigmatic witness to the nature of divine saving action. The earlier author finds here a virtually unqualified distinction between God's saving action towards the holy people and his punitive action towards their enemies. By way of the technique of displacement, the narrative is rewritten along these lines. In contrast, Paul chooses not to conceal the fact that the gift bestowed at Sinai led immediately to catastrophe, but rather to highlight it and to find paradigmatic significance in it. The catastrophe is the subversion of the law's conditional promise that "the one who does these things will live by them", an offer that was immediately overtaken by the reality of sin and death. Against this dark background, the unconditional divine promise to Abraham and to the whole world stands out all the more brightly. Numbers represents the negative corollary of Genesis. Together, these texts speak not of the saving benefits bestowed on the holy nation, but of the justification of the ungodly.

Part Four

Last Words

Chapter 9

Deuteronomy (1)

On eight occasions, Paul explicitly quotes texts from Deuteronomy, introducing them with his standard citation formula ("as it is written ... ") or some variant of it. In addition, there are at least five clear allusions, several of which are virtually indistinguishable from citations – apart from the lack of an introductory formula. There is also the anomalous case in which the words of Deuteronomy are placed in the mouth of a personified theological concept, the Righteousness of faith. Arranged in their original scriptural order, the thirteen Deuteronomy passages fall into two main categories. Paul draws five of his citations and allusions from Moses' long second address to "all Israel", especially from its later chapters (Deut.5– 26). The remaining eight are drawn from the final chapters of the book (Deut.27–34), which constitute a "testament of Moses" consisting of farewell addresses within a narrative framework. These citations can be further subdivided: some are drawn from the warnings and appeals of chapters 27–30, others from the "Song of Moses" (ch.32). Paul's interest in the closing chapters of Deuteronomy is already evident. In these chapters, it becomes clear that the promised land is already forfeit. On the verge of the land and at the culmination of the pentateuchal story, the hope of possessing the land is already undermined by the certainty that the land will be lost.

The ending of any text may be expected to have particular significance, as resolution is achieved, or a pattern brought to completion, or a crucial point reinforced. The ending is the point at which the reader may contemplate the significance not just of the individual parts but also of the whole. It is no surprise, then, that Paul and his contemporaries pay close attention to the ending of the complex text they know as "the Law of Moses". As the completion of his own life drew near, what did Moses have to say to his contemporaries and to later generations? Granted the diversity of his recorded utterances from this time, where are his readers to place the emphasis? Moses' last word to the people of Israel might be found in "the curse of the law", the theme that dominates Deuteronomy 27–29. Or it might be found in the hope that, beyond the curse and the exile and dispersion to which it leads, the law's blessing will finally be realized as the nation at last returns to the law (Deut.30). Or it might be found in the Song of Moses, where the sombre picture of national apostasy is transformed not by a return to the law but by the saving intervention of Israel's God (Deut.32). These alternative construals of the ending of Torah, Pauline and otherwise, will be the main concern of this chapter and the following one.

Deuteronomy is more than an ending, however. Paul also draws from it rules of conduct for the guidance of the Christian community.

The Commandments of God

The citations or allusions Paul draws from Moses' second address (Deut.5–26) all relate to individual laws. In four out of five cases, these are laws or commandments with direct practical applications within the Christian community (Deuteronomy 21.23, cited in Galatians 3.13, is the exception). Thus, the Corinthians are to love the Lord their God (Deut.6.5; 1 Cor.8.3); they are to expel notorious evildoers from their midst (Deut.13.7; 1 Cor.5.13); their guilt must be confirmed by two or three witnesses – that is, by two or three Pauline visitations (Deut.19.15; 2 Cor.13.1); and they are not to muzzle a threshing ox – that is, withhold material support from itinerant evangelists (Deut.25.4; 1 Cor.9.8–10). Paul's appeal to these texts may be related to his paradoxical claim that "neither circumcision counts for anything nor uncircumcision, but keeping the commandments of God" (1 Cor.7.17). On the one hand, the Corinthians are subject to the commandments of God, as recorded in the Law of Moses. On the other hand, they are not necessarily subject to them in their literal form – as the claim about the indifference of circumcision already indicates, and as the later citation of commandments about oxen and witnesses will confirm. The difference between the treatment of the law in 1 Corinthians and in Galatians and Romans may be related to the fact that, in the former, three of the four Deuteronomy citations or allusions are drawn from Moses' second speech, whereas in the latter, six out of seven citations are drawn from the concluding "testament".[1]

---

1. According to J. W. Drane, the Paul of Galatians presents himself as an apostle of "freedom", whereas in 1 Corinthians his stance is that of a "legalism" with a tendency towards "early catholicism" (*Paul: Libertine or Legalist?*, *passim*; see H. Hübner's positive assessment, *Law in Paul's Thought*, pp. 7–10). While Drane's terminology and conceptuality are now dated, the difference he notes is real. It stems in part from the different type of scriptural material employed, and the different uses to which it is put.

(i) Deuteronomy 6.4b–5

In Deuteronomy this passage follows the recitation of the ten commandments that opens Moses' second speech, together with some further
reflection on the circumstances in which the commandments were first
uttered (Deut.5). The commandment to love the one God of Israel is not
an addition to the decalogue. Rather, it has to do with the fundamental
orientation towards the God who speaks in the decalogue and in the
further commandments, which have not yet been specified:

> Hear, Israel: the Lord our God is one Lord *[heis kurios estin]*. And you
> shall love the Lord your God with your whole heart and your whole soul
> and your whole strength.[2]

Paul alludes to this passage as he opens his discussion of "food offered to
idols" *(eidōlothuta)* in 1 Corinthians 8. A Corinthian claim to "know"
that there is one God, and that the deities represented by the idols are non-
existent, is subjected to criticism. What matters is (as Deuteronomy says)
to *love* the God who is one: "If anyone loves God, that person is known by
him" (1 Cor.8.3). Despite the oneness of "the Lord our God", a distinction
is drawn between the "one God" and the "one Lord Jesus Christ" (v.6).
An allusion to Deuteronomy is clearly present here, in spite of the absence
of the distinctive imperative, "Hear".[3] A connection might be made with
the Israel typology that Paul later develops in his discussion of food
offered to idols (1 Cor.10.1–22).

(ii) Deuteronomy 13.6, etc.

A false prophet or a dreamer of dreams, who proposes the worship of
other gods, supporting his proposal with signs and wonders, represents a
divinely ordained test of loyalty. He is to be put to death: in that way,
"you shall remove the evil *[ton ponēron]* from your midst" (Deut.13.6).
This concluding phrase is repeated with minor variations in other cases
where the death penalty is imposed: in the case of the man or woman who
worships other gods (17.7), the person who disregards the verdict of priest
or judge (17.12), the false witness (19.19), the stubborn and rebellious son
(21.21), the non-virginal bride (22.21), the partners in adultery (22.22–24

---

2. The inclusion of *estin* in v.4 LXX resolves the ambiguity of the Hebrew syntax (on
which see R. D. Nelson, *Deuteronomy*, pp. 89–91), and represents an early interpretation of
the Hebrew.

3. N. T. Wright argues that Paul here "glosses 'God' with 'the Father', and 'Lord' with
'Jesus Christ', adding in each case an explanatory phrase" – thereby producing a
christological redefinition of the *Shema* (*The Climax of the Covenant*, p. 129).

[×2]), and the one who forcibly enslaves a fellow-Israelite (24.7).[4] In 1 Corinthians 5.13, Paul applies this stock phrase from Deuteronomy to a case of *porneia* in which "a man has had intercourse with his father's wife" (v.1);[5] he replaces the second singular future introduced by *kai* with a second plural aorist imperative, but otherwise cites it verbatim.[6] There is no citation formula.[7] Paul claims that this case contravenes even the normally low moral standards of the Gentiles, but he may also have Leviticus 20.11 in mind: "If anyone lies with his father's wife, he has uncovered his father's nakedness; let them both be put to death, they are guilty" (cf. also Lev.18.8; Deut.27.20). The offender is to be formally expelled from the congregation and delivered to Satan, and it is here that Paul has recourse to the text from Deuteronomy: "Remove the evil from your midst" (1 Cor.5.13). Both in Deuteronomy and in Paul, this instruction concludes the discussion of the particular case, and expresses a concern to preserve the purity of the community, which the offender has compromised.[8]

(iii) Deuteronomy 19.15

When a person is charged with an offence, the testimony of a single witness is not sufficient: "By the mouth of two witness, and by the mouth of three witnesses, shall every accusation be established." Paul quotes this text, in slightly abbreviated form and without a citation formula, in 2 Corinthians 13.1. He himself charges the Corinthians with a variety of crimes (cf. 12.21). The third witness may be the third visit he is about to make (13.1); alternatively, or additionally, it may take the form of the present letter, following as it does upon the second visit. Since the Deuteronomy text speaks of the "mouth" of the witnesses, Paul

---

4. A different verb is used in 13.6 LXX; "from Israel" rather than "from among you" in 17.12, 22.22.

5. For this sense of *echein*, cf. 1 Corinthians 7.2.

6. It is not clear that Paul takes *ton ponēron* to refer to "the evildoer" rather than, "the evil".

7. Did Paul expect his readers to recognize the Deuteronomy allusion, in the absence of a citation formula? According to Christopher Tuckett, "it is hard to see that this would have been picked up in any way by Paul's audience..." ("Paul, Scripture and Ethics", p. 416). But if the Corinthian congregation consisted largely of Gentiles who had been on the fringe of Judaism (p. 411), it is not at all unlikely that they should have recognized what is, after all, a stereotyped formula in Deuteronomy.

8. So Brian Rosner, *Paul, Scripture, and Ethics*, pp. 61–64. Rosner also shows that the vices listed in 1 Corinthians 5.11 can be correlated with the various contexts in which the cited phrase, "Remove the wicked person from among you" (v.13) occurs in Deuteronomy: this may be applied to the *pornos* (Deut.22.21), the idolator (Deut.17.3, 7), the reviler (Deut.19.18–19), the drunkard (Deut.21.20–21), and the thief (Deut.24.7) – leaving only the *pleonektēs* unaccounted for (*ibid.*, p. 69).

emphasizes that, whether present or absent, he still "speaks" to those who have sinned – in person or in writing (v.2). Multiple accusations from a single witness are, however, obviously not the same thing as a single accusation from two or three witnesses. Paul can therefore place little argumentative weight on the scriptural text, which he uses for rhetorical effect.[9]

(iv) Deuteronomy 21.23

As noted above, laws to which the death penalty is attached frequently conclude with the formula, "And you shall remove the evil from your midst". That is the case with the law of the stubborn and rebellious son, publicly branded by his own parents as "a glutton and a drunkard" who refuses to obey them (Deut.21.18–21). A further law is appended to this, which concerns the corpse of the executed person:

> And if there shall be in any person an offence bearing the death penalty, and he dies, and you hang him upon the wood, his body shall not remain all night upon the wood, but you shall bury him that same day: for accursed by God is everyone hanged upon the wood *[kekatēramenos hupo theou pas kekramenos epi xulou]*. And you shall not defile the land, which the Lord your God gives you for an inheritance. (Deut.21.22–23)

In the statement cited by Paul, "everyone hanged upon a gibbet" (LXX) is fuller than the Masoretic text's single-word reference to the hanged person *(tlwy)*. Both the Hebrew and the Greek terms are broad enough to cover either a "tree" or a wooden artefact such as a pole, a gibbet or a cross. In both cases, it is assumed that the death penalty has already been carried out by means other than hanging – for example, by stoning, as in the case of the rebellious son (Deut.21.21). The five kings of the Amorites have already been put to death, presumably by the sword, when Joshua hangs them upon five trees or gibbets. Joshua ensures that the law is strictly observed:

> And they hung upon the gibbets until evening. And when the sun went down, Joshua gave orders, and they removed them from the gibbets and threw them into the cave in which they had taken refuge, and they rolled stones against the mouth of the cave, to this day. (Josh.10.26–27)

Similarly, Joshua hanged the king of Ai "upon a gibbet *[epi xulou didumou]*", once again removing the body before sunset (Josh.8.29); it is

---

9. V. P. Furnish argues that "in Palestinian Judaism the Deuteronomic rule was widely used to support the requirement that persons suspected of wrongdoing should be carefully forewarned about the possibility of punitive action against them", and that "Paul's quotation of the rule makes good sense" (*II Corinthians*, p. 575). The Qumran texts cited (p. 569) do not appear to bear out this claim.

probably assumed that death took place prior to hanging, although this is not entirely clear. In both cases, Joshua's scrupulous observance of the law contrasts with David's apparent ignorance of it when he handed over members of Saul's family to be hanged by the men of Gibeon (2 Sam.21.1–14). As this latter story shows, the expectation was that a corpse that remained exposed would be devoured by wild animals and birds of prey. The Deuteronomy law thus ensures that the executed person receives a proper burial, even though that is not its primary purpose.

The extension of this law to those who are put to death by hanging or crucifixion occurs by way of a piece of legal exegesis that can now be reconstructed. The exegetical logic of this move can be traced by comparing the commandment in its Masoretic form to the equivalent passage in the *Temple Scroll*. In the translations that follow, italics represent the words that are not common to both passages; curved brackets identify a passage that is transposed in the later text; and empty square brackets indicate a Hebrew connective which must be omitted in translation for the sake of the sense.

> *And* if there shall be in any person an offence bearing the death penalty, {and he shall die}, and you shall hang him upon a tree, [ ] his body shall not remain all night upon a tree, for you shall bury him that same day; for accursed of God is the hanged person. And you shall not defile the land, which the Lord your God gives you for an inheritance. (Deut.21.22–23 MT)

> If there shall be in any person an offence bearing the death penalty, *and he escapes among the Gentiles and curses his people, the children of Israel,* [ ] you shall hang him *also* upon *the* gibbet, {and he shall die}; and his body shall not remain all night upon the gibbet, for you shall bury him that same day; for accursed of God *and humans* is the person hanged *upon the gibbet*. And you shall not defile the land, which I give you for an inheritance. (11Q19 lxiv.9–13)[10]

An initial interpretative problem stems from the lack of any clear linguistic marker for the beginning of the apodosis, the sequel to the protasis or conditional clause that opens this passage. The *ky*- clause is followed by a series of clauses introduced by the connective *w*-, with no indication where description stops and prescription begins. The Septuagint assumes (like the above translation of the MT) that prescription begins with "his body shall not remain all night … ", which therefore lacks a connective. In the *Temple Scroll*, on the other hand, "you shall hang him … " is already prescription,

---

10.   The insertion of the definite article in all three occurrences of *'s* justifies the translation "gibbet" rather than "tree". In the inclusion of "on the gibbet" in the reference to the curse, the *Temple Scroll* agrees with LXX against MT.

not description, as is, "… and he shall die". We might describe this as a "maximalist" (or maximally prescriptive) reading of the Deuteronomy text, in contrast to the Septuagint's "minimalist" reading.[11]

In the *Temple Scroll*, the second main interpretative move in relation to the scriptural exemplar is the specification of a distinct situation: an individual has sought to evade a merited death penalty by taking refuge among Gentiles and renouncing his own people. The individual has presumably been apprehended, and is now liable to the death penalty.[12] Since it is no longer assumed that criminals (or their corpses) will be hung on a gibbet as a matter of course, actions must be identified that merit this scripturally warranted punishment. This leads to the third element in the interpretation, the transposition of "and he shall die", on the assumption that hanging is a mode of execution, not just of exposure. Hermeneutically, the transposition operates on the basis of an analogy between the situation explicitly covered by a law and the situation for which one now seeks to legislate. In this case, an analogy is assumed between the corpse that is exposed on a tree and the person who is hung alive on a gibbet or cross. The analogy is deduced from the statement that the hanged person is accursed by God, understood now as a general principle that applies to a living person enduring execution as well as to the corpse specified in scripture.

This deuteronomic law, extended to apply to crucifixion, may be presupposed in the gospel accounts of Jesus' burial – although Mark and John, who are the most explicit at this point, attribute Joseph of Arimathea's action to the imminence of the sabbath (Mk.15.42, Jn.19.31, cf. Lk.23.54).[13] Be that as it may, a tradition about Jesus' burial on the evening after he died may underlie Paul's appeal to Deuteronomy 21.23 in Galatians 3.13. In Paul's citation, "Cursed by God…"

11. That the *Temple Scroll* takes the apodosis to begin at "you shall hang…" is evident from the parallel case in 11QT lxiv.6–8, where "you shall hang…" can only be prescription rather than description (lxiv.8).

12. This is actually the second such case to be described. The preceding lines speak of a person who "passes on information against his people, and betrays his people to a foreign nation, and does evil against his people"; here too, the reference to hanging precedes the reference to death (11QT lxiv.6–8). In lxiv.8–9, the deuteronomic order is restored: on the evidence of two or three witnesses, "he shall die and they shall hang him on the wood". Here, "they shall hang" specifies the mode of death, rather than the sequel to an execution carried out by other means. "Also" in lxiv.10 refers back to this previous case.

13. In the *Gospel of Peter*, the law from Deuteronomy is conflated with the presentation in the canonical gospels. At the request of Joseph, and before Jesus has been crucified, Pilate asks Herod for the body, so that Joseph may bury it. Herod is here seen as representing "the Jews" who are solely responsible for Jesus' crucifixion (cf. 1.1). He replies: "Brother Pilate, even if no one had requested him, we should bury him, since the Sabbath is drawing on. For it is written in the law: The sun shall not set on one who has been put to death" (*Gospel of Peter*, 2.5).

[kekatēramenos hupo theou] is replaced by "Cursed..." *[epikataratos]*, which assimilates this passage to the opening words of Deuteronomy 27.26 (cited in Galatians 3.10): "Cursed is everyone... *[epikataratos pas...]*" The connection between the two Deuteronomy texts is essential to Paul's argument at this point.[14] A curse is pronounced on "everyone who does not abide by all things written in the book of the law to do them", but a curse is also pronounced on "everyone who is hanged upon the wood". The former text underlies the claims that "Christ redeemed us from the curse of the law"; the latter supports the claim that he did so by "becoming a curse for us" (Gal.3.13).

Deuteronomy 21.23 enables Paul to speak of the *manner* of the redemption achieved by Christ – in particular, that this involves his entering fully into the dire state of those needing to be redeemed. In his crucifixion, Christ himself was subject to the very curse from which he seeks to liberate others: and Paul *learns* this from the Deuteronomy text, rather than merely using it to confirm what he already knows.

As in the other passages that Paul draws from Moses' second speech, the scriptural text functions as a valid piece of legislation and not as a prophecy of Christ.[15] Rather than speaking directly of Christ, it refers to *everyone* hanged upon the wood – including Christ. Of course, not everyone who is hanged upon the wood becomes a curse *for us*, as Christ does; Paul cannot extract the saving significance of the crucifixion from Deuteronomy. What he can do is to reflect on the scriptural connection between public execution and the divine curse, and to ask what light that connection sheds on the redemption Christ has achieved. The Christ who is subject to the divine curse disclosed in the law is a Christ who is himself "under law" (Gal.4.4) – a Jewish Messiah in solidarity especially with "those who are of works of law", who are subject to the curse the law pronounces on all who transgress it (cf. 3.10).[16] If those who seek to observe the law are accursed, they are for that very reason Christ-like, participating in the costly sacrificial act that secures the redemption of the world. Although Paul himself does not draw attention to this point, it is an obvious corollary of his juxtaposition of the two Deuteronomy

14. So J. D. G. Dunn, *Galatians*, pp. 177–78. The omission of the reference to God also corresponds to "the curse of the law" in v.13a, which may imply some distinction between the agency of the law and that of God, as in Romans 8.3–4 (so J. L. Martyn, *Galatians*, pp. 320–21). See the fuller discussion of both points in B. H. McClean, *The Cursed Christ*, pp. 134–38. For further indications of assimilation between the Deuteronomy passages and Leviticus 18.5, see D.-A. Koch, *Die Schrift als Zeuge des Evangeliums*, p. 120.

15. The retention of *pas* implies that Paul does not read 21.23 as straightforward prophecy, as argued by J. M. Lieu, *Neither Jew nor Greek?*, pp. 157–58.

16. A "substitutionary" interpretation of "for us" (as advocated by B. H. McClean, *The Cursed Christ*, pp. 126–27, and others) would seem to undermine that solidarity.

texts.[17] If "those who are of works of law" may be identified with "Israel, who pursued the law of righteousness", but did so mistakenly, "as if by works" (Rom.9.31–32), then "Israel" is subject to the divine curse not on its own but by virtue of its fleshly and spiritual kinship to the cursed Christ. Without Deuteronomy 21.23, however, we would know nothing of a cursed Christ.

(v) Deuteronomy 25.4

In both asserting and renouncing his right to material support from the congregations he founds, Paul does not rely merely on human and pragmatic considerations, but can also appeal to what is said by "the law", to what is written "in the Law of Moses" (1 Cor.9.8–9a). The argument assumes the divine authorship and the enduring validity of the law. It also indicates that Paul's normal term, "the law", can be seen as an abbreviation of the full title of this text, which is "the Law of Moses" – a phrase unattested elsewhere in Paul. The specific law cited here states: "You shall not muzzle the threshing ox" (1 Cor.9.9b).[18] The humane principle underlying this commandment is that "the one who ploughs should plough in hope, and the one who threshes, in hope of partaking" (v.10). Paul assumes that the commandment is to be understood analogically – a standard hermeneutical move when interpreting a legal text. Yet he also assumes that the analogy cancels out the primary meaning: God is *not* concerned about oxen, but God *is* concerned that those who labour in his service should have their material needs met. The meaning of the commandment is that those who labour in God's service are not to be deprived of their material requirements; positively formulated, "Let those who are taught the word share all good things with their teacher" (Gal.6.6). The law's commandment is still normative, but it is so only in the form it assumes as a text written "entirely for our sake" (1 Cor.9.10).[19]

Paul's repeated claim that the commandment in question was written "for our sake" may be compared to his later assertion that the story of

17. The solidarity between Israel and Christ is also implied in Romans 11.15, where Israel's temporary rejection *(apobolē)* leads to the world's reconciliation – just as in the case of Christ himself (cf. Rom.5.10). On this see N. T. Wright, *The Climax of the Covenant*, p. 248.

18. Paul's citation corresponds exactly to the LXX form of this commandment – if, with P[46], א and the majority, we read *phimōseis* rather than *kēmōseis* (B D F G). In the parallel at 1 Timothy 5.19, D (or its exemplar) has unquestionably replaced *phimōseis* with *kēmōseis*.

19. Remarkably, Paul chooses not to obey this normative commandment, but rather "allows the *imitatio Christi* paradigm (renunciation of privilege for the sake of others) to override all particular ethical rules and prescriptions, even when the rule is a direct command of scripture" (R. Hays, *Echoes of Scripture*, p. 225n).

Israel's experience in the wilderness "was written for our instruction, upon whom the ends of the ages have come" (1 Cor.10.11). On this view, the scriptural texts have a unique applicability to the present eschatological moment, which enables them to speak out their true meaning and to disclose their real significance as never before. In so doing, the texts abandon any claim to recall us to a normative and sacred past; rather, they come to meet us in a normative present, and this present must determine how they are to be understood. The present moment marks the eschatological turning-point between the old order that is passing away and the dawning of the new age (cf. 1 Cor.7.29–31). If it can be said of "food" and "the stomach" that "God will destroy both the one and the other" (6.13), and that "flesh and blood cannot inherit the kingdom of God" (15.50), the same can also be said of the ox and the grain it threshes. At this critical turning-point, material things are significant only insofar as they further the service of God: that is the hermeneutical assumption underlying Paul's appropriation of the Deuteronomy text.[20]

Although Paul believes that the Deuteronomy text concerns not oxen but Christian ministers such as himself and Barnabas, he also offers a secondary or intermediate interpretation in which the text applies not to oxen but rather to human agricultural labourers. After claiming that the text expresses the divine concern not for oxen but for "us", Paul continues: "For on our account it was written that in hope should the ploughman plough, and the thresher in hope of a share" (1 Cor.9.10). This statement recalls the rhetorical questions of v.7: "Who plants a vineyard, and receives no share of its fruit? Or who tends a flock, and receives no share of the milk?" While the examples of the ploughman and the thresher make exactly the same point, they are introduced with the phrase, "it was written that...". Since the statement that follows corresponds to no known scriptural text, it is best understood as an interpretative paraphrase of the Deuteronomy text just cited.[21] On the basis of "You shall not muzzle a threshing ox", Paul arrives at the positive corollary that the (human) thresher should participate in the fruit of his labours, and likewise the ploughman. This transfer of the commandment from the animal into the

---

20. Paul's appropriation of this text may have been influenced by its complete isolation within its context in Deuteronomy, where it stands between passages on corporal punishment (Deut.25.1–3) and levirate law (25.5–10); so R. Hays, *First Corinthians*, p. 151. Attempts to connect v.4 to its context (see R. D. Nelson, *Deuteronomy*, pp. 295–97) are unconvincing.

21. Most commentators separate the reference to scripture from the examples of the ploughman and thresher, translating *hoti* as "for" rather than "that": "For our sake it was written – for..." But *egraphē hoti* introduces a scriptural citation in Romans 4.23–24 (again with *di' hēmas*) – in spite of G. Fee's assurance that "nowhere else does Paul use the aorist passive as an introductory formula to a quotation" (*1 Corinthians*, p. 409n); and *gegraptai hoti* introduces a summary rather than a citation in Galatians 4.22.

human sphere represents an intermediate step in Paul's eschatological interpretation of this text.

Of these five texts from Moses' second address (Deut.5–26), only one is cited in the context of the Pauline discussion of the law as a theological problem (Deut.21.23; Gal.3.13). Indeed, it is drawn into that context on the basis of a text from the concluding chapters of Deuteronomy (Deut.27.26; Gal.3.10), chapters which form one of the primary sources of Paul's conviction that Israel's relationship to the law is fundamentally problematic. Yet there is nothing problematic about the application to the Christian community of laws relating to the love of the one God, communal purity, multiple testimony, and the care of oxen. Like the stories of Exodus and Numbers, the laws of Deuteronomy "were written for our instruction..." (1 Cor.10.11) – that is, for practical guidance in matters of everyday conduct. It is likely that these and other scriptural laws have exercised a far more pervasive influence over Pauline parenesis than the small number of explicit citations and direct allusions would suggest.[22] Naturally, these laws must be interpreted flexibly – for "the command-ments of God" are not always identical with their literal sense (cf. 1 Cor.7.19). Above all, they must be correlated with the requirements of the Christian gospel. Yet, subject to this all-important christological proviso, it would seem that Moses' instructions to Israel in the land of Moab are still valid for Christian communities at Corinth and elsewhere.[23]

There is a striking discrepancy between this parenetic use of texts from Deuteronomy and the motif of "the curse of the law", which likewise appeals to Deuteronomy. How can it be that laws which continue to guide individual and communal conduct are at the same time the bearers of a curse? This is one of the more obvious examples of a real "contradiction" within Paul's understanding of the law. It cannot be resolved by distinguishing the different theologies of the various letters, for it repeatedly occurs *within* an individual letter. In 1 Corinthians, we encounter not only a relatively positive attitude towards "the command-ments of God", but also the claim that "the sting of death is sin, and the

22. As argued by Brian Rosner, *Paul, Scripture, and Ethics, passim.*

23. E. P. Sanders is therefore right to argue that, for Paul, "the law should be fulfilled" (*Paul, the Law, and the Jewish People*, pp. 93–122. "In discussing the behavior appropriate to being Christian, Paul saw no incongruity between 'living by faith' and 'fulfilling the law'. Doing the commandments (1 Cor.7:19) is integral to living by faith" (p. 114). The tension with Paul's "not by works of law" statements cannot be resolved by asserting that "the law is not an entrance requirement", however (pp. 17–64). If Christians are to fulfil the commandments at all, then a commitment to do so would seem to be some kind of entrance requirement. In reality, "not by works of law" represents an entire scriptural hermeneutic, and a praxis based on it.

power of sin is the law" (15.56 – an interpretative gloss on a text from Hosea). In Galatians and Romans, love of neighbour summarizes the whole law and is obligatory for Christians (Gal.5.14; Rom.13.8–10), and yet Christ must free us from "the curse of the law" (Gal.3.13), enabling us to die to the law and to belong instead to himself (Rom.7.1–6).[24]

While this contradiction is no doubt generated by Paul's christology, this christology is itself generated by the interplay of gospel and scripture. If so, it may again be possible to discover the roots of a Pauline "contradiction" within scripture itself. The basis for this particular contradiction emerges from Paul's reading of Deuteronomy. In the central section of this book (chapters 5–26), laws are promulgated which will guide Israel's life within the land, and which can be adapted for use within the Christian community. In the concluding section (chapters 27–34), Israel's future under the law is a future under the law's curse.

Israel's Predicament

The long central section of Deuteronomy consists of a single address comprising a reminder of the ten commandments and of the various disasters of the wilderness period, general instructions and exhortations, and (from chapter 12 onwards) the specific commandments that form the heart of the book. With only one minor exception (10.6–9), second person discourse is unbroken here; no narrator intervenes to interrupt Moses' monologue. In the concluding chapters of the book, the narrator gradually becomes more prominent (Deut.27–34).[25] Three main sections can be identified here. First, instructions are given about a liturgical action that is to be performed at Mount Ebal and Mount Gerizim (Deut.27); this leads directly into the blessings and curses of chapter 28. Second, an address that further develops the theme of the blessing and the curse is introduced as "the words of the covenant which YHWH commanded Moses to make with the people of Israel in the land of Moab" (29.1 EVV; 29.1–30.20). Third, Moses' words and actions in preparation for his imminent death are recounted, followed by the account of his death and the summary of his

---

24. As H. Räisänen states: "Paul has two sets of statements concerning the validity of the law for Christians. According to one set the law has been abrogated once and for all. According to the other the law is still in force, and what it requires is charismatically fulfilled by Christians" (*The Torah and Christ*, p. 10).

25. The strong thematic links between Deuteronomy 27–28 and 29–30 suggest that 27.1 marks the end of the speech that began in 5.1, rather than 29.1 (as assumed by W. Brueggemann, *Deuteronomy*, p. 17). It is notable that the "editorial voice" returns at 27.1a, 9a, 11a for virtually the first time since 5.1a (10.6–9 being the sole exception); on this see G. von Rad, *Deuteronomy*, pp. 164–65. Most significant from a Pauline perspective is the fact that the motif of the "curse" occurs throughout Deuteronomy 27–30.

achievements with which the book closes (31.1–34.12). The "Song of Moses" (32.1–43) and Moses' final blessing (33.2–29) form two discrete literary units within this section. All three sections focus on the people's future in the land, and all of them strike a surprisingly pessimistic note. Repeated warnings of the fate decreed for the disobedient tend to lose their conditional character, and to present judgment and exile not just as a possibility but as a certainty. It seems that, at the very moment when the people of Israel are poised to enter the land, the land is forfeit.

These chapters represent the conclusion not just of Deuteronomy but also of the Torah as a whole. As Moses himself is finally refused entry into the land, so the Law of Moses leaves its readers outside the land promised to the fathers, threatened indeed by the divine curse whose ongoing effect within the history of Israel is all too obvious. Deuteronomy brings the people of Israel to the verge of the promise's fulfilment, and yet, at the very end, it throws that fulfilment into serious and fundamental doubt. The Torah concludes not with the enjoyment of the land flowing with milk and honey, but with an agonizing question. That is the essential difference between a pentateuch and a hexateuch.[26]

Quotations from and allusions to these chapters are found in four of Paul's extant letters (Galatians, Romans, 1 Corinthians, Philippians). Most tend to highlight the negative tone of the scriptural text, and they carry noticeably more weight in Paul's argument than the material he draws from elsewhere in Deuteronomy. Paul's use of these chapters is not uniform, however. In particular, material relating to "the curse of the law" (Deut.27–30) is treated differently from material drawn from the "Song of Moses" (Deut.32). Paul is also aware that, according to Deuteronomy 30, the predicament created by the law's curse is to be resolved by way of the law itself. That was also the view of many of Paul's contemporaries, and his divergence from their readings of Deuteronomy is especially clear at this point. To a considerable extent, Paul's engagement with Deuteronomy is determined by these attempts to identify Moses' final, all-encompassing word to his people.

(i) Deuteronomy 27.26

In Galatians 3.10, Paul derives his claim that "those who are of works of law are under a curse" from the statement of Deuteronomy: "Cursed be everyone who does not remain in everything written in the book of the law, to do them." Paul here appears to universalize a scriptural statement which refers *prima facie* to only one of the two main categories of those addressed by the law: those who transgress it, as opposed to those who observe it.

---

26. This difference is the central focus of James A. Sanders' book, *Torah and Canon*; see also B. Childs, *Introduction to the Old Testament as Scripture*, pp. 131–32.

For Paul, those who do not remain in the things written in the law include those who are of works of law. Far-reaching consequences follow from this universalizing reading of the Deuteronomy text. If those who are of works of law are under a curse, then it is clear that, through the law, no-one is justified before God: and this claim is supported by the citation of a second text (Hab.2.4; Gal.3.11). Thus the law and the prophet agree. The law pronounces a curse on those who are of works of law, the prophet announces that the righteous will live by faith, and between them they demonstrate that "we are justified by faith of Christ and not by works of law" (Gal.2.16).[27]

On the other hand, this way of harmonizing the law and the prophets creates a severe internal tension within the law itself. On the *prima facie* reading of the Deuteronomy text, there is no tension whatever between the "life" promised to those who observe the law and the "curse" threatened against those who do not. As Moses himself says,

> I call heaven and earth to bear witness to you this day: Life and death I have set before you, the blessing and the curse. Choose life, so that you may live, and your offspring... (Deut.30.19)

There is apparent harmony, then, between the statement of Leviticus 18.5, that "the one who does these things will live by them", and the statement of Deuteronomy, which pronounces a curse on "all who do not remain in the things written in this book, to do them". Life and blessing, death and the curse are respectively correlated with doing or not doing what is written in the law. In Galatians 3.10–12, however, Paul appears to adopt a *consecutive* reading in which the law's earlier promise of "life" (Leviticus) is overtaken by the universal scope of the "curse" (Deuteronomy). Detached from the Leviticus text, the Deuteronomy text is now the obverse of the one from Habakkuk.

For modern readers, this reading of Deuteronomy may seem even more problematic than the one in which Paul eliminates the threshing ox. Here it

---

27.   Why does Paul cite a scriptural passage that appears not to say what he wants it to say? According to E. P. Sanders, the answer is to be found in the verbal link in Deuteronomy 27.26 between "law" and "curse": Paul "wants a passage which says that the *nomos* brings a curse, and he cites the only one which does" (*Paul, the Law, and the Jewish People*, p. 21). Sanders here opposes the conventional reconstruction of Paul's argument, which runs: (1) Those who seek to observe the law are under a curse, for (2) scripture says that those who fail to fulfil everything written in the law are under a curse, and (3) in fact no-one does fulfil the entire law. In this conventional reconstruction of Paul's logic, point (3) has been added as "the unexpressed premise of the argument" (E. D. Burton, *Galatians*, p. 164). Sanders wishes to eliminate point (3), and to reduce point (2) to a scriptural echo of point (1). In the reading that follows, the "unexpressed premise" is that the law's curse is extended to include all Israel within its original context in Deuteronomy. It is not a matter of Paul "wanting a passage" to confirm what he can already say independently of that passage.

is no mere ox that is sacrificed on the altar of eschatological conviction; rather, it is the person who seeks to observe the law, in the belief that the way of the commandments is the way to life. In the one case as in the other, it is tempting to conclude that Paul's eschatological convictions have generated an interpretative high-handedness which can eliminate a text's primary meaning and compel it to assert its very opposite.[28] The text that expresses God's care for oxen can only be understood when we accept that God does not care for oxen. The text that pronounces a curse on the disobedient can only be understood when we accept that the corresponding promise of life to the obedient is actually a dangerous illusion.[29]

A negative assessment of Paul's interpretation of Deuteronomy 27.26 is understandable, but it is not justified. Paul practises a consecutive reading of his texts from Leviticus and Deuteronomy, in which the latter effectively cancels out the former. In doing so, he identifies a severe internal tension within the crucial closing chapters of Deuteronomy: the tension between conditional statements, which imply that the choice between blessing and curse, life and death is genuinely open, and statements of prophetic denunciation, in which the realization of the curse has become a certainty.

The text Paul cites is the last of a series of twelve curses that are to be proclaimed by the Levites when the people pass over the Jordan and arrive at Mount Gerizim and Mount Ebal (Deut.27.11–26).[30] Apart from the final

28. Compare J. Rohde's comment: "Im Urtext sagt das von Paulus angeführte Wort das Gegenteil von dem, was Paulus hier herausliest: Die *nicht* alles tun, was im Buch des Gesetzes geschrieben steht, sind unter dem Fluch" (*Galater*, p. 140n). Rohde resolves the problem in the usual way, arguing that for Paul the law requires a perfect fulfilment that is never actually forthcoming (p. 141).

29. Christopher Stanley argues that to be "under a curse" is merely to be *threatened* by a curse, rather than for the curse to be already realized ("'Under a Curse': A Fresh Reading of Galatians 3.10–14", p. 500). On this view, Paul warns his readers in v.10 that "[a]nyone who chooses to abide by the Jewish Torah in order to secure participation in Abraham's 'blessing' is placed in a situation where he or she is threatened instead with a 'curse'..." (*ibid.*). The scriptural proof is completed in vv.11–12: "Having broached the topic of the *negative* potentiality of Torah-observance in the previous verse in order to *affirm* it, Paul turns now to the question of its *positive* potentiality (the implied promise to 'justify' [v.11] and to 'give life' [v.12], only to *deny* it" (p. 502; italics original). If, however, the law does not give life, then the curse of the law must be universal and inevitable, at least from the standpoint of vv.11–12. In addition, vv.13–14 show the curse to be a reality that had to be removed in order for the blessing to be realized.

30. In Deuteronomy 27.12–13, six tribes are associated with Mount Gerizim and the blessing, and six with Mount Ebal and the curse. The result of the ceremony will be that "Segen und Fluch liegen... auf den weithin sichtbaren Bergen bereit, um auf Israel je nach dessen Gehorsam oder Untreue gegenüber Jahwe herabzukommen" (G. Braulik, *Deuteronomium*, p. 201). It is striking that the Levitical liturgy of vv.14–26 is wholly devoted to the curse, with no further reference to the blessing.

one, these curses are directed against specific forms of behaviour. Several are closely related to the decalogue (27.15, 16, 24: idolatry, dishonouring of parents, murder), while others refer to a range of sexual offences (27.20–23).

The concluding curse summarizes all the preceding ones: "Cursed be the one who does not confirm the words of this law by doing them" (27.26). Here, it is certainly not those who practise works of the law who are under this curse. Yet in the wider context of the concluding chapters of Deuteronomy, things are not so straightforward. In these chapters, the curse that is initially directed against law-breakers is extended so as to encompass all Israel.

Up to this point, there has been little in Deuteronomy to suggest that the people will inevitably fail to do what the Lord requires of them – apart from their past history (cf. 9.4–10.22). Moses' long second speech (Deut.5–26) is characterized throughout by the language of exhortation rather than condemnation. If the people of Israel maintain their vigilance and learn from their former mistakes, a bright future awaits them in the land of promise. And yet the curse on all law-breakers (27.26) heralds the intrusion of prophetic denunciation into this context of instruction and exhortation. The twelve curses of Deuteronomy 27.15–26 are prefaced by the words, "And Moses charged the people the same day, saying..." (27.11), and this same speech of Moses continues until the end of Deuteronomy 28, without a break. In this lengthy chapter, an exposition of the blessings consequent upon obedience (vv.1–14) is far outweighed by the exposition of the curses that will befall a disobedient nation (vv.15–68). The conditional clause with which this long section opens ("If you will not obey the voice of the Lord your God...", v.15) is repeated only once (v.58). Everywhere else it appears that the curses of plague, famine, defeat and exile are an inevitable fate corresponding to an inevitable disobedience:

> All these curses shall come upon you and pursue you and overtake you, till you are destroyed, because you did not obey the voice of the Lord your God, to keep his commandments and his decrees which he commanded you. (Deut.28.45)

Here, "because you did not obey *[hoti ouk eisēkousas]*" takes the place of "if you do not obey *[ean mē eisakousēs]*" (v.15), as warning gives way to denunciation.[31]

---

31. The distinction is equally clear in MT. According to the analysis of G. Seitz, "der bedingte Fluch" predominates in vv.15–46, 58–68, and "der begründete Fluch" in vv.47–57 (*Redaktionsgeschichtliche Studien zum Deuteronomium*, pp. 276–302). Even in the outer sections, the opening conditional statements (vv.15, 58) do not dispel the impression that the realization of the curse is certain (cf. v.45).

It is evident from the form of Paul's citation of Deuteronomy 27.26 that he has in mind more than an isolated proof-text. His version differs significantly from the Septuagint:

> Cursed is everyone who does not continue in all things written in the book of the law *[pasin tois gegrammenois en tō bibliō tou nomou]*, to do them. (Gal.3.10)

> Cursed is every person who does not continue in all the words of this law, to do them. (Deut.27.26 LXX)

The most significant difference between the two renderings of this curse lies in the substitution of "all things written in the book of the law" for "all the words of this law". It cannot be Paul's intention here to emphasize the written character of the law in contrast to the divine speaking that occurs in the gospel; for, two verses earlier, it is "the scripture" *(hē graphē)* which preached the gospel beforehand to Abraham (Gal.3.8). Instead, the alteration draws on phraseology derived from elsewhere in the later chapters of Deuteronomy and beyond:

> If you do not obey and do all the words of this law written in this book *[panta ta rēmata tou nomou toutou ta gegrammena en tō bibliō toutō]* . . . (Deut.28.58)

> And every sickness and every affliction that is not written in the book of this law the Lord will bring upon you, until he destroys you. (28.61)

> And the Lord will single him out for evil from all the children of Israel, according to all the curses of the covenant written in the book of this law *[hai gegrammenai en tō bibliō tou nomou toutou]*. (29.20, cf. also vv.19, 26)

> . . . if you obey the voice of the Lord your God, to keep and do all his commandments and his decrees and his judgments that are written in the book of this law. (30.10)

Three of these four passages share the phrase *en tō bibliō tou nomou* with the Pauline rendering of Deuteronomy 27.26. A shift occurs here from law as oral proclamation ("the words of this law", 27.26) to an identification between law and the Book of Deuteronomy itself.[32] Thus, in the second, third and fourth passages, the term "law" is detached from its previous connection to the divine "words" (27.26, 28.58) and attached instead to the term "book": the resulting phrase, "the book of this law", is the origin of

32. Even in 27.26, "the words of this law" refers back not just to the series of curses but also to the law that is to be written on plaster-covered stones in 27.8.

Paul's "the book of the law". (He naturally omits the self-referential "this".) In each case, "the book of this law" is associated with the threat – and indeed the certainty – that the law's curse represents the destiny of the entire people, and not just of individual law-breakers.[33] That is the final truth conveyed by the law in its written form as the Book of Deuteronomy, which here stands for the Pentateuch as a whole.[34] As "the book of this law", Deuteronomy is above all and in the end the book of the law's curses – the book that announces the catastrophe that is to befall the people of Israel. Paul's use of this phraseology as he quotes Deuteronomy 27.26 confirms that he understands this text within its wider context in the final chapters of the Pentateuch. All who stand within the sphere of the law are under its curse: at the very least, there is significant overlap at this point between Paul and Deuteronomy.[35]

Also relevant here is Joshua 8.30–35 (LXX: 9.2a–2f), which tells how Joshua carried out the covenantal ceremony prescribed in Deuteronomy 27. After the destruction of Jericho and Ai, Joshua built an altar to the Lord at Mount Ebal, writing on it a copy of the law of Moses in the presence of "all Israel" (8.30–32). As instructed by Moses, the people were assembled on opposite sides of the ark of the covenant, half in front of Mount Gerizim and half in front of Mount Ebal, to be blessed by the priests and Levites (8.33). After that, evidently on his own initiative,

> Joshua read all the words of this law, the blessings and the curses *[tas eulogias kai tas kataras]*, according to all things written *[kata panta ta gegrammena]* in the law of Moses. There was not a word of all that Moses commanded Joshua that Joshua did not read in the hearing of the whole congregation of the sons of Israel, men and women and children and proselytes who had joined themselves to Israel. (Josh.9.2e– 2f [8.34–35 EVV])

In place of "all things written in the law of Moses", MT has "all things written in the book of the law" *(kl hktwb bspr htwrh)*, which is particularly close to Paul's phraseology. This narrative underlines the link between the "blessings and the curses" of Deuteronomy 28 and the ceremony at Mount Gerizim and Mount Ebal prescribed in the previous chapter (Deut.27.1–

---

33. 29.20 is not an exception to this, as its context shows.

34. "It almost seems as if the writer of this stratum . . . considered this curse to be the real purport of Deuteronomy" (G. von Rad, *Deuteronomy*, p. 180).

35. There is therefore no reason to suppose that Paul is compelled to cite this text because his opponents have done so (the view of J. L. Martyn, *Galatians*, pp.309, 324–25). It is not the case either that "the threatened curse of Deut 27:26 fits the Teachers' theology hand in glove", or that "Paul interprets Deut 27:26 in a way that is the precise opposite of its literal meaning" (p. 309).

26; cf. 11.26–32).[36] Israel's entire existence in the land promised to the forefathers is to stand under the dual possibility of blessing and curse declared by Moses and enacted by Joshua at the time of the conquest. Thus the blessing and the curse reach into Israel's future. As the Deuteronomic history will eventually show, it is the curse that finally prevails as Jerusalem and the temple are destroyed and the people are exiled from the land of promise, in punishment for their failure to observe "all things written in the law of Moses".[37] The Pauline claim that "those who are of works of law are under a curse" (Gal.3.10) derives not from the assumption that the law requires an impossible sinless observance, but from the deuteronomic interpretation of Israel's history.[38]

Neither the deuteronomic history nor Deuteronomy itself regard the fulfilment of the curse as the end of God's relationship with Israel. In a crucial and widely influential passage (Deut.30.1–10), Israel under the divine curse is invited to return to the law, and so receives a second chance to attain the fullness of the divine blessing by way of law observance. It is likely that "those who are of works of law" (Gal.3.10) refers not just to Israel as such, but to those who understand their law observance as the way out of a past determined by the curse into a future determined by the divine blessing. Moses' words are now addressed to a future Israel that has experienced the full force of the divine curse:

> ... For the Lord your God will turn *[epistrepsei]* to rejoice in you for good, as he rejoiced in your fathers – if you obey the voice of the Lord your God, to keep and to do *[phulassesthai kai poiein]* all his commandments and his decrees and his judgments which are written in the book of this law; if you turn *[ean epistraphēs]* to the Lord your God with your whole heart and with your whole soul. (Deut. 30.9b–10)

---

36. It is notable that the Levitical curses of Deuteronomy 27.14–26 are absent from the Joshua passage. Its author also appears to assimilate the stones on which the law is to be inscribed to the stones that form the altar (Josh.8.31–32 MT): so J. A. Soggin, *Joshua*, p. 243.

37. In Deuteronomy 28, however, the "curses" amount to a return to Egypt, and thus to a clearer *reversal* of salvation history than in the deuteronomic history (cf. Deut.28.27, 60, 68). On this point, see J. G. Millar, *Time and Place in Deuteronomy* (with J. G. McConville), pp. 76–77.

38. For a thorough investigation of Paul's use of Deuteronomy 27.26 along these lines, see James M. Scott, "'For as Many as are of Works of the Law are under a Curse' (Galatians 3.10)"; more briefly, N. T. Wright, *The Climax of the Covenant*, pp. 144–48. As Wright argues, the crucial point is that Paul is *not* here asserting "a truth about salvation or justification which could be expressed in principle without reference to the story of Israel..." (*ibid.*, p. 144). In a well-known article, Martin Noth argues for a similar approach to Paul's reading of Deuteronomy 27.26 within the context of the deuteronomistic history ("For All who Rely on Works of the Law are Under a Curse", in his *The Laws in the Pentateuch and Other Studies*, pp. 118–31).

If, for Paul, "those who are of works of law" refers to those who strive to make this return to the Lord, then he and they are agreed that the law's curse has been realized within the history of Israel and continues to determine Israel's present. Disagreement would then concern the viability and appropriateness of the return to the law as the way out of the curse. It is Paul's view that the repeated association of "the book of the law" with the divine curse (Deut.28.58, 61; 29.19, 20, 26) is necessary and inevitable, and that the hope of salvation by returning to the law is illusory. Those who are of works of law have not arrived at a turning-point between the curse and the blessing. They continue to stand under the curse. Their situation is defined not by Deuteronomy 30 but by Deuteronomy 27–29.

The curse that Paul cites is, then, very far from being a mere proof-text detached from its total scriptural context. On the contrary, it identifies the fundamental dynamic of the entire scriptural history of Israel as the people of God. This interpretation of Paul's citation from Deuteronomy 27 will be confirmed by his treatment of closely related material from the chapters that follow.

(ii) Deuteronomy 29.3 (4 EVV)

Paul's citation in Romans 11.8 draws on Isaiah as well as Deuteronomy. The citation follows the statement that "what Israel sought it did not attain", and that, although "the elect obtained [it], the rest were hardened" (11.7; cf. 9.31). Isaiah contributes much less to the citation than Deuteronomy:

> For the Lord has caused you to drink *a spirit of sleep*, and he will close your eyes and the eyes of your prophets and your rulers, which behold the secret things. (Is.29.10)

> And the Lord your *God* did not *give* you a heart to know, *eyes to see or ears to hear, to this day*. (Deut.29.3)

> ... as it is written: God gave them a spirit of sleep, eyes that do not see and ears that do not hear, to this day. (Rom.11.8)

Paul inserts Isaiah's "a spirit of sleep" in the process of recasting the negative statement of Deuteronomy ("the Lord your God did not give *[ouk edōken]* ...") into an affirmative one ("God gave *[edōken]* ..."). The negation is thus displaced into the phrases about eyes and ears. Rather than negating "a heart to know" along similar lines, Paul replaces this with the more vivid Isaianic "spirit of sleep", which fits well with the image of unseeing eyes and unhearing ears. This is not so much a composite citation as the recasting of a single text which draws part of its phraseology from another text. In other words, it really is Deuteronomy 29.3 that is cited here.[39]

In Paul's reading of this text, the Israel of his own day is in exactly the same situation as the Israel addressed by Moses in the land of Moab. The text occurs in the context of the "covenant which the Lord commanded Moses to make with the sons of Israel in the land of Moab, beside the covenant that he made with them at Horeb" (28.69 LXX [29.1 EVV]).[40] More precisely, the text occurs as a parenthesis within the historical retrospect that opens Moses' covenantal address:

> And Moses called all the sons of Israel and said to them: You have seen everything that the Lord did in the land of Egypt, in your presence, to Pharaoh and to his servants and to all his land, the great trials which your eyes saw, the signs and those great wonders. *(And the Lord your God did not give you a heart to know, eyes to see or ears to hear, to this day.)* And he led you forty years in the wilderness. Your garments did not become old, and your sandals have not worn out upon your feet. You did not eat bread, or drink wine or strong drink – so that you may know that he is the Lord your God. (29.1–5)

From the past, Moses' address moves on to the present moment, as the entire people stands ready to "enter into the covenant of the Lord your God, and into its curses, which the Lord your God imposes upon you today" (29.11). Instead of a detailed statement of the terms of the covenant, there follows a warning against an individual act of idolatry that unleashes "all the curses of the covenant written in the book of this law" (29.20; cf. vv.19, 26). The resulting future takes the form of a national devastation

---

39. According to Ross Wagner, Paul reads Moses and Isaiah together in Romans 11.8 just as in 10.19–21 (*Heralds of the Good News*, p. 241). Wagner acknowledges that Isaiah 29.10 contributes only a single phrase to the citation, but argues that it also accounts for the claim that "Israel's insensibility has been directly caused by God", which is not present in the original Deuteronomy text (pp. 243–44). It is more likely that the formulation has been influenced by Psalm 68.23–24, cited in Romans 11.9–10. As Wagner himself notes (p. 244), *skotisthēsan hoi ophthalmoi tou mē blepein* (Ps.68.24; Rom.11.9) is a plausible source for the negative *ophthalmous tou mē blepein* in the Deuteronomy citation. In that case, Isaiah is less relevant here. A tendency to assimilate adjacent citations is also evident in Galatians 3.10, 13 (Deut.27.26, 21.23: *epikataratos pas . . .*).

40. This statement is an introduction rather than a conclusion: so G. von Rad, *Deuteronomy*, pp. 178–79, who finds elements here of the familiar "covenant pattern", with its opening historical summary (cf. 29.1–7) and closing blessing and curse (cf. 30.16–18). In contrast, W. Brueggemann argues that 29.1 EVV serves the same retrospective function as 4.44–49 (*Deuteronomy*, p. 258). The explicit reference to entry into a covenant "this day" (29.10–15, cf. 30.11) confirms the first interpretation. In 5.1–3 (the beginning of the speech that is concluded in 29.1, according to Brueggemann), there is no suggestion of a second covenant, but rather a reference back to the covenant at Horeb which the Lord made "not with our fathers, but with us".

that recalls the fate of Sodom and Gomorrah (29.22–28) and a dispersion that offers the opportunity of repentance and restoration (30.1–10).

In spite of the eloquent final appeal to choose life and blessing rather than death and cursing (30.11–20), nothing is said about the people's response – in contrast to the covenant-making ceremonies at Sinai (Ex.24.3–8) and later at Shechem (Josh.24.16–28), where the people explicitly accept the terms and conditions of the covenant: "All that the Lord has spoken we will do" (Ex.24.7). When Moses makes a covenant in the land of Moab, the people are completely silent. It is as though they have not heard. The reason for this is stated in Deuteronomy 29.3: the people addressed by Moses have to this day not been given a heart to know, eyes to see, or eyes to hear. Moses addresses them, but it is as if they are asleep: "God gave them a spirit of sleep ... " (Rom.11.8). Neither the threats nor the concluding eloquence succeeds in rousing them. Even as he begins his opening historical retrospective, Moses knows that the people understand nothing of what he says to them.

According to Paul, this is "to this day" the position of "Israel" – with the exception of the elect remnant, which corresponds to the seven thousand in Elijah's time who did not bow the knee to Baal (11.1–7).[41] An uncomprehending people will inevitably fall victim to the law's curse (cf. Deut.29.15–27): what Paul says about Israel on the basis of Deuteronomy 29.3 is closely related to his use of Deuteronomy 27.26 in Galatians 3.10. That the later text applies not just to pre-exilic Israel but also to the present generation is confirmed by Moses himself, who announces that the covenant in the land of Moab includes not only "those who are here with us this day before the Lord our God" but also "those who are not with us this day" (Deut.29.14; cf. 5.3). In Paul's view, the incomprehension to which Moses refers now takes the specific form of a hermeneutical error: the failure to see that scripture attests an unconditional divine saving action, universal in its scope and now realized in Christ.

(iii) Deuteronomy 30.11–14

This passage marks the beginning of the final exhortation that concludes Moses' "covenant address" in Deuteronomy 29–30. After the extensive account of a future characterized by devastation and exile, but also by the possibility of repentance and restoration (29.17–30.10), the passage

---

41.　Compare the use of "to this day" in 2 Corinthians 3.14, 15. In both cases, Paul's point is that the Israel of his own day may still be identified with scriptural Israel, with its hardness of heart and unseeing eyes. Contrary to its own self-understanding, the Israel of the present has not succeeded in putting right its relationship with God (along the lines of Deuteronomy 30.1–10).

ostensibly marks a return to the present. In it, Moses seeks to persuade his addressees that the way of the commandments that he has outlined is not impossibly difficult but easy and straightforward:

> For this commandment, which I command you this day, is not too exalted, nor is it far from you. It is not in heaven above, saying, "Who shall ascend for us into heaven, and bring it to us, so that hearing it we may do it?" Nor is it beyond the sea, saying, "Who will cross the sea for us, and bring it to us, and enable us to hear it so that we may do it?" The word is very near you, in your mouth and in your heart, and in your hands, so as to do it. (Deut.30.11–14)

In chapter 8, we analysed the careful rewriting of this passage that Paul ascribes to "the Righteousness of faith" (Rom.10.6–10). Essentially, the purpose of the rewriting is to substitute faith in Christ for the doing of the commandment. Only by way of this rewriting does the passage create the required contrast between the righteousness of faith and righteousness by the law, as articulated in the preceding citation from Leviticus 18.5 (Rom.10.5). In its original form, the Deuteronomy passage would simply confirm Leviticus 18.5. To the person setting out to fulfil the commandments as the way to life, the Deuteronomy passage offers counsel and encouragement. Choosing life rather than death, blessing rather than curse is, it tells us, almost absurdly simple – since the requirements on which this choice must be based are not remote and inaccessible but manifest, already familiar, and easy to practise. If that is actually the truth about the law, then (from a Pauline perspective) Christ would have died in vain (cf. Gal.2.21). Because Christ cannot have died in vain, what Moses here teaches cannot be the truth about the law.[42]

The Pauline rewriting respects the original text in the sense that it can reappropriate much of its language. Yet the impression remains that, here at least, Paul is imposing an *a priori* christology on a scriptural text, in defiance of that text's plain meaning. Indeed, Paul even seems to acknowledge that this is exactly what he is doing. And if such a hermeneutic is explicitly employed here, perhaps it is also employed in contexts that are less hermeneutically self-conscious?

The context of this passage is again Moses' "covenant address" in the land of Moab (Deut.29.1–30.20), in which it forms part of the concluding exhortation. At the outset, Moses has acknowledged that his teaching will

---

42. Facile harmonization of Deuteronomy and Paul is rightly rejected by Richard Hays, who writes: "It will not do ... to read Deuteronomy as a simple precursor of the doctrine of faith. The problem, from the point of view of Pauline theology, is that God's gracious action creates in Deuteronomy a covenant that is rigorously conditional in character and that pronounces terrifying curses upon Israel for disobedience. How can this text, the source of 'the curse of the law', serve as a prefiguration of Paul's gospel?" (*Echoes of Scripture*, p. 163).

fall upon deaf ears: for "the Lord your God has not given you a heart to
know, eyes to see or ears to hear, to this day" (Deut.29.3; cf. Rom.11.8).
The address proceeds to describe the grim future that awaits a community
deaf to the voice of God (29.17–27), but then unexpectedly offers a second
chance to realize the divine blessing through law observance. If, in
dispersion and under the curse, Israel turns to God and his law, God will
turn towards his people and restore their fortunes (30.1–10). Ostensibly
addressed to Moses' own contemporaries, the implied readership of this
address is to be found in a later generation whose situation is still
determined by the catastrophic loss of the land and its blessings. The
address closes with the passage about the easy availability of the
commandment (30.11–14) and the final eloquent appeal to choose life
and blessing rather than death and the curse (30.15–20). This concluding
section (vv.11–20) ostensibly marks a return to the situation of "this day"
(v.11), the time that Moses shares with his own contemporaries. And yet
the central section of the address (29.17–30.10) has been dominated by the
prospect of future dispersion and return; Moses' final words are therefore
to be understood as directly addressed not only to his contemporaries but
also to a later Israel, in dispersion and yet invited to return to the law. Here
if anywhere in Deuteronomy, Moses' voice achieves a total contemporaneity with later readers of his text. These readers hear Moses' words in the
consciousness that the curse he predicted has now been realized, and yet,
throughout Deuteronomy 30, they are invited to recapitulate the situation
of Moses' contemporaries; they are given a second chance to choose life
rather than death, blessing rather than curse. The commandment is so easy
and so well known that there is no question of an inability to obey – as
Israel's past history might otherwise suggest (30.11–14).

It is because he cannot accept this teaching that Paul rewrites the
passage as the utterance of the Righteousness of faith. As we have seen,
"those who are of works of law" remain entangled in the curse of
Deuteronomy 27–29 (Gal.3.10); the identity between Israel now and Israel
in the land of Moab consists only in unseeing eyes and deaf ears
(Deut.29.3; Rom.11.8). Hints of a divine action in which "the Lord your
God will purify your heart" (Deut.30.6) are not developed further in
Moses' closing words, in which fulfilment of the law is eloquently
represented as a real and urgent human possibility.[43]

43. In v.6, LXX reads "the Lord God will purify your heart . . . "; MT, "YHWH your God
will circumcise your heart . . . " M. Brettler finds here a formulation influenced by the
Jeremianic "new covenant" and at odds with the usual Deuteronomic assumption that
conduct is determined by human freedom rather than divine grace ("Predestination in
Deuteronomy 30.1–10", pp. 172–74). Brettler also argues that, if Deuteronomy 30.1b–2 is
understood as the apodosis of v.1a (rather than vv.3–9 of vv.1–2), the whole passage views
repentance as enabled by divine grace (pp. 174–79). The syntactic ambiguity is occasioned by

Paul rewrites this passage on the basis both of what God has done in Christ, and of the theological logic of the Book of Deuteronomy. In the light of the terrible history foreshadowed in Deuteronomy 27–29, there is little reason to suppose that all will be well if Israel is given a second chance. For Paul, Moses' over-optimistic claim to that effect stands in need of correction. Indeed, as we shall see, Moses himself later attained to a higher level of insight, testifying in his "Song" (32.1–43) to a divine rather than a human solution to Israel's predicament.

Israel's Hope

Moses' discourse on the blessings and curses of the covenant (Deuteronomy 27–28) concludes with a description of national catastrophe and the dispersion of the few survivors to the ends of the earth (28.62–68).[44] The address that follows (Deuteronomy 29–30) begins by presenting an equally bleak picture of the people's future under the curses of the covenant (cf. 29.12, 20, 21, 27); but the possibility of restoration is now envisaged (30.1–10), and the conclusion goes further still in suggesting that the choice of life and blessing rather than death and the curse is still open (30.11–20). In Paul's view, such optimism is only justified if the passage is rewritten from the standpoint of righteousness by faith. As the broader context shows, optimism for the future is otherwise unwarranted.

A comparable balancing of hope and despair is evident in chapters 31–34. These chapters are dominated by Moses' approaching death, announced for the first time in 31.1–2. Moses is not permitted to lead the people across the Jordan, and so a successor must be named (cf. Num.27.12–23; Deut.1.34–40, 3.23–28, 4.21, 32.48–52). Joshua's appointment is announced to the people (Deut.31.1–6), and confirmed first by Moses (31.7–8) and then by the Lord himself, who appears within the tent of meeting and addresses Joshua in very similar language to Moses's (31.14–15, 23). Moses is more than just a leader, however; he is also and above all the one who declares and expounds God's will to the people. This has been his primary role in Deuteronomy as a whole, which tells how "beyond the Jordan, in the land of Moab, Moses undertook to explain this

the series of *waw*-clauses in vv.1b–3, among which must be found the apodosis for the protasis introduced by *ky* (v.1a). The ambiguity is reproduced in the LXX, and the usual translation of v.3 ("*then* the Lord God will heal...") presupposes a decision about the location of the apodosis. Yet the statement about divine action in v.6 does not seem emphatic enough to determine the interpretation of the whole passage – especially in the light of the resulting tension with 30.11–20.

44. In Deuteronomy, the catastrophe is understood as "dispersion" rather than simply exile; Deuteronomy 30.4 is actually the origin of the term *diaspora* (cf. the use of the cognate verb in 28.64).

law... " (1.5). In this role, Moses' place will be taken not by a living successor but by a book, which Moses himself is to write. What he writes is "this law" – referring initially to Deuteronomy itself but subsequently to the Pentateuch as a whole. This is entrusted to "the priests the sons of Levi", with the instruction that "all the words of this law" are to be read to the assembled people every seventh year at the feast of booths (31.9–13). The two themes – appointing the successor, writing the law – are interwoven; the initial account of the writing of the law occurs between Moses' commissioning of Joshua (31.7–8) and God's (31.14–15, 23). This still leaves two passages unaccounted for, however. In the tent of meeting, before anything is said to Joshua, Moses is entrusted with a third task: the composition of a song, which is to be taught to the people of Israel so that in days to come it will serve as a witness against them (31.16–22). Next, in a second account of the writing of the law and its being handed over to the Levites, it is said that the law itself will serve as a witness against Israel (31.24–29). Since the only material Paul cites from Deuteronomy 31–34 is taken from the "Song of Moses" (chapter 32), this relationship between the Song and the law as a whole is of particular significance.[45]

The composition of the Song is set against the background of the certainty of national apostasy following Moses' death. Already in chapters 28–29, as we have seen, the curses of the law are presented not as one of two possible futures but as the actuality of Israel's future history. In chapter 31, this becomes still clearer:

> And the Lord said to Moses: Behold, you will fall asleep with your fathers; and this people will get up and fornicate with the strange gods of the land into which it is going; and they will abandon me and break my covenant which I made with them... So now, write the words of this song *[ōdē]* and teach it to the sons of Israel and put it in their mouth, so that this song may be a witness for me among the sons of Israel. (Deut.31.16, 19)

The possibility of future apostasy here becomes a certainty: for a text is to be composed and handed on that is intended not for the present but for the time when the curses released by that apostasy have been realized. Once Moses has taught the Song to the people, it will remain "unforgotten in

---

45. According to R. D. Nelson, the preamble to the Song in 31.16–22 is a later addition, based on the description of the warning role of the law itself in vv.24–29, and breaking the original connection between vv.14–15 and v.23 (*Deuteronomy*, pp. 355–56). In the final form of the text, however, what is said about the law in vv.24–29 is modelled on what is said about the Song in vv.16–22. Nelson also argues that the chapter as a whole represents the resumption of the deuteronomic history, which was broken off at the end of chapter 3 when its opening section was combined with the deuteronomic law-code (pp. 354–55). Yet the account of the writing of the law (31.9–13, 24–29) serves to explain the earlier references to "the book of this law" (28.61; 29.19, 20, 26; 30.10).

their mouth and in the mouth of their seed" (v.21); but its meaning and significance is held in reserve for a quite specific future moment.

Moses duly writes the Song and teaches it to the people (31.22) – but its text is not given at this point, as one might have expected. Instead, there follows the passage about the divine commissioning of Joshua (31.23), and a second account of the writing of the law (31.24–29). Only then is the full text of Moses' Song given (31.30–32.43). In the initial passage about the writing of the law, it is handed over to the Levites to be read every seven years at the Feast of Tabernacles (31.9–14). In the second passage, the law is described in terms that closely resemble what has already been said about the Song. The Levites are instructed:

> Take this book of the law and set it beside the ark of the covenant of the Lord our God, and it shall be there among you as a witness. For I know your rebelliousness and your hardness of heart. For if while I am alive among you this day you have been rebellious towards God, how much more after my death! (31.26–27)

Once again, future apostasy is here a certainty. What is striking, however, is that the Book of the Law has now acquired exactly the same role as the Song of Moses: to serve as a witness, testifying on God's behalf against a sinful people.[46]

This pessimistic view of Israel's future life under the law contrasts sharply with the previous account of the writing of the law, where the seven-yearly reading of the law ensures that future generations "may hear and learn to fear the Lord your God" (31.13). According to the later account, Moses already knows that these future generations will do no such thing: the rebelliousness that he himself has had to endure will inevitably become still worse after his death. But that is simply to negate the more optimistic view that law observance remains a genuine possibility, and that nothing stands in the way of its realization. The initial description of Moses' arrangements for life in the land after his departure (31.1–15) is overtaken by an overwhelmingly negative portrayal of a future in which Moses' texts serve simply as a witness *against* the people (31.16–29). Nothing is said here about a possible future return to the law. If there is still ground for hope, this must lie exclusively in God, and not in the human capacity for the good to which Moses earlier appealed (30.11–20).

---

46. As R. Wagner has shown, the parallel between the law and the Song is further developed in LXX (*Heralds of the Good News*, p. 200). At the conclusion of the Song, MT tells how "Moses came and spoke all the words of this song in the ears of the people, he and Hoshea *[sic]* son of Nun" (Deut.32.44). According to LXX, however, "Moses wrote this song in that day and taught it to the sons of Israel [cf. 31.22]. And Moses came and spoke all the words of this law in the ears of the people, he and Joshua the son of Naun."

Therein lies the significance of Moses' Song, at least for one of its early readers.[47]

The Song of Moses is primarily about God – the only God, the God who kills and makes alive and who wounds and heals (cf. Deut.32.39). Like the Suffering Servant of deutero-Isaiah, Israel's path to life lies only through death and dereliction. For Paul, the passage from death to life is the passage from the law to Christ, by way of Christ's own death and renewed life. His fragmentary references to the Song of Moses understand this text as a witness against Israel only insofar as it is also and more fundamentally a witness to God's saving mercy in its universal scope.[48]

(i) Deuteronomy 32.5

The Song of Moses opens with an appeal to heaven and earth to give heed to the speaker, whose words will be like rain that waters the face of the earth, since their subject matter is the greatness of "our God" (Deut.32.1–3). In striking contrast to this lyrical exordium, there follows a passage in which the faithfulness of God is starkly juxtaposed with the faithlessness of God's people. This passage introduces the issue that runs throughout the poem, underlying the story it tells about Israel's history:

> This God, true are his works,
> and all his ways are judgments,
> a faithful God, in whom there is no unrighteousness,
> a righteous and holy Lord.
> They sinned, they are not his children, they are at fault *[ouk autō tekna, mōmēta]*, a crooked and perverse generation *[genea skolia kai diestrammenē]*. (Deut.32.4–5)

It is the paradox of Israel's election that, from the start, it generates this apparently unbridgeable chasm between the divine and the human.

Paul alludes to this passage when he describes his Philippian readers as "children of God, faultless in the midst of a crooked and perverse generation" (Phil.2.15). For "they are not his children", Paul substitutes, "children of God"; for "at fault" *[mōmēta]*, he substitutes "faultless" *[amōma]*; and the insertion of "in the midst of" *[meson]* effects a distinction between these faultless ones and the "crooked and perverse

---

47. For a wide-ranging survey of the use of the Song of Moses within early Jewish and Christian literature, see Richard Bell, *Provoked to Jealousy*, pp. 209–69.

48. As Bell argues, the Song enables Paul to show how "the disobedience of Israel, the inclusion of the Gentiles, the provoking to jealousy of Israel, and the final salvation of Israel all belong together" (*ibid.*, pp. 112–13).

generation".[49] There is no indication that Paul applies this latter phrase to the contemporary Jewish community; his Philippian readers live in the midst of a primarily Gentile society, not a Jewish one. Paul may here reapply words originally descriptive of the people of Israel to the wider world, in the belief that Israel's position of guilt before God is paradigmatic for the whole of humanity. On the other hand, an allusion such as this does not need any overarching account of its transfer from its original context into a new one.[50] Other evidence would be required in order to settle the question whether Paul could see a representative dimension in Israel's situation, as depicted in the Song of Moses.

A tentative answer to this question may be found in Romans 3.1–8, where the Song's juxtaposition of divine faithfulness and human guilt (Deut.32.4–5) finds a close analogy. Although this passage does not contain any direct reminiscences of vv.4–5a, its language has apparently been decisively influenced by v.4 – as a line-by-line treatment will demonstrate:

(1) This God, true are his works *[alēthina ta erga autou]*,
(2) and all his ways are judgments *[kriseis]*,
(3) a faithful God *[theos pistos]*, in whom there is no unrighteousness *[kai ouk estin adikia]*,
(4) a righteous and holy Lord.
(5) They sinned *[hēmartosan]*, they are not his children, they are at fault . . .

In line 1, the emphasis on divine truthfulness is echoed in Paul's plea, "Let God be true *[alēthinos]*!"), and in his reference to "the truth of God" *[hē alētheia tou theou]*" (Rom.3.4, 7). The reference to God's "judgments" in line 2 may be compared to Paul's use of the corresponding verb (Rom.3.6, 7). Line 3 is echoed in two of the questions Paul places in the mouth of his imaginary interlocutor: "Does their faithlessness nullify the faithfulness of God *[tēn pistin tou theou]*?" (Rom.3.3), and, "Is God unjust *[mē adikos ho theos]* to inflict wrath?" (3.5). To the confession that God is truthful and faithful line 4 adds that God is righteous and holy: and Paul similarly adds a reference to "the righteousness of God" to his preceding references to God's faithfulness and truthfulness (3.5). Finally, the bald statement that "they sinned" in line 5 creates a dichotomy between divine righteousness

---

49. Thus, as E. Lohmeyer states, the use of these scriptural terms "steht . . . in einem deutlichen und wohl bewussten Gegensatz zu ihrem ursprünglichen Zusammenhang" (*Philipper*, p. 107). Lohmeyer finds in the distinction here between community and world an analogy with Johannine dualism (p. 108).

50. F. W. Beare suggests that Paul alludes to the Song because he too, like Moses, is facing the prospect of death (*Philippians*, p. 89).

and human wickedness which is mirrored in the structure of the Pauline argument.

Paul draws on the language of the Song as he seeks to demonstrate that human wickedness can coexist with the divine faithfulness and truthfulness (Rom.3.3–4) – a point that Deuteronomy 32.4–5 is ideally suited to illustrate, also enabling a shift in focus from "the advantage of the Jew" (Rom.3.1) to the entanglement in sin and falsehood that the Jew shares with the non-Jew. The real concern here is to show that, in the face of human sin, the divine faithfulness, truthfulness or righteousness can only take the form of judgment (3.4).[51] This claim is further elaborated in opposition to a perverse conclusion drawn from the juxtaposition of divine truth and human falsehood in v.4 – that God would be unjust to punish a human sinfulness that actually serves to enhance the divine glory (3.5–8). In this difficult passage, Paul seeks to demonstrate his opposition to arguments of the "let us do evil that good may come" variety, which have been falsely ascribed to him (3.8; cf. 3.23–24, 5.20–6.2, 11.32). His interlocutor in 3.5–8 is none other than the distorted image of himself created by his theological opponents – a Paul for whom human sin leads not to judgment but to grace. Paul intends here to reassure his readers that his stark juxtaposition of the divine righteousness and human sinfulness implies no weakening of belief in divine judgment (cf. 2.16) – which will indeed befall those who maliciously distort his views (3.8).[52] The fact that the juxtaposition can be expressed in familiar scriptural language is already an indication of his orthodoxy.

The passage develops out of the recognition that some Jews are guilty of "unfaithfulness" *(apistia)* (v.3): as the Song of Moses puts it, they are "sons in whom there is no faithfulness *[pistis]*" (Deut.32.20). This rapidly escalates into the assertion that every human is false and liable to the righteous divine judgment (Rom.3.3–4), which lays the foundation for the later claim that Jews as well as Greeks are all under sin (v.9). All this

51.   In the citation from Psalm 50(51).6, *en tō krinesthai se* is probably passive rather than middle (against Cranfield, *Romans*, 1.182n): the second line of the citation (". . . and prevail when you are judged") is explained by the first line ("so that you may be justified in your words"), which refers to the human acknowledgment of the righteousness of the divine verdict (cf. Rom.3.19b).

52.   This reading of 3.1–8 now seems to me to be preferable to one in which the interlocutor represents an extreme form of Jewish covenant theology – a view for which I argued in *Paul, Judaism and the Gentiles*, pp. 124–31 (following D. R. Hall's article, "Romans 3.1–8 Reconsidered"). That view originated in a (broadly correct) "mirror-reading" of Romans 2 as directed against a supposed *Jewish* theology of "salvation by grace alone" (pp. 109–15). In extending this reading into Romans 3.1–8, insufficient weight was given to the shift from the faithlessness of "some" Jews (v.3) to the falsehood of *pas anthrōpos* (v.4). It appears to be Paul's statements about universal human guilt that underlie the caricature he identifies in 3.8, and just such a statement is found in v.4.

suggests that, when Paul reads the words, "they sinned, they are not his children" in Deuteronomy 32.5, he understands them to refer to Israel as a paradigm of the human condition.

A similar interpretative move may underlie the allusion to the "crooked and perverse generation" in Philippians 2.15. Gentile society here takes on the role of sinful Israel in the Song; and a contrasting role is created for the Christian community by rewriting "they are not his children, they are at fault", as, "children of God without fault". What Israel should have been is realized in the Philippian community, on the basis of the righteousness not of the law but of faith in Christ (Phil.3.9). Without that extrinsic righteousness, however, members of the community are simply part of the "crooked and perverse generation" – the human situation before God as disclosed in Israel.[53]

(ii) Deuteronomy 32.17

As the Song proceeds, the perverse and crooked generation is reminded of its true identity as "Jacob" or "Israel", uniquely privileged among the "sons of Adam" in being the Lord's heritage – rather than being ruled by one or other of the "angels of God" like the other nations (vv.6–9 LXX). It is reminded of the divine care that preserved "Jacob" (cf. v.15) in the wilderness, and brought him into an earthly paradise full of all good things to enjoy (vv.6–14). At that time, "there was no strange god with him" (v.12): in the Song, the wilderness period represents the original perfection of the covenant relationship – a view in some tension with Deuteronomy and the Pentateuch as a whole.[54] As Jacob prospered, however, "he forsook the God who made him" (Deut.32.15). Indeed, "they sacrificed to demons and not to God *[ethusan daimoniois kai ou theō]*" (v.17).

Paul alludes to this last statement in the context of his discussion of food offered to idols. His readers are to "flee idolatry" (1 Cor.10.14), that is, they are not to participate in sacral meals in pagan temples: for "what they sacrifice, they sacrifice to demons and not to God *[daimoniois kai ou theō thuousin]*" (10.20). Those who participate in the cup of the Lord at the Lord's table cannot possibly participate in a demonic cup at the table of demons (10.21). Such behaviour will "make the Lord jealous *[parazēlou-men]*" (10.22). This is a further allusion to the Song, where God says,

53. Thus, "it is not the Pharisaic ideal of being better than the wicked world that Paul is proclaiming here" (K. Barth, *Philippians*, p. 76).

54. G. von Rad sees here a vestige of an old, non-exodus tradition in which YHWH "found" Israel in the wilderness: cf. also Hos.9.10, Jer.31.2–3 (*Old Testament Theology*, 1.177n). LXX's insertion of *autarkēsen* (v.10) may reflect a "correction" to this tradition originating in a transposition of letters in the Hebrew exemplar (cf. R. D. Nelson, *Deuteronomy*, p. 376).

"They made me jealous *[parezēlōsan me]* with what is no god"
(Deut.32.21). As in Deuteronomy, Paul's "demons" are simply the gods
of the Gentiles.[55] The allusion to the Song of Moses follows Paul's
typological reading of Israel's disastrous experiences in the wilderness (1
Cor.10.1–11), but the sacrifices to demons are here ascribed not to Israel but
to the Gentiles. Of Israel it is said: "Consider Israel according to the flesh –
are not those who eat the sacrifices participants in the altar?" (10.18). It is
the Gentiles who sacrifice to demons,[56] just as it is they who are a crooked
and perverse generation (Phil.2.15). At Corinth, it is the Gentiles who pose
a threat to the Christian community, and not "Israel according to the
flesh". Yet the sin known as "idolatry" comes into being only within the
sphere of the law, and the idolatry spoken of in the Song discloses the true
nature of the otherwise impressive religious rituals of the Greek world.

(iii) Deuteronomy 32.21

In headlong rebellion against God, the people of Israel "sacrificed to
demons and not to God", thereby showing themselves to be "a crooked
and perverse generation" (Deut.32.17, 5). There is a symmetry to the
divine response. The punishment fits the crime:

> They have made me jealous *[parezēlōsan me]* of what is no god *[ep' ou
> theō]*, they angered me with their idols.
> So I shall make them jealous *[parazēlōsō autous]* of what is no nation
> *[ep' ouk ethnei]*, with a foolish nation I shall anger them. (Deut.32.21)

Later in the poem reference will be made to Israel's enemies, who would
have brought death and final destruction to the people of Israel had there
not been a need to curb the triumphalistic claim that "it is my uplifted
hand that did all these things, and not the Lord" (v.27). It is generally
assumed that the "foolish nation" (v.21) is to be identified with this enemy,
and that the Song here takes up the traditional claim that God uses foreign
nations such as Assyria to punish his people (cf. Is.10.12–19; Deut.28.47–
51).[57] It is not said that the "foolish nation" is an aggressor, however, or
that it is commissioned by YHWH for punitive purposes.[58] Neither

---

55. The equation is succinctly expressed in Psalm 95.5 LXX: "All the gods of the Gentiles
are demons."

56. Although the reading, "... but that what *the Gentiles* sacrifice" (P[46] א A C *al*) is
probably not original (so B. Metzger, *Textual Commentary*, pp. 560–61).

57. See the commentaries of von Rad, Nelson, and Brueggemann, *ad loc.*

58. The "foolish nation" of v.21 need not be identified with the "nation without
understanding" of v.28, which is probably a reference to Israel itself. While vv.32–33 are
concerned with Israel's enemy, there is no good reason to read that back into vv.28–29 *(contra*
R. D. Nelson, *Deuteronomy*, p. 375). The third plural in v.30 refers to Israel, and the same is
true of vv.28–29.

"jealousy" nor "anger" need suggest foreign invasion (but cf. 28.33–34). The symmetry of the statement suggests that, as Israel has transferred its allegiance from YHWH to other gods, so YHWH will transfer his affection from Israel to another people. The fact that Israel becomes "jealous" at this point is, perhaps, a faint sign of hope.

Deuteronomy 32.21b is quoted in Romans 10.19, after Paul has claimed that the gospel message has been heard to the ends of the earth – even if it has not been universally believed (Rom.10.16–18).[59] The argument requires a contrast between the Gentile world and Israel:

> But I ask, have they not heard? Indeed they have: for, "Their sound has gone forth into all the earth, and their words to the ends of the world." [Ps.18.5] But I ask, did Israel not know? First, Moses states: "I will make you jealous of what is no nation, with a foolish nation I shall anger you." (Rom.10.18–19)[60]

What Israel knew, or should have known, is not simply the gospel in a general sense, but rather the divine plan that the message of salvation should extend to the furthest corners of the Gentile world.[61] The question about Israel must relate both to what precedes it (the citation from Psalm 18) and to what follows it (the citation from Deuteronomy 32). Paul's meaning is that God's plan to extend the scope of his saving action into the Gentile world is the fulfilment not only of the psalm text but also of Moses' prophecy about Israel's jealousy of what is "no nation" – the Christian community, composed of Gentiles as well as Jews (cf. Rom.9.24–26). "Israel" here refers to those who were "hardened", as opposed to the remnant (cf. Rom.11.7), and the "jealousy" of non-Christian Israel is the reaction that Paul himself seeks to evoke among his fellow-Jews by way of his Gentile mission:

> By their trespass salvation has come to the Gentiles, so as to make them jealous *[eis to parazēlōsai autous]*. (11.11)

> I speak to you as Gentiles: inasmuch as I am apostle of the Gentiles, I magnify my ministry, in the hope of making my "flesh" jealous and saving some of them. (11.13–14)

---

59. Romans 10.14–18 is to be understood as referring to the Gentile mission, not to the Jewish one: so N. T. Wright, "The Messiah and the People of God", pp. 178–79, followed by my own *Paul, Judaism and the Gentiles*, pp. 164–68.

60. Paul's substitution of "you" for "them" (MT, LXX) may suggest that the generation has now arrived for whom the Song was once written (for the Song's orientation towards the future, cf. Deuteronomy 31.16–21). Richard Bell rejects this possibility, on the grounds that Paul here "is primarily addressing Gentiles and certainly not non-Christian Jews" (*Provoked to Jealousy*, p. 96n). Yet Romans 10.19–21 is clearly direct address to non-Christian Israel, although in reported speech.

61. So R. Bell, *ibid.*, pp. 96–103.

Paul draws from Deuteronomy the idea that God has transferred his favour from Israel to the "foolish nation", and that this naturally arouses Israel's "jealousy". Yet this jealousy is overcome as soon as it arises, for it is nothing other than the recognition of the fulfilment of Israel's ancestral blessings in the midst of the Gentile world – and to recognize this is already to participate in it and so to be "saved". By virtue of its non-recognition of the Christ, unbelieving Israel is temporarily excluded from the fullness of its own heritage. Yet the exclusion is of such a kind that re-inclusion always remains a possibility and will finally become a reality (cf. 11.17–32). For Paul, "jealousy" is the dawning of the moment of saving insight. The making-jealous is the way to the divine compassion, which is all-embracing in its scope (cf. Rom.11.32). Through this scriptural motif, supersessionism is itself superseded.

Paul may have identified the "non-nation" of the Deuteronomy text with the Gentile Christian community by association with the "not-my-people" of his earlier citation from Hosea (Rom.9.25). Alternatively, or additionally, he may have been influenced by the one explicit reference to the Gentiles within the Song itself: "Rejoice, Gentiles, with his people" (Deut.32.43) – a text that Paul himself will later cite (Rom.15.10). As we shall see, there are text-critical indications that this exhortation was not an original part of the Song. It is difficult, if not impossible, to harmonize it with the theme of God's vengeance on his and his people's enemies that otherwise dominates the Song's conclusion (vv.35–43). The "jealousy" text raises the question of the identity of the "non-nation"; the call for Gentile rejoicing raises the question of what the Gentiles have got to celebrate; and Paul conflates the two questions and arrives at a single, comprehensive answer. The Gentiles exhorted to rejoice are the Gentile worshippers of the God of Israel whom God has called to take the place of the disobedient majority in Israel. They are to rejoice "with his people" because, in the divine plan, the event of supersession has as its goal the evoking of jealousy as the first step towards salvation. In his olive tree image, Paul articulates and criticizes the already typical supersessionist consciousness of the Gentile Christian: "Branches were broken off so that I might be grafted in" (Rom.11.19). The Gentile Christian is not wholly wrong at this point. Paul himself has laboured to show how the apparent divine change of plan is consistent with the true scriptural doctrines of election (Rom.9.6–29) and of faith (9.30–10.21). What the Gentile Christian should not suppose, however, is that this new development within the divine plan of election is in any way final and an end in itself. On the contrary, it is the means that God has devised to bring about the salvation of his people Israel. The "jealousy" that is initially a mark of exclusion (10.19) is in fact an element in God's comprehensive saving action (cf. 11.14). To recognize oneself as excluded is the first step on the way to inclusion: and that is the case for Jews as well as for Gentiles.

"Jealousy" represents a necessary moment of dawning insight. It is the beginning of the process that will lead Gentiles and Jews to celebrate together the inexplicably comprehensive scope of the divine mercy (cf. 11.28–36). If Paul has learned all this through a "mystery" or special revelation (11.25), the revelation has come to him in and through his meditation on the Song of Moses.

(iv) Deuteronomy 32.35

In Paul's reading of the Song of Moses, two mutually interpreting texts are thought to provide the hermeneutical key to the eschatological purpose of God: the jealousy text, and the exhortation to Gentiles (Deut.32.21, 43). These texts are said to testify to the universal scope of the divine mercy; and this creates a tension with the Song itself, where the Lord's vindication of his people means the punishment of their enemies (Deut.32.35–43). In due time, the Lord will turn his anger away from his people onto their enemies:

> In the day of vengeance I will repay *[en hēmera ekdikēseōs antapodosō]*,
> in the day when their foot shall slip.
> For near is the day of their destruction,
> and what is prepared for you is at hand.
> For the Lord will give judgment for his people,
> and for his servants he shall be comforted *[paraklēthēsetai]*.
> For he beheld them powerless,
> and abandoned to captivity and forsaken. (Deut.32.35–36)

The Lord will come to the aid of his people only when they are on the verge of extinction. As he says of himself, "I kill and I make alive" (v.39).

In Romans 12.19, Paul cites the statement about the divine vengeance as a reason for human forbearance:

> Do not take revenge, beloved, but give place to the [divine] wrath: for it is written, "Mine is revenge, I will repay *[emoi ekdikēsis, egō antapodosō]*, says the Lord."

Paul's reading is closer to MT than to LXX in the opening phrase, but corresponds to LXX in presupposing a verb *('šlm)* rather than a noun *(šlm,* "recompense") in the second phrase. The additional "says the Lord" occurs nowhere in the Song of Moses, but has the effect of marking a distinction between the Deuteronomy text and the passage from Proverbs 25.21–22 cited immediately afterwards: "But if your enemy is hungry, feed him . . . " (Rom.12.20). Paul takes the phrase, "Mine is revenge" to mean that revenge is a prerogative that humans should cede to God. It is not clear how far Paul intends his readers to take comfort in the prospect of their enemies' punishment at the judgment – as the Song intends its own readers to do.[62] In the citation although not in the original, the point is simply to forbid a particular human action on the grounds that revenge is an exclusively divine prerogative. It is possible to detect here a subtle marginalizing of the Song's teaching on the divine vengeance. The teaching is acknowledged, but it is given a highly specific function as part of a *prohibition* of revenge. If Christians are not to seek revenge but are to "overcome evil with good" (12.21), modelling their conduct on "the mercies of God" (12.1) as expounded in chapter 11, then it is hard to imagine that God will, at the last, seek to overcome evil with evil.

(v) Deuteronomy 32.43

Paul's third citation from the Song of Moses in Romans continues to follow the original order (Rom.10.19, 12.19, 15.8 = Deut.32.21, 35, 43). It is drawn from the concluding verse of the Song, where the opening call to worship is extended over four lines in LXX, in contrast to MT's single line. The italicized material has no equivalent in MT:

> *Rejoice, heavens, with him,*
>   *and let all the sons of God worship him.*
> Rejoice, Gentiles, *with* his people,
>   *and let all the angels of God ascribe power to him.*
> For he avenges the blood of his sons,
>   and he will take vengeance *and execute judgment* on his enemies,
>   *and those who hate him he will recompense.*
> And the Lord will purify his people's land. (Deut.32.43 LXX)

The similarity of lines 2 and 4 suggests that lines 3–4 may represent a doublet of lines 1–2. This is confirmed by a Qumran Deuteronomy text, which here reads:

> *Rejoice, heavens, with him,*
>   *and let all* gods *worship him.*
> For he avenges the blood of his sons,
>   and takes vengeance on his enemies
>   *and those who hate him he will recompense,*
>   and will make atonement for his people's land. (4QDeut^q)

While this is generally in agreement with LXX against MT (as the italicizations indicate), the LXX's lines 3–4 ("Rejoice, Gentiles, with his

---

62. The references to "giving place to [the] wrath [of God?]" (Rom.12.19) and to the "coals of fire" (12.20) might suggest that abstaining from revenge leaves the way open for the (far more effective) divine vengeance. That would hardly be an overcoming of evil with good, however (12.21, cf. v.17); Paul would be instructing his readers in the most effective way of overcoming evil with evil.

people, and let all the angels of God ascribe power to him") are conspicuously absent. Further evidence of a doublet here may be seen in the fact that "with him" *('mw)* in line 1 of the Qumran text is consonantally identical with "his people" *('mw)* in line 1 of MT:

> Rejoice, heavens, with him *('mw)* ... (4QDeut^q)[63]

> Rejoice, Gentiles, his people *('ammô)* ... (MT)

Thus, lines 1 and 3 of the LXX rendering are closer in the underlying Hebrew than in Greek: the first and last words *(hrnynw, 'mw)* are identical, and only the middle one differs *(šmym; gwym)*. Lines 3–4 LXX may therefore stem from a Hebrew exemplar in which an original two-part call to rejoicing (attested in 4QDeuteronomy^q and lines 1–2 LXX) was expanded. The original expansion could have occurred through dittography, lines 1–2 being accidentally copied twice. If so, a later scribe then addressed the problem of the repetition not by eliminating the added lines but by introducing variations – notably "Gentiles" in place of "heavens", together with alternative terms relating to the angelic worship. The resulting line 3 would now read, "Rejoice, Gentiles, with him" *(hrnynw gwym 'mw)*. Here, the consonantal text could also be taken to mean, "Rejoice, Gentiles, his people", as in MT.[64] Aware of the ambiguity, the LXX translator gets the best of both worlds by combining "with him" and "his people" to give "with his people". This results in the exhortation cited by Paul: "Rejoice, Gentiles, with his people."[65]

If this reconstruction is correct, then 4QDeuteronomy^q represents the earliest accessible Hebrew text, and LXX an accidental expansion of this Hebrew text, subsequently rationalized. The short MT reading might stem from a text resembling the LXX's exemplar, lines 1, 2 and 4 of which are eliminated on the grounds of their theological unorthodoxy.[66] This would mean that the exhortation Paul cites had no place in the earliest accessible Hebrew text of the Song, and that it entered the text owing to an accident of transmission subsequently rationalized by a Hebrew copyist and by the

---

63. The translation assumes that the Qumran copyist understood *'mw* in his line 1 to mean "with him", as the LXX translator did *(hama autō)*. This reading produces a more intelligible sense.

64. Is it supposed to mean, "Praise his people, O you nations" (RSV)?

65. Other reconstructions are possible. P.-M. Bogaert argues for an original text close to MT, except that the opening line reads: "Rejoice, gods (heavens?), with him ... " ("Les trois rédactions conservées et la forme originale de l'envoi du Cantique du Moïse (Dt 32, 43)", p. 333). A two-line opening call to worship seems more probable on form-critical grounds. See also A. van der Kooij, "The Ending of the Song of Moses: On the Pre-Masoretic Version of Deut.32:43"; A. Rofé, "The End of the Song of Moses (Deuteronomy 32:43)", in his *Liebe und Gebot: Studien zum Deuteronomium*, pp. 164–72.

66. So R. D. Nelson, *Deuteronomy*, p. 379.

Septuagint translator. Both rationalizations are essential to Paul's citation. Only if the call to worship is addressed to "Gentiles" rather than "heavens", and only if they are called to rejoice "with his people", is this text usable for his purposes.

Paul cites this text in Romans 15.10, in the context of a series of citations supporting his expression of hope that Gentiles and Jews will worship together and accept one another (cf. 15.5–7). The Deuteronomy text balances the preceding citation from Psalm 17.50: "Therefore I will confess you among the Gentiles, and sing to your name" (Rom.15.9). The Jewish worshipper must worship God in the company of Gentiles; the Gentile worshipper must worship God "with his people". In the Deuteronomy text as in the psalm text that follows (Ps.116.1; Rom.15.11), the scriptural motif of the call to praise can be applied to the Gentiles. Paul finds here the basis for his eirenical vision of a common worship addressed to a God whose saving action is universal in its scope. Indeed, as we have already seen, this text probably accounts for Paul's earlier reading of the passage on the "foolish nation" (Rom.10.19; Deut.32.21) as referring to Gentile salvation.[67] If, at the end, Gentiles are to rejoice with God's people, this suggests that they too have cause for celebration. Nothing in the Song's robust descriptions of the divine vengeance on Israel's enemies gives Gentiles any obvious reason to rejoice (cf. Deut.32.35–43). In this context the reference to Gentile rejoicing seems thoroughly out of place (as indeed it is, from a text-critical standpoint). While Paul notes the Song's testimony to the divine judgment (cf. Rom.12.19), he is much more interested in its testimony to universal reconciliation. From the Song Paul learns that God has caused a no-people consisting of Gentiles to enter the fullness of the blessing promised to Israel. He also learns that Israel will gradually recognize this and, becoming jealous, will find its own way back to its ancestral heritage. Thus, beyond the jealousy and the hostility, Gentiles and Jews will together praise the one God of Israel.[68]

67. The connection that Paul finds between vv.21, 43 of the Song is rightly noted by R. Wagner, *Heralds of the Good News*, pp. 315–17.

68. In opposition to the assumption that the "weak" of Romans 14–15 are Jewish Christians, and that their weakness comes to expression in a scrupulous observance of the law, Mark Nanos has suggested that they are in fact non-Christian Jews (*The Mystery of Romans*, pp. 85–165). Nanos argues that the distinction between the weak and the strong in faith (Rom.14.1–2, 15.1) corresponds to the use of the same terminology in Romans 4.19–21, where Abraham "did not weaken in faith" but, on the contrary, "grew strong in faith" (pp. 139–43). "Weakness" is, then, the condition of those who "cannot see clearly and 'stumble over the stumbling stone' of whether Jesus is the promised Christ who brings the fulfillment of Abraham's promises, and thus over the inclusion of gentiles as equal co-participants in God's blessings without becoming Jews" (p. 143). One problem for this reading is that the "weak" and the "strong" seem already to participate in Christian communal life and worship; thus Christ is the Lord of the weak just as he is Lord of the strong (Rom.14.4–9). For a thorough

The Song of Moses speaks of the sin of Israel and of the divine saving action beyond the inevitable judgment. Paul alludes three times to the Song's treatment of the former topic (Phil.2.15; Rom.3.1–8; 1 Cor.10.20–22), but his three citations in Romans 10–15 relate to the latter and carry greater weight in his argument. In the allusions, there is a tendency to cast the Gentiles in the role assigned in the Song to sinful Israel. Since the main complaint in the Song is of Israel's idolatry, it is easy enough for Paul to see Israel's sin as paradigmatic of the original sin of the entire world (cf. Rom.1.18–25). Yet, in his two most significant citations, Paul preserves the Song's own specific reference to Israel, finding in its utterances the key to God's strange work with God's own people and with the world. In particular, Deuteronomy 32.21 plays a crucial role in the move *beyond* the concept of supersession – the very concept that Paul has taken such pains to elaborate and to defend exegetically in Romans 9–10. Indeed, its citation in Romans 10.19 marks the beginning of a great turning-point in the argument.

Interpreted along these lines, the Song represents a second Pauline attempt to articulate Moses' final, definitive word to the people of Israel. Where Moses is identified with the law that bears his name, his final word is found in the curse that comes to expression in Deuteronomy 27–29. In spite of appearances, Israel's predicament is not resolved by the return to the law called for in chapter 30. Indeed, the surface meaning of that chapter is misleading. Resolution must come not from a new start in relation to the law, following the execution of the law's curse, but from a divine word spoken long before the law, at the very dawning of the history of election: the unconditional, yet-to-be-fulfilled promise that God gave to Abraham on behalf of all who are his descendants. In his office as lawgiver, Moses knows nothing of any such promise. On the other hand, the Moses who speaks in the Song speaks not as lawgiver but as prophet, alongside Isaiah and others (cf. Rom.10.19–21). The theme of his prophetic testimony is the unconditional divine saving act, in spite of the apostasy of God's people and of the world. Here too, what Moses says requires careful interpretation. In particular, his enthusiasm for the divine vengeance on Israel's enemies must be subordinated to the clear hints in his words of a final comprehensive mercy, encompassing a recalcitrant Israel and the "non-nation" of the Gentiles alike.

In Paul's reading of the closing chapters of Deuteronomy, the Torah has two endings. Moses' ministry as lawgiver concludes with the terrible,

critique of Nanos's position, see Robert Gagnon, "Why the 'Weak' at Rome Cannot Be Non-Christian Jews". If the more usual view is correct, and conservative Jewish Christians are in mind, these are nevertheless *representative* of Israel as a whole (cf. 11.1–6), just as Gentile Christians are representative of the non-Jewish world. The fact that both groups are Christians does not eliminate the universal scope of Paul's appeal, or of the scriptural texts he cites (15.9–12).

unforeseen pronouncement of the curse that is to engulf Israel's entire future. Afterwards, however, Moses dons the mantle of the prophet, and is enabled to see beyond the curse of the law and the limiting of the divine blessing to a single nation. At this point, Moses speaks of a strange divine work that aims at a homecoming for Jews and Gentiles alike (admittedly with some crucial help from his copyists and translators). The insight is fragmentary, but it is truly to be found. These two accounts of the ending of the Torah are at odds, however, with the teaching of Deuteronomy 30 – part of which Paul goes to the lengths of rewriting. This is arguably the single most important chapter in the entire Torah for many of Paul's contemporaries. In his alternative, twofold identification of the ending of the Torah, Paul therefore *contests* this exegetical and hermeneutical issue with other readers of the Torah. The radicality of his conclusions will come more clearly to light if they are set alongside the dominant non-Pauline view, according to which the solution to Israel's predicament is and remains the law.

The Return to the Law

The Song of Moses can be a source of hope for Paul because it finds the ground of hope in the God who kills and makes alive, and not in the observance of the law. Deuteronomy 30 presents a rather different scenario, however. Although the history of Israel under the law has been a history of disaster, the law's offer of life to the one who observes it remains open; and this is the key to a future in which the blessings that God has always intended for his people are finally realized. Here, the actualizing of the curse in exile and dispersion is not the end of God's relationship with Israel, but rather the opportunity for a new beginning:

> And when all these words *[rēmata]* come upon you, the blessing and the curse, which I have set before your face, and you receive them in your heart among all the nations *[en pasin tois ethnesin]*, wherever the Lord may have scattered you, and you turn to the Lord your God and obey his voice in all that I command you this day, with all your heart and with all your soul, then the Lord your God will heal *[iasetai]* your sins and have mercy on you, and he will gather you again from all the nations where the Lord your God scattered you. Even if your dispersion *[hē diaspora sou]* is from the end of heaven to the end of heaven, from there the Lord your God will gather you, and from there he will fetch you; and the Lord your God will bring you into the land which your fathers inherited, that you may inherit it ... And the Lord your God will purify your heart and the heart of your seed, to love the Lord your God with all your heart and with all your soul, that you may live *[hina zēs su]* ... And you shall turn, and you shall hear the voice of the Lord your

God, and you shall do his commandments which I command you this day. (Deut.30.1–8)

Paul too knows of a life beyond the curse of the law, but for him this is a life originating in the resurrection of Jesus, a life of freedom from the law. In Deuteronomy, the turning to the Lord and his commandments leads to a return to the land and to a cleansing of the heart that ensures continued obedience and therefore life. From the standpoint of dispersion and its ongoing reality, the curse of the law represents the past whereas the law's promise of life represents the future. The present is, potentially, the turning-point between that past and that future, the moment in which dispersed Israel is challenged to return to the law, turning from a past of disobedience and death to a future of obedience and life.

This deuteronomic schema is elaborated with great clarity by the (Greek) book of *Baruch*.[69] This work, which may have been written as an adjunct to the LXX translation of Jeremiah, consists of a lengthy confession of sin, followed by a wisdom poem and a passage of prophetic consolation. As we shall see, there is a logic to this arrangement, which should not too quickly be subjected to source-critical disintegration into originally independent fragments.

Like the book of Daniel, this book is set against the background of the Babylonian exile.[70] Baruch, Jeremiah's former scribe (cf. Jer.32.12; 36 *passim*; 43.3; 45.1–5), is said to have written a book in Babylon at the time of the fall of Jerusalem, and to have read it to those who were already in exile (Bar.1.1–4). The exilic community agrees to send this book to the priests and people who remain in Jerusalem, together with a request that sacrifice and prayer be offered on behalf of Nebuchadnezzar and his son Belshazzar, under whose rule the community hopes to live in peace and

---

69. The significance of this work in this connection is rightly noted by James M. Scott, "Galatians 3.10", pp. 201–203. Scott points out that this and other texts indicating "a prolonged disruption in the covenantal relationship" are largely absent from the work of E. P. Sanders (*ibid.*, p. 202n).

70. Texts that adopt the deuteronomic schema presuppose that "exile" is ongoing, and some of them therefore provide a fictional exilic setting (e.g. Daniel, Tobit, *2 Baruch, 4 Ezra*) which is understood as closely analogous to the present. Alternatively, the exile and the final return may be presented as the goal of a history revealed in advance, whether to Enoch (1 En. 93.8–10) or to Moses (Jub.1.5–18). The exile may be extended to seventy weeks of years (Dn.9.24–27), or to 390 years (CD i.3–11; cf. Ezek.3.5, 9). The significance of this theme has been brought out by N. T. Wright, in his *The New Testament and the People of God*, pp. 268–79. For Wright, it is basic to "Israel's worldview" at this time that "we are still in exile" (p. 243), and that the history of God's covenant relationship with his people awaits a definitive conclusion in which YHWH will come to Zion and the exile will be brought to an end. It may, however, be an exaggeration to ascribe this belief to "most Jews of this period" (p. 268). It should also be noted that the Babylonian exile often serves as a metaphor for *diaspora* or "dispersion" (the term used in Deuteronomy 30.4).

security (1.5–13). The book is to be read in the house of the Lord (which still appears to be standing), and it is in the first instance a book of confession (1.14). Baruch confesses that the present disasters manifest God's righteousness, since the people have consistently disobeyed the voice of the Lord from the exodus onward, and have succumbed to the curse of which Moses warned (1.15–2.5). Even now, there has been no true repentance (2.6–10). Turning from confession to supplication, Baruch asks for deliverance from the total destruction that threatens, and thus for favour in the eyes of those who carried the people into exile. Alongside the earlier request for sacrifices and prayers on behalf of the Babylonian rulers, this prayer marks a turning away from the earlier refusal to obey the divine command to serve the king of Babylon, which had such dire consequences (2.11–26). Baruch's long confession appeals to Moses' promise that exile would lead to repentance and return (2.27–35), before concluding with final pleas and expressions of confidence that it is God who has now moved the community to repent and to call upon his name (3.1–8).

The second part of the book opens abruptly by addressing itself no longer to God but to Israel (3.9–4.4). The idiom is now that of the wisdom literature rather than Deuteronomy, but the identification of wisdom and law ensures thematic coherence with the first part. A depiction of the world's fruitless quest for a wisdom known only to God, but revealed in the gift of the law (3.15–4.1), is enclosed within pleas to Israel to find in the law the way to life (3.9–14; 4.2–4). The third and final section of the book speaks of the people's sinful past and future glory from the standpoint of Jerusalem, portrayed as a mother who has lost her children because of their disobedience, but who now joyfully anticipates their return (4.5–5.9). The idiom here shows the influence especially of Isaiah 40–66. Thus the book as a whole moves from a confession oriented towards the past to a consolation oriented towards the future, by way of an appeal to live here and now as worthy recipients of the gift of the law, the embodiment of wisdom. The three parts of the book have their respective backgrounds in the law, the wisdom literature, and the prophets – that is, in all three sections of the scriptural canon. What is striking about this text is not its incoherence but, on the contrary, its synthesis of diverse material derived from a remarkably broad scriptural background. This short book represents in outline a reading of scripture as a whole. As we shall see, however, scripture as a whole is read from a controlling deuteronomic perspective.

Whether or not any part of the book predates its present context, our concern is with its final form.[71] Although it is often thought to be a

---

71. In spite of the consensus that *Baruch* is a composite work (so e.g. C. A. Moore, *Additions*, pp. 258–59), there is no reason why a single author should be incapable of imitating

translation from a Hebrew original, arguments for this hypothesis are unconvincing.[72] Passages which are said to reflect Hebrew idiom can more satisfactorily be explained as deriving from earlier Septuagintal texts (notably Jeremiah).[73] At two points at least, there is unambiguous evidence of dependence on the Greek version of the Book of Daniel ascribed to Theodotion.[74] Qumran has produced no trace of a Hebrew original for

different biblical idioms. O. Steck's comment is apposite: the problem with theories of disunity is, "dass sie mit dem Leitbild eines Autorindividuums operieren, dem stilistische und thematische Vielseitigkeit nicht zugetraut werden kann, dass anderwärts belegte – man denke nur an Sir oder Qumrantexte – theologiegeschichtliche Komplexität zur Abfassungszeit von Bar nicht in Rechnung gestellt wird, und vor allem, dass die Frage nach einer ganz Bar tragenden theologischen Leitkonzeption ausser Betracht bleibt" (*Das apokryphe Baruchbuch*, p. 254).

72. The assumption of a Hebrew original derives from the monograph of J. Kneucker, *Das Buch Baruch* (1879), which is based on a reconstructed Hebrew text. The continuing influence of this methodologically flawed approach is still evident in O. Steck's major monograph of 1993. (Steck's main concern is to present *Baruch* as the mediator of a now normative and canonical tradition to a readership that remains "in exile".)

73. Examples of "translation Greek" given by O. C. Whitehouse (*APOT* i.572) may be explained as deriving from the LXX rather than a Hebrew original. For example, the phrase *peri hamartias* in *Baruch* 1.10 is no more a sign of a Hebrew original than it is in Romans 8.3; and *poiēsate manna* here is influenced by Jeremiah 48.5 LXX. In *Baruch* 2.26, *ton oikon hou epeklēthē to onoma sou ep' autō* is a Hebraism paralleled in LXX Jeremiah 7.14, 30; 39.34; 41.15. It is often suggested that "the prayer of the dead in Israel" (Bar.3.4) represents a mistranslation of *mty* as "dead" rather than "men"; yet Israel is "counted among those in Hades" in 3.11. Although points like these are said to show that a hypothesis of a Hebrew original is "incontrovertible" (so C. A. Moore, *Additions*, p. 257), the hypothesis appears to be based on a simple methodological error. While E. Tov explains the links between LXX Jeremiah and Baruch by postulating that the same translator was responsible for both (*The Septuagint Translation of Jeremiah and Baruch*, pp. 111–33, 165), the influence of LXX Jeremiah is a more likely explanation for the points of contact. Tov's hypothesis would entail an early dating for *Baruch*, which seems to be ruled out on other grounds (see below).

74. Daniel 9.15 (Theodotion) is reproduced almost *verbatim* in *Baruch* 2.11 (although some supplementary material is added); likewise Daniel 9.7–8 in *Baruch* 1.15–16 (where there is also material unique to each text). In these passages there is exact correspondence for 25 and 24 words respectively, and almost exact correspondence for several others. There is also a nine-word correspondence between *Baruch* 2.14 and Daniel 9.17 (Theodotion). All this cannot be a coincidence, and neither can it stem from the independent faithfulness to the Hebrew Daniel 9 both of a Hebrew Baruch and of Theodotion (the view of O. Steck, *Das apokryphe Baruchbuch*, p. 95, who refers to "occasional" agreements with Theodotion but does not identify or discuss them). *Baruch* 2.12a comprises three verb forms identical to Daniel 9.5a LXX, which may suggest that the author – like Origen (*ad Afric.* 2) – was already familiar with both early Greek translations of Daniel. While this matter requires further investigation, the evidence of dependence on the Theodotion translation is in itself sufficient to rule out a Hebrew original. Steck lists a number of cases in which Baruch is supposed to agree with MT against LXX and Theodotion/Daniel (p. 251n). The instances cited consist of individual words or short phrases, and they are unconvincing. For example, in *Baruch* 2.19, *ouk epi ta dikaiōmata [tōn paterōn]* does not agree with *l' 'l sdqtynw* against *ouk epi tais dikaiosunais*

Baruch. As regards dating, the relationship to Daniel-Theodotion rules out a date in the second century BCE.[75] On the other hand, the attempt to date the first part (and therefore the final redaction as well) after the destruction of Jerusalem in 70 CE is implausible.[76] The reference to Nebuchadnezzar and his son Belshazzar (1.11) is probably drawn from the book of Daniel, and there is no need to see an allusion here to Vespasian and Titus. Allusions or quotations in a range of patristic writers (Athenagoras, Irenaeus, Clement, Origen, Hippolytus and others) indicate that *Baruch* held a secure place within the Septuagintal texts by the later second century CE, making a relatively early dating more likely.[77] In contrast to the eschatological concerns of late first or early second century texts such as *4 Ezra* and *2 Baruch*, the author of *Baruch* follows his scriptural exemplars in omitting all reference to individual resurrection. Above all, the author (or final redactor) does not appear to respond to an acute crisis such as that of 70 CE. The emphasis falls not on the physical destruction of temple or city but on the long-term reality of dispersion and exile. Indeed, despite the reference to the Chaldean destruction of Jerusalem (1.5), the temple is still in operation as the place where sacrifices are offered and confession is repeatedly to be made (1.10–14). Priests and people are instructed by the exiles to use Baruch's book "to make your confession in the house of the Lord on the days of the feasts and at appointed times" (1.14). There is no good reason to suppose that this book is to be dated later than 70 CE.

hēmōn (Dan.9.16). In *Baruch* 2.30, 32, *en gē apoikismō* does not clearly agree with *m'rṣ šbym* in Jeremiah 46.47 (an otherwise unrelated passage) over against *ek tēs aichmalōsias autōn* (Jer.26.27 LXX – the same passage). It is true that *aischunē tōn prosōpōn* (Bar.1.15; cf. 2.6) reproduces the plural in *bšt pnym* (Dan.9.7, 8), whereas *aischunē tou prosōpou* does not; but this hardly outweighs the indisputable dependence on Daniel-Theodotion in precisely this passage (Bar.1.15–16; Dan.9.7–8). Steck concedes the widespread Septuagintal influence on *Baruch* but ascribes this to the Greek translator (pp. 251–52), or, in the case of Jeremiah 29–52 LXX, to the Hebrew *Vorlage* of this text. The more obvious conclusion is simply that *Baruch* was composed in Greek.

75.   The crucial issue would seem to be the dating of the translation of Daniel ascribed to Theodotion. The current consensus is that, in the case of Daniel and other parts of the Hebrew Bible, "a translation very similar to Theodotion's was already in use in the first century B.C.E." (K. H. Jobes and M. Silva, *Invitation to the Septuagint*, p. 42; see the literature cited there).

76.   This late dating was favoured by O. C. Whitehouse, *APOT* 1.574–75, who presented this as the consensus position, and by W. O. E. Oesterley (*Introduction to the Books of the Apocrypha*, p. 260).

77.   Details of patristic usage of this work are given in *APOT* i.580–81. Two early citations (Irenaeus, *AH* v.35; Clement, *Paed.* i.10.91–92) ascribe the book to Jeremiah – presumably on the assumption that Baruch continued to act as Jeremiah's secretary. This tends to confirm the suggestion that *Baruch* never existed apart from LXX Jeremiah. In *2 Esdras* 2.2–4, material from *Baruch* 4.11–19 is redeployed to further the author's supersessionist argument.

As we have seen, the three parts of the book have their respective background in each of the three major divisions of the scriptural canon. Yet, in the second and third parts, the influence of texts and themes from Deuteronomy is still perceptible. The wisdom poem and the prophetic consolation are both subjected to the fundamental deuteronomic schema of law-sin-exile-repentance-return. It is this deuteronomic schema that gives an apparently disparate text its remarkable underlying coherence.[78] Since Paul too remains dependent on this schema even as he breaks with it, our study of the book of *Baruch* will focus on its use of texts drawn from Deuteronomy.

(1) Baruch's confession (1.15–3.8) opens with an acknowledgment of God's righteousness and of Israel's guilt (1.15–18). Israel's entire history is a history of disobedience:

> From the day when the Lord brought our fathers out of the land of Egypt until this day, we have been disobedient to the Lord our God and have neglected to hear his voice. And, to this very day, the evils and the curse [*ta kaka kai hē ara*] have clung to us, which the Lord commanded through Moses his servant in the day in which he brought our fathers out of the land of Egypt to give us the land flowing with milk and honey. And we did not hear the voice of the Lord our God in all the words of the prophets, which he sent to us... (Bar.1.19–21)

The "curse" here is the curse of Deuteronomy 27.26 ("Cursed be every person who does not remain in all the words of this law, to do them"), as elaborated into a series of specific evils in the following chapter (28.15–68) and summarized in the choice of life or death, good or evil, blessing or curse in the concluding exhortation (30.15–20; cf. also 29.20–28). Of the alternative future histories set forth long ago by Moses, it is the history of disobedience, culminating in death, evil and the curse, that has been realized. The prophets were sent to repeat and reinforce Moses' warnings, but they were not heeded any more than he was. In both its written and its oral forms, the voice of the Lord has been ignored, and Israel now suffers the consequences. Exactly the same deuteronomic interpretation of the history of Israel occurs in the prayer in Daniel 9 that was the model for Baruch's confession:

> To the Lord our God belong mercies and forgiveness, for we have rebelled and have not listened to the voice of the Lord our God, to walk in his law which he gave us by the hands of his servants the prophets. And all Israel transgressed your law and turned aside so as not to hear your voice, and there came upon us the curse and the oath that are

---

78. So G. Nickelsburg, "The Bible Rewritten and Expanded", p. 145; O. Steck, *Das apokryphe Baruchbuch*, p. 266. Both scholars reject the more usual assumption of multiple authorship.

> written in the Law of Moses the servant of God *[hē katara kai ho orkos*
> *ho gegrammenos en nomō Mōuseōs doulou tou theou]* – for we sinned
> against him . . . As it is written in the Law of Moses, all these evils came
> upon us . . . (Dan.9.9–13 Thdt.)

In Daniel as in *Baruch*, the disasters that have now taken place show that
the curse of the law is the controlling factor of Israel's whole history, from
the exodus to the present.[79] Paul is not alone in claiming that the whole of
Israel's existence is subject to the curse of the law (Gal.3.10).

In the earlier writers, the fulfilment of Moses' warnings serves to confirm
his authority. Thus Baruch rewrites Daniel 9.12–13 so as to bring out the
fact that what has happened in Jerusalem fulfils Moses' prophecies to the
letter – in this case, his gruesome prophecy that during the siege of
Jerusalem parents will eat their own children (Deut.28.53–57, cf.
Lev.26.29):

> And under the whole heaven it has not been done as he [the Lord] did in
> Jerusalem, according to what is written in the Law of Moses, that we
> should eat one man the flesh of his son and another the flesh of his
> daughter. (Bar.2.2–3)

Similarly, Josephus tells of an incident during the siege of Jerusalem in 70
CE in which a once wealthy woman named Mary daughter of Eleazar
killed, roasted and ate her own infant son – to the horror of both the
besiegers and the starving inhabitants of Jerusalem (*BJ*. vi.199–219). This
is presented as an isolated incident, "an act unparalleled in the history
either of Greek or of barbarians" (vi.199). Although Josephus does not
draw attention to its scriptural background, it is likely that he expects
informed Jewish readers to make the connection and to draw the
appropriate conclusion about the fulfilment of Moses' prophetic word.[80]
The *Baruch* text speaks not of an isolated incident but of a practice that is
assumed to have been commonplace during Nebuchadnezzar's siege, but
here too the emphasis falls on the unprecedented nature of this practice.
Daniel's confession had spoken in general terms of the evils that occurred
in Jerusalem, in fulfilment of what Moses wrote; and Baruch, rewriting and
expanding Daniel's confession, seizes on perhaps the most horrible of the

---

79. Motifs shared by Daniel and *Baruch* occur at Bar.1.15–16, Dan.9.7–8 (divine
righteousness, human confusion); Bar.1.17–18, 21, Dan.9.5–6 (confession of sin); Bar.1.20,
Dan.9.11, 13 (Mosaic curse); Bar.2.2–3, Dan.9.12–13 (destruction of Jerusalem); Bar.2.11,
Dan.9.15 (exodus as basis for confession); Bar.2.13, Dan.9.16 (plea for end of divine anger);
Bar.2.14, Dan.9.17 (plea to be heard, for God's own sake); Bar.2.19, Dan.9.18 (prayer not
based in our own righteousness). It is notable that *Baruch* presents this material in the same
order as in Daniel 9 – with the exception that Daniel 9.5–6, 7–8 are reversed.

80. Despite emphasizing the "unparalleled" nature of this act, Josephus elsewhere retells
the story of the similar incident recorded in 2 Kings 6.24–31 (*Ant.* ix.64–67).

many evils foreseen in Deuteronomy 28 and claims (on the basis of Lamentations 2.20, 4.10?) that it actually took place, thereby confirming the authority of Moses' prophecy.[81] It was the Lord who brought it about that, during the siege, parents ate their own children, as he had warned through Moses. The divine curse envisaged the whole of what Israel suffered at that time, down to the last terrible detail.

In a third appeal to Moses, Baruch now finds in his final speeches an expression of hope for a future beyond the curse. A free paraphrase of Deuteronomy 30.1–10 is presented:

> Yet you acted towards us, O Lord our God, in accordance with your gentleness and your great compassion, as you spoke by the hand of your servant Moses in the day when you commanded him to write your law before the sons of Israel, saying: If you do not hear my voice, this great multitude will surely become a small number among the nations where I shall scatter you. For I knew that they would not hear me, for they are a stubborn people. And they will turn in their heart in the land of their exile, and they will know that I am the Lord their God. And I shall give them a heart and ears that hear, and they will praise me in the land of their exile, and they will remember my name, and they will turn from their stubbornness and from their evil deeds, for they will recall the way of their fathers who sinned before the Lord. And I shall bring them back to the land which I swore to their fathers, to Abraham, Isaac and Jacob, and they will rule over it. And I shall multiply them, and they will not be diminished. And I shall establish with them an eternal covenant, to be God to them and that they should be my people. And I will not again remove my people Israel from the land which I gave to them. (Bar.2.27–35)

Here, the introductory reference to "the day when you commanded him to write your law before the sons of Israel" suggests that Baruch has in mind the depiction of a future beyond the curse in Deuteronomy 30.1–10. In the following chapter, Moses writes "this law" (31.9, 24), and is also commanded to write the song which will serve as a witness against future generations (31.19–22). It is therefore the passage in the preceding chapter that is foremost in the author's mind. The main themes of Baruch's paraphrase correspond to Deuteronomy 30, although it also incorporates material drawn from elsewhere: the diminishing of the great multitude into a tiny remnant (Deut.28.62, with an ironic allusion to the patriarchal promise); the people's stubbornness (Deut.9.13; 32.20); their repentance in exile (Deut.30.1–2; Lev.26.40–41); their coming to know the Lord (Ezek.36.11); the gift of a new heart (Deut.30.6; Ezek.11.19, 36.26);

---

81. The point here is not that consuming one's own child is "the culmination of Israel's sinfulness" (so D. J. Harrington, *Invitation to the Apocrypha*, p. 95), but that Moses' authority has been confirmed by the fulfilment of his prophecy.

rejection of the sinful ways of preceding generations (Zech.1.2–6); return to the land in accordance with the promise to the patriarchs (Lev.26.42–43; Jer.30.3); an increase in numbers (Deut.30.5); and the everlasting covenant (Jer.31.33; Ezek.36.28). Baruch's paraphrase differs from Deuteronomy in connecting the exiled people's repentance with the divine gift of a new heart and of ears that hear. In Deuteronomy, the repentance takes place in exile (30.1–2) and the circumcision (MT) or purification (LXX) of the heart occurs after the return (30.6). The three distinct phases of exile, transformation and return are more clearly demarcated in *Baruch* than in Deuteronomy, and the use of prophetic material to reinforce Moses' testimony recalls the implication of *Baruch* 1.20–21, that the role of the prophets is to repeat and amplify what has already been said through Moses. There is a parallel here to Paul's ascription of quotations from the psalms and the prophets to the voice of the law (Rom.3.9–20).

Baruch's confession – which, we recall, is to be read regularly in the temple (Bar.1.14) – enacts the transformation of which it speaks. At the end of the confession, the community acknowledges that

> you have set the fear of yourself in our heart, so that we may call upon your name; and we shall praise you in our exile, for we have put away from our hearts all the wickedness of our fathers who sinned before you. (3.7)

Just as the curse of which Moses warned has been fulfilled (1.20–2.3), so now the promised future beyond the curse begins to take shape, precisely in the act of confession and praise. All three elements here – the new heart, the praise of God, the turning from the sins of the fathers – correspond closely to the new beginning that God promised through Moses:

> I shall give them a heart and ears that hear, and they will praise me in the land of their exile ... and they will turn from their stubbornness and from their evil deeds, for they will recall the way of their fathers who sinned before the Lord. (Bar.2.32–33)

The act of confession is itself seen as the fulfilment of this promise, which opens up the possibility of a new future in the land. Confession originates not in despair but in hope. The acknowledgment that the past has been determined by the law's curse derives from the hope that the future will be determined by the law's blessing. Moses' offer of two hypothetical possibilities – blessing or curse, life or death – is realized in the form of two consecutive histories, the past history of the law as the bearer of death and curse and a future history of the law as the bearer of life and blessing. The confessing community stands at the turning-point between these two histories.

Like Baruch, Paul too sees the history of Israel as a history under the law's curse. "Those who are of the law *[hoi tou nomou]*" are identical to those who are subject to the curse the law pronounces on transgressors (Gal.3.10; Deut.27.26). Paul, again like Baruch, has reached this conclusion on the basis of the concluding chapters of Deuteronomy (and of the Torah as a whole). For both writers, the Torah's conclusion is their own starting-point. Neither is interested in the ups and downs of Israel's canonical history, from the conquest to the exile and partial restoration. In both cases, a drastic foreshortening takes place as the rebellion of the wilderness period becomes a paradigm for the entire history. It is the deuteronomic curse that bestows this paradigmatic status on events at the beginning of Israel's history – events that might otherwise have been no more than unfortunate aberrations:

> From the day when the Lord brought our fathers out of the land of Egypt and until this day, we have been disobedient to the Lord our God and have neglected to hear his voice. And, to this very day, the evils and the curse have clung to us, which the Lord commanded through Moses his servant... (Bar.1.19)

Thus, the entire history of Israel is already contained *in nuce* within the Torah itself, and the writings of the "former prophets" are no more than commentary on this.[82] Indeed, the history of Israel has been so compressed that it is not clear whether Israel still *has* a "history" at all. History as the unfolding succession of events is reduced to its essence, which is the state of perpetual disharmony between Israel and its God – a problem crying out for a resolution.

Paul's characteristic terse formulations are making closely related points: "the law brings wrath" (Rom.4.15); "law came in to increase the trespass" (Rom.5.20); "the power of sin is the law" (1 Cor.15.56); "the letter kills" (2 Cor.3.6). Such statements as these reflect not only the distinctive Pauline problematizing of the law, but also its scriptural roots in the concluding chapters of Deuteronomy – where the law itself announces the nexus of law, sin and death that will determine Israel's future.

Baruch and Paul also agree that Deuteronomy not only poses Israel's fundamental dilemma but also points towards its divine resolution. Baruch finds this resolution in the prospect opened up in Deuteronomy 30.1–10 of a life subject at last to the law's requirements. This passage announces that

---

82. Compare the confession in Nehemiah 9, which lacks the explicit reference to the curse of the law and gives an extended account of God's dealings with his people, from the call of Abraham to the conquest, the period of the judges, and the constant rebellions that provoke the divine wrath (vv.7–31). The presentation balances an emphasis on the divine mercy and grace with an acknowledgment of Israel's constant tendency to rebel. In the later confessions of Daniel and Baruch, the motif of the law's curse creates both a foreshortening of this history and a bias towards its negative side; here, Israel's history is no longer – or not yet – *Heilsgeschichte*.

there is, after all, a life beyond the law's curse, although it is still determined by the law; the curse and the blessing are not alternative but consecutive futures. In contrast, Paul finds the resolution of Israel's dilemma in the Song of Moses, which speaks not of a final turning to the law but of a definitive act of God for Israel's vindication – a strangely circuitous act that also encompasses the "foolish nation" of the Gentiles, so that, in the end, the praise of God may be universal (cf. Rom.10.19, 15.8; Deut.32.21, 43). In the Song, the Torah points to a resolution lying beyond its own horizons, in the act of the God who kills and makes alive, who wounds and heals, and who consigns all to disobedience so that he may have mercy upon all (cf. Deut.32.39; Rom.11.32).

In citing Deuteronomy 27.26, however, Paul finds the resolution of the dilemma posed at the end of the Torah in the blessing pronounced near its beginning (Gal.3.6–14). For Paul, it is the Christ-event that marks the turning-point between a history of death and the curse and a history of life and blessing. Life and blessing are no longer the gifts of the law; realized in Christ, they actually predate the law, in the form of the unconditional promise. The deuteronomic ideology that shapes Baruch's confession has no room for an unconditional promise; for, in both the old and the new histories, possession of the land promised to the fathers is dependent on faithful observance of the law.[83] In one case, the turning-point between the old and new is a matter of appropriate *human* action, beginning with confession and determined by the law. In the other case, the turning-point is a matter of definitive, unsurpassable *divine* saving action, which reorients human action towards itself and so represents a breach with the law. The antithesis between human and divine action is by no means absolute. The return to the law is a human action inspired by God (Bar.2.31–33; 3.7), and the divine action in Christ intends the human action of faith that corresponds to it and acknowledges it. Yet, although the return to the law is achieved only with divine assistance, the law's basic premise, that the divine blessing is conditional on human obedience, remains intact. The offer is made of a second chance to realize the blessing through observing the law. The old history, recorded in scripture, is significant chiefly as a permanently valid warning of the danger of disobedience, an ever-present

---

83. The relationship between Deuteronomy and the Genesis promise is acutely analysed by Robert Polzin, who writes: "The distinction between the covenant with the fathers and the covenant at Horeb is absolutely basic to the ideological tension within this book. The presence in an utterance in Deuteronomy of a phrase such as 'the God of our fathers' or 'the covenant made with the fathers' or 'the oath which God swore to our fathers' brings with it associations of mercy, grace, and divine election that are at odds with the ultimate viewpoint of the book on the [retributive] justice of God" (*Moses and the Deuteronomist*, p. 54). Polzin argues that, in passages such as Deuteronomy 13.17–18, the unconditional connotations of the patriarchal promise are "neutralized" by the addition of a necessary condition of obedience (p. 53).

memorial of disobedience – like the pillar of salt that was once Lot's wife. It is an extended cautionary tale, from which the community must learn to be different from its forebears (2.33; 3.7).

Paul understands the scriptural history not primarily as a cautionary tale but as an indirect testimony to Christ. Still more emphatically than Baruch, he believes it to be a history of disaster; but he also believes that, precisely as such, it is also of the greatest positive significance. In the light of God's life-giving action in Christ, the law discloses the limits and limitations of a human action that intends the life that the law itself conditionally offers. Thus, the fact that the law has in practice generated an *Unheilsgeschichte* is no accident. Rather, it is the law's own confirmation of the gospel's claim that life-giving saving action is the prerogative of God alone. In Deuteronomy 30, Moses announces that the problem posed by the old history can be solved by the offer of a second chance to secure life under what is still essentially the old regime. Baruch follows him in this. For Paul, that is to miss the final significance of the scriptural rendering of Israel's history, in which the curse of the law is in the end the negative corollary of the blessing of Abraham.

(2) According to the wisdom poem that follows the confession (Bar.3.9–4.4), the way to understanding (*phronēsis:* 3.9, 14, 28), wisdom (*sophia:* 3.12, 23) or knowledge (*epistēmē:* 3.20, 27, 36) is known to God alone, and humankind is ignorant of it (3.15–36). Yet God has imparted "the whole way of knowledge" to Israel, in the form of "the book of the decrees of God, the law which endures for ever" (3.37, 4.1).[84] The main body of the poem (3.15–31) depicts human ignorance of the way in terms reminiscent of Job 28. In both cases, the question about the way to wisdom ("Where shall wisdom be found...?" [Job 28.12]; "Who has found her place...?" [Bar.3.20]) leads to an acknowledgment of human ignorance (Job 28.13 LXX; Bar.3.31), and to a confession that the way is known only to God (Job 28 23–27; Bar.3.32–35), who nevertheless imparts this way to humans in the form either of the announcement that the fear of the Lord is wisdom (Job 28.28), or of the giving of the law to Israel (Bar.3.37; 4.1). In Baruch though not in Job, the contrast between human ignorance and divine knowledge is at the same time a contrast between the ignorance of Gentiles (3.16, 22–23, 27) and the divinely imparted knowledge possessed by Israel. The theme of the poem is in fact the election of Israel to be the people to whom the law was given. As in the well-known case of Sirach 24, the

---

84. References to the conclusion of *Baruch* 3 follow the enumeration of the verses in the Greek rather than in the English translations. *Baruch* 3.34–35 LXX corresponds to 3.34 EVV, with the result that 3.36–38 LXX corresponds to 3.35–37 EVV.

language of the wisdom tradition is now deployed in order to glorify the gift of the Torah to Israel.[85]

Besides making the identification of wisdom and law clear at the outset, the poem's opening exhortation serves to connect it with the confession that precedes it:

> Hear, O Israel, the commandments of life, give ear to know understanding. Why is it, O Israel, why is it that you are in the land of your enemies, that you grow old in a strange land, that you are defiled by the dead, that you are counted among those in Hades? You forsook the fountain of wisdom! If you had walked in the way of God, you would have dwelt in peace for ever. Learn where there is understanding, where there is strength, where there is insight, so as to know where there is both longevity and life *[makrobiōsis kai zōē]*, where there is light for the eyes and peace. (Bar.3.9–14)

Here, the claim that Israel finds itself in exile because of its apostasy from "the way of God" repeats in different language the fundamental premise of the preceding confession. The identification of Israel with the dead (3.10–11) recalls the reference in 3.4 to "the prayer of Israel's dead" (a connection that is hard to explain on the assumption that the confession and the wisdom poem were originally entirely independent of one another). Most important of all, the opening exhortation is linked with the confession's announcement and enactment of the turning away from the sins of the fathers (3.7), as foreseen by Moses (2.27–35). This is to be a turning from the law's curse to the law's blessing, from death to life – and it is therefore appropriate that Israel should now be exhorted to "hear the commandments of life", recognizing that exile and death are not what the law intends (3.9–11). In the poem as a whole, the wisdom tradition serves to highlight the fact that Israel's possession of the law is not a burden but a privilege and a gift, truly the way to life. The wisdom tradition is employed here to communicate a more positive message about the law as the means to national salvation.

This co-opting of the wisdom tradition into the service of deuteronomic ideology is evident from the poem's opening words: "Hear, O Israel, [the] commandments of life, give ear to know understanding" (Bar.3.9). The form of this call to attention in two-part parallelism is derived from the wisdom literature; to the reader familiar with this literature, Baruch's sudden change of idiom is immediately perceptible. Yet there is also a significant difference. In parallel passages in Proverbs, the call to "hear" is accompanied by the vocative, "son[s]": "Hear, my son, your father's

---

85. The parallel is particularly close in *Sirach* 24.23 and *Baruch* 4.1, where wisdom – bestowed uniquely upon Israel (Sir.24.8–12; Bar.3.36) – is finally identified with the book of the law. On this see E. J. Schnabel, *Law and Wisdom from Ben Sira to Paul*, pp. 95–99.

instruction, and do not reject your mother's precepts" (Prov.1.8). Where the term "commandment" is used, the reference is typically to "*my* commandment[s]" – as in Proverbs 7.2, "Keep my commandments and you shall live" (cf. Prov.2.1; 7.1). Thus, in the call to attention that opens Baruch's wisdom poem, a reference to the commandments addressed by God to Israel supplants the traditional reference to the instructions of a parent to a child. This point is underlined by the fact that "Hear, O Israel" alludes to Deuteronomy 6.4: "Hear, O Israel, the Lord our God is one Lord." The result is that the second part of the call to attention ("Give ear to know understanding"), which in itself reproduces exactly the idiom of Proverbs (cf. Prov.4.1b), acquires a new meaning: it is the Law of Moses that will convey understanding to those who heed its appeal and attend to its voice. The sapiential style clothes a deuteronomic substance; but what is emphasized is now the positive message, that the commandments continue to point the way to life.

The commandments, then, are "commandments of life" (Bar.3.9). Israel's descent into the realm of the dead has been contrary to the divine intention that by observing the commandments Israel would dwell securely in the land for ever (3.10–13). Even now, the situation can easily be remedied, if Israel will only learn where wisdom and life are to be found (3.14). The author's reworking of the traditional motif of wisdom's inaccessibility leads him once again back to Deuteronomy. According to Deuteronomy 30.12–14, the life-giving commandments are easy and ready-to-hand, and need not be sought in inaccessible locations above the sky or over the sea. Echoing this passage, *Baruch* at first seems to envisage precisely the inaccessibility that Deuteronomy rules out:

> Who ascended into heaven, and took her, and brought her down from the clouds? Who crossed over the sea, and found her, and will buy her for choice gold? (Bar.3.29–30)

In Deuteronomy, the future tenses ("who will ascend?", etc.) imply a search for a volunteer (cf. Is.6.8). The point of the instruction, "Do not say ... " is that there is no need for anyone to undertake any such arduous quest, since the law has already been given and made accessible. In contrast, the substitution of aorist tenses in *Baruch* assimilates the language of Deuteronomy to the traditional claim that wisdom is humanly inaccessible (cf. Job 28.12–28). Here, however, this claim serves simply to emphasize that God has already bestowed this otherwise inaccessible wisdom on the people of Israel, in the form of the law. God

> found the whole way to knowledge, and gave her to Jacob his servant, and to Israel whom he loved ... This is the book of the decrees of God and the law which exists for ever. All who hold fast to her will live *[pantes hoi kratountes autēs eis zōēn]*, but those who forsake her will die

[hoi de kataleipontes autēn apothanountai]. Turn, O Jacob, and take her, walk towards the shining of her light. Do not give to another your glory, or your privileges to a foreign people. Blessed are we, O Israel, for what pleases God is known to us. (3.37–4.4)[86]

The past has been erased, for the law permits a new start in which the recipients of the law learn to rejoice in it and to regard it as the unique privilege that it truly is, and not as an unwelcome imposition. Israel is to be reconstituted on the basis of this new joy in the law, which will set those who observe it on the way to "life" – the life of those who have been gathered in from the places of their exile, and who now dwell securely in the land promised to the fathers. That is also the theme of the third and final section of this book.

(3) *Baruch* concludes with a section of prophetic consolation (4.5–5.9), in which the personified Jerusalem is first the speaker (4.9–29) and then the addressee (4.30–5.9). After a brief introduction, in which the people are yet again reminded of their sin and consequent exile (4.5–8), there follows a speech in which Jerusalem begins by lamenting her widowhood and the loss of her sons and daughters (4.9–20; cf. Lam.1.11–22). Yet, in an abrupt transition, lamentation gives way to an expression of hope (Bar.4.21–29). Shortly after the despairing dismissal of her sons and daughters as they go forth into exile ("Go, my children, go, for I have been left desolate" [4.20]), they are exhorted to "be of good courage", confident that "he will deliver you from the power and hand of the enemy" (4.21). An explanation is given for the change of tone:

> For I have put my hope in the Eternal One for your salvation, and joy came to me from the Holy One because of the mercy which will quickly come to you from your Eternal Saviour. (4.22)

Unexpectedly, God has transformed the widow's grief into a joy which is the harbinger of her children's imminent return. Her own expression of hope is taken up by a prophetic voice which addresses her in words inspired especially by the oracles addressed to Jerusalem in Isaiah 40–66. Common themes include: God as the comforter of Jerusalem (Bar.4.30; Is.49.14–16); Jerusalem's sight of the returning exiles (Bar.4.36–37, 5.5; Is.49.18, 60.4–5); her reclothing herself in beautiful garments (Bar.5.1–2; Is.52.1); the exiles' triumphant arrival (Bar.5.6; Is.49.22–23); and the levelling of mountains and valleys to ease their journey (Bar.5.7; Is.40.4).[87]

---

86. According to the omitted verse, "Afterward she appeared *[ōphthē]* upon earth and lived among humans" (3.38). This may be a Christian gloss.

87. The concluding verses (Bar.5.5–9) are closely related to *Psalms of Solomon* 11, with several verbal links that cannot be explained by the common dependence on deutero-Isaiah

And so the text completes its movement from confession of past sins through recognition of a privileged present to anticipation of a glorious future – a movement that encompasses the law, the wisdom writings, and the prophets.

Like the wisdom motifs in the central section of the book, the prophetic themes are reinterpreted in the light of the deuteronomic framework established in the opening confession. The question is whether this deuteronomic theology is capable of sustaining the prophetic visions that conclude the work, or whether it actually undermines them. The continuing influence of Deuteronomy is felt especially in the introduction to this final section (Bar.4.5–8) and in Jerusalem's initial lament (4.9–20). The introduction includes an unmistakable allusion to the Song of Moses, with its denunciation of an idolatrous people:

> For you provoked *[parōxunate]* the one who made you, sacrificing to demons and not to God; you forgot the eternal God who brought you up *[epelathesthe de ton tropheusanta humas theon aiōnion]* ... (Bar.4.7–8)

> They provoked me *[parōxunan me]* with strange gods..., they sacrificed to demons and not to God...; God, who begot you, you forsook, and you forgot God who brought you up *[kai epelathou theou tou trephontos se]*. (Deut.32.16–18)

In alluding to this text, the author of *Baruch* returns to the outlook of the opening confession, and so to a past determined by the divine curse. The past also casts its long shadow over the first part of Jerusalem's speech, where, with another reference to Deuteronomy, Jerusalem acknowledges that her exiled sons and daughters fully deserved their fate:

> They did not acknowledge his decrees nor did they walk in the ways of God's commandments, nor tread the paths of training in his right-eousness... [So] he brought upon them a far off nation *[ethnos*

(Bar.5.5, Ps.Sol.11.3; Bar.5.7, Ps.Sol.11.5; Bar.5.8, Ps.Sol.6b–7a). O. Steck argues for the dependence of the psalm on *Baruch* (*Das apokryphe Baruchbuch*, pp. 240–42), C. Moore for the reverse (*Additions*, pp. 314–16). The latter view seems more plausible to me. After Jerusalem's address to her children (Bar.4.9–29), Jerusalem herself is addressed in a poem in three stanzas of equal length. The first stanza celebrates the downfall of Babylon (4.30–35); the second appeals to Jerusalem to prepare herself for her children's return (4.36–5.4); and the third describes the return itself (5.5–9). The parallel with *Psalms of Solomon* 11 occurs in this third stanza, whose opening appeal ("Arise, O Jerusalem... and see your children gathered from west and east"; cf. Is.40.9 + 49.18) is closely related to the opening of the second stanza (Bar.4.36–37). It seems likely that the author of *Baruch* initially formulates 4.36–37 under the influence of *Psalms of Solomon* 11.2, and subsequently decides to make further and more direct use of the psalm in his final stanza. It should be noted that the verbal links occur at the level of the Greek text, and are difficult to reconcile with the hypothesis that the secondary, dependent text is a translation of a Hebrew original.

makrothen]; a nation without shame *[ethnos anaides]* and of a strange language, who showed no respect for an old man nor mercy to a child... (Bar.4.13, 15)

The Lord will bring upon you a far off nation *[ethnos makrothen]*, from the ends of the earth, swift as an eagle; a nation whose language you do not understand; a nation without shame *[ethnos anaides prosōpō]*, which will not respect the person of the old man nor show mercy to the young... (Deut.28.49–50)

If the wisdom poem was an attempt to exorcise the memory of the past, the author nevertheless remains fixated on that past, and on the scriptural language that interprets remembered violence and atrocity – at precisely the moment when he turns to the future for consolation. This fixation on the past is symptomatic of an unspoken anxiety about the hoped-for future. If the experience of violence at the hands of a foreign conqueror is interpreted as divine retribution for transgression, what guarantee can there be that the cycle of law, transgression and judgment will not be repeated? And how can there be any real confidence in the Isaianic vision of Jerusalem's glory when it remains subject to the condition: *if* you keep my commandments...? Jerusalem's address to her children concludes with the appeal:

Take courage, my children, and pray to God, for the one who brought this upon you will remember you. For as your purpose was once to go astray from God, so now return with tenfold zeal to seek him *[dekaplasiasate epistraphentes zētēsai auton]*. For the one who brought evil upon you will bring upon you eternal joy with your salvation. (Bar.4.27–30)

The Isaianic vision is subject to the deuteronomic condition of the turn from past error, which has already supposedly been enacted in the confession. (Compare *Baruch* 4.2: "Turn, O Jacob...") It seems that this act of repentance must yet again be repeated. But how can Jerusalem be so confident that, this time at last, the return to the law will be sufficient? If the Isaianic vision is subjected to a deuteronomic condition, it threatens to become a groundless fantasy.

Throughout his work, the author of *Baruch* betrays the influence of Deuteronomy 30.1–10, where he finds nothing less than the hermeneutical key to scripture as a whole. In that passage, in what is almost his last word to the people of Israel, Moses teaches that the way out of the law's curse is provided by the law itself. It is this view of the ending of the Torah that Paul rejects, arguing instead for a dual ending that is to be found both in the curse motif and in Moses' final prophetic insight into God's unconditional, all-comprehending saving action. Yet the passage in chapter 30 is integral to the theology of Deuteronomy as a whole, and cannot be dismissed as an aberration. In effect, it offers a "second chance" – a motif that the Book of Deuteronomy develops in a number of ways.[88] In order further to clarify the view of the Torah's ending that Paul rejects and Baruch accepts, we must reflect briefly on the role of this motif in Deuteronomy itself.

As the Book of Deuteronomy opens, Israel finds itself for the second time on the verge of the promised land. What went wrong at Kadesh Barnea, nearly forty years previously, is now to be put right in the land of Moab (cf. 1.2, 19–46). Just as the broken stone tablets were once replaced by a second set (cf. 9.6–10.11), so there is now to be a second chance to secure the fulfilment of the promise of the paradise-like land. In both cases, the people wilfully disobey the divine commandment, suffering punishment in consequence; and yet, their punishment completed, they are restored to their prelapsarian relationship to a divine word that remains to be obeyed. Finding this theology of "recapitulation" within the traditional stories of Israel in the wilderness, the deuteronomic narrator develops from it not only an additional covenant alongside the covenant at Horeb (29.1 EVV), but also a hermeneutical framework for the whole book. For the narrator, Israel in the land of Moab is not an object of purely historical interest but represents the situation of the Israel of his own day – in dispersion, outside the land, awaiting the realization of the promise. That is the clear implication of Deuteronomy 27–30, chapters which shed retrospective light on the book in its entirety. The divine curses culminate in a return to Egypt, a reversal of the exodus (28.68); and yet this reversal is itself reversed in a re-enactment of the exodus, a second chance to hear and obey the divine voice and to secure the blessings of the land (30.1–10). The geographical location in "the land of Moab" symbolizes and dramatizes the juncture at which Israel now stands, in the time of the narrator. In its final form, the implied setting of the book is one of exile and dispersion: the narrator uses Moses' speeches to address his own contemporaries, whose situation is analogous to that of Israel "in the land of Moab".[89] Moses' exposition of the law defines, with all possible clarity, the return to the law that must take place here and now (cf. 30.2). In that sense the book as a whole is truly a *deuteros nomos*, in which the same law

88. So J. G. Millar, *Time and Place in Deuteronomy* (with J. G. McConville), pp. 29, 60–61, 67. The discussion that follows is indebted to this work.

89. The analogy is only effective from the "post-exilic" standpoint implied in Deuteronomy 28–32; it is not clear how a setting "in the land of Moab" would be appropriate in a document composed during the period of Manasseh and Josiah. This is a problem for the standard view that Deuteronomy served as "the foundation for Josiah's reform", and that thereafter "its text would have remained more or less stable", with the exception of the later expansions in chapters 27–34 (R. D. Nelson, *Deuteronomy*, p. 8).

is enacted for a second time – a repetition represented within the text by the distinction and the identity between Horeb and the land of Moab (cf. 5.3; 29.1, 10–15). If the post-exilic turning-point of Deuteronomy 30.1–10 represents the narrator's present, this would account both for the persistent indications of historical distance between the narrator and Moses, and for the direct relevance of Moses' speeches to a later generation.[90] To read and understand the end of this book is also to arrive at its starting-point in the land of Moab, and to know the place for the first time.

The implied location of the deuteronomic narrator is identical to that of *Baruch* and its implied author (cf. Bar.1.1–14). Although *Baruch* is ostensibly dated to the time of the destruction of Jerusalem, the third person narrative with which it opens (1.1–14) serves to distance the situation within the narrative from that of the narrator.[91] While the entire book ostensibly deals with the immediate aftermath of the event of 587 BCE, this setting during the reign of King Nebuchadnezzar serves to symbolize and to interpret the situation of the author's own day. The event of exile is a vivid metaphor for that situation, determined as it is by the divine curse (Deut.28) and the exhortation to return to the law (Deut.30) – scriptural motifs representing the realized past and the possible future that intersect in the present moment. Since Baruch's situation symbolizes that of the implied author and readers of this book, they too are located at that point of intersection. That is also the location that Deuteronomy constructs for its own implied readers. Whether the readers of these texts are transported to Moab or to Babylon, the message is the same: that the promise of the land still awaits its fulfilment, and that this can only be secured by way of a return to the law. Nothing of substance has changed between the earlier and the later texts. Israel appears perpetually poised on the verge of the land, like Moses glimpsing it from afar but unable to enter. Constantly repeated exhortations raise the question whether the always-future moment of return to the law can ever be realized, and whether there really is a way out of a present determined by the divine curse. *Baruch*

90. As R. Polzin writes: "The hero of Deuteronomy and his audience are in Moab, that is, outside the land, hoping to possess it with God's power and mercy; the author of Deuteronomy and *his* audience are apparently in exile, that is, also outside the land, hoping to get in once more with God's mercy and power..." (*Moses and the Deuteronomist*, p. 72).

91. The introduction of *Baruch* begins with the announcement, "These are the words of the book which Baruch... wrote in Babylon, in the fifth year..." (1.1–2), but proceeds to a lengthy description of the book's original context. The book itself only begins in 1.15 – assuming that "And you shall say..." (v.15) corresponds to "And you shall read this book which we are sending you..." (v.14). The implied author of 1.1–15a is therefore someone other than Baruch. While the effect of this passage may be "one of awkwardness and imprecision in both style and content" (C. A. Moore, *Additions*, p. 275), it remains important in mediating between Baruch in Babylon and the book's actual readers.

represents a reading of Deuteronomy in which the text has become frozen at chapter 30 – leaving open the possibility only of endless reiteration. We recall that Baruch's book is appointed to be read within the public liturgy – over and over again (cf. 1.14). The turning-point from the curse to the blessing proves to be a moment of stasis.

Paul finds a resolution of this impasse within Deuteronomy itself – in the Song of Moses, where the execution of the law's curse is followed by the announcement not of blessing conditional on obedience but of unconditional and assured divine saving action. It is Paul's claim that, after the extended reflection on the blessing and the curse that occupies Deuteronomy 27–30, Moses is enabled to see beyond his own announcement of conditional future blessing, and to envisage an alternative future determined by God alone. When, in the aftermath of his great Song, Moses is instructed to ascend Mount Nebo, so as to see the land without entering it (32.48–52), what he will see is a future *certainty*, and not just a possibility dependent on an ever more problematic act of choice. It is Moses' own final insight that leads Paul to rewrite what Moses had earlier written about the law's easy way to life (30.11–14; Rom.10.6–9). Thus the citation from the Song needs no rewriting (Rom.10.19); Moses here speaks in the full authority of prophetic foreknowledge. For Paul, no exhortation to return to the law will ever produce the conduct that is the precondition for the blessing. Moses himself was aware that the people to whom he appealed were blind and deaf, and this remains the condition of subsequent generations included within the covenant (Deut.29.3, 13–14; Rom.11.8). At best, the law's proclamation of good and evil leads to a longing for the good that is undermined by the inescapable human propensity for evil (Rom.7.13–25).

As represented by Paul, the non-Christian Israel of his own day is characterized by the ever-renewed attempt to enact the return to the law by zealous practice of the law's works. This is the theological programme of Deuteronomy 30, and, from a Pauline perspective, its failure is confirmed by the simple fact that God has chosen to act differently. As a reader of Deuteronomy, Paul's advice to other readers such as Baruch is simply to *keep reading* – not to come to a halt at the end of chapter 30, but to read on into chapter 32. There, Moses sees that God's saving action will be manifested in a different form and on a different basis to what he has previously imagined. Israel must learn this from and with the Gentiles; but also from and with Moses, retracing his own movement beyond the conditional logic of the blessing and the curse to a final insight into the unconditional basis of divine saving action.

Chapter 10

Deuteronomy (2)

The Torah ends with the death of Moses, but its ending may also be sought among Moses' last words to his people before his ascent of Mount Nebo, or Pisgah. If the Song of Moses and the final blessing of the twelve tribes are regarded as appendices, then Moses' last words may be found in Deuteronomy 30. Here, the "curse" that has dominated the preceding chapters begins to recede. After the deluge, signs of hope begin to reappear – like the olive leaf and the rainbow at the time of the Flood. The curse is not Moses' last word, nor is it God's. A return to the law, enabled in part by the divine purification of the heart, will bring an end to dispersion and a realization of the blessings of the land. Moses envisages the future history of Israel as determined first by the curse of the law, but then by its blessing (Deut.29.16–30.10). As Moses continues to speak, the perspective of the audience within the text is merged with that of a readership that sees itself in a condition of dispersion or exile. A "fusion of horizons" takes place, in which Moses, still ostensibly speaking to his contemporaries, simultaneously addresses his final eloquent appeals to those who read his words rather than hearing them. Here, more clearly than anywhere else in Deuteronomy, the "land of Moab" is a metaphor for the state of dispersion. In both locations, the law is offered as the key that gives access to the land and its blessings. Moses speaks of the ease and the accessibility of the commandment (30.11–14); and he concludes by confronting his hearers or readers with the great act of choice they must make, either rejecting the commandment and falling victim to death and the curse, or observing it and finding it to be the way of life and blessing (30.15–20). If the ending of the Torah is the point where the most fundamental truths are most clearly articulated, then its ending is here:

> I call heaven and earth to witness to you this day: Life and death I have set before you, blessing and curse. Choose life, so that you may live, you and your seed, to love the Lord your God, to obey his voice, and to cling to him. For this is life and length of days for you, so that you may dwell in the land which the Lord swore to give to your fathers Abraham and Isaac and Jacob. (Deut.30.19–20 LXX)

In spite of the reasonableness of the appeal to "choose life", Paul does not find Moses' eloquence to be irresistible. On the contrary, his one citation from this chapter is so extensively rewritten and corrected that it can no longer be ascribed to Moses' authorship. The Righteousness of faith speaks through Moses' words, but also against them (cf. Rom.10.6–10). The disagreement is profound, and is not simply a matter of minor adjustments or reinterpretations. If Moses is right, and if the question of life or death hinges on law observance, then Christ died and rose in vain. The truth in Moses' words is to be found only in their almost inaudible anticipations of the righteousness of faith. As they stand, they threaten to undermine the very truth of the gospel. Their teaching is summarized in the text Paul likes to cite from Leviticus: "The one who does these things shall live by them" (Lev.18.5; Gal.3.12, Rom.10.5). Conversely, Moses' farewell discourse in Deuteronomy 30 can be seen as commentary on this earlier saying. Either way, these texts reveal the extent to which "the law is not of faith" (Gal.3.12). Faith refers back to the life-giving act of God in the raising of Jesus, whereas the law teaches that observance of its own commandments is the one divinely appointed way to life. This is the teaching that Moses seeks to inculcate as he approaches his end – in spite of his foreknowledge of the effect of the law's curse.

The question is whether Paul, as a Jewish reader of Jewish scripture, is unique in finding a problem in the Torah's conclusion and summation. And the answer is that he is not. For the author of *4 Ezra* too, the Moses of Deuteronomy 30 poses an almost insuperable difficulty in the dialogue between Ezra and Uriel, his angelic conversation partner. While deuteronomic influence is less pervasive in *4 Ezra* than in *Baruch*, the book's most distinctive dialogue is generated by Moses' concluding appeal to choose obedience to the commandments as the way to life. Stark implications for eschatological destiny are drawn out by Uriel; Ezra finds them unacceptable, and appeals to other scriptural material in support of his case. The debate seems interminable, and Ezra and Moses remain unreconciled. All this invites a comparison with Paul, who engages in an equally critical dialogue with Moses' final utterances – and for some of the same reasons.

The Desolation of Zion

As the Ezra apocalypse opens, we find ourselves on terrain that is already familiar from *Baruch*. The setting is again Babylon, and although it is now thirty years since "the desolation of Zion" – and so thirty years after Baruch wrote his own book (Bar.1.1–2) – Ezra's preoccupation with that event is no less intense than Baruch's. The exilic setting already implies the deuteronomic view of Israel's past, present and future, and one would therefore expect Ezra's opening address to the deity to take the form of a confession (cf. Dan.9.3–19, Bar.1.5–3.8). Ezra's survey of scriptural history from creation to Sinai (4 Ezr.3.4–19) is initially suggestive of this genre – for the normal role of such a survey is to highlight the divine faithfulness towards Israel, in order then to contrast it with Israel's unfaithfulness towards God. The only oddity here is the surprisingly negative statement about Adam as the bringer of death into the world (4 Ezr.3.7). Otherwise, the election of Noah, Abraham and the other patriarchs out of the *massa damnata* of humankind proceeds as one would expect, as does the exodus from Egypt and the arrival at Sinai. The author seems to take the confession attributed to Ezra in Nehemiah 9 as the model for this new confession of Ezra: in both cases, Ezra starts from creation and proceeds to the covenant with Abraham, the exodus, and the arrival at Sinai. The earlier confession also speaks of the miraculous divine provision in the wilderness; the later one, of Adam, Noah, and the spread of ungodliness; but they share the movement from creation through the patriarchs and the exodus to Sinai. If the later confession continues to follow its scriptural model, it will at this point make the turn from divine faithfulness to the faithlessness of Israel. The scriptural confession of Ezra tells how, in spite of the constant divine favour,

> our fathers became proud and stiffened their neck and did not hear your commandments; and they refused to listen, and did not remember your wonders which you had done for them... (Esd.B 19.16–17 LXX = Neh.9.16–17)

The persistent refusal to obey, in defiance of all the prior divine goodness and faithfulness, naturally provokes God's wrath. Thus the people are delivered into the hands of their enemies; and that is the situation that the speaker seeks to remedy through the act of confession. The logic is thoroughly deuteronomic, although Ezra's confession differs from those of Daniel or Baruch in lacking the characteristic foreshortening created by the motif of the law's curse.

In the Ezra apocalypse, however, Ezra's confession diverges so completely from this scriptural model that it ceases to be a confession at all, and becomes a complaint. Furthermore, the object of this complaint is nothing other than the sin which, under the deuteronomic schema, ought rather to be confessed. From Sinai onwards, the people of Israel did indeed sin persistently and grievously; yet the responsibility lies not so much with the people as with God, who at Sinai gave a law that lacked the power to eradicate the sinful tendency inherited from Adam. Sinai was nothing less than the meeting-point of heaven and earth, for there the divine glory was manifested in fire and earthquake, wind and ice, in order to communicate the gift of the law (4 Ezr.3.18–19). And yet, unaccountably and in spite of this impressive theophany, you did not remove from them the evil heart *[cor malignum]*, so that your law might bear fruit in them. For, burdened with an evil heart, Adam was the first to transgress and to be overcome, but also all who were descended from him. And the weakness *[infirmitas]* became permanent, and the law co-existed with the evil of the root *[cum malignitate radicis]* in the heart of the people, and what was good departed and evil remained. (4 Ezr.3.20–21)[1]

Owing to this evil heart inherited from Adam, it was inevitable that the people should continue to transgress and that the holy city should fall in consequence (3.25–27). To speak of this as a "punishment" would presuppose that the people actually had a choice and were responsible for their transgression. In fact, the choice and the responsibility lie with God. In the situation of exile, it is God who is indicted and not the people of Israel.

Ezra's argument here appears to be profoundly anti-deuteronomic; its full implications will emerge later. It is of course a question how far the author of this text identifies himself with the dangerous thoughts he puts into Ezra's mouth.[2] Yet Ezra's complaint is surely in a quite different category to the atheistical speech that the author of the *Wisdom of Solomon* puts into the mouths of the ungodly (Wis.2.1–20). The scriptural Ezra is "a scribe skilled in the law of Moses, which the Lord God of Israel gave", and his vocation is "to study and to observe the law, and to teach its decrees and judgments in Israel" (Esd.B 7.6, 10). At the end of the Ezra apocalypse, he will be entrusted with the work of restoring the lost Torah (4 Ezr.14). The reader is entitled to expect that what Ezra says will be basically trustworthy. Of course, the angel Uriel will on occasion tell him that he is in error. Yet, even in the face of these angelic reproofs, the author permits his Ezra-figure to persist in a "heterodox" point of view long enough to be able to state it in its most powerful and compelling form. Unlike the angel's answers, Ezra's objections are always framed in a manner likely to engage the reader's sympathy.[3] If Ezra becomes more

---

1. Translations are from *Biblia Sacra Vulgata*, checked against the information from the other versions contained in M. E. Stone's commentary.

2. W. Harnisch argues that the author of *4 Ezra* uses the angel to represent his own views and Ezra to represent his sceptical opponents (*Verhängnis und Verheissung der Geschichte*, pp. 60–67). The author/Uriel identification is also maintained by E. Brandenburger, who writes: "Die Meinung des Verfassers ... kommt im Dialogteil fast ausschliesslich in den Offenbarungsreden Uriels, des Boten der himmlischen Welt, zum Ausdruck. Nur ganz vereinzelt und davon abhängig hören wir seine Meinung auch im Munde Esras..." (*Die Verborgenheit Gottes im Weltgeschehen*, p. 150).

3. Thus, E. P. Sanders can speak of Ezra's prayer of 7.132–40 as "his most moving appeal, based as it is on the entire Jewish conception of the mercy of God and his steadfastness toward his chosen people" (*Paul and Palestinian Judaism*, p. 414). Sanders does not explain why an author supposed to be identified with Uriel gives the best and most scriptural arguments to

compliant in the final chapters of the book, there is still a total absence of Job-like contrition for having spoken rashly (cf. Job 40.3–5; 42.1–6).[4] On several occasions, Ezra's piety is emphatically endorsed (6.31–33; 7.76–77; 8.48–49). At the very least, the author of this dialogue intends Ezra to raise serious theological problems that cannot lightly be dismissed.

At this point, however, the anti-deuteronomic complaint about the inescapably evil heart is a subordinate motif. Ezra's opening address to the deity culminates in a rather different complaint, to the effect that the exile is an excessive punishment for what were actually relatively minor sins – especially in comparison with the gross sins of the Gentiles (3.28–36). Despite what was earlier said about the evil heart, the emphasis now lies on Israel's relative success in observing the commandments and acknowledging the one true God. The state of exile is now construed not as merited punishment but as unjust suffering, and this is the true starting-point for both of the first two dialogues (3.1–5.20; 5.21–6.34).[5] The full significance of the evil-heart motif will only emerge in the longer and more radical third dialogue (6.35–9.25), which includes a sustained critique of the deuteronomic schema, interpreted now in terms of individual rather than national destiny. In the opening statements of the first two dialogues, what is emphasized above all is that Israel's sufferings in exile are incompatible with her covenant status (3.4–36, 5.23–30). In the first passage, it is Israel's relative success in living out this covenant status that is highlighted, whereas the second speaks of the covenant from the standpoint of the divine love that is expressed in it. Either way, the sufferings of Israel in exile are unjust:

> Has Babylon behaved better than Zion? or has any other nation known
> you more than Israel has? or which tribes have believed the covenants as

Ezra. The problem recurs in Richard Bauckham's analysis. Ezra's argument is "based on the Torah's own revelation of God's character", and is "presented so sympathetically, even persuasively, that it must be part of the book's rhetorical strategy to allow this view its full weight" ("Apocalypses", p. 164). Yet Bauckham assumes that (from the author's perspective) Ezra is in error, being as yet "unconverted".

4. C. Rowland rightly notes that "the book of Job is an obvious antecedent to the questionings which emerge in the apocalypses, 4 Ezra and Syriac Baruch" (*The Open Heaven*, p. 207). This makes the absence of contrition in *4 Ezra* all the more striking.

5. The Ezra apocalypse consists of three "dialogues", three "visions" and a conclusion. While revelations occur in both dialogues and visions, it is not appropriate to describe all seven sections as "visions" (as do J. M. Myers, *I & II Esdras*, pp. 108–12, M. E. Stone, *Fourth Ezra*, pp. 24–30, and others). In the dialogues, the visual element has been reduced to vanishing point. The angelic revelations are heard, and there is no evidence that Ezra "sees" anything at all – except perhaps the angel (cf. 5.14–15). In 6.33, "show" *(demonstrare)* is metaphorical: the request, "show thy servant..." (6.12) is answered by a divine voice (6.13–17).

those of Jacob, whose reward has not appeared and whose labour has not borne fruit? (3.31b–33)

From every forest of the earth and from every tree you have chosen a single vine... and from all the flocks that have been made you have provided yourself with a single sheep, and from all the multitudes of the peoples you have acquired for yourself a single people, and you have given the law approved by all to this people whom you loved. And now Lord, why have you handed over the one to the many, and dishonoured the one root among all others, and scattered your only one among the many? (5.23, 26b–28)[6]

On the grounds both of Israel's conduct and of the electing divine love, present suffering is incomprehensible. At this point, the problem of the evil heart has dropped out of sight. Even in the first dialogue, Ezra's summary of his initial complaint mentions only the problem of Israel's unmerited sufferings (4.23–25) – although the evil-heart motif is subsequently taken up by the angel (4.28–32). Throughout the first two dialogues, the fundamental problem is the "desolation of Zion", in its apparent contradiction to the "everlasting covenant" in which God promised Abraham that he would never forsake his descendants (3.2, 15).

The first two dialogues follow a common pattern. Ezra asks why God has handed over his beloved people to such suffering (3.1–36; 5.21–30). The initial response is negative: as God's representative, the angel Uriel seeks to persuade Ezra that all such matters lie far beyond his comprehension (4.1–25; 5.31–40), pointing to his ignorance even of things that lie near to hand (4.3–9; 5.36–37).[7] Ezra replies passionately that a life without comprehension would not be worth living (4.12; 5.35). Despite the

---

6. In the Latin text of 5.28, the word translated "dishonoured" is actually *praeperasti* ("you have prepared"). This stems from a misreading of the Greek *ētimēsas* as *hētoimasas*, and is clear evidence that the Latin is a translation of a Greek exemplar (so G. H. Box, *APOT*, 1.546). Equally clear evidence for this is found in 7.26, where the error in question is attested in the Syriac as well as the Latin, and must be ascribed to a Greek copyist rather than to the Latin translator. Here, *et apparebit sponsa apparescens civitas* ("the bride will appear the city appearing") represents a misreading of *kai phanēsetai hē nun mē phainomenē polis* ("and the city that is now invisible shall appear"), *hē nun mē* being read as *hē numphē* (*ibid.*). The correct reading is preserved in Armenian and Arabic translations (see Stone, *Fourth Ezra*, pp. 6, 8). On the other hand, the appeal to Hebraisms as evidence for a Hebrew original (*APOT*, 1.547–49; Myers, *I & II Esdras*, pp. 115–19) suffers from the usual failure to consider whether these might stem from the influence of the LXX on a Jewish author writing in Greek. Stone is partially aware of the problem (p. 9), but gives only a brief discussion of "the Hebrew theory" (pp. 10–11).

7. Uriel speaks with Ezra as one sent by God (4.1, 52; 5.31, 33; 7.1), and as other than God, whom (like Ezra) he refers to as "the Most High". In 6.13–34, however, there is direct divine utterance, distinguished from that of the angel; and in 6.1–6, 7.11, 9.7–22 (cf. 8.63) the angel speaks as God (see Stone, *Fourth Ezra*, p. 199, for further references).

initial angelic refusal, and in response to Ezra's urgent pleas, the dialogues now take a more positive turn. The solution to the problem of Israel's unmerited suffering lies in the end that God has secretly decreed. The first piece of information that Ezra elicits from the angel is the fact that "the age hastens swiftly to its end" (4.26), and in both dialogues this leads to a series of overlapping questions and answers (4.33–52; 5.41–6.10). In the first dialogue, Ezra asks when the end will be (4.33), whether human sin might bring about its delay (4.38–39), and whether more time has already passed than is still to come (4.44–46). In the second dialogue, he asks why the slow succession of generations is necessary at all (5.41–45), whether the earth as our common mother has now entered her old age (5.50), whether God has delegated the end to any subordinate agent (5.56), and what the division will be between the present age and the age to come (6.7). He is assured that the end will come at its appointed time, which is indeed approaching. The image of the womb is employed in both dialogues, to show that the time of the end is fixed (4.40–43), and to explain why all humans could not have been created simultaneously (5.48–49) and why their quality is declining (5.51–55). After both series of questions and answers, there follows an account of the signs that precede the end, of which the second is the continuation of the first (4.52–5.13a; 6.11–28). These dialogues close with a command to prepare for further revelations (5.13b; 6.29–34). Each of them has completed a movement that takes in the opening complaint, the initial refusal to respond to it, and the subsequent disclosure of crucial secrets about the end. Although there is no concrete information about how the "desolation of Zion" will be rectified in the end-time, that end is also identified as "the goal of the love [*finem caritatis*] that I have promised my people" (5.40). To that extent, the initial complaints are answered to Ezra's satisfaction. As for the (anti-deuteronomic) complaint about the "evil heart" as the cause of Zion's desolation (3.20–27), this might be the object of the warning at the close of the second dialogue: "Do not be quick to think vain things about the former times, lest you be hasty about the last times" (6.40).[8]

---

8. Whatever may be true of some other apocalypses, this one is dominated by questions and answers relating to eschatology. According to Christopher Rowland, in *4 Ezra* "the interest in eschatology is matched by another issue, the nature of man and the reason for the desperate straits in which the people of God found themselves" (*The Open Heaven*, p. 135). In *4 Ezra*, however, reflection on the covenant and human destiny occurs within a consistently eschatological framework, and not as a separate topic alongside eschatology. The false dichotomy here stems from Rowland's attempt to define "apocalyptic", or rather the apocalyptic genre, in terms of its form – heavenly secrets disclosed by revelation – rather than its content. While this is a valuable corrective to the conventional "indifference to the fact that apocalyptic is concerned with the revelation of a variety of different matters" (p. 71), an orientation towards *ta eschata*, broadly and variously construed, is characteristic of many if not all of the texts belonging to the apocalyptic genre.

Moses, Daniel, and the End

It is in the third dialogue (6.38–9.25) that Ezra's engagement with Moses comes to a head. In one of only two scriptural references in this book, Uriel cites Deuteronomy 30.19 as warrant for the claim that it is only those who have fully observed the law who will attain to salvation in the world to come. As a result, and to Ezra's intense distress, it emerges that only a tiny minority will be saved:

> For this is the way that Moses spoke to the people while he was alive, saying: Choose for yourself life that you may live *[elige tibi vitam ut vivas]*. Yet they did not believe him, nor the prophets after him, nor myself, who spoke to them; so there is no sorrow in their perdition, just as there shall be joy over those to whom salvation is assured. (7.129–31)

As interpreted by Uriel, the Deuteronomy text articulates and summarizes the stark message of salvation by strict law observance that lies at the heart of this dialogue. Ezra's (scripturally based) objections to this harsh teaching are addressed in the first instance to Uriel, but also indirectly to Moses.[9]

Ezra's third dialogue is equal in length to the first and second dialogue and the first vision combined.[10] At the conclusion of the second dialogue as of the first, he is promised "greater things than these" *(horum maiora)* in the dialogue that is to follow (6.31; cf. 5.13), and in this case the "greater things" consist in a mass of new eschatological information – about the temporary messianic kingdom, the judgment, the intermediate state, and so on – all of which is subject to the proviso that law observance is the sole criterion for attaining to eternal life, just as disregard for the law condemns one to eternal torment. The concern in the first two dialogues about the timing of the end gives way to a much fuller account of the form of that end. An all-important distinction is now established between the

---

9. The Latin form of the citation, *elige tibi vitam ut vivas*, betrays the influence of Deuteronomy 30.19 LXX in its use of the imperative (Greek, *eklexai*) rather than a finite verb (MT, *wbḥrt*), in the absence of a preposition preceding *vitam* (MT, *bḥyym*), and in the present subjunctive *ut vivas* (LXX, *hina zēs*; MT, *lm'n tḥyh*). The additional *tibi* may stem from the second singular pronoun that follows "that you may live..." in both the Hebrew and the Greek. The citation does not support the hypothesis that *4 Ezra* was written in Hebrew.

10. To find the heart of the book in the third dialogue is not necessarily to divide structure and meaning (as argued by E. Breech, "These Fragments I Have Shored Against My Ruin: The Form and Function of 4 Ezra", p. 269): the disproportion between the third dialogue and the other sections of the book is, after all, a structural feature. Breech argues that the function of the visions that follow is to administer consolation, although he has to admit that "[n]either the dream visions nor the interpretations actually answer Ezra's initial questions" (pp. 273–74).

temporary this-worldly end or goal of history, and the transcendent end of the present world order marked by a universal resurrection to final judgment.[11]

The this-worldly end has to do with the deliverance of the righteous from the trials and tribulations of the last days, anticipated in the current sufferings of Israel in exile. This is a "national" eschatology that serves as an interim solution to the problem of the "desolation of Zion" (3.2; 12.48). It will be the theme of the visions that tell of the transfiguration of mother Zion (9.26–10.59), the eagle and the lion (11.1–12.51), and the man from the sea (13.1–58). More precisely, it may be described as a "Zion eschatology" (cf. 4 Ezr.12.44, 48; 13.35–36). While its scriptural roots lie in the old tradition of the divinely guaranteed sanctity of Zion as the "city of David" (cf. Ps.132), this Zion eschatology is here mediated through the Book of Daniel. Like Ezra, Daniel too is preoccupied with "the end of the desolations of Jerusalem" (Dan.9.2). It is no doubt for that reason that he customarily faces towards Jerusalem as he prays (Dan.6.10). In Daniel's account of King Nebuchadnezzar's dream, "the stone that struck the image" and "became a great mountain" (Dan.2.35, cf. vv.44–45) is an obvious reference to Zion. The author of the Ezra apocalypse has this passage in mind as he describes the "man from the sea" carving out for himself a great mountain that appears to have fallen from heaven (4 Ezr.13.6–7, 35–36). Just as in Daniel "a stone was cut from a mountain by no human hand" (Dan.2.45), so in *4 Ezra* Zion is to be "manifested to all people" as a "mountain carved without hands" (4 Ezr.13.36). As a further indication of Danielic influence, it is significant that the second of the two explicit scriptural references in the Ezra apocalypse is to the "fourth kingdom which appeared in a vision to your brother Daniel" (12.11; cf. Dan.7.23). The focus on the time and the signs of the end in the first two dialogues is also broadly Danielic (cf. Dan.12.1, 5–13).

Yet it is not the Book of Daniel but Moses' farewell appeal to the people of Israel that represents the primary scriptural source for the eschatology of Ezra's third dialogue. This is an eschatology determined not by the divine commitment to Zion or by membership of the covenant people, but by observance of the law. Within the Ezra apocalypse, the conventional distinction between "national" (or "this-worldly") and "transcendent" (or "other-worldly") eschatologies is also a distinction between a Zion

---

11. This distinction between two types of future expectation is intended to apply specifically to *4 Ezra*. In general, the conventional distinction between "this-worldly" and "other-worldly" eschatologies may not be particularly helpful – as John Barton has argued (*Oracles of God*, pp. 206–208). See also C. Rowland, *The Open Heaven*, pp. 37–38.

eschatology and an eschatology of law observance. One is drawn from Daniel, the other from Moses.[12]

In contrast to the first two dialogues, the structure of the third dialogue is complex, and there are indications of redactional activity. In 8.19b, Ezra's prayer for the unrighteous is introduced with the words: "The beginning of the words of Ezra's prayer, before he was taken up [*priusquam adsumeretur*]" (8.19b). This insertion undermines the chronological framework of the third dialogue, and creates a connection with the concluding chapter, where Ezra is promised, "You shall be taken up [*recipieris*] from among humans, and henceforth you shall live with my son and with those who are like you until the times are ended" (14.9). It is possible that the insertion is confined to 8.19b, and that it reflects the independent use of this prayer for liturgical purposes.[13] On the other hand, the insertion may include the entire prayer that follows the introductory statement (8.20–36), which, with its elaborate invocation of the deity (8.20–23) in a context in which Ezra is already at prayer (8.6–19), fits awkwardly into its present context. The angels's response (8.37–40) comments more appropriately on 8.15–19 than on the prayer of 8.20–36.[14]

More significant is the anomalous reversion to the motif of signs of the end towards the conclusion of the third dialogue (9.1–8). This has to do with the "national eschatology" of the messianic kingdom, and with those who "will survive the predicted dangers and will see my salvation within my land and within my borders, which I have sanctified for myself from the beginning" (9.8). This topic is out of place in a context dominated by Ezra's intense concern with the fewness of those who are to be saved at the final judgment. Its introduction in 8.61–62 is incongruous, and its sequel (9.9–13) follows seamlessly from 8.61. This section (8.62–9.8) may have been inserted so that the close of the third dialogue would include a discussion of signs of the end, just as the first and second dialogues did (4.51–5.13, 6.11–28).[15]

12. This distinction between Daniel and Moses is drawn by *4 Ezra* itself (7.129; 12.11–12). Of course, the theme of resurrection, which belongs here to the "Mosaic" eschatology, is in reality dependent on Daniel rather than Deuteronomy. For the author of *4 Ezra*, however, this doctrine was already taught by Moses.

13. So G. H. Box, *APOT*, 1.594. The versions indicate that the introduction to the prayer was already present in the Greek.

14. The future tense in 8.19a ("I will speak before you") is not incompatible with the suggestion that Ezra's (already lengthy) address to God concludes at this point. Similar usage in vv.15, 17 seems to refer to Ezra's present utterance, not to a prayer that is still to come (note the "now" in v.15, *et nunc dicens dicam*).

15. Compare G. H. Box, *APOT* 1.598, who proposes a slightly longer insertion (8.63–9.12) – a fragment of an older "Ezra apocalypse" (together with 4.56–5.13a; 6.11–28), later inserted into the "Salathiel apocalypse" (cf. 3.1) preserved in the rest of chapters 3–10 (*APOT*, 1.549–52).

In principle, there is no incompatibility between "national" and "transcendent" eschatologies. The scenario in which signs of the end give way to the messianic kingdom, which itself gives way to the universal judgment, is in itself reasonably coherent (7.26–44).[16] Yet it is still noteworthy that *4 Ezra* as a whole is largely concerned with the national eschatology that addresses the problem of "the desolation of Zion"; that it develops the individual and transcendent eschatology of the judgment almost exclusively in the third dialogue;[17] that Ezra himself vehemently protests against this eschatology; that, as a result of his protests, the third dialogue is extended to such inordinate length as to unbalance the structure of the entire book;[18] and that fragments of extraneous material have apparently been inserted into it. It is tempting to propose a redaction-critical hypothesis at this point, and to suggest that, in the third dialogue, material originally concerned with the destiny of the people of Israel was rewritten and expanded, in the light of a new concern with transcendent individual destiny as determined by the law.

In that connection, one might also take up the suggestion of earlier source criticism that the pseudonymous author's self-introduction – *ego Salathihel qui et Ezras* (3.1) – implies a complex redactional history. Salathiel is Shealtiel, son of the exiled King Jehoiachin or "Jeconiah the captive" and father of Zerubbabel (1 Chron.3.17–19; cf. Matt.1.12, Lk.3.27). This Salathiel or Shealtiel is a much more plausible resident of Babylon "in the thirtieth year after the destruction of our city" than Ezra, who is associated with the Persian era (Ezr.7.1; cf. 6.14).[19] As a royal figure who experiences the Babylonian exile, Salathiel has an obvious affinity with the "Zion eschatology" that predominates almost everywhere in *4*

16.   The sequence, signs – messianic kingdom – universal judgment, is also attested in *2 Baruch* 27–30, a section that is independent of *4 Ezra* and perhaps more primitive. The sequence is clear and (in its own way) rational; R. H. Charles' source-critical dismemberment is unconvincing (*APOT* 1.475–76, 496–98).

17.   Outside the third dialogue, material relating to this theme is found in the first dialogue (3.7, 10, 20–22, 26; 4.28–32), and in the transition to the first vision (9.31–37).

18.   That the third dialogue is the climax and centre of the book in its present form is confirmed by the promise of "greater things" at the end of the first and second dialogues (5.13; 6.31); the promise is not repeated at the end of the third (cf. 9.25). The view that the visions of 9.26–13.58 provide an answer to the problem posed by the third dialogue is rightly criticized by E. P. Sanders, *Paul and Palestinian Judaism*, pp. 416–18.

19.   The Latin translator takes "Salathiel" directly from his Greek exemplar, which in turns derives it from LXX (cf. 1 Chron.3.17, 19; Esd. B 3.2, 8; 5.2; 22.1 LXX). Interest in the otherwise obscure Salathiel may be related to the enhanced role assigned to his son Zorobabel (= Zerubbabel) in *1 Esdras* 3–4, where he is responsible for obtaining from King Darius permission to rebuild Jerusalem; Zorobabel is described as "Zorobabel [son] of Salathiel, of the house of David" (1 Esd.5.5). It is likely that the identification with Ezra is influenced by 1 Chronicles 3.17 LXX *(kai huioi Iechonia Asir Salathiel huios autou . . .)*, where LXX reproduces the Hebrew *'sr* ("captive") as a personal name – attested also in 1 Chronicles 6.7, 8

Ezra apart from the third dialogue. On the other hand, Ezra has an obvious affinity with a transcendent individual eschatology dependent on law observance. We might therefore conjecture that an original Salathiel apocalypse was subjected to extensive rewriting and expansion in the case of the third vision; and that material in the first dialogue relating to the "evil heart" and the universal judgment was also added, so that crucial themes of the third dialogue should be anticipated at the beginning of the book. This rewriting of the original would then be symbolized by the intrusion of "Ezra" into a text originally assigned to "Salathiel". It is consistent with this that, after 3.1, Ezra is named only in the third dialogue (7.2, 25, 49?; 8.1, [19])) and in the final chapter (14.1, 38), where his virtual identification with Moses is clearly related to the more problematic Ezra/Moses relationship of the third dialogue.[20]

A redaction-critical hypothesis along these lines would encounter significant difficulties, however. If the third dialogue had been "rewritten", one would expect to find traces of the original text preserved within it. Yet the most likely candidate for such a scenario – the "signs" passage in 8.62–9.8 – is evidently a later insertion. If it belonged to an earlier form of the third dialogue, it was first excluded from it and only subsequently reincorporated. On a more substantive level, the Zion eschatology of the second and third visions (11.1–13.58) does not appear to be complete; it describes the messianic overthrow of Gentile dominion, but it has little to say about what follows. Without the additional eschatological material from the third dialogue, it would be no more than a torso. For such reasons as these, the redaction-critical hypothesis seems doubtful. On the other hand, even a rejected source- or redaction-critical hypothesis can still produce useful insights. In this case, the figures of Salathiel and Ezra can be employed to identify and to distinguish the two eschatological strands in this text: the Zion eschatology, and the eschatology determined by law observance. In these representative figures, the text acknowledges its own dual concern with Zion and with the law.

As we have seen, the eschatology that Uriel outlines and defends in the third dialogue is presented as exegesis of Moses' farewell appeal in Deuteronomy 30.19: "Choose for yourself life, that you may live" (4 Ezr.7.129). Deuteronomy is now understood in the context no longer of a

in the context of a Levitical genealogy. Yet it is one thing to identify Salathiel as Asir, another to identify Asir as Ezra. LXX provides the occasion for the identification, but not the motivation.

20. The classical source-critical analysis (see *APOT*, 1.549–62) fails to connect its Salathiel and Ezra material to the biblical portrayal of these figures. Their detachment from their scriptural roots would represent a departure from apocalyptic convention, as evident in the cases of Enoch, Abraham, Baruch, Daniel, and others.

national eschatology, as in the case of *Baruch*, but of a universal individual eschatology focused on "the day of judgment". In contrast, the national eschatology of *4 Ezra* is oriented not towards Deuteronomy but towards Daniel. The fundamental difference between national eschatologies inspired respectively by Deuteronomy and Daniel is that, in the one case, national salvation is conditional on the return to the law (cf. Deut.30.1–10), whereas, in the other case, its time is already unconditionally determined (cf. Dan.9.24–27).[21] The decision for Daniel rather than Deuteronomy at this point is encapsulated in a passage in the first dialogue, where Ezra asks whether the time of salvation has been delayed on account of human sin, and is told that the time is unconditionally determined – like the nine months of pregnancy (4 Ezr.4.38–43). In Ezra's three visions, all of which are focused on the messianic kingdom, the deuteronomic claim that national salvation is dependent on a prior return to the law is entirely absent. In the third dialogue, the timing of the Messiah's coming and of the universal judgment that later follows is again unconditionally determined: what remains conditional, for each individual, is the outcome of the judgment that all must undergo. Both Baruch and Ezra appeal to the conditional element in Moses' final speeches, but in the one case this is applied to national salvation, in the other to individual salvation.

In *4 Ezra*, Deuteronomy 30 no longer serves to undergird a national eschatology based on the return to the law; the "life" and "death" of which it speaks are the eternal life or death of the individual. In *Baruch*, the prophetic certainty of the restoration of Zion is undermined by the deuteronomic condition, whereas in *4 Ezra* that prophetic certainty is reinstated; and yet the deuteronomic condition returns here in still more menacing form, as the sole criterion for the final judgment of the individual. We may observe this interpretative shift taking place in another text ascribed to Baruch, the *Syriac Apocalypse*, or *2 Baruch* – a text with close affinities to *4 Ezra*.[22]

---

21. As the example from Daniel 9 illustrates, this apocalyptic "determinism" stems from the conviction that the promise of salvation in the prophetic books is certain of fulfilment. It is thus the product of a developing "canonical consciousness", which may relate specifically to the prophets (cf. Dan.9.1–2; Tob.14.4–8; Sir.36.15–17), but also to scriptural narrative (cf. Judt.9.2–6; CD ii.7–iii.12; 1 En.93.1–8). This canonical consciousness is also expressed in the "pseudonymity" of the apocalypses, or, more positively expressed, their attribution to great figures of the scriptural past. The "determinism" of the apocalypses need not reflect a disillusionment with the historical realm deriving from bitter post-exilic ideological conflicts – the view of P. D. Hanson, *The Dawn of Apocalyptic*, pp. 405–406.

22. Debate about the relationship between *2 Baruch* and *4 Ezra* has been inconclusive; see the summary in W. Harnisch, *Verhängnis und Verheissung der Geschichte*, pp. 11–12. A possible solution might be along the following lines. In the narrative framework of the Ezra apocalypse, the seven episodes are marked off from each other by references to the passage of

The Baruch apocalypse concludes with a letter that Baruch sends to the ten (or nine and a half) lost tribes (2 Bar.78–87), conveyed to them by an eagle. The letter is written at the suggestion of the people who remain in the land after the fall of Jerusalem, who propose that Baruch should write to "our brothers in Babylon" before he dies (77.12). Baruch agrees to do so, but also decides to write a similar letter to the lost tribes; it is the text of this second letter that is given in the final chapters of this apocalypse. In his final dialogue with the people, Baruch assures them in good deuteronomic fashion that "if you direct your ways aright, you will not go as your brothers went; but they will come to you" (77.6). We have here the familiar motif of a national salvation following exile and conditional on a return to the law, extensively developed in the earlier Baruch text. Salvation will take the form of a return to the promised land, where the promised blessings will at last be realized (cf. Deut.30.1–10). Thus, in the letter to the lost tribes, Baruch recalls Moses' final words to his people:

> Remember how Moses at one time summoned heaven and earth to witness against you, and said, If you transgress the law you will be dispersed, but if you keep it you will be planted. (2 Bar.84.2)[23]

The allusion to Deuteronomy 30.19 is clear ("I call heaven and earth to witness to you this day: Life and death I have set before you, blessing and curse..."). The conditional statement that follows is a summary of Deuteronomy 28–30 as a whole, and the reference is apparently to the fortunes of the nation. And yet this straightforward literal interpretation of Deuteronomy becomes less clear in the statements that follow. After Moses' death, his people rejected what he had taught them and fell victim to the curse of the law:

time (5.13–20; 6.31–35; 9.23–27; 10.58–11.1; 12.28–13.1; 13.58–14.1). In four of the six passages, there is a chronological interval of seven days (11.1 and 13.1 being the exceptions), and in the first two Ezra mourns and fasts. A similar framework is present in *2 Baruch* (5.6–7; 9.2; 12.5; 21.1; 35.1; 47.2), where seven-day intervals (12.5; 21.1; 47.2), mourning (5.6; 9.2; 35.1) and fasting (5.7; 9.2; 12.5; 21.1; 47.2) are also to be found. Here, however, the framework is relatively arbitrary: the resulting seven sections are of unequal length and contain disparate material. This suggests that the framework may have been imposed in the course of a later redaction influenced by *4 Ezra*. Passages in *2 Baruch* that echo the dialogues between Ezra and Uriel (14.1–23.7; 41.1–42.8; 48.1–52.7) may tentatively be assigned to this redactional stratum, alongside passages that recall the angel's transcendental eschatology (4.2–6; 44.8–15; 48.48–50; 83.1–23; 85.1–15), or Ezra's view of the role of Adam (54.15–19; cf. 48.42–47). Some of this "secondary" material may represent a rewriting of existing material – in which case precise differentiations will not be attainable.

23. I have used the translations of R. H. Charles, revised by L. H. Brockington, in H. F. D. Sparks (ed.), *The Apocryphal Old Testament*, pp. 835–95; and of A. F. J. Klijn, *OTP* 1.615–52.

Moses told you beforehand, so that it might not befall you; and, behold,
it did befall you, because you forsook the law. And now I tell you, after
you have suffered, that if you obey what I have said to you, you shall
receive from the Mighty One everything that has been prepared and
preserved for you. (2 Bar.84.5–6)

This no longer sounds like a restoration to the land. The addressees are to
"remember" Zion and the holy land, but it is not said that they will return
there. The deuteronomic condition is now applied to a different
eschatology. Zion has been lost, and there remain to us only God and
his law: and yet, "if we direct and dispose our hearts aright, we shall
retrieve everything that we have lost" – or rather, we shall gain "many
more and much better things than we have lost", things incorruptible
rather than corruptible (2 Bar.85.4–5). The passage as a whole illustrates
the transition from the Deuteronomy interpretation of the earlier Baruch
text to that of *4 Ezra*.[24] As reinterpreted in the later texts, the choice
between "life and death" refers to individual rather than national destiny.[25]

For and Against Moses

Ezra's third dialogue with Uriel opens like the first two, with a complaint
relating to Israel's situation in the world. At the beginning of the first
dialogue, Ezra attributed the disasters of Israel's history to the God who
elected the patriarchs, brought the people from Egypt, bestowed the gift of
the law at Sinai – and yet failed to remove the evil heart inherited from
Adam, and treats his people more harshly than others (3.4–36). The second
dialogue opened in similar vein, with Ezra lamenting the divine
dishonouring of the one people elected from all the peoples of the world
(5.23–30). In the third dialogue, the opening complaint consists of a
rehearsal of the six days of creation, culminating with the appointment of
Adam as ruler of the world – a role which should have been inherited not

24. Cf. 2 Bar.19.1–3; 59.2. If the theory sketched in note 21 above is correct, this shift
would be explicable along redaction-critical lines.

25. A further example of this interpretative move occurs in *4 Maccabees* 18.18–19, which
tells how the father of the seven martyred brothers "did not neglect to teach you the song that
Moses taught, which says, "I shall kill and I shall make alive; this is your life and length of
days." The quotation conflates Deuteronomy 32.39 and 30.20. The phrase, "this is your life
and length of days" is here transplanted into a context in which it refers to a life beyond death
– if, that is, we take "I shall kill and I shall make alive" to refer to a single object, first put to
death and then raised by the Lord. God has put the martyrs to death in the sense that it is
God's law that requires them to die rather than to transgress, but God has also made them
alive by bestowing on them "souls holy and immortal" (4 Macc.18.23). The "life and length of
days" promised by the law is understood here as the eternal life of those who, beyond death,
"live to God".

by the Gentiles but by Israel, the elect nation (6.38–56). The problem is this:

> On the sixth day you commanded the earth that it might bring forth before you cattle, wild animals and reptiles, and Adam to be over them, whom you established as leader *[ducem]* over all that you had made, and from whom we have all come as the people you have chosen. All these things I have spoken before you, Lord, because you have said that for our sake *[propter nos]* you created the original world. For you have said that the other nations born from Adam are nothing and that they are like saliva, and you have compared their abundance to a drop from a bucket. And now Lord, see how these nations, which are regarded as nothing, domineer over us and devour us. But we, your people whom you called your firstborn, your only one, full of zeal for you and beloved – we are handed over into their hands! And if you created the world on our behalf, how is it that we do not possess our inheritance, which is the world? How long will these things be so *[usquequo haec]*? (6.57–59)

Ezra's argument is based on a typological interpretation of Adam's dominion over the animals as foreshadowing Israel's dominion over the Gentiles; the present situation, in which the Gentiles "domineer over us and devour us", is thereby interpreted as contravening the original order of creation.[26] Otherwise, this third complaint is similar to the first two in the contrast it draws between Israel's elect status and current suffering, and in its implied plea that the divine election should be manifest to all.

On this occasion, however, Uriel gives a quite different response to Ezra's complaint. This difference represents nothing less than a paradigm shift, from an eschatology based on the covenant to one based on law observance. Ezra is now taught that it is no longer a matter of patiently waiting for salvation to come from God. Israel's suffering loses its specificity, and becomes a metaphor for an active endurance of hardship in this world that is the precondition for entry into the next. This teaching is conveyed by way of a pair of closely related parables, in the first of which the inheritance is symbolized by a broad sea, in the second by a city:

> There is a city built and set on a plain, full of all good things. But the way to it is narrow and set in a steep place, with fire to the right and deep water to the left. There is a single path set between the two (that is, the fire and the water), and the path is not able to support more than

26. There is a closely analogous argument in Daniel 7 (on which see the comments of N. T. Wright, *The New Testament and the People of God*, pp. 266–67). Without this typology, Ezra's *Hexaemeron* is really superfluous – as it is for Stone, who comments: "Something of a mystery surrounds the precise conceptual connection between creation of the world and election of Israel" (*Fourth Ezra*, p. 182). The use of the term *devorare* in v.57 indicates that the typology is still in mind.

one person walking on it *[vestigium hominis]*. If the city is given to someone as an inheritance, yet he does not pass through the danger set before him, how will he enter into his inheritance? (7.6–9)

This, then, is Israel's situation in the world: no longer the passive object of unjust suffering, patiently awaiting future vindication, but a people summoned to an arduous journey which will either reach a successful conclusion or end in disaster – depending on the care that is taken on the narrow and precipitous path between the abysses of fire and water. Every member of the people of Israel must undertake that journey, and must do so as an individual.

This dangerous path between fire and water is the way of the divine commandments. Uriel's parable is inspired by Deuteronomy 5.32–33:

And you shall be careful *[phulaxesthe]* to do whatever the Lord your God has commanded you *[soi]*. You shall not turn to right or to left in all the way that the Lord your God commanded you to walk in, so that he may give you rest and you may live long in the land which you shall inherit.

In this utterance of Moses, the journey through the desert to the promised land has become a metaphor for the way of obedience to the commandments; and this way is seen here not as the means of maintaining possession of the land but of gaining possession of an inheritance that lies at the end of a way still to be traversed.[27] In the Greek text although not in the Hebrew, the pronouns are singular while the second person verbs are plural; the metaphor here acquires an individual as well as a national dimension. The Deuteronomy passage is the source of Uriel's image of the pathway to the inheritance, with disaster threatening to right and to left. The dangers are now specified and heightened; the precipitous terrain in which the path is located is no longer the wilderness but the present world; and the inheritance is no longer the land promised to the fathers but the life of the world to come. Above all, the metaphor of the path is radically individualized – a possibility already suggested by the Septuagint's singular pronouns. The path described by Uriel is so narrow that one must walk it alone. One does not journey as part of a company of pilgrims, conscious of a shared status as the elect people of God and trusting the accompanying divine presence to bring them safely to their destination. The journey can only be a solitary one, since every individual is subject to the law's demand – as though the divine voice were addressed to him or her personally – and will finally be judged on that basis. In *4 Ezra* as in Deuteronomy, the way

27. The "right or left" metaphor recurs in Deuteronomy 17.11, 20; 28.14. The more literal usage in Moses' messages to local kings (Num.20.17, Deut.2.27; cf. also Num.22.26) reveals the roots of this metaphor in the narrative of Israel's journey towards the promised land.

has a beginning as well as an end. The original metaphor follows the rehearsal of the ten commandments and the reminder of the occasion on which they were uttered – which was the one occasion on which God addressed the people directly, without intermediary (Deut.5.1–31). In this context, the way *to* the promised land is also the way *from* Horeb or Sinai, and it is the divine utterances heard there that constitute this way. To turn from it to right or to left, falling headlong into the abyss of fire or of water, is simply to disobey the divine voice that spoke at Sinai.[28] Though dangerous, the path is so clearly marked that those who fall have only themselves to blame.[29]

This, says Uriel, is "Israel's portion" in a world determined not only by Israel's election but also by Adam's sin. Initially, Adam's sin is connected not to the issue of law observance but to the immediate divine punishment, the hardships and sufferings imposed on the entire human race (cf. Gen.3.14–19):

> For their sake *[propter eos]* indeed I made the world, and when Adam transgressed my statutes what was made was judged. And the entrances of this world *[introitus huius saeculi]* were made narrow and sorrowful and laborious, few and evil and full of dangers and involved in great hardships. But the entrances of the greater world are broad and secure and bring forth the fruit of immortality. If, then, those who live do not enter these difficult and vain things *[angusta et vana haec]*, they cannot receive what has been set aside for them. (4 Ezr.7.11–14)

A slippage has occurred between the parable (7.6–9) and its sequel. In the parable, this world offers a single, narrow entrance to the next; but now it is "the entrances of this world" that are "narrow", whereas "the entrances of the greater world are broad". It appears that the term "entrance" *(introitus)* now serves simply as a metaphor for "this world" or "the greater world", and is no longer the point of passage from the one to the other. The general sense of this passage is clear, however. Ezra has asked: "If the world was indeed created for us, why do we not possess our world as an inheritance?"(6.59). He has appealed to Adam's dominion over the world, a role which should devolve to Israel, since other nations descended from Adam are as nothing before God (6.53–56). Uriel's answer is that the world was indeed created for Israel, but that Adam's significance lies not in

28. For "fire and water" in this sense, compare *Sirach* 15.11–20, where there is also an allusion to Deuteronomy 30.19 (so Stone, *Fourth Ezra*, p. 197).

29. The image of the narrow way between fire and water underlies the description of Christian's passage through the Valley of the Shadow of Death in Bunyan's *Pilgrim's Progress*. Bunyan could have read *4 Ezra* as *II Esdras*, in either his Geneva Bible or his King James Version. (For Bunyan's use of these versions, see Christopher Hill, *A Turbulent, Seditious, and Factious People: John Bunyan and his Church*, p. 169.)

his dominion over the animals (foreshadowing Israel's dominion over the Gentiles), but in his transgression of the divine commandments.[30] At this point, it is the immediate consequence of Adam's action that is emphasized: the world has become a place of hardship and suffering, exemplified in the struggle to obtain subsistence from the ground cursed by God, and in the pain of childbearing (Gen.3.16–19). In this respect, "Israel's portion" is no different to anyone else's. If the elect people are to gain access to the spacious life of the greater world, they must endure the common human lot in this world. The implication may be that they should not think of their sufferings as a special, unique case; "the desolation of Zion" is simply a particular manifestation of that common human lot. The motif of the divine curse that followed Adam's "fall" (*casus*, 7.118) subverts or relativizes a fundamental premise of the covenantal theology to which Ezra has appealed in all three of his complaints: that the suffering of the elect people contravenes the order established by God. Far from guaranteeing its world dominion, Israel's Adamic descent is turned against it.

All this has to do with the present *(quod in praesenti)*, yet it is the eschatological future *(quod futurum)* that really matters (7.16). Rather than agonizing over the present reality of the desolation of Zion, Ezra should concern himself with the last things: heaven and hell, death and judgment. If there is a "greater world" in which one may enjoy "the fruit of immortality", then the *only* important questions to put to an angelic instructor relate to the way from this world to the next. In comparison, Israel's subservience to the Gentiles is a decidedly secondary matter. So Ezra devises a question that links the issues of present sorrow and eternal life:

> Sovereign Lord, behold, you have ordained in your law that the righteous will inherit these things *[iusti heritabunt haec]*, but that the wicked will perish *[impii autem peribunt]*. So the righteous endure hardships *[angusta]* hoping for times of ease *[spatiosa]*, whereas those who live wickedly both suffer hardships and fail to obtain the times of ease. (7.17–18)

Ezra's concern for the unrighteous is to be understood in the light of the preoccupation with intercession that will later come to dominate this dialogue (cf. 7.102–8.62). At this point he seems to have in mind the

---

30. Uriel's view of Adam recalls Ezra's own statements in the opening speech of the first dialogue (3.4–7, 21; cf. 4.30). As we have seen, that opening speech (3.4–36) is characterized by a tension between the appeal to the covenant and the acknowledgment of the human condition (on which see also B. Longenecker's helpful analysis, *Eschatology and the Covenant*, pp. 50–65). In the third dialogue, this tension is developed in such a way that Ezra represents the appeal to the covenant, Uriel the universal anthropological reality.

unrighteous in Israel, rather than the unrighteous generally – who, we recall, are "nothing" before God (6.56–57; cf. 8.15–17). The law, then, makes a division within Israel, decreeing that those who observe it in the midst of the hardships of this world will inherit eternal life, whereas those who fail to observe it suffer now and will be further punished hereafter. Although the parables of the narrow entrances (7.3–9) are followed by a discussion of present hardship based on Genesis 3.14–19, their primary subject matter is the law as the narrow way from this world to the next; the law must therefore be brought into the centre of the debate.

While Ezra does not identify a specific text from the law, he surely has in mind Moses' final appeal to the people of Israel, in which they are offered a choice between life or death, good and evil (Deut.30.15; cf. v.19). As we have seen, a text from this passage is cited later in the dialogue (4 Ezr.7.129; Deut.30.19). The assertion that the righteous "will inherit" while the unrighteous "will perish" echoes Deuteronomy 30.16–18, where obedience leads to long life in the land which "you enter in order to inherit it *[eis to klēronomēsai autēn]*", whereas the disobedient are warned that "you shall surely perish *[apōleia apoleisthe]*". Precisely these Greek verbs must underlie the translator's Latin rendering here.[31] Ezra's reference to what God has ordained in his law alludes specifically to this crucial passage at the law's conclusion; and he immediately signals his difficulty with the apparent scriptural teaching that all Israel will *not* be saved.[32] From this point on, the problem for this dialogue is no longer Israel's subservience to the Gentiles – as in the otherwise dominant Danielic strand in this text. Israel's real problem is not the Gentiles but Moses. The Gentiles subject Israel to temporal suffering in this world, but Moses condemns the majority in Israel to eternal suffering in the next. A Danielic covenant theology is subverted by a Mosaic eschatology derived especially from Deuteronomy. At least, that is what Ezra fears. And the angel's uncompromising response shows that his fears are well founded: "Let many perish who now live, rather than that the law of God set before them be disregarded!" (4 Ezr.7.20). The majesty of the law's demand must prevail, even over Israel's other sacred traditions.

That is indeed the central theme of the entire lengthy dialogue. Out of the Deuteronomy passage, seen as summarizing the whole law, Uriel develops a view of the law as absolute and unlimited in its scope. The law's scope is universal, for it stands at the beginning of every human life: in it, "God strictly commanded those coming into the world, when they came,

---

31. This is a more likely scriptural background here than the combination of Deuteronomy 8.1 and Psalm 37.9 suggested by Stone (*Fourth Ezra*, p. 199).

32. The deuteronomic background suggests that Ezra still has Israel in mind here (against B. Longenecker, *Eschatology and the Covenant*, p. 79).

what they should do in order to live." While Ezra's concern is primarily with the unrighteous in Israel (cf. 8.15–17), the angel speaks of the law without any reference to the covenant. Under the regime of the law, there seems to be no fundamental difference between Jews and Gentiles, for all alike are exposed to the same unbending demand. Extended across the whole of space, the law is also extended across the whole of time. It was there in the beginning, for when Adam sinned it was "my statutes" that he transgressed (7.11). It will be there at the end, on "the day of judgment" (7.38), when the entire human race will be restored to life, and when "compassion shall pass away and patience shall be withdrawn, and judgment alone *[iudicium solum]* shall remain" (7.33–34). On that day the Most High will address the resurrected nations (presumably including Israel), and confront them with himself as the giver of the law, and with the fate that awaits them in consequence of their neglect of the law (7.37–38). For humankind the law is omnipresent. In it we live and move and have our being; there is no place of refuge from its sway.

> Those who dwell in the earth will be tormented *[cruciabuntur]*, since having understanding they committed iniquity, and though receiving the commandments *[mandata]* they did not observe them, and though they obtained the law they dealt faithlessly *[fraudaverunt]* with what they received. And what will they have to say in the judgment, or how will they reply in the last times? (7.72–73)

Here, at the close of the first section of this dialogue (7.1–74), the absolute status of the law's demand is established without any qualification. Ezra's passionate protests (to which we shall return) achieve not the slightest modification to a hardline position stated at the outset and repeated at the conclusion. At this stage in the dialogue Uriel has established, to his own satisfaction if not to Ezra's, that at the day of judgment the law's universal claim will finally be vindicated. If only a few will be saved, so be it. After all, precious stones and precious metals are rare (cf. 7.49–61). When Moses offered a choice between life and death, he meant what he said.

The next two major sections of this dialogue arise out of Ezra's further questions. He asks, first, whether the experience of torment will begin immediately at death or only at the final judgment (7.75); and second, whether at the last judgment the righteous will be permitted to intercede for the unrighteous (7.102–3). The questions are similarly introduced, and are clearly intended as structural markers. The answer to the first question produces a description of the immediate *post mortem* experience of unrighteous and righteous souls (7.76–101); the answer to the second is that no intercession will be possible, since the point of the judgment is to disclose the choice of life or of death that has in each case already been made (7.104–132). Ezra's questions and objections merely enable the angel to fill out his initial account of the law's universal and unqualified sway.

The law is omnipresent, and yet it is not recognized as such by the majority of humans. Immediately after death, however, the unrighteous will be compelled to recognize the authority of the law and of the God who gave it. Their doom is now irrevocably sealed, and for seven days they will wander aimlessly, tormented by the knowledge that "they have scorned the law of the Most High *[legem Altissimi]*" and that "they cannot now make a good repentance so that they may live" (7.81, 82). We recall that Moses' choice between life or death is by no means incompatible with repentance: it is possible to choose death in the first instance, but subsequently to repent and to choose life instead (cf. Deut.30.1–10). As for the righteous, they experience a similar revelation of their true position – of how they served the Most High and endured constant danger "that they might perfectly keep the Lawgiver's law *[uti perfecte custodirent legislatoris legem]*" (4 Ezr.7.89).[33] Unrighteous and righteous alike experience for seven days an anticipation of the eschatological realities, before oblivion descends (cf. 7.100–1).[34] The righteous and the unrighteous are distinguished above all by their *attitude* towards the law and to the divine lawgiver – an attitude expressed, of course, in their conduct. The unrighteous despise and reject the law, the righteous honour it and live by it. If, during their earthly lives, the unrighteous are always at liberty to repent and to turn from death to life, this is surely also the case in the event of the righteous falling inadvertently into sin. During this life, the divine patience and mercy does allow for the forgiveness of sins; the scriptural teaching to that effect is acknowledged. The righteous individual must, like Ezra, accumulate "a treasure of works stored up with the Most High *[thesaurus operum repositus apud Altissimum]*" (7.77); yet not every deed that is done need be a further addition to that treasure. This text does not teach "perfectionism", but is concerned above all with the fundamental and final orientation of an individual's life.[35] There is no reason to think that Uriel (or the author of *4 Ezra*) would have dissented from the rhetorical question posed by Ezekiel: "Have I any pleasure in the death of the wicked, says the Lord God, but rather that he should turn from his way

33. This passage refers to the *aspiration* of the righteous, but does not mean that even Uriel requires a lifelong sinless perfection – as Sanders argues, as evidence for his view that *4 Ezra* is the one extant witness to a Jewish "legalistic works-righteousness" (*Paul and Palestinian Judaism*, pp. 416, 418). The angel requires a level of obedience to the law that demonstrates that loyalty to the law is the fundamental orientation of one's life.

34. Both the righteous and the unrighteous are conscious of their situation for only seven days, after which they presumably pass into unconsciousness until the resurrection. This would conflict with the view of 4.35–37, where the souls of the righteous remain conscious enough to express their impatience for the coming of the end (cf. Rev.6.9–11). This passage alludes to an earlier tradition, however (so Stone, *Fourth Ezra*, pp. 96–97).

35. So Richard Bauckham, "Apocalypses", in *Justification and Variegated Nomism*, ed. D. A. Carson *et al.*, p. 172.

and live?" (Ezek.18.23). Yet, by the end of a person's life, an irrevocable
choice will have been made, and there only remains a day in which "I will
judge you, O house of Israel, everyone according to their ways"
(Ezek.18.30); a day when the individual's final decision for life or for
death will be revealed and put into effect. In spite of the time for
repentance and amendment of life that has been conceded by the divine
mercy, Ezra and the angel take it for granted that those who are to be
saved will be few.

Because the final decision for life or for death is irrevocable, there will be
no possibility for the righteous to intercede for the unrighteous on the day
of judgment (7.102–31). Ezra's own role as mediator and intercessor is
strictly for this life only. For the moment exiled Israel may have been
entrusted to his care (cf. 5.17–18), but at the last Ezra will stand before the
divine judgment seat as a solitary individual, without any role in relation to
anyone else. The same will be true of the other great scriptural intercessors,
Abraham, Moses, Joshua, Samuel, David, Solomon, Elijah and Hezekiah
(7.106–10). They interceded for people threatened with temporal disaster,
and they were heard. At the Last Judgment, however, every individual is
held fully accountable for his or her actions, as the ties that bind one
person to another are finally severed. Ezra envisages a possible scenario,
poignant and intimate, in which the righteous pray for the unrighteous,
"fathers for sons, sons for parents, brothers for brothers, relatives for their
kin, friends for those who are most dear to them" (7.103). Here, the
unrighteous are not a collectivity somewhere out there. Rather, they are
persons bound to other persons in family love or friendship, while, perhaps
unknowingly, the choice for death is gradually realized in the one case and
the choice for life in the other. Yet these ties to others are finally irrelevant
to the great question that is to be settled only on the day of judgment.
Ezra's possible scenario is unreal; there will be no comfort in solidarity.[36]

This refusal of the role of the intercessor provokes a further eloquent
lament from Ezra (7.116–26). But all his horror at the terrible fate of the
excluded cannot alter the human situation – which is just what Uriel said it
was at the outset, in the parables of the narrow entrance (7.3–9). In
bringing Ezra back to that starting-point, the angel explicitly cites a text
from the Deuteronomy passage that underlies the entire argument:

> This is the meaning of the contest in which every person born on earth
> takes part: that if he is overcome he will suffer what you said, whereas if

36. Passages such as this make it difficult to accept Philip Esler's dogmatic claim that
there cannot be any "individualism" in *4 Ezra*, since this is a modern concept with no place in
the "social system of the first-century Mediterranean world" ("The Social Function of *4
Ezra*", pp. 119–20). In *4 Ezra*, individualism (of a kind) is entailed in the concept of universal
judgment.

he overcomes he shall receive what I say. For this is the way that Moses announced to the people while he was yet alive, saying: "Choose for yourself life, that you may live." But they did not believe him, or the prophets after him... (7.127–30)

The earlier image of the heir's perilous journey is here replaced by the image of life as a contest, in which the opponent is presumably one's own "evil heart" (cf. 7.48) – although the earlier image continues to echo in the reference to *"the way* that Moses announced..." (cf. Deut.5.32–33). Whatever the image, the message is the same. All Ezra's ragings cannot alter what Moses said, which is so transparently clear and reasonable that the majority who are to perish will have only themselves to blame. Those who are to perish are, in the first instance, the majority in Israel who disbelieved Moses and the prophets; but their situation also represents the situation of the majority of the human race before God. Contrary to the implication in Ezra's laments, God is here exonerated. All that could be done for humankind has been done, and yet they still obstinately persist in fleeing from life into the arms of death. We have here an early example of the theodicy now known as the "free will defence": the claim that God cannot be held accountable for the manifold evils that humans bring upon themselves by the perverse exercise of their God-given freedom to choose. In this version at least, the free will defence is a paraphrase of Deuteronomy.[37]

The Deuteronomy citation brings Uriel's discourse back to its starting point, and marks its intended conclusion. In the fourth and final part of the dialogue, which constitutes its actual conclusion (7.132–9.25), Ezra seizes the initiative and takes upon himself the role of the intercessor that will be denied him at the judgment. If he cannot intercede for the unrighteous then, he will do so now (7.132–40; 8.4–36; 9.14–16). It is not enough to lament the fate of sinful humankind; one must strive through prayer to change it. But there is no indication that anything does change. In contrast to Ezra's scriptural predecessors, from Abraham to Hezekiah, his own act of intercession evokes no positive divine answer. What is more significant is the fact that Ezra maintains his resistance to Uriel (and to Moses) to the very end of the dialogue. Twice, he is invited to forget about the fate of the unrighteous and to ask about the glories that await him, as a member of the select group of the saved (8.51–55; 9.13). On both occasions, he refuses to abandon the solidarity with the unrighteous that is essential to his role as intercessor. The second refusal is especially striking. Initially, the speaker is Uriel, who (unsettled perhaps by Ezra's obstinate refusal to shift his ground) offers him all the information he cares to ask for about the salvation of the righteous:

---

37. Compare also *Sirach* 15.11–20.

"... So do not still be curious about how the ungodly *[impii]* will be tormented, but inquire how the righteous will be saved, and to whom the world belongs and for whose sake the world was made, and when these things shall be." I answered and said: "I said before, and I say now, and I will say again, that those who perish are more than those who will be saved, as a wave is greater than a drop of water." (9.13–16)

In refusing Uriel's offer of unlimited information about the state of the saved, Ezra also refuses to abandon his solidarity with the unrighteous majority. For him, it seems that the glory that awaits the righteous few is bought at too high a price, and it is therefore of no interest to him. While Ezra's attempts to diminish the rigour of the angel's Mosaic eschatology end in failure, the angel's attempts to persuade him to accept this eschatology also fail. Moses proclaims a way to life that the "evil heart" renders impossible to all but a few; and Ezra's last word in this dialogue is to reassert his initial objection to this, and to announce that he will never withdraw that objection. As the dialogue closes, Ezra and Uriel-Moses are no closer to reconciliation than at the beginning. If anything, attitudes have hardened. If Uriel and Moses are utterly intransigent, Ezra also knows how to be intransigent. At the beginning of the dialogue, Ezra and the angel play the parts of disciple and teacher. By the end, they are antagonists.[38]

Uriel presents himself as Moses' true interpreter, and Ezra too avails himself of scriptural resources in his resistance to the world-view developed out of the Deuteronomy passage. In particular, he appeals to a scriptural understanding of (1) creation, and (2) the divine character.

(1) The third dialogue has opened with a paraphrase of Genesis 1, posing the question why the typological significance of Adam's rule over the animals has not been realized in Israel's rule over the nations (6.38–59). In the new, deuteronomic framework initially outlined in Uriel's parables of the narrow entrance (7.3–9), Adam's significance changes dramatically. He is the type no longer of the world-ruler but of the sinner, who not only brings temporal sufferings to his descendants (7.11–14; cf. Gen.3.14–19) but also implicates them in his "fall" (7.118). As the dialogue develops, Ezra continues to draw on the opening chapters of Genesis, arguing now that it would have been better for us if creation had never taken place. In the first of two lamentations (7.62–69), he alludes both to the creation of humankind from the dust and to its promised dominion over the animals:

---

38. It is formally true that "[s]tets ist es Uriel, der das letzte Wort behält" (W. Harnisch, "Der Prophet als Widerpart und Zeuge der Offenbarung", p. 463); cf. *4 Ezra* 9.17–25. Yet, in this case, there is no indication that the angel's last word is convincing to Ezra (cf. 9.14–16).

O earth, what have you brought forth *[O tu terra, quid peperisti]* – if indeed the mind *[sensus]* is made from dust like the other creatures? For it would have been better if the dust itself had not been born, so that the mind might not proceed from it. But now the mind grows with us, and therefore we are tormented, since we know that we perish. Let the human race lament, but let the beasts of the field be glad! Let those who have been born lament, but let the four-footed animals and the flocks rejoice! (7.62–65)

Apart from the passing allusion to the "dust" of Genesis 2.7, the primary scriptural background here is the account of the work of the sixth day in Genesis 1.24–31 (earlier summarized in *4 Ezra* 6.53–54). In Genesis 1.24, the earth is commanded to bring forth living creatures, and duly does so; and Ezra now appeals to the earth – who here takes on the role of mother-figure elsewhere assigned to Zion – to reflect on the appalling consequences of her own fecundity. The "mind" here is the faculty that differentiates humans from animals; this term seems to represent an interpretation of the "image of God" motif in Genesis 1.26–27. In an interestingly materialistic rendering of this motif, Ezra assumes that the earth "brings forth" humans, minds as well as bodies, just as she brings forth animals. "Let us make..." (Gen.1.26) continues to entail, "Let the earth bring forth..." (Gen.1.24). This corresponds exactly to Ezra's earlier summary of the sixth day of creation, according to which God commanded the earth "to bring forth... cattle, beasts and creeping things, and over these Adam" (4 Ezr.6.53–54). The earth plays the same maternal role in the production of humans as of animals, even though humans are endowed with under-standing whereas animals are not.[39] The problem with the human mind lies in its capacity to comprehend the divine command, but also to choose to transgress it and to become aware of the eternal consequences of doing so. A unique honour is bestowed on the human creature, which is the addressee of a divine command calling for conscious, voluntary obedience; and yet this unique honour proves to be its downfall. The result is that the dominion of humans over animals is again reversed – but now literally rather than typologically. The animals, who are not burdened with understanding or with the possibility of transgression and its conse-quences, are far better off than humans. The continuing influence of Genesis 1 is indicated by the terminology used for the animals: "beasts of the field" *(agrestes bestiae)* and "four-footed animals" *(quadrupedia)* recall the *thēria tēs gēs* and the *tetrapoda* of Genesis 1.24 LXX.

---

39. The point is lost in the RSV translation of *4 Ezra* 6.54, where it is not clear that the earth's maternal role extends also to Adam. For the image of the earth as a mother or a womb, see Stone, *Fourth Ezra*, pp. 98–99.

Ezra's lament is addressed to mother earth, who is exhorted to mourn her bringing forth of the human creature on the sixth day of creation. Yet it was God who "commanded the earth to bring forth..." (4 Ezr.6.53). Ezra's address to the earth is indirectly addressed to God; it is a divine work that he is criticizing. This is crucial for the interpretation of Ezra's claim that "it would have been better *[melius erat]* if the dust itself had not been born, so that the mind might not proceed from it" (7.63; cf. 7.116). The production of "earth" or "dust" is the work of the third day, and, as in the case of the other days, it is said that "God saw that it was good" (Gen.1.10). When Ezra claims that it would have been better if the dust had not been produced, he directly contradicts the divine approval of the works of creation. If the creation of earth or dust leads to the creation of humans, which leads in turn to their transgression and to everlasting torment, then it can no longer be said that the creation of earth is good. It is important to note that this is a criticism of the divine work of creation only on the premise that Uriel's Mosaic eschatology is true. Although Ezra seems here to accept that premise, he later rejects it as he adopts the role of intercessor. With a little bit of interpretative licence, it is possible to see Ezra's lament as the *reductio ad absurdum* of the hard-line theology of Uriel and Moses. If Uriel is right, then the creation of humans was a manifestation not of divine goodness but of divine malice. But if Genesis 1 is right in its presentation of a creation approved by God, then Uriel's interpretation of Deuteronomy 30 cannot also be right. The beginning and the end of the Torah appear to be in tension with one another.

(2) Ezra's anti-deuteronomic argument also draws on scriptural material relating to intercession, and so to the divine character. His question about intercession on the day of judgment has received a negative answer. He has been told that the great scriptural examples of intercession (Abraham, Moses and so on) are irrelevant to the present issue, since their intercessions related only to the conditions of the present life (cf. 7.102–15). Undeterred, Ezra does take upon himself the role of intercessor in the closing section of the third dialogue (7.132–8.45), refusing to abandon his solidarity with the unrighteous even when encouraged to concern himself instead with the glories in store for the righteous (8.46–9.25).

Abraham "prayed for the people of Sodom", and Moses prayed "for our fathers who sinned in the desert" (7.106). Like Moses, Ezra is concerned primarily with the unrighteous within Israel rather than with the unrighteous as such (cf. 8.15–18, 26–31) – although his argument from creation applies in principle to humankind as a whole.[40] In the Golden Calf

---

40. According to Longenecker, Ezra in the third dialogue is no longer merely "Israel's defender", as in the first two, but rather "the defender of the human race" (*Eschatology and*

story, Moses intercedes to prevent the destruction of the entire people by
the divine wrath (Ex.32.11–13), and, subsequently, to ensure the ongoing
divine favour and presence (Ex.32.30–32; 33.12–16). Having obtained what
he asked for, Moses also requests and receives a revelation of the divine
character as merciful and gracious, slow to anger and abounding in
steadfast love and faithfulness (Ex.33.18–23; 34.5–9). All this is in the
background of Ezra's intercession. Immediately after Uriel's citation from
Moses' final appeal, Ezra finds the resources he needs for his own act of
intercession in the revelation to Moses of the divine character:

> I know, Lord, that the Most High is now called compassionate
> *[misericors]*, in that he shows compassion to those who have not yet
> come into the world; and merciful *[miserator]*, in that he is merciful to
> those who are converted to his law; and patient *[longanimis]*, since he
> shows patience to those who have sinned, as to his own workmanship;
> and generous *[munificus]*, since he wills to give rather than to take
> away; and of much mercy *[multae misericordiae]*, since he greatly
> multiplies mercies to those now living and to those who have lived and
> to those who will live. (4 Ezr.7.132–37)

Here, the divine attributes are drawn from God's self-revelation to Moses.
The terms *misericors, miserator, longanimis* and *multae misericordiae*
correspond precisely to the Septuagintal *oiktirmōn kai eleēmōn, makrothu-
mos kai polueleos* (Ex.34.6). The additions, introduced by "in that" or
"since", are Ezra's exegetical glosses on the scriptural language. To these
scriptural terms are added three closely related terms – "generous"
(munificus), "giver" *(donator)*, and "judge" *(iudex)* – which are all
similarly glossed (4 Ezra 7.135, 138–40). A further allusion to Exodus
occurs in the second of these glosses, where God is said to act in such a way
that "those who have committed iniquities might be relieved of them",
without which "not one ten-thousandth part of humankind would have
life" (7.138). This recalls the statement that the Lord "acts in mercy for
thousands, removing their iniquities *[anomias]* and injustices and sins"
(Ex.34.7). This scriptural revelation of the divine character is utterly
incompatible with the near-universal destruction of the human race – the
grim prospect that Uriel has conjured out of Moses' statement from
Deuteronomy 30. The scriptural basis for Ezra's statements about God is
also implied in the claim that "the Most High is now called *[nunc vocatus
est]* compassionate", and so on: "now" may be a concession to Uriel's
view that the divine mercy is only temporary (cf. 7.33), but "is called"

---

the Covenant, p. 88). This seems unlikely in view of the explicit denial of a concern for
humankind as such in 8.15–16. In Longenecker's reading of *4 Ezra*, Ezra's roles as advocate
first of Israel and then of the human race are *both* based on a false premise – a trust in the
divine mercy, which he will later abandon under the impact of Uriel's arguments.

502 *Paul and the Hermeneutics of Faith*

refers to a traditional knowledge of the divine character that is derived from scripture. In this way, the divine self-revelation to Moses is directly opposed to Moses' own farewell speech, as understood by his angelic interpreter. The disagreement between Ezra and Uriel is a contest between exegetes.[41]

Recollection of the divine self-disclosure to Moses gives Ezra the courage to take on the role of the intercessor, in spite of Uriel's warning that "many have been created, but few shall be saved" (8.3). As practised by Moses or Abraham, intercession is an argument to the effect that a proposed punitive action is incompatible with the divine character or reputation. Thus Ezra appeals to the patient divine care that goes into the production of the individual human being, and asks, "If you suddenly destroy the one who was formed with such labours at your command, to what purpose was he made?" (8.14). In the awkwardly inserted prayer of 8.19b–36, the conviction is expressed that "your righteousness and goodness will be declared... when you show mercy to those who do not have a store of good works" (8.36). Here and elsewhere in this prayer, there is explicit appeal to the divine character as known through the revelation to Moses (cf. 8.31–32). As the prayer of Ezra "before he was taken up" (8.19b), this passage demonstrates that he remained faithful to his role as intercessor until the end of his life, undeterred by the angelic conviction that intercession is pointless. Like Genesis 1, Exodus 34 provides Ezra with the resources to counter Uriel's assumption that Deuteronomy 30 is the last word on the divine–human relation.[42]

It is not clear why the author of this remarkable third dialogue should have written as he did. It is unsatisfactory to assume that he takes one side over against the other – for example, that his own view coincides with Uriel's, and that he puts into Ezra's mouth the objectionable views of his theological opponents.[43] If, however, this text cannot be read as a polemic against the views attributed to Ezra, neither can it be read as a polemic against the views attributed to Uriel. One does not put objectionable views

41. The connection between the two appeals to scripture is rightly noted by Longenecker, *Eschatology and the Covenant*, p. 86.

42. In contrast, Sanders' assessment implies that the angelic perspective consistently maintains an effortless superiority. Summing up *4 Ezra* as a whole, but alluding specifically to this passage, Sanders writes: "One has here the closest approach to legalistic self-righteousness which can be found in the Jewish literature of the period; for only here are the traditional characteristics of God – he freely forgives and restores sinners and maintains the covenant promises despite transgression – denied" (*Paul and Palestinian Judaism*, p. 418). Such a view misses the drama and the subtlety of the clash of perspectives.

43. Advocating this view, W. Harnisch writes: "Mit dem geplanten Ausgang einer Kehre des Geschehens... in der Hinterhand kann er es sich leisten, gerade Esra, der zu Grossem berufen ist (5,17), zum Sprecher einer religiösen Opposition zu machen, die sich durch die

into the mouth either of a revered figure from the past or of an angel. It seems that what the author intended is identical to what he actually achieved – a dramatic, tense confrontation between two theological positions which respectively assert the ultimacy of the divine justice or of the divine mercy, with no attempt at a resolution.[44] There is little further reflection on these matters elsewhere in this text. In the concluding visions (9.26–14.48) as in the first two dialogues (3.1–6.34), the concern is with "the desolation of Zion" and with the messianic kingdom that will bring about the long-awaited restoration. In the third dialogue, the messianic kingdom is merely an interim arrangement between the close of the present age and the dawning of the universal day of judgment (7.26–30). In spite of its close connections with the rest of *4 Ezra*, the third dialogue remains distinctive. For our purposes, it represents a remarkable analogy to the Pauline claim that we must be *liberated* from a law understood along the lines of Moses' concluding utterances. As such, it may help us to understand the deeper motivations of Paul's reading of the Pentateuch.

Paul and Ezra

In Romans 2, Paul addresses one who presumes upon God's kindness, forbearance and patience, confident that the threat of divine judgment on human sinfulness is directed against others. Insisting that God will judge everyone according to their works, and that Jews can claim no advantage at this point over non-Jews, Paul appears here to adopt a Uriel-like

autoritativen Weisungen des Engels anfechten und überholen lassen muss" ("Der Prophet als Widerpart und Zeuge der Offenbarung", p. 477). This view is effectively criticized by A. P. Hayman, "The Problem of Pseudonymity in the Ezra Apocalypse", pp. 50–53.

44. The visions that follow the dialogues are concerned with the desolation and restoration of Zion (cf. 10.20–24, 38–54; 12.46–48; 13.35–36), rather than with universal judgment. The first vision is the means by which Ezra is diverted from his obsession with the fewness of the saved and brought back to his initial concern with the desolation of Zion. In his opening statement, the theme is still the universal condemnation brought about by the law (9.29–37); in his second statement, the Zion theme is introduced alongside the judgment theme (10.6–17); in his third statement, the judgment theme has dropped out entirely (10.20–24). The shift is occasioned by the appearance of a bereaved mother, whom Ezra reprimands for her self-centred grief, and who is suddenly transformed into a city – Zion restored. It is possible to understand this first vision as "a description of a major religious experience, a conversion" (Stone, *Fourth Ezra*, p. 32). As E. Brandenburger puts it, "In der Zionepisode ereignet sich, noch in der Weise der Erscheinung, das Mysterium der Verwandlung Esras und damit verschlungen die Ingangsetzung der kritischen Tröstung Zions" (*Die Verborgenheit Gottes im Weltgeschehen*, p. 86). Yet Ezra himself states simply that, interrupted by the woman, "I abandoned the matters with which I had been engaged" (10.5). There has been no solution to the theological problem he raised, as Ezra's final prayer indicates (cf. 8.19b): rather, in the Zion vision, Ezra is brought back into the sphere of the community and its concerns. The vision marks a shift in the subject matter, but not a resolution of Ezra's problems.

rigorism. He does not at this point suggest that, on this basis, only few will be saved. His major concern is to suggest that, if the judgment is truly universal and impartial, the saved might include Gentiles whereas the condemned might include Jews. In spite of the single reference to Christ as agent of judgment (Rom.2.16), the criterion of judgment is the divine law, whether in written or unwritten form. As for the divine attributes, the kindness and patience evident in God's present dealings with humanity will give way on the day of judgment to the single attribute that characterizes God as judge – impartiality (2.11). While Jews are the privileged recipients of "the oracles of God" (3.2), that in no sense gives them immunity from the final judgment. Deeds alone are what count, and the deeds of many Jews as well as most Gentiles are evil. The judgment will pitilessly expose this fact, and will determine the final destiny of all humans accordingly. This judgment is universal in its scope, and does not concern only those who are alive at the coming of the Messiah; it therefore entails a universal resurrection. In Romans 2, there is little for Uriel to criticize or correct.[45]

By the end of Romans 11, however, Paul has reached a position that goes far beyond even Ezra in its absolutizing of the divine mercy: just as humankind is universally subject to sin, so too it is universally the object of God's mercy. Like the author of *4 Ezra*, Paul can comprehend both opposing points of view, incorporating them into a single theological discourse – although without finally resolving the question how they are to be reconciled. Again like the author of *4 Ezra*, Paul develops a theological position shaped by his reflection on the texts of scripture – above all, the Pentateuch. The question is whether Deuteronomy 30 plays the crucial role for Paul that it does for the author of *4 Ezra*, and, if so, whether it represents a position *against which* formidable and equally scriptural arguments can be mounted. There are three points where Paul's engagement with Moses' final address can usefully be compared with Ezra's.

---

45. According to Longenecker, both the Uriel of the third dialogue and the Paul of Romans 2 "engineer the collapse of ethnocentric covenantalism, and maintain that the escape from the anthropological condition is by means of one's works" (*Eschatology and the Covenant*, p. 184). Correlations between Paul's understanding of grace and Ezra's appeal to divine mercy are here ruled out, however; for, in Longenecker's "conversionist" reading of the Ezra apocalypse, Ezra is persuaded by Uriel to *abandon* his former belief in the covenant with Israel and in the saving power of the divine mercy. On that view, which I believe to be incorrect, the main analogy between Paul and Ezra is that both receive a divine revelation that converts them from their former "ethnocentrism" (p. 269). "What animates Romans 1–11 and *4 Ezra* is primarily the repudiation of Jewish ethnocentrism and, consequently, the revaluation of the law and the people of God" (p. 282).

(1) In the eschatology developed by Uriel in the third discourse, the key text is Deuteronomy 30.19: "Choose for yourself life, that you may live." The choice of life is realized in law observance, which is the appointed way to life. Paul finds just this point articulated in Leviticus 18.5, according to which the person who does the things prescribed in the law will live by them (cf. Gal.3.12, 21; Rom.7.10, 10.5). In both cases, law observance is the way to life; in both cases, the "life" in question is resurrection life, on the far side of the universal judgment; and in both cases, this clear scriptural teaching constitutes a problem. The texts are in fact interchangeable. In Galatians 3.12 and Romans 10.5, Paul might have cited the Deuteronomy text rather than the Leviticus one without seriously damaging his argument; the Leviticus text is no doubt preferred because the issue of law observance is explicit in the text itself, and not just in its context. Leviticus and Deuteronomy agree that law observance is not an end in itself but the way to a desirable goal, that of "life", and, conversely, that the way to "life" is the way of law observance. Ultimate human destiny is determined by the law.

In their different ways, Paul and Ezra both resist the testimony of these texts. In Paul's case, this is evident in the stark opposition he finds between the Leviticus text and Habakkuk 2.4 (Gal.3.11–12). More subtly, Paul finds an equivalent opposition between Leviticus and Deuteronomy (Rom.10.5–9) – but a Deuteronomy fundamentally rewritten so as to articulate the proclamation of the righteousness of faith. As we saw in chapter 7, the rewriting is occasioned by the fact that, as it stands, Deuteronomy 30.12–14 is in complete harmony with Leviticus 18.5. Moses teaches that the commandment is not far off, and that it does not need to be fetched from heaven or from beyond the sea in order to be heard and performed. Rather, it is already heard and known, and easy to perform. The person who does these things will live by them, and the choice of life rather than death, blessing rather than the curse, is or should be a straightforward one. In rewriting this passage as the utterance of the Righteousness of faith, Paul suppresses all three of its references to law observance, replacing them with references to Christ. Thus, this passage can no longer be assigned directly to Moses – in contrast to Leviticus 18.5 (Rom.10.5). In effect, the rewriting acknowledges the complete agreement of the texts in their original form: Deuteronomy is simply commentary on Leviticus. Paul shows his awareness of this intertextual relationship even as he tries to disrupt it. Like the author of *4 Ezra*, he too ascribes fundamental significance to Moses' farewell appeal to choose life rather than death.

Paul's rewriting of Deuteronomy replaces the doing of the law with God's definitive saving action in the resurrection of Christ, which reaches its goal in its acknowledgment as such – that is, in "faith". This faith is not extraneous to the raising of Jesus; rather, this self-revelatory dimension is

constitutive of the divine action, which is nothing other than an
"apocalypse" (cf. Rom.1.17, 3.21; Gal.1.16, 3.23) in which the final,
eschatological sense of scripture is disclosed. Paul and Ezra are both
recipients of apocalypses, disclosures of the eschatological sense of
scripture. The difference between them is that Paul is fully persuaded by
his own apocalypse, whereas Ezra resists the apocalypse he receives with
all the rhetorical force and scriptural argumentation that he can muster.
Even here, however, the two visionaries are secretly at one. According to
Paul's apocalypse, eternal life as the pure gift of God is *not* finally
conditional on law observance – precisely the assurance that Ezra sought
but failed to obtain from Uriel. It may be significant that the agent as well
as the content of the Pauline apocalypse is Jesus Christ, and not an angel
(cf. Gal.1.1–12): for the law was mediated by angels, and they remain its
guarantors (cf. 3.19–20; 4.1–11). If an angel from heaven proclaims that
law observance is the way to life – let him be anathema (1.8)! While Ezra
cannot carry his resistance to Uriel so far as this, his intransigent refusal to
abandon his solidarity with sinners amounts to a refusal of the eternal life
that his own law observance merits.

(2) Summing up his farewell addresses, Moses sets before the people of
Israel "life and death, good and evil" *(tēn zōēn kai tēn thanaton, to agathon
kai to kakon)*, and exhorts them to "choose life" (Deut.30.15, 19).[46] He sets
before them life and death, good and evil, by virtue of his role as lawgiver;
for it is the law that offers life and good to those who observe it, and that
threatens death and evil to those who do not. In v.19, "life and death" is
supplemented by a third pair of opposites, "blessing and curse", which is
clearly equivalent to "life and death" in identifying the two outcomes of
the two possible modes of conduct in relation to the law. In v.15, however,
"good and evil" might be taken to refer not to these outcomes but to the
modes of conduct themselves, which are defined by the law as "good" or
evil". Moses would then be summarizing the law in terms of the outcomes
of obedience or transgression ("life and death"), but also in terms of their
character ("good and evil").

These four co-ordinates (life and death, good and evil) determine Paul's
analysis of life under the law in Romans 7.7–25. As we saw in chapter 8,
Paul alludes to the Exodus and Numbers narratives of death in the desert
in telling of his own life under the law, marked as it is by a constant bias
away from life and the good and towards death and evil. In speaking of
the law as being "unto life" (Rom.7.10), he alludes in the first instance to
Leviticus 18.5. In their abstract form, however, the four co-ordinates

---

46. In Deuteronomy 30.15 MT, the pairs are "life and good, death and evil"; in v.19 the
LXX and MT pairs correspond. The LXX order is crucial for the present argument.

appear to derive from Deuteronomy 30.15. Thus, the first part of Paul's analysis is determined by the life/death polarity (Rom.7.7–12), whereas the second part is determined by the good/evil polarity (7.13–25). Vv.12–13 represent the transition between the two, since "good" occurs in v.12 and again in v.13, and "death" occurs twice in v.13. In spite of this overlap, however, the distinction of usage is clear. In constructing his argument along these lines, Paul follows his scriptural exemplar in presenting the outcomes of the two possible modes of conduct ("life and death") before characterizing the modes of conduct themselves ("good and evil").

In vv.7–13, the connection with the Deuteronomy text is clearest in v.10, which tells how the commandment which promised life led in fact to death. The singular "the commandment" may be influenced not only by the tenth commandment, cited in vv.7–8, but also by the unusual use of the singular to speak of the entire law in the preceding verses of Deuteronomy (30.12–14, the very passage that Paul will later rewrite in Romans 10.6–9). Because he is narrating an actual history, Paul prefers the concretion of verbs ("I died", v.10; "sin... killed me", v.11) to the more abstract noun, "death". Yet he reverts to the noun in the transitional v.13, asking whether "what was good brought death to me". Whether by way of verbs or nouns, the structural significance of the deuteronomic life/death polarity is clear in vv.7–12. The Deuteronomy text teaches that death as well as life is a possibility generated by the law. It does not explain the actuality of the catastrophic event that Paul narrates, but it does account for its possibility.

The term "good" *(agathon)* is initially used of the law itself (vv.12, 13; cf. *kalos* in v.16), but is more characteristically used – in conjunction with "evil" *(kakon)* – in connection with the law's fundamental categorization of modes of conduct. There is, of course, a close link between the two: if the law itself is good, then what it prescribes is also good. Paul again tells of a bias towards the negative side of a deuteronomic polarity. He fails to do "the good" *(agathon)* that he wishes and that is prescribed in the law, and finds himself doing instead "the evil" *(kakon)* that he does not wish and that the law prohibits (v.19; cf. vv.18, 21, where *to kalon* is used). This bias towards the negative is caused by "another law", a sinister parody of the law of God, inescapable since it is located in the human body: "the law of sin which is in my members" (v.23). The Deuteronomy text cannot in itself explain the negative experience that Paul here reports, but it again provides the basic categories – "good" and "evil" – that make that experience possible. Paul's analysis of life under the law is organized on the basis of the law's own categories, as articulated in the four co-ordinates of Deuteronomy 30.15. Moses offers life or death; Paul finds that the commandment that promised life brings him death (Rom.7.10). Moses defines good and evil; Paul finds that, wishing to perform the good, he actually performs only the evil (7.19). In Romans 7.7–25, the construction of Paul's argument mirrors exactly the pairs of opposites with which Moses summed up the meaning of the law.[47]

Precisely these four co-ordinates are also fundamental to Ezra's third dialogue with Uriel. Uriel's citation of Deuteronomy 30.19 ("Choose for yourself life, that you may live") entails the polarity of life and death, and of the deeds that issue in the one or the other (4 Ezr.7.129). In Uriel's argument, the co-ordinates are asserted in their abstract form: every human being who comes into the world is confronted with the choice between pursuing the good as defined in the law, and so attaining life, or of pursuing the evil defined in the law that leads to death (cf. 7.127–28). Ezra's counter-argument is based on the concrete reality of the inexorable bias towards the negative occasioned by "the evil heart" – an equivalent of the Pauline law of sin in the members (cf. 7.48, 68). Paul shares with the Ezra apocalypse the distinction between the law's abstract reality, as defined in Deuteronomy 30, and the law in its concrete reality for inherently sinful human beings.

For Ezra and for Paul, the gulf between the abstract and concrete forms of the law is a cause for lamentation. The concrete remains subject to the abstract: the law lays out the possibilities of life and death, good and evil, and the reality of an already actualized choice of evil and death appears inescapable. Paul's lament is first person singular in form, Ezra's laments are typically in the first person plural:

> For what good is it to us, if an eternal age has been promised us, but we have performed works that bring death *[opera mortalia]*? And what good is it that an everlasting hope has been promised us, but we have miserably failed? (4 Ezr.7.119–20)

The first plural usage stems from Ezra's role as intercessor, which presupposes that, while identifying himself with the unrighteous majority, he himself is righteous. In him as in a few others, the *cor malignum* has somehow been neutralized, and this enables him to assume a role that, from a Pauline and Christian perspective, could only be taken by Jesus himself. The Paul of Romans 7 is in no position to intercede for others, for the category of the righteous minority – still operative in *4 Ezra* – has here

---

47. Romans 7 thus draws on all five books of the Pentateuch: Genesis, in the Adamic allusions of vv.9–11; Exodus, in the citation of the tenth commandment (v.7); Leviticus, in the reference to the law's promise of life (v.10, cf. Rom.10.5); Numbers, in the linkage of law, desire and death (vv.7–11); and Deuteronomy, in the pairings of life and death, good and evil, that underlie the whole passage. Genesis is not here differentiated from the rest of the Pentateuch, since Paul understands Genesis 3 as a unique anticipation of the Sinai event (cf. Rom.5.12–14, 20). Käsemann's claim that the story told in Romans 7.9–11 "can refer strictly only to Adam" (*Romans*, p. 196) ignores even the explicit citation, as well as the allusions.

been closed down. Righteousness under the law's regime is not simply difficult, as Ezra thinks; it is impossible. At best, the person under the law can affirm the law's abstract goodness – a goodness that cannot be concretely realized within the conditions of human life. Indeed, Ezra too can on occasion acknowledge that the guilt disclosed by the law is universal:

> For all who have been born have become entangled in iniquities and are
> full of sins and burdened with transgressions. (4 Ezr.7.68)

In the face of this pessimistic insight, it is only the great figures of the scriptural narrative who ensure that the category of the righteous minority remains viable for Ezra.

Ezra's radical doctrine of the "evil heart" has a scriptural basis. It is associated specifically with Adam (3.20–22; 4.30), but it also serves to explain the disaster of Israel's history after Sinai, culminating in the Babylonian exile (cf. 3.25–27). Here, the "evil heart" represents a radicalizing of the deuteronomic motif of the "curse". The curse is realized in Israel's history, as in Deuteronomy 28, but it is realized on the basis of an inescapable bias towards evil that is inherited from Adam and that the law is powerless to eradicate. For Ezra, the evil heart excludes the possibility of the return to the law enjoined in Deuteronomy 30.1–10 and echoed by Baruch.

The deuteronomic curse motif is equally significant for Paul. In Galatians 3.10, he cites the curse of Deuteronomy 27.26 as encompassing all who live under the law's regime. As we have seen, the form of his citation indicates that this is to be understood not as an isolated proof-text but as summarizing the curse motif developed throughout Deuteronomy 27–30 and beyond. Thus, Paul draws from Deuteronomy not only the law's abstract co-ordinates: life and death, good and evil, blessing and curse (Deut.30.15, 19). He also exploits the fact that, in Deuteronomy itself, these co-ordinates occur not just in abstraction but also in the concrete form of the prophetic certainty that it is the negative possibility that will be realized in Israel's history.

In the context of the pessimism that pervades the closing chapters of Deuteronomy, Moses' exhortation to "choose life" rings hollow. Even as he utters the words, Moses knows that the people will inevitably choose death rather than life, the law's curse rather than the law's blessing. Paul and the Ezra apocalypse are both marked by the sharp disjunction between the abstract and concrete that comes to light in the Torah's conclusion. In the later text, the irreconcilable difference between Ezra and Uriel is in part the product of this disjunction. For Paul, the disjunction is writ large across the entire Pentateuch from the Sinai event onwards. From the very outset, the law's conditional offer of life (Leviticus) is nullified by the pervasive reality of death (Exodus, Numbers, Deuteronomy). Ezra believes something very similar (cf. 4 Ezr.3.20–23; 9.30–37).[48]

(3) For both Paul and Ezra, lamentation occurs in the broader context of resistance to the law's final offer of life only on impossibly difficult terms. Both of them appeal to earlier scriptural material that is at variance with this unacceptable final offer. The exalted status bestowed on Adam at his creation makes it hard to believe that he and almost all of his descendants will be subjected to an eternity of punishment (Gen.1). In the promise to the fathers, God unconditionally guarantees the final well-being of their descendants and of the world itself (Gen.12–18). In the revelation of the divine character to Moses, mercy predominates over strict justice (Ex.34). The God actually made known to Adam, Abraham and Moses is difficult to reconcile with the God revealed by Uriel, in spite of the angel's plausible appeal to Mosaic authority. In their different ways, Paul and Ezra are agreed in claiming that the authority of what is early (Genesis; Exodus?) cannot be annulled by what is late (Deuteronomy). Faced with a problematic text from Deuteronomy, they too avail themselves of the hermeneutical principle that "from the beginning it was not so" (cf. Matt.19.8).

In appealing to this principle, both Paul and Ezra are exposed to the same objection: that the plight of Israel and the world in the aftermath of Sinai was anticipated at the beginning, in the figure of Adam. Ezra finds it particularly difficult to counter the objection that Adam's significance for us lies not in his created glory, but in his role as the bringer of sin and death into the world:

> O Adam, what have you done? For though it was you that sinned, what took place was not your fall *[casus]* alone, but also ours who came forth from you. (4 Ezr.7.118)

Although Ezra earlier appealed to Adam's world-rule as the basis for Israel's (6.53–56), he cannot escape the simple fact that "Adam transgressed my statutes" (7.11). The problem for Ezra and for Paul is that a conjunction between commandment, transgression and judgment is already present in the figure of Adam, and that this conjunction may plausibly be seen as paradigmatic for the universal human condition. If

---

48. Such similarities do not entitle us to conclude that views later articulated in *4 Ezra* were a presupposition of Paul's conversion; that, as C. H. Dodd put it in an early work, "it was out of some such position as this that Paul advanced into Christianity" (*The Meaning of Paul for Today*, p. 76n). Given its early second century date, it is more likely that the Ezra apocalypse is indirectly influenced by the emergent Pauline tradition. The apocalypse's remarkable disjunction between divine mercy and justice might even be located somewhere on the trajectory between Paul and Marcion.

law, sin and judgment go back to the beginning, then one cannot appeal to the beginning of the Torah in opposition to its ending. What is there at the end is already present in the beginning. If so, the scope of the condemning law would be universal, so that (as in Uriel's discourse) there would be no place to stand outside its omnipresent, all-inclusive reality. Romans 5.12–21 represents an attempt to resolve this dilemma – following the contrast in chapter 4 between the beginning represented by the Genesis promise and a later law issuing only in "transgression" and "wrath" (Rom.4.15). Romans 5 was not actually written in opposition to Uriel, but it might have been.

In Romans 4, the promise to Abraham and to the world is said to have occurred in a context characterized by the righteousness of faith alone, in the absence of law, wrath and even of transgression (Rom.4.13–15). The familiar Pauline insistence that the law is a relative latecomer again comes to expression here. It is claimed that law, transgression or wrath are absent from the Abraham narratives; and this claim has a real basis in the Genesis text, where the relationships between God, Abraham, his family and indeed their Canaanite neighbours are largely unaffected by those deuteronomic themes.[49] If one wishes Genesis to harmonize with Deuteronomy, then one will have to rewrite it – as the author of *Jubilees* does. As it stands, the earlier text displays a significantly different theological logic, and this difference is the fundamental premise of the entire Pauline reading of the Pentateuch. The claim that law, wrath and transgression are absent from Genesis is exposed to an obvious objection, however. It can plausibly be argued that these realities are integral to the human condition, and are not purely historical phenomena; they therefore predate Abraham, and are found already in Genesis 2–3. Universal sin presupposes a universal law, and both must go back to the beginning: that is the problem Paul must address, if his own appeal to the beginning over against the end is to be persuasive.

The complexity of the interpretative issue is mirrored in the complexity of the syntax in Romans 5.12–21. In v.12, "as" *(hōspēr)* appears to introduce a comparison, to be completed by "so" – a comparison of the kind that Paul earlier developed in 1 Corinthians 15.22, where he wrote: "For as in Adam all die, so also in Christ shall all be made alive." The intention here is to present Adam as a type of Christ, the point of analogy being that in both cases a single person's action determines the eschatological destiny of all. Since the antitype is greater than the type, and since Christ's act actually reverses the effect of Adam's, the typological

49. "The possibility of curse as well as blessing, as regularly presented both in the law codes and in prophetic literature (e.g., Deut.30:15–20; Hos.4:1–3), is nowhere alluded to in the patriarchal traditions... [T]he overall ethos of the story... entirely lacks the emphasis upon sin and judgment and the corresponding need for moral choice that is characteristic of Mosaic Yahwism" (R. W. L. Moberly, *The Old Testament of the Old Testament*, p. 98).

analogy serves to limit the otherwise universal scope of what takes place in Adam. Universal human destiny is now determined not by Adam but by Christ, of whom Adam is a type; Paul will make that point in Romans 5.15–19. Ezra's lament about universal human involvement in Adam's "fall" would be entirely out of place here, for humanity is now – universally, it seems – "in Christ".[50]

In Romans 5.12, however, Paul suspends this analogy and leaves it uncompleted until vv.18–19: and he does so in order to make an important point about the period between Adam and Moses, covered by the Book of Genesis (vv.13–14). The basic concern here is to reassert the secondariness of the law, and to rule out the Uriel-like claim that law, transgression and judgment are original elements of the human condition. And so Paul insists that the universality of sin and death in the pre-Mosaic period is unrelated to law, and that the law is a latecomer.[51] The "sin" of the people of this period was not regarded as sin in the absence of law (v.13), and the "death" they experienced was more like a natural occurrence than a punishment for transgression (cf. v.14).[52] If Adam died on account of his "transgression" *(parabasis)* of a specific commandment, that is not true of any of his pre-Mosaic descendants. In other words, the conjunction of commandment, transgression and death in the case of Adam is entirely atypical. No-one else in Genesis is given a commandment to observe on pain of death. Adam is the historical point of entry of sin and death into the world, and he can therefore serve as a type of Christ on the basis of the universal scope of his action. Yet, in the absence of law between Adam and Moses, sin and death are hardly the central focus of the Genesis narrative as a whole. The characters that populate it are not confronted either with the demand that they should choose life rather than death, or with the judgment that they have already rejected life and blessing and chosen death

---

50.   A full discussion of Paul's Adam-Christ typology is unfortunately not possible here, where the focus will be on the problematic passage in Romans 5.13–14. R. Bultmann pronounces v.13 "completely unintelligible" (*Theology of the New Testament*, 1.252), failing to grasp the significance of the Pauline insistence on the secondariness of the law. Adam's legacy to his descendants is sin and death, but not law.

51.   E. Brandenburger rightly argues that the point here is to establish the priority of sin and death over law, and to deny the universal scope of the latter (*Adam und Christus*, p. 203). Paul here rejects the tradition that knowledge of the law was accessible prior to Moses, since he is concerned to avoid everything, "was diesen Nomos zu mehr als einer zwischenzeitlichen Grösse stempeln könnte" (p. 205).

52.   The claim that sin "was not reckoned" may allude to the tradition that a heavenly record is kept of all sinful actions, ready to be produced in evidence on the day of judgment (so G. Friedrich, "Röm 5,13", pp. 525–28; on this tradition, see also G. Nickelsburg, *1 Enoch 1*, pp. 478–80). Thus, in *Jubilees* 4.23–24, Enoch is translated to the Garden of Eden, where his role is to "keep a record of all the deeds of every generation till the day of judgment". From a Pauline perspective, Enoch has nothing to write until the law is given at Sinai.

and the law's curse. Even the Flood narrative concludes with a covenant of pure grace whose logic is that of the Abrahamic promise rather than of Sinai (cf. Gen.9.8–17). Genesis as a whole gives little occasion for the lament, "O Adam, what have you done?" Sin and death only become serious later, with the coming of the law – and it is just there, through the coming of Christ into the sphere of the law, that "grace abounded all the more" (Rom.5.20).

In their immediate context, the statements of Romans 5.13–14 are intended to reaffirm the secondariness and the belatedness of the law, and to disallow the claim that humanity as such is subject to a law-like regime from Adam onwards. Genesis is not a theologically empty space, however: for Paul has already shown that it is above all the site of the divine promise, the point at which scripture testifies most clearly to the unconditional divine saving action that has now been realized in Christ. In the stringent and pessimistic form it assumes in the final chapters of Deuteronomy, the law is enclosed and limited by the Genesis promise on one side and its fulfilment in Christ on the other. Within such a perspective, Ezra's despair at the human predicament is without foundation.

Conclusion

Paul's "view of the law" is his reading of a text – the composite text comprising the five books from Genesis to Deuteronomy. His "theology of justification" is a scriptural hermeneutic, antithetical in form and itself constructed from selected scriptural texts, which aims to show how the true meaning of scripture is its testimony to God's unconditional saving action, now realized in Christ. The dynamic of Pauline scriptural interpretation comes most clearly to light within the context of other contemporary readings of the same scriptural texts. Through their common concern with the interpretation of scripture, Pauline and non-Pauline writings constitute a single intertextual field, rather than indicating an immediate "parting of the ways" between two monolithic entities labelled "Christianity" and "Judaism". We started out from claims such as these, and the time has come to see how far we have been able to substantiate them.

One obvious objection must be taken very seriously. We have said that, at the heart of Pauline scriptural interpretation is a reading of a complex fivefold text: the Torah. Yet, the objection would run, it is one thing to demonstrate that, in different contexts, Paul draws on material from all five books of the Torah. It is another thing to claim that this amounts to a (presumably singular) "reading" of the Torah as a whole. Arguably, the only extant readings of the entire Torah from this period are Philo's *Exposition of the Law* and the first four books of Josephus's *Antiquities*. Other texts focus selectively on certain parts of the scriptural exemplars, but do not attempt a comprehensive treatment of the whole: we learn little about Genesis from *Baruch*, or about Deuteronomy from the *Wisdom of Solomon*. Although Paul himself does draw on each of the five books, his treatment of them is highly selective. Huge tracts of scriptural material are passed over with barely a mention. There is in Paul no reference to the Flood narrative or the story of Joseph; most of the Sinai legislation is passed over in silence, as are the preparations for the conquest. Paul never indicates that he would like to speak of such things but is hindered by constraints of time, space and subject-matter, in the manner of the author to the Hebrews (cf. Heb.9.5; 11.32). Hebrews (and indeed Barnabas and Justin) may approximate more closely to a reading of the Pentateuch as a whole than Paul does. In Paul, intense engagements with particular passages are often succinct to the point of obscurity, and there is little attempt to co-ordinate what is said about one passage with what is said about another. In addition (this is still our hypothetical objector speaking), the relevant interpretations are scattered among various letters and are occasioned by a variety of contingent situations. The pieces at our disposal are simply not made to be fitted together: not surprisingly, as they belong to different puzzles. Given the nature of the material, a "Pauline reading of the Pentateuch" will be an artificial construct, no doubt bearing telltale signs of some contemporary theological agenda but telling us little about the real Paul.

So far the objector. By way of preliminary clarification, it is important to note that the term "reading" is being used here to refer to a construal of the whole from a particular perspective.[1] Unlike an "exegesis", a "reading" does not have to account for everything in a text. It is the product of an actively engaged reader; it is not simply a self-effacing reproduction of an original by way of transcription, translation or paraphrase. In this sense, a reading (or two conflicting readings) of the entire Pentateuch may be found in *4 Ezra* no less than in Philo or Josephus. But do the surviving fragments of Pauline pentateuchal interpretation amount even to a "construal of the whole"?

It is hard to know how else to describe Paul's argument in Galatians 3, where material drawn from Genesis, Exodus, Leviticus and Deuteronomy is co-ordinated with Paul's christological proclamation. Detached fragments of scriptural interpretation can be found here only if we abstract the various citations and allusions from the total context in which they are set. Paul's reading or construal of the Pentateuch here includes the following elements:

(i) Material drawn from the Genesis Abraham narrative (Gal.3.6–8, 14–18). In Paul's reading, the "soteriology" of Genesis 15.6 is first universalized by way of Genesis 12.3, and then formally ratified in the "covenant" of 15.7–21, where the promise of the singular seed (cf. "your own son shall be your heir" [Gen.15.4]) is a typological anticipation of Christ. Through Christ,

---

1. The terminology is David Kelsey's. According to Kelsey, "[W]hen a theologian appeals to scripture to help authorize a theological proposal, he appeals, not just to some aspect of scripture, but to a *pattern* characteristically exhibited by that aspect of scripture, and in virtue of that pattern, he construes the scripture to which he appeals as some kind of *whole*" (*The Uses of Scripture in Recent Theology*, p. 102; italics original). Kelsey shows that an implicit "construal of the whole" may be reconstructed from a theologian's actual *use* of scripture, in relation to which it serves as a kind of hermeneutical framework. There is no reason why this should not apply also to Paul.

Christians belong to the "seed of Abraham" to whom eschatological salvation is promised.

(ii) An attempt to co-ordinate the promise motif of Genesis with the Sinai event of Exodus (Gal.3.15–18). The main point here is a negative one: that what takes place at Sinai, 430 years after the promise, does not affect the terms of the promise. A similar concern underlies the allegory of Galatians 4.21–31, where a connection between Abraham and Sinai can only be made by way of Hagar and Ishmael, and not through Sarah and Isaac.

(iii) Interpretative statements about the Sinai event (Gal.3.17–20). The cryptic reference to the law's plural, angelic authorship may imply that Paul finds indications of difference in the texts. The most striking element here is the insistence on the particular event in which the law originated, which has its own specific time (430 years after the promise), place (Sinai, a mountain in Arabia [4.25]) and *dramatis personae* (the angels, the mediator).

(iv) The law's promise of life to the one who observes its requirements, as articulated in Leviticus 18.5 (Gal.3.12). Paul believes this statement to be at odds with the gospel (3.12) and to be untrue in itself (cf. 3.21–22). Otherwise expressed, he believes that there is some limited scriptural warrant for a soteriology at odds with the gospel. If it seems incredible that Paul should have believed any such thing, we may recall Ezra's dogged resistance to a similar scriptural statement about law observance as the way to life, which is again bound up with an angel.

(v) The curse on all transgressors, announced in Deuteronomy 27.26 and amplified in later statements (Gal.3.10). Like Baruch (and Deuteronomy), Paul believes that this encompasses all Israel: this is "the scripture" that "consigned all things to sin" (Gal.3.22). Unlike Baruch (and Deuteronomy), Paul does not believe that the blessing that is to follow the curse can be attained by way of the law itself. That would conflict with the promise of universal blessing in Genesis 12.3.

(vi) The Christ-event (Gal.3.13–14, 16, 22–29). This is the extra-scriptural point of reference that interprets scripture and is itself interpreted by scripture. Scripture is interpreted as pointing towards this event, and scripture thereby interprets the event itself – which is, from Paul's Christian standpoint, the only reason for being concerned about scriptural interpretation in the first place. The Christ-event is not a pure datum whose meaning is unilaterally imposed on the text. On the contrary,

meaning flows simultaneously in both directions. Scripture is promise and law, and Christ is the promise's fulfilment and the law's end.[2]

For present purposes, it does not matter if any of this seems remotely plausible as an interpretation of the Torah. The point is simply that, in outline, Galatians 3 *is* an interpretation of the Torah, a construal of the shape and logic of its fivefold form. The texts cited from Genesis, Leviticus and Deuteronomy are not isolated proof-texts: rather, they are each cited so as to articulate a broad complex of scriptural material, from, respectively, the Torah's beginning, its middle and its end. Turning Galatians 3 into an outline construal of the Torah requires only minimal intervention by the interpreter. Essentially, it is just a matter of bringing the Pauline order, Genesis-Deuteronomy-Leviticus-Exodus (Gal.3.6–20) into conformity to the canonical order. This modest interpretative achievement bears no obvious traces of that "contemporary theological agenda" darkly alluded to by our purely fictitious objector – who seemed unaccountably alarmed at the suggestion that Pauline scriptural argumentation might actually be reasonably coherent, at least on its own terms. (An *ad hominem* riposte: if anything betrays a contemporary agenda of an objectionable kind, it is the insistence on fragmenting Paul's scriptural argumentation, thereby delegitimizing him as a Jewish interpreter of Jewish scripture and reducing his christology to an arbitrary personal conviction.)

This analysis of Galatians 3 can serve as a template for much if not all of the scriptural argumentation of Romans and the Corinthian correspondence.

(i) In Romans 4, the crucial soteriological statement of Genesis 15.6 is initially discussed in relative isolation from the promise motif (Rom.4.1–12). As in Galatians, however, the fundamental concern is to establish that the scriptural statement is universally normative for Jews and Gentiles alike. In 4.16–23, an argument based on the order of the scriptural narrative (4.9–12) is supplemented by an appeal to the promise that Abraham will be "father of many nations/Gentiles" (Gen.17.5), which here takes over the role assigned to the promise of universal blessing in Galatians. In comparison to Galatians the scriptural argumentation is more free-standing, with the *a posteriori* christological dimension introduced only at the end of the chapter, in order to identify the event that occasions the promised worldwide dawning of faith (4.23–25). Also to

---

2.   The scriptural matrix of Paul's christological statements belongs to the "coherent core" of his gospel, not just to the "situational contingency" of a "Judaizing scheme of synthesizing Abraham, Torah, circumcision, and Christ", to which Paul is compelled to respond (against J. C. Beker, *Paul the Apostle*, p. 56).

be noted is the recurrence of the Genesis promise motif in Romans 9.6–9, in a passage that corresponds closely to Galatians 4.21–31.

(ii) Having greatly expanded his treatment of Genesis 15.6, Paul devotes correspondingly less space to the relationship of promise to law: Romans 4.13–15 is, in effect, a summary of the fuller discussion of this issue in Galatians 3.15–22. In Galatians, the opposition between promise and law is occasioned both by the law's demand, which would illegitimately introduce a condition into an absolute and unconditional promise (cf. Lev.18.5), and by the fact that the outcome of this demand is to subject all who encounter it to the law's curse (cf. Deut.27.26). In Romans 4, Paul repeats the latter point but not the former, when he states succinctly that "the law brings wrath" (v.15).

(iii) The particularity of the event of the law's origin is strikingly illustrated by Paul's interpretation of Exodus 34.29–35 (2 Cor.3.1–18). The close connection and parallel with the Golden Calf story (Ex.32) enables Paul to develop his claim that the law brings death (or wrath, or the curse) on the basis of the Exodus story itself – as it were, without waiting for Deuteronomy. Also present here is a further acknowledgment of the scriptural warrant for a reading according to which the Torah is genuinely and enduringly the way to righteousness and life. The symbol of Moses' veil, which conceals the fading of the glory on his face, plays a role related to Leviticus 18.5 elsewhere. The Torah is not everywhere clear about its own soteriologically necessary limits.

(iv) In writing as he does in Leviticus 18.5, Moses articulates the soteriological rationale for the law that underlies and warrants non-Christian Israel's zeal for God, its pursuit of law observance as the way of righteousness and life. It seems that Moses writes here as the agent of the divine predestination, which hardens some and extends mercy to others (Rom.9.14–18). Moses continues to write along similar lines in Deuteronomy 30.12–14, another text presumably preordained to mislead, which can only be brought into line with the gospel when drastically rewritten by Paul (Rom.10.6–10). In Romans 7, however, it becomes clear that the Leviticus text (with its elaboration in Deuteronomy 30.15–20) misleads only in the sense that its promise of life is immediately overtaken by the reality of sin and death. Divine preordination and human sinfulness are to be seen as two sides of a single explanation for the failure of the soteriological programme outlined in the Leviticus text – not as alternatives.

(v) The role assigned to the deuteronomic curse motif in Galatians is taken over by the first person meditation on the realities of life and death under the law in Romans 7.7–25. As a comparison with 1 Corinthians 10 indicates, this meditation is informed by the Israelites' experience of death in the desert. The people who stand before YHWH at Mount Sinai are doomed to die before reaching the promised land; and in several of the post-Sinai stories in the book of Numbers, the law itself is instrumental in defining and enabling the sin that leads to their death. In addition, Romans 7 is structurally dependent on Moses' farewell appeal, with its offer of life or death, good or evil (Deut.30.15, 19). Paul here argues that, in concrete experience of the law, the choice for evil and for death has always already been realized, in spite of an enduring longing for good and for life. Of the explicit citations of Deuteronomy in Romans, one is closely related to the curse motif (Deut.29.4; Rom.11.8), while the others are drawn from the Song of Moses in chapter 32 (Rom.10.19; 12.19; 15.10). In Pauline perspective, the Song marks a point at which Moses ceases to be wholly identified with the law and speaks as a prophet like Isaiah or David.

(vi) In Romans 4, 7 and 9, Paul's construal of the Torah as a whole might seem to leave christology in a relatively marginal position, especially in comparison to Galatians (cf. Rom.4.24–25; 7.25a; 9.33). Yet each of these scriptural meditations is followed by a christologically rich sequel (Romans 5, 8 and 10); and each of them is oriented towards the claims of the gospel from the very outset. The christological reticence is striking, however, especially when Romans 1.16–3.31 is added into the picture. Paul in Romans respects the indirectness of the scriptural testimony to Christ, and eschews the christological equations – Abraham's singular seed, the rock in the desert – that occasionally occur elsewhere (cf. Gal.3.16; 1 Cor.10.4). That does not mean that in Romans scripture and christology come apart. Scripture is still wholly oriented towards God's future, definite act of salvation, universal in scope; yet the difference must be marked between the prophetic writer's antecedent knowledge of this event and the apostle's *a posteriori* knowledge of it. Prophetic and apostolic discourse converge upon this event, but the difference between them is not dissolved.

At each point, and in spite of additional complexities, the correspondence with the template provided by Galatians 3 is clear: Romans in particular further elaborates the reading of the Torah outlined in the earlier text. It seems, then, that Paul *should* be seen as a reader of the Torah as a whole, and not as an exploiter of isolated proof-texts. A further problem remains, however. In Romans and elsewhere, there are a significant number of scriptural citations that do not correspond closely to this outline; many if not all of them have been discussed, at least in passing, in earlier chapters.

Do these citations in any way threaten the stability of the outline? Or does it remain flexible enough to accommodate them? This is not a question that can be answered in general terms, so two specific examples must suffice.

The first is Leviticus 19.18: "You shall love your neighbour as yourself." This text can serve to represent all other commandments of the Torah that Paul regards as normative for Christian congregations. For Paul himself, it summarizes the second table of the decalogue and indeed "any other commandment" (Rom.13.8–10), among which we might include the various Deuteronomy allusions or citations in 1 Corinthians 5–9 (see chapter 9, above). Paul twice cites this text after previously citing a neighbouring text, Leviticus 18.5, as a summary of the law's unchristian soteriology (Gal.3.12, 5.14; Rom.10.5, 13.9). Both Leviticus texts summarize something absolutely fundamental to the law: its soteriological rationale and its interpersonal ethic. Yet there would seem to be a serious tension between them, as they are understood by Paul: for one of them remains normative for Christians, whereas the other does not. In Galatians 5, the problem is exacerbated by the claim that observing the commandment to receive circumcision (cf. Lev.12.3) actually causes one to forfeit one's salvation.

This is one of those *prima facie* contradictions within Paul's view of the law that lead exegetes to conclude that he was either a deeply confused or a profoundly dialectical thinker.[3] Both conclusions are inappropriate here. The solution to this problem is simply that Paul believes that he hears a plurality of voices within the Torah itself: the text that derives from the Sinai event is multiple and not singular in its origin (cf. Gal.3.19–20). From one angelic voice we learn that the person who does these things will live by them; from another we learn that all who are of works of law are under a curse; a third instructs us to love our neighbour as ourselves; a fourth is concerned with the observance of sacred times and seasons (cf. Gal.4.9–10). None of the voices that speak in these laws has anything directly to say about the unconditional promise. Indeed, they almost give the impression that it has been forgotten, or cancelled – an impression that Paul strives hard to counter (cf. Gal.3.15–22; Rom.4.13–15). Once again, contradictions in Paul's view of the law derive from contradictions in the law itself, as Paul reads it. It should be noted that this textual confusion remains subject to the divine providential ordering (cf. Gal.4.1–3), and that even within the confusion much is said that can and should be appropriated by Christians, either directly or indirectly. The crucial point, however, is that tensions and anomalies are built into the basic Pauline

---

3. For examples of the respective positions, see H. Räisänen, *Paul and the Law*, pp. 62–64; H. Hübner, *Law in Paul's Thought*, pp. 36–42.

construal of the Torah, and that the citation of certain commandments as still normative is in complete harmony with it.

A second example of a Pauline citation that may not fit the proposed outline of Paul's reading of the Torah occurs in Romans 9. In his treatment of scriptural material relating to election, Paul moves directly from Abraham and his children (9.6–9; cf. Gal.4.21–31) to Jacob and Esau (9.10–13), and to Moses on Mount Sinai: "I will have mercy on whom I have mercy, and I will have compassion on whom I have compassion" (Rom.9.15; Ex.33.19). In conjunction with the negative figure of Pharaoh (Rom.9.17; Ex.9.16), this divine utterance confirms the model of election and rejection that Paul finds in his Genesis examples. Here, at least, there is no disjunction between the Genesis promise and the Sinai revelation. While this presentation does indeed differ from the outline reading of the Torah in Galatians 3, it harmonizes fully with the more complex version of this outline found in Romans. Here, Moses serves a dual role both as the mediator of a law which wrongly claims to be the way to life, and as a prophetic figure who, in the Song and elsewhere, reveals God's future ways with the world just as Isaiah does. The Exodus text exemplifies this prophetic side of Moses's person. The image of Moses veiled and unveiled serves as a scriptural warrant and a theoretical basis for this two-sided portrayal (cf. 2 Cor.3).

Paul's basic reading of the Torah seems to be flexible enough to accommodate all his citations from it, although some are more fundamental to it than others. Removal of Leviticus 18.5 would affect its whole structure, whereas removal of Leviticus 19.18 would not. It seems unlikely that the picture would be changed much if we took fuller account of Paul's scriptural allusions, as well as his citations. Paul's allusions have played a lesser role in this book than in Richard Hays' *Echoes of Scripture*, where they serve to establish a theory of intertextuality drawn in part from literary theory, subsequently adapted to cover specific citations.[4] It is possible that the present account of Paul's reading of the Torah would be enriched by bringing his allusions more fully into play. This might, for example, bring the exodus into greater prominence as the event in which the fulfilment of the promise is typologically foreshadowed.[5]

A further confirmation that a particular construal of the Torah lies at the heart of Paul's theology may be found in the hermeneutic that serves as

---

4. But note Ross Wagner's observation that, "[w]hile attention has naturally focused on the figure of echo in Hays' work and on his criteria for discerning echoes, the extent to which his study relies on indisputable instances of citation and allusion often goes unnoticed" (*Heralds of the Good News*, p. 10n).

5. On this see S. C. Keesmaat, *Paul and his Story*. If the present reconstruction of Paul's reading of the Torah is accepted, it might form a framework for further study of Pauline allusions.

the framework for his exposition of righteousness by faith in Romans 1–3. As we have seen, this exposition originates in the text from Habakkuk 2.4 cited in Romans 1.17: "The one who is righteous by faith will live." It is this text that underlies the discussion in Romans 3.21–31, where the prophetic soteriology is contrasted with an alternative soteriology summed up in the phrase, "works of law" (3.28; cf. v.20). This alternative soteriology is grounded in the law, yet, more importantly, it is disowned by the true voice of the law that speaks through early commentators such as David and Isaiah, who reveal that, even in the sphere of the law, no-one is righteous (cf. 3.9–20). It is clearer here than anywhere else how Paul can understand the negative voice of the law as harmonizing with his own soteriological proclamation of faith (cf. also Gal.3.21–22). For present purposes, what is significant is the abstracting of the faith/law antithesis from its original context within Paul's reading of the Torah (cf. Gal.3), and its assignment instead to the voices of Habakkuk on the one hand, David and Isaiah on the other. The positive voice of the law – its proclamation of the "works" it prescribes as the way to life – is played down here. Thus, points drawn in Galatians from Genesis (righteousness by faith) and Deuteronomy (the curse of the law) are echoed in Romans 1–3 by prophetic commentators, who form a kind of bridge between the Torah and Paul himself. This commentary consists essentially in scriptural passages suggesting that Israel's guilt is exposed by the law as incurable, and that Israel must therefore await a salvation that is to be wholly God's act. "Faith" is the orientation of life towards that salvation, and is evoked by the written prophetic message (cf. Hab.2.1–4). As the argument of Romans unfolds, this faith/law antithesis serves as a hermeneutical grid for the outline reading of the Torah that occurs especially in Romans 4, 5 and 7. In Galatians, the Habakkuk citation is subordinated to Genesis 15.6. In Romans, it is Habakkuk who has precedence.

Paul, as we have seen, is a reader of the Pentateuch alongside other readers. He can claim no monopoly on it, for he is himself a member of a reading community characterized by ongoing debate about scriptural meaning and significance. Disagreement does not cut him off from that reading community, even when community can only take the form of mutual antagonism. Disagreement can only take place on the basis of an agreed frame of reference, without which it dissipates into incommensurability and indifference. How are we to sum up the disagreement and the agreement, the divergence and the convergence, that have been the theme of this book?

We start out from the remarkable fact that Paul not only acknowledges the reality of interpretative disagreement but actually finds a basis for it in the Torah itself, where Moses, veil firmly in place, writes of a righteousness attainable through the law: "The person who does these things shall live by them." Shortly before his death, Moses elaborates the point. The law's commandment is fully accessible, easy to understand and to obey, and it offers us a stark choice between life and death, good and evil, blessing and curse. From this perspective, the law may be described as "the law of life".[6] This is the view, grounded in the Torah, that Paul disputes. This view is articulated in specific passages, but it also represents a reading of the Torah as a whole: that communal practice of reading "Moses" or "the old covenant" in which the meaning of the text – its testimony to its own eclipse in the glory of Christ – is concealed behind Moses' veil (cf. 2 Cor.3.14–15). The Torah as the law of life is a Torah which has mysteriously concealed its own face behind a veil, creating the illusion that its glory is abiding and eternal. The question is whether anything corresponding to this law-centred soteriology, as identified by Paul, is actually attested in the surviving Jewish texts.

In the Habakkuk pesher, it is the interpretation not of the law but of the prophets that is at stake. Nevertheless, a reference to the law is inserted into the scriptural statement that "the righteous one will live by his faith". This text refers to "all who observe the law in the house of Judah, whom God will deliver from the house of judgment on account of their labour and their faith in the Teacher of righteousness" (1QpHab viii.1–3). The law here is the Torah as interpreted and practised by the pesherist's community. Right interpretation, practice and belief belong together, ensuring that the righteous person will live – that is, he will be delivered from "the house of judgment". The Torah here is clearly "the law of life", with the proviso that it is a Torah read and practised in distinctive ways. From a Pauline perspective, it is as though the Habakkuk text has been infiltrated by Leviticus 18.5. The pesherist fuses the texts, while Paul insists on a sharp disjunction (cf. Gal.3.11–12). Yet interpretative disagreement always occurs within an agreed framework. Paul and the pesherist both read Habakkuk 2.4 as a soteriological statement of fundamental importance; they agree that its true meaning has been disclosed in a definitive interpretative event originating in God, they agree that the interpreter must explain how "faith" relates to the practice of the law, and they agree in envisaging a final salvation towards which faith is oriented.

Paul explicitly acknowledges the possibility of an alternative construal of the Abraham narrative in terms of "righteousness by works" and "boasting" (cf. Rom.4.1–2). The reference is to a reading that identifies

---

6. The phrase is drawn from *Sirach* 17.11, which derives from the allusion to Deuteronomy 30.19 in *Sirach* 15.17. Compare *Sirach* 45.5 ("the law of life and knowledge"); *Baruch* 3.9 ("Hear the commandments of life, O Israel"); and *Baruch* 4.2 (Wisdom is "the book of the commandments of God, and the law that endures for ever; all who hold her fast will live").

Abraham as an exemplary figure whose deeds of heroic piety are to be recounted and celebrated. Such a reading would show forth the possibility of a life lived in conformity with the law, even before the law was fully disclosed. It could also claim to follow the Genesis text in celebrating the departure from Chaldea as the beginning of Abraham's life of faithful obedience, and the offering of Isaac as its culmination. Readings along these lines are in fact to be found in *Jubilees*, in Philo's *On Abraham*, and in Josephus's *Antiquities*. They are intended to glorify Abraham, and, indirectly, Abraham's God, whose law – already inscribed on heavenly tablets or in nature and the soul – brought forth such fruit in him. The Abraham narrative is a story about "righteousness by works" in the sense that the divine call liberates Abraham from the idolatry of Chaldea and calls him to a life of righteousness, piety *(eusebeia)* and virtue *(aretē)* that remains exemplary for his descendants and for the world. Paul's reading diverges from this by presenting Abraham purely as the addressee of the unconditional divine promise, and by detaching the faith that was reckoned to him as righteousness from the indications of supreme faithfulness or virtue that other readers find in his story. Yet Paul's reading and the others all register the discrepancy between the patriarchal narratives of Genesis and the Sinai revelation narrated in Exodus. The discrepancy can be overcome by projecting the law back into Genesis, or it can be used to assert the absolute significance of the promise: in either case, it is the same textual phenomenon that generates the divergent readings. All of the readings agree that the fundamental dynamics of the divine–human relationship are disclosed here in exemplary fashion, at the very beginning of the chosen people's history.

At the heart of the book of Exodus is the complex event of the giving of the law – an event in relation to which even the life of Abraham might seem to be merely commentary. This event includes the divine recitation of the ten commandments in the hearing of the people, Moses' communion with God on the mountain top, and his double descent bearing the inscribed stone tablets in wrath or in glory. The diversity of material in Exodus 19–34 will tend to result in selective readings that highlight some themes at the expense of others. The key to Paul's reading in 2 Corinthians 3 is to be found in his insistence that the giving of the law should not be abstracted from its initial impact on those who found themselves addressed by it. As a result of their idolatry with the Golden Calf, the law was initially experienced not as a law of life but as the bringer of death. Through a conflation of Moses' two descents, the glory of the transfigured Moses is represented as a deadly glory; for, as the remaining books of the Pentateuch will show, the law's initial fatal impact on its addressees is a paradigm rather than an exception. A far more optimistic reading of this section of Exodus is also possible, however. For Philo, Moses' glory is the after-effect of his mystical communion with the deity; Moses on the mountain top establishes a pattern for mystical experience, and in so doing fulfils his vocation as high priest and mystagogue. The Golden Calf incident simply illustrates the exposure of the would-be mystic to the downward pull of political affairs. The stone tablets are not relevant to this presentation, for the law is given supremely in the divine utterance of the ten commandments, not in the act of inscription. Since the ten commandments are addressed as directly to ourselves as to the people gathered at Mount Sinai, the question of the law's impact on its first addressees is of no real significance. This law remains the law of life, leading us directly to the knowledge of the one who truly is. As in the Genesis examples, the different readings are generated in part by decisions about which strands within the text are to be developed, and which are to be passed over.

In the book of Leviticus, Moses articulates for the first time the intended outcome of law observance, which is simply "life" (Lev.18.5). For Josephus as for Paul, the law's conditional promise relates to individual rather than to national destiny, and speaks of immortality and resurrection; but it also summarizes the wholly admirable and praiseworthy way of life that characterizes the entire Jewish people. In principle, this conditional promise of life could be understood in a perfectionist sense as referring to a total, sinless observance of the law: Josephus can appear to take it in this sense, although allowance must be made for his use of hyperbole for rhetorical effect. Yet, of all the books of the Torah, Leviticus has most to say about the means of atonement for sin, and it is unlikely that either Josephus or Paul seriously believe that the Jewish people are committed to the pursuit of a "sinless perfection". Josephus tends to assimilate the Jewish belief that law observance leads to life to the Greek belief that eternal life is the reward of the life of virtue, and there is a partially analogous argument in Romans 2 – subsequently undermined, however, by the claim that what the law actually discloses is the universality and all-pervasiveness of sin. At this last point, Paul and Josephus finally part company. On broader scriptural grounds, Paul is pessimistic about human capacity for the law whereas Josephus is optimistic. A measure of agreement about the law's conditional promise of life coincides with irreconcilable disagreement about whether life can actually be attained by this route. This coincidence of agreement and disagreement is an extreme example of the dialectical relationship between Pauline and non-Pauline scriptural readings that is also evident elsewhere.

With the book of Numbers, we return to the issue of the impact of the law on its first addressees. Numbers begins with preparations for the departure from Sinai; before it concludes, the generation of those who stood before YHWH at Sinai has perished under the divine wrath in the wilderness. In several cases, cited by Paul in 1 Corinthians 10, it is precisely the encounter with the law that proves to be their undoing. Superficially, the Leviticus promise of life to the law observant coheres well with the account of the destruction of a disobedient generation in Numbers. At a deeper level, the contrast is unsettling. Faced with this textual problem, readers move in different directions. In Romans 7, for example, Paul highlights the disjunction between Numbers and Leviticus as sharply as he elsewhere highlights the disjunction between Genesis and Exodus. In contrast, the author of the *Wisdom of Solomon* seeks to minimize the post-Sinai death motif, displacing it into the plague cycle so that it is Egyptians and not Israelites who die at the hand of the Lord. His presentation is determined by the conviction that Israel is the holy nation, untainted by the degrading superstition and moral anarchy of the Gentile world. As such, the holy nation must be shown to be uniquely and consistently favoured by God – at which point Paul intervenes with what appears to be an explicit rejoinder, brusquely asserting that the supposedly holy nation is in fact as implicated in idolatry and ungodliness as anyone else. Like Paul, however, the author of *Wisdom* draws on narrative material from Genesis, Exodus and Numbers, and finds in this narrated past the key to God's definitive saving action in the eschatological future.

Paul and the author of *Baruch* are agreed that the motif of the curse, developed in Deuteronomy 27–30, is the key to understanding the history of the people of Israel. For other readers also, this scriptural passage seemed crucially important both in explaining the elect nation's current sufferings, symbolized in the Babylonian exile, and in pointing ahead to a future characterised by blessing rather than the curse – a future attainable by way of a wholehearted return to the law (cf. Deut.30.1–10). At this point Paul parts company with Baruch: for him, salvation takes the form not of the law's blessing but of Abraham's, and the way from the law's curse to Abraham's blessing has been realized in the death and resurrection of Jesus Christ and in the outpouring of his Spirit (Gal.3.10–14). In Romans, however, Paul does find testimony to divine saving action in Deuteronomy itself, in the Song of Moses (Deut.32). Here there is no further mention of a return to the law, and salvation is accomplished by God alone. *Baruch* is unable to substantiate the claim that a return to the law is the true path to salvation, and this uncertainty is expressed in the sharpest form – and within a rather different theological framework – in *4 Ezra*. Ezra struggles with a rigorist though non-perfectionist interpretation of the law's conditional offer of life (Deuteronomy), appealing to the scriptural testimony to creation (Genesis) and to the revelation of the divine character (Exodus). What is remarkable here is not the angel's insistence that law observance is the appointed way to life, but rather the fact that a figure of the stature of Ezra can find this scripturally based teaching utterly unacceptable. The suggestion of a fundamental tension within the Torah itself is closely analogous to Paul (and may indeed have been indirectly influenced by him).

At a certain level of generality, these diverse non-Pauline readings do appear to conform to Paul's own account of a reading of the Torah, warranted by the text and realized in practice, that he himself rejects. For these readings, the Torah is above all the law of life. At its heart lies the concern to articulate the pattern of conduct appropriate to the holy nation, on the assumption that this conduct is the appointed way to national and/ or individual salvation (however understood). That is not at all to say that there is no place for divine mercy and human repentance in these texts, or to insinuate that these realities are acknowledged only on their margins. In texts that appeal to Deuteronomy 30.1–10, repentance and divine mercy are indispensable elements in the call for a return to the law; and there may also be scope for the concept of a divine transforming power. In non-deuteronomic texts such as *The Wisdom of Solomon*, the scriptural paradigms of divine mercy and power, exercised for the benefit of the elect people, are heightened and celebrated. In texts commemorating the lives of figures such as Abraham, there is not the slightest intention of detracting from the glory of God, which is in fact disclosed precisely in the glory of such human lives. If these readings understand the Torah as elaborating the principle that "the person who does these things shall live by them", they can certainly not be *reduced* to that abstract principle. Indeed, it is only from the perspective of a different reading of the Torah, oriented towards the unconditional divine saving action associated with the promise motif, that a "common denominator" of these readings comes to light at all. Only from the standpoint of this self-consciously different reading do they appear to be essentially the same. And only from that standpoint can it be said that these readings are theologically deficient.

Similarity and difference are relative and not absolute concepts. We may recall the readings of the Abraham narrative in Romans 4, Philo's *On Abraham* and the book of *Jubilees*. From the perspective of a Pauline reader, the obvious differences between Philo and *Jubilees* will be less interesting than what they have in common, which is that they both celebrate Abraham's faithful obedience with little reference to the divine promise. But the same will be true, *mutatis mutandis*, from a Philonic perspective. For a Philonic reader, what Paul and Jubilees have in common is their ignorance of the ontological presuppositions of Abraham's life of piety and virtue. It is this shared ignorance that underlies their equal and opposite errors – the supposition of a time and place without law in the one case, the projection of the Sinai revelation back into Genesis in the other. And how would a convinced reader of *Jubilees*, at Qumran or elsewhere, react to the Pauline and Philonic readings? Such a reader might identify a pernicious common error, the shared assumption that the stipulations revealed at Sinai do *not* correspond, precisely and literally, to the eternal and universally valid will of God. (Both readers have no doubt been corrupted by living among Gentiles.) At this point we may introduce a fourth, uncommitted reader, for whom all three readings are legitimate – but only relatively so, from the standpoint of the particular truth-claim on which each is based. We should not conclude that this fourth reader, being uncommitted, displays greater hermeneutical acumen than the other three: for the pluralist conclusion may itself be based on another particular truth-claim, in the shape of the sceptical assumption that the text cannot and should not be seen as articulating a single normative truth. From this standpoint, the three committed readings are all guilty of the same hermeneutical error in presupposing that reading a text must also be an exercise in dogmatic construction.[7] There is, then, no way out of the relativity of judgments of similarity and difference. The familiar debate about whether, at a purely factual level, Paul's view of Judaism is correct or incorrect should be reformulated accordingly.[8]

Granted this qualification, it can be simply stated that Paul's controversy with "Judaism" (Christian or otherwise) is in fact a conflict about the interpretation of the Torah; that the disputing parties agree that the Torah, correctly understood, is soteriologically normative; and that the question at issue is whether interpretive priority is to be given to a particular mode of divine agency (the making of an unconditional promise) or of human agency (the observance of the commandments). The radical difference between the two readings is, however, constructed *within* the Pauline reading. Projected onto the non-Pauline texts, this construct has evoked clear echoes: Paul's claim that contemporary understanding of the Torah is determined by the soteriological principle articulated in Leviticus 18.5 is not a pure fabrication. Yet the difference between the readings cannot be absolutized, as though a necessary "parting of the ways" between Pauline Christianity and "Judaism" could be confirmed independently of Paul's own perspective.

---

7.   My own partial identification with this uncommitted reader is occasioned by the quest for analytical clarity and not by theological scepticism. For a defence of the view that theological construction is an entirely proper activity for a biblical interpreter, see my *Text, Church and World* and *Text and Truth*.

8.   Both E. P. Sanders and J. D. G. Dunn argue that Paul understands Judaism as they themselves do, in terms of the priority of election, covenant and grace. As Sanders states, "This is both the position which, independently of Paul, we can know to have characterized Judaism and the position which Paul attacks" (*Paul, the Law, and the Jewish People*, p. 46; original italicized). Räisänen is a dissenter here, concluding that Paul *did* "treat the law as the Jewish way of salvation, detached from God's covenantal grace", and that "the Apostle either gives a totally distorted picture of Judaism or else bases his portrayal on insufficient and uncharacteristic (even though authentic) evidence" (*The Torah and Christ*, pp. 39, 32). What is problematic here is the assumption that an empirical account of a singular "Judaism" is attainable, and that Paul's own statements can be straightforwardly tested against this for accuracy. There is a hermeneutical innocence about these assumptions which a more careful reading of Bultmann might have helped to dispel.

This brings us to another possible objection to the case that has here been argued. It might be said that the analysis so far has exaggerated the extent to which Paul is a "reader", and underplayed the fact that he is an apostle with a message to proclaim about the crucified and risen Jesus. Paul reads the texts of the Torah only in the light of the event of Jesus' death and resurrection. For Paul, an event has taken place that illuminates the texts but which also interposes itself between himself and the texts. And so he proclaims Christ, not Torah. He practises the reading of the Torah not for its own sake but for the sake of the gospel of Christ as he understands it. In this respect at least, his reading of the Torah is fundamentally and absolutely different from other contemporary readings, where no Christ-event has intervened between the reader and the text. There is direct continuity between text and reading in these cases, but only an indirect and disrupted continuity in the case of Paul. Scriptural interpretation does *not*, therefore, constitute the common field on which Pauline Christian and non-Christian Jewish theological construction takes place. Paul's allegiance to Christ displaces him into a different field.

This objection derives its apparent plausibility from unexamined essentialist assumptions about the nature of "Christianity" and of "Judaism". Two points may be made in response. First, it is not true that Paul proclaims "Christ, not Torah" (we recall that "Torah" properly includes Genesis). The Christ Paul proclaims is a Christ attested by the law and the prophets; Christ and scripture reciprocally interpret one another. In all its concreteness and historical particularity, the Christ-event can therefore be described as a hermeneutical event. For Paul, the light of the risen Christ is at the same time the illumination of scripture, a scripture reordered so as to form the interpretative matrix within which the Christ-event takes shape and discloses itself as the particular event it is.[9] When Paul moves to and fro between scriptural interpretation and explicitly christological discourse (e.g. in Romans 4–5), he is not changing the subject.

Second, it is not true that the non-Pauline readings are in direct continuity with the scriptural text, without the interposition of a realized saving event. The Habakkuk pesher tells of precisely such an event, focused on the persecuted and vindicated individual in whom God has disclosed the true meaning of scripture for the sake of our salvation. In *The Wisdom of Solomon*, the writer has himself experienced Sophia's transforming illumination, reading scripture in the light of it and thereby

---

9. As Paul Ricoeur writes: "The very originality of the event requires that it be transmitted by means of an interpretation of preexisting significations – already inscribed – available within the cultural community" ("Philosophical Hermeneutics and Biblical Hermeneutics", in his *From Text to Action*, pp. 89–101; p. 94).

giving particular form and content to the illumination itself (cf. Wis.10). In these cases as in the Pauline one, interpreters move freely between the transforming event, its attestation in scripture, and its eschatological realization. In each case, the transforming event occurs *within* the field constituted by scriptural normativity, although it comes onto the scene "vertically, from above" and is not simply the product of this field. In no case is the transforming event simply a means to the end of understanding scripture, lacking significance in its own right. The analogies are not exact, of course. The Teacher of Righteousness is not crucified, nor is he raised on the third day. Sophia bestows her radiance on her initiates without identifying herself with the life and destiny of a single individual. But analogies never are exact. That is what makes them analogies.

There is, then, no absolute breach between the Pauline and the non-Pauline readings, occasioned by Paul's christological convictions. For Paul, the saving event illuminates and is illuminated by scripture, and is therefore a hermeneutical event. Parallels to the Pauline concept of the saving event may be found in other texts. Pauline and non-Pauline theological construction occurs within a single intertextual field.

Is this model of the single intertextual field undermined by the fact that the readings in question are intended for quite different communities? In Romans and Galatians, Paul is addressing largely Gentile communities. By a divine grace that is contrary to nature, Gentile Christians have been grafted into the ancestral olive tree that is the historic life of the people of Israel (Rom.11.17-21). As an apostle who is himself an "Israelite" (Rom.11.1), it is Paul's calling to welcome the incoming Gentiles and to find a secure place for them within the narrative of the Torah as he understands it in the light of God's saving intervention. Pauline scriptural interpretation in its entirety has this specific communal context and rationale. Yet these Gentiles remain Gentiles. In contrast, the non-Pauline readings are primarily or exclusively intended for Jews, not for Gentiles. Given this fundamental difference of communal setting, can the various readings still be seen as occurring within a single intertextual field?

In reality, the social setting of these readings is far too complex to be captured in any simple differentiation between a Gentile-dominated Christian community on the one hand, and "the Jewish community" (or "the synagogue") on the other. The Pauline Gentiles are indeed Gentiles; and yet they have been brought into Israel's ancestral heritage, as mediated through the earliest Jewish Christian or Christian Jewish community, to which Paul belongs and to which he remains to some degree accountable (cf. Rom.11.1-6, 15.25-32; Gal.2.1-10; 2 Cor.8.1-9.15). From many points of view, they are converts to a variant or deviant form of "Judaism". In spite of tensions reflected in Galatians and Philippians, the Pauline "Gentile" communities appropriate not only Jewish scripture but also the characteristic Jewish orientation towards Jerusalem as the spiritual centre of their developing worldwide community – a Jerusalem associated with the first followers of Jesus rather than the Temple establishment. Gentile Christians later lost this orientation to Jerusalem, but so too did non-Christian Jews, and for similar historical reasons. If Gentile Christian communities in Asia Minor, Greece or Rome exist in a state of "sectarian" separation from local Jewish communities and their synagogues, the separation nevertheless occurs within the common field constituted by Jewish scripture and its interpretation and realization in practice. If this is the case with the Judean communities centred on Qumran, it is also the case with those geographically more diverse communities that locate their own alternative establishment in Jerusalem itself. There can be no simple dichotomy between the social contexts of the Pauline and the non-Pauline readings.[10]

In this book, it has not been possible to take full account of the historical and social reality of the communities in and for which scriptural interpretations were produced. This whole dimension has been neglected not because I regard it as unimportant or uninteresting, but because one has to set limits somewhere. The reason for touching on this issue here is simply to show that Paul's largely "Gentile" communities can be accommodated without difficulty in the model of the single intertextual field. It cannot be said that the model has led to a neglect of historical context *per se*, however, for the intertextual field is absolutely fundamental to the historical context of a text such as Galatians. One does not exhaust the historical context of Galatians when one has located its addressees in the north or south, or pieced together one more possible profile of Paul's opponents. Even from a purely historical standpoint, that is merely to scratch the surface. There is nothing "purely historical" about being oblivious to theory.

So has this work been an exercise simply in theoretically informed history? What has become of theology? Theology as I understand it is present everywhere and nowhere in this book. It is present nowhere in the sense that the book contains no specifically theological strand to be clearly distinguished from a variety of non-theological emphases. As far as I am aware, there is no point at which a boundary is crossed between "descriptive" and "confessional" statements – to invoke another problematic dualistic schema. Theology is everywhere, however, in the sense that

---

10. A further dimension of this complexity is identified by John Barclay: Paul "radically expands – indeed threatens – the boundaries of [the Jewish] community", yet is "far less open to... cultural engagement" than fellow-Jews such as Aristeas, Philo and Josephus (*Jews in the Mediterranean Diaspora*, p. 389). In certain respects, Paul the Jew is a remarkably conservative figure.

at every point matters of real theological concern are raised.[11] Theology has a special although not exclusive concern with the "canonical form" of scriptural texts, since it is in this form that texts became communally normative and have helped to shaped enduring forms of communal life. From this perspective, even the laborious piecing together of textual fragments in quest of the canonical form of the Book of the Twelve has potential theological significance. More obvious theological potential is to be found in the fivefold canonical form of the Torah or Pentateuch, as read by its early readers, and in the disjunctions within this canonical form that occasion some of their most important interpretative decisions. In the Pauline reading of the Torah, the conjunction between text and gospel produces a highly distinctive understanding of divine agency, with direct relevance to questions about divine identity. The attempt to rethink the "doctrine of justification by faith" along hermeneutical and intertextual lines may have a contribution to make to ongoing theological discussion of this topic – if the question how we are most fruitfully to understand Paul's texts is still relevant here, as it should be. The emphasis on the textual matrix of christology might lead to a critical assessment of the assumption that christology is a self-sufficient discourse with a purely internal rationale, or that its primary interpretative matrix is some construal or other of the needs of the contemporary world. At every point, possible future theological conversations may be envisaged.

If there is a central theological question running through the whole, it has to do with "Christian" and "Jewish" identity and their relation to one another. If, at the turn of the eras, Christian and non-Christian Jews are reading the same texts, interpreting them in the light of some kind of revelatory hermeneutical event in order to interpret the world itself, where does this leave the assumption that to be "Christian" is one thing while to be "Jewish" is another? May we perhaps understand the Christian community itself as just another Jewish sect? To raise these questions is not at all to suggest that we can or should erase the difference between Pauline Christian Judaism (for want of a better expression) and non-Christian Judaisms. Well-intentioned arguments to the effect that what unites is more important than what divides are beside the point, and lack both historical and theological integrity. As our readings of early readings of

---

11. It is probably not possible to eradicate the prejudice that theologically interesting exegesis is *ipso facto* bad exegesis, and that, abjuring theology once and for all, we must strive to be even more "purely historical" than before. ("Purely historical" is of course an oxymoron.) For a recent discussion of this issue, see the "Essay on Interpretation" that opens Troels Engberg-Pedersen's *Paul and the Stoics* (pp. 1–31). Engberg-Pedersen initially proposes an approach that is to be historical-critical "*and not* theological" (p. 2; italics original), but concludes by outlining a cautiously theological reading with strong affinities with Bultmann (pp. 28–31). It is precisely this theological dimension that makes his book so provocative.

scripture have shown, the difference is ineradicable – the difference summed up in the Christian invocation of Jesus as Lord. What these readings may suggest is a possible non-reductionistic way of negotiating that difference.

Bibliography

Apocrypha and Pseudepigrapha of the Old Testament, 2 vols., ed. R. H. Charles, Oxford: Clarendon Press, 1913

The Apocryphal Old Testament, ed. H. F. D. Sparks, Oxford: Clarendon Press, 1984

Biblia Hebraica, ed. R. Kittel, Stuttgart: Württembergische Bibelanstalt, 1937[3]

Biblia Sacra iuxta Vulgatam Versionem, Stuttgart: Deutsche Bibelgesellschaft, 1994[4]

The Book of Ben Sira in Hebrew: A Text Edition of all Extant Hebrew Manuscripts and a Synopsis of all Parallel Ben Sira Texts, VTSup, Pancratius C. Beentjes, Leiden: Brill, 1997

The Dead Sea Scrolls: Study Edition, 2 vols., ed. F. García Martínez and E. J. C. Tigchelaar, Leiden: Brill; Grand Rapids: Eerdmans, 1997–98

The Dead Sea Scrolls in English, ed. Geza Vermes, London: Penguin, 1995[4]

Discoveries in the Judean Desert, II: Les Grottes de Murabbaïat, ed. P. Benoit, J. T. Milik and R. de Vaux, Oxford: Clarendon Press, 1961

Discoveries in the Judean Desert, V: 4Q158–4Q186, ed. J. M. Allegro and A. A. Anderson, Oxford: Clarendon Press, 1968

Discoveries in the Judean Desert, VIII: The Greek Minor Prophets Scroll from Naḥal Ḥever (ḤevXIIgr), ed. E. Tov, Oxford: Clarendon Press, 1990

Discoveries in the Judean Desert, XV: Qumran Cave 4, X: The Prophets, ed. E. Ulrich et al., Oxford: Clarendon Press, 1997

Encyclopedia of the Dead Sea Scrolls, ed. Lawrence H. Schiffman and James C. VanderKam, 2 vols., Oxford and New York: Oxford University Press, 2000

Eusebii Praeparatio Evangelica, tr. and ed. E. H. Gifford, Oxford: Oxford University Press, 1903

Die Fragmente der griechischen Historiker, IIIC, ed. F. Jacoby, Leiden: Brill, 1958

Gesenius' Hebrew Grammar, ed. E. Kautsch and A. E. Cowley, Oxford: Clarendon Press, 1909[2]

Josephus, Loeb Classical Library, 10 vols., ed. H. St.J. Thackeray *et al.*, London: Heinemann; Cambridge, Mass.: Harvard University Press, 1926–65

Luther's Works, Philadelphia: Fortress; St Louis: Concordia, 1955–

The Mishnah, trans. Herbert Danby, Oxford: Oxford University Press, 1933

Old Testament Pseudepigrapha, 2 vols., ed. James H. Charlesworth, London: Darton, Longman and Todd, 1983–85

Philo, Loeb Classical Library, 10 vols. and 2 supps., ed. F. H. Colson *et al.*, London: Heinemann; Cambridge, Mass.: Harvard University Press, 1929–62

Septuaginta: Vetus Testamentum Graecum Auctoritate Academiae Scientiarum Gottingensis editum, Göttingen: Vandenhoeck & Ruprecht
    Vol. I Genesis, ed. J. W. Wevers, 1974
    Vol. II, 1 Exodus, eds. J. W. Wevers and U. Quast, 1991
    Vol. II, 2 Leviticus, eds. J. W. Wevers and U. Quast, 1986
    Vol. III, 1 Numeri, eds. J. W. Wevers and U. Quast, 1982
    Vol. III, 2 Deuteronomium, eds. J. W. Wevers and U. Quast, 1977
    Vol. XII, 1 Sapientia Salomonis, ed. J. Ziegler, 1980^2
    Vol. XIII Duodecim Prophetae, ed. J. Ziegler, 1967^2
Septuaginta, ed. A. Rahlfs, Stuttgart: Deutsche Bibelgesellschaft, 1935
Die Texte aus Qumran: Hebräisch und Deutsch, ed. E. Lohse, Munich: Kösel-Verlag, 1981^3
Theological Dictionary of the New Testament, 10 vols., Eng. tr., Eerdmans: Grand Rapids, 1964–76

Alexander, Philip	"Torah and Salvation in Tannaitic Literature", in *Justification and Variegated Nomism: Volume 1 – The Complexities of Second Temple Judaism,* eds. D. A. Carson, Peter T. O'Brien and Mark A. Seifrid, Tübingen: Mohr-Siebeck; Grand Rapids: Baker Academic, 2001, pp. 261–301
Andersen, Francis I.	*Habakkuk: A New Translation and Commentary,* AB, New York: Doubleday, 2001
Avemarie, Friedrich	"Bund als Gabe und Recht: Semantische Überlegungen zu b°rît in der rabbinischen Literatur", in *Bund und Tora,* eds. F. Avemarie and H. Lichtenberger, WUNT, Tübingen: Mohr-Siebeck, 1996, pp. 163–216
Avemarie, Friedrich, and Lichtenberger, Hermann (eds.)	*Tora und Bund: Zur theologischen Begriffsgeschichte in alttestamentlicher, frühjüdischer und urchristlicher Tradition,* WUNT, Tübingen: Mohr-Siebeck, 1996
Badenas, Robert	*Christ the End of the Law: Romans 10:4 in Pauline Perspective,* JSNTSup, Sheffield: JSNT Press, 1985
Barclay, John M. G.	*Jews in the Mediterranean Diaspora, from Alexander to Trajan (323 BCE–117 CE,* Edinburgh: T. & T. Clark, 1996
Barrett, C. K.	*A Commentary on the First Epistle to the Corinthians,* BNTC, London: A. & C. Black, 1971^2
—	*Essays on Paul,* London: SPCK, 1982
Barth, Karl	*The Epistle to the Philippians,* ET Louisville: WJK, 2002^2

Barton, John — *Oracles of God: Perceptions of Ancient Prophecy in Israel after the Exile*, London: Darton, Longman and Todd, 1986

Barton, John, and Muddiman, John (eds.) — *The Oxford Bible Commentary*, Oxford: Oxford University Press, 2001

Bauckham, Richard — "A Quotation from 4Q Second Ezekiel in the Apocalypse of Peter", *RQ* 15 (1992), pp. 437–45

— "Apocalypses", in *Justification and Variegated Nomism. Volume 1: The Complexities of Second Temple Judaism*, eds. D. A. Carson, Peter T. O'Brien and Mark A. Seifrid, Tübingen: Mohr Siebeck; Grand Rapids: Baker Academic, 2001, pp. 135–87

Baumgarten, Albert I. — "The Perception of the Past in the Damascus Document", in *The Damascus Document: A Centennial of Discovery*, STDJ, eds. Joseph M. Baumgarten, Esther G. Chazon and Avital Pinnick, Leiden: Brill, 2000, pp. 1–15

Baumgarten, Joseph M., Chazon, Esther G., Pinnick, Avital (eds.) — *The Damascus Document: A Centennial of Discovery. Proceedings of the Third International Symposium of the Orion Center for the Study of the Dead Sea Scrolls and Associated Literature, 4–8 February 1998*

Beall, Todd S. — *Josephus' Description of the Essenes Illustrated from the Dead Sea Scrolls*, SNTSMS, Cambridge: Cambridge University Press, 1988

Beare, F. W. — *The Epistle to the Philippians*, BNTC, London: A. & C. Black, 1959

Begg, Christopher T. — "The Golden Calf Episode according to Pseudo-Philo", in *Studies in the Book of Exodus: Redaction-Reception-Interpretation*, ed. M. Vervenne, Leuven: Leuven University Press, 1996, pp. 577–94

Beker, J. Christiaan — *Paul the Apostle: The Triumph of God in Life and Thought*, Edinburgh: T. & T. Clark, 1980

Bell, Richard H. — *Provoked to Jealousy: The Origin and Purpose of the Jealousy Motif in Romans 9–11*, WUNT, Tübingen: Mohr-Siebeck, 1994

— *No One Seeks for God: An Exegetical and Theological Study of Romans 1.18–3.20*, WUNT, Tübingen: Mohr-Siebeck, 1998

Belleville, Linda   *Reflections of Glory: Paul's Polemical Use of the Moses-Doxa Tradition in 2 Corinthians 3.1–18*, JSNTSup, Sheffield: Sheffield Academic Press, 1991

—   "Tradition or Creation? Paul's Use of the Exodus 34 Tradition in 2 Corinthians 3.7–18", in *Paul and the Scriptures of Israel*, eds. C. A. Evans and J. A. Sanders, Sheffield: Sheffield Academic Press, 1993, JSNTSup, pp. 165–86

Ben Zwi, E.   "Twelve Prophetic Books or 'The Twelve': A Few Preliminary Considerations", in *Forming Prophetic Literature: Essays on Isaiah and the Twelve*, eds. J. W. Watts and P. R. House, JSOTSup, Sheffield: Sheffield Academic Press, 1996, pp. 125–56

Berger, Klaus   "Abraham in den paulinischen Hauptbriefe", *MTZ* 17 (1966), pp. 47–89

Bernstein, Moshe   "Introductory Formulas for Citation and Re-citation of Biblical Verses in the Qumran Pesharim", *DSD* 1 (1994), pp. 30–70

Betz, Hans Dieter   *Galatians: A Commentary on Paul's Letter to the Churches in Galatia*, Hermeneia, Philadelphia: Fortress, 1979

Blum, E.   "Das sog. 'Privilegrecht' in Exodus 34,11–26: Ein Fixpunkt der Komposition des Exodusbuches?", in *Studies in the Book of Exodus: Redaction-Reception-Interpretation*, ed. M. Vervenne, Leuven: Leuven University Press, 1996

Boccaccini, Gabriel   *Middle Judaism: Jewish Thought 300 BCE–200 CE*, Minneapolis: Fortress, 1991

Bogaert, P.-M.   "Les trois rédactions conservées et la forme originale de l'envoi du Cantique du Moïse (Dt 32, 43)", in *Deuteronomium: Entstehung, Gestalt und Botschaft*, ed. N. Lohfink, Leuven: Leuven University Press, 1985, pp. 329–40

Borgen, Peder   *Early Christianity and Hellenistic Judaism*, Edinburgh: T. & T. Clark, 1996

—   *Philo of Alexandria: An Exegete for his Time*, NovTSup, Leiden: Brill, 1997

Bornkamm, G.   *Das Ende des Gesetzes: Paulusstudien*, Munich: Chr. Kaiser Verlag, 1966[5]

Boyarin, Daniel	*A Radical Jew: Paul and the Politics of Identity*, Berkeley, Los Angeles, London: University of California Press, 1994
Brandenburger, E.	*Adam und Christus: Exegetische und religions-geschichtliche Untersuchungen zu Röm 5,12–21 (1 Kor 15)*, WMANT, Neukirchen: Neukirchener Verlag, 1962
—	*Die Verborgenheit Gottes im Weltgeschehen*, AThANT, Zürich: Theologischer Verlag, 1981
Braulik, G.	*Deuteronomium*, NEBKAT, 2 vols., Würzburg: Echter Verlag, 1986–92
Breech, Earl	"These Fragments I Have Shored Against My Ruins: The Form and Function of 4 Ezra", *JBL* 92 (1973), pp. 267–74
Brenner, Athalya	"An Afterword: The Decalogue – Am I an Addressee?", in *A Feminist Companion to Exodus to Deuteronomy*, ed. A. Brenner, Sheffield: Sheffield Academic Press, 1994, pp. 255–58
Brettler, Marc Zwi	"Predestination in Deuteronomy 30.1–10", in *Those Elusive Deuteronomists: The Phenomenon of Pan-Deuteronomism*, eds. Linda S. Schearing and Steven L. McKenzie, JSOTSup, Sheffield: Sheffield Academic Press, 1999; pp. 171–88
Brooke, George J.	*Exegesis at Qumran: 4QFlorilegium in its Jewish Context*, JSNTSup, Sheffield: JSOT Press, 1985
—	"*E Pluribus Unum*: Textual Variety and Definitive Interpretation in the Qumran Scrolls", in *The Dead Sea Scrolls in Their Historical Context*, ed. T. H. Lim et al., Edinburgh: T. & T. Clark, 2000, pp. 109–19
Brooke, George J., with García Martínez, Florentino (eds.)	*New Qumran Texts and Studies: Proceedings of the First Meeting of the International Organization for Qumran Studies, Paris 1992*, STDJ, Leiden: Brill, 1994
Brownlee, William H.	*The Text of Habakkuk in the Ancient Commentary from Qumran*, JBLMS, Philadelphia: Society of Biblical Literature and Exegesis, 1959
—	"The Placarded Revelation of Habakkuk", *JBL* 82 (1963), pp. 319–25
—	*The Midrash Pesher of Habakkuk*, SBLMS, Missoula: Scholars Press, 1979

Bruce, F. F. — *The Epistle to the Galatians: A Commentary on the Greek Text*, NIGTC, Exeter: Paternoster, 1982

Brueggemann, Walter — *Deuteronomy*, AOTC, Nashville: Abingdon, 2001

Budde, K. — "Die Bücher Habakuk und Zephanja", *ThStKr* 66 (1893), pp. 383–93

Bultmann, Rudolf — *Primitive Christianity in its Contemporary Setting*, Eng. tr, London: Thames and Hudson, 1956

Theology of the New Testament, 2 vols., Eng. tr., London: SCM Press, 1952

Burkes, Shannon — "'Life' Redefined: Wisdom and Law in Fourth Ezra and Second Baruch, *CBQ* 63 (2001), pp. 55–71

Burrows, Millar — *The Dead Sea Scrolls*, London: Secker and Warburg, 1956

Burton, E. D. — *A Critical and Exegetical Commentary on the Epistle to the Galatians*, ICC, Edinburgh: T. & T. Clark, 1921

Byrne, Brendan — *Romans*, SP, Collegeville: Liturgical Press, 1996

Calvin, John — *The First Epistle of Paul to the Corinthians*, Eng. tr., Grand Rapids: Eerdmans, 1960

Campbell, Douglas — *The Rhetoric of Righteousness in Romans 3.21–26*, JSNTSup, Sheffield: Sheffield Academic Press, 1992

— "The Meaning of ΠΙΣΤΙΣ and ΝΟΜΟΣ in Paul: A Linguistic and Structural Perspective", *JBL* 111 (1992), pp. 91–103

— "Romans 1:17 – A *Crux Interpretum* for the ΠΙΣΤΙΣ ΧΡΙΣΤΟΥ Debate", *JBL* 113 (1994), pp. 265–85

Campbell, Jonathan G. — *The Use of Scripture in the Damascus Document 1–8, 19–20*, BZAW, Berlin: de Gruyter, 1995

Carroll, Robert P. — *When Prophecy Failed: Reactions and Responses to Failure in the Old Testament Prophetic Traditions*, London: SCM, 1979

Carson, D. A., O'Brien, Peter T., and Seifrid, Mark A. (eds.) — *Justification and Variegated Nomism. Volume 1: The Complexities of Second Temple Judaism*, Tübingen: Mohr-Siebeck; Grand Rapids: Baker Academic, 2001

Charlesworth, James H. — *The Pesharim and Qumran History: Chaos or Consensus?*, Grand Rapids: Eerdmans, 2002

Cheon, Samuel	*The Exodus Story in the Wisdom of Solomon: A Study in Biblical Interpretation*, JSPSup, Sheffield: Sheffield Academic Press, 1997
Childs, Brevard	*Exodus: A Commentary*, OTL, London: SCM Press, 1974
—	*Introduction to the Old Testament as Scripture*, London: SCM Press, 1979
—	*Biblical Theology of the Old and New Testaments: Theological Reflection on the Christian Bible*, London: SCM Press, 1992
Childs, Brevard S.	*Isaiah*, OTL, Louisville: WJK, 2001
Coats, George W.	*Rebellion in the Wilderness: The Murmuring Motif in the Wilderness Traditions of the Old Testament*, Nashville & New York: Abingdon Press, 1968
—	*The Moses Tradition*, JSOTSup, Sheffield: Sheffield Academic Press, 1993
Conzelmann, Hans	*1 Corinthians*, Eng. tr., Hermeneia, Philadelphia: Fortress, 1975
Cranfield, C. E. B.	"St Paul and the Law", *SJT* 17 (1964), pp. 43–68
—	*Romans* (2 vols.), ICC, Edinburgh: T. & T. Clark, 1975–79
—	*On Romans and other New Testament Essays*, Edinburgh: T. & T. Clark, 1998
Davids, Peter H.	*The Epistle of James: A Commentary on the Greek Text*, NIGTC, Grand Rapids: Eerdmans, 1982
Davies, Philip R.	*The Damascus Covenant: An Interpretation of the "Damascus Document"*, JSOTSup, Sheffield: JSOT Press, 1982
—	*Behind the Essenes: History and Ideology in the Dead Sea Scrolls*, Atlanta: Scholars Press, 1987
—	*In Search of 'Ancient Israel'*, Sheffield: Sheffield Academic Press, 1992
—	"The Judaism(s) of the Damascus Document", in *The Damascus Document: A Centennial of Discovery*, eds. J. M. Baumgarten, E. G. Chazon, and A. Pinnick, STDJ, Leiden: Brill, 2000, pp. 27–43
Davis, Stephan K.	*The Antithesis of the Ages: Paul's Reconfiguration of Torah*, CBQMS, Washington, DC: Catholic Biblical Association of America, 2002

Dimant, Devorah	"An Apocryphon of Jeremiah from Cave 4 (4Q385^B = 4Q385 16)", in *New Qumran Texts and Studies*, eds. G. J. Brooke with F. García Martínez, STDJ, Leiden: Brill, 1994, pp. 11–30
Dinkler, Erich	*Signum Crucis: Aufsätze zum Neuen Testament und zur Christlichen Archäologie*, Tübingen: Mohr-Siebeck, 1967
Dodd, Brian	*Paul's Paradigmatic 'I': Personal Example as Literary Strategy*, JSNTSup, Sheffield: Sheffield Academic Press, 1999
Dodd, C. H.	*The Meaning of Paul for Today*, London: George Allen & Unwin, 1920
—	*The Epistle of Paul to the Romans*, London and Glasgow: Collins, 1959^2
—	*Historical Tradition in the Fourth Gospel*, Cambridge: Cambridge University Press, 1963
Douglas, Mary	*Leviticus as Literature*, Oxford: Oxford University Press, 1999
Dozeman, Thomas B.	"Masking Moses and Mosaic Authority in Torah", *JBL* 119 (2000), pp. 21–45
Drane, John W.	*Paul: Libertine or Legalist? A Study in the Theology of the Major Pauline Epistles*, London: SPCK, 1975
Driver, S. R.	*An Introduction to the Literature of the Old Testament*, Edinburgh: T. & T. Clark, 1913^9
Dunn, J. D. G.	*Christology in the Making: An Inquiry into the Doctrine of the Incarnation*, London: SCM Press, 1980
—	*Romans* (2 vols.), WBC, Dallas, Texas: Word Books, 1988
—	*Jesus, Paul and the Law: Studies in Mark and Galatians*, Louisville: WJK Press, 1990
—	*The Epistle to the Galatians*, BNTC, A. & C. Black, London: 1993
—	*The Theology of Paul the Apostle*, Grand Rapids: Eerdmans, 1998
Durham, John I.	*Exodus*, WBC, Waco, Texas: Word Books, 1987

Paul and the Hermeneutics of Faith

Ego, Beate	"Abraham als Urbild der Toratreue Israels: Traditionsgeschichtliche Überlegungen zu einem Aspekt des biblischen Abrahambildes", in *Bund und Tora*, eds. F. Avemarie and H. Lichtenberger, WUNT, Tübingen: Mohr-Siebeck, 1996, pp. 25–40
Eichrodt, Walther	*Theology of the Old Testament*, vol.1, Eng. tr., London: SCM Press, 1961
Eissfeldt, Otto	*The Old Testament: An Introduction*, Eng. tr., Oxford: Blackwell, 1965
Emerton, J. A.	"The Textual and Linguistic Problems of Habakkuk II. 4–5", *JTS* n.s. 28 (1977), pp. 1–18
Endres, John C.	*Biblical Interpretation in the Book of Jubilees*, CBQMS, Washington, DC: Catholic Biblical Association of America, 1987
Engberg-Pedersen, Troels	*Paul and the Stoics*, Edinburgh: T. & T. Clark, 2000
— (ed.)	*Paul beyond the Judaism/Hellenism Divide*, Louisville: WJK, 2001
Engel, Helmut	*Das Buch der Weisheit*, Neuer Stuttgarter Kommentar, Stuttgart: Verlag Katholisches Bibelwerk, 1998
Esler, Philip	"The Social Function of *4 Ezra*", *JSNT* 53 (1994), pp. 99–123
Evans, Craig A., and Sanders, J.A. (eds.)	*Paul and the Scriptures of Israel*, JSNTSup, Sheffield: Sheffield Academic Press, 1993
Fee, Gordon D.	*The First Epistle to the Corinthians*, NICNT, Grand Rapids: Eerdmans, 1987
Feldman, L. H.	"Abraham the Greek Philosopher in Josephus", *TAPA* 99 (1968), pp. 143–56
Fitzmyer, Joseph A.	"Habakkuk 2:3–4 and the New Testament", in his *To Advance the Gospel*, New York: Crossroad, 1981, pp. 236–46
—	*Romans: A New Translation with Introduction and Commentary*, AB, New York: Doubleday, 1992
Fretheim, Terence E.	"Numbers", in *The Oxford Bible Commentary*, eds. John Barton and John Muddiman, Oxford: Oxford University Press, 2001, pp. 110–34

Friedrich, G.   "αμαρτια ουκ ελλογειται Röm 5,13", *TLZ* 77 (1952),
                       pp. 523–28

Fuller, Russell E.   "The Form and Formation of the Book of the
                       Twelve: The Evidence from the Judaean Desert", in
                       *Forming Prophetic Literature: Essays on Isaiah and the
                       Twelve in Honor of John D. W. Watts*, eds. J. W.
                       Watts and P. R. House, JSOTSup, Sheffield: Sheffield
                       Academic Press, 1996; pp. 86–101

Furnish, V. P.   *II Corinthians*, AB, New York: Doubleday, 1984

Gadamer, H.-G.   *Truth and Method*, Eng. tr., London: Ward and
                       Sheed, 1961

Gager, John G.   *Reinventing Paul*, New York: Oxford University
                       Press, 2000

Gagnon, Robert A. J.   "Why the 'Weak' at Rome Cannot Be Non-Christian
                       Jews", *CBQ* 62 (2000), pp. 64–82

Gaston, Lloyd   *Paul and the Torah*, Vancouver: University of British
                       Columbia, 1987

Gathercole, Simon J.   *Where is Boasting? Early Jewish Soteriology and
                       Paul's Response in Romans 1–5*, Grand Rapids:
                       Eerdmans, 2002

—   "A Law unto Themselves: The Gentiles in Romans
                       2.14–15 Revisited", *JSNT* 85 (2002), pp. 27–49

—   "Torah, Life, and Salvation: Leviticus 18:5 in Early
                       Judaism and the New Testament", in *From Prophecy
                       to Testament: The Function of the Old Testament in the
                       New*, eds. C. A. Evans and J. A. Sanders, Peabody,
                       Mass.: Hendrickson, forthcoming, pp. 131–50

Georgi, Dieter   *Jüdische Schriften aus hellenistisch-römischer Zeit*,
                       III.4, Gütersloh: Gerd Mohn, 1980

—   *The Opponents of Paul in Second Corinthians*, Eng. tr.,
                       Edinburgh: T. & T. Clark, 1987

Goldstein, Jonathan A. *I Maccabees: A New Translation with Introduction and
                       Commentary*, AB, New York: Doubleday, 1976

Goodenough, E. R.   *An Introduction to Philo Judaeus*, Oxford: Basil
                       Blackwell, 1962

Gunkel, Hermann   *Genesis* Eng. tr., Macon, Georgia: Mercer University
                       Press, 1997

Hafemann, Scott J.	*Paul, Moses, and the History of Israel: The Letter/Spirit Contrast and Argument from Scripture in 2 Corinthians 3*, WUNT, Tübingen: Mohr-Siebeck, 1995
Hall, D. R.	"Romans 3.1–8 Reconsidered", *NTS* 29 (1982–83), pp. 183–97
Hanson, A. T.	*Studies in Paul's Technique and Theology*, London: SPCK, 1974
Hanson, Paul D.	*The Dawn of Apocalyptic: The Historical and Sociological Roots of Jewish Apocalyptic Eschatology*, Fortress: Philadephia, 1979[2]
Harnisch, Wolfgang	*Verhängnis und Verheissung der Geschichte: Untersuchungen zum Zeit- und Geschichtsverständnis im 4. Buch Esra und in der syr. Baruchapokalypse*, FRLANT, Göttingen: Vandenhoeck & Ruprecht, 1969
—	"Der Prophet als Widerpart und Zeuge der Offenbarung. Erwägungen zur Interdependenz von Form und Sache im IV. Buch Esra", in *Apocalypticism in the Mediterranean World and the Near East*, ed. D. Hellholm, Tübingen: Mohr-Siebeck, 1983, pp. 461–93
Harrington, Daniel J.	*Invitation to the Apocrypha*, Grand Rapids: Eerdmans, 1999
Hayman, A. P.	"The Problem of Pseudonymity in the Ezra Apocalypse", *JSJ* 6 (1975), pp. 47–56
Hays, Richard B.	"Psalm 143 and the Logic of Romans 3", *JBL* 99 (1980), pp. 107–15
—	*The Faith of Jesus Christ: An Investigation of the Narrative Substructure of Galatians 3:1–4:11*, SBLDS, Chico, CA: Scholars Press, 1983
—	"'The Righteous One' as Eschatological Deliverer: A Case Study in Paul's Apocalyptic Hermeneutics", in *Apocalyptic and the New Testament*, eds. J. Marcus and M. L. Soards, JSNTSup, Sheffield: JSOT Press, 1988, pp. 191–215
—	*Echoes of Scripture in the Letters of Paul*, New Haven and London: Yale University Press, 1989

— "On the Rebound: A Response to Critiques of *Echoes of Scripture in the Letters of Paul*", in *Paul and the Scriptures of Israel*, eds. Craig A. Evans and James A. Sanders, JSNTSup, Sheffield: JSOT Press, 1993, pp. 70–96

— *First Corinthians*, Interpretation, Louisville: John Knox Press, 1997

— "The Conversion of the Imagination: Scripture and Eschatology in 1 Corinthians", *NTS* 45 (1999), pp. 391–412

Hempel, Charlotte — "The Place of the Book of *Jubilees* at Qumran and Beyond", in *The Dead Sea Scrolls in Their Historical Context*, ed. T. H. Lim *et al.*, Edinburgh: T. & T. Clark, 2000, pp. 187–96

Hengel, Martin — *Judaism and Hellenism: Studies in their Encounter in Palestine during the Early Hellenistic Period*, 2 vols., Eng. tr., London: SCM Press, 1974

— *Die Zeloten*, Leiden: Brill, 1961

Hill, Christopher — *A Turbulent, Seditious, and Factious People: John Bunyan and his Church*, Oxford: Oxford University Press, 1989

Hooker, Morna D. — *From Adam to Christ*, Cambridge: Cambridge University Press, 1990

Horbury, William — "The Wisdom of Solomon", in *The Oxford Bible Commentary*, eds. John Barton and John Muddiman, Oxford: Oxford University Press, 2001, pp. 650–67

Horgan, Maurya P. — *Pesharim: Qumran Interpretations of Biblical Books*, CBQMS, Washington, DC: The Catholic Biblical Association of America, 1979

House, Paul R. — *The Unity of the Twelve*, Sheffield: Almond Press, 1990

Hübner, Hans — *Law in Paul's Thought*, SNTW, Eng. tr., Edinburgh: T. & T. Clark, 1984

— *Die Weisheit Salomons*, ATD Apokryphen, Göttingen: Vandenhoeck & Ruprecht, 1999

Jobes, Karen H. and Silva, Moisés — *Invitation to the Septuagint*, Grand Rapids: Baker; Carlisle, Paternoster, 2000

Jöcken, Peter — *Das Buch Habakuk: Darstellung der Geschichte seiner kritischen Erforschung mit einer eigenen Beurteilung*, BBB, Köln-Bonn: Peter Hanstein Verlag, 1977

Johnson, Luke T.   "Rom 3:21–26 and the Faith of Jesus", *CBQ* 44 (1982), pp. 77–90

—   *The Letter of James*, AB, New York: Doubleday, 1995

Johnstone, William   *Exodus*, Old Testament Guides, Sheffield: Sheffield Academic Press, 1990

Jones, Barry Alan   *The Formation of the Book of the Twelve: A Study in Text and Canon*, Atlanta: Scholars Press, 1995

Käsemann, Ernst   *Commentary on Romans*, Eng. tr., Grand Rapids: Eerdmans, London: SCM Press, 1980

—   *Perspectives on Paul*, Eng. tr., Philadelphia: Fortress, 1971

—   *New Testament Questions of Today*, Eng. tr., London: SCM Press, 1969

Keck, Leander A.   "The Function of Rom 3:10–18: Observations and Suggestions", in *God's Christ and His People: Studies in Honour of Nils Alstrup Dahl*, eds. J. Jervell and W. A. Meeks, Oslo/Bergen/Tromsö: Universitetsforlaget, 1977, pp. 141–57

Keesmaat, Sylvia C.   *Paul and his Story: (Re)Interpreting the Exodus Tradition*, JSNTSup, Sheffield: Sheffield Academic Press, 1999

Keller, Carl.-A.   "Die Eigenart der Prophetie Habakuks", *ZAW* 85 (1973), pp. 156–67

Kelsey, David H.   *The Uses of Scripture in Recent Theology*, London: SCM Press, 1975

Kister, M.   "Barnabas 12:1, 4:3 and 4Q Second Ezekiel", *RB* 97 (1990), pp. 63–67

Kneucker, J. J.   *Das Buch Baruch: Geschichte und Kritik, Übersetzung und Erklärung auf Grund des wiederhergestellten hebräischen Urtextes*, Leipzig: F. A. Brockhaus, 1879

Knox, W. L.   "Abraham and the Quest for God", *HTR* 28 (1935), pp. 57–60

Koch, D.-A.   *Die Schrift als Zeuge des Evangeliums: Unter-suchungen zur Verwendung und zum Verständnis der Schrift bei Paulus*, BHT, Tübingen: Mohr-Siebeck, 1986

—   "Der Text von Hab 2,4b in der Septuaginta und im Neuen Testament", *ZNW* 76 (1985), pp. 68–85

van der Kooij, A.

"The Ending of the Song of Moses: On the Pre-Masoretic Version of Deut.32:43", in *Studies in Deuteronomy*, ed. F. García Martínez *et al.*, VTSup, Leiden: Brill, 1994, pp. 93–100

Kuhn, Heinz-Wolfgang

"Die Bedeutung der Qumrantexte für das Verständnis des Galaterbriefes, aus dem Münchener Projekt: Qumran und das Neue Testament", in *New Qumran Texts and Studies*, eds. G. J. Brooke with F. Garcia Martínez, pp. 169–221

Kümmel, W.-G.

Römer 7 und die Bekehrung des Paulus, Leipzig: Hinrichs, 1929 (reissued Munich: Kaiser, 1974)

Lambrecht, Jan, S.J.

Second Corinthians, SP, Collegeville: Liturgical Press, 1999

Lietzmann, H.

An die Galater, HNT, Tübingen: Mohr-Siebeck, 1971[4]

Lieu, Judith M.

Neither Jew nor Greek? Constructing Early Christianity, SNTW, Edinburgh: T. & T. Clark, 2002

Lightfoot, J. B.

Saint Paul's Epistle to the Galatians, Cambridge and London: Macmillan, 1865

Lim, Timothy H.

"The Wicked Priests of the Groningen Hypothesis", *JBL* 112 (1993), pp. 415–25

—

Holy Scripture in the Qumran Commentaries and Pauline Letters, Oxford: Clarendon Press, 1997

— (ed.)

The Dead Sea Scrolls in their Historical Context, Edinburgh: T. & T. Clark, 2000

—

"The Wicked Priest or the Liar?", in *The Dead Sea Scrolls in their Historical Context*, ed. Timothy H. Lim, *et al.*, Edinburgh: T. & T. Clark, 2000, pp. 45–51

—

Pesharim, Sheffield: Sheffield Academic Press, 2002

Logan, Alastair H. B.

Gnostic Truth and Christian Heresy: A Study in the History of Gnosticism, Edinburgh: T. & T. Clark, 1996

Lohmeyer, Ernst

Der Brief an die Philipper, KEKNT, Göttingen: Vandenhoeck & Ruprecht, 1953[9]

Longenecker, Bruce W.

Eschatology and the Covenant: A Comparison of 4 Ezra and Romans 1–11, JSNTSup, Sheffield: Sheffield Academic Press, 1991

—

The Triumph of Abraham's God: The Transformation of Identity in Galatians, Edinburgh: T. & T. Clark; Nashville: Abingdon: 1998

— (ed.)   *Narrative Dynamics in Paul: A Critical Assessment*,
                                Louisville and London: WJK, 2002

Longenecker, Richard N.   *Galatians*, WBC, Dallas: Word Books, 1990

MacIntyre, Alasdair   *After Virtue: A Study in Moral Theory*, London:
                                Duckworth, 1985[2]

Martin, Dale B.   "Paul and the Judaism/Hellenism Dichotomy", in
                                Paul beyond the Judaism/Hellenism Divide, ed. T.
                                Engberg-Pedersen, Louisville: WJK, 2001, pp. 29–61

Martin, Ralph P.   *2 Corinthians*, WBC, Waco, Texas: Word Books, 1986

—   *James*, WBC, Waco, Texas: Word Books, 1988

Martyn, J. Louis   *Galatians: A New Translation with Introduction and
                                Commentary*, AB, New York: Doubleday, 1997

Matera, Frank J.   *Galatians*, SP, Collegeville: Liturgical Press, 1992

Matlock, R. Barry   *Unveiling the Apocalyptic Paul: Paul's Interpreters and
                                the Rhetoric of Criticism*, JSNTSup, Sheffield:
                                Sheffield Academic Press, 1996

—   "Detheologizing the ΠΙΣΤΙΣ ΧΡΙΣΤΟΥ Debate:
                                Cautionary Remarks from a Lexical Semantic
                                Perspective", *NovT* 42 (1999), pp. 1–23

McClean, B. Hudson   *The Cursed Christ: Mediterranean Expulsion Rituals
                                and Pauline Soteriology*, JSNTSup, Sheffield: Sheffield
                                Academic Press, 1996

McConville, J. G.,   *Time and Place in Deuteronomy*, JSOTSup, Sheffield:
  and Millar, J. G.   Sheffield Academic Press, 1994

McGlynn, Moyna   *Divine Judgement and Divine Benevolence in the Book
                                of Wisdom*, WUNT, Tübingen: Mohr-Siebeck, 2001

Metzger, Bruce M.   *A Textual Commentary on the Greek New Testament*,
                                London and New York: United Bible Societies, 1975

Milgrom, Jacob   *Leviticus: A New Translation with Introduction and
                                Commentary* (3 vols.), AB, New York: Doubleday,
                                1991–2000

—   *Numbers*, JPS Torah Commentary, Philadelphia and
                                New York: The Jewish Publication Society, 5750/1990

Moberly, R. W. L.   *The Old Testament of the Old Testament: Patriarchal
                                Narratives and Mosaic Yahwism*, OBT, Fortress:
                                Minneapolis, 1992

Moo, Douglas J.   "Israel and Paul in Romans 7.7–12", *NTS* 32 (1986),
                                pp. 122–35

—   *The Epistle to the Romans*, NICNT, Grand Rapids:
                            Eerdmans, 1997

Moore, Carey A.   *Daniel, Esther and Jeremiah: The Additions*, AB, New
                            York: Doubleday, 1977

Munck, Johannes   *Paul and the Salvation of Mankind*, Eng. tr., London:
                            SCM, 1959

Murray, John   *The Epistle to the Romans* (2 vols.), NICNT, Grand
                            Rapids: Eerdmans, 1959–65

Myers, Jacob M.   *I & II Esdras: A New Translation, Introduction and
                            Commentary*, AB, New York: Doubleday, 1974

Nanos, Mark C.   *The Mystery of Romans: The Jewish Context of Paul's
                            Letter*, Minneapolis: Fortress, 1996

—   *The Irony of Galatians: Paul's Letter in First-Century
                            Context*, Minneapolis: Fortress, 2002

Nelson, Richard D.   *Deuteronomy*, OTL, Louisville: WJK Press, 2002

Nickelsburg, G. W. E.   "The Bible Rewritten and Expanded", in *Jewish
                            Writings of the Second Temple Period: Apocrypha,
                            Pseudepigrapha, Qumran Sectarian Writings, Philo,
                            Josephus*, ed. Michael E. Stone, Assen: Van Gorcum;
                            Philadelphia: Fortress, 1984, pp. 89–156

—   *1 Enoch 1: A Commentary on the Book of 1 Enoch,
                            Chapters 1–36; 81–108*, Hermeneia, Minneapolis:
                            Augsburg Fortress, 2001

Nogalski, James D.   *Redactional Processes in the Book of the Twelve*,
                            BZAW, Berlin: de Gruyter, 1993

Nogalski, James D.,   *Reading and Hearing the Book of the Twelve*, Atlanta:
and Sweeney,   Society of Biblical Literature, 2000
Marvin A. (eds.)

Noth, Martin   *Exodus: A Commentary*, OTL, Eng. tr., London:
                            SCM Press, 1962

—   *The Laws in the Pentateuch and Other Studies*, Eng.
                            tr., Edinburgh and London: Oliver & Boyd, 1966

—   *Leviticus: A Commentary*, OTL, Eng. tr., London:
                            SCM Press, 1977

—   *Numbers: A Commentary*, OTL, Eng. tr., London:
                            SCM Press, 1968

Nygren, Anders   *Commentary on Romans*, Eng. tr., London: SCM
                            Press, 1952

Paul and the Hermeneutics of Faith

Oesterley, W. O. E. — *An Introduction to the Books of the Apocrypha*, London: SPCK, 1935

Olson, D. T. — *The Death of the Old and the Birth of the New: The Framework of the Book of Numbers and the Pentateuch*, Chico, CA: Scholars Press, 1985

Polzin, Robert — *Moses and the Deuteronomist: A Literary Study of the Deuteronomic History. 1. Deuteronomy, Joshua, Judges*, Bloomington and Indianapolis: Indiana University Press, 1990²

Porter, Stanley E. — "The Use of the Old Testament in the New Testament: A Brief Comment on Method and Terminology", in *Early Christian Interpretation of the Scriptures of Israel: Investigations and Proposals*, eds. Craig A. Evans and James A. Sanders, JSNTSup, Sheffield: Sheffield Academic Press, 1997, pp. 79–96

Provan, Iain W. — "Ideologies, Literary and Critical: Reflections on Recent Writing on the History of Israel", *JBL* 114 (1995), pp. 585–606

von Rad, Gerhard — *Old Testament Theology*, 2 vols,, Eng. tr., London: SCM Press, 1965–75

— *The Problem of the Hexateuch and other Essays*, Eng. tr., Edinburgh and London: Oliver and Boyd, 1966

— *Genesis: A Commentary*, OTL, Eng. tr., London: SCM Press, 1972²

— *Deuteronomy: A Commentary*, OTL, Eng. tr., London: SCM Press, 1966

— *Wisdom in Israel*, Eng. tr., London: SCM Press, 1972

Räisänen, Heikki — *Paul and the Law*, Eng. tr., Philadelphia: Fortress, 1986

— *The Torah and Christ: Essays in German and English on the Problem of the Law in Early Christianity*, Helsinki: Finnish Exegetical Society, 1986

Rendtorff, Rolf — *Das Alte Testament: Eine Einführung*, Neukirchen-Vluyn: Neukirchener Verlag, 1983

Ricoeur, Paul — *From Text to Action: Essay in Hermeneutics II*, Eng. tr., London: Athlone Press, 1991

Rieger, Hans-Martin — "Eine Religion der Gnade. Zur 'Bundesnomismus'-Theorie von E. P. Sanders", in *Bund und Tora*, eds. F. Avemarie and H. Lichtenberger, WUNT, Tübingen: Mohr-Siebeck, 1996, pp. 129–61

Roberts, J. J. M.
Nahum, Habakkuk, and Zephaniah: A Commentary, OTL, Louisville, Kentucky: WJK Press, 1991

Rofé, A.
Liebe und Gebot: Studien zum Deuteronomium, FRLANT, Göttingen: Vandenhoeck & Ruprecht, 2000

Rohde, Joachim
Der Brief des Paulus an die Galater, ThHKNT, Berlin: Evangelische Verlagsanstalt, 1989

Rosner, Brian S.
Paul, Scripture, and Ethics: A Study of 1 Corinthians 5–7, Grand Rapids: Baker, 1999

Rowland, Christopher
The Open Heaven: A Study of Apocalyptic in Judaism and Early Christianity, London: SPCK, 1982

Rudolph, W.
Micha – Nahum – Habakuk – Zephanja, KAT, Gütersloh: Gerd Mohn, 1975

Sanday, W., and Headlam, A. C.
The Epistle to the Romans, ICC, Edinburgh: T. & T. Clarke, 1902[5]

Sanders, E. P.
Paul and Palestinian Judaism: A Comparison of Patterns of Religion, London: SCM Press, 1977

—
Paul, the Law, and the Jewish People, Philadelphia: Fortress, 1983

Sanders, James A.
Torah and Canon, Philadelphia: Fortress, 1972

—
"Habakkuk in Qumran, Paul, and the Old Testament", repr. in *Paul and the Scriptures of Israel*, eds. C. A. Evans and J. A. Sanders, JSNTSup, Sheffield: Sheffield Academic Press, 1993, pp. 98–117

Sandmel, Samuel
Judaism and Christian Beginnings, New York: Oxford University Press, 1978

Schart, Aaron
Die Entstehung des Zwölfprophetenbuchs. Neu-arbeitungen von Amos im Rahmen schriftenübergreifender Redaktionsprozesse, BZAW 260, Berlin: de Gruyter, 1998

Schlier, Heinrich
Der Römerbrief, HThKNT, Freiburg, Basel, Wien: Herder, 1979[2]

Schnabel, Eckhard J.
Law and Wisdom from Ben Sira to Paul, WUNT, Tübingen: Mohr-Siebeck, 1985

Schnelle, Udo
"Transformation und Partizipation als Grundgedanken paulinischer Theologie", *NTS* 47 (2001), pp. 58–75

Schreiner, Stefan
"Erwägungen zum Text von Hab 2 4–5", *ZAW* 86 (1974), pp. 538–42

Schroer, Sylvia — "The Book of Sophia", in *Searching the Scriptures: A Feminist Commentary*, ed. E. Schüssler Fiorenza, London: SCM Press, 1994, pp. 17–38

Schürer, E. — *The History of the Jewish People in the Age of Jesus Christ*, 3 vols. (rev. G. Vermes, F. Millar and M. Goodman), Edinburgh: T. & T. Clark, 1973–86

Schüssler Fiorenza, Elisabeth (ed.) — *Searching the Scriptures: A Feminist Commentary*, London: SCM Press, 1994

Schweitzer, Albert — *Paul and his Interpreters: A Critical History*, Eng. tr., London: A. & C. Black, 1912

— *The Mysticism of Paul the Apostle*, Eng. tr., London: A. & C. Black, 1931

Schwemer, Anna Maria — "Zum Verhältnis von Diatheke und Nomos in den Schriften der jüdischen Diaspora Ägyptens in hellenistisch-römischer Zeit", in *Bund und Tora*, eds. F. Avemarie and H. Lichtenberger, WUNT, Tübingen: Mohr-Siebeck, 1996, pp. 67–109

Schwenk-Bressler Udo — *Sapientia Salomonis als ein Beispiel frühjüdischer Textauslegung: Die Auslegung des Buches Genesis, Exodus 1.1–5 und Teilen der Wüsten-tradition in Sap 10.19*, Beiträge zur Erforschung des Alten Testaments und antiken Judentums, Frankfurt am Main: Lang, 1993

Scott, James M. — "'For as Many as are of Works of the Law are under a Curse' (Galatians 3.10)", in *Paul and the Scriptures of Israel*, eds. C. A. Evans and J. A. Sanders, JSNTSup, Sheffield: Sheffield Academic Press, 1993, pp. 187–221

Seebass, Horst — *Numeri IV/2.3*, BKAT, Neukirchen-Vluyn: Neukirchener Verlag, 2001

Segal, Alan — *Paul the Convert: The Apostolate and Apostasy of Saul the Pharisee*, New Haven and London: Yale University Press, 1990

Seifrid, Mark A. — *Christ our Righteousness: Paul's Theology of Justification*, Leicester: Apollos, 2000

Seitz, Christopher R. — *Isaiah 1–39*, IBC, Louisville: John Knox Press, 1993

Seitz, Gottfried — *Redaktionsgeschichtliche Studien zum Deuteronomium*, Stuttgart: Verlag W. Kohlhammer, 1971

Smith, Ralph L. — *Micah-Malachi*, WBC, Word Books: Waco, Texas, 1984

Soggin, J. Alberto	*Joshua: A Commentary*, OTL, London: SCM Press, 1972
Spilsbury, Paul	*The Image of the Jew in Flavius Josephus' Paraphrase of the Bible*, TSAJ, Tübingen: Mohr-Siebeck, 1998
Stanley, C.D.	"'Under a Curse': A Fresh Reading of Galatians 3.10–14", *NTS* 36 (1990), pp. 481–511
—	*Paul and the Language of Scripture: Citation Technique in the Pauline Epistles and Contemporary Literature*, SNTSMS, Cambridge: Cambridge University Press, 1992
—	"'Pearls Before Swine': Did Paul's Audiences Understand His Biblical Quotations?", *NovT* 41 (1999), pp. 124–44
Steck, Odil Hannes	*Das apokryphe Baruchbuch: Studien zu Rezeption und Konzentration "kanonischer" Überlieferung*, FRLANT, Göttingen: Vandenhoeck & Ruprecht, 1993
Stockhausen, Carol K.	"2 Corinthians 3 and the Principles of Pauline Exegesis", in *Paul and the Scriptures of Israel*, eds. C. A. Evans and J. A. Sanders, JSNTSup, Sheffield: Sheffield Academic Press, 1993, pp. 143–64
—	*Moses' Veil and the Story of the New Covenant: The Exegetical Substructure of II Cor.3.1–4.6*, AnBib, Rome: Pontifical Biblical Institute, 1989
Stone, Michael E. (ed.)	*Jewish Writings of the Second Temple Period: Apocrypha, Pseudepigrapha, Qumran Sectarian Writings, Philo, Josephus*, Assen: Van Gorcum; Philadelphia: Fortress, 1984
—	*Fourth Ezra*, Hermeneia, Minneapolis: Fortress, 1990
Stowers, Stanley K.	*A Rereading of Romans: Justice, Jews, and Gentiles*, New Haven and London: Yale University, 1994
Talmon, S.	"Yom Hakkippurim in the Habakkuk Scroll", *Biblica* 32 (1951), pp. 549–63
—	"The Desert Motif in the Bible and in Qumran Literature", in *Biblical Motifs, Origins and Transformations*, ed. A. Altman, Cambridge, Mass.: Harvard University Press, 1966, pp. 31–63
Theissen, Gerd	*Psychological Aspects of Pauline Theology*, Eng. tr., Philadelphia: Fortress, 1987

Thielman, Frank	*From Plight to Solution: A Jewish Framework for Understanding Paul's View of the Law in Galatians and Romans*, NovTSup, Leiden: Brill, 1989
Thompson, Thomas L.	*The Historicity of the Patriarchal Narratives: The Quest for the Historical Abraham*, Harrisburg: Trinity Press International, 2002[2]
Thrall, Margaret E.	*A Critical and Exegetical Commentary on the Second Epistle to the Corinthians*, volume 1: I–VII, ICC, Edinburgh: T. & T. Clark, 1994
Tomson, Peter J.	*Paul and the Jewish Law: Halakha in the Letters of the Apostle to the Gentiles*, Assen/Maastricht: Van Gorcum; Minneapolis: Fortress, 1990
Tov, Emanuel	*The Septuagint Translation of Jeremiah and Baruch: A Discussion of an Early Revision of the LXX of Jeremiah 29–52 and Baruch 1:1–3:8*, Missoula: Scholars Press, 1976
—	"Three Fragments of Jeremiah from Qumran Cave 4", *RQ* 15 (1992), pp. 531–41
—	*Textual Criticism of the Hebrew Bible*, Minneapolis: Fortress, 2001[2]
Trebolle-Carrera, Julio	"Qumran Evidence for a Biblical Standard Text and for Non-standard and Parabiblical Texts", in *The Dead Sea Scrolls in their Historical Context*, ed. Timothy H. Lim *et al.*, Edinburgh: T. & T. Clark, 2000, pp. 89–106
Trible, Phyllis	*Texts of Terror: Literary-Feminist Readings of Biblical Narratives*, Philadelphia: Fortress, 1984
Tuckett, Christopher	"Paul, Scripture and Ethics", *NTS* 46 (2000), pp. 403–24
VanderKam, James C.	*Textual and Historical Studies in the Book of Jubilees*, Missoula: Scholars Press, 1977
Vanhoozer, Kevin	*Is there a Meaning in this Text? The Bible, the Reader, and the Morality of Literary Knowledge*, Grand Rapids: Zondervan, 1998
Van Seters, Jan	*Abraham in History and Tradition*, New Haven: Yale University Press, 1975
—	*Prologue to History: The Yahwist as Historian*, Louisville: WJK, 1992

—
"Cultic Laws in the Covenant Code (Exodus 20,22–23,33) and their Relationship to Deuteronomy and the Holiness Code", in *Studies in the Book of Exodus: Redaction-Reception-Interpretation*, ed. M. Vervenne, Leuven: Leuven University Press, 1996, pp. 319–45

Vervenne, Mark (ed.)
Studies in the Book of Exodus: Redaction-Reception-Interpretation, Leuven: Leuven University Press, 1996

Wacholder, B. Z.
Essays on Jewish Chronology and Chronography, New York: Ktav, 1976

Wagner, J. Ross
Heralds of the Good News: Paul and Isaiah "in Concert", NovTSup, Leiden: Brill, 2002

Wagner, V.
"Zur Existenz des sogenannten 'Heiligkeitsgesetzes'", *ZAW* 86 (1974), pp. 307–16

Walter, N.
"Zur Überlieferung einiger Reste früher jüdisch-hellenistischer Literatur bei Josephus, Clemens und Eusebius", *Studia Patristica* 7, TU 92, 1966, pp. 314–20

Ward, William Hayes
A Critical and Exegetical Commentary on Habakkuk, in J. M. P. Smith, W. H. Ward and J. A. Bewer, *Micah, Zephaniah, Nahum, Habakkuk, Obadiah and Joel*, ICC, Edinburgh: T. & T. Clark, 1912

Watson, Francis
"2 Cor. X–XIII and Paul's Painful Letter to the Corinthians", *JTS* n.s. 35 (1984), pp. 324–46

—
Paul, Judaism and the Gentiles: A Sociological Approach, SNTSMS, Cambridge: Cambridge University Press, 1986

—
Text, Church and World: Biblical Interpretation in Theological Perspective, Edinburgh: T. & T. Clark, Grand Rapids: Eerdmans, 1994

—
Text and Truth: Redefining Biblical Theology, Edinburgh: T. & T. Clark, Grand Rapids: Eerdmans, 1997

—
Agape, Eros, Gender: Towards a Pauline Sexual Ethic, Cambridge: Cambridge University Press, 2000

—
"The Triune Divine Identity: Reflections on Pauline God-language, in Disagreement with J. D. G. Dunn", *JSNT* 80 (2000), pp. 99–124

—
"Is There a Story in These Texts?", in *Narrative Dynamics in Paul*, ed. Bruce W. Longenecker, Louisville and London: WJK, 2002, pp. 231–39

Watts, James W., and House, P. R. (eds.)	*Forming Prophetic Literature: Essays on Isaiah and the Twelve in Honor of John D. W. Watts*, JSOTSup, Sheffield: Sheffield Academic Press, 1996
Watts, John D. W.	*Isaiah 1–33* WBC, Waco: Word Books, 1985
Westerholm, Stephen	*Israel's Law and the Church's Faith: Paul and his Recent Interpreters*, Grand Rapids: Eerdmans, 1988
Westermann, Claus	*Genesis 12–36: A Commentary*, Eng. tr., London: SPCK, 1986
Wevers, John W.	*Notes on the Greek Text of Exodus*, Septuagint and Cognate Studies 30, Atlanta: Scholars Press, 1990
Whitehouse. O. C.	*Baruch*, in *APOT*, ed. R. H. Charles, Oxford: Clarendon Press, 1913, i.569–95
Whitelam, Keith W.	*The Invention of Ancient Israel: The Silencing of Palestinian History*, London: Routledge, 1996
Wilckens, Ulrich	*Rechtfertigung als Freiheit: Paulusstudien*, Neukirchen-Vluyn: Neukirchener Verlag, 1974
—	*Der Brief an die Römer*, EKK VI/1–3, Zurich, etc.: Benziger, Neukirchener, 1978–82
Williams, David S.	*The Structure of 1 Maccabees*, CBQMS, Washington: Catholic Biblical Association of America, 1999
Williamson, Paul R.	*Abraham, Israel and the Nations: The Patriarchal Promise and its Covenantal Development in Genesis*, JSOTSup, Sheffield: Sheffield Academic Press, 2000
Windisch, Hans	*Der Zweite Korintherbrief*, Meyer, Göttingen: Vandenhoeck and Ruprecht, 1924[9]
Winston, D.	*The Wisdom of Solomon*, AB, New York: Doubleday, 1979
Wolff, Christian	*Der erste Brief des Paulus an die Korinther*, ThHKNT, 2 vols., Berlin: Theologische Verlagsanstalt, 1982
Wolff, H.-W.	*Hosea*, Eng. tr., Hermeneia, Philadelphia: Fortress, 1974
van der Woude, A.S.	"Wicked Priest or Wicked Priests? Reflections on the Identification of the Wicked Priest in the Habakkuk Commentary", *JJS* 33 (1982), pp. 349–59
Wright, N. T.	"The Paul of History and the Apostle of Faith", *TynB* 29, 1978, pp. 61–88
—	"The Messiah and the People of God", unpublished D.Phil. thesis, Oxford, 1980

—   *The Climax of the Covenant: Christ and the Law in Pauline Theology*, Edinburgh: T. & T. Clark, 1991

—   *The New Testament and the People of God*, London: SPCK, 1992

—   *The Resurrection of the Son of God*, Minneapolis: Fortress, 2003

Zenger, E.   "Wie und wozu die Tora zum Sinai kam: Literarische und theologische Beobachtungen zu Exodus 19–34", in *Studies in the Book of Exodus: Redaction-Reception-Interpretation*, ed. M. Vervenne, Leuven: Leuven University Press, 1996, pp. 265–88

Zimmerli, Walther   *Ezekiel 1: A Commentary on the Book of the Prophet Ezekiel Chapters 1–24*, Eng. tr., Hermeneia, Philadelphia: Fortress, 1979

Index of Biblical References

bar

Index of Subjects

Index of Authors